The Thought of Jonathan Edwards

The Thought
of Jonathan Edwards

Miklos Veto

Translated into English by
Philip Choinière-Shields

Forewords by
Harry S. Stout
and
Wilson H. Kimnach

WIPF & STOCK · Eugene, Oregon

THE THOUGHT OF JONATHAN EDWARDS

Copyright © 2021 Miklos Veto. All rights reserved. Except for brief quotations in critical publications or reviews, no part of this book may be reproduced in any manner without prior written permission from the publisher. Write: Permissions, Wipf and Stock Publishers, 199 W. 8th Ave., Suite 3, Eugene, OR 97401.

Wipf & Stock
An Imprint of Wipf and Stock Publishers
199 W. 8th Ave., Suite 3
Eugene, OR 97401

www.wipfandstock.com

PAPERBACK ISBN: 978-1-4982-2624-0
HARDCOVER ISBN: 978-1-4982-2626-4
EBOOK ISBN: 978-1-4982-2625-7

01/20/21

Contents

Foreword: The Jonathan Edwards Classic Studies Series by Harry S. Stout | vii
Foreword by Wilson H. Kimnach | ix
The author's preface to the American edition of his book | xi
Abbreviations | xiii
Introduction | xv

1 From Being to Grace | 1
2 The Will | 65
3 God and the Evil Will | 127
4 The Evil in Good | 188
5 Spiritual Idea and Natural Knowledge | 245
6 The Knowledge of Spiritual Things | 292
7 The Two Beauties | 331
8 The Whole and the Essential | 363
   Conclusion | 391

APPENDIX 1: CAN MAN WISH TO BE DAMNED? | 403
APPENDIX 2: SAINTS AND DAMNED | 409

Chronology | 414
Bibliographic Notice | 418
Concordance | 424
Bibliography | 453
Scripture Index | 479
Name Index | 481
Subject Index | 489

Foreword

The Jonathan Edwards Classic Studies Series

THE JONATHAN EDWARDS CENTER at Yale University is pleased to offer this volume, in grateful cooperation with Wipf & Stock Publishers, as part of its mission to encourage ongoing research into and readership of one of American's most original thinkers and one of its most significant historical and cultural figures. As much as the Edwards Center is devoted to presenting Edwards's own writings in a comprehensive and authoritative online format, which can be assessed at edwards.yale.edu, we also see providing secondary resourses as vital to supporting an ongoing understanding of Edwards's extensive and varied corpus.

Writings about Edwards's life, thought, and legacy continue to accumulate from authors representting a broad range of disciplines and agendas. Within the voluminous secondary literature, the Edwards Center recognizes the importance of insuring that certain key works are easily assessible. Up until now, we have focused in this series on new editions of out-of-print landmark studies. With this current volume, we for the first time present an English translation of a major interpretive work, *La pensée de Jonathan Edwards*, first published in French in 1987 and then again in 2007. Writing from a European perspective, and bringing to bear an impressive knowledge of classical and Christian theological and philosophical history, Prof. Veto, in a detailed manner seldom if ever paralleled, shows the ways in which Edwards was part of long intellectual traditions but also how he was innovative, even brilliant.

Harry S. Stout, Director
Jonathan Edwards Center
Yale University

Foreword

FIRST PUBLISHED IN FRANCE in 1987, Miklos Veto's *The Thought of Jonathan Edwards* was recently updated for a second French edition and is now translated for this first American edition. Originally intended to introduce Edwards to a European audience by explaining and reconstructing his thought within its historical background of sixteenth- and seventeenth-century Continental religious thought and Reformation theology, Veto's study has resulted in a path-breaking addition to the renaissance of Edwardsian studies of the past thirty years.

A former Yale professor, a philosopher and noted historian of philosophy in Europe, having published on thinkers from Kant and Schelling to Simone Weil, Miklos Veto was arrested by the metaphysical brilliance of Jonathan Edwards's philosophical theology only after he left America. Frequent returns to New Haven enabled him to become acquainted with the team of editors who were then producing the new Yale Edition of Edwards's writings, including much material that had never before been published. Subsequently, he has kept in touch with the evolving resources of the Yale Edwards, making use of the most recently published materials, as well as those of the classic texts and editions of Edwards's writings. Indeed, his study is text-centered and remains closely focused upon Edwards's writings throughout its exposition.

The argument of this book is predicated upon the notion that the immense corpus of Edwards's writings can best be reconstructed in the light of three major themes: being and grace, the will, and spiritual knowledge. Inasmuch as Edwards's ontology is deeply influenced by his theology, the conceptual landscape of his sermons and treatises is dominated by the presence of Infinite Being—not sheer necessity, but Being grounded in a dynamic goodness, experienced as a fountain of benign creativity. Over against this ontological theme of being stands the idea of willing. Edwards analyses the will in order to defend the Christian doctrine of Original Sin, yet he ultimately rethinks the will in its pure immanency and homogeneity, thereby renewing it as a philosophical concept. Finally, in the course of his analysis of religious experience, Edwards elaborates a profound theory of knowledge in which spiritual, aesthetic, and moral elements are constantly interwoven with epistemology *stricto sensu*. Taken as a whole, this body of writing establishes Edwards as the first important philosopher and theologian of America, who has exerted a powerful influence over generations of American thinkers, stimulating debate and controversy to this day.

Miklos Veto's own heritage—born into a Hungarian Jewish milieu, converted to Roman Catholicism as a youth, moved to France at the age of twenty—combined with his more recent deep interest in Protestant thinkers, has equipped him with a rich cultural foundation that enhances his professional discipline as he engages the thought of Edwards.[1] His insights are thus not necessarily aligned with the Anglo-American sensibility usually found in studies of Edwards, although he certainly appreciates Edwards's intellectual life within the Puritan culture of eighteenth century New England.

Preparing this complex metaphysical argument for an American audience has not been without its difficulties, but what has been achieved is largely the result of the talent and diligence of Canadian translator Philip Choinìere-Shields. He and Professor Veto have often hammered out the text phrase by phrase through transatlantic internet dialogue. While a few American scholars have already made use of the original French text, it is hoped that for the monolingual this publication will provide new perspectives on the study and understanding of Edwards's thought.

Of course, all this has not been done without cost, and thus it is a pleasure to acknowledge the initiating grants from James M. and John H. Edwards, lineal descendants of Jonathan Edwards, without which the entire project would have remained a mere good intention. Once begun, the project has also benefited from the sustained technical facilitation of Kenneth P. Minkema in The Jonathan Edwards Center at Yale University. For all such kinds of support, we are deeply grateful.

Wilson H. Kimnach
Presidential Professor of Humanities, Emeritus, University of Bridgeport
Editorial Board, *Works of Jonathan Edwards*

---

1. Submerged within the broader currents of his heritage and yet significant in its influence is that historic moment of the tragic 1956 Hungarian uprising against Soviet Russian domination, Veto's participation in which resulted in his having to flee his homeland and spend months in a Yugoslavian refugee camp. American readers today are unlikely to remember this dark moment when our government decided not to risk intervention on behalf of an oppressed people, a decision bitterly memorialized by E. E. Cummings in his poem, "Thanksgiving (1956)." See for all this a very recent autobiography, *From Budapest to Paris (1936–1957). An Autobiography*.

The Author's Preface to the American Edition of His Book

ALL BOOKS HAVE A history and the present one is not an exception. A specialist of post-kantian idealism, I was teaching for many years German and French philosophies at Yale. As a fellow of Jonathan Edwards College at that great university, I had no idea who this harsh preacher was whose portrait hung on a wall of the Junior Common Room, except that he was the favourite butt of undergraduate jokes. But one day, shortly before we left America, I entered Barnes and Nobles in New York and fell upon a nice black-covered copy of the treatise on Free Will. I bought the book for the sum of two dollars and forty-five cents and took it with me to Abidjan, in the Ivory Coast where I was to teach at the French-speaking university. And there, under the West-African tropics, I began to read Edwards and the American Puritans. A many years interlude of my life resulted in the publication of the first French edition of this book, *La pensée de Jonathan Edwards*. Unfortunately few people read it. The French language public is very moderately interested in Edwards and the American scholars, working on the Puritans... well, the working knowledge of the French language is not one of their strengths! So the book was to receive a few eloquent reviews, but one could not even say that it has become forgotten. For this, it should have been known before...

For some time, I tried to find a translator but with no success. However some twenty years after the publication of the French language study, Wilson Kimnach convinced me to rework it for a second, corrected and slightly enlarged edition in Paris, with the ultimate perspective of an American translation and edition. It is also thanks to Kimnach that Yale's Jonathan Edwards Center so aptly led by Kenneth Minkema, agreed to sponsor the publication of this big book. It is first to Kimnach, the best contemporary scholar of Edwards Studies that I would like to express my grateful thanks. After him, I wish to thank Philip Choinière-Shields who, besides rendering in a magnificent English this bit of French academic prose, called to my attention the imperfections of the work and rectified a large number of incorrect quotes and references. I would also thank Nathanael Antiel, helpful in correcting a number of footnotes. Finally, I desire to invoke the memory of Thomas Schaefer, perhaps the most knowledgeable person in the world of Edwards's texts who allowed me to read his transcriptions of the *Miscellanies* which would appear only ten or twenty years later in the *Works of Jonathan Edwards* of Yale University Press. It is the publication of the twenty-six printed volumes, followed by a publication on an online which is still ongoing, that has made possible the extraordinary renewal and blossoming of Edwards studies in the last thirty or forty years. I hope that my book, work of a European philosopher, is going to contribute in its way to a deeper understanding of the thought of the first great philosopher-theologian of America.

Miklos Veto

Abbreviations

1–26	*The Works of Jonathan Edwards.* 26 vols.
I–X	*The Works of President Edwards.* 10 vols.
Dw. I.	*The Works of President Edwards with a Memoir of His Life.* Vol. 1.
W 1, 2, 3	*The Works of President Edwards, in Four Volumes. A Reprint of the Worcester Edition.*
WJE	"Works of Jonathan Edwards Online."
Bl.	*The Blessing of God. Previously Unpublished Sermons of Jonathan Edwards.*
Salv.	*The Salvation of Souls: Nine Previously Unpublished Sermons on the Call of Ministry and the Gospel by Jonathan Edwards.*
MO	*Miscellaneous Observations on Important Theological Subjects, Original and Collected, by the Late Reverend Mr. Jonathan Edwards.*
Ms.	"Manuscript."
Ak.	Kant, *Gesammelte Schriften.*

Introduction[1]

Jonathan Edwards died in 1758 at fifty-four years of age. At seventeen, he wrote his first sermons; at nineteen, he began his Miscellanies and, in the years that followed, started work on a huge construction site of preparatory texts: *Notes on the Bible, Notes on the Apocalypse, Images and Shadows of Divine Things*, and *The Mind*. He was barely thirty when a collection of his theological *Discourses* was ready for publication. Some ten years later, he wrote his classic *Treatise Concerning Religious Affections*. The last decade of Edwards's life—spent in exile in the missionary parish of the Indians at Stockbridge—saw a burst of literary creativity with the composition of his great treatises *Freedom of the Will, Original Sin, The End for Which God Created the World*, and *The Nature of True Virtue*. These treatises, the clarified works of a mature mind, represent the finest fruit of his reflections. Though they give evidence of an accomplished subtlety of argument and great mastery of thought and writing, the first signs of these accomplishments, and even their basic themes and theses, were already evident in his early work. In 1733, when he preached his great sermon *A Divine and Supernatural Light* to the congregation at Northampton, Edwards gave a summary version of his ideas about spiritual knowledge. Eighteen years later, he would return to this in his Newark homily *True Grace Distinguished from the Experience of Devils*. However, an even somewhat attentive reading shows that the essence of these two famous sermons was already present in *A Spiritual Understanding of Divine Things Denied to the Unregenerate*, which he had preached at the age of twenty.

The central themes of Jonathan Edwards's reflection, which touched on most areas of theology and philosophy, were present right from the outset. His contemporaries, however, had only a fragmented, unbalanced image of

1. The Introduction to the North American edition covers just some key moments from the much longer Introduction to the French edition (*La pensée de Jonathan Edwards*, 13–67), which was written for a reading public with only scant knowledge of the life and thought of 18th century colonial America.

this great thinker. Considered one of the most important preachers of his time, his sermons and discourses were read beyond the confines of New England, on the other side of the Atlantic and especially in Scotland, although his great treatises—even those published before his death—initially enjoyed only limited recognition. During his lifetime, Edwards was seen primarily as the theoretician of the Christian renewal movement, the Awakening that began to affect English-speaking America in the 1730s. Things had already begun to change during the last ten years of his life and, following the posthumous publication of his treatises, Edwards was recognized as the greatest English-speaking theologian of the eighteenth century[2] as well as one of America's "representative philosophers."[3] However, the publication of his treatises, the renowned *Life* by the faithful Samuel Hopkins, and important selections from Edwards's sermons and Miscellanies in the decades following his death in Princeton took place during an Age of Enlightenment whose luminaries would ultimately penetrate even distant America. This explains the discordant notes, rifts and rebuffs that marked the "reception" of his work, an often violently negative view of its significance that persisted until almost the middle of the twentieth century. Edwards was deemed a reactionary ideologist of the Pietistic uproar, a preacher of hell-fire, and although they could not fail to recognize the dialectical brilliance of his argument in the *Enquiry into Freedom of Will*, he was primarily seen as the archetypal representative of a bygone world, that of Calvinism's abstract and absurd dogmas.

Jonathan Edwards was indeed the theologian of Calvinist orthodoxy. Now, while intending to remain faithful to the positions of his Puritan predecessors, he formulated and presented dogmas using the philosophical concepts and terms of his time and, in particular, by getting back to the basics of spiritual experience, notably that of the Awakening. The Pietism that swept over eighteenth-century Protestantism was a resurgence of Christian fervor in the face of the subversion and aggression of the Enlightenment, and the Awakening in the British colonies of North America was part of that renewal. However, although Pietism saw itself in a combat against the anti-Christian sentiment of the Enlightenment, it had very little to do with dogma, centered as it was on prayer and the Christian life. American Christianity is virtually the only exception to this disinterest in doctrine: on its home ground, spiritual renewal went hand-in-hand with a vigorous reaffirmation of dogma. "New Divinity"—also known as "New England Theology"—is the foundation of this active and creative synthesis of spiritual

2. Hopkins, *Life*, 83.
3. Royce, *Basic Writings*, 1:207.

experience and theological doctrine. It originated with Jonathan Edwards and was cultivated by his students and disciples. It was both a renewal and a return to the roots of Calvinism, and Edwards was, in fact, called "the metaphysician of Calvinism."[4] Of course, the assessment of the work and the thought of Edwards depends greatly on the position adopted with respect to this reincarnation of the Reformation.

Edwards was violently criticized, initially by his contemporary adversaries (such as Chauncy and Mayhew), then by nineteenth-century liberal thinkers, and even into the middle of the twentieth century. He seemed to have become the very symbol of everything that the descendants of the Enlightenment felt they had to reject. The preacher of Enfield was reproached for terrorizing the Christians of his day and of later times. He was called a true "theological Torquemada,"[5] a dogmatician who would have watched the damnation of his own daughter with equanimity if that had been the outcome of his system.[6] He would not hesitate to repudiate his brothers in order to glorify his God, but the worst is that his efforts ended in blasphemy! He loudly and emphatically confessed the unlimited sovereignty of God, yet how could the Christian notion of a God of Love be reconciled with the image of a tyrant who freely and gratuitously elected and condemned His creatures? To defend moral purity, the rational humanism of the Christian religion, curses were invoked upon the pastor from Northampton, while other readers were even more radical and squarely attacked Edwards for his attachment to Christianity and religion. Jonathan Edwards was "the last medieval American," the author of a work that was merely a monument to a lost cause.[7] Of course, he left us a few remarkable texts, but they are sullied and contaminated by the unhealthy outworking of horrible dogmatics. Afflicted, Edwards is made out to be a hybrid monster, "a kind of Spinoza-Mather," a strange intellectual phenomenon combining "the logical keenness of the great metaphysician with the puerile superstitions" of a colonial pastor.[8] An optimistic reader of Edwards certainly thought that "the cloud of old Puritan fear still veiled his firmament, but the light and warmth of the sun penetrated somewhat the gloom."[9] However, it was much more common to hear lamenting about the crushing failure and bankruptcy of a great mind that provoked his strange attachment to Calvinist dogma. We read

4. Osgood, "Jonathan Edwards," 367.
5. Thompson, "Edwards, Character, Teaching and Influence," 815.
6. De Normandie, "Jonathan Edwards at Portsmouth," 20.
7. Gay, *Loss of Mastery*, 88–89.
8. Stephen, "Jonathan Edwards," 230.
9. Channing, "Edwards and the Revivalists," 383.

that Edwards was like Pascal, whose great career in theoretical physics was checked by the influence of a gloomy religion.[10] It was his conversion that diverted him from his true path and left his philosophical insight "buried under the ruins of his religion."[11] The genius who might have become an Aristotle had made a fatal compromise in his intellectual life, and the result was failure.[12] Of course, a man can be great—independently of his beliefs—and, in the case of Edwards, his philosophical thought transcended the narrow limits of his own credo.[13] Nonetheless, this great mind had "squandered his talents on theological trifles,"[14] and we would never be able to measure what America had lost by his enslavement to Calvinist dogma.[15]

Edwards remains a great historical figure and, along with Franklin, the most important personality in colonial America.[16] He is an outstanding, almost mythic figure of the American conscience,[17] yet his thought and teaching are forgotten or rejected. Positivism and scientism certainly exercised less magisterial authority in America than in other Western countries, but even those speaking from a Christian viewpoint despairingly underlined how rarely they engaged in "abstract speculation" or age-old ecclesial dogmatics. Wasn't it stated at a meeting devoted to Edwards's memory that his views on predestination, original sin, and the efficacious action of grace are topics that are now very rarely raised and given little thought? What counts, what matters, are not these dogmas but rather the three virtues of faith, hope, and charity![18] Yet others, freed from any connection to Christian thought, regarded Edwards's ideas as vestiges of a bygone past and historical curiosities. Andrew MacPhail deemed "his course of reasoning as sinuous, his conclusions as unintelligible as those of any pioneer into the Teutonic mysteries." In any event, "it does not interest us now whether the will be free or not, or what may be the nature of true virtue; no one now defends or

---

10. Suter, "American Pascal," 338.

11. Schneider, *Puritan Mind*, 155.

12. Angoff, *Literary History of American People*, vol. 1, in Manspeaker, *Jonathan Edwards*, 9.

13. Royce, *Basic Writings*, 1:207.

14. Evans, "Jonathan Edwards," 57.

15. Muirhead, *Platonic Tradition in Anglo-Saxon Philosophy*, 307.

16. Stephen, "Jonathan Edwards," 219.

17. In 1900, only G. Washington received more votes than Edwards in a public opinion survey regarding the establishment of an American Hall of Fame. MacCracken, "The Hall of Fame," 567.

18. S. Edwards Tyler Henshaw, "Memorial Poem," in Woodbridge, *Memorial Volume*, 169.

attacks the proposition of original sin, or claims that one is sometimes three. It may be so, but we have other things to bother about."[19]

These lines were written more than a century ago and, since then, the *Weltgeist* has entered a new era. What evidently lacked interest for this British historian has newfound relevance for a great number of our contemporaries and, of particular interest to us, has become the subject of what is often high-level research and inquiry. Shortly after his death, it was written that he was "the greatest divine that ever adorned the American world"[20] and, at the end of the nineteenth century, it was thought that he could be designated "the most acute . . . thinker that Colonial New England produced."[21] He had sparked a true restoration of Calvinist theology[22] and was considered "the ablest metaphysician of the period from Leibniz to Kant."[23] We could cite many similar, often excessively flattering remarks.[24] They were frequently made by less distinguished writers and, more importantly, did not constitute a genuine historiography. Much has certainly been written on Edwards over the last two hundred years, although all of these historiographical works—with very few exceptions[25]—did not really contribute to a better understanding of America's first great thinker. This situation only changed with the renewal of Puritan studies led by a great historian, Perry Miller, towards the middle of the twentieth century.[26] While his most important works deal with the period prior to Edwards, his impressive books and articles restored the intellectual respectability of the entire Puritan world and opened a new era of scholarly studies of the Puritans.[27] Miller also devoted some of his works to Edwards himself. He published previously unpublished works, directed the critical Yale Edition until his death, and is most famous for writing *Jonathan Edwards* (1949), a work that rehabilitated this "inflexible logician of Calvinism"[28] as the greatest intellectual figure of his time. This book undoubtedly puts excessive emphasis on the "modernity"

---

19. MacPhail, "Jonathan Edwards," in *Essays in Puritanism*, 36.

20. Ryland, "Preface," in Lesser, *Jonathan Edwards*, 15.

21. Pancoast, *Introduction to American Literature*, 63.

22. Warfield, *Studies in Theology*, 532.

23. Dexter, *Biographical Sketches*, 218.

24. For an anthology of flowery praises, see the new French edition of this book, *La Pensée de Jonathan Edwards*.

25. In particular, the works of A. V. G. Allen, E. Smyth, G. P. Fisher, and L. H. Atwater.

26. Miller's work is "der bedeutendste Werk geistesgeschichtlichen Forschung [the most important work of intellectual history research]" in America (Brumm, *Puritanismus und Literatur in Amerika*, 87).

27. McGiffert, "American Puritan Studies in the 1960's," 64.

28. Leroux, "Pensée philosophique aux États-Unis," 129.

of the "last medieval American" and his indebtedness to Newton and Locke while presenting more of an intellectual portrait than a systematic exposition of thought "according to the order of reasons." Nevertheless, Miller did, in a manner of speaking, open the way to a renewal of this historiography. Since the 1950s, a great number of articles, an uninterrupted flow of theses and several good books have marked the new attention given to this great thinker of the colonial period. Once described by Santayana as "the greatest *master* in false philosophy,"[29] Edwards continues to be the subject of serious university studies that strive to portray the subtle coherence of his speculation and attempt to reconstruct the great themes of his thought. Conrad Cherry produced an insightful study on the formulation of the Protestant doctrine of justification by faith in Edwardsian theology.[30] In vigorous, subtle analyses, James Carse addressed the Edwardsian theory of supernatural manifestations.[31] Roland André Delattre undertook a profound reconstitution of the aesthetic-based ontology underlying the entire Edwardsian speculation.[32] These works attempted, in varying ways, to stake out the ground of Edwards's entire body of work while addressing the implications of certain major themes.

In their own way, they indeed succeeded in shedding light on the profound intelligibility of this immense and disparate body of work. However, with the possible exception of a work by Robert W. Jenson,[33] each of these recent historiographical works has a fundamental limitation. While these works, in particular the work by Delattre, clearly adhered to genuinely rigorous standards, their otherwise legitimate choice of a single line of inquiry—while helping to uncover connections and discern the profound logic underlying this proliferation of various treatises, sermons, and notes—did not allow for a systematic portrayal of Edwardsian thought in terms of its great conceptual themes. What mattered, they thought, was to carve out a drivable road through this forest of writings—a wide, solid road with narrower paths going off in all directions—but with hardly any ambition to establish a network covering the entire forest.[34] The forest is immense, the

29. Santayana, *Character and Opinion*, 5.
30. Cherry, *Theology of Jonathan Edwards*.
31. Carse, *Visibility of God*.
32. Delattre, *Beauty and Sensibility in Edwards*.
33. Jenson, *America's Theologian*.
34. More recent significant works deserving of mention include *The Philosophy of Jonathan Edwards: A Study in Divine Semiotics*—a book by S. Daniel that views Edwards from a "post-modern" perspective—and *Jonathan Edwards and the Bible*, a wonderful study by Robert E. Brown. We must also mention the introduction, appendices and the wealth of notes in vol. 8 of the Yale Edition by the late, lamented P. Ramsey and the

species of trees in it are quite varied, and its layout has no apparent organic homogeneity. Nonetheless, we think that this great vastness hides a latent, inner unity. In other words, as Thomas A. Schafer explained it, Edwards's body of work is indeed a system.[35] While it cannot claim the status of a Hegelian encyclopedia or a Scholastic *summa*, it is no less unified a project than the other great monuments of Western philosophic-religious speculation, a designation needed to underline both the claims and the limits of our intentionally systematic interpretation.

For Edwards, whom compatriots celebrate as one of the great figures of Protestant history, the role philosophy played was important for reasons other than those of the Reformers. Even if his Christian piety and dogmatic concerns determined the spirit and themes of his reflections, and Biblical references and reminiscences are omnipresent in his writings, the primitive make-up of his thought and the logic of his reflection had more in common with metaphysics than theology or, rather, he appeared to espouse an original, unified combination of theology and metaphysics. Although he professed irreproachable Calvinist orthodoxy and regularly dealt with the usual themes of Reformed dogmatics, the deep structures of his mind put Jonathan Edwards closer to Saint Augustine or Saint Thomas Aquinas than to Calvin or Barth. While *The Mind* is traditionally cited, with respect to Edwards, to support a claim of chronological priority for philosophy, a reading of his early Miscellanies nonetheless reveals a level of conceptual brilliance and depth in purely religious and theological texts that is in no way inferior to the originality and penetration of *The Mind*. Interpreters of Edwardsian thought often recall the apparent disappearance of philosophical concerns during the quarter century of his Northampton pastorate and then draw attention to the final, great concert of metaphysical treatises during his Stockbridge years. However, these conjectures cannot withstand even the most elementary overview of Edwardsian literary production. During his "pastoral period" at Northampton, the Miscellanies regularly returned to philosophical themes and it was in them that the teaching in the "majestic dissertations of the 1750s"[36] was developed and clarified. Conversely, at least one of these great works of maturity, namely *The Great Christian Doctrine of Original Sin Defended*, is purely theological in character.

It is scarcely possible to explain the deployment of Edwardsian thought using comments of a chronological nature because issues can become blurred, with theology and metaphysics sometimes being juxtaposed

---

"General Introduction to the Sermons," in vol. 10 by W. Kimnach.

35. Schafer, "Being in Edwards," 377.
36. Heimert and Miller, *Great Awakening*, xlii.

or, much more commonly, combined into one harmonious synthesis. Nonetheless, on the level where concepts and texts begin, we can speak of a certain priority that is not temporal but rather transcendental or metaphysical. From the outset, Jonathan Edwards struggled with the great themes of Protestant theology, such as self-will, justification by faith alone, election and reprobation, as well as the inspiration of the Scriptures, the role of the minister, and ecclesial discipline; and yet, right from the beginning, his formulations were developed on a metaphysical level. Of course, the designs and material teleology of this theology were dogmatic in nature, but its formal unity was metaphysical. Metaphysical illumination therefore offers the most opportunities to get a global vision of Edwards's work and understand the systematic unity of his thought. Although Edwards deploys dogmas from the Scriptures and reads quite exclusively from the Bible, his explanations follow a logical order that is metaphysical in nature. This philosophico-religious speculation is one in which a great apologist of the Christian faith used reason to develop the profound implications of dogmas. It was certainly not the "natural reason" so favored by his contemporaries, but rather the high rationality of metaphysics. That said, this emphasis on the originally metaphysical nature of Edwardsian reflection has its limits. Although conceptual construction played a preponderant role in his thought, it wasn't the only, exclusive way in which this great thinker expressed himself. The profound Biblicism of "this great religious light" of America is also demonstrated by a logic of images that mostly resist being reduced to metaphysical conceptuality. [37] Entire swaths of the Edwardsian corpus are difficult to subject to metaphysical illumination: scriptural notes and comments that are strangely literal, apocalyptic speculations that are often primitive, and especially its admirable typology. It was a previously unknown example of Christian symbolism where "the images and shadows of divine things," i.e., "types" of a scriptural or natural order mingle and complement one another to give our fallen understanding a spiritual *episteme sui generis* that defies all conceptual interpretation and integration.

However, as long as these limitations are taken into account and the autonomy of the "colorful" elements is respected, a metaphysical study of the foundations of Edwards's thought will lead to a genuine reconstruction of his dogmatic and spiritual theology and, in the final analysis, to a systematic exposition of the main conceptual themes of his work, which seems like an original reformulation of the great Augustinian dogmas or one of the great metaphysico-theological syntheses of Christian teaching. It came at a singular moment in history—when eighteenth-century Protestantism

---

37. Parton, *Life and Times of Burr*, 1:127.

found itself at the intersection of the Enlightenment and Pietism—although the phenomenon is important enough in itself to discourage explanations using literary sources, quite apart from the difficulties faced by the historical exegesis of a thinker who read few of his great predecessors and didn't quote his sources as a matter of principle. Everything in Edwards's work is too brilliantly original for us to ascribe much importance to textual influences, which can clarify points of detail but hardly make an essential contribution to a systematic interpretation. Historical connections certainly exist, but they are more transcendental than chronological in nature. Affinities, while noticeable, are portrayed in terms of conceptual relationships. Although the context for presenting and illustrating the deployment of Edwardsian ideas takes obvious historical considerations into account, it essentially focuses on the logic of thematic and conceptual affinities.

Edwards is first and foremost an active representative of Puritan Calvinism. Quotes from Calvin and other, mainly English-speaking, Calvinist writers, as well as from continental European dogmaticians, are scattered throughout this book.[38] Potential textual influences are not of concern. Irrespective of what Pascal thought of it, Calvinism sees itself as the continuation of Augustine[39] and, less explicitly and consciously but nonetheless in a real way, as heir to the medieval *summas* and disputations.[40] Edwards quoted Saint Augustine and, less frequently, Saint Thomas Aquinas, even though he likely never read them in the original. Moreover, though not personally a practitioner of Scholastic Protestantism, Edwards was immersed in its teaching and may have somewhat unknowingly assimilated the post-Cartesian rationalism from it that has marked Christian theologies ever since the middle of the seventeenth century. Because of this, Descartes, Malebranche, and Leibniz are quoted from time to time. Beyond a direct influence from Theophilus Gale,[41] there is a certain affinity with the religious approach and concerns of Jansenism; a Jansenist, after all, is just a Calvinist who says Mass![42] On a few rare occasions, we refer to the classics of Jan-

---

38. For the theological background and context of Edwardsian dogmatics, see Wilson, *Virtue Reformed*.

39. See "*Calvin* has no conformity with Saint *Augustine* and differs from him in every way from *start* to finish" (Pascal, "Writings on Grace," 225).

40. We should certainly reject the "absurdity of the . . . abstruse distinctions of the school divines [Scholastics]," but why "discard those that are clear and rational . . . ?" (19, 795).

41. See Gale, *Court of the Gentiles*. Edwards began citing this work in 1742–1743 (20, 222). For Gale in Fiering, *Moral Philosophy at Seventeenth Century Harvard*, 279–80.

42. Sainte-Beuve, *Port-Royal*, 2:953.

senism.[43] Lastly, we make some connections to Kant, who brought issues of Protestant theology to a conclusion and whose philosophy was inspired by the Reformation's logic of piety. However, we do not pretend, or make any hidden claim whatsoever, that these citations are the work of a historian or a study of the historical formation of Edwardsian thought. Our work is a reconstruction of the conceptual framework of Edwards's system, which basically amounts to following the metaphysical approach he took when developing his themes.

---

43. For a deeper understanding of the metaphysical implications of Edwardsian theology, it is very worthwhile to read Laporte, *La doctrine de Port-Royal*.

1

From Being to Grace

1. The three major spheres of the Edwardsian system

AN EARLY HISTORIAN OF American philosophy identified three distinct phases in the development of Edwardsian thought: idealism, Calvinism, and pantheism.¹ The first phase was represented by *The Mind*; the middle phase, by a mass of sermons and treatises of a theological and ecclesial nature; and the last phase, by *The End for Which God Created the World*. The inadequacy of this kind of categorization is apparent, even from a strictly chronological perspective, because Jonathan Edwards wrote texts during each of these literary production periods that covered the entire range of his intellectual interests. Moreover, does it make sense to juxtapose metaphysical doctrines with the positive theology of a particular Christian confession? Lastly, as we will shortly see below, Edwards was only an idealist in a very limited sense, while his supposed pantheism was more literary expression than a substantial formulation of a speculative position. On the other hand, he was a Calvinist in the most systematic and orthodox way, and it is only his Calvinism that allows his "idealism" and "pantheism" to be interpreted in such a productive way.

Chronologically dividing the work of a great thinker is always a risky endeavor. In Edwards's case, the essential continuity of his reflection cannot be overstated. Rather than attempting to divide Edwards's thought into sequential phases, it would be better to distinguish simultaneously co-existing realms of reflection. From a metaphysical perspective, the Edwardsian

1. Riley, *American Philosophy*, 127.

system had three main realms: *being, willing,* and *knowing.* The realm of being was concerned with the mutual relations between God and creature, the difference and identity of infinite being with finite being, and the question of the divine foundation of Creation. The foundation of knowing also falls within this realm. However, an unbroken passage from being to knowing is rendered impracticable by the will or, more specifically, by the fact that the created will is fallen right from the beginning. The second part of Edwards's metaphysical system therefore dealt with studying the fallen will and the various forms that its subjugation to evil assumes. Moreover, the effect of the fall is felt even within the realm of being, where it provides an opportunity, so to speak, to characterize creative goodness as redemptive grace. Knowing, the third realm of Edwards's thought, initially appears in a form or rather at a level determined by the Fall, functioning within the world of sin. It then assumes in its regenerate form, having attained an intuitive and complete grasp of reality, the primary beauty that constitutes the essence and brilliance of God and divine things.

2. Idealism

It's in this first realm of Edwards's reflection that we discern what can most properly be termed metaphysical questions, and it is also where we first encounter the philosophical speculation that earned Edwards the title of idealist, pantheist, or monist. Critics have tried to establish links between the young author of *The Mind* and Berkeley,[2] as well as Norris and Collins.[3] Other, very legitimate attempts have been made to situate Edwards within the grand Neo-Platonist tradition.[4] However, Edwards's idealism, monism, or rather his pantheism can only really be understood in light of the theological ends of his thinking. In fact, idealism and pantheism—especially insofar as *The Mind* is concerned—are only important or significant in terms of these theological ends. Sereno Dwight's publication of Edwards's earliest writings helped spread the legend concerning the precocious genius of this Yale student, who was supposed to have developed an idealist system at 16 years of age. There are two good reasons why this story is well and truly a legend. First, as Thomas Schafer's patient work has demonstrated, *The Mind* was written while Edwards was a pastor in New York and already

---

2. For the latest developments, see Anderson, "Introduction" in 6, 36, 102–1, 123, and Fiering, *Edwards's Moral Thought*, 39–40.

3. Morris, *Young Jonathan Edwards*; Stewart, *Progress of Metaphysical, Ethical and Political Philosophy*, 150.

4. See, for example, Whittemore, "Edwards and the Sixth Way," 68.

twenty years old. Second, and more importantly, his notes don't even outline a real philosophical system. There undoubtedly were a number of troubling similarities between the ideas of this "poor country Berkeley" and the actual Bishop of Cloyne.[5] But even if it could be proven that the Irish philosopher had a direct influence on this American student, Edwards's dazzling fragments cannot be compared to Berkeley's richly elaborate thought. Echoed in a few fleeting lines scattered within Edwards' immense corpus,[6] these notes amount at best to brilliant intuitions that would most likely not even have been noticed had they not come from the "greatest American theologian."[7] Of course, it was through his idealism that Edwards "deduced" the immortality of man and founded his typological theology. But these are only the implications or consequences of such thinking. In and of itself, his idealism didn't have any potential for conceptual development. While certainly profound and fascinating, this rough draft wasn't developed in a systematic, detailed way. Edwards returned to these notions from time to time in brief comparisons or allusions, yet he never explicitly integrated them into his mature reflection. Edwards's idealism remained, as it were, buried in the nurturing soil of his thought and only surfaced through adaptation or transformation.

Proper philosophical questions may indeed have influenced or even given rise to Edwardsian idealism. Nevertheless, it is no exaggeration to say that its true significance lies in the theological-religious domain.[8] If such is the case, then his basic intuition and deepest motives were not in fact epistemological. There are, of course, purely epistemological passages dealing with colors (6, 350) or the structure of bodies (6, 215), and these notions develop and define Edwards's theory regarding the essentially mental character of all real existence. Nonetheless, his conclusion is grounded on a more general principle: nothing can be without being known.[9] This principle—an elementary intuition of a young pastor—seemed to have all the clarity of a deep, existential truth: "How doth it grate upon the mind, to think that something should be from all eternity, and nothing all the while be conscious of it" (6, 203). This principle is also found in Miscellany pp, another text from the New York period written just prior to *The Mind*: "For how doth one's mind refuse to believe, that there should be being from all

---

5. Lowell, "Edwards in Western Massachusetts," 41.

6. See 6, 398; 13, 258, 327, 360, etc.

7. See *supra*, p. xviii.

8. For the theological origins and ends of Edwardsian idealism, see McClymond, *Encounters with God*, 34.

9. Anderson, "Introduction," 6, 75–7.

eternity without its being conscious to itself that it was" (13, 188). And then, on a more general level, Edwards formulated a question that sounded like a categorical judgment: "In what sense may those things be said to exist which are supposed, and yet are in no actual idea of any created minds?" (6, 356).

The deployment of this basic metaphysical principle leads to idealism, although this can only be understood by clarifying the metaphysical status of both material and spiritual beings. If nothing exists except insofar as it is known, then the existence of a (known) being depends upon the being that knows it. Such dependence can be explained comparatively: material things are like the shadows of spiritual things. The word "shadow" expresses a kind of negative evaluation of the consistency and subsistence of the thing in question, but also implies its participation in the being of which it is the shadow. In other words, though admittedly an imperfect reflection or representation of the original (15, 247), the shadow of a thing is nonetheless a reproduction of it, albeit in a particular way. This more "positive" vision of the state of material things lies at the heart of typological theology, which is founded on the premise of an analogical relation between the spiritual world and the exterior world (8, 564). To use the language of the Miscellanies, God "communicates... a shadow... of His excellencies to bodies" (13, 279) and, by this very fact, the world is given the ability and authority to represent and typify spiritual realities.[10] For Edwards, as for Berkeley before him, this vision leads to a sort of grammatical theology[11] in which nature is viewed as the language of God, because language is not only what is spoken or heard, but also includes signs (18, 427–8). At the same time, this vision of the material world is laden with an ambiguity that is even expressed by the title of Edwards's typological notes: *Images and Shadows of Divine Things*. Material things can be understood either as "images" of spiritual things or as their mere shadows. This notion is based upon a strict interpretation of the principle that "nothing can be without being known," i.e., a reading which rejects that material things have any authentic reality.

3. All existence is mental

If things only exist insofar as they are known, then they only exist "there," i.e., where they are known. As a result, they don't exist in and of themselves but only in terms of others outside of themselves. This amounts to saying that material things do not exist materially. Notwithstanding all the precautions that Edwards felt obliged to take in a domain where the highly

---

10. 8, 564; 11, 53, 69, etc.
11. Gueroult, *Berkeley*, 186.

abstract nature of speculation can easily trigger scorn (6, 353), he didn't hesitate to declare that bodies have no proper substance and, in spite of their hardness and solidity, "no matter is, in the most proper sense, matter" (6, 238). As we will see later, this conclusion was based on and supported by a physics theory in which bodily existence is identified with solidity and resistance, and—drawing on Newton—is one in which the resistance of bodies consists in the "immediate exercise of God's power" (6, 215). Speculation in physics and metaphysics is therefore converging towards direct proportionality between what is spiritual and what is substantial. It is a gross mistake of common thinking to perceive spirits as kinds of shadows. It is actually physical bodies which are the shadows of spirits, the only substantial realities in existence (6, 206). Although this idealist identification of substantiality with spirituality would not be fully developed prior to the arrival of the great post-Kantian systems, the intuition that "only that which is spiritual can be substantial" already dominated Edwards's ontology. In other words, the only proper and real beings are those that perceive (6, 343). For a metaphysical idealist, being and perceiving are ultimately synonymous, so that things that do not perceive, but are only perceived, can only be said to exist insofar as they belong to the mental universe of an intelligent being. Although already anticipated by Leibniz, this was a Berkeleyan theme and it was Berkeley who concisely defined it: "Nothing properly but persons i.e. conscious things do exist, all other things are not so much existences as manners of ye existence of persons."[12] The reflections of young Edwards led him to the same conclusion. Only our wild imagination prevents us from realizing that material things exist only to the extent that they are perceived by a conscious being (6, 204). In other words, "the material universe ... is absolutely dependent on the conception of the mind for its existence" (6, 368). Or again, as stated in a much later note, "real existence depends on knowledge or perception" (6, 398). If such is the case, we are forced to conclude that "all existence is mental" (6, 341) and that "the existence of all corporeal things is only ideas" (13, 327).

This vision of the world, in which the physical universe is emptied of all reality in order to transpose it into the spiritual domain, serves as a kind of metaphysical justification for Christian anthropomorphism. "Understanding and will are the highest kind of created existence" (8, 454), Edwards explains, and thus, "the intelligent part of the world ... is transcendently the most important" (23, 255).[13] We are now in a better position

---

12. Berkeley, *Philosophical Commentaries* 24, *Works*, 1:10.

13. See "the volitions of moral agents ... are the most important events of the universe, to which all others are subordinate" (1, 395).

to understand the assertion that man, who "was made in the image of God [and] placed here as God's vicegerent" (24, 478), is "the head and the end of the system" (23, 64),[14] and that, on a more general level, the moral world should be considered as the end for which the material world was created (1, 395). The "focal" situation of the thinking creature—the only means by which other creatures can exist (see 6, 206)—puts the thinking creature in a privileged relation with God. The end of Creation is the glorification of God, whose greatness material beings can neither comprehend nor communicate because they do not really even exist, being deaf and dumb. Like the eyes and mouth of Creation, human souls contemplate, celebrate, and praise God (25, 66) because their spiritual nature makes them the only suitable receptacles for communicating the excellence of God and His only true "images."

Elevating the intelligent creature's cosmic status is not exclusively positive because it can also call his metaphysical autarchy into question. Edwards repeatedly affirmed that spiritual beings are the only real beings and that their existence does not depend on "other minds" (6, 368). But are these created spirits truly independent if their "real" existence is situated beyond themselves, namely "in" God? In other words, is Edwardsian thought a true form of subjective idealism, or would it be better qualified as a metaphysics of the Absolute Spirit? Let's remember that the defining principle of such thinking is that "all existence is mental." If all existence is mental, things only truly exist within the conscious mind. The conscious mind is human, *ergo* human consciousness exists. At the same time, it is precisely this mental characteristic of all things that forces our thinking in this domain to go beyond finite, subjective idealism in order to arrive at what might be called the idealism of divine understanding. As previously stated, things only exist to the extent that they are perceived by a finite consciousness. But then, what exactly happens to things when that consciousness ceases to perceive them; and what were they before they were perceived by a finite consciousness? Can the mental existence of things be explained in terms of the conscious mind, which is itself a mental reality that is dependent on non-mental factors for its own existence? Edwards's response was that ideas (i.e., things), because of their strict interdependence and the prevailing "gravity" that draws them together (6, 377), practically constitute a system of inter-relating essences, even if there is no finite mind to effectively perceive them. In a supreme fiction for the Being of beings, God, who "supposes" that created beings exist, gives birth to and sets in

---

14. See Pauw, *Supreme Harmony of All*, 135. Note that, while at Stockbridge, Edwards had intended to write a "treatise on human nature" (10, 70).

motion the chain of ideas as if they had arisen from and were unfolding within created minds (6, 354). Strictly speaking, it is created minds that think of ideas of things, and yet, in practice—because of their dispersion in time and space—they cannot think *all the time* or even less think of *all the ideas*. Only God can bridge such discontinuities. In the final analysis, ideas that cannot be effectively thought of by finite minds are thought of by an infinite mind, that of God himself (see 6, 204). As Edwards writes in a later Miscellany (#94), "those things that are in no created consciousness have no existence but in the divine idea" (13, 258). At the same time, the "divine consciousness" (6, 204), God's understanding, should not be mistaken for a stand-in that fills the gaps or intervals between those moments when finite minds are working. If God's understanding contains all ideas that are not perceived by any finite minds, then it must also conceive of or contain them while they are being thought of by finite minds. In other words, just as there is a continuing physical creation, there is also a continuing mental creation (see 6, 204). However, if this is the case, then all of reality is nothing other than the thought of God. As Edwards put it in a well-known passage of *The Mind*, "That which truly is the substance of all bodies is the infinitely exact and precise and perfectly stable idea in God's mind" (6, 344). But if all material reality exists in God's mind, what is left for human consciousness, which only perceives the exterior world intermittently?

On a purely metaphysical level, a sort of nominalism with links to John Locke's empiricism forced Edwards to conclude that if a body is only a specific kind of perception, then the mind itself is nothing but a composition or series of perceptions (6, 398). In the final analysis, there doesn't appear to be any significant difference between what is only found in the understanding of God and what is supposed to exist independently of all other consciousness. Elsewhere, Edwards asserts that the mind is nothing without its properties (13, 273), but would it be something without its content? In other words, wherever the reality of its content is to be found, the reality of the consciousness itself is also to be found. Edwards certainly continued to affirm the distinction between the things perceived and the finite minds that perceived them and—except perhaps in an eschatological context—never expressly asserted that finite minds are contained within the Mind of God. Finite minds can only be considered truly void of reality to the extent that there is metaphysical continuity between God and souls because of their common spirituality. Confining the reality of material things entirely within God might even lead to the absolute monism that A. V. G. Allen claimed to find in Edwards's thought.[15] On the other hand, portraying the reality

---

15. Allen, *Jonathan Edwards*, 316.

of beings as the communication, radiation, or image of God leads towards an open-ended form of pantheism. Instead of concentrating and confining all things in God, God is expanded through the assertion of continuity between beings and Being.

4. The problem of Edwardsian pantheism

Jonathan Edwards was a Calvinist, and two aspects of the Calvinist doctrine of God—the absolute sovereignty of God and the universality of divine causation—could be understood to imply the negation of finite beings and their integration and dissolution into the Absolute.[16] And yet, even as God's absolute sovereignty spread its wide shadow over all his "perceptions," it was always metaphysically counterbalanced by Edwards's elementary intuition of absolute Being. The opuscule "Of Being"—said to contain the whole of Edwards's future system of thought[17]—begins with this sentence: "That there should absolutely be nothing at all is utterly impossible" (6, 202).[18] If Frederick Denison Maurice is to be believed, the notion of being was as sacred for Edwards as it was for Spinoza.[19] Edwards seems to have been obsessed and fascinated by the idea of the necessity of existence and the impossibility of nothingness. Even at the end of his life, he regarded it as an essential task for him to demonstrate "How existence in general is necessary" (6, 398). This intuition was clearly existential in nature, a fundamental axiom that the thinker sought to formulate through conceptual demonstration. The ontological proof he used for this was the impossibility of nonexistence, a notion derived from the logico-metaphysical "fact" that it is impossible for absolute Being to have an opposite. Nonexistence and nothingness were terms that could be applied to particular beings, but certainly not to "being, absolutely considered" (6, 207). Simply trying to think of nothingness "puts the mind into mere convulsion and confusion" (6, 207). The idea of nonexistence is contradictory to the nature of the soul and even thinking about nothingness in a particular place is perturbing (6, 202). As for the state of absolute nothingness, it is the aggregate of all the most absurd contradictions and is even an absolute contradiction itself. It is a state in which every proposition in Euclid is not true, in which all eternal truths are neither true nor false, and a state of which a complete idea can only be formed if we "think of

---

16. See Stephen, "Jonathan Edwards," 230.
17. Warfield, *Studies in Theology*, 519.
18. See 1, 182.
19. Maurice, *Moral and Metaphysical Philosophy*, 4:473.

the same thing that the sleeping rocks dream of" (6, 206).[20] The very fact that we think we can "imagine" nothing can only be explained by the "miserableness" of our understanding (13, 436). In reality, we cannot conceive of nothing, because being and nonexistence do not constitute a "disjunction." Nonexistence is not the true opposite of being because, in the final analysis, being does not have any opposite at all. All things that appear in mutually opposite pairs fall under the same category, but being, as the ultimate category, cannot be classified under any other heading and, strictly speaking, has no alternative or opposite.[21]

When first formulated, this "proof" only concerned being in general, but was applied to God in a text that appeared very shortly thereafter. The existence of God is necessary because there cannot be any alternative that would "make a disjunction" (18, 122). This logical proof starts from an absolute to show that there is nothing else besides it. However, right from the outset, this sort of descending or deductive reasoning has its complement in an ascending or inductive demonstration. In fact, from a chronological perspective, Edwards seems to have used induction before deduction. The inductive proof of pantheism—the divine omni-reality—is the metaphysico-physical counterpart of the metaphysico-epistemological intuition of idealism. Like Henry More and Isaac Newton, Edwards meditated upon the existence of bodies and came to the conclusion that he could reduce them to being nothing more than an exercise of God's omnipotence. Bodies are nothing more than solidity, and solidity is resistance. Resistance cannot be anything other than the exercise of an infinite power, because there is no secret, inaccessible substratum hidden somewhere in the distant depths of things. For if things had a "substratum," it would be their solidity, which is the "constant" and "immediate exercise of God's power" (6, 214–15).[22] This redefinition of corporeal reality in terms of the infinite power of God is reinforced by idealistic considerations. If corporeality is nothing but resistance, and if resistance itself is ultimately a function of mind, then once again we arrive at the conclusion that "the world is therefore an ideal one" (6, 351). Physical and epistemological speculations both seem to lead to pantheism. Whether portrayed as ideas or resistances, bodies only exist within the Divine Being and minds are at best its emanations. We are forced to conclude, in all "metaphysical strictness and propriety," that "the great

20. These arguments, in addition to those pertaining to the non-validity of Euclidean positions in nothingness, were perhaps inspired by Locke's *Essay Concerning Human Understanding* (4. 10. 3, 4, 8).

21. Anderson 6, 70–2.

22. On the role of gravity in Edwardsian thought, see Miller, *Jonathan Edwards*, 79–80.

original Spirit" exists, that "He is, as there is none else" (6, 364). This notion of the exclusivity of the Divine Being led to two types of declarations: those concerned with absolute being itself and those dealing with other beings, their status, and how they are derived from being in general. At age twenty, Edwards used inductive physical proof to show that the only true substance is God himself (6, 215). Some fifteen years later, he declared that God "must comprehend in Himself all being" (18, 281). At the end of his life, in his so-called pantheistic phase, he took up this theme again, adding nuance to the claim that "God is as it were the only substance" (6, 398). Everything real exists immediately within the first being (6, 238) and "God and real existence are the same" (6, 345). Such radical declarations made it tempting to reinterpret other statements regarding the Divine Being's relationship with his creatures: God, the Being of beings (8, 550), "depends on nothing but Himself" (8, 450). He is incessantly making us, but it is "in Him that we live, move and have our being" (6, 216). Expressed in the erudite terminology of speculative theology, this "effulgence or communication [of God's glory] is the fullness of all intelligent creatures, who have no fullness of their own" (8, 521, n.3).

The life-giving continuity linking the Creator to his creatures allowed Edwards to formulate the co-essentiality between God and creature in both negative and positive terms. In the former, co-essentiality is affirmed at the expense of the creature's autarchy; in the latter, through an emphatic celebration of the creature's participation in God. In developing this positive approach, Edwards took the surprisingly bold step of presenting the distinction between God and intelligent creatures in purely quantitative terms (13, 295). Edwards explained elsewhere that, because our knowledge is an image of God's knowledge, the two are not really so different (13, 257). We read in the Miscellanies that finite minds are simply communications of God and, as such, add nothing new (18, 282). Their mental operations, and consequently the very exercise of their existence, are to be perceived as rays of light sent out from the Sun itself (8, 441). Like the planets orbiting the Sun, human minds also have a certain degree of autonomy, although Edwards would probably agree with the great American Calvinist poet, Edward Taylor, who said, "Life from thy Fingers ends runs, and ore spred Itselfe through all thy Works."[23] Whether situated literally within the understanding of God or understood as rays emanating from Him, spiritual and material beings are both comprehended in the fullness of God.

The preceding statements—and many others that could easily have been added to the list—appear to justify a pantheistic interpretation of

---

23. Taylor, *Poems*, 107.

Edwardsian thought.[24] However, a closer reading of such language—one that gives greater consideration to the various contexts in which it occurs—reveals that it is not as significant as we might initially assume. From a metaphysical standpoint, Edwards was part of a neo-Platonist tradition which had nourished Christian philosophy and theology through the ages and come down to him in diluted form. He quoted leading Platonists from the work of T. Gale. Plato, he wrote, considered the "great object" of his philosophy to be divinity, conceived of as "Being itself." As for Jamblique, he taught that only spiritual beings exist and that Plato himself "proved that nothing properly is, but God." Lastly, he linked a Delphic inscription to Plato's *to on* and concluded that *You are*—understood to mean "the true being"—was the most appropriate epithet and the most perfect title that could be attributed to God. Edwards quoted these passages from pagan philosophers as part of a commentary on a famous verse from the book of Exodus, because the real Being of whom Plato spoke is the same One who revealed Himself to Moses using the name "I AM THAT I AM." (15, 418)[25] This parallel between the God of Moses and the Being of the ancient philosophers, which incidentally is a very traditional one, sheds light on the real meaning and applicability of Edwardsian expressions, which are more in line with the venerable biblical tradition of divine sovereignty than with any kind of pantheism along the lines of what Spinoza had proposed.

---

24. It was always thought that Edwards's pantheism could be proved by studying the terminology of his texts. Sometimes the difference between God and others appeared to be only a matter of degree (13, 295). God is designated "an all-comprehensive being" (18, 281), and elsewhere the young preacher exclaims with joy that "here are the beauties and glories of Jehovah Himself in this lily" (10, 613). The expression, "partakers of the divine nature" (2 Peter 1:4) is frequently quoted by Edwards (8, 132; 21, 122; etc.) and according to a Northampton "conference," when Christ gathers "all things in God" together in heaven, it will bring "the actual union between God and man to a final completion" (*Bl.*, 323). But such linguistic ambiguities can be easily clarified. In the language of the *Treatise Concerning Religious Affections*, God can "communicate ... His own nature" to men, yet "nature" does not signify "essence" but rather an attribute or a quality (8, 638). The saints have not been "godded," but "merely" receive the spiritual beauty of God (2, 203)! To be sure, Edwards uses distinctly ontological terminology to describe God, especially at the very beginning and end of his career, but the context in which he uses such terms remains resolutely theistic, not pantheistic. "Being in general" is synonymous with "Creator" (8, 461–2); the "Deity" is "the prime ... of all beings" (6, 355); the "great Being" of the fragment on Sarah Pierrepont is the One who "made and rules the world" (16, 789). All this was practically foreshadowed by his first sermon, in which Edwards expresses "The pleasures of loving and obeying, loving and adoring, blessing and praising the Infinite Being, the Best of Beings, the Eternal Jehovah" (10, 305).

25. Here Edwards is using biblical language (8, 632n.3). Elsewhere, the formulation from Exodus signifies the perfect self-sufficiency and faithfulness of God (9, 525; 4, 337).

There were basically three ways in which Edwards came to the conclusion that God exists. First, from an epistemologico-metaphysical point of view, all ideas are to be found in God; second, from a physical perspective, all corporeality is reduced to an immediate exercise of God's power; and third, from a logico-metaphysical standpoint, it is impossible to imagine any disjunction that would lead to actual non-existence. The first two lines of thinking culminate in New Testament-based affirmations, and one of the most basic formulations of the third is also expressed in biblical terms.

In the fifteenth section of *The Mind*, where Edwards declares that "God and real existence are the same," he identifies all truth and all existence with God's ideas, concluding in a corollary "how properly it may be said that God is, and that there is none else, and how proper are these names of the Deity: 'Jehovah' and 'I Am That I Am' " (6, 345). In a series of observations on *Natural Philosophy*, Edwards sums up the results of his thinking on physical matter. Since bodies have no substance apart from their solidity, and since this solidity is not really their own, they must be considered as void of all reality. Hence, God is "*ens entium*," the Being of beings, and "it may be said, in a stricter sense than hitherto, 'Thou art and there is none else besides Thee'" (6, 238). In the end, this biblical expression is nothing less than one of the most ancient formulations of the impossibility of non-existence. Edwards wrote that God is a necessary being because it is a contradiction to suppose that He could not be. Absolute non-existence is the very essence of all contradictions, whereas "being includes in it all that we call God, who *is*, and there is none else besides Him" (13, 213).[26]

Rather than interpreting Edwards's statements in a superficial, literal way in order to prove that he was a pantheist, it would be better to understand them as a rhetorical expression of *analogia entis*, that great metaphysical *analogy of being*, in the sense that it conveys the deep religious intuition of the essential indigence of all creatures. In fact, the young writer was overwhelmed with a desire to humble himself before God: "My heart as it were panted after this, to lie low before GOD, and in the dust; that I might be nothing, and that God might be all; that I might become as a little child" (16, 796). And if a creature could be exalted in some way, it should only be in and through Jesus Christ, not at all in itself, so that "its absolute infinite dependence on the Creator" (18, 242) should never be forgotten. Much later, in *The End for Which God Created the World*—a major treatise that earned him the reputation of a pantheist—Edwards used the imagery of a king and his subjects in a significant exposition of the theme of God and

---

26. In its definitive formulations, the concept of disjunction includes no biblical references. God must exist "because there is nothing else supposable . . . There is no other way" (18, 122).

His creatures. He makes a clear distinction between the Supreme Being and creation, declaring that "the whole system of created beings in comparison of the Creator would be found as the light dust of the balance (which is taken no notice of by Him that weighs) and as nothing and vanity" (8, 424). Again, the creature's lack of proper reality can be interpreted in both negative and positive terms, although this time we will clearly see that we are dealing with metaphors from the comparative world of rhetoric and not, strictly speaking, ontological notions. Expressed negatively, the creature's lack of reality is less of a pure void than a "precarious, fluctuating, unstable" condition that does not deserve the designation of "being," a word with great significance. It is the "vanity" that profound scriptural references clearly associate with the influence of sin and its consequences. It is therefore not a coincidence that this rhetoric of divine exclusivity reappears in the context of an exposition on the misery of the damned. The damned see the greatness of God and nothing can help them to endure the apprehension of his wrath: he will appear at that time as "immensely the greatest being," and even as "the comprehension of all being" (13, 349). The damned, living in the intensely tortuous presence of one another, will not arrive at the strictly metaphysical conclusion of the exclusivity of God; only their terror before the extent of his wrath will open their eyes to the fact that this greatest of beings encompasses all being. Now turning to the "positive" interpretation of the creature's lack of reality as compared to the Most High, it must be kept in mind that Edwards did not seek self-annihilation, but only to become like "a little child." The basic intuition of his pantheistic statements is not a vision of peaceful continuity between God and creature, but that of a radical difference expressed through the terror of the damned or the trusting nature of little children. In Edwards's thought, as Thomas Schafer rightly put it, it is the infinite gap between God and others that causes God to appear as the only being.[27]

5. The immediacy of divine action

Even in what seemed to be his most idealist or pantheistic endeavors, Edwards constantly resorted to biblical quotations and not just as a form of literary expression. While Edwards seems to profess his belief in the continuity between God and creation, this continuity is paradoxically the result of an extreme difference. It is precisely because the creature is nothing and vanity in itself that it appears invisible in the presence of God and in uninterrupted continuity with Him. The radical preponderance of the Creator in

27. Schafer, "Being in Edwards," 139–40.

relation to the creature should not be understood in terms of a pantheistic ontology, but rather that of a Bible-based theology. It is not a matter of an impersonal Absolute which subsumes and contains all, but rather of a God who creates and dominates finite creatures. The sovereignty of the God of the Scriptures is the hidden force behind Edwards's pantheistic statements and what has to be sought out are the conceptual structures he used to reformulate and integrate this doctrine into his metaphysics.

The radical indigence of the creature does not imply its total absorption *into* this infinite Being, but rather its dependence *on* this Being. God creates beings and also maintains them in existence through the continuation or incessant renewal of that same operation. This sovereignty leads to an understanding of God as "that almighty Being, who made and rules the world" (16, 789), which is to say that sovereignty implies both creation and its conservation through incessant repetition. Sovereignty implies that nothing can come between the Great Being and his creation, not even creation itself as something already constituted. God acts immediately, i.e., directly and without any intermediary. Beginning with this concept, the vast perspectives of Edwards's system unfold and, despite their radical difference, they reveal how the worlds of creation and redemption, the works of nature and grace are subsumed under this great, overarching principle of the immediacy of God's existentializing action. More precisely, divine action in the two realms of nature and grace also occurs without any real intermediary, though its immediacy is of a more radical nature in its gracious operations. Despite natural man's innate tendency to push God out of the world or to put him out of sight as far as he can, the need for God's immediate influence on the beings of our universe is as rational as it is scriptural. God created the world immediately and out of nothing. All things owe their very being to the immediate, free and voluntary action of the Almighty. Although God appears to exercise dominion over material things through a network of secondary causes that he himself instituted, his sovereignty over intelligent beings—those who are most similar and dear to Him—operates in a radically immediate manner (see 21, 275). This immediacy is especially evident in the realm of religion and morality, the privileged sphere of action for that spiritual creature called man.

Edwards espoused the Calvinist doctrine which affirms that "grace... is immediate... [and] not gradually" acquired (W 2, 552), but rather, "in the twinkling of an eye,"[28] i.e., that it is communicated immediately. It is therefore only logical to carefully avoid any naturalization of grace or attempt to hypostatize it into a permanent state (21, 196–7). Grace is an absolutely new

---

28. Stoddard, *Treatise Concerning Conversion*, A 2 recto.

entity and, to remain so, must act in its entirety at all times. It was Emmons who later explained in great detail that there is no immanent link between "successive exercises of grace."[29] This basic intuition of divine sovereignty over all of man's spiritual actions—which portrays the free nature of grace in the total absence of any permanent human causality—can already be found in Edwards's early writing: "if it were not for His mere grace, one might be a very good man one day, and a very wicked one the next" (16, 760). This is the pious Protestant formulation of an absolutely fundamental component of religious consciousness, namely our radical dependence on God. French philosopher Simone Weil would later say that we cannot "stock up" on grace and Edwards emphasized in one of his sermons that we "stand in need of daily supplies from God" (VII, 446). The attitude we adopt therefore has to be that of "an humble, daily and continual dependence on God" (4, 467), because just as "grace is at first from God, so 'tis continually from him, and is maintained by him, as much as light in the atmosphere is all day long from the sun, as well as at first dawning, or at sunrising" (17, 206).

Developed under the influence of the Augustinian-Calvinist doctrine of the radical sovereignty of gracious exercises, the metaphysical foundation for Edwards's teaching on the immediacy of divine action was based on the idea that the natural order of causes depends on God to freely and unceasingly sustain it (see 6, 359). This does not mean that anything can derive from anything else, nor that anything can be connected to anything else, but rather that the actual fact and effective reality of the mutual relationships between things depends on the sovereign will of God. While we might well find reasons immanent to ideas, and consequently to physical things, to explain how they could or should be as they are and not otherwise, they are only as they are because God continues to uphold them at every moment. Edwards, a fervent reader of the venerable Sir Isaac Newton, wrote in an early sermon of his Northampton pastorate, "Nothing except God Himself is more constant and unchangeable than the course and laws of nature," (17, 311) and even drew a parallel between the "laws of nature and the laws of Christ" (12, 570). Nevertheless, even this deferential recognition of nature's power and regularity should not be taken in a deistic sense, in

---

29. See "gracious exercices are not necessarily and inseparably connected with each other, and, of consequence, they may at any time be interrupted by totally sinful affections. They have no permanent source or fountain of holiness within themselves, from which a constant stream of holy affections will necessarily flow. As one holy affection will not produce another, so they are immediately dependent upon God for every holy affection. The moment he withdraws his gracious influence, their gracious exercises cease, and sinful exercises instantly succeed. And in this case, they are no more able to renew the train of holy affections, than they were to begin it at first" (Emmons, *The True Character of Good Men Delineated, Works*, 5:213). See also 21, 196.

contrast to Pascal's critique of Descartes for asserting that God ceased to intervene after He had initially established order in the universe. The God that Edwards worships is no *Deus otiosus* (idle god) and his high esteem for nature is based on the assumption that it is under the direct control of God. Edwards remains faithful to the Augustinian tradition in which God's will is understood as "the 'nature' of . . . nature"[30] and for him the natural order was, to quote Milton, "the mysterious power and efficacy of that divine voice which went forth in the beginning, and to which, as to a perpetual command, all things have since paid obedience."[31] Edwards would also agree with Berkeley's affirmation about "Nature" being for him nothing "but the Ordinance of the free Will of God."[32] Indeed, it was Samuel Hopkins who perhaps best expressed the thought of his Master when he wrote that, in nature, we must see only "the immediate exertion of divine power, which is the proper efficient cause of every event."[33]

Edwards first formulated his doctrine of immediate divine causality in nature while reflecting on physics. "The laws of nature" are but "the stated methods of God's acting with respect to bodies" because, as we know, the very substance of bodies is nothing more than "the immediate exercise of God's power." Only the immediate application of God's power can keep "two atoms being together." In fact, all the solidity and resistance that constitutes corporeality results from this immediate exercise.[34] Edwards later explained that the solidity-resistance relation is identical to gravity; and gravity, which is "universally admitted," depends on God's immediate influence. If it were possible for gravity to be withdrawn from the world, the entire world would simply disappear and vanish into nothingness. Thus, it is not only the manner in which things are, i.e., their established order, that depends on divine influence, but even their very being itself (6, 234–5). All of creation, as well as its preservation, is sustained by the immediate activity of God. It is in this dynamic sense that the statement quoted above needs to be understood: "all that is real, it is immediately in the first being" (6, 238).[35] The influ-

---

30. Saint Augustine, *City of God*, 21. 8.

31. Milton, *On Christian Doctrine*, 1. 8.

32. Berkeley, *Philosophical Commentaries* 794, *Works*, 1:95.

33. Hopkins, *System of Doctrines*, *Works*, 1:244. See also "All creatures are dead ciphers . . . they are as Pictures and Idols, that can let out no Efficacy, except he acts upon them." (Willard, *Compleat Body of Divinity*, 105).

34. See 6, 214–6. According to C. Faust, Edwards's physics is nothing more than an application of the Calvinist doctrine of the immediate sovereignty of God to the world of atoms ("Science in the Interest of Religion," in Opie, *Edwards and the Enlightenment*, 46).

35. The need for divine causality is not only applicable to the domain of efficient

ence of God's infinite presence is a reality at the very moment that a being is constituted and likewise in every succeeding moment. Although being and perseverance in being are philosophically the same thing (6, 211), the first immediate exercise of divine power that brings forth a body is what we commonly call creation (6, 215). Every moment that follows is but a reflection of that same exercise, "according to certain fixed and exact established methods and laws" (6, 344). All of which led the young Edwards to conclude that "what divines used to say concerning divine concourse had a great deal of truth lay at the bottom of it" (6, 216).

Jonathan Edwards arrived at the doctrine of continuous creation through speculation on the physical world, although he greatly expanded it at a very broad metaphysical level. As Samuel Willard put it, the basic religious intuition is that "the whole world is a sucking infant depending on the breasts of divine providence."[36] But before it could be verified and confirmed in systematic theology, this intuition had to be grounded in the crucible of metaphysics. If the world resembles a child nursing at its mother's breast, it is simply because everything relies on the life-giving activity of God. Things are not maintained in existence by any principle immanent in creation, but freely by the transcendent work of a sovereign God, which is why "all union and all created identity is arbitrary" (6, 398). Union and identity are arbitrary because they are rooted more in the great Being than in finite substances. Because finite substances are constantly coming into being, they cannot be considered to exhibit any ontological permanence whatsoever. This is why Edwards wrote that "'Tis certain with me that the world exists anew every moment, that the existence of things every moment ceases and is every moment renewed" (13, 288). Every finite being "is created out of nothing every moment; and if it were not for our imaginations, which hinder us, we might see that wonderful work performed continually, which was seen by the morning stars when they sang together" (6, 241). As with all major theologians, Edwards's nominalism stemmed from a radical doctrine of God's sovereignty in which the existence of finite beings was only conceivable in terms of an immediate and arbitrary constitution. Moreover, "immediate" and "arbitrary" are ultimately synonymous (23, 208), because both terms indicate a situation in which God relates to the creature without the intervention of any third reality. God's will is arbitrary in the sense that it is free and sovereign, i.e., it does not need to take any exterior circumstances whatsoever into account. God's actions are immediate in the sense that they

---

causality, but also to that of final causality. Matter is not only void of being, but also of form and order, for such order must be established by God (18, 392–3). See also 20, 333–5.

36. Lowrie, *Shape of the Puritan Mind*, 71.

apply directly to the creature without involving any intermediary reality. Immediate constitution not only applies to bodies but also to spirits. Furthermore, it not only accounts for the unity and identity of our conscience, but also for the unity and identity of our religious and moral character.

6. Dependent identity

Locke taught that identity is only an "impression" of the mind.[37] Hume and then Kant—each in his own way—subjected this assertion to a radical critique, yet both located identity entirely within the sphere of the mind in order to demonstrate that it doesn't come from the outside, i.e., doesn't correspond to anything in the objective world. Edwards also rejected any realist conception of identity, although he did so in order to anchor all identities—more specifically, those of free, intelligent creatures—in the sovereign will of God.

Edwards first stated the essential points of this doctrine in *The Mind* and his early Miscellanies, although it was only in his last major work, *The Great Christian Doctrine of Original Sin Defended*, that he formulated it in a clear and systematic way. The essence or philosophical core of this work, which is primarily an exegesis of Scripture, is the rejection of any efficient causal relation between physical things. This position leads Edwards to ascribe the appearance of new things, or even more importantly, every moment in the continuing existence of any thing, to the immediate influence of God. The present existence of the body we call the moon, he explained, cannot be an effect of its antecedent existence because "no cause can produce effects in a *time* and *place* in which itself is *not*. . . . But the moon's past existence was neither *where* nor *when* its present existence is. . . . The past moment is ceased and gone, when the present moment takes place; and does no more coexist with it, than does any other moment that had ceased twenty years ago" (3, 400). The same argument holds for any attempt to explain the cause-effect relation spatially: even the closest temporal and spatial contiguity between two different states or elements of the same thing cannot be interpreted as a veritable efficient cause. Rejecting the legitimacy of any autonomous causality in the domain of what is traditionally known as "secondary causes" led Edwards to emphasize the radical newness of every successive moment of the same substance. Moonlight may well seem permanent—like something that is always there—when, in fact, it is only reflecting the light rays emanating from the sun. Because these rays are individually different, each of the sensorial impressions they produce within

---

37. Locke, *Essay*, 1. 4. 4.

us is a new effect. Numerically speaking, the luminosity of the moon now is just as discontinuous with what existed a moment ago as "the sound of the wind that blows now, is individually the same with the sound of the wind that blew just before" (3, 402, n.5). Likewise, the images we see in a mirror appear to stay the same, yet "philosophers" know very well that they are constantly being renewed by the impact and reflection of new rays of light. This constantly regenerated image has no more numerical identity than "if it were by some artist put on anew with a pencil, and the colors constantly vanishing as fast as put on" (3, 402, n.5). The fact that they are instantaneously renewed does not make them any more identical than if the same phenomenon occurred at intervals of one hour or even an entire day. The current image cannot be derived from the one that preceded it because, if something placed between the object and the mirror blocks the stream of light rays, the image immediately disappears and is no longer reflected in the mirror. The image's past existence has no capacity to influence or preserve itself for even one second, and therefore only continues to exist because it is being renewed at every moment. Like the image in the mirror, the continuing existence of any finite being does not depend on anything immanent or on its own efficiency. A majestic tree is considered one and the same with the little sprout from which it came; and yet they might not possess a single atom in common (3, 397). Union and identity of finite substances are, so to speak, nothing but an immense fiction, "the *arbitrary* constitution of the Creator; who ... *treats them as one*," (3, 403) even though they really are not.

Creation is not self-perpetuating. Its continuance—this "present, remaining act" (13, 418)—resides not in itself but in "this great ... Being, who made and rules the world" (16, 789). The identity of the world is entirely dependent on the "pleasure and sovereign constitution" of Almighty God (3, 400). In a manner perfectly in keeping with the thought of David Hume, Edwards, a Calvinist theologian, rejects any belief in the objective continuity of worldly phenomena. "All dependent existence whatsoever is in a constant flux, ever passing and returning; renewed every moment, as the colors of bodies are every moment renewed by the light that shines upon them." This "indigence" or need, so to speak, obliges finite creatures to constantly look to God for their continuing existence. Here then is why we join with the Apostle Paul in affirming that "In Him we live and move and have our being" (3, 404).

Edwards rounds out his doctrine of the creature's entirely dependent identity with a reflection on the immediate, arbitrary act of God's constitution of Adam's union with his posterity through sin. This line of thought was first expressed in Miscellany 18, entitled "Adam's Sin." Edwards posits that "remembrance, consciousness, love, likeness" (13, 210) do not owe their being, i.e., their continuity, to anything immanent in themselves, but only to conditions established by the sovereign God. Edwards, as we recall, was certain that the world is being renewed at every moment, an intuition first formulated in the same Miscellany: "For we are not the same we were in times past, any other way than only as we please to call ourselves the same. For we are anew created every moment" (13, 210). Edwards developed this metaphysical notion of an entirely dependent identity from the *theologoumena* of the constituted, arbitrary identity of Adam and his descendants, for if "all creatures and all the operations of the universe are only the immediate influence of God" (13, 326), then the immediacy of divine action is most fully revealed in the sphere of spiritual communication. The Great Being who created the world literally created it *ex nihilo* in what was "the only divine operation that [is] absolutely arbitrary" (23, 204). In organizing the natural world, however, his sovereignty is asserted through laws that govern phenomena. Though instituted by God himself, these laws allow him to dispense with constant personal intervention in that domain.

At the same time, the higher we ascend the ladder of creation, the clearer we see the "more immediate hand" of God in it (6, 265). The human realm is where divine action is the least tied to any particular, permanent law (13, 327). Because intelligent creatures are at the summit of creation and therefore closest to God, it is fitting, in God's relations with intelligent beings, that divine action—itself one and simple—to be communicated in the least fragmented form possible (23, 206). The creation of the material world *ex nihilo* was, of course, an immediate operation but, following this initial intervention, the Creator's arbitrary action is covered by natural laws, right up to the moment when the first man appears. Here again we have a new, immediate act of creation—the souls of Adam and Eve—an intervention God repeats in the creation of each new soul and also at each man's moment of death, "in disposing of that soul that He infused in his birth" (23, 209).[38] With material beings, the Creator maintains a multiplicity of laws as a screen between himself and his handiwork, yet intervenes directly at least twice in the existence of each creature made in his own image. Immediate divine intervention is first about bringing the intelligent creature's soul into being and then about his final destiny beyond the grave. In the first case, life also brings with it the possibility of a spiritual existence; in the second, it is purely a matter of spiritual history. As we shall see below, immediate influence is particularly prevalent in the realm of spiritual operations. Since nothing is more spiritual than God's grace, it can only be communicated

---

38. Immediate creation also occurred "with respect to the greater part of the body of Eve" (23, 209).

immediately (21, 165). Before the fall, grace indwelt man by virtue of a constant law and, simply by persevering, a man could have improved and perfected himself, and grown in grace. Now, even perseverance is no longer possible, except "by the spirit of grace" in an "arbitrary and sovereign way" (18, 278).[39] Justification by faith, that grand scheme by which redemptive grace saves the sinner, is an immediate operation, having no dependence whatsoever on either exterior or interior "means" (18, 87).[40]

According to the Edwardsian system of thought, there is a direct, quasi-proportional relationship between the immediacy of divine action and the spiritual character of those beings who are its objects.[41] Philosophical idealism and the biblical doctrine of God's absolute sovereignty converge. The only real beings are spiritual ones (3, 279) and therefore—*stricto sensu*—only they can be objects of divine action, which is the creation/production of being out of chaos. But the true order conferred is always the encompassing and "informing" of a being's multiplicity by unity. This "information" is the same thing as the omnipresence of the center within a particular being, an indication of spirituality. Spirituality is therefore synonymous with unity, which is why truly immediate action can only result in the creation of beings who are one, i.e., simple, and identical. If these beings were not truly one and identical, God would not have fully created them and His action would therefore have remained imperfect. Conversely, the creation of a being who is one and identical requires an undivided action. Given the mutual implications of the immediacy of divine action, and the one and identical state of its true object (the spiritual creature), constituting the identity of man—the only spiritual being recognized in philosophy—must play a paradigmatic role in any study of dependent identities.

Edwards develops man's personal identity through reasoning on several different levels. As a distant heir of the Cartesian tradition, Jonathan Edwards was firmly convinced that the union of body and soul is due solely to its "arbitrary" institution by God (see 21, 210). Nothing in the nature of these two substances explains the correspondence between their respective moments of occurrence or the relations between a perception and a movement. The "vital communication" between these two parts of the human composite can therefore only be founded on and maintained by the

---

39. "[I]f God should take away His Spirit out of the soul, all habits and acts of grace would of themselves cease as immediately as light ceases in a room when a candle is carried out" (21, 196). In fact, since the Fall, man depends more immediately on God (VI, 442).

40. See also 18, 157.

41. See "the prophecies represent the Messiah as suffering from the immediate hand of God" (11, 311).

exertion of "immediate divine efficacy" (13, 394).⁴² Beyond what might be called the horizontal identity between the body and the mind, there is the vertical identity of the conscience itself. Edwards addresses the latter in his development on the doctrine of original sin, beginning with the arbitrary divine constitution of the first man's union with his posterity. The whole philosophical problem of identity and unity, which stems from theological considerations, illustrates the essential conjunction between the immediacy of divine action and the spiritual character of its object. The very notion of dependent identity in Edwards's thought arises from the question of personal identity, which can only then be understood in terms of the sin identity shared by Adam and his posterity.⁴³ In other words, the metaphysical doctrine of dependent identity is but a reflection on man's identity as a spiritual being. This spiritual identity is expressed, so to speak, through spiritual considerations of a second order, namely moral considerations.

7. Sovereignty and covenants

The convergence of philosophical idealism with the Calvinist doctrine of divine sovereignty led Edwards to construct a metaphysics in which all created identity depends on continuous creation for its very being. The supreme example of dependent identity is that of a human being for whom personal identity only takes shape and actually becomes real through the union in sin that each of us shares with Adam, a union that Edwards the theologian believed was established by a deliberate and positive act of God.⁴⁴ In other words, the most significant manifestation of immediate divine action is not the spiritual realm itself, but rather that realm as seen from a moral perspective. Moreover, the fact that the cosmic outworking of immediate divine action takes place in a moral context sheds new light on God's sovereignty.

God's unlimited sovereignty is, of course, a leitmotiv of Calvinist preaching. While this sovereignty is undoubtedly radical, is it *nuda potestas* (raw power) or can it be reconciled with order and goodness? Some claim that Calvinism necessarily leads to pantheism. To counter any such accusation, it might be tempting to take refuge in the notion of an unlimited will

---

42. See also 3, 398; 21, 176; etc.

43. See *infra*, p. 76ss.

44. "For the corruption of all mankind in the person of Adam alone did not proceed from generation but from the ordinance of God." (Calvin, *Commentary on John 1-10*, 66). See "It was the divine constitution, and not any divine law or covenant, that connected the moral character of Adam with the moral character of his posterity." (Emmons, *The Law of Paradise, Works*, 4:468).

whose very irrationality and absolute disinterestedness preclude the possibility of melting into the diffuse placidity of an omnipresent Absolute or dissolving into the homogeneity of a veritable univocity with its own creatures. But would God's unlimited arbitrariness or irrationality suffice to ensure his transcendence? Would it not be better to find a formulation of divine sovereignty that implied intelligibility and order? Could we not try to understand divinity in terms of a harmonious synthesis of goodness and power?

Although the origin of Edwards's notion of dependent identity is to be found in his teaching on the union in sin that binds Adam to each one of us, his brilliantly expressed vision of sovereignty emerged especially from the Augustinian-Calvinist doctrine of predestination. Speculative theologians try to develop this notion in terms of omnipotence, but its origin is really found in considerations regarding election and reprobation. Although the *potestas* (power) of God might seem like a philosophical notion, it is nevertheless a metaphysical translation or sketch of God's good pleasure as expressed in predestination. For Edwards, the original object of his critique was the "doctrine of God's sovereignty, in choosing whom He would to eternal life, and rejecting whom He pleased" (16, 792). While Edwards enumerated in detail the domains in which divine sovereignty operates more or less fully, i.e., more or less immediately, and reminded his readers that the *creatio ex nihilo* (see 21, 159–60) is the original manifestation of this arbitrary sovereignty, we nevertheless find—at the core of his thinking—the image of a "potentate" (8, 451), the long shadow of "the mere arbitrary will, and uncovenanted unobliged forbearance of an incensed God" who sinners apprehend with terror (22, 409). It was this vision of God's unlimited sovereignty in predestination that led the theologian to explore God's sovereignty in creation and preservation. Beginning with disquieting meditations on predestination, he sought to conceptualize the relations prevailing between what is immediate and what is arbitrary, the intelligible order and the display of God's power through his actions. Edwards's reflections on this problem touched upon God's relation to events or essences. The former dealt with divine governance over the world; the latter, with the relation of truth to the will of God.

The discussion surrounding the link between God and eternal truths is a key element of Cartesian and post-Cartesian metaphysics. Descartes, as we know, did not hesitate to declare God the master of truth, whereas for Berkeley, the *aeternae veritates* (eternal truths) simply "vanish."[45] In one way or another, what we have here are nominalist, Ockhamistic positions that we might expect to encounter in Calvinist theology, but reality turns out to be

---

45. Berkeley, *Philosophical Commentaries 735*, Works, 1:90.

quite different. The Reformed position on this issue was determined by Calvin himself who, while clearly affirming the unlimited sovereignty of God, had such a radically acute view of God's divine perfection that he could not admit the possibility that God might effectively deviate from goodness and order. Speaking of God, Calvin wrote: "sed quia certissima iustitiae regula est eius voluntas [but because His will is the most certain rule of perfect equity],"[46] yet rejecting "that absolute will, indeed, of which sophists prate, when by a profane and impious divorce, they separate his justice from his power."[47] "There is no use," he wrote, "in absurdly disputing concerning the power of God in opposition to his truth,"[48] for "we do not imagine God to be lawless" but "a law unto himself."[49] In fact, all the most prominent Reformed theologians reiterate the idea that although God is not subject or tied to any norm whatsoever—either without or within Himself—He nevertheless constitutes the norm of all truth and is the crux of all meaning.[50]

Now as for God and events, the connection between them takes two forms: first, the relation between the Great Being and nature, and second, his relation to intelligent creatures. As far as the creation and preservation of nature was concerned, Calvinism assimilated what had already been established by medieval philosophers, namely, the notion of a permanent natural order established by God. Because of this, Calvinists would have little difficulty reconciling the "Natural philosophy" of the modern age with Newtonian thought. The Puritans were undoubtedly more inclined to point out God's immediate manifestations in the course of events—divine "signs and providences"—than Newton, that great commentator on Revelation, or his disciples. Nevertheless, the Puritans also believed that, while God remains the master of all events within the universe he freely created by his own, sovereign will, his interventions are essentially limited to "common concourse" and sustaining the network of secondary causes to which he confides the production and direction of world events. In other words, while simultaneously affirming the unlimited character of the Power who created and governs the world, the Calvinists also underlined the limits within which this Power has agreed to remain by respecting the system that he himself imposed upon the functioning of world events.

46. Calvin, *Consensus Genevensis*, in Niemeyer, *Collectio*, 305.
47. Calvin, *Institutes*, 1. 17. 2.
48. Calvin, *Institutes*, 2. 7. 5.
49. Calvin, *Institutes*, 3. 23. 2.
50. In one of the most successful formulations of Reformed dogma, the origin of all truths is said to be found in the quintessence of God, which is his holiness, defined as the primordial synthesis of his goodness and his strength, or again his glory, defined as the expression of this same synthesis (Heppe, *Dogmatics*, 92–3).

Although, within the domain of the divine governance of nature, Calvinism did not make any particularly unique contribution to Western religious thought, its meditation on divine sovereignty led to new teachings regarding God's relation with intelligent creatures. Following the federal theology of Coccejus and his disciples, Puritan writers developed the famous doctrine of the Covenant. God—the Master of all that is (being) and is not (non-existence), of good and evil—condescends, through His own free will, to enter into a covenant with his creatures and agrees to its terms. Thus, while we must not "tie [God] . . . to His own prescript," for he "with His own laws . . . can best dispense" as he pleases,[51] the ruler of the world has nevertheless sworn to follow a certain course of action with regard to his people, to guide them openly, to reveal his will to them, and "He cannot be a covenant breaker." God must remain faithful to his word—*se ipsum negare non potest* (because he cannot deny himself) (2 Timothy 2:13)—otherwise man could "sue" him on the basis of "His own bond written and sealed."[52]

In this case, we are dealing with a *theologoumenon* that was explicitly set out in the context of biblical revelation and only concerns the history of Christian congregations. And yet, on a purely conceptual level, it shares the same structure as the common concourse of God in changing the world. In both cases, we are confronted with the great paradox of divine sovereignty and, in both cases, our attempts to portray it are but poor approximations. It's a game of catch-up and we are constantly falling behind. We begin by positing God's unfathomable freedom to do what He wants, both in creating the world and in governing the lives of men, and then allude to a kind of discipline which God agreed to abide by from the very start. When the theologian's concern to respect God's sovereignty pushes him to situate the point when God chose to accept or adopt this discipline in a second phase, i.e., after that of God's own being, he infringes upon God's perfection to a certain extent. Again, when respect for the radical sovereignty of God makes us want to push forward the moment of God's choosing this order to a time subsequent to his being, this choice appears so contingent that it doesn't seem to have flowed freely from the heart of the Divinity. As a result, the only way to save the perfect sovereignty of God is to integrate the choice to accept this discipline and establish order into the very being of God. In other words, we do justice to the Calvinist vision of God by situating order and goodness at the level of a primordial synthesis of power and order within God himself and not in some subsequent, contingent choice.

51. Milton, *Samson Agonistes*, 308, 314. *Works*, 1. 2. 348.

52. Bulkeley, *Gospel-Covenant*, 321; Preston, *New Covenant*, 477, in Miller, *Errand into the Wilderness*, 72.

Inspired by the goal of the reformer, Edwards formulated a doctrine of sovereignty in which the immediacy and arbitrary nature of God's acts are in harmony with his wisdom and goodness. He also adheres to the great biblical doctrine of the covenant and its promises. God promised salvation to those who believe in Jesus Christ and damnation to those who sin against the Holy Spirit and he must keep his promise (X, 303–4). At the same time, this quasi-necessity in which he must act according to his word is not the result of a mutual agreement between man and God. God is constrained by nothing other than his own attribute of "truthfulness"[53] and, as we know, his attributes are co-essential to his being. Therefore, the obligation under which God acts according to his promise is the perfect expression of his very essence, the fullness of his sovereignty (X, 303–4). God's law is certainly "that eternal and immutable rule of righteousness," although this rule "between Him and mankind" (22, 406) has been established by God himself.

While keeping in mind that the regularity and order in nature originated in an absolute, immediate and arbitrary act, Edwards did not seek to explain it in terms of absolute power but instead tied it into the profound doctrine of God's having created the world with a view to his own free and intelligible glory. The rules of nature, he wrote, "are entirely at the pleasure of Him that establishes them" (13, 326). Nature owes its existence to the absolutely arbitrary operation of *creatio ex nihilo*; its essential force is gravity, "arbitrarily" established by God (20, 282); and, generally speaking, the functioning of nature depends upon these arbitrary operations (23, 203–5). At this point, it might seem like we have arrived back at the notion of *nuda potestas*, yet this is not the case at all. For Edwards, "arbitrary" stands for that which is the opposite of "an operation confined to . . . those fixed establishments and laws commonly called the laws of nature" it is not in any sense opposed to "an operation directed by wisdom" (23, 202). Beyond the level of physical nature, i.e., in more general, metaphysical terms, a constitution is arbitrary when it depends solely on God's will, whereas the Divine Will itself depends upon wisdom (3, 403). As a great Miscellany (1263) puts it, "'Tis the glory of God that He is an arbitrary being, that originally He, in all things, acts as being limited and directed in nothing but His own wisdom, tied to no other rules and laws but the directions of His own infinite understanding" (23, 202–3). Here we are back to the primordial synthesis of power and order within God, which allows us to avoid the "profane and impious divorce" that "separate[s] his justice from his power."[54] Beginning

---

53. Gerstner, *Steps to Salvation*, 185; see also Bogue, *Edwards and the Covenant of Grace*, 198–9.

54. Calvin, *Institutes*, 1. 17. 2.

with his earliest works, Edwards acknowledged that "infinite wisdom" was inseparable from "infinite power" in the creation of the world's very being (6, 246), yet he never explicitly developed the theme of God's relation to eternal truths. However, he did adopt a position worthy of Calvin himself with regard to the primordial relation between God's sovereignty and wisdom. Moreover, his views were not based on a doctrine of divine attributes, but instead on inquiries regarding the end for which God created the world and speculative meditations on God's fullness and glory.

8. Creation and Trinity

Edwards taught the doctrine of God's radical sovereignty with no less fervor than the classic treatises of Reformed dogmaticians, but he realized that in order for this sovereignty to be truly free, it had to be inseparably linked to the notion of order.[55] If the definitive proof of the goodness of God's works is ultimately to be found only in the fact that he effectively performed them (8, 427), then on a more general level, the good that God does is good not only because it is he who does it, but because everything he does is orderly. God is not beholden to anyone for his own being (10, 419), nor does he depend on anything else, yet if his acts were unlimited and arbitrary, he would lack autarchy, so to speak, inasmuch as he would be beyond his own control. To be truly free, his sovereignty must conform to some kind of order or itself be a form of order. If this is not the case, we arrive back at the position where sovereignty and order are located at different levels within God and, by making one level dependant on the other, we break God's homogeneity and ultimately the absolute perfection of his being.

The sovereignty of God, by its very definition, can only truly be understood in terms of a relation between God and something other than himself. As Newton explained, God's domination implies that there is something he dominates. Since only God existed in the beginning, it was necessary for something else to be brought into existence in order for him to relate to it. There had to be a sort of diversification, the establishment of some difference or disjunction between God and something else, and hence there needed to be creation. Sovereignty can therefore be viewed as creation (and conservation), yet to be an expression of sovereignty, creation cannot be imposed upon God. There are two reasons for this. On the one hand, for the act of creation to be truly free, it has to come from "within" the divinity, i.e., emanate from God himself. On the other hand, when this immanent outpouring is granted, the threat to divine freedom does not entirely disappear.

---

55. "God is not a wilderness, or a land of darkness" (22, 258).

Even if we grant that the Creator is free from all external conditioning, he remains subject to internal necessity. Indeed, the creative act could be portrayed as a kind of irresistible impulse, an outburst whose very spontaneity was practically forced on God by his very nature. In other words, from a theological perspective like that of Edwards, creation can never be seen as akin to any necessary process or emanation in the strict, metaphysical meaning of that term.[56] If creation was nothing more than a necessary emanation for God, it would pertain to his very being, be part of his perfection (which is identical to him) and therefore God would be imperfect had he not created the world. For this reason, creation should not be understood in terms of any necessity whatsoever—even one that is immanent and proper to God—because it would only serve to fulfill a need and thereby confirm the existence of an imperfection. Moreover—and this is very logical—it should also not be understood as a free outburst with the goal of deriving some sort of satisfaction or joy from its results, because God is perfect in himself and consequently does not experience any enlargement or fulfillment, i.e., any kind of improvement, through something other than himself. If creation is to be seen as a real expression of God's sovereignty, it cannot be expressed in terms of an immanent impulse where God is enlarged, so to speak, by what he produces, nor can it be the fruit of some sublime servitude that the Almighty can only overcome through his act of creation.

And so we find ourselves caught between Scylla and Charybdis: sovereignty implies creation, yet creation cannot be portrayed in terms of any kind of necessity. It can neither emanate from an immanent need, nor aim at any external satisfaction. In other words, creation is neither emanation nor alienation; and neither can it be represented as an action that ultimately returns into itself, nor as an operation that becomes lost, as it were, in what it produces. What remains to be done is to find a formula that reconciles the effective foundation of new things with the essential immutability of God while excluding any notion of a need to be fulfilled. God the creator must be portrayed as calling autonomous beings into existence who, even in exercising their autonomy, return fivefold to God what his creative act granted to them. To put it in Edwardsian terms, we are dealing with emanation and re-manation (8, 531), which are neither simple duplications of one another nor repeat operations with the same content and materially identical but moving in opposite directions. It implies actual creation, i.e., creating something

---

56. "God created the world not from any necessity, but because it pleased Him; and He created it as it pleased Him" (24, 1213). As used by Edwards, the term "emanation" is sometimes rather imprecise and indicated "a participation of the Deity" (17, 422), but also an *ad extra* communication (8, 433). Elsewhere, emanation is the equivalent of shadow (13, 279).

new, although it must be possible to portray the process as the culmination of something new, and its return as something new and therefore free within the Creator. As Hopkins wrote, "Absolute, uncontrollable sovereignty may be considered as included in the moral character of God.... Omnipotence is indeed a natural perfection; but benevolence, clothed with omnipotence or doing what it pleases, is the essence of God's moral perfection."[57] In other words, to consider the problem in its broadest terms, we are to understand God's sovereignty ultimately as His goodness or, in Edwardsian terms, the revelation of "God's moral character."[58] Sovereignty is a kind of unlimited effusion or overflow that nevertheless conforms to a certain type of order precisely to avoid the limit inherent to any action beyond the control of its author. We should therefore understand sovereignty as love, because love—even unconditional love—is not meaningless. This sense of love is not immanent and therefore not egotistical, because sovereignty, as "exuberant goodness" (6, 167), actually produces the "being and well-being" of the creature (6, 235). Insofar as it establishes well-being, and incarnates and expresses a *telos*, creation becomes a transparent reflection of God himself and consequently returns to him.

When viewed from the perspective of creation, the doctrine of God's sovereignty is seen to unfold in three phases. First, we notice that God, by his very nature, has a diffuse disposition. Second, we see that this disposition is not a necessary process or a blind outflow, but rather a free self-communication. Third, because it is free, this self-communication is not simply a gratuitous exercise of divine omnipotence but rather the actualization of his goodness. In other words, we first have to show that the very essence of God's character is diffusive. We then need to explain that God is not under any obligation to disseminate himself or, in particular, to disseminate aspects of his nature *beyond* himself. Lastly, building on the results of the previous two developments, we need to show the essential correspondence between God's diffusiveness and his goodness, including the way in which the outworking of this goodness climaxes with the effective calling into existence of free creatures, abiding images of his perfection in whom he delights, yet without annihilating his works or losing himself in them. Strictly speaking, the term "creation" is the production of free beings whose essential activity or purpose in life is "devotion" (13, 189–91), the glorification of the Creator. However, having completed this magnificent theological journey, we realize that the end is somewhat tainted by the intelligent creature's refusal to perform his task. Man refuses to engage in devotion and

---

57. Hopkins, *System of Doctrines*, 1:69.
58. See Bellamy, *The Wisdom of God in the Permission of Sin, Works*, 2:94n.

shirks his duty to glorify God. The ultimate product of emanation, he hinders even the slightest gesture of remanation. In accordance with the same dialectic of goodness and freedom that led God to create in the first place, the Creator—who, according to the Scriptures, is "faithful"—undertakes the work of redemption. In other words, while the remanation of the creature to God is made *possible* by the diffusion of God's being, it can only be *realized* through the communication of his Spirit.

The religious intuition of God's sovereignty is expressed through the representation of divinity as having a "diffusive disposition" (8, 434). In a perfect being, diffusiveness does not infer a kind of displacement or outflow of his being, but rather a kind of self-presentation or manifestation. However, this manifestation doesn't stem from a pathological need for self-exhibition; on the contrary, it implies the self-sufficiency of the divinity itself. In fact, it is this perfect self-sufficiency that leads to the exercise of divine attributes *ad extra*, because part of the very nature of fullness is to transmit itself. God has an essential inclination towards self-communication (*Bl.* 346-7): "the glory of God is the shining forth or effulgence of His perfections" (13, 361), the "shining forth or flowing out of God's infinite fullness" (23, 152), for "it is a becoming and condecent and worthy thing for infinite and supreme excellency to shine forth" (13, 410). Edwards seemed to immediately and obviously transition from sufficiency to fullness and from self-diffusion to self-communication. In fact, he accomplished an important work of speculation in establishing the efficacy of the immediate exercise of God's act as the source and foundation of God's transitive act of self-diffusion. Although the diversification implied in sovereignty was initially understood to be almost self-evidently inherent in creation, it has now become necessary to refer back to the Trinitarian procession—a more primordial form of diversification because it is immanent in God—precisely in order to better establish creation as effective diversification.

Edwards repeatedly stated that even though the *ad extra* manifestation of His glory and radiance is essential to God, this still does not imply in any way that God is therefore "in need" of the world or has to call creation into existence so that he can communicate with it. In fact, God is continually causing the world to rise up and giving himself over to the work of creation and conservation—which constitutes his emanation *ad extra*—yet none of this is actually necessary for God to be happy, harmonious or at peace, because his desire for self-diffusion was anticipated by and founded upon an *ad intra* emanation, an even more primordial form of self-communication (23, 153). In his youth, Edwards had written that "God has appeared glorious to me, on account of the Trinity" (16, 800), and it was this central Christian dogma, "the greatest and the most glorious of all mysteries" (13, 393), that enabled him to portray creation as the free outworking of God's superabundant goodness.[59]

At the end of several, rather abstract speculations, Edwards abruptly concluded that "Jehovah's happiness consists in communion" (13, 264). Much later, he returned to this theme in his *Treatise on Grace*, observing that the "happiness of the Deity, as all other true happiness, consists in love and society" (21, 187).[60] God is a communicative being and, as such, yearns with all his being for society. Nevertheless, it is essential to understand that God does need not go outside of himself to enjoy the company of other persons, for "He hath in His Son an adequate object for all the desires of this kind that are in His heart" (12, 151). This amounts to saying that God's *ad extra* communication is preceded and greatly exceeded by his *ad intra* communication, i.e., that God's inclination towards the world is only secondary to the mutual love of the divine persons among themselves (8, 557). Far from being a necessary end of God's "need for communication," the world can only truly be understood from the starting point that this "need" has already been adequately met within the divinity itself, "a kind of social happiness, in the society of the persons of the Trinity" (16, 415). It is for this reason that Edwards's great Miscellany on the Trinity (94) declares that "the perfect energy of God with respect to Himself is the most perfect exertion of Himself, of which the creation of the world is but a shadow" (13, 262).

According to the Old Testament, during his consecration as High Priest, the anointing oil "ran down upon the beard" of Aaron and "down to the skirts" of his priestly garments (Psalm 133:2). Because the nature of this holy oil is "diffusive," it is entirely appropriate that it should represent the "Spirit that is the Deity, breathed forth or flowing out" (21, 184). A little further on, Edwards compares the precious oil to the pure river which, according to the Book of Revelation, flows forth from the throne of the Father and the Son, as well as to the "infinite delight" described in Psalm 36:8. The river of life is "typified" by the anointing oil. Both oil and river allude to God's own, ultimate pleasure by virtue of their being the natural manifestations of this outflowing, primordial diffusion founded in the very essence of God. The fact that the anointing oil ran down on the fringes of the High Priest's garments signifies that "the divine essence entirely flows out and is breathed forth . . . from the Father and the Son." Edwards emphasized the total and complete character of this flow, which is the Holy Spirit, the supreme bond between the Father and the Son. However, while this entire

---

59. Concerning the Trinity as a paradigm of first beauty, see *infra*, p. 346ss.

60. See also "the eternal, infinite happiness of the divine being seems to be social, consisting in the infinitely blessed union and society of the persons of the Trinity" (25, 662).

flow first takes place within the Trinity itself, the divinity also flows "secondarily" and "freely" towards the creature (21.186).[61]

9. Sovereignty as goodness

If the divine persons of the Trinity mutually possess—each within the other—adequate objects for their desire to communicate, then why would this primordial flow be repeated in a secondary form? What is the motive behind the *ad extra* emanation of a deity who already enjoys perfect happiness (8, 445–7)? It is customary to point out the philosophical problems posed by the notion of creation. It is often said that creation is the manifestation of an imperfection, betrays a lack of some sort or reveals a deficiency. But is it an "argument of the emptiness or deficiency of a fountain that it is inclined to overflow" (8, 448)? Here Edwards followed in the footsteps of innumerable Christian apologists who have said with John Smith, the Cambridge Platonist, that "God Himself being infinitely full, and having enough and to spare, is always overflowing."[62] It is his infinite plenitude that overflows into the creature, because God, as Wollebius said, does not create out of need, but out of excess.[63] This supreme paradox, which is at the very root of the theory of *ad extra* emanation, is found in *Charity and Its Fruits*. Because God is an all-powerful and "unchangeable" Being, it follows that he is "a full and overflowing and an inexhaustible fountain of love" (8, 369).[64] There would appear to be a contradiction in this passage between the unchangeable and overflowing aspects of God's nature, which is seen in the transition from all-sufficiency to fullness. However, once fullness is reformulated in terms of goodness, this seeming contradiction is resolved and disappears.

Edwards began mediating on this question in his youth and situated it in the province of the Trinity. As early as Miscellany 104, he held that God's entire *ad intra* communication is the key to understanding creation. However, it was only after Edwards had composed some forty-five Miscellanies

---

61. The best study of Edwardsian teachings on the Trinity is by Pauw, *Supreme Harmony of All*.

62. Smith, *Select Discourses*, 142. On Edwards and Smith, see Kimnach, "General Introduction to the Sermons," in 10, 6–9.

63. Wollebius, *Abridgment of Christian Divinity*, 57. See also "God did not make the world out of need or to better His own happiness," (Willard, *Divinity*, 273).

64. Divine, "self-sufficient" (10, 383) goodness is an "inexhaustible, infinite fountain" (22, 351), a "river which ever runs" (8, 383), "full of water ... overflow[ing] all its banks" (14, 481). The young Edwards contrasts the "bottomless gulf of misery" in hell with the "rivers of pleasure forevermore" in heaven (10, 510).

on this subject that its definitive formulation appeared in his impressive treatise, *The End for Which God Created the World*. Written at Stockbridge around the same time as its purely philosophical counterpart, *The Nature of True Virtue*, this treatise would also not be published during the author's lifetime. In this "most sublime piece of colonial literature"[65]—the most audacious speculative work written in English in the eighteenth century[66]— Edwards succeeded in "neo-Platonizing Calvinism"[67] by identifying God's fullness with the natural and moral good within Him (8, 433n.7).

The fullness of God is the totality of all that is good in God, and yet this totality should not be understood as merely the sum of individual good aspects. All that is in God *is* God and therefore, in the final analysis, what is good in God is his own goodness. Identified elsewhere with the Holy Spirit, who is the outflow or diffusion of the divinity (21, 186–7), the fullness of God expresses his goodness. The notion of sufficiency still has almost pejorative connotations. The idea of fullness almost inevitably evokes the notion of overflowing. As Supreme Intelligence and Supreme Power are involved, this overflow of fullness cannot be a kind of accidental or fortuitous spillover, i.e., an aimless process devoid of any meaning rather than a form of self-communication. In the last Miscellany on the end for which God created the world, written just before the treatise itself, Edwards copied a passage from the works of Goodwin: "*bonum est sui communicativum* [the sharing of oneself is good], and it is the nature of perfection also to be *manifestativum sui* [making oneself known], and that not because any perfection is added to it when made known . . . but that they might perfect others."[68] Edwards would only revisit this text in his mature years, but the idea was already explicitly present in the Miscellanies of his youth. As early as 1725, he wrote that "this is the notion of goodness, an *inclination* to show goodness" (13, 252). Elsewhere, he wrote "To be perfectly good is to . . . delight in making another happy" (13, 263). We seem to be dealing with a tautology: to be good is to communicate that which is good. Worse yet, this tautology seems to refer back to the affirmation of that pure diffusiveness that we were expressly trying to avoid. However, a short sentence—itself also somewhat tautologous in appearance—allows Edwards to avoid the risk of repeating the same idea: "The degree of *free goodness* is in proportion to the *freeness*

---

65. Heimert, *Religion and the American Mind*, 218. The first part of this work is purely metaphysical and constitutes, as Miller put it, "Edwards' explanation of explanations," *Jonathan Edwards*, 298.

66. Gardiner, "Early Idealism of Edwards," 594.

67. Elwood, *Philosophical Theology of Edwards*, 81.

68. Goodwin, *Works*, 1. 2. 246, cited by Edwards in 23, 223.

of the goodness" (20, 447). In other words, the very degree of free goodness, i.e., authentic goodness, depends on the degree of freedom in that goodness.

Because goodness is not truly good unless it is free, the reality of goodness depends on the reality of the freedom. Simple diffusion or mere overflowing is not quite goodness, since only a freely desired emanation is good. All freely desired diffusion is intended to transmit something to something else, and so both the "something" and the "something else" must be included in it. In other words, the free diffusion of goodness implies that such diffusion has meaning. Consequently, when we read that the definition of God's goodness is His "disposition to . . . cause His own infinite fullness to flow forth" (8, 460), we have to realize that this goodness, which is not indigence but rather indulgence, is both free and meaningful; and because divine sovereignty is freedom and order, sovereignty is identical to goodness. Sovereignty is goodness insofar as goodness is self-diffusion. While self-diffusion is undoubtedly directed towards something else, it relates to that something else as goodness, i.e., without expecting anything in return, without being motivated by any ulterior motive, and without pursuing any quest for satisfaction or hope of reward. It is "a manifestation of a greater fullness of . . . goodness . . . when the principle flows out of itself . . . with little or nothing from without to attract it" (20, 449). The highest degree of fullness is therefore that in which the being that overflows not only has no object that he seeks to attain by overflowing, but also never had any such object prior to overflowing, so that the being must produce this object himself (8, 542).

When Edwards clearly affirms that God's purpose in creating the world was communication in general and not the production of particular things (8, 433–5), we might think that we have just fallen back into the realm of unlimited emanation and a meaningless sort of sovereignty, whereas nothing could be farther from Edwards's mind. If true goodness is a desire to communicate without being motivated by any particular end, then the true freedom of God's action is precisely His self-communication. God's goodness consists in the fact of His self-communication: "The one last end of all things . . . is that the infinite good might be communicated" (20, 525). Rather than diminishing God's sovereignty, the fact that he actually produces something and enters into a relation with something other than himself—which seems extremely hard to reconcile with the fullness and perfection of God in his self-communication—instead ends up being the most dazzling manifestation of those very same characteristics. God wishes to communicate himself because he is good, but he must find another being to do so. Yet God can only find one if he makes it himself. "The spring of God's beneficence," wrote Edwards in one of his major Northampton sermons, "is within Himself only" (VI, 505), and this is precisely why his beneficence is so radically effective. The permanent, *ad extra* emanation of his works is made possible by a divine self-diffusion whose motivation is absolutely immanent, because it is the absolutely immediate character of the divinity's desire for self-communication that leads to effective creation. Since God has no need to create (18, 237-9), it can only be that he does it out of pure generosity.[69] As the outcome of God's gratuitous act, creatures who would otherwise recede back into God can continue to exist. As Kierkegaard would later explain, God's omnipotence is so radical that it can turn back into itself even while offering itself up for another—i.e., God is capable of imparting his own being without continuing or extending ontologically into another.[70]

Unlike that last great Edwardsian, Nathanael Emmons, who held that God cannot create beings independent of himself,[71] Edwards viewed the liberty of spiritual beings as precisely the reflection of God's image. While God's sovereignty is manifested most spectacularly in the "arbitrary" character of his operations, intelligent creatures possess a "secondary and dependent arbitrariness" (23, 203). God does not only love his creatures "metaphorically" (8, 449-50), nor is he inclined towards an "ineffectual exertion" of his Spirit (23, 153). Since "He delights in His own light, He must delight in every beam of that light" (8, 441-2). God makes sure that these rays spread out effectively and have their own proper existence.[72] Of course, this very traditional image of the sun and its rays is not exempt from ambiguity. It was therefore no coincidence that *The End for Which God Created the World*—even more so than *The Mind*—would give rise to accusations of pantheism. Such critiques may not be entirely without foundation, although the distinction between material and spiritual things found in Edwards's early writings was sufficient to deflect most of their substance. As for created minds, which do not need to be perceived by another mind in order to exist, Edwards seems to have clearly established the proper substantiality of the creature. However, it should be understood that idealism which excludes all substantiality other than that of intelligences has, as a corollary, the recognition of a certain continuity between the Great Being and individual intelligences. If the emanation, multiplication and even the increase

69. God created the world to communicate himself, not to receive anything (25, 116), with the communication of God being "the fullness of all intelligent creatures who have no fullness of their own" (24, 634).

70. Kierkegaard, *Journal 2*, 62-63.

71. Emmons, *Works*, 2:431, in Haroutunian, *Piety Versus Moralism*, 247.

72. "The main end of His shining forth is not that He may have His rays reflected back to Himself, but that the rays may go forth" (13, 496).

of goodness (8, 433) are required by the doctrine of effective creation, it must not be forgotten that "The Lord hath made all things for Himself."[73] Continuity between God and his creatures, who are co-essential to a certain extent because they are spiritual beings, is implied by the finality of his action.

10. Glory and newness

Edwards's idealism and pantheism were undoubtedly structural elements, i.e., important points in time when he explained his theology, theory of prayer, or teaching on "devotion." By no stretch of the imagination, however, could they be considered conceptually adequate to account for his vision of the relation between God and his creatures—especially free, intelligent creatures—much less the entire continuity between the Creator and his creatures. With goodness as its central truth, the ontological category of diffusiveness is supposed to be the key to this theology—with its emphasis on the absolute sovereignty of the Great Being and the radical difference between him and that which is not he—and also explain the appearance of other autonomous beings with their own authentic teleology. However, even if this vision of Divine Being as goodness justifies creation and maintaining the existence of what has been created, it must also have an ontological dimension that renders the Most High capable of acting effectively and of producing something new. However, the dogmatics that Edwards inherited was too devoted to a pseudo-Aristotelian necessitarianism, an ontology buttressed by an absolute distinction between actuality and possibility, to be able to envisage a genuine reconciliation of immutability and newness, of impassibility and creative love. Edwards undoubtedly found himself confronted with a similar dilemma while developing the notion of the Deity's diffusiveness. In that instance, the paradigm of the Trinity, a specifically Christian religious theme, had proved helpful to him. Yet another biblical, religious theme—that of God's glory—now allowed him to free the Divine Being from the straitjacket of necessity, an actuality that would imprison God in his own perfections.[74]

God's glory is a biblical notion that assumed increasing importance in Edwards's metaphysical reflection[75] and perfected his explanation for the

---

73. Prov 16:4, in 8, 467.

74. For Edwards's widening and transformation of the central notions of Scholastic ontology, see the works of Sang Hyun Lee, in particular, *Philosophical Theology of Edwards*.

75. For an explanation and interpretation of the notion of "glory," see Ramsey's

advent of beings other than God. The brightness and fullness of God—his glory—express the intuition of a manifestation of God that signifies being "enlarged" (8, 527), although without the need to split it in two or effectively separate themselves from him. Glory, which can be associated with the Godhead as a whole or with one of its divine persons, denotes the excellency and greatness (8, 514) or fullness of God (see 8, 438). In preaching, glory is equated with the greatness, holiness, and even the goodness of God (19, 456). It denotes divine attributes so fundamental that they express the divine in the Deity, so to speak, though always with an overarching connotation of turning towards or of showing favor.[76]

The glory in and by which God expresses or manifests himself implies something in God that is external to God (13, 252–53), i.e. that radiates *ad extra* when he acts. It enables the inclusion, and even the integration, of time in eternity, progress in perfection, and weakness in strength. The Christian theologian's major preoccupation is to reconcile the immutability of the Divine Being with the joy he experiences as a result of events in the history of salvation (*Salv.* 91n.3); to include what is new in God without it seeming to be "random" and incompatible with "a necessary being" (*Bl.* 114). A necessary being is a being who is act; and God is act, a pure act, and nothing but a pure act (13, 260). However, the purity of actuality is not something static or fixed, but ultimately reverts back to action, its original dimension. The truth of actuality is activity. According to young Edwards, the Christian loves Christ with "an active love" (10, 615); the saints in heaven "shall be active as angels; their souls shall be full and overflowing with an active, sprightly holiness" (10, 527). In short, they will be "transformed into love... become activity itself" and be "changed into mere ecstasy" (13, 260).

Designating actuality as ecstasy testifies to the efforts of Edwardsian metaphysics to overcome confinement within the ontological self, to unlock actuality, and to "open" being. This New England theologian tried to extricate himself from the grip of Parmenides and, in his own way, worked to rehabilitate "becoming." To be glorified doesn't simply mean coming out of oneself or turning to another; rather, "going further" implies real progress and actual growth. Of course, heaven is the ultimate state of the blessed, although this doesn't mean that all movement is stopped or frozen. The happiness of the elect is "progressive" (13.478).[77] The saints's faculty for enjoy-

---

wonderful notes and appendices in vol. 8 of the Yale Edition.

76. The *theologoumenon* of "the brightness of His glory" is not merely a "property or virtue of the Divine Being" but implies a reference to the incarnation (25, 519). The "*Logos* of God" is his glory (24, 483); and the fullness of God, i.e., his glory, dwells in the Messiah (24, 413).

77. The misery of the damned is also "progressive" (18, 507).

ment is constantly being "enlarged" (18, 53) and "their number of ideas shall increase to eternity" (13, 275). In heaven, the union of the saints with God is never perfect, but always "increasing" (8, 535). The saints will see the glory of Christ's body "increasing" more and more (20, 48), and those glorifying God will "be increasing in their knowledge of His glory, and so in the degree of their love" for him (20, 485).

Jonathan Edwards integrated growth in actuality. Now, the inclusion of becoming in being is not limited to the redemption of progress; it also results in changes and affections that are not merely quantitative in nature but which can also lead to oppositions and ruptures. If "sinless perfection ... admits of infinite degrees" (20, 199), then change isn't incompatible with perfection. The state of the elect angels is perfect and no "evil changes" can affect it, yet it is "subject to great changes and revolutions of the contrary nature," i.e., the "increase of their holiness." (18.497)[78] This change—a good one—represents growth and development,[79] yet leaves the way open for alterations and even mutations. If "God's perfections" are not to lie "eternally dormant and ineffectual" but bear "fruit" (8, 527), then divine action cannot only be concerned with the enlargement and increase of what is given, but must also lead to the arrival of new realities.

The incarnation of the Word, the life of Christ, presents theologians with the enigmatic arrival of something new, not only with respect to men but also with respect to God. It is primarily preachers who venture to talk about this novelty, the mystery that "Christ had some excellencies in His human nature of a different denomination than any in His divine nature" (*Bl.* 168), whereas philosophers reflect on the significance for God of his action in time and space, and the joy he takes in the love and faith of his creatures (8, 448). As for elect creatures, the blessed in heaven, "new beauties are continually discovered" (13, 337), and they will have "new occasions" on which to feel "new joys" (13, 444).[80] The state of the blessed is one of "perfect contentment," yet it does not "exclude all hope." On the contrary, "part of that happiness" will consist precisely "in the sight of what is future" (13, 443).

Christian theology thinks of hope as an innate virtue, i.e., a perfection we cannot acquire by our own efforts and therefore one for the continuity

---

78. The happiness of pure beings is not "immovable and immutable" because—before their election was "confirmed"—the elect angels experienced "trouble," "uneasiness," and "fear" (20, 197–98).

79. Even "growth" does not have a narrow, quantitative, material sense. The blessed will no longer "crave" greater happiness, joy, and knowledge but will have a desire to grow (18, 53). See Sermon on Rom. 2:10 in 8, 723–24.

80. See *infra*, p. 306ss.

of our finite being. There is something novel here. Now, in the final analysis, the most radical meaning of novelty isn't to simply go beyond the qualitative order, nor to go back to the coming of something that didn't previously exist. According to its own truth, novelty isn't just concerned with the coming of nothingness to being but—in what is perhaps the most authentic sense of that notion—is also manifested in the acceptance, to varying degrees, of non-being by being. If creation is a prime example of the coming of something new, the incarnation appears to be an even more extreme one. The incarnation is "the most wonderful" form of divine "condescension" (25, 671), in and by which God "humbles Himself" (*Bl.* 85). God in Jesus Christ, the one who is fullness, perfectly "self-sufficient" and who has set his love on "low and despicable" beings (*Bl.* 290), condescends to talk to us, tries to persuade us, and knocks at our door "till His head is wet with the dew, and His locks with the drops of the night" (10, 441).

Edwardsian formulations resort to this kenotic conception of divine love, which is not unrelated to the ancient tradition of Christian mysticism in which the relationship between God and man is expressed in the language of human affection. According to an early Miscellany (z), the "love of God, as it is in the divine nature, is not a passion . . . but by the Incarnation is really become passionate" (13, 176). The love that Christ bears for his church is pictured as "our love to anyone of the other sex,"[81] and "Christ's heart is as it were ravished with the graces and holy exercises of His saints" (14, 340).[82] More than its vehemently passionate character, it's the non-reciprocity and gratuitous character of this relationship that puts the final touch to the Edwardsian subversion of ontological impassibility-immutability by envisioning Being as glory. God takes more pleasure in communicating to the creature than in receiving from the creature (8, 448); the stream of love that flows from his heart towards us is stronger than the stream flowing from our heart towards him (22, 240). In short, the motivation for Christ's love to men is not found in them or their merits but "in Himself." Instead of only loving the best, the perfect, his "overflowing benevolence . . . extends to those who have no beauty or excellence" (*Bl.* 282),[83] no "greatness or goodness" (19, 782).[84]

The advent of the new, the non-reciprocity of relationships and the various instances of divine condescendence are outcomes of the ontological

81. Sermon on Eph. 5:30. Sweeney, "The Church," 178.

82. Also see the wonderful texts brought together in Sweeney, "The Church," 178–9.

83. The love of saints who are "superior" towards those who are "inferior" to them (8, 376).

84. For glory, goodness, and fullness, see 8, 527n.5; see "fullness" and "sweet" in 22, 292.

unlocking that results from reading Being as glory. God descends and the creature welcomes, although this welcome is not only made possible but required, called for, and even virtually implied by the descent. Glory is the manifestation, the communication of God, albeit a manifestation related to a term in which it manifests itself and a communication that can only occur with the coming of a counterpart, a partner of the Deity. Glory is not a burst of sterile brilliance, nor a gleam of light with nowhere [nothing] to reflect it. Because "goodness has no existence but with relation to perception" (18, 395), "there is no glory without perception" (13, 428). Some imputed pantheism to Edwards; others were mesmerized by his idealism. In reality, if there is any continuity between the Creator and the creature, it's that glory wants to be perceived; and perception requires beings capable of having "knowledge of God's excellency" (8, 521) and a willingness to respond to his call. Hence the need to conceptually deduce this immortal, spiritual, finite being and religion.

11. Immortality and religion

Edwardsian theology has two major, complementary requirements: (1) the creation of beings independent and autonomous enough for them to be an appropriate end for the Creator's communication and (2) sufficient affinity between the Creator and his creatures for them to be a medium for the return of God back to himself. God's communication of himself culminates with the being and action of the creature, but rather than keeping this radiation of God in himself, the creature must be "actively . . . promoting" its return to God (18, 95). A wonderful passage in Edwards's treatise on *The End for Which God Created the World* aptly summarizes this issue: "In the creature's knowing, esteeming, loving, rejoicing in, and praising God, the glory of God is both *exhibited* and *acknowledged*; His fullness is received and returned. Here is both an *emanation* and *remanation*. The refulgence shines upon and into the creature, and is reflected back to the luminary. The beams of glory come from God, and are something of God, and are refunded back again to their original. So that the whole is *of* God, and *in* God, and *to* God; and God is the beginning, middle and end in this affair" (8, 531).[85] The majestic beauty of these sentences attests to a vision where theologico-religious intuition takes precedence and determines its metaphysical conception or, more precisely, where Edwardsian idealism and pantheism appear with the

---

85. This ontological "definition" has its spiritual counterpart in the description of Sarah Edwards's experience: "a constant flowing and reflowing from heart to heart" (4, 332; see *Dw.*, I, 178).

full splendor of their theological finality. This theological issue is the reason why Jonathan Edwards only conceded true substantiality to spiritual beings, because they alone can be in true continuity with God. The deep design, the true finality of divine emanation is remanation, and therefore any creature that cannot actively participate in it is smitten with ontological worthlessness. If the material world doesn't have real existence, it's because it cannot contribute from itself to the great process of remanation. If minds are recognized as having substantiality, it's because they effectively return God's self-communication to himself.

The idealistic texts of the Edwardsian corpus are rather uncertain in their use of the terms "shadow" and "image" to designate material things. In truth, however, each of these two expressions is legitimate. In themselves, material things are only shadows, although they are indeed images for minds that view them as types of God. In themselves, material beings cannot stop or restrain God's communication of himself because they lack a mind, i.e., a core ontological *pour-soi*. In themselves, they are not true ends of divine self-communication and only become so though the mediation of minds. If the being of physical things only truly exists in minds (6, 206), it's because only minds can interpret their message. Natural things are authentic manifestations of God's glory—outpourings of the "innumerable streams" of God's love (8, 373)—yet, in themselves, they can never act as types. Man can be designated the eyes and mouth of creation,[86] because it is in and through man that dumb and passive creatures are referred to God and participate in the great cosmic reflection that is the hidden design of the universe, the immense process of remanation.[87] At this moment, we realize that man's existence, and even his immortality and religion, are deduced, so to speak, from the very dialectic of God's self-communication inasmuch as it culminates in true remanation.

Philosophers generally allow that man is the end of creation, but are they right to place his end in with the good of the rest of creation? If material beings have their end in man and man has his end in them, then creation is deprived of any ulterior end and doesn't refer to anything outside of itself (13, 189–91). It is God who created all things and though he certainly created them for themselves, they ultimately exist for him.[88] Now,

---

86. See *supra*, p. 6.

87. The things of nature are, in themselves, only capable of reflecting a "passive" glory to their creator (10, 427).

88. "God in seeking His glory, therein seeks the good of His creatures" (8, 459). However, God's respect to the creature's good, and his respect to himself, is not "a divided respect" (8, 533). "God has not forgot Himself, in the ends which He proposed in the creation of the world" (8, 425). He delights "in the happiness of His creatures

if the world has no essential purpose beyond its momentary existence, why would God want to create it? God would only want to effectively deploy his power in order to accomplish something for himself, a fact that implies the presence of a being in the world, one in whom the world finds its profound meaning and in whom it subsists. Man is the consciousness of the world (13, 272) and if, at death, he wholly ceases to exist, the world of which he was the conscience will—after a short moment of existence—likewise cease to exist. And so, with the universe sinking into black nothingness, it will be as if the work of God never existed (22, 234)!

God created the world for a purpose. The world is like God's chariot and its wheels, after they have revolved a thousand times, don't remain just where they were at first, "without having carried the chariot nearer to a journey's end" (20, 108). There has to be some progress in the state of the universe (15, 375). Nature, the physical world, is a place of constant revolutions that repeat without truly renewing themselves and, but for its material nature, the world wouldn't come to an end. The creation therefore has to end with a being who doesn't always perform the same movement but knows how to progress, a being who doesn't simply abide in nature but progresses in history. Man is the foundation of this world, the one in whom the rest of creation finds its meaning; yet it is not enough that man exist and reflect the world for only a short time. For man's presence to be a true accomplishment, he needs to remain and his mind—the consciousness of the world—must subsist. Otherwise, the world would be in vain and may as well not exist (13, 197). If creation was only temporary and if man did not endure, God would have obtained nothing from the world that was "worthy of Him" (20, 334). If the main creature eternally ceased after having existed and acted for a short period of time, then "nothing in any respect new . . . remains" (20, 335) and God would have "no benefit . . . has gained no knowledge, no new idea, by all that has happened" (18, 95). Generally speaking, if "the perception and intelligence of the world don't remain after the world comes to an end, then . . . God . . . reaches nothing, He accomplishes nothing; but only is just where He was before He made the world" (18, 94). Edwards returned frequently to this deduction on the survival of man as a *conditio sine qua non* of the intelligibility of Creation—from the perspective of the formal cause and final cause—but here again, he is simply developing an intuition from his youth. "If there were not intelligent beings," he wrote in one of his very first Miscellanies (gg), "all the world would be without any end at

---

. . . for 'tis to be resolved into the delight that He has in His own goodness" (18, 238). "And though God in seeking this end, seeks the creature's good; yet therein appears His supreme regard to Himself" (8, 531).

all . . . for God could neither receive good himself nor communicate good." He continued: "It follows from this that we must be immortal" (13, 185).

Man's immortality is therefore implicitly deduced from God's effective and fruitful self-communication, but it shouldn't be construed simply as an infinite continuation of a mind that reflects the glory of God, a mechanical deciphering of the images and types of nature. Man only actively reflects the glory of God when he doesn't just think of it but perceives it with joy (14, 144 n.). Man does not become the seat of God's glory purely by being a mirror of nature, because then what would distinguish him from that same dumb nature? God created the world so that the creature would welcome his glory and that glory is to be received by both the understanding and the will (20, 517). The Creator is glorified when his glory is beheld and also when man rejoices in it; and he is glorified more by rejoicing than by mere beholding (18, 495). If this is so, then man cannot be just a receptacle for the rays of God's glory, but a true agent of divine worship, i.e., of "devotion" to God. The voluntary character of man's soul, in itself, distinguishes him from beasts and is what makes man capable of morality and "capable of religion," i.e., of communication that glorifies God (6, 374). If man or, more precisely, immortal man, is deduced from the very essence of remanation, he is therefore deduced as a religious being, as the supreme instrument for contacts and communications with God. The Miscellany that concluded with immortality also concluded that "religion must be the end of creation" (13, 185). Moreover, in this Miscellany, religion is the primary conclusion, while immortality not only follows it but is consecutive to it. Man is not initially deduced as an immortal mind and then, secondarily, as a religious immortal mind. Rather, based on the demonstration that religion is the end of creation, man is deduced from the very start as immortal because he is religious. Ultimately, it is not just man's immortality that is deduced in this way from religion, but also his very existence itself.

In a Northampton sermon we read that, in the world, every creature has its end in another creature, whereas only man has his end in God. If this end did not exist, if creation did not imply the glorification of God as its essential end, then there would be no reason for man to exist (VI, 537–8).[89] However, if man is deduced from the ontological requirement of devotion, and if this higher creature's existence is therefore just an instance where this religious function is realized, then the religious function itself derives from man's ontological status. Each creature has his end in another immediately above it on the scale of beings and with which it is directly related,

---

89. If religion hadn't been his proper, "immediate occupation," there "would have been no need of introducing the animal in the image of God in the world at the end of the six-day work" (*Bl.*, 91).

i.e., without an intermediary. Because man is the pinnacle of creation, there is no created being over him, and he consequently finds himself in direct relation to God himself. In a manner of speaking, devotion is man's natural activity and God, for his part, "immediately influences the soul" (13, 191). The creature's participation in God and the spiritualization of the creation by divine indwelling are thus portrayed in terms of an ontology of divine glorification. Even idealism plays a role in this presentation, as an indispensible way to explain this glorification in moral terms. While nature also glorifies God, it ultimately only does so through the mediation of man, an intelligent, moral being in communication with God (23, 348).[90] The religion that Edwards deduced as the proper end of creation is not a reality of a cosmic order but consists in the intellectual-personal relationship linking God and his creatures. God's communication encounters a communication from the creature. This emanation and remanation are essentially an exchange of signs and words, i.e., a mutual exchange of personal expressions.

12. Revelation and the Church

Edwards, who from his youth had emphasized the immense importance of "conversation" in religious and moral matters,[91] used this term to describe the intellectual and spiritual exchanges between intelligent beings, i.e., their "communion" (13, 399).[92] There are two ways in which intelligent beings can reveal or show themselves to others: by *mediate* or *immediate* signs. Mediate signs allow us to philosophically decipher our interlocutor's ideas, whereas immediate signs disclose the mind and intentions. Immediate signs, which voluntarily signify your intentions to others, are known

---

90. Edwards quotes Goodwin who wrote that God, in making man, wanted to create a being "unto whom He might as it were unbosom Himself" (*Works*, 1. 3. 63 in 23, 223). God delights in his creation, and especially in his intelligent creation, but his happiness does not depend on it (18, 237–39), because "although the dispositions and voluntary actions of His creatures are made the means of it, yet these are perfectly in God's hands" (23, 138). Ultimately, with respect to communication, "God takes delight . . . But this delight is not properly from the creature's communication to God, but in His to the creature" (13, 496).

91. See 16, 784, 797.

92. Edwards used the term "conversation" in a Biblical context. He mentioned the "vain conversation" of 1 Peter 1:18 in 24, 222, which the English Bible took from the "*vane conversatione*" in the Vulgate. It refers, of course, to a man's conduct and behavior among other men. This is why we read that "the moral . . . and the conversible world, are the same thing" (23, 349). In a narrower sense, "conversation" simply means the faithful and natural expression of our personality (2, 102). Moral government is exercised "in way of conversation" (23, 353).

as "conversation" (23, 346).[93] According to a great metaphysical principle which states that the law of mediacy reigns in the physical nature, while immediacy applies in an ever-increasing degree as we approach the Absolute Spirit, conversation doesn't exist in the material world because it requires a certain "union of wills" (20, 104) that is signified by the signs given. In a full and proper sense, there is only conversation among men—intelligent and moral beings—and, among them, it's most authentic expression is found in their moral actions (23, 348–9). A vehicle proper to moral ideas and a supreme instrument of inter-human relationships, conversation is also used to designate the exchanges between God and man.[94] Though partners devoted to an intimate friendship, God and man nonetheless have a very different dignity and character. When it emanates from God, conversation is known as revelation, and if rising up from the human mind, as prayer (23, 349–50).

Living in an era in which deists of various persuasions constantly sought to make breaches in even the very principle of revelation itself, Edwards deduced it from God's very essence and his infinite desire for communication, which would not be fruitful without an interlocutor. Of course, in a broad sense, nature and the types hidden in it are also a revelation. However, *stricto sensu,* only divine communication addressed to an intelligent creation is revelation.[95] "There must be some Word of God," we read in the notes of a sermon to the Indians in Stockbridge. "'Tis unreasonable to think that God would always keep silence and never say anything

---

93. Conversation is not limited to exchanges with other beings. A man can have a conversation with his own idea, i.e., with himself, whom he knows adequately (13, 260).

94. When he is in "immediate communication" with man, God is said to be "conversing with him" (21, 177).

95. Strictly speaking, divine revelation "is that discovery of truth that God had made by His own immediate instructions . . . supernaturally given to the world in His word" (19, 723). However, since the essence of God is communication, there is revelation in nature, a cosmic revelation which "the whole creation" preaches (10, 440). The types that Edwards found scattered throughout the universe are all examples of this communication. Nature is a "voice of God," a "manifestation and declaration" to "intelligent creatures" (23, 374); the universe is "full of images of divine things," as full as a language is of words (11, 152); in fact, it is a language in which God is wont to speak to us (11, 150). Moreover, types are just natural realities that Edwards also discerns in history: God disposes things in world events in such a manner as "to represent divine things and signify His mind as truly as His Word." Of course, inasmuch as Christ is, properly speaking, the communication of the Deity and "the substance of all the types and shadows" (9, 218), this typology cannot but have implications for Biblical revelation. See Brown, *Edwards and the Bible,* 132, 144. For Edwards, however, these types or images constituted "the Book of . . . Common Providence" (11, 50); they did not count as "means" with respect to the work of saving grace. For the best work on Edwardsian types and typology, see Knight, "Typology," 190–209.

to mankind."[96] It's from the eternal emanation of the Word, and therefore from an ontological communication, that revelation is conjectured as a divine activity of conversation. At every level, the Word, the Verb serves to explain and clarify the thought of the one from whom it emanates and, in the context of glorification, the Word is emanated so that its recipient can freely reflect it back to God. This return of the Word—remanation—takes place through man as a moral being; and a moral being must know the laws and precepts he has to follow in his life. He also has to know "divine history," because only the reading of divine history, i.e., the history of salvation, will enable him to understand the meaning and principles of God's government of the world (23, 352).

However, God is not only the supreme legislator and sovereign monarch of the moral universe, but also our "infinitely . . . gracious friend." He therefore asks us to not only know and obey his laws but also to rejoice in his designs. Communication not only serves to mediate and maintain unity between intelligent beings but is also how "the felicity of friendship is tasted and enjoyed" (23, 350, 353). For man, communication does not consist in a mere return, a simple reflection of the types in nature in their archetype (God), but in an admiring and always amazed reading that moves the heart and ends in prayer.

When God's creatures freely communicate with him in prayer they remanate God's communication of his own glory. The individual, scattered rays of the sun alone cannot reflect the fullness of God's glory; remanation must instead begin from an organic coming together of its rays, ensuring the total reflection of the infinite brightness that is the glory of God. In other words, if the cosmic totality of nature is not the place and vehicle of remanation, in the strict sense of that term, then the organic totality of intelligent creation can and must be that place and vehicle. Consequently, the holy conversation of men among themselves and with God must take place and find its fulfillment in the church.

To emphasize the truly moral and intelligent character of this kingdom of beings who converse with God, Edwards resorted to wonderful images drawn from physical nature to represent and typify the community of those who pray. Referring to the period of his own conversion, Edwards wrote: "The soul of a true Christian . . . appeared like such a little white flower, as we see in the spring of the year; low and humble on the ground, opening its bosom, to receive the pleasant beams of the sun's glory; rejoicing as it were, in a calm rapture; diffusing around a sweet fragrancy; standing peacefully and lovingly, in the midst of other flowers round about; all in like

---

96. Edwards, *Selections from the Unpublished Writings*, 191.

manner opening their bosoms, to drink in the light of the sun" (16, 796). In his *Personal Narrative*, which contains an almost literal copy of the very first Miscellany, Edwards again emphasized the open and humble way in which individual souls receive grace. Of course, even though these flowers were among other flowers and each opened in the same way to welcome the rays of the sun, there still wasn't any image to represent the mutual relation between these souls and the community they formed. It went differently when this same imagery was later transposed into the allegory of the rainbow, traditionally understood as the symbol of God's covenant with men. In a long note on Genesis 9:12–17, we read that the rainbow is light, the symbol of God's communication with those who are the objects of his favor. It appears from a cloud, a cloud of rain, and the drops of rain that reflect the light of the sun also symbolize the life-giving influence of the church of Christ. The light originating from the sun is one and unvaried but, when reflected from the clouds, appears in great variety. In like manner, the glory of God, which is simple, is reflected from the saints in various graces. The rainbow is composed of innumerable bright drops that represent the church of the saints. All of these drops are like so many beautiful images of the sun reflected in the multiplicity of the creatures. However, the individual drops not only represent an instance of God's light but also symbolize it by the way in which they relate to one another. The drops represent the saints, and the sun is Christ, through whom the Deity relates to the creation. "They are in the most apt order with respect to the sun, all opposite to him, and so placed in a fit posture to view the sun, and to receive and reflect his rays, all at an equal distance from the sun, and all in a sense round about him, to testify their respect to him, and yet none behind him, but all before his face, and all in the most apt order to behold and reflect light on, and converse together, and assist and rejoice one another" (15, 332).

This multiplicity of intelligent creatures only arises by virtue of an *ad extra* deployment of God; and the end of God's self-communication to the world is the return of the deployed—as deployed—to God. God considers the emanation of his glory as belonging to his own fullness, "as though He were not in His complete state without her," i.e., as though the fullness of God would be incomplete without the church (8,440).[97] Because of his self-communication in creation, God dwells in this world and his most perfect dwelling is the church.[98] God's perfect communication in the world is

97. "The church is said to be the completeness of Christ" (13, 272); see also 24, 1096.
98. The church is a "glorious society of created beings" (8, 431) and God's "special aim" in creating the world was this "one spouse and body of His Son for the adequate displays of His unspeakable and transcendent goodness and grace" (23, 179). The church constitutes, so to speak, "God's family" (25, 588) and God prefers it even "above the

directly related to the active welcome which intelligent creatures give it. The union of minds is the moment when this welcome is made complete. This union takes place in the church; and it is the church that remanates God's glory (8, 431). It is as the Church in heaven—the perfect, undivided society of the blessed who freely converse with God (X, 337)—that the world is returned perfect to God.

13. Providence and redemption

Edwards deduced man's existence from the religious function itself but later remarked in the same sermon that even though man had the most exalted task of all the creatures, he alone can neither perform this task nor indeed fulfill it (VI, 548). The purpose of God's communication, of the entire creation, is to return to God and be "swallowed up" in him (8, 443), but sin is an obstacle to this return and hinders remanation. The intelligent creature is at the summit of creation and through his proper task—devotion—might have been able to ensure perfect continuity between God and the world, but sin broke this continuity and seems to obstruct the realization of God's designs. The nature of God is to love himself, and it was as if everything involved in that love, especially the intelligent creature's love for him (8, 437), had to start over and be moved to a new creation in order to ensure the unobstructed emanation and effective remanation of his glory. This second creation is redemption (23, 622).

In redemption, God as it were "revised" his first indistinct action where bringing the world back to him would have involved all intelligent beings. He did not, of course, renounce the attainment of his fullness, but rather its accomplishment by means of an *ad extra* diffusion which moreover, from the outset, he had only advocated by a free decision that he could well have avoided. Instead of all intelligent creatures, only "elect creatures" (23, 157) would henceforth be involved. The absence of a real disjunction between God and the creature made his first communication—creation—total. Now that the creature had provoked a (vicious) disjunction, the unlimited goodness of God no longer has its end in the entire mass of intelligent beings. Redemption therefore appears under the sign of election. Redemption is also an integral exercise of God's sovereignty, even if exercised in an intensified

---

angels" (24, 212). "Every event in the universe" serves the good of the church (24, 315). The primary expression of divine glory in the creation is the community of consenting beings to divine being. Of course, God elects individuals, yet he does so on the basis of their union with the "mystical body" of Christ, the invisible church (24, 1122), which he will admit "into the society of the blessed Trinity" (*Bl.*, 179).

or reinforced way (see 15, 513). In creation, the goodness of God was deployed under the sign of sovereignty and is moreover its real outcome; in redemption, where exclusion is involved, this goodness must now be expressed in terms of choice. Expressed and deployed as the predestination unto life of the elect and without losing any of its sovereign generosity, divine goodness is displayed within limits it has chosen and assumed for itself and in meticulous agreement with order. More precisely, in God's creative emanation, and in his wisdom, the gift of being did not depend in any way on an order that constituted, or rather preconstituted, the essence of the creatures. God's even greater generosity in redemption seems to take the creature's moral and religious *quiddity* (whatness) into account, even if the constitution of this quiddity reflects God's sovereign goodness. The essential challenge in redemption is how to reconcile God's justifying goodness as narrowly as possible with this suitability for salvation that God's justifying will creates. Justification should also be a direct emanation of God's *potestas* (power), an immediate exercise of his will. In his *Treatise on Grace*, Edwards wrote that "the Holy Ghost . . . flows out primarily towards God, and secondarily towards the elect that Christ came to save"; and he added "freely" to describe this secondary outflow (21, 186). God's love is only for creatures "united" to Christ (21, 158), i.e., to those who have espoused Christ and form this "glorious society" to which God unceasingly communicates his fullness (8, 443–4).

If the free flow of the Spirit in redemption—the second creation—only indeed concerns elect creatures, this discrimination has its metaphysical origin and anticipation in creation, which is not a blind outflow but has meaning inasmuch as it is goodness. Creation isn't just an instanteous overflow, but a continuous process and preservation where preservation has two aspects: the uninterrupted exercise of primitive power that forged the world out of nothing and the Creator's care for this world whose existence he maintains. Consequently, God is not only the Creator of this world, but also its governor (20, 95). God's creating and preserving work is expressed and reflected in a multiplicity of actions and gestures that address various moments and elements of creation. To employ a Kantian term, the creative understanding contains the transcendental totality of the predicates that constitute the world, a fact the religious conscience expresses with belief: no sparrow lives or no hair of our head falls apart from his will.[99] In other words, while the preservation aspect of Creation is understood as general providence, what matters for the religious conscience is that it also finds

---

99. "God governs the spring of every motion" (22, 348).

expression in particular, i.e., special, providence.[100] Nothing happens apart from the particular will of God, "the great Governor of the world" (16, 442), and everything that comes to pass happens because of it.

The Puritans of New England were very expert at interpreting "signs and providences"[101] and, in doing so, they were putting a fundamental teaching of Calvin into practice. The reformer would not suffer those who, in speaking of God, despoiled him of his "justice and providence" and shut him up "idly in heaven."[102] Since creation is also preservation, we need to see "the presence of divine power shining as much in the continuing state of the universe as in its inception." Preservation means the active governing of particular things. God not only drives "the heavens . . . by producing a kind of general motion"[103] but also specifically directs "the action of every creature"[104] in "the disposing and directing of everything to its proper end by incomprehensible wisdom."[105] Calvin and his Puritan descendants took pleasure in retracing God's acts of providence in the events of the created world, but since preservation concerns all finite beings, providence primarily extends like a reading of natural history from the perspective of human history. "As we know," wrote Calvin, "that it was chiefly for the sake of mankind that the world was made, we must look to this as the end which God has in view in the government of it."[106] Because the significance attributed to nature is so deep and full of meaning, it is incorporated into a total history in which God follows, supervises, punishes and rewards the activity of his creatures.

Edwards also saw the world of nature and that of history as forming one great continuity (see 15, 373–4) and, as a good naturalist, was fascinated to observe spiders, "these wondrous animals . . . from whose glistening webs

---

100. Providence is the end of creation (9, 118).

101. Edward Johnson (*Wonder-Working Providence*, 79) interpreted the increased mortality of the Indians due to an epidemic as a sign of providence, as did W. Bradford (*History of Plymouth Plantation*, 92–3) when he wrote about the unexpected death of "a proud and very profane yonge man." Regarding that same era, English author K. Thomas (*Religion and Decline of Magic*, 88) wrote that it was relatively rare for lightning to strike the elect. Almost a century later, Jonathan Edwards didn't hesitate to point out signs of providence in the life of his congregation and in the historic events of his time. However, he also cautioned his readers that "there are innumerable ways that persons may be misled, in forming a judgment of the mind and will of God, from the events of providence" (4, 451).

102. Calvin, *Institutes*, 1. 4. 2.

103. Calvin, *Institutes*, 1. 16. 1.

104. Calvin, *Institutes*, 1. 16. 4.

105. Calvin, *Institutes*, 1. 16. 4. 227 n.c.

106. Calvin, *Institutes*, 1. 16. 6.

so much of the wisdom of the Creator shines" (6, 169). He praised "the exuberant goodness of the Creator, who hath not only provided for all the necessities, but also for the pleasure and recreation of all sorts of creatures, even the insects" (6, 167). However, having deduced particular providence from God's desire for self-communication (8, 412), Edwards was especially thinking here of the "fatherly kindness" the Lord shows towards his intelligent creatures. "God," he wrote, "is not regardless how things proceed here upon the face of the earth" (14, 516), and he assures us that the "wheels of providence are not turned round by blind chance, but they are full of eyes round about, as Ezekiel represents; and they are guided by the Spirit of God" (9, 519); and those eyes are set on the destiny of mankind. Having created the world primarily for mankind (20, 95) and mankind for himself, God cannot be an indifferent spectator of his creature's behavior, especially when it comes to his religious and moral conversation and his love and hate for God (20, 101). The purpose of creating the world and, more specifically, man is to enable and encourage remanation, i.e., for the emanation of God's glory to be reflected back to him. The fall of man hindered the "natural" reflection of this glory. In consequence, God adjusted how he acted and, caring even more intensely, transposed providence into redemption.[107] And redemption is understood in the light of justification.

14. Justification

For Puritan theologians, the *Epistle to the Romans* represented "the Quintessence and perfection of saving Doctrine" and its eighth chapter, which deals with justification, "is like a conduit conveying the waters of life."[108] Justification by faith alone is the material principle of the Reformation, i.e., its principle teaching. To quote Luther, it is the *"fundamentum Novi Testamenti, ex quo tanquam ex patenti fonte omnes thesauri divinae sapientiae profluunt* [the foundation of the New Testament, from which all the treasures of divine wisdom flow forth as from an open source]."[109] Elsewhere, Luther wrote that "*Articulus justificationis est magister et princeps, dominus, rector et iudex super omnia doctrinarum, qui conservat et gubernat omnem doctrinam ecclesiasticam* [The article of justification—the master

---

107. See V, 279. It's in this sense that redemption is an even higher manifestation of God's greatness than creation (19, 776), i.e., that all of God's other works are but "appendages" to redemption (18, 284).

108. Haller, *Rise of Puritanism*, 87.

109. Luther, *In Esaiam Prophetam Scholia, Werke*, 25:332. Our attention to this text by Luther and to those following it was drawn by Barth, *Kirchliche Dogmatik*, 4. 1. 581.

and prince, lord, ruler and judge of all learning—preserves and governs all ecclesiastical doctrine]."[110] The reformer knew perfectly well that "*Amisso articulo justificationis amissa est simul tota doctrina Christiana* [without the article of justification, all Christian doctrine would be lost as well]."[111] For Christians, it's the doctrine of justification that distinguishes them from the followers of all other religions, because "*soli enim christiani hinc locum credunt et sunt iusti non quia ipsi operantur, sed quia alterius opera apprehendunt, nempe Passionem Christi* [For only Christians come to that place where they believe and are justified, not because of their own works, but because they apprehend the work of another, namely the Passion of Christ]."[112] Justification, as Calvin said, "is the principal ground on which religion must be supported,"[113] which is why the Devil, the moral enemy of all religion, fights more against it than any other affirmation of our faith.[114] It is the most concise and most characteristic expression of God's sovereign mercy, and "the Gospel declares nothing more than that sinners, without any merit of their own, are justified by the paternal indulgence of God."[115] In a direct line from the Reformation, Edwards constantly meditated and wrote on this subject and thought that the first "great harvest" in Northampton was "a remarkable testimony of God's approbation of the doctrine of justification by faith alone" (19, 795).[116] Edwards was convinced that no one doctrine in the Bible "is more fully asserted, explained, and urged" than the doctrine of justification (19, 232). Later in the same "Discourse," he made the profound observation that the doctrine of the Trinity was seemingly revealed for us to better understand that justification teaches the respective roles of the divine

---

110. Luther, *Die Promotionsdisputation von Palladius und Tilemann*, Werke, 39:1. 205.

111. Luther, *In Epistolam S. Pauli ad Galatas, Commentarius*, Werke, 40:1. 48. "Von diesem Artikel kann man nicht weichen oder nachgeben, es falle Himmel und Erde oder was nicht bleiben will . . . auf diesem Artikel stehet alles, das wir wieder den Papst, Teuffel und Welt lehren und leben [Of this article nothing can be yielded or surrendered . . . even though heaven and earth, and whatever will not abide, should sink to ruin . . . And upon this article all things depend which we teach and practice in opposition to the Pope, the devil, and the world]" (*Die Schmalkaldischen Artikel*, Werke, 50:199–200).

112. Luther, *In Esaiam Prophetam Scholia*, Werke, 25:330.

113. Calvin, *Institutes*, 3. 11. 1.

114. Calvin, *Commentarii in Quinque Libris Mosis, Opera*, 23, 211.

115. Calvin, *Institutes*, 2. 10. 4.

116. The enemies of the Great Awakening are those who preach justification by faith alone in theory but do not accept it in practice—see Heimert, *Religion and the American Mind*, 55.

persons in "the great affair of our salvation" (19, 239).[117] If the satisfaction of Jesus Christ "is . . . the centre and hinge of all doctrine of pure revelation," (MO 398) then justification, which expresses what is essential about man, is the keystone of Christian theology, "the highest glory of the gospel and the delight of the Scriptures" (14, 60).

Reformed dogmatics frequently makes a distinction between election, justification, and sanctification. Election precedes justification outside of or before time, i.e., with God in eternity. It is that mysterious moment when the universal, saving will of God—addressed to drops of the rainbow, all at an equal distance from God and facing him (15, 332)—is transposed into a choice, a selection. Conversely, sanctification follows justification and deploys, frames, and develops it in the lives of the saints. As for justification, it is that instanteous and indivisible act by which grace, "a sovereign thing . . . bringing good out of evil," (3, 110)[118] changes the status of children of wrath into that of adopted sons and transfers the elect from the family of the devil to the household of God.[119] The act of justification, which is absolutely free and expresses the overflowing goodness of God, is not contingent upon any interior or exterior qualification of man,[120] nor does it require any active collaboration on his part. Justification, as an ecclesial document puts it, is "an effective call" in radical discontinuity with "the common operations of the Spirit,"[121] i.e., the general convergence of actions that God takes with respect to his rational creatures. The actions of this general, common convergence can be retroactively seen as many moments of preparation and saving grace, although they only seem so from the effective call of this grace, always a "particular work of God" that alone produces our salvation (*Salv.*, 47). In themselves, these means of preparation—the various

---

117. See also "Man in integrity might be happy in the enjoyment of one God; but fallen men cannot be recovered without a Trinity" (Willard, *Divinity*, 100). E. Beecher would later say of his contempories that they rejected the doctrine of the Trinity because of its relations with the teaching on man's "natural depravity" (*Conflict of Ages*, 121). Barth thought that if the eighteenth century rejected the doctrine of the Trinity, it was because it referred back to the being and action of God within himself, without considering the preoccupations of humanistic morality (*Protestant Theology in Nineteenth Century*, 106).

118. See also ". . . this thing is formed by the Holy Ghost . . . It is the proper work of this infinite, divine, holy energy to bring good out of evil . . . holiness out of impurity" (18, 414).

119. Taylor, *Poems*, 524. For the various stages of this process, see the description of the "morphology of conversion" developed by Puritan theologians in Morgan, *Visible Saints*, 66–67.

120. For this topic, refer to Cherry, *Theology of Jonathan Edwards*, 61–62.

121. Walker, *Creeds and Platforms*, 378–79.

phenomena that accompany and mark the process of "awakening" and "conviction" that are even found in the behavior of hypocrites—are nothing but the tempestuous manifestations of a fallen nature unable to escape or surpass itself (3, 433n.3) and vainly yearning for the descent of grace.

To mark the efficacy and radical novelty of this operation, dogmaticians describe conversion—a general expression for justification—from the perspective of the human subject, and not just as a divine operation of a "moral" order, but as a real, physical action of the Holy Spirit.[122] To underline the radicality of the change it effected, Calvinist writers took pleasure in comparing justification to creation, but as a second creation that takes place in fallen beings; a comparison with the resurrection of the dead might be more appropriate. The change from sin to grace is not a movement that goes from zero to plus, but rather an operation that starts with negative numbers and ends with positive numbers. Calvin wrote that when God illuminates us, "he is said to raise us from the dead [John chapter 5, verse 25], and make us new creatures [Second Corinthians, chapter 5, verse 17]."[123] In a being who up until that point had constantly consented to sin, there was no internal inclination to turn towards holiness, so the start of this new existence in the spirit of grace had to have an external cause. (18, 230)[124] It is a complete break-away, and what makes it so radical is that we cannot discern any intermediate moment in it. The conversion that results from justification is a *creatio ex nihilo*, a passing from death to life (*Bl.* 223), and there is no intermediate moment between death and life (21, 159–60). Given the maximum immediacy of operations in the religious and moral universe, justification seems like a leap into conversion, like a change that is not gradual but done in one and the same act.[125] It is with one great step that we cross the gaping fault that separates good from evil.[126] The radical immediacy of justification imitates that of the first creation, because it also doesn't end with its first founding moment but continues on in every moment thereafter (22, 190). Of course, in a certain manner, perseverance is implied by the first moment of grace (19, 203) although, as Augustine wrote, it is not a mechanical

---

122. Heppe, *Dogmatics*, 177–8. According to Emmons, the actions of God upon the hearts of his elect are produced by the same physical force ("almighty power") which he exerted in creating the world and in raising Christ from the dead (*On the Special and Irresistible Grace of God in the Conversion of Sinners*, Works, 5:102). This teaching is radically at odds with Edwardsian doctrine, *infra*, p. 232.

123. Calvin, *Institutes*, 3. 14. 5.

124. Justification must have "some extrinsic cause" (18, 65).

125. See 18, 230; see also Amesius, *Medulla Theologica*, 122.

126. Miller, *New England Mind*, 2:58.

inclination or a natural result of justification, but a free gift of God.[127] Beginning and persevering in grace is also beyond the scope of our autonomous will[128] and this commonplace notion in Christian preaching appears in a sermon from Edwards's youth: "We are dependent on free grace, even for ability to lay hold in Christ already offered" (10, 395).[129]

This radical dependence of the creature, even to continue receiving the grace already bestowed, shows that justification still doesn't abolish the distance between the Great Being and the works of his hands. Because perseverance in grace is also a gift and even the meritorious character of works is from the Lord (13, 322), grace is not a type of delegation or alienation of an attribute of God but rather God himself acting (21, 194). According to Samuel Willard's definition, "grace is God willing to exalt a residue of fallen men to a state of life . . . for his own sake."[130] In the best tradition of Christian theology, this Harvard dogmatician did not define grace as something that comes from God but as something in God himself. It is God himself who emanates and communicates and, by virtue of the total immeasurability between the Creator and the term of his emanation, which he freely constitutes, nothing in the creature can determine God's action towards him. The insistence of the reformers on the fact of simply being *declared* just by God and not on actually *becoming* just reflected their intuition of the radical impossibility that the creature could influence God in any way. In justifying sinners, God—as Luther put it—covers his eyes[131] and decides to ignore the corruption that still exists in the fallen creature. Regarding the justified person, Calvin wrote that God "judges of his happiness from this, that in this way he is righteous not in reality, but by imputation."[132] It is not a matter of "becoming or being absolved by the judgement of God."[133] Justification in no way implies that we are innocent; rather, "God justifies us . . . so that though not righteous in ourselves, we are deemed righteous in Christ."[134] The Savoy Declaration, a major exposition of the Calvinist doctrine of "sovereign free grace," explains that God does not justify sinners by

127. Saint Augustine, "Admonition and Grace," 6. 10—7. 15.

128. Donne, "we are so far from being able to begin without grace, as that when we have first grace, we cannot proceed to the use of that, without more" (*Works*, 5:577).

129. See "If God should withdraw his continued operation, godly men would fall away from grace" (*Bl.*, 217).

130. Willard, *Divinity*, 87.

131. Luther, *Ein Sermon von dem Heiligen Hochwürdigen Sakrament der Taufe*, *Werke*, 2:731.

132. Calvin, *Institutes*, 3. 11. 11.

133. Calvin, *Commentarius in Harmoniam Evangelicam*, *Opera*, 45, 345.

134. Calvin, *Institutes*, 3. 11. 3.

infusing His righteousness into them, but by pardoning their sins, and by accepting them "not for anything wrought in them, or done by them, but for Christ's sake alone."[135]

The Augustinian intuition of sin that is merely covered but not erased is a striking testimony to the absence of any real difference between those whom God justifies and those he leaves in bondage to wrath. Before justification, all men are indeed sinners; and justification itself—to paraphrase Luther—is but a cloak that God spreads over the sinner to hide his filthiness. Of course, even if the acts of the unjustified have any value in and of themselves, the extraordinary preponderance of corruption in every natural man is such that the authors of those acts will never deserve to be treated differently from others for having done them (19, 212–3). Even if, after justification, God closes his eyes to residual corruption, justification itself is not motivated by any pre-existing good (20, 392). There is no virtue or good that God sees or foresees in man that arouses the Lord to do good to him; God always "prevents him," i.e., comes first to man, "by free liberality."[136] God's generosity is free. He is not a mere demiurge, either in the first creation or in the second. He therefore does not decide to elect by foreseeing the creature's future merits as material for his recreation. By their own actions, the drops of the rainbow that were initially equidistant from the sun can move closer or further away and yet, in relation to the infinite distance separating God and man, the minute changes in the creature's situation are entirely insignificant to God.

Pelagians in every age have emphasized the creature's merits, as did one contemporary of Edwards who, before his illumination during the Great Awakening, wrote: "yet something I had [been] secretly imagining, *that there was something in Men to begin with, and that Gospel Grace came to make perfect*"[137] However, this view is diametrically opposed to Calvinism, because it makes man only partially and not totally dependent on God (VI, 477).[138] The Arminians—the Pelagians of that era—resurrected the oldest heresy in the world: the belief that man could rely on works-righteousness. "For," as Calvin said, "as we have been formed by nature, sooner shall oil be

---

135. Walker, *Creeds and Platforms*, 379. Conversely, although there is indeed something in (the elect) man that is good, it cannot be accepted by God prior to justification because man's infinitesimal goodness bears no proportion to his sin" (19, 164).

136. Calvin, *Institutes*, 3. 14. 5.

137. *Christian History*, 203, in 4, 6.

138. The Lord did not say, "'Without me you can with difficulty do something,' but said, *Without me you can do nothing*" (Saint Augustine, "Answer to Letters of the Pelagians," 2. 18).

extracted from a stone than good works from us."[139] Sinners cannot prepare their own (re)creation[140] and, unless God regenerates them, they neither will nor are able to return to God. In short, they have to know and confess with Brainerd, a young missionary to the Indians of whom Edwards published a famous biography, that whatever man enjoyed that is "better than Hell, is free grace" (7, 172). Hell is not only the place of future punishment, but also man's natural state before justification (see 22, 405–6). Justification therefore isn't simply moving from point zero, but rather the abolition of a pre-existing, wicked state. In justification, we exit ourselves, although this exiting amounts to tearing, which does violence to our nature.

15. Grace

In Edwards' rainbow metaphor, the rainbow represents the church. The bow is a complete image of the sun's disc, but when this disc is fully visible and filled with light around its entire circumference, the rainbow itself is empty and only filled from without by the sun's radiance. The rainbow symbolizes an empty container that can only be filled by the "communication of Christ" (15, 330). The cloud from which the rainbow appears is also an image or type of the church. It softly reflects the light from the sun but, in itself, the cloud is only an insubstantial, evanescent thing. It lacks light and is obscure by nature (15, 330). The dark, obscure nature of the rainbow lets us complete our analysis of this metaphor of grace. The rainbow that represents the church is, in itself, a passive yet faithful image of the sun. After all, the rainbow is only the unity of its moments because the radiance of the sun's light maintains it. The elements of the rainbow—its individual drops—represent the saints in whom good doesn't merely fill emptiness but instead overcomes active opposition. The drops of the rainbow are fire and water, which are opposing principles, and the saints also consist of opposites, i.e., the spirit and the flesh. Saints have nothing spiritual in them. They have no brilliance or light other than what they receive "immediately from heaven, from the Sun of Righteousness" (15, 334). This sun of righteousness is Christ, by whose death the saints receive new life (15, 330). The church, that fullness of God, is born of God's fullest self-communication, the death of Christ. By Christ's death, the supreme moment of God's

---

139. Calvin, *Institutes*, 3. 14. 5.

140. "all men are conceived in sin . . . indisposed to all saving good . . . without the grace of the regenerating Holy Spirit, they neither are willing nor able to return to God, to correct their depraved nature, or to dispose themselves to the correction of it" (*Synod of Dort*, 294).

emanation *ad extra*, "His fullness is abundantly diffused in many streams; and expressed in the beauty and glory of a great multitude of his spiritual offspring" (8, 440n.8). This outflow of God's glory in many streams consists in a multitude of justified creatures. They are like many different refractions of the light from the sun of righteousness, each reflecting the glory of God in its own way (15, 330–31). But why is this or that creature elected, i.e., chosen before the death of Christ to bear fruit in that person's life? In other words, how do we account for the fact that the "arbitrary, self-determined, self-possessed" sovereign will of God (21, 238) in the "free" movement of his second outflow seems—from man's perspective—to be a selection?

In the best tradition of Christian theology, Jonathan Edwards tried to portray this choice and selection as one essentially made in accordance with the sovereignty of God and only secondarily in terms of the creature's "qualifications." God did not elect this or that creature for his own aptitudes or merits, but rather because God's choice was best suited to fulfill the designs of his wisdom. It was only secondarily, and not out of any immanent necessity, that God considered the creature's aptitudes and actions. Of course, the creature's merits and actions are virtually required in any election, although only by virtue of the good pleasure of God, that "sovereign, arbitrary agent" (18, 530) who made them normal concomitants and not a required condition of his choice.[141]

Every time Christian thinkers find themselves confronted with the question of God's choice, i.e., why God did this or willed that or, more precisely, why God elected one person and left another in the "mass of the damned," they get cornered by the words of the Apostle Paul (Romans 9:20–21): God treats the creature as the potter treats the clay. Now, the metaphor of the potter still does not imply arbitrariness. Of course, it is most often used in the sense given, for example, by Madame de Sévigné, a critic of Malebranche: "St. Paul and St. Augustine," she wrote, "never scruple to assert, that God disposes of his creatures as the potter does of his clay; some he chooses, some he rejects."[142] However—as Karl Barth observed—though the potter is indeed the sovereign master of his works, he treats them as a reasonable, experienced craftsman. God sovereignly disposes of his creature, yet does so according to his wisdom.[143] The anti-Pelagian polemic of

---

141. See 20, 451–52; see also "God does not require that men should be first willing and then come: it is a concomitant willingness only that God does require, not an antecedent: for indeed no man . . . is truly willing to believe in Christ, until he does so" (Stoddard, *Day of Judgment*, 305).

142. Madame de Sévigné, *Letters*, 419.

143. Barth, *Kirchliche Dogmatik*, 2. 2. 212.

the theologians never abandons its defense that this election has meaning, even though there might be very little or no understanding of it.

The doctrine of justification by faith alone is founded on the satisfaction of Christ, the "centre and hinge" of all revealed teaching on grace. God, the master of his grace (see VI, 486–7), does not owe it to a penitent man but, in a certain manner, does owe it to Jesus Christ and therefore ultimately to himself.[144] By grounding justification in Jesus Christ, and therefore ultimately in God himself, the Edwardsian argument ensured that election and justification would be acquitted of the charge of arbitrariness while not making them dependent on any intrinsic quality in the creature. An implacable enemy of the indifferent will, Edwards fought it at every level—even the divine—and rejected the idea that God, whose freedom is limitless, would have made an absolutely arbitrary choice, i.e., that did not take account of any difference between the objects involved in that choice.

Edwards developed his argument by resorting to what Leibniz called the "principle of indiscernables." God's will cannot find itself in a situation of indifference. It cannot apply to two absolutely similar objects for the good reason that there aren't two objects in the world that are absolutely similar. However, the principle of indiscernables is not being applied here to the objects of divine volitions but rather to the volitions themselves. He didn't question the possibility that two objects, or two aspects of one object, might share one complete identity, but he refused to accept the possibility that both could be the object of one and the same divine volition. If need be, God can will one and the same thing at two different moments but that doesn't mean that one is a double of the other. Conversely, the will of God cannot be exercised twice in and by the same act of volition. When God wills twice, he wills in two distinct volitions and these volitions must have different motivations (1, 384–5). As for election (and justification), the subject that serves as the context for this argument, you have to distinguish between the object's merit and divine favor, i.e., between a moral qualification of the creature that would attract divine favor and the natural aptitude of this determination of the act of divine goodness to respond to the particular designs of God's wisdom (1, 394).[145] God undoubtedly considers the qualification of the creature he chooses, but not for its own merit. God considers the accomplishments and dispositions of his creature so that, when electing and consequently justifying this or that creature, the inclinations of infinite mercy are best served (1, 395). God does not have to accept the creature's

---

144. Bellamy, *A Careful and Strict Examination of the External Covenant, Works*, 3:281.

145. For the more specific context of justification, see 19, 156.

works as meritorious, but only considers them in light of his own designs. The profound and ultimate end of creation is to promote God's full self-communication and only his wisdom can judge what best contributes to that end. The final destiny of the elect is to be "swallowed up" in the fullness of the Omega God (see 21, 191) and, consequently, the law governing the *ad extra* emanations of God can only be contingent on the first immanent outflow of the Deity, the Trinitarian procession.

Experience undoubtedly shows that, in bestowing grace, God considers the means that he himself instituted, namely the sacraments and the preaching of the word. However, even though they might be the most frequently used means of grace, they are not a condition for bestowing it.[146] Edwards would not have gone as far as Bushnell, who later said that "the sovereignty of God has always a relation to means,"[147] but he would certainly approve of Stoddard's position: "God's way is to bless suitable means."[148] However, Stoddard knew very well that although God used means, they were not the proper causes of the effect that is justification. When God plays music in our hearts, he makes it resound on heart strings,[149] because although men are not saved on account of their works, neither are they saved without them. For "our own care and diligence is as much the proper and decreed means of perseverance, as of conversion" (13, 475); but these are only proper means because they have been so decreed. "According to a divine constitution, salvation is to be conferred in connection with means," but this constitution is only contingent upon the sovereign considerations of God's wisdom.

In and beyond the various means that God uses like "golden pipes" to diffuse his grace,[150] faith is the essential moment of justification, the faith that unites the believer to Jesus Christ. However, Edwards unceasingly stresses the fact that faith doesn't justify as a condition but rather as a privileged opportunity. He wrote that "there is a difference between being justified by a thing, and that thing universally, and necessarily, and inseparably attending, or going with justification" (19, 151). Faith infallibly accompanies justification, yet for all that is not its cause. It is undoubtedly faith that makes us "fit" to be justified (19, 154), although we need to distinguish between two kinds of fitness: a moral fitness and one that is only natural. A person has moral fitness for a certain state or circumstance when his moral excellence

---

146. Miller, *New England Mind*, 1:290.

147. Bushnell, *Christian Nurture*, 37.

148. Stoddard, *Presence of Christ*, 27 in White, "Stoddard's Theories of Persuasion," 249.

149. See Taylor, *Poems*, 11.

150. Taylor, *Poems*, 453.

makes him worthy of attaining it. On the other hand, natural fitness is where access to a state is not due to a person's moral qualifications, although a sort of natural concord between the state in question and that person's qualities makes it appropriate for that individual to attain that state. In the case of justification, faith is not the expression of a moral fitness which, in itself, would render us worthy to actually receive the righteousness of Jesus Christ. Faith in Christ only expresses a natural agreement with the justified state that simply allows God to look on it as "fit by a natural fitness, that he whose heart sincerely unites itself to Christ as his Savior, should be looked upon as united to that Savior, and so having an interest in Him" (19, 159).[151] Edwards wanted to avoid, at all costs, the final and supreme temptation of *Werkheiligkeit* (works-righteousness), which renounces moral works while seeking to make faith itself a work. Faith can only be "the socket for the jewel" of justification (18, 53). In a manner of speaking, justification marries the contours of the socket, which serves as a worthy recipient, yet cannot produce it. Of course, we frequently see a sort of empirical succession between human efforts and the manifestations of God's mercy, but this order is only apparent. In reality, "God has been pleased to constitute prayer to be an antecedent to the bestowment of mercy, and [he is] very often pleased to bestow mercy in consequence of prayer as though He were prevailed on by prayer" (VI, 505). If God decides on deployment, he does so to shatter the harmony between the creature's efforts and the help that he himself sends to the creature. "God decrees rain in drought because He decrees the earnest prayers of His people." Likewise, "when He decrees diligence and industry, He decrees riches and prosperity." Lastly, "when He decrees conformity to His Son, He decrees calling; and when He decrees and when He decrees calling, He decrees justification; and when He decrees justification, He decrees everlasting glory" (13, 216–7).

Edwards was confronted with the supreme theological problem of reconciling the absolute sovereignty of God's merciful will with the fact that it is commonly addressed to individuals who demonstrate piety and moral rectitude. Wanting to avoid any position where works or faith itself might seem like conditions for justification (see 19, 151–52), Edwards advocated a concomitant situation for faith with respect to justification and wrote

---

151. See 21, 368; 20, 451; etc. Another explanation of this question is given in a sentence that Edwards bracketed and deleted from his manuscript: "I conclude that there is a propensity in the divine nature to communicate happiness to that which is holy, because it is in itself absolutely a beautiful thing that that which is holy should be happy" (13, 396 n.). For an excellent summary explanation of how the notion of natural fitness reconciles the freedom and rationality of grace in justification, see Miscellany 1346 from Stockbridge (23, 381).

about the "congruity" of our spiritual-moral state and the communication of grace (see 18, 466). Elsewhere, he observed that the means of grace are not causes, but only "occasions" of its dispersion (18, 157). However, even the term "occasion"—found in circles influenced by Malebranche's "occasional cause"—overstates the autonomy or pre-existence of the creature's contribution in justification and it is rather the notion of "matter" that best corresponds to the Edwardsian vision.

Equating the means of grace with its matter also implies taking the absolute sovereignty of God's efficacious work and the proper structure of the human contribution into consideration. The means of grace are "the Word and ordinances . . . of God" which, properly speaking, produce the "matter" of grace in our souls, i.e., religious notions and even a deep sense of natural good and evil. Such feelings, ideas and conceptions regarding the things of religion, God and Jesus Christ, the world to come, etc., constitute the very matter on which grace acts. While they still don't constitute grace itself, grace has no opportunity or occasion to act without them (18, 84–86). Even though Edwards only used this notion of matter within the context of justification in the preparatory Miscellanies of his great *Discourse*, it is a valuable formulation of his intuition. Form and matter have traditionally been represented as parallel but distinct realities. More in-depth study shows that form should not be understood as a type of frame applied from without to a pre-existing matter but as an organizing power that unifies it. Instead of merely containing and defining matter, form reunites, gathers, and structures it. Form is not a receptacle but rather a force that penetrates the raw material of sensible impressions, giving it order and—to use a Scholastic dictum—being. The relationship of grace to matter is not one of gradual fashioning, but rather of immediate bringing together. This process unfolds in time and yet, from a purely metaphysical point of view, it is simple and undivided (see 18, 231) and, strictly speaking, the matter did not truly exist before the form took charge of it.

This is most clearly seen in the work of creation in which God's action simultaneously plays the role of efficient cause and formal cause. Matter did not exist before it was created, and it was created by being formed. Creation was an immediate operation. It gave things their being and essence, instituted their existence and constituted them in terms of their quiddity (see 6, 246). Redemption, the second creation, certainly begins with a pre-existing matter, albeit one that transgression had rejected in circumstances that could be considered worse than nothing (13, 323). God's action not only addresses the absence of being and order, but also confronts disorder within a kind of being. By itself, disorder can never become order, either immediately or gradually. God alone can perform this operation and he performs it immediately. This is why, in moments when the creature is "restored," "virtue and holiness are given by way of immediate emanation from God" (13, 331).

The various elements that constitute the matter of justification—good works, receiving the sacraments and faith itself—are but disparate factors or raw, sensible impressions awaiting unification which, like the Kantian *a priori*, implies an *a posteriori* operation in time. Even if an empirically unverifiable, unlocalizable act of God could be situated in time, the temporal posteriority of the act of justification with respect to faith and works would not change the fact that good will and justification are, so to speak, parallels in the decree of God, or rather, what man might judge to be posterior is actually anterior from an ontological perspective. Though good in themselves, works cannot please God, i.e., he only considers them or accepts them as good retroactively from justification (see 19, 211–12). This entire complicated dialectic—one where anteriority and posteriority alternate depending on the respective positions from which they are viewed—is overshadowed by a consequent interpretation of the divine operation whereby a new denomination, i.e., that of "spiritual," is brought about by grace (2, 201–2). God's operation in the second creation was immediate and, as in the first creation, this immediate operation repeats and continues itself. At every moment, God recreates the man he justified as a justified man. Edwards wrote of the justified state which grace, that "sovereign agent," has made a "natural principle" (4, 454), but there is an essential restriction here. Grace always remains a free outflow of the Spirit, which God can withdraw at any moment. This is why perseverance is as much from God as conversion and is also the result of a "divine constitution" (19, 203).

At this point, we realize that what might be considered difficulties of Edwardsian metaphysics reappear at the level of the doctrine of justification and that the key problem of pantheistic ontology has its counterpart in that of divinization by grace. An insistence on the crushing superiority of Being over beings had the paradoxical result of showing too great a continuity between God and the intelligent creature; and now that sin had lowered the value of the creature with respect to the creator, their continuity was strengthened as a result. A product of God's desire for self-communication, the creature only seemed to be a mere prolongation of God's being. Now that it pulls the creature away from sinking into evil, grace pays for his deliverance at the cost of an even more radical dependence. Justifying grace "divinizes" the creature and, in a very real way, subsumes him under God. An ontological analysis of the structures proper to this divinization and subsumption would shed light on the dangers of the neo-Platonic conceptual mould for the transcendence of God in Augustinian Calvinism. However, our subject is not ontological and so will limit ourselves to studying the regenerated state, knowledge, and will of the justified and sanctified man.[152] In the meantime, however, we need to explore this huge aside between creation and redemption due to the fall of the will, which was analyzed and developed by Jonathan Edwards with a degree of power and subtlety that is perhaps unequaled in the history of Protestant thought.

---

152. For more on these issues, see the descriptive phenomenological analysis and its implications *infra*, p. 111, 125, 303ss.

2

The Will

1. The corruption of human nature

THE SECOND MAJOR AREA of Edwardsian thought concerns the will. In itself and in the strict sense of the term, the will is but one of our natural faculties and, as such, should only be subjected to investigations of an epistemological nature. Nevertheless, in the history of Western thought, statements regarding the will quickly acquire metaphysical significance and, as we have just seen in the case of Jonathan Edwards, the impact of events in the sphere of the will extends even to the order of Being. The fall of the creature is not just a "wound" that is limited and "local" in scope,[1] but a cataclysm in which creation itself is qualified for and transposed in redemption. The Fall was an act of the will. However, it was not a random event but rather a full and complete exercise of the will and, as such, concerned the total condition of the finite creature, a voluntary being. The Fall continues in the corruption of the creature and it is this stark portrayal of permanent and voluntary corruption that underlies Calvinism's theological thinking. This is not morbid pessimism but rather a type of Christian realism. Harriet Beecher-Stowe wrote that "the great fundamental facts of nature are Calvinistic, and men with strong minds and wills always discover it."[2] Indeed, the novelist's rigid

---

1. See Milton, *Paradise Lost*, 12. 387, *Works*, 2. 2. 392.
2. Beecher-Stowe, *Sunny Memories of Foreign Lands*, 2:277. See A "Calvinistic sense of Innate Depravity and Original Sin, from whose visitations, in some shape or other, no deeply thinking mind is always or wholly free" (Melville, "Hawthorne and His Mosses," *Works*, 13:129).

Calvinist is but an echo of Jonathan Edwards.³ "In this country," wrote Edwards, "we think that human nature is corrupt" (V, 517)⁴ and, if New England's Puritan preachers have always taught this doctrine, it is because they feel themselves in close continuity with the primitive sources of the Reformation.

The Heidelberg Catechism states that man is prone by nature to hate God and his neighbor,⁵ because—and now we hear Calvin—"there is no part in which it is not perverted and corrupted."⁶ Man is overwhelmed by sin, "deluged," "from the crown of the head to the sole of the foot,"⁷ and "everything in us consists of evil."⁸ Because "the whole man is in himself nothing else than concupiscence," the extent of our corruption is not static but dynamic. "Our nature is not only utterly devoid of goodness, but so prolific in all kinds of evil that it cannot be idle"; it "constantly produces new fruits . . . just as a lighted furnace sends forth sparks and flames."⁹ This corruption causes a serious defect in our basic faculties. The light of understanding is "so smothered by clouds of darkness" and the will is "so enslaved by depraved lusts as to be incapable of one righteous desire."¹⁰

The declarations made in these vigorously worded statements by the master of Geneva remained the *leitmotiv* of his Puritan descendants' preaching. Treatises, sermons and catechisms were saturated with the doctrine of total depravity. In *The Foundation of Christian Religion*, "pious" Perkins succinctly wrote: "Every man is by nature dead in sin as a loathsome carrion, or as a dead corpse lieth rotting and stinking in the grave, having in him the seed of all sins."¹¹ Considering this state made Thomas Hooker exclaim: "good Lord, how can a man in his naturall condition sleepe quietly?" If you think about what the Lord has revealed concerning natural man, "why it is enough to make thee goe sighing to they grave." Therefore, you "that are natural goe into corners and mourne for your selves and those that belong unto you. . . . Parents . . . when thou lookest upon thy child whom thou

---

3. Hopkins, *Life*, 52.

4. See also "Our fathers were not fools . . . Their fundamental maxim was, that man is desperately wicked" (Beecher, *Reformation of Morals* in May, *Enlightenment in America*, 319).

5. *Heidelberg Catechism*, 9.

6. Calvin, *Institutes*, 2. 3. 1.

7. Calvin, *Institutes*, 2. 1. 9.

8. Calvin, *Sermons on the Book of Job, Opera*, 33, 728.

9. Calvin, *Institutes*, 2. 1. 8.

10. Calvin, *Institutes*, 2. 2. 12.

11. Perkins, *The Foundation of Christian Religion, Workes*, 1:3–4.

dearly lovest," consider that it is "a damned child."[12] As for "sweet" Shepard, he wrote with bitterness that "every natural man and woman is born full of all sin . . . as full as ever his skin can hold; . . . so that if thou hast any good thing in thee, it is but as a drop of rosewater in a bowl of poison."[13] It is undoubtedly possible for natural men to do good, so that they appear momentarily pious and virtuous but, according to Solomon Stoddard, the person who taught "the best philosophy . . . of original sin" that Edwards had known (13, 387), natural men remain under the reigning power of sin: "their corruptions are stunded but not mortified, they are restrained but not killed, they are like Vermin in Winter, stupifyed but not dead."[14]

This vigorous denunciation is omnipresent in Puritan literature, but the consensus began to crack at the beginning of the eighteenth century and the Edwardsian reaffirmation of innate depravity would be only a vigorous jump start to a Calvinism declining against the spirit of the times. In England, Toland denied that man is necessarily destined to sin and that his understanding contains faults and imperfections other than those he himself acquired during his lifetime.[15] In 1717, American pastor J. Wise wrote that "whatever has happened since his Creation" man remains "a Creature of a very Noble Character."[16] In the wake of Locke, the primacy of the being's human reason[17] was slowly but surely recognized and elevated as a criterion and judge of revelation. In this spectacle exalting the progress of science and the easing of morality, the immense choir of voices singing with ever-increasing fervor of nature's goodness and the power of reason expressed the feelings of a world yielding to serene optimism. It was the great Leibniz who succinctly expressed this vision: "how slender is the entity of evil."[18] While the entity of evil may have seemed slender to the author of the *Théodicée*, his spiritual progeny is not content with minimizing evil, but is still trying to "exterminate it out of existence."[19] Did we not see a great mind such as Shaftesbury demonstrate by a sort of reverse ontological proof that

---

12. Hooker, *Application of Redemption*, in Hooker, *Three Sermons*, 35, 37–38.

13. Shepard, *The Sincere Convert, Works*, 1:28.

14. Stoddard, *Treatise Concerning Conversion,*, 3.

15. Toland, *Christianity Not Mysterious*, 59.

16. Wise, *Government of New England Churches*, in Miller and Johnson, *Puritans*, 1:261.

17. Shaftesbury, *Characteristics*, 2:112; see "reason is the eldest child of men's nature" (24, 191).

18. Leibniz, *Theodicy*, 3. 378.

19. According to the old translation of *De Malorum Subsistentiae*, by Taylor, *Fragments of Proclus*, 79.

if it was *possible* that evil did not exist, then evil could not actually exist?[20] The Shaftesbury "argument" is nothing other than the extreme formulation of this effort to eradicate evil. At first it was said that evil was not all that bad. Then it was explained that there was really no such thing as true evil. Finally, it was insinuated that, as a necessity in the best of worlds and consequently a servant and auxiliary of right, evil is ultimately good.[21] The great Leibnizian apologetic was diluted into theodicies of all stripes and, rather than foretelling with the prophets that, in some distant eon, the wolves would live side by side with the lambs, the increasingly unrestrained optimism of the Age of Enlightenment taught—as K. Barth noted—that the wolves are the lambs.[22] This victorious naturalism washed even those distant shores of Protestant Christianity, the New England colonies. The powerful preaching of Jonathan Edwards, with its vigorous reiteration of the great dogma that all men are sinners and that every sinner is under the curse of God (3, 115), arose to hold back its waves.

This is certainly not a matter of morbid pessimism or flesh-slaying Gnosticism. Protestant preachers took pleasure in severely denouncing Man's weakness and corruption, although the theologians themselves resorted to the celebrated axiom "*gratia non tollit naturam sed perficit*,"[23] implying that nature is not absolutely evil. As Luther himself admirably put it, "grace does not hinder or destroy nature and her work, but rather improves and promotes it, as if naturally nourishing it with milk from her breast."[24] Some one hundred and sixty years later, Samuel Willard, with characteristic simplicity, declared that "grace doth not destroy but rectify nature."[25] In spite of the corruption after the Fall, there are still "some *remainders* of the Image of God in men,"[26] because the Fall did not cause us to lose the substance of our soul but merely "the purity or integrity of its nature."[27] Though we are undoubtedly taught about divine things by revelation alone and justified by faith alone, natural prudence is a gift of God[28] and, in spite

20. Shaftesbury, *Characteristics*, 2:109.

21. See Veto, *Le mal*, 203-4.

22. Barth, *Kirchliche Dogmatik*, 3. 3. 363.

23. See Pierre Lombard, "natural goods became corrupt in man and the goods of grace were taken away . . . *wounded* in his natural goods, of which he was not deprived, otherwise [his] reparation could not occur; but *despoiled* of the goods of grace, which had been added to the natural ones through grace" (*Sentences*, 2. 25. 7).

24. Luther, *Evangelium in der Christmess, Werke*, 10:1. 1. 67.

25. Willard, *Spiritual Desertions*, 71.

26. Mather, *Sermon Occasioned by Execution*, in Miller, *New England Mind*, 1:187.

27. Perkins, *Graine of Mustard-Seed, Workes*, 1:637.

28. Calvin, *Commentary on Corinthians*, 1:112-13.

of its pagan origin, philosophy must be counted among those activities in which "man's efforts [human understanding] are not so utterly fruitless as not to lead to some result."[29] Man must resort to his natural faculties and gifts to arrange and construct his daily existence but his mind also serves his religion. The Puritans refused to preach "an irrational Gospel"[30] and it is the profound rationality of the good news that is highlighted by the use of our mind in studies. This is why "the interest of religion and good literature has risen and fallen together."[31] While reason may only be the soul's left hand—faith being its right hand[32]—it is still an irreplaceable instrument of our encounter with him and God, who is himself "abstract wisdom" and rejoices "to see His creatures seek this wisdom."[33]

Jonathan Edwards is resolutely aligned with this great Christian tradition that celebrates nature and reason, acknowledges the beauty of the world and appreciates spiritual things. He thought that nature is "nothing but the established order of the agency and operation" of God (3, 385) and admired "this noble fabric of glorious bodies"(6, 235)[34] In short—as Niebuhr said—he had a "sacramental sense of all existence."[35] Edwards's *Personal Narrative* shows the immense importance that contemplating and experiencing nature had in each step of his spiritual development and, notably in his Miscellanies, he has left us some marvelous descriptions that are true hymns to nature. Moreover, the beauty and grandeur of nature were not only powerful drivers of his religious imagination but, when understood as "images and shadows of divine things," enabled the deciphering of a "kind of voice or language of God" (11, 67) in the created universe and the development of a "typological theology."[36]

Like the Cambridge Platonists, Edwards saw Reason as "the candle of the Lord," a guide implanted by God in man to light his existence here

---

29. Calvin, *Institutes*, 2. 2. 13. See also Vincent, *L'herméneutique du discours théologique*, 432–33.

30. Miller, *New England Mind*, 1:68.

31. Mather, *Danger of Apostasy*, in Miller, *New England Mind*, 1:84.

32. Donne, *Poems*, 1:189.

33. Miller, *New England Mind*, 1:69. On the importance of education for the Puritans, see, for example, Cremin, *American Education*, 177, 197–98, etc. J. Elliott, the apostle to the indians, translated a treatise on logic into Algonquin "to initiate the Indians in the knowledge of the Rule of Reason" so that they would better understand the Bible (Miller, *New England Mind*, 1:114).

34. For the marvels of the human body, see 14, 480.

35. Niebuhr, *Kingdom of God in America*, 116.

36. For Edwards's typology, see *supra*, p.45 n.95.

below and raise him up towards him (17, 67).³⁷ Human understanding is one of the supreme perfections of the created universe (8, 454),³⁸ a precious instrument to receive and understand the truth and, in particular, the essential truths regarding divinity. Heir to the Christian tradition of rational optimism, Edwards began his earliest known sermon with the words "Reasonable beings" (10, 296) and had immense confidence in the power of reason and the fruit of reflection. However, Edwards the theologian also knew that reason had been harmed by the fall and had lost its original vigor. Though created to understand divine things, human reason without the glorious light of the Gospel falls into gross idolatry (9, 399) because all of man himself is fallen and covered in corruption (3, 229).³⁹

Christian preachers should certainly not resort to overly harsh language when exhorting their neighbors and yet, if men could see their hearts, "they would see themselves as beasts, snakes and devils" (4, 420). Unregenerated by grace, natural man is in a terrible state.⁴⁰ Our "heart is a mere sink of sin, a fountain of corruption, whence issue all manner of filthy streams" (X, 115). And Edwards is not afraid to say with Illyrius Flaccus and Ursinus—and also with Calvin himself⁴¹—that because the image of God in man is effaced, the image of the devil is therefore sealed on the heart of man (X, 115);⁴² man "bears the image and deformity of the Devil" (19, 317) and is a genuine "devil incarnate" (24, 136).

---

37. This biblical expression (Prov 20:27) was recognized in philosophy by Cambridge Platonist Benjamin Whichcote, in Tulloch, *Rational Theology and Christian Philosophy*, 2:99.

38. The soul of man, the rational soul, is "by far the most glorious piece of divine workmanship" (20, 327).

39. The corruption of man that is taught in Scripture is corroborated by experience and even attested beyond the confines of Christian dogmatics. The rabbis profess that man is corrupt from infancy (23, 299); and, though "miserably bewildered in all their researches after the chief good" (23, 457) after vainly seeking the nature of ultimate happiness for six hundred years (9, 278), even ancient philosophers were not unaware of our fallen state. Gale wrote that "Jansenius breaks forth into a rapture upon observing these philosophers speak more truly about the corruption of man's nature than Pelagius and others of late" (23, 177). Plato taught that the cause of vice, or of a vicious nature, is "from our parents" (20, 241). Edwards also quoted Horace: "For no one is born without defects" (20, 456).

40. Because sin is "naturally dear" to us (24, 496), we find ourselves "naturally opposite to God" and in a state of radical "alienation and emnity" (25, 212).

41. Laporte, *La doctrine de Port-Royal*, 32n.2; Ritschl, *Dogmengeschichte des Protestantismus*, 264. The impious are recognized "as the children of Satan, from having degenerated into his image" (Calvin, *Institutes*, 1. 14. 18).

42. For parallels between Edwards and Illyrius Flaccus, see Crabtree, *Edwards' View of Man*, 26.

But what exactly is implied by this radical downfall of natural man? Aside from the deterioration of the human body, "an alteration of its sweet composition" that prevents it from faithfully submitting to the mind's commands and from following and carrying them out (13, 325),[43] and the weakening and darkening of the mind itself (19, 382–3), man's corruption primarily consists of an inveterate hatred of God and unbounded malice towards his neighbor. Natural men are "inveterate enemies" of God[44] who hatefully desire, as it were, "to destroy the essence of the Almighty" himself.[45] We have an innate tendency to turn against and oppose God and—the crucifixion of Jesus Christ confirms the basis of this observatio—we would kill him if we could (V, 292). Men are also one another's implacable adversaries and their vicious self-love pushes them to sin against their neighbor.[46] In this latter instance, there is no being as dangerous to a man as another man (3, 165).[47]

The seriousness of man's depravity arises first and foremost from his opposition to God because the least sin against an infinitely holy being is an infinite offense.[48] In the authentic line of a tradition which, stretching from

43. See *infra*, p.358 n.61. Ever since the Fall, our nature is polluted (24, 413) and in a "mean, defaced, broken, infirm, ruined state" (18, 208). For the curse on nature following the fall of man, see 22, 304; 5, 344–45; etc. Moreover, because the forces of nature have been subject to sin ever since, God's creation serves "men's wickedness" (24, 1015).

44. Calvin, *Institutes*, 3. 14. 6.

45. Hooker, *Application of Redemption*, in Miller and Johnson, *Puritans*, 1:295.

46. In their natural state, without a government to keep them in order, the members of a human society are "continually making a prey one of another . . . every one acting the part of an enemy to his neighbor, every one's hand against every man, and every man's hand against him; going on in remediless and endless broils and jarring" (25, 321). E. W. Hankamer, who quotes this passage, notes its Hobbesian affinities (*Das Politische Denken von Jonathan Edwards*, 224; see 177, 187). The stuttering starts of an unregulated market economy led the preacher to explore the classic theme of men acting "like wolves one to another" (Valeri, "Economic Thought of Edwards," 42–43). All of this seemed to anticipate the "intersubjectivity" of hell: "instead of the damneds' being comforted in each others' company, t'is probable that they will be as coals or brands in a fire, that heat and burn one another" (18, 357). Indeed, such corruption isn't limited to intersubjective transgressions, but also affects the political realm: "this world . . . has been filled with irregularities and confusion ever since the fall . . . all societies of men in all ages have been full of public irregularities" (14, 516) and, consequently, "the proceedings of kings and earthly judges may be inquired into" (14, 517).

47. Although man's hatred against God is undoubtedly greater than that against his neighbor (V, 293), there is a certain link between the respective transgressions against these two great commandments. The unpardonable sin—against God as God, i.e., in terms of his holiness—represents implacable opposition to the Trinitarian God of redemption, who has manifested and revealed himself, and therefore ordinarily implies the persecution of Christians who profess the holiness of God (18, 330).

48. See 2, 326; 3, 130; etc. This idea, which is only mentioned very briefly by the

Augustine to Schleiermacher, taught that there was no middle way between heaven and hell,[49] that "every interruption of religion is irreligion,"[50] that "the hypothesis of an intermediate state between the regenerate and unregenerate should not even be made,"[51] Edwards resisted every attempt to quantify or calculate the weight of sin and professed with Calvin that a sin is only venial by virtue of the gracious mercy of God.[52] By itself, every sin is mortal[53] and merits damnation (3, 114)![54] This indivisible character of evil excludes even the possibility of acts that are part good and part evil. Just as there is no middle way between life and death, Man in his natural fallen condition does not have gracious affections to any degree (18, 232–3), nor is his enmity against God diluted by any addition of love (V, 290). There are saints and sinners, friends and enemies of Christ (25, 525), and "the Bible does not recognize any neutral or third kind" (12, 216)[55]

In contrast to someone like Bishop Butler, seeing this radical dichotomy in human existence prevented Edwards from reducing vice to the simple absence of virtue.[56] Echoing Calvin, who scolded Augustine himself for having professed a purely negative view of evil,[57] Edwards refused to identify evil with simple non-being (17, 205) and taught that all men are constantly challenged to choose between good and evil. Choosing cannot be avoided and natural man's depravity essentially implies that he has always opted for evil. All of humanity is subject to this corruption and, "since the beginning of the world, the Devil has reigned peacefully" in the recently discovered Americas (5, 143),[58] and even in ancient Christian lands, "all men

---

young Edwards (13, 187), is discussed later in more detail (18, 341–42). As Foster observed in *A Genetic History of New England Theology*, 85, this argument harkens right back to Saint Anselm of Canterbury (*Why God Became Man*, 1. 21).

49. Saint Augustine, *Sermo*, 334. 3; see Kant, "Religion within Boundaries of Reason," 6:60n [Academy pagination].

50. Schleiermacher, *On Religion*, 118.

51. Heppe, *Dogmatics*, 519; see *Dogmatik*, 25, 598, 683, etc.

52. Calvin, *Institutes*, 2. 8. 59; see also "No sin of its own nature is so venial, or so small as not to merit damnation" (Wollebius, *Abridgment of Christian Divinity*, 84).

53. Moltmann, *Prädestination und Perseveranz*, 100. In a related context, see also Baius, *Dictionnaire de Théologie Catholique*, 3, 93.

54. Compare with "he that offends in one point is guilty of all" (20, 179). See *infra*, p. 377–78.

55. "There can be no neutral moral exercises" (Hopkins, *System of Doctrines, Works*, 1:236). "The human heart is either a heart of stone . . . or a new heart" (Hopkins, *System of Doctrines, Works*, 1:368).

56. Butler, "Nature of Virtue," 248. Edwards mentioned Butler in 21, 297, 315, etc.

57. Calvin, *Consensus Genevensis*, in Niemeyer, *Collectio*, 299.

58. A lot has been written about the attitude and conduct of the Puritans towards

immediately sin as soon as they are capable of it" (3, 135n.2)[59] Perversity is never idle; man's depraved nature not only has a virtual disposition towards

---

the Indians. In spite of J. Cotton's exhortation: "Offend not the poor natives, but as you partake in their land, so make them partakers of your precious faith" (Emerson, *John Cotton*, 53); in spite of a declaration in one of the very first colonial church documents regarding "the Indians whose good we desire to promote" (Walker, *Creeds and Platforms*, 118), and in spite of a reminder that "the first planters of this colony did ... come into this land with a design to convert the heathens to Christ," the 1679 Synod had to admit that the Indians had been treated "deceitfully and oppressively" (Walker, *Creeds and Platforms*, 430–1). For T. Shepard, the Indians were "unclean spirits" and "the ruins of mankind" (Youngs, "Indian Saints of New England," 242). They were the most degenerate of men (Slotkin, *Regeneration Through Violence*, 195). Even for someone like Franklin, they evoked images of hell (Slotkin, *Regeneration Through Violence*, 212; see also 251). For Cotton Mather, the massacre of the Indians was "a sweet sacrifice" to God, whereas Increase Mather went as far as to write this about his compatriots: "They did sometimes unhappily shoot men instead of Indians" (Heimert, "Puritanism, Wilderness, Frontier," 372). When applying *Paradise Lost* to the conditions in Massachusetts, C. Mather replaced the devils, horsemen fallen in a great angelic battle, with "Sygamore" Indians (*Magnalia Christi Americana*, 2:568). Barely 70 years later, an English writer made this ironic remark: "Naturalists have often puzzled themselves in endeavouring to account for the peopling of America; they may spare their future labours, for the late President of the college of New Jersey tells us it was colonised by the Devil!" ("History of Redemption," 120). Indeed, Jonathan Edwards subscribed to the belief that the Devil had led America's aboriginal inhabitants there so "that they might be quite out of the reach of the gospel, that here he might quietly possess them, and reign over them as their god" (9, 434). It helps to recall an example of a "copulative [or conjunctive] syllogism" proposed by young Immanuel Kant during the same period as Jonathan Edwards, pastor to the Indians, was writing his treatise on original sin: "Niemand dient Gott und dem Teufel zugleich; atqui die amerikaner dienen dem teufel, also nicht Gott [No one serves God and the Devil at the same time; if indeed the Americans serve the Devil, then they are not serving God]" (*Ak.*, 16, 749). Edwards, of course, called the Indians "barbarously ignorant" (10, 360), denied they had the light of grace before the coming of Christianity (3, 323), but after witnessing the astonishing influence of the Great Awakening on these "dregs of mankind" (4, 329), he could only hope for their ultimate conversion (7, 533). In the meantime, especially during his early years in Stockbridge, he fought unceasingly in defense of the Indians, helping them withstand the greed and negligence of the colonists exploiting them by buying their furs at dirt cheap prices, and especially by selling them rum in vast quantities to stupefy and defraud them (16, 437). He fervently pursued projects for the instruction of the Indians. While a village judge, "a professed deist," was suing them for their lands (16, 270), Edwards sent his own ten year old son two hundred leagues away to a missionary school among the Indians (Marsden, *Jonathan Edwards*, 404), he looked for a music instructor to teach the Indians how to sing in church (16, 597) and foresaw that these "savages" would one day study theology (16, 444).

59. See "sinning is infallibly connected with their existence" (Hopkins, *System of Doctrines, Works*, 1:220). In his sermons to the Indians, Edwards emphasized their depravity, yet as a case of the universal depravity of Adam's descendants that implied the equality of all men (Wheeler, "Friends to Your Souls," 749); compare with 3, 424.

evil but also a constant tendency to do it and to intensify his evil conduct (3, 136).

Voices would arise to accuse Puritan preachers of painting too somber a picture of man's natural condition, of ignoring what was good or rather that "good" would ultimately prevail over evil. In light of thefts, frauds, and murders, it is certainly tempting to believe that humanity is wicked—wrote the worthy George Turnbull—but why study the healthiness of the climate in a hospital or the moral condition of men in a court of law? Should we not instead consider the fact that honest townsfolk and farmers far outnumber the criminals and even the latter commit more innocent acts than blameworthy ones? Instead of obstinately emphasizing deplorable examples of moral depravity, shouldn't we instead focus our attention on "the innocence, natural good, diligence, happiness and gladness of heart that prevails among the great majority of men"?[60] What matters, however—observed Edwards—is not the fact that men accomplish more good deeds than evil ones, but the disposition that dominates and governs the heart, which alone determines their moral condition and consequently decides their eternal destiny. Would a boat be called fit "to cross the Atlantic" when it had not held together for the entire crossing but instead foundered and sank on the way, on the pretext that it had completed a large part of the trip before sinking (3, 219)?[61] Those who insist on our marked preponderance of good deeds should ask themselves if they could say that a lady was a worthy and faithful wife "if she had committed adultery from time to time with scoundrels and slaves, though less often than she had fulfilled her duties as a spouse." Since the greatest kindness cannot outweigh the least lapse with respect to an infinite being, humanity accordingly appears to have a flawless inclination to do moral evil that infinitely surpasses all the good that may be found in it (3, 132). This flawless inclination is due to original sin.

---

60. Turnbull, *Principles of Moral Philosophy*, 289 in 3, 108–9; see also Holbrook, "Introduction," 3, 38n.4, and 70–71. This sort of numerical apologetics was even practiced by Voltaire. Thefts and assassinations are rather rare; exceptional epidemics and cataclysms, together with wars—though frightening—only kill several thousand of some hundred million Europeans every century (*Extraits de la Bibliothèque Raisonnée*, *Œuvres*, 39:440). In a later period—and despite having read Edwards "with care" (*Dw.*, I, 543)—W. Paley began to study hospital statistics and, to prove the immense superiority of the good in this world over the bad, reported that, out of 6,420 patients admitted in a given period, 5,476 had been healed fairly quickly and only 234 had died (Cherry, *Nature and Religious Imagination*, 98).

61. See *infra*, p. 204. The argument harkens back to Plutarch ("Common Conceptions," 10).

2. Identity in Adam

If we are to believe Coleridge, original sin is the only unexplainable mystery of Christianity and yet one that explains all of the others.[62] After 35 years of writing and preaching theology with human corruption as one of its fundamental tenets, Edwards felt obliged to devote his last great treatise to "the defense of the great Christian doctrine of original sin and the demonstration of its truthfulness."[63] Essentially polemic in character, this book was written to refute the pernicious teachings of John Taylor that were corrupting the religion of the Christians in New England.[64] As usual, Edwards mostly cited contemporaries or relatively recent authors in this treatise and rarely mentioned the great theologians of the past. In reality, however, he accepted their teachings as given. Notwithstanding the presence of some novel ideas, the polemic character of the treatise did not prevent discussion of classical themes in the least.

The theologians of the Reformation were unanimous in emphasizing the positivity of original sin. Beginning with his course on the *Epistle to the Romans*, Luther reminds us that our hereditary corruption is not simply the absence of a quality of the will or a loss of the light of understanding, but a violent upset of our outer and inner faculties. It is "an affective inclination to evil, an aversion to good, an opposition to light and wisdom, a dilection for error and darkness."[65] Original sin is a propension as positive as the mag-

---

62. A century later, Chesterton observed that original sin was the only Christian dogma that could be empirically demonstrated (*Orthodoxy*, 22).

63. The preface is dated May 26, 1757 (3, 104). Edwards was able to correct the proofs but the book only appeared after his death. Among the major Edwardsean treatises, this one seems to be most unequal in philosophical and theological importance. A Scottish theologian observed that it was a work "whose defense of the doctrine of original sin contains the fullest and acutest answers . . . to the objections commonly urged against that doctrine" (Hill, *Lectures in Divinity*, 2:336). If H. Rogers is to be believed, the work in question is "the ablest exposition of the calvinistic doctrine on this point, ever written" ("Genius and Writings of Edwards," xl). But E. A. Park would be obliged to admit that this book, written by a man with a "constitution shattered by the fever and ague," showed "signs of hurried composition" ("New England Theology," 208). Violently hostile voices were never lacking. We could simply quote W. E. H. Lecky's designation of the work as "one of the most revolting books that have ever proceeded from the pen of man" (*Spirit of Rationalism in Europe*, 1:368n). Church historian W. Walker wrote: "Of all his works none is more ingenious or intellectualy acute, but none met so little acceptance" ("Jonathan Edwards," in Levin, *Jonathan Edwards*, 112). However, as already predicted in a very ancient recension: "His scheme . . . will be unintelligible.and useless to the bulk of the people" ("Doctrine of Original Sin Defended," 20).

64. See 3, 102; see also 12, 449, 501–2; for John Taylor, refer to C. A. Holbrook's Introduction (3, 68–70).

65. Luther, *Ad Romanos*, *Werke*, 56:312.

netic force of a magnet—to echo Melanchthon—and as effective as the sins themselves.[66] Or, to quote a definition by Calvin: "Original sin, then, may be defined a hereditary corruption and depravity of our nature, extending to all the parts of the soul, which first makes us obnoxious to the wrath of God, and then produces in us works which in Scripture are termed works of the flesh."[67] Original sin is therefore an effective reality and not a simple virtuality; not only "the omission of original good but also the commission of evil, its opposite."[68] It penetrates and corrupts the entire man and puts him in a situation where he is incapable of not sinning.[69]

Edwards, it should be repeated, wrote a polemic treatise that does not emphasize each element of ecclesial doctrine in the same way. He was primarily interested in proving the universality of sin, a task he believed he could accomplish using an "empirical" method. It was the universality of depravity that led to his conclusions about the inevitability of sin and, once reached, he wanted to show that corruption, though inevitable, was no less voluntary. Edwards defined original sin as "the innate sinful depravity of the heart," but he immediately added that "the subjection ... of Adam's posterity ... to the chastisement for this sin" (3, 107–8) is commonly included under this notion. Edwards found that the doctrine of original sin "conformed to experience" (23, 61), by which he meant the witness of Scripture and the facts of human life. The text of the treatise is stuffed with biblical citations and his conclusion is that there might not be any other theological doctrine—perhaps not even the teaching on the nature of God—that is so "clearly and explicitly" attested to by Scripture as the one dealing with original sin (3, 427).[70] With regard to the observation of human life, Edwards provides many examples of corruption in the conduct of men and their irresistible inclination to sin as soon as they are capable of it. Arguing from the principle that "a constant effect pleads for a constant cause" (3, 121), he concludes from the ever-repeated transgressions of men in favor of a firm determination of the human soul by and towards evil (3, 144). However, if the never-failing repetition of bad deeds demonstrates the immutable determination of the will towards evil, how can we continue to speak of any responsibility? Like Saint Augustine, Saint Thomas Aquinas, and Calvin

---

66. Melanchthon, *Commonplaces*, 37. There is no real difference in us between original sin and actual sin: "There is strictly speaking no other sin but actual sin" (Hopkins, *System of Doctrines, Works*, 1:224.)

67. Calvin, *Institutes*, 2. 1. 8.

68. Wollebius, *Abridgment of Christian Divinity*, 79.

69. For "representative" formulations of original sin in orthodox Calvinism, see Heppe, *Dogmatics*, 330–31.

70. See also *supra*, p. 53 n.117.

before him, Edwards believed that sin was only voluntary,[71] but how could this voluntary choice of evil be reconciled with the impossibility of not succumbing to temptation?

Jonathan Edwards devoted his most celebrated writings to showing that the subjection of man's will to evil is perfectly compatible with his full responsibility and this same doctrine is found in his discussion on original sin. If he ignored (or rather rejected) the idea of natural man's *physical* depravity, it was to highlight the firmly voluntary nature of each man's original sin,[72] and this preoccupation pushed him to specify that every man willed the Adamic transgression as much as Adam himself in his own time. Consequently, it wasn't simply a matter of following his example but one of effectively making his sin our own (3, 407–8). Well, in that case, he needed to prove that man willed and acted as Adam himself willed and acted. The depravity of the heart affects his posterity in the same manner as it affected our forefather; the tree exists in each of its buds and everything that happens in the roots immediately impacts even the branches (3, 379–80). A distinction should be made in every man between the cropping up of the first disordered movement and its subsequent confirmation in a bad moral disposition. Every man's first depraved movement has exactly the same consistency as Adam's sin. With the evil disposition of his heart, each descendant also fully approves of the sin that his forefather committed in his own time; his responsibility is his alone inasmuch as the evil disposition acts in his own being and rises up in his own heart (3, 390). Edwards literally believed that "all men sinned in Adam," but also did not take the firmly voluntary nature of every sin any less literally. To resolve this contradiction, he then only had to posit the metaphysical unity of every man with his forefather.

It is this doctrine of the real unity of every man with Adam that made Edwards a figure of theological innovation. Here he raises "the profound and difficult article" of the transmission of original sin[73] and his line of argu-

---

71. See 13, 521. As they are not dispossessed of their will but of their ability to will "a movement towards goodness" (Calvin, *Institutes*, 2. 3. 5), men never fail without its being willful and of their own accord (*Sermons sur l'épître à Tite*, Opera, 54, 383). Even what a man is compelled to do unwillingly, he does, if he does it, by his volition (Saint Augustine, "Spirit and Letter," 53).

72. This understanding—that original sin was profoundly voluntary—pervaded all New England theology and culminated in the famous text by N. W. Taylor, *Concio ad Clerum*, in Ahlstrom, *Theology in America*, 213–49.

73. Willard, *Divinity*, 198. As W. Whitacker put it, "Quaemadmodum ab Adamo ad posteros peccatum propagatum fuerit magis melius intelligitur quam explicatur [How sin spread from Adam to his descendants is better understood than explained]" (Heppe, *Dogmatik*, 276). Or, more popularly, from W. Perkins, "whereas the propagation of sin is as a common fire in a town, men are not so much to search how it came,

ment is based on an explanation of the sovereignly divine constitution of each finite individual's identity. Edwards starts with the fact that all identity is dependent and cannot be explained in terms of itself but only with reference to a divine action. In the latter case, all substance depends on God for its continuity and identity and this is *a fortiori* true for human beings who, as spiritual creatures, are subject to the immediate exercise of divine causality. And why not then find an analogy between the sovereign establishment of a person's identity and the "arbitrary" constitution of Adam's unity with each of his descendants? In the same way that continuity between two moments of one and the same person's conscience is possible because of a continuing creation that allows the attribution of guilt to a given individual, it is also quite possible to conceive of a similar sovereign constitution of God dealing with Adam's identity and continuity with each of his descendants (3, 389–90).

The essence of this doctrine was already stated in a Miscellany from Edwards's youth.[74] It would only be completed in one respect, i.e., subsuming both the notion of the individual's personal identity and that of his identity with his forefather under the general doctrine of continuing creation. Edwards builds on Locke, referencing a chapter of his *Essay* (6, 342) when first mentioning the problem of personal identity. Contrary to the Scholastics, John Locke did not consider the notion of personal identity to be self-evident and even used it as one of his very first examples of the absurdity of the theory of innate ideas.[75] The notion of personal identity itself had to be distinguished from that of a particular material substance. A person is a conscious being whose identity is wholly dependent on the unity and continuity of a conscience which, if really necessary, can be covertly "annexed" to several substances, just as a man can remain the same person "while wearing different clothes today than he wore yesterday."[76] Personal

---

as to be careful how to extinguish it" (*A Golden Chaine or the Description of Theology*, *Workes*, 1. 20).

74. "It is no more reasonable that we should be guilty of Adam's first sin, than that we should be guilty of our own that we have been guilty of in times past. For we are not the same as we were in times past, any other way than only as we please to call ourselves the same. For we are anew created every moment; and that is caused to be this moment, is not the same that was caused to be the last moment, only as there is such a relation between this existence now and a certain existence in time past as we call sameness; such as remembrance, consciousness, love, likeness, a continuation of being both as to time and place without interwal, etc.: which relations the sovereign God has constituted stated conditions of derivations of guilt. What relations he will constitute to be such conditions, is entirely at his will and pleasure" (13, 210).

75. Locke, *Essay*, 1. 4. 4.
76. Locke, *Essay*, 2. 27. 10.

identity is not the identity of the substance but of the conscience and "if Socrates and the current mayor of Queinborough agree, they are the same person." On the other hand, "if the same Socrates waking and sleeping do not partake of the same consciousness, Socrates waking and sleeping is not the same person."[77]

Edwards initially adopted Locke's definition (6, 342–43) but, after deep reflection that would last decades, he perceived its imperfections and ultimately expressed and explained his disagreement with it. The identity of the conscience—he wrote—is an insufficient basis for personal identity, which requires the unity of the being, i.e., of the substance (6, 385–86). A conscience is certainly an essential thing for a person's identity (3, 398), but there is always the possibility that God might annihilate me and then create another with the same ideas as those that presently fill my mind. Or again, God might very well create someone right now with the same conscience as mine, although he and I might be unaware of one another's existence and not experience our respective joys and sorrows. So then, in what sense would we be the same person (6, 386)?

3. The will and its object

In his definitive thought, Jonathan Edwards refused to explain our identity in terms of the continuity of our mental content. In other words, he did not want to reduce a person to memory. Unlike Locke's system, where philosophy had psychology as a paradigmic discipline, the logic underlying Edwards's metaphysics was theologico-moral in nature. The question that sparked this reflection was on the unity in sin of all men with Adam and this unity cannot be reached by studying the individual conscience. The real unity of all men with their forefather cannot be rendered plausible by psychological reflections. Philosophy can only express it in metaphysical terms. This is why Edwards integrates this question into his own version of continuing creation, i.e., the theory of immediate and arbitrary divine action. Jonathan Edwards began his meditations on the problem of identity in the context of the dogmatic fact of original sin and, so that he could explain it conceptually, he eventually developed a metaphysical view of identity under which he subsumed the dogmatic fact. Edwards developed his thesis of the sovereign constitution of Adam's identity with his descendants to demonstrate the genuinely voluntary character of every man's corruption, but this *theologoumena* also had a bearing on his theodicy. If there is an analogy between the constitution of the identity of Adam and his descendants on

77. Locke, *Essay*, 2. 27. 19.

the one hand and that of any other substance on the other hand, then, in a manner of speaking, God's positive intervention in the transmission of sin becomes of less importance. While the arbitrariness of divine agency is shown in a particularly striking way, the operation by which God established the unity in sin of all men with Adam only appears to arise from the general context in which this Great Being created all things and maintains their existence, which therefore makes it easier to affirm a genuine resumption of each individual's depravity for his own benefit.[78]

The first end of Edwards's theory was to provide a plausible explanation of the dogma on the transmission of original sin while also enabling this "rigid Calvinist" to accomplish the *tour de force* of minimizing divine responsibility for our corruption, even despite the insistence that "the human race has not naturally derived corruption through its descent from Adam; but that result is rather to be traced to the appointment of God."[79] Edwards accordingly succeeded in practicing theodicy through the very act of professing the positive intervention of God in the advent of every man's corruption. A third, significant outcome of Edwards's theory as a means of providing a metaphysical explanation of the dogma and formulating a theodicy was a reworking of the "science of the will" (1, 133), that fundamental level of man's very own being, i.e., his fallen state.

Edwards exalted the importance of the science of the will but did not practice it for purely theoretical reasons. A theologian, observer and interpreter of our corrupt condition, he wanted to base the notion of fallen nature in metaphysics and show that if all men without exception sin, it is because their will necessarily predisposes itself to evil. Individual good is the object of the individual will and philosophers have always taught that this individual good, though partial and limited, can nonetheless be the object of a legitimate desire and can also develop into an egotistical individual good where the absence of universality becomes opposition to universality. What Jonathan Edwards taught—in line with Saint Augustine, Saint

---

78. We might indeed wonder about the great philosophical fragility of speculative thinking that "subverts all our ideas" (Hodge, *Systematic Theology*, 2:222) and yet, from the perspective of a metaphysical view founded on the sovereignty of God, it presents a plausible "solution" to the inextricable problem of hereditarily transmitted sin that nonetheless remains voluntary. Having said that, C. Chauncy judged Edwards's thesis to be "as absurd as . . . the doctrine of transubstantiation" (*Five Dissertations*, 271–72). In more moderate terms, it was called a theory that "differs from and opposes all the rest" (Beecher, *Conflict of Ages*, 315).

79. Calvin, *Commentaries on First Book of Moses*, 156. Compare with "The cause of the contagion is neither in the substance of the flesh nor the soul, but God was pleased to ordain that those gifts which he had bestowed on the first man, that man should lose as well for his descendants as for himself" (*Institutes*, 2. 1. 7).

Thomas Aquinas, and Calvin—is that it is not only possible for individual good to become opposed to the common good, but that it is actually and even necessarily opposed to it and has, in a manner of speaking, a metaphysical calling to make this transition to evil and ultimately *is* itself evil. Man's natural condition is not only virtually but also truly evil, and this is explained not only by spiritual and moral considerations, but can also be demonstrated on a strictly metaphysical level.

In its attempts to explain the concept of man's naturally sinful condition, Christian thought has to avoid several pitfalls. On the one hand, it should not attempt to state the issue in ontological terms; good and evil, regenerated condition, and natural condition are not different levels of being but states into which the subjectivity of the mind is changed. On the other hand, this change should not be seen as originating from the outside, but instead as a movement springing from the most active core of the mind. In the latter case, if the corruption is to be envisaged as a truly existential change, it should never be represented in temporal dispersion, like an unmediated series of successive moments. This natural condition is a change that bears the whole weight of being and emanates from the very core of the mind. In other words, this natural condition can be understood as an effective, instantaneous passage from limitation to perversion, from privation to transgression. And this passage is the very being of the will.

The will is the only reality that involves a true change without temporal dispersion. It is present in each of its moments in its entirety and renews its entire work in every instant. Kant later wrote that "every evil action [volition] must be so considered, as if the human being had fallen into it directly from the state of innocence,"[80] an intuition that expresses the Christian vision of the natural condition as an instantaneous and constant passage from individual good (if starting with limitation) to active opposition or from evil to the common good. The instant character of the passage of the will to evil is a veritable *leitmotiv* for Edwards, who untiringly repeats that the will does not have to be explained in terms of its antecedent causes but only in terms of its present volitions. The passage of the mind from individual good to evil does not occur within the space of a moment, but instead necessarily takes place at every instant of that moment. Only these will-based interpretations account for the dialectic of an inevitable passage of the mind from limitation to corruption, from its primitive condition of weak light to its present reality of "contrary light."[81]

---

80. Kant, "Religion within Boundaries of Reason," 6:41.
81. Hopkins, *System of Doctrines, Works*, 1:400.

The contrary light that characterizes this natural condition is a function of the immediate and necessary transposition from individual good to evil. From time immemorial, philosophers have delighted in baptizing the object of the will with the name "good," a term that couldn't be more ambiguous. Calvin had already complained about assigning "good" as the natural object of the will. Philosophers—he wrote—tirelessly repeat "that all things seek good through a natural instinct," but this still does not mean that the human will is naturally inclined towards genuine good. And actually—adds Calvin—"if you attend to what this natural desire of good in man is, you will find that it is common to him with the brutes. They, too, desire what is good; and when any semblance of good capable of moving the senses appears, they follow after it." Here the will is only taken to be a natural inclination and the good it desires has nothing to do with "virtue or righteousness."[82] Edwards himself also wanted to avoid the pitfalls of a terminology where a naturalist metaphysic of desire surreptitiously became an ethic of the will. He strove to develop a definition of the will and its object in a way that exorcised it of all ethical ambiguity.

For Edwards, the will is determined by the strongest motive and he used "motive" to describe everything that excites and moves the will. Consequently, what the mind perceives as its motive is viewed as something good; it can then be said that "the will is always like the greatest apparent good" (1, 142). It is important not to lose sight of the word "apparent." The "good" in question here is not the good itself but rather something that excites the natural appetite of the mind. To dispel any ambiguity, Edwards immediately remarked that he used the term "good" as a synonym for "agreeable" and understood "evil" as referring to what was "disagreeable" (1, 287).[83] Thus far—as can be observed—Edwards has remained on common philosophical grounds, the omnipresent and fairly innocuous heritage of Western thought, and this seemingly neutral and very traditional doctrine appears to have governed Edwards's reflections from his distant beginnings. Don't we read in *The Mind* that Edwards understood "good" to be what "agrees with the inclinations and dispositions of the mind" (6, 376)? In reality, what appears to be a very classic and ordinary definition is given new meaning, because Edwards agreed with the Scriptures that "the imagination of man's heart is evil from his youth." Since a corrupt mind can only agree with evil dispositions, an evil disposition leads to evil!

---

82. Calvin, *Institutes*, 2. 2. 26.
83. For natural good and evil as pleasure and pain, see 18, 462.

4. The mechanics of egoism

The proper object of the mind's natural dispositions is individual good as opposed to any other good. This is a dogmatic teaching of the Calvinists, but also one that is justified by empirical developments. The great sin of pride is self-exaltation, but since a person can only exalt himself in relation to other people, pride is therefore a "comparative exaltation of oneself" (20, 209). The adjective "comparative" denotes the metaphysical fact that man is only man through interaction with other men, but this essential conditioning of his existence is vitiated from the start. Man can only be man through and with other men, but as soon as he is man, he also finds himself opposed to other men. We read in a Miscellany that self-love without restraint—exercised without the transcendent influence of a higher power—will incline us "to delight in another's misery, because self-love seeks its own comparative happiness . . ." by putting others down and "will delight in cruelty and putting others to pain, because it appears to it as an exercise of power" (18, 478).

Here we have a sort of physics of evil, where the elevation of one being has its counterpart in the abasement of another, and where the power of one can only be deployed by oppressing the power and being of another. People are not in a neutral space where they are separated from one another by so many peaceful *no man's lands*. There isn't enough space for all men and, by moving, i.e., existing, they cannot avoid infringing on others. Self-love is necessarily opposed to the good of others, and man has a natural inclination within him to transgress against his neighbor.[84]

Writing in an era in which the relationship of selfless love to self-love never ceased to be debated and compared to Fénelon by his posterity, Edwards resolutely took a "hedonist" position. The only motive that can motivate natural man, self-love, was initially understood as only an inclination to pleasure and a hatred of pain, i.e., nothing other than "a capacity for enjoyment or suffering." The proper object of self-love is therefore man's proper good—and here is the heart of the problem—because it can extend in two directions: (a) Every good a person enjoys and every thing in which he delights, and (b) "a person's proper good, i.e. his own and separate good" (18, 73). In the first acceptance of this term, proper good is defined positively and as something in itself and, in the second, negatively and relative to others. In the first case, "proper good" doesn't yet have any moral qualifications; in the second, it constitutes the very essence of the offense and transgression and becomes the metaphysical presupposition for all moral reflection.

---

84. See *supra*, p. 71–72.

An optimistic view of man holds that he can secure his good without detriment to the interests of others, whereas a realistic view of our nature reveals that seeking our own good necessarily means opposing the good of others. The adversaries of Calvinism reproach it for having an overly rigid view of natural man's inability to feel genuine love for God and his neighbor, but the objection itself betrays a flawed metaphysic that only retains the primary, positive sense of proper good while ignoring its negative, comparative aspect. Natural self-love is incompatible with true love because proper good, in the negative sense that characterizes man's natural condition, is in opposition to common good. Because there are two goods, there are two loves. On the one hand, general benevolence, with the Universal Being as its object; on the other hand, private affection, which turns towards one or more individual beings. And private affection is not merely different from general benevolence, but directly opposed to it.

Affection—wrote Edwards—for a particular object not only sets us in opposition to the supreme object of virtuous affection, but "would become *itself* an opposition to that object."[85] Private affection, if not subordinate to general benevolence, is not only liable to issue in enmity to Being in general, but will necessarily result in it. An affection detached from general benevolence is not only independent of it, but also opposed to it. If it is the case, by virtue of immanent necessity, that private affection is condemned to end in opposition to Being in general, then this flows from the nature of its object. The object of self-love and all private affection in general is its proper good; the object of general benevolence is the Universal Being, the Supreme Good, and any elevating the individual above the Universal Being is also in opposition to it. If we can only exalt individual beings, such as our haughty selves, to the detriment of other individual beings, how much more sinful must it be to forsake the Universal Being, the Supreme Good! We pretend not to turn away or set our attention on a particular object. However, this pretence of neutrality is pure fiction because those who neglect the Sovereign Good are *eo ipso* opposed to him. Making a subject, a mere individual, the object of their affections "puts down Being in general." When the good from which we seek to break away is the Supreme Good, separation amounts to opposition (8, 554–56)!

The moral physic applies to the relationships between individual good and common good even more clearly than the mutual relationships between particular goods. It amounts to a metaphysical "deduction" in man's natural blindness in matters of religion and morality and a philosophical conceptualization of the Christian doctrine of the mind's naturally wicked

---

85. For private affection as evil, see *infra*, p. 205–6.

disposition and of the universally observable fact that "there is a strong tendency in Man to seek his good in the creature, to remain apart from God, in opposition to the general union and dependence on God that is the goal of the Gospel" (24, 1025). Indeed, precisely because it concerns a disposition of the mind, a sphere that involves the will and therefore intention and responsibility, this necessary physico-metaphysical demonstration of opposition between particular good and common good ultimately seems insufficient. To illustrate the immanent corruption of the mind by the sin of Adam, we could evoke the image of a mechanism where the movement of a spring automatically causes a change in the forces within the entire system (see 3, 50 and n.8) but, to be specific, translating a moral process into quasi-physical terms has serious drawbacks. Since the essence of all moral reality is individual responsibility, would the necessary interaction of physico-metaphysical forces allow the establishment of such responsibility? If responsibility presupposes a requirement for liberty—for so we are told— how do we find liberty within a necessary movement? In other words, if the human will opposes the common by the simple act of tending towards its object and sins by the simple act of existing, can it still be considered a free faculty? Since, like Descartes, we have traditionally thought that "voluntariness and freedom are one and the same thing,"[86] how can we affirm the free character of actions done out of necessity? The problem of the identity of necessity and liberty has haunted Western thought since the Stoics and been compounded by Christian reflections on man's original corruption involving a necessity that the will freely imposes on itself.

Edwards's task is therefore to prove that the inevitable and necessary character of the transgression does not negate liberty, i.e., the responsibility of the willing agent.[87] The dogmatic solution to this problem was presented by the *theologoumenon* of a divine constitution under which every man takes personal responsibility for the sin of his forefather. Yet this was only a dogmatic solution presented as a hypothesis that speculative theologians formulated to their liking, without any demonstrative or empirical justification. However, it is nothing of the sort, because this hypothesis is found in a work on original sin that came out within a period of a few years after the *Enquiry into Freedom of Will*, a book overflowing with arguments and proofs that would make this most audacious of Edwards's theses appear plausible and sensible. The imputation of the transgression to each individual by an arbitrary divine constitution is but the crown on a whole chain

---

86. Descartes, "Third Set of Objections with Replies," 7:191 [Adam and Tannery pagination].

87. For this, see M. Veto, "La Mauvaise Volonté selon Jonathan Edwards," in Veto, *Le mal*, 213–40.

of reflections that exerted every effort to formally prove the possibility that an individual could be held entirely responsible for a volition and action which that individual could not avoid choosing. This is again the problem of justifying the imputation of a transgression to someone without the power to not commit it. In the case of original sin, the act in question took place in the distant past and issued from another individual. On the contrary, in the inquiry on the will found in every man, we are dealing with acts being performed *now* by an author who is also their *present* subject. Nonetheless, this lapse in time and difference in subject do not in any way change the fact that both cases involve the same speculative model. That the volition is separated from the action by all of history or the shortest moment, or that the physical author of the act is another or myself has no effect whatsoever on the apparent absence of liberty in the action performed (see 3, 387–8). This is the same metaphysical model of a necessarily performed act found in original sin and in our present sins, and Edwards's basic preoccupations tend to prove that, notwithstanding its necessary character, the agency defined by the model continues to incur responsibility, i.e., the fact that this liberty excludes free will does not in any way change human responsibility, which saves the moral character of the willing subject without removing him from a necessary determination of his volition and consequent action.

5. The *Enquiry into Freedom of Will*

In 1746, after having written a certain number of Miscellanies on the problem of free will during his youth,[88] Edwards told his friend and disciple J. Bellamy of his intent to publish something on this subject (16, 218) and, in the following year, stated in a letter to Erskine that the context for the work was the controversy over Arminianism (*Dw.*, I, 250). Edwards was seriously concerned about the threat that the Arminian stranglehold on the mind of New England represented and his polemic against these modern Pelagians aimed to reaffirm Calvinist teachings on the sovereignty of God via a vigorous defense of its corollary, the mystery of the will under bondage.[89] After

---

88. See 13, 208, 217, 238, etc.

89. The Arminian deluge that swept over New England (Bellamy, *True Religion Delineated*, Works, 1:49) arose from the teachings of Arminius, who had been condemned by the Synod of Dort, although orthodox Calvinism used the term "Arminian" to describe all those who professed "a charming Religion," i.e., one that rejected or watered down the great dogmas of regeneration by grace, original sin, and natural depravation (Bellamy, *True Religion Delineated*, Works, 1:116–17). For Arminians in America, refer to Wright, *Unitarianism in America*. The essential difference between Arminians and Calvinists is that "the grace or virtue of truly good men not only differs from the

reflecting at length on this subject and studying the best Arminian writers, Jonathan Edwards began to write his major work in 1752 and finished it at the beginning of the following year.[90] Only appearing in Boston in 1754, the book began a triumphant run that extended to some twenty editions.

The *Enquiry into Freedom of Will* is the best known, most admired, and most loathed work by Jonathan Edwards. It was this text that, in a manner of speaking, brought America into the history of philosophy,[91] as well as being practically the first work written by an author born in the New World that Protestant theologians in Europe would deign to study. Read, reread, praised, and commented upon *ad nauseam*[92] in America, this work was long used as a teaching manual,[93] with summaries and refutations of it constantly being published. It was the logical power and virtuosity of the argument[94] that most elicited the greatest admiration. It was a work—we read—that elevated its author to the same rank as Leibniz and Locke, and it was thanks to it that Edwards surpassed Kant and Spinoza![95] In philosophy, Jonathan Edwards is forever known as the author of the *Enquiry* and it therefore comes as no surprise that critical publishing at Yale began with this work. Moreover, the work was never viewed simply as a study of a technical

---

virtue of others in *degree*, but even in *nature and kind*" (7, 523). The great majority of Anglicans have become Arminians (9, 431–32) and every Arminian is three-quarters Papist (G. Tennent, *The Necessity of Holding Fast the Truth*, in Heimert and Miller, *Great Awakening*, 514n.3); the system of Arminius is "almost Catholic" (Brémond, *Sentiment Religieux en France*, 1:164). Arminianism is essentially a variant of the Pelagian doctrine that denied original sin and the Holy Spirit's influence in conversion and affirmed the power of free will (9, 406). Like Chauncy, modern Pelagians teach that "there is . . . a certain *fitness* or *unfitness* of conduct . . . antecedently to, and independently of, all will whatsoever, not excepting even the will of God Himself" (*Benevolence of the Deity*, 34). At the root of all that lies the "diabolical arrogance" of a belief in free-will (Calvin, *Sermon sur L'épître aux Éphésiens*, *Opera*, 51, 597). For a comparison of Arminianism, Pelagianism, deism, and atheism, see *infra*, p. 271 n. 87.

90. Ramsey, "Introduction," 1, 7.

91. See Parain, *Histoire de la Philosophie*, 1032.

92. Hopkins, "one of the greatest efforts of the human mind, that has appeared, at least in this century" (*Life*, 85); "the greatest work which the century produced on this subject" (Miller, *Retrospect of the Eighteenth Century*, 2:30, etc.). Eugène Vail echoes this praise in France: "The *Inquiry* is one of the finest expositions of metaphysical philosophy ever written" (*Hommes de lettres des états-Unis*, 209).

93. Gohdes, "Aspects of Idealism," 549, n.54.

94. Rogers, "Genius and Writings," xxi. His argumentation "has never been equaled in power, and certainly has never been refuted" (Huxley, *Hume*, 194–95). This argumentation, in and of itself, serves to glorify God (Schlaeger, "Edwards' Theory of Perception," 67–8).

95. See *supra*, p. xxi. Compare with "the one large contribution which America has made to the deeper philosophical thought of the world" (Allen, *Jonathan Edwards*, 283).

problem of philosophy but, starting with its publication, was understood for its broader significance, namely as a vigorous reaffirmation of the spirit and letter of Calvinism and as a profound apology for the doctrine of the Reformers in the difficult era of the Enlightenment.

Writing during the great New Theology period, Jonathan Edwards the Younger explained that American Protestants were beginning to be ashamed of their own faith and were on the point of abandoning the Calvinist doctrine of liberty and necessity, which could have irreparably compromised the essential doctrines of orthodoxy. It was the *Enquiry* that put an end to the apparent triumph of the Arminians.[96] With the possible exception of the *Theodicy* of Leibniz, it is perhaps the greatest effort the human mind has ever made "to get rid of the seeming antagonism between the scheme of necessity and the holiness of God"[97] and is more suitable than any book outside of Scripture to illuminate the mysteries of Calvinism.[98] Of course, this "*Principia* of Calvinist theology"[99] did not only elicit praise, but, over and beyond objections of a logical and metaphysical order,[100] the "greatest American theologian" was accused of having destroyed human morality and blasphemed the holiness of God. If a text from the end of the eighteenth century is to be believed, Edwards "removed Man's free agency and made God the author of all the sins of men and angels."[101] A slightly older pamphlet expressed the opinion that if Edwards's thesis was correct, "then we are no more susceptible to virtue or vice than a hatchet, sword or gun," which amounts to "acquitting men and devils of all responsibility and blame and casting the entire burden on the ever-blessed God." The author concludes that Edwards's theses "go against all morality and religion and encourage an

---

96. J. Edwards, *Remarks on the Improvements Made in Theology by his Father, President Edwards*, in Edwards, *Works*, 1:482. The *Enquiry* is a "monument" against the errors of the time (West, *Essay on Moral Agency*, x). With it, "he effectively redeemed the doctrines called Calvinist from the scorn" of their adversaries (Isaac Taylor, quoted by Miller, *Jonathan Edwards*, 229–30).

97. Bledsoe, *Theodicy*, 98.

98. The reference, given by A. V. G. Allen (*Jonathan Edwards*, 285) to Chalmers, *Works*, 1, 318 is incorrect.

99. Parton, *Life and Times of Burr*, 1:29.

100. This "essay that splits hairs in four, finely chops trifles" (Channing, "Edwards and the Revivalists," 374–94), where Edwards subjugates rational arguments to the "chimera of Calvinist orthodoxy" ("Review of 'Freedom of the Will,'" 434–38). Others wrote of "a logical failure on a grand scale" (Foster, *History of New England Theology*, 75); of "logomachy" (Plues, *Spurgeon and His Brethren*, in Lesser, *Jonathan Edwards*, 64); of being a "Boa Constrictor" in logic (Cheever, "Review of Tappan's Works," in Lesser, *Jonathan Edwards*, 44); of using an overabundant flow of arguments that fatigued readers without convincing them (King, "Edwards as Philosopher and Theologian," 37).

101. Smith, *Fall of Angels and Men*, iii.

atheistic life under the pretext of philosophy."[102] The accusation against this work's "false and blasphemous doctrines" echoed until the middle of the nineteenth century, a time when A. Bledsoe felt compelled to remark that, with his book, Jonathan Edwards had "dealt a mortal blow to the vital and fundamental principles of all religion."[103]

This highly praised and disparaged work contains one of the most complete expositions ever on the "science of the will" and it is hard to find a development of the dialectic of the will under bondage that is as powerful and detailed as the one he presents. In a firestorm of arguments, the author seeks to prove several essential theses, which are always the same. The will—he taught—is a faculty whose essence is not a so-called liberty of indifference to choose but the effective power to choose. Free will is only a philosophical myth; in reality, the will always wills necessarily. However, the fact that it was determined by an antecedent cause still does not negate the will's free and accountable character since it is defined by the nature and not the cause of its volition. Because the whole man—and not a remote intention—is the moral subject, such determination by an antecedent cause does not detract in any way from the merits of virtue or the demerits of vice.[104]

6. Will and liberty

Locke's influence on Edwards shows throughout his entire theory of knowledge and also in his doctrine of the will. Locke taught that man is free insofar as he is able to make an action happen or not happen by so choosing in his mind. In other words, I am free when, by my own volition, I can make something exist or not, for who is freer than someone who has the power to do what he wills?[105] However, men moved by a desire to dismiss all thoughts of guilt are not content with this basic and clear concept of freedom but hold that a man is only truly free when he is as free to *will* as he is to *act* what he wills. It is therefore not enough for a man to have the power to act since he

---

102. Newtoun, *Against the Doctrine of Fate* in Haroutunian, *Piety Versus Moralism*, 235. Edwards was hailed as "a powerful coadjutor" by the apostles of modern unbelief, who triumph with the help of the *Enquiry*, that veritable "text-book of infidelity" (Taylor, *Logic and Other Essays*, 20, 12, 38).

103. Bledsoe, *President Edwards' Inquiry*. With "this naked and physical view of the question of human liberty" (Blakey, *History of Philosophy of Mind*, 4:498), Edwards led man to "cast off all solicitude about his moral *conduct*" (Newtoun, *Against the Doctrine of Fate*, quoted in Boller, *Freedom and Fate*, 21).

104. For a description of the Edwardsian doctrine of the will and its metaphysical implications—of "the will in itself"—see Veto, *La naissance de la volonté*, 151–80.

105. Locke, *Essay*, 2. 21. 21.

must also have power over his own volition; and we know perfectly well that the will does not have such freedom because, in any particular case, a man must unavoidably choose one thing or another.[106] Moreover, it is said that the will is only free if it can choose either of the two given courses of action. We must not lose sight of the fact that *"freedom consists in the dependence of the existence, or non-existence of any action, upon our volition of it; and not in the dependence of any action, or its contrary, on our preference."* A man standing on a cliff is at liberty to leap sixty feet downwards into the sea, not because he has the power to do the contrary action, which is to leap sixty feet upwards, but because he has the power to leap or not to leap. But if a greater force than his either holds him fast or tumbles him down, he is no longer free in that case.[107] Freedom does not consist in the capacity to determine our will, but in the power to govern our actions.[108]

Edwards frequently referred to Locke in the context of his discussions on freedom and the will,[109] and he fully agreed with the *Essay* that freedom was the effective power exerted by the will to bring something to pass in the world. Moreover, he even surpassed the English philosopher in his efforts to negatively define freedom as the absence of constraints on action. Freedom—he said—is "the power, opportunity, or advantage, that any one has, to do as he pleases. Or in other words, his being free from hindrance or impediment in the way of doing, or conducting in any respect, as he wills." Or again: "the proper and original sense of a man's liberty . . . is being in a state where he can act according to his good pleasure and do as he wants" (18, 197). Philosophers have always defined the will in terms of its immediate effectiveness, but Edwards now included liberty in this immediate effectiveness and without regard to either the suspension of attention or the capacity to choose. The brutal and unconditional subsumption of liberty under the will allowed this Calvinist theologian to develop a metaphysical and moral theory where the absence of any choice, indetermination, or indifference does not compromise moral responsibility. The *Enquiry* advocated a formal and not merely a material identity of the will and liberty and, in so doing, took inspiration from Locke's rejection of faculty psychology, which it did not fail to generalize on a metaphysical level.

While Locke wanted to avoid breaking up the mind into isolated functions, Edwards went further in also refusing to distinguish faculties from

---

106. Locke, *Essay*, 2. 21. 22, 23.

107. Locke, *Essay*, 2. 21. 27.

108. Regarding this position in the history of Western philosophy, see Arendt, *Life of the Mind*, vol. 2.

109. See 1, 138–40, 143, 164, 171, 353, 377n, etc.

their own acts. Just as the subject *is* its faculties, the faculties *are* their acts. In other words, just as a subject should not be made subordinate to its faculties or precede them, faculties should not be represented as a substratum or support for their various acts.[110] The profound finality of this position was to disallow the infinite regression of the causes of a voluntary action and, in so doing, make the total attribution of the action to its effective agent possible. Another consequence of this position was the introduction of an ethic where every voluntary act fully expressed its subject, ultimately leading to a theological metaphysic where man's condition, i.e., his naturally sinful condition, became as though it had been willed and assumed by him at every moment.

This is one of the metaphysical models that is characteristic of Edwardsian speculation. It was already present in his ontology, namely in the pantheistic developments on the continuity of God and the creature, and would also appear in his epistemology: when there is true knowledge, the mind is one with its object and, in a manner of speaking, even *is* its object.[111] With regard to the will, this perfect correlation (of choice) with its object, already noted by an old commentator,[112] is seen on two levels. When analyzing an act of the will, Edwards insisted on the fact that its object is not external but rather its own act. The will always "chooses" what pleases it the most; for example, what is most agreeable to a drunkard is not the alcohol but his own act of drinking (1, 143). However, we shouldn't speak of choosing insofar as this notion involves an expectation, a suspension of judgment, a deliberation or especially the possibility that its term might be extended. It is said that the object of the will is its good. It is the greatest good that determines the will or, to be more precise, the greatest apparent good (6, 348). If, in *The Mind*, Edwards emphasized the dynamic character of the factors that determine the will, it was to highlight all the more the continuity or absence of hiatus between the will and its object. Thirty years later, he tried again and improved his definition. Rather than stating that the will is determined by the greatest apparent good, we should instead say that "the will always is as the greatest apparent good, or, as what appears most agreeable" because "an appearing most agreeable to the mind, and the mindss preferring, seem scarcely distinct" (1, 144). The conscious omission of the word "determined" clarified and highlighted the immediate character of the will and the need to avoid all external factors likely to engender an idea of distance, i.e., duality. Good is therefore what is most agreeable to the

---

110. For this, see Edwards, "Liberty and Necessity," in Edwards, *Works*, 1:295-98.
111. See *infra*, p. 250-51.
112. Tappan, *Edwards's "Inquiry into the Will,"* 31.

dispositions of the mind (6, 371) and is not the fruit of a long process, but immediately and directly imposes itself on the mind.

However, if the choice imposes itself on the will, in what sense can it be said to be free? This question confronts us with the famous notion of *liberty of indifference* which, in a manner of speaking, Leibniz had pulverized but which the Arminians continued to brandish against the Calvinists. It held that, to be truly free to choose, the will must be in a state of indetermination. When called upon to choose a possible action, the will must be in state of indifference with respect to what it actually chooses. However, this theory involves two contradictions. On the one hand, it requires the subject making the choice to remain indifferent, i.e., to be indeterminate when making a determination and, on the other hand, to be indeterminate when making a commitment to something determinate. With respect to the first contradiction, Edwards explained that, at any given moment, the will can do anything it wants. The will wills its act and is incapable of not willing its present act (1, 305). Seventeenth-century Thomism and also Descartes had already taught that, when choosing its act, the will cannot be indifferent in any way. What is done cannot remain undone at the time when it is done and, at the very instant when the will chooses a particular act, it cannot choose another. Freedom does not therefore consist in the power to turn from an act but only in the ease with which it is determined.[113] As for this so-called indifference, it requires the subject to will and not will an act at the same moment. The will chooses according to its good pleasure and, to be able to act as it pleases, it is said that the will must act indifferently. However, this pleasure is always caused by a preponderant motive which, to be precise, is absent in a state of indifference.

To say that the will—when indifferent—can act according to its good pleasure is tantamount to saying that "it can act according to its good pleasure when it has no such good pleasure." A man is in a state of indifference when he has to choose between two absolutely similar cakes and may only choose between them by preferring one over the other. But exactly how it is possible to prefer one thing over another when the two are identical? Drawing on the principle of the identity of indiscernibles,[114] the conclusion of this development was that those led by "a false sensation of seeming experience"[115] to promote a liberty of indifference condemn man to "choose without a choice" (1, 198). The other contradiction is "objective." As every volition requires the willing of a determined act, how is it possible to derive

---

113. Gilson, *La liberté chez Descartes et la théologie*, 430–31.
114. See *supra*, p. 59–60.
115. Hume, *Enquiry*, 103n.7.

a determined act from an indeterminate subject? Uninterrupted continuity of cause and effect is required and this is exactly what is lacking between an undetermined agent and a determined agent.[116]

In any event, the reasoning of those holding to a liberty of indifference is based on a mistake regarding the time of choosing. They stress the willing subject's indifference at the exact moment of choosing, i.e., of volition, so that the subject can commit to his choice in complete liberty. However, we cannot ask the subject to be indifferent at the very moment of choosing, because then he wouldn't make a choice! The act of choosing, wrote Edwards, "may be immediately after a state of indifference, but has no coexistence with it" (1, 207). There may be indifference before but not during determination and, what interests us is not the past but the present—not the antecedents of the exercise of the will but its effective exercise.

Using a wealth of brilliant arguments, Edwards exposed in detail the logical absurdities concealed in the notion of a liberty of indifference and, rather than limiting his critique to the sphere of logic, also drew frequently on arguments of a moral nature. Defenders of a liberty of indifference want to preserve liberty, i.e., responsibility, and yet that very liberty of indifference is not defensible from a moral point of view. Arminians—"who seem the most jealous of the rights of free will"[117]—teach that an act must have been chosen by a completely indeterminate will in order for it to be free. However, this radical indetermination amounts to a perfect contingency and, as such, is hardly suited to a moral faculty. Here Edwards is referring to Locke (21, 225–26), though he is also and more particularly following in the wake of Leibniz, who so eloquently explained the incompatibility of liberty of indifference with any type of moral responsibility. Leibniz was up against the zealous defenders of divine omnipotence, which apparently would be mutilated by any determination, even a determination towards good. For this philosopher, "the highest freedom to be impelled to the best by a right reason. Whoever desires any other freedom is a fool."[118] Acting according to his nature, which is goodness itself, is a happy necessity for God. "Is it to be desired that God should not be bound to be perfect and happy? Is our condition, which renders us liable to fail, worth envying? And should we not be well pleased to exchange it for sinlessness . . . ? One must indeed be weary of life to desire the freedom to destroy oneself and to pity the Divinity for

---

116. "To claim that a determination comes from a complete indifference absolutely indeterminate is to claim that it comes naturally from nothing" (Leibniz, *Theodicy*, 3. 320.

117. Descartes, "To Elizabeth," 4:316 [Adam and Tannery pagination].

118. Leibniz, "To Magnus Wedderkopf," 146–47.

not having that freedom."[119] For God to be moved to act by something other than goodness would not only be an imperfection but evil itself. "To do less good than one could is to be lacking in wisdom or in goodness."[120] And, at the end of his life, Leibniz exclaimed in one of his letters to Clarke: "it is the most perfect liberty not to be hindered from acting in the best manner!"[121]

7. Liberty and necessity

Edwards, who had read Clarke's work and had at least a secondhand knowledge of the theses of his correspondence with Leibniz,[122] frequently noted the absurdity of depriving God of his goodness and wisdom on the pretext of saving his sovereign freedom, although in the *Enquiry* he particularly emphasized the moral absurdity involved in a liberty of indifference. If human freedom is the unlimited power to act without any constraint or reflection, according to every possible whim and against the wise advice of the understanding, then it is difficult to see how it could have any moral significance. "The notion mankind have conceived of liberty, is some dignity or privilege, something worth claiming. But what dignity or privilege is there in being given up to such a wild contingency as this, to be perfectly and constantly liable to act unintelligently and unreasonably, and as much without the guidance of understanding as if we had none, or were as destitute of perception as the smoke that is driven by the wind" (1, 273)? Using both logical and moral arguments, Edwards dismissed a liberty of indifference and, as a philosopher, resolved to define the will under bondage as a determined will. Commentators were not slack to often sharply criticize this notion of the will or liberty which, voided of any real significance and existing in name only,[123] was a type of synonym for necessity. Edwards found himself in the camp of those who identified necessity and liberty but he did not adopt the classic solution for interpreting this identity. Unlike the Stoics, this Protestant theologian was not inclined to seek liberty in recognized

---

119. Leibniz, *Theodicy*, 2. 191; see also "The sweetest and highest libertie is to have no power to sin" (Gale, *Court of the Gentiles*, 4:90 in Fiering, *Moral Philosophy at Seventeenth-Century Harvard*, 289). See "liberty from sin" vs. "liberty to sin" (24, 216).

120. Leibniz, *Theodicy*, 2. 201.

121. Leibniz, *Fifth Paper. Schriften*, 7. 390. As Locke observed, to be determined to good is perfection (*Essay*, 251 § 30). Augustine said of the elect, "The souls in bliss will still possess the freedom of will, though sin will have no power to tempt them. They will be more free than ever—so free, in fact, from all delight in sinning as to find, in not sinning, an unfailing source of joy." (*City of God*, 22. 30).

122. Fiering, *Edwards's Moral Thought*, 295.

123. Bledsoe, *President Edwards' Inquiry*; see Coleridge, *Aids to Reflection*, 107.

necessity, because this would have made Christian liberty too external and "objective." Rather than baptize liberty entirely as necessity insofar as it is integral to the spirit, Edwards preferred to distinguish two sorts of necessity and only kept one of them.

Scholastic Catholics and Protestants make a distinction between absolute or simple necessity—which is, properly speaking, necessity—and hypothetical necessity. This necessity of consequence or *ex hypothesi* "is the unchangeability of the effects that follow the fact that things are put in place: the effect must follow, but the causes themselves may not exist or be changed."[124] The truth does not come "from the nature of the thing itself, but from the supposition of something before, which determines the event . . . cannot be otherwise."[125] That Christ died on the cross does not flow from his nature but from his will which, in turn, was determined by consideration of the fact that only his passion could satisfy the conditions required for the redemption of fallen humanity.[126] A reader of the dogmatic controversies of his day, Leibniz himself was largely impressed by the spirit of this line of argument when he distinguished between absolute or metaphysical necessity and contingent or purely moral necessity. An absolutely necessary reality is one which—for logical, metaphysical or mathematical reasons—must be and exist in every possible world. On the other hand, a hypothetical or moral necessity is one in which an event must take place in *this* world, established by the will of God, but which might otherwise have remained in a virtual state for eternity if the divine *fiat* had called another universe into existence. Five times five equals twenty-five in all possible universes. On the other hand, while Judas Iscariot certainly could not but betray Christ in this world, his betrayal would never have occurred if the divine decree had established a world other than our own. In his effective context, Judas was undoubtedly unable to not betray his master, yet his betrayal was only constrained by hypothetical or moral necessity as the opposite of his action would have been logically possible! Without going into the complicated details of how Leibniz believed he could demonstrate that the necessity of his betrayal did not affect Judas's moral responsibility in any way, what emerges and truly matters is that, for the Scholastics and also for Leibniz, the essential difference between these two types of necessities is to be sought in the action's chain of logical-metaphysical premises and not in the nature of the agency itself. Heir to the dogmatics of the Leibnizian era, Edwards also recognized two sorts of necessity, though he based them more solidly on the

124. Heppe, *Dogmatics*, 267.
125. Willard, *Reply to Keith*, 10, in Lowrie, *The Puritan Mind*, 73.
126. Willard, *Divinity*, 377.

immanent nature of the recognized necessary action. Here again, he is in the line of Calvin. A reader of Saint Bernard, the Reformer taught that man's will is naturally subject to necessity, though without ceasing to be voluntary and therefore accountable. The opposite of necessity is not freedom but compulsion, and not recognizing this distinction had led Pierre Lombard, the Master of Sentences, to give "occasion to a pernicious error" of thinking that man could avoid sinning because he sinned freely![127] This distinction between necessity on the one hand and force or compulsion on the other is not a function of the modalities or degrees of chaining between an action and its cause but is instead based on an analogy between the condition of the subject and the action, which is the same consideration that determines Edwards's line of argument.

By necessity—he wrote—is meant "an infallible connection of the things signified by the subject and predicate of a proposition." (1, 156) Necessity can be either natural or moral. By natural necessity, as applied to men, is meant such necessity as men are under through the force of natural causes. For example, they feel pain when their bodies are wounded; they see the objects presented before them in a clear light when their eyes are opened; and they assent to the truth of certain propositions as soon as they understand their terms. In contrast, Edwards used "moral necessity" for "that necessity of connection and consequence which arises from such *moral causes*, as the strength of inclination, or motives, and the connection which there is in many cases between these, and such certain volitions and actions" (1, 156). Moral necessity is not only relative but absolute. It is 'a certainty and inclination of the will itself, which does not admit of the supposition of a will to oppose and resist it" (1, 159). In other words, moral necessity is as absolute as natural necessity, i.e., the effect is no less rigorously or unconditionally connected with its moral cause than a natural necessary effect is with its natural cause. We might be tempted to attribute a certain contingency to the world of the will. In reality, however, motives and prejudices, biases and habits can be so strong and solid that the will cannot escape their grasp. However, if moral necessity can be as categorical as natural necessity—which is the most original thesis of the *Enquiry*—the difference "does not lie so much in the nature of the connection as in the two terms connected" (1, 158).

At first glance, this appears to be a truism because, after all, what should distinguish moral necessity from any other kind of necessity if not

---

127. Calvin, *Institutes*, 2. 3. 5. see also "liberty is not opposed to necessity but to force: the will cannot be forced by any external violence, but it may be necessitated by reason and conviction: natural men sin voluntarily yet necessarily" (Stoddard, *Day of Judgment*, 230).

the moral character of the causes that determine it? However, affirming a connection, i.e., a determination of the same order as natural necessity, which is supposed to be absolute, seemed absurd and unleashed criticism. The Edwardsian position was very clear: those acting out of moral necessity always act willingly and they therefore also act freely. On seeing a beverage, a drunkard may find himself under the control of a moral necessity to want to drink. Notwithstanding the violent inclination for alcohol that he might experience, he cannot raise the glass to his lips if he doesn't want to drink. To put this in the strictest sense of the term, "a man has a thing in his power, if he has it in his choice... and a man cannot be truly said to be unable to do a thing when he can do it if he will" (1, 162). The drunkard would not drink if he didn't want it, but he does *want* to drink. As a result, he drinks and all other considerations regarding this person and the various antecedents of his volition may only concern what preceded the volition, without in any way influencing the fact that he actually wanted to drink. The drunkard wants to drink and is therefore free to drink, because a person is free who has the power and opportunity to act as he wills, without any consideration whatsoever of the circumstances that led him to this volition (1, 164).

The critics raged against this line of argument. They accused him of reducing the will and freedom to the level of a bodily movement or the descent of a waterfall,[128] and of limiting his analysis to the external fact of the performance of an action without scrutinizing its deeper motivation.[129] The critics let loose against the seeming blindness of the *Enquiry* to the essentially inner character of the will and its refusal to treat the will in terms of intention. The critics accused Edwards of only dealing with the external phenomenon of the will and therefore of focusing his attention on what was not truly the will itself. In reality, the critics were making the very mistake they attributed to the author of the *Enquiry*. Edwards was reproached for ignoring the ultimate cause of the volition, i.e., the intention, even though individuals form their own intention as the efficient cause of their volition, i.e., as something that precedes the volition, which is then lost from sight simply by analyzing the intention.[130]

---

128. Bledsoe, *President Edwards' Inquiry*, 189–90.

129. McClelland, *Predestination and Election Vindicated*, 19–20.

130. "Wer also dem Willen eine Ursache sucht, lässt den Willen aufhören, Wille zu sein [If anyone seeks a cause for the will, the will ceases to be the will]" (Baader, *Erläuterungen zu Sämtlichen Schriften von Louis Claude de Saint-Martin, Werke*, 12:92). Baader may have been "influenced" by Edwards through reading W. Goodwin, (*Erläuterungen zu Sämtlichen Schriften von Louis Claude de Saint-Martin, Werke*, 12:138, and *Tagebücher aus den Jahren 1786–1793, Werke*, 11:210–11). Concerning Edwards and Goodwin, see Aldridge, "Edwards and Godwin on Virtue," especially 317–18.

8. Criticism of efficient causality

The rejection of a causal explanation in the sphere of the will was initially justified by general preoccupations of a metaphysical nature and then in due form by analyzing the moral character of the voluntary phenomenon. Like all great philosophers, Edwards himself also rejected reductionism. The paradigm of all reductionisms is an obsession with explanations based on efficient causality. Anticipating another Calvinist theologian, Schleiermacher, for whom everything had its own reality within itself, where everything is "a self-contained work without connections with others or dependence upon them," knowing "nothing about derivation,"[131] Edwards taught that, in the sphere of what truly constitutes real knowledge, we should always seek to understand something directly and by itself. Edwards undoubtedly kept resorting to the demonstration method because the cause-effect relationship is a basic law of reality (13, 416), although he did confine it to the sphere of notional and historic knowledge, i.e., to the imperfect knowledge of fallen man[132] and, like Luther, refused to apply it to religious and moral realities.[133] Causality is certainly useful for explaining phenomena contrived according to their superficial appearance, but it has nothing to do with a body of knowledge where the subject becomes its object, nor *a fortiori* with the will, a faculty that nothing separates from its own act. The immediacy and indivisibility of the will are the immanent reasons why it is impossible to fragment it into efficient causal relationships, although there is an even more eloquent argument against the projection of good and evil in past intention.

Edwards began the fourth part of his *Enquiry* with a rebuttal of an absurd doctrine that would have sought the essence of vice and virtue in the cause rather than in the nature of the dispositions and acts of the will. If the good or evil character of the will does not reside in the will itself but in its origin, we are led to conclude that good and evil are not a quality of the action but rather of something that precedes it. This is equivalent to saying that the moral element is projected into what precedes the action for the simple reason that it precedes the action! Good and evil have nothing to do with the fact that there is a temporal (or logical) antecedent, and it shouldn't be possible to account for or explain a moral reality using what foregoes it. Of course, something can be blamed as the cause of vice and

---

131. Schleiermacher, *On Religion*, 26.

132. For notional and historic knowledge, see *infra*, p. 261–62.

133. "Nulla forma syllogistica tenet in terminis divinis [No syllogistic form is valid when applied to divine terms]" (Luther, *Disputatio contra Scholasticam Theologiam*, 47, *Werke*, 1:221).

it may be wickedness in the cause that produces wickedness in the effect. However, these two are not the same individual wickedness. The wicked act of the cause producing the wickedness in the effect is one wickedness and the wickedness produced is another. In consequence, the wickedness of the latter does not lie in the former, because wickedness only resides in the evil nature of the things which are themselves wicked (1, 337-9). A good or evil volition have, respectively, a certain inherent beauty or deformity. There is evil in the nature of the evil volition itself and not wholly in some foregoing act which is its cause, otherwise the evil volition which is the effect would be no moral evil, any more than sickness or some other natural calamity that arises from a morally evil cause (1, 340).

All of these absurdities that Edwards took pleasure in enumerating led to the conclusion that good and evil are not found in the cause of the volition but in the volition itself. All men undoubtedly have a common inclination to seek the morality of an act in its foregoing cause, but Edwards believed he could clarify the origin of this widespread misconception. Human common sense teaches—with good reason—that the moral good and evil associated with external actions is not found in the actions themselves but in the internal dispositions and volitions that cause them. However—and this is already an illegitimate procedure—the vast difference between external and internal actions is overlooked and the search is continued for an external cause of actions that contain their cause within themselves (1, 341).[134]

---

134. The entire Augustinian tradition is in agreement. It is not the intention but the content that makes an action sinful (Baius, *Dictionnaire de Théologie Catholique*, 3, 15). Rather than going back to another, antecedent volition, we need to appreciate the freedom of the volition itself (Jansenius, *Augustinus,*). See also, from a moral point of view, "For I can be quite indifferent as to the origin of my state in which I am now to act" (Kant, "Review of Schulz," 8:13 [Academy pagination]). We are still dealing with operations of the will and "there is nothing that is so much in our power as the will itself" (Saint Augustine, *Retractions*, 1. 21. 4 in Pascal, *écrits sur la Grâce, Œuvres*, 324). Moved by invincible determination, the will is "infallibly" drawn in a particular direction and yet, in terms of desire, the movement remains ours (Pascal, *Provincial Letters*, 448). After all, "to say that it does not belong to our will that we want to be happy" doesn't in the least change the voluntary nature of that desire (Saint Augustine, "Nature and Grace," 46. 54 paragraphs]). This is why it's enough that an act is voluntary for it to be imputable (Jansenius, *Augustinus*, 3, 6. 4. 260-61). This is not a paradox of faith but rather, as Edwards taught, a realization of the fact that, to be good or bad, the internal act of the will doesn't need to be preceded by a volition because willing is the very spontaneity of man, i.e., something that arises immediately of itself. We accordingly understand that "while Edwards taught that volitions necessarily agree with the inclination and have no power over it, he also taught that the inclination itself is free, not necessitated agency" (Shedd, *Dogmatic Theology*, 2:206-7).

It was in these few unpretentious lines, added as a sort of modest appendix to a chapter of brilliant logical demonstrations, that Edwards succeeded in putting the finishing touches to his doctrine of the will and freedom. If moral good and evil are not to be sought in the cause of the volition but rather in willing itself, it is because the universe of the will, the moral world, is radically different from the physical world. The latter is subject to the system of efficient causality because, to paraphrase Kant, it is only a chain of phenomena that follow or are deduced from one another and do not have their meaning and significance within themselves.[135] In contrast, the will is fully present whenever it is exercised. Accused of depriving human agency of all true liberty, Edwards felt able to retort pointedly that his was the greatest conceivable notion of liberty (1, 454) and, by refusing to divide up the will, he successfully propounded a doctrine where morality, though founded on the most intimate core of the subject, nonetheless remained obvious and visible.[136] Shortcutting all infinite regression in the determination of the will that would have definitively driven freedom beyond the confines of this world (1, 211), Edwards finds all of the willing agency in the current volition. In this he anticipated Kant, who separated the will from any temporal succession and conceived of it as present at all times with all of its prerogatives, undivided at every instant, and an ever-intact possibility of another beginning.

Critics fault Edwards for having obscured the root cause of moral phenomena by limiting the moral to the apparent will and agency. In fact, he challenged even the very idea of such a distinction. The volition is never a pure phenomenon, nor just the facade of a hidden *Hinterwelt*, and if there is anything behind it, that could only be itself.[137] Instead of relativizing and limiting human morality, Edwards generalized and deepened it by refusing to separate appearance and reality, the phenomenon and the noumenon in the moral sphere. Edwards knew that, at every breathing moment, a man is a moral being[138] and that every human agency has moral significance. However, this universal "moralization" of human activity (see 21, 274)—a total "presentification" of the will in each human volition—can lead to two diametrically opposed doctrines. It can either lead to integral nominalism or integral realism, with the former dispersing the will into its periodic

---

135. It was this "natural necessity" that Kant characterized as merely "a heteronomy of efficient causes" ("Groundwork of Metaphysics of Morals," 4:446 [Academy pagination]).

136. See Carse, *Visibility of God*, 60.

137. In this regard, see the important developments by Ramsey, "Introduction" in 1, 11–12, as well as the criticism by Morris, "Reappraisal of Edwards," 515–25.

138. Davidson, "From Locke to Edwards," 363.

exercises, the latter perceiving each exercise as an adequate translation of overall moral disposition. Edwardsian thought—both of Edwards himself and his disciples—developed these two opposing doctrines to their logical conclusion, thereby framing two archetypal possibilities of Protestant theology in moral matters that also have their counterpart in the history of post-medieval philosophy.

These two opposing models of the will and therefore of morality were espoused by Hume and Kant, the two most important philosophers of Edwards's century. Transferring his atomism and nominalism into the sphere of the will, Hume saw the will merely as a discontinuous succession of an infinite quantity of individual volitions. The will only exists in the volition; there is therefore no distinct, permanent faculty hidden behind periodic acts and it is scarcely possible to speak of a moral subject underlying voluntary actions. Kant—whose main ambition was to reconstitute the permanent subject on new, more solid grounds—rescued the will from dispersal by locating it in an atemporal sphere, sheltered from all succession because of efficient causality, and viewed intention as only a manifestation or expression of the entire will. For Hume, the absence of any permanent subject meant there could only be periodic acts, whereas for Kant there was no such thing as a periodic act because every act contained the subject in its entirety within itself. From a purely religious perspective, the Kantian model seems to correspond to the Augustinian vision of the person as pure interiority and will in a personal face-to-face with God. However, Augustinianism also had another dimension: the intuition of God's absolute sovereignty. In light of this sovereignty, which bears down on all finite existence, wouldn't it be tempting to relativize the creature's own continuity and autarky? This is the very logic of divine omnipotence that circuitously led to the nominalism of the late Middle Ages and would then resurface in the religious vision of the Reformers. The basic experience of sin and corruption that dominates the thinking of a Luther or Calvin fits very well with underscoring responsibility by insisting on the continuity and unity of the moral subject. On the other hand, the creature's worthlessness before God militates in favor of a nominalist version of the subject and his will. The resolution of this contradiction is found in the Calvinistic doctrine of predestination, which profoundly reconciles nominalism and realism. Since man must be responsible for his acts, it is therefore necessary that his will have unfailing continuity. However, a human being's radical worthlessness is expressed as the impossibility for him to be the artisan and master of this continuity. This contradiction leads, so to speak, to its dialectical resolution in the eternal counsels of God, who predestines man to virtue or vice. Man is predestined to be virtuous or vicious, i.e., to be unified by moral determination—the metaphysical power accomplishing the underlying unity of disparate volitions—and yet, precisely because he is *predestined*, man owes this unity and continuity to God and not to himself. This ensures the unity and continuity of the will and, consequently, of man's responsibility, but without man's being the author of it.

9. Freedom and responsibility

We said that realism and nominalism were logical outcomes of Edwardsian thought and, in fact, both were developed by Edwards and his disciples. Edwards himself, Bellamy, and Hopkins professed an intransigent realism of the will, whereas Nathanael Emmons, the most original of the Edwardsians, developed integral nominalism.[139] While both equally legitimate, these two opposing developments did not appear randomly, but were outcomes of the perspective and dialectical context adopted. If the perspective is purely theological, this leads into nominalism which, with its principle of the purely intrinsic unity of the will to create, provides a better explanation of the sovereignty of God. On the other hand, if the point of view of moral philosophy is adopted, the tendency is invariably towards realism and the immanent unity of the will. Since this was evidentially a case of authors who were both theologians and philosophers at the same time—or rather those for whom moral philosophy was identical to heology[140]—they could be found expressing both visions in parallel or together. As for Edwards himself, nominalism and realism were both essential constituent elements of his thought. His interpretation of the transmission of original sin in terms of a sovereign, divine constitution is close to nominalism. God grants only external support to the identity and permanence of the universe and that same external support, like a type of individual *fiat*, presides over the coming into existence of the individual moral subject. However, when the inquiry is then situated within the context of moral philosophy, Edwards opted for a realism of the will as the only approach capable of providing a philosophical explanation for unconditional responsibility in the moral sphere. The arbitrary constitution of the individual's identity with Adam that is the basis of his own identity and unity is a tribute of a metaphysical nature to the profound intuition of God's absolute sovereignty, while the indivisibility of the will—its integral efficiency at every moment—marks the creature's theological understanding of autarky and autonomy.

139. The best portrayal of the Edwardsian school's nominalism is by Breitenbach, "New Divinity Theology." See also Atwater, "Edwards and the New Divinity," 601–2.

140. See Hopkins, *Life*, 6.

The Edwardsian doctrine of the will is the masterpiece of an entire anthropology teaching the unity of man and specifically with the will as its seat and vehicle. Obviously, the will is to be understood in a broader sense, such as for Augustine, for whom *voluntas* was not a mere faculty but the entire person.[141] Christian literature acknowledged this broadening of the notion of the will by translating it using the popular, prephilosophical term "heart." Preachers use this term as an equivalent for the will *stricto sensu*[142] or for man as a whole.[143] J. Owen gave it a more technical definition: "the heart . . . is the effective acquiescence of the will and affections to the object proposed to them."[144] This extension of the notion in relation to the will dominates the thought of T. Hooker: "Heart in Scripture . . . applies to the will of man or to that aptitude whereby he wants or rejects something . . . and with the joy, pleasure, hate and regret that accompany this will."[145] These ideas were essentially those of Edwards, who frequently identified the will with the heart[146] and—starting from his youth—referred to the Bible to justify this use of the term[147] and who, with regard to the exercises of the faculty of inclination and volition (2, 96-97), would later define the mind as the heart. This latter definition is found towards the beginning of *A Treatise Concerning Religious Affections*, a work intended to explain the greatest manifestations of the conscience—where theoretical knowledge is made subject to energy emanating from the whole person—and one in which Edwards designates "sense of the heart" as the highest form of this "sensible" knowledge.[148] This is a powerful evocation of the moral character

---

141. See Rist, "Augustine on Free Will and Predestination," 220-21 and Veto, *La naissance de la volonté*, 39-40.

142. Cotton, *Way of Life*, 127 in Scheick, *Will and Word*, 49n.15.

143. Scheick, *Will and Word*, 57n.16.

144. Owen, *Pneumatologia*, 212.

145. Hooker, *Unbeleevers Preparing for Christ*, 137-9 in Pettit, *Heart Prepared*, 96.

146. See 18, 462; 2, 226; 25, 511. See also "heart or life" (2, 102), and the synonomy of "heart" and "glory" (24, 482).

147. See 6, 362. The books of the Bible make abundant use of the word "heart" and with a full range of meanings. The word "heart" represents the whole man from a moral and religious point of view. Good or bad acts come from the heart like fruit from a tree (Lk. 6:44) and the evil thoughts, lies, adulteries, and everything that defiles a man proceed from the heart (Mt. 15:19). The heart is the opposite of the appearance (Jer 15:16-17) and the vehicle of an existential relationship with God (Jer. 30:21). It is by the heart that we know God (Jer 24:7) and pay attention (Prov 23:26). It is in the heart that God instills one's new covenant faith (Jer 32:39) and in the heart that we believe in the resurrection that will save men (Rom. 10:9). Terms such as "pure heart," "heart of stone," and "heart of flesh" also form essential moments in biblical preaching.

148. See *infra*, p. 257-58. For a sense of "cordial" in contexts ranging from total engagement to the regenerated state, see *infra*, p. 365-366.

of an active totality—man and his common sense—to which Edwards frequently makes apologetic references, using the terms "good heart" or "evil heart" to judge the whole man without regard to subtle distinctions between antecedent intention and consequent volition. When a common man wants to recall a man's depravity, the blameworthy character of his conduct, he doesn't burden himself with questions regarding the determination or autodetermination of the will but simply maintains that a person who has "an evil heart or conceives wickedness in his heart" merits reproach (1, 357). We give praise or assign blame according to the heart, which represents the whole man, and God himself reads the heart to judge all men. "A man is like his heart,"[149] but *why* does a man have such a heart? The question which persistently comes up is as follows: Is man responsible for the evil that arises in his evil heart and, consequently, for his evil heart?

This issue clearly has universal moral implications but is of more immediate relevance to the controversy between Calvinists and Arminians. Orthodox Calvinism teaches that all of us are implicated in Adam's sin, inclined to evil, and "all the virtue of our free will consists only of throwing wicked affections—like darts—in every direction."[150] Some will certainly be saved but only because of God's sovereign election, while the others will be confirmed in their sins and consequently suffer a terrible fate because of another divine decision that is apparently as gratuitous as election, namely reprobation.[151] To Arminians, fiery champions of human liberty and fervent defenders of God's justice, this doctrine seems to be the height of absurdity and injustice, for how could men be judged for acts they were unable to avoid committing? The heart is given by God and given as either good or evil. Man can do nothing to accept or reject it. In a manner of speaking, being externally given a good heart prevents man from freely desiring what is good, i.e., by himself, while being given an evil heart by God makes God seem unjust. God makes us commit unrighteousness—or so it seems—and subsequently condemns us for the evil he imposed on us.[152] Putting aside the complex question of divine cooperation with our will, we will content ourselves here with reproducing Edwards's arguments regarding God's every right to punish us, even when it seems that God himself has predetermined us to be wicked.

---

149. Cotton, *Way of Life*, in Scheick, *Will and Word*, 56n.17.
150. Calvin, *Commentarius in Epistolam Pauli ad Romanos*, *Opera*, 49, 122.
151. For election and reprobation, see *supra*, p. 48, 51; *infra*, p. 154.
152. See Schneider and Schneider, *Samuel Johnson*, 3:193-94.

Like Locke, Arminians think that "God . . . does not require more of us than we are capable of doing"[153] and make the will of God dependent on man's faculties, whereas the Augustinian tradition leans heavily in the opposite direction. Calvin spoke angrily of the "devilish opinion, that God commandeth not anything which is not possible for men to do."[154] Stoddard's comment was both blunt and concise: "That though he [man] has lost his power to obey, yet God has not lost his right to command."[155] And N. Emmons, always inclined to be paradoxical and blunt, exclaimed: "a heart is something that God requires, whether he gives it or not."[156] While these comments were inspired by a sense of the absolute sovereignty of God and a rejection of any attempt to weaken man's responsibility, a theologian would not be content with religious rhetoric but must still find arguments to explain the paradox that, regardless of what Locke thought, God asks us to do things that we are incapable of doing (12, 497) and even has the right to punish us if we don't accomplish them. The theologian's task is therefore to show that our inability to do good and avoid evil is "our own fault."[157]

10. Moral inability

Some claim that being unable to do or not do something frees an individual of any responsibility for a task and from having to accomplish it or not. Natural and moral necessity certainly exist, but so also do natural and moral inability. This distinction is very essential to Edwardsian thought, allowing this Calvinist theologian to explain how it is possible to have a rigorous determination of the will that still does not deprive it of moral responsibility. As in cases of moral and natural necessity, the difference between natural and moral inability does not depend on a difference in the logico-metaphysical connection between terms but on the nature of these terms. We are naturally incapable of something "when we cannot do what we want to do" because our physical nature prevents us from doing it, i.e., we are subject to an external constraint. On the other hand, moral inability involves opposition or a lack of inclination towards something. Moral inability is not lower

---

153. Locke, *Essay*, 2. 21. 53.

154. Calvin, *Sermons on Deuteronomy*, 22:1–4[whereby the numbers indicate biblical chapter and verse, and the quoted words have been modernised for contemporary readership].

155. Stoddard, *Guide to Christ*, 90. Here Stoddard is directly inspired by Owen, *Pneumatologia*, 249.

156. Emmons, *Excuse of Sinners*, *Works*, 6:93.

157. Calvin, *Institutes*, 2. 8. 2.

in degree than natural inability; its character is different (see 1, 159). Moral habits and dispositions can provoke consequences just as surely as a change in the atmosphere or blood circulation. An affectionate and obedient child cannot desire to kill his father, nor is it very likely that an evil man would perform charitable acts towards his enemies. In like manner, a chaste and honorable woman has a real moral inability to prostitute herself with a slave (1, 160).[158] Theoretically, of course, a man whose heart is hardened could desire to do good to his neighbor, just as a woman of great virtue could prostitute herself with her slave but, in reality, this power is scarcely real. To use R. Hooker's terminology, itself inspired by medieval Scholasticism, the will "tends" to will other than what it truly wants but is "incapable" of doing so.[159] Edwards himself described this daily paradox in detail, which is confirmed by observing the human condition, and summarized it as follows: "Many things are [entirely] in our power that are impossible because of our dispositions" (13, 239). To those who consider this definition too abstract or who would say with Channing that the distinction between moral and physical inability is "a distinction without a difference,"[160] Edwards cites the example of two rebel prisoners.

The first rebel is a man who, having offended his sovereign, is thrown into a prison where he languishes for a long time. One day the king has pity on this man and calls for him in order to set him free on condition that he humbly pleads for forgiveness. The man really wanted to accept this generous offer and run into his master's presence but "was held captive by strong fortification walls, bronze doors and iron bars." The other rebel was someone with wicked and hateful dispositions, devoid of any feeling of thankfulness or gratefulness. He conspired day and night against his master who, exasperated, finally had him placed under arrest. Well, the king also had compassion on him. He gave orders to remove his chains and open the prison gates so that he too could go before his sovereign to ask for clemency. But this second rebel was full of pride, evil, and hate that prevented him from taking advantage of his master's offer and going into his presence. In both of these cases, the sovereign's call clearly had the same negative outcome because equally irresistible constraints prevented the two prisoners from seeking the promised pardon. But does this mean that we cannot distinguish between the physical powerlessness of the first rebel—who sincerely repented—and the moral powerlessness of the second rebel with a

---

158. The connection between the character of a man who lacks love and his refusing to give his estate to his neighbor is of the same order as one between two mathematical phenomena (18, 112).

159. Hooker, *Laws of Ecclesiastical Polity*, Works, 4:101.

160. Channing, *The Moral Argument Against Calvinism*, Works, 460.

hardened heart? The first prisoner suffered because of a natural impossibility; the second was controlled by a moral impossibility. The first should be lamented, the second condemned (1, 362–3).

This demonstration regarding moral inability is underpinned by an Edwardsian understanding of the will as a faculty that is immediately free and self-contained. The essence of this argument—one in which Edwards finds himself in direct continuity with Augustine and Calvin—is that being voluntary is sufficient for an act to be considered free. The will is the heart and someone with an evil heart wills and does evil. While this is evidently not the sort of liberty that throws "wicked affections—like darts—in every direction," it is nonetheless enough to assign responsibility. The essential thesis is that we are still responsible for evil, even if we cannot avoid willing it. We then need to ask how it was that we got into a situation where we are incapable of changing our moral orientation. This raises the entire paradox of the will under bondage. We are only able to will evil and are condemned for desiring evil. Our enslaved will can only tend towards evil and yet this enslavement can only come from within the will itself. Since the will is always responsible, it is seen as effectively enslaved at every moment, as passing at every instant—to speak like Kant—from innocence to guilt, from freedom to slavery. Incapable of imagining the world outside of temporal schemes, human reason posits a state of freedom prior to servitude but is then obliged to designate a point in time when this freedom becomes enslavement. However, it is logically impossible to indicate a moment when a reality, namely the will, is simultaneously something and its opposite and, consequently, to specify a point where freedom and servitude meet. This impossiblity which, in the domain of natural phenomena, Kantian philosophy resolves by becoming, could not be overcome by logical reasoning and can only be solved using the analogies of a pictorial language. Saint Augustine wanted to use suicide to illustrate the mystery of the will under bondage. The man killing himself is alive. He is still alive when taking his life but, once dead, can no longer come back to life. His act is irrevocable and yet he is no less responsible for doing it.[161] Almost fifteen centuries later, Kierkegaard resorted to a parable about children who got money from their parents to buy school books but who, on their way to school, were drawn to a shop where they spent all of their money on toys. After a good playtime, they became afraid and wanted to return the toys in exchange for their money but the merchant refused to do this for them. You spent your money just as you wanted, he told them, and now it is no longer possible for you to get it back.[162] The issue

---

161. Saint Augustine, *Enchiridion*, 30.
162. Kierkegaard, *Philosophical Fragments*, 20n.4.

here is the very historicity of freedom itself. If the will could be exercised and renounced at any moment, how could it be taken seriously and what weight could be given to any decision taken? The essence of the teaching on the will under bondage is that decisions taken that specifically involve the entire will can no longer be called into question. Given this alienation, how then do we explain the will's ability to engage in evil?

11. Culpable ignorance

Our thoughts now turn to the mystery of ignorance. That man can now only do evil due to some past determination is because that determination was not chosen with full knowledge of the facts but rather in ignorance. That man can no longer free himself from the iron mesh of the moral necessity of sin is perhaps because he got entangled without truly realizing it. This hellenistic dilemma was not unknown to Christianity, which had to regard it with deep distrust. Christian theologians question its supposedly invincible character and attempt to avoid responsibility, even through genuine ignorance. In fact, the distrust of theologians regarding the excuse of ignorance is found in the recesses of even the most secular thinking. The French civil code begins with the famous phrase "Ignorance of the law is no excuse" and John Locke, patron saint of the Age of Enlightenment, likewise refused to acquit criminals on the pretext that they were ignorant of the law. Of course, the will always follows "that which is judged good by his understanding, yet it excuses him not, because, by a too hasty choice of his own making, he has imposed on himself wrong measures of good and evil. . . . He has vitiated his own palate, and must be answerable to himself for the sickness and death that follows from it."[163] Indeed, philosophers have never accepted ignorance as a peremptory excuse for any sort of lapse. After all, had not Plato already remarked to Socrates: "is not a soul equally to be deemed halt and lame which hates voluntary falsehood and is extremely ignorant at herself and others when they tell lies, but is patient of involuntary falsehood, and does not mind wallowing like a swinish beast in the mire of ignorance . . . ?"[164] This is not invincible ignorance—that raw reality of a lack of knowledge, of not having any effective means to incur guilt—but rather any sort of ignorance which an individual could have willingly avoided or, worse, which he willingly caused.[165]

---

163. Locke, *Essay*, 2. 21. 56. Edwards himself refers, through T. Gale, to Socrates, who affirmed that "all sin proceeds from a conceited ignorance" (20, 251).

164. Plato, *Republic*, 535e.

165. Pascal referred to Aristotle to prove that ignorance of the good and evil in an

The paradigm of this sort of reflection is presented to Christian thought by Scripture. The book of Proverbs declares: "If anyone turns away his ear from hearing the law, even his prayer is an abomination" (Prov 28:9); and yet the wicked say to God: "Depart from us! We do not desire the knowledge of thy ways" (Job 21:14). The Bible knows the iniquity of the heart and also knows that ignorance is quite often deliberate or at least vaguely desired. Scholasticism handled this problem using logical distinctions which nonetheless reproduced the essence of the inspired word portrayed by the writers of holy Scripture. The subtle analyses of Saint Thomas Aquinas, in particular, describe the subterfuges of the heart, which disguises itself with ignorance or unconsciousness in order to give over body and soul to sin. Moralists are often tempted to draw too fine a dividing line between the conscious (for which we are answerable) and unconscious (for which we are not answerable). There are levels of unconsciousness where the conscious is actively engaged. In a way, the unconscious individual's blindness is willed and therefore he is guilty;[166] "whoever sins from habit sins with resolute malice."[167] A habit is something acquired in the past but forged by a conscious operation. The conscious fact remains, even through the opacity of what has become an involuntary gesture or tick.[168]

Scholastic theologians carried out fine, detailed studies to more closely define man's responsibility for his ignorance, and the Puritans—those masters of practical theology—didn't lose their opportunity to address this

---

action is worthy of blame and not excusable (*Provincial Letters*, 191). He also quoted Augustine: "qu'il est impossible qu'on ne pèche pas quand on ne connoît pas la justice: *Necesse est ut peccet, à quo ignoratur justicia* [It is impossible not to sin when we do not know righteousness]" (*Pascal, écrits sur la Grâce, Œuvres*, 343). All Augustinian theologicans, and especially Jansenists, used prodigious rational and scriptural arguments to show the inexcusable nature of ignorance in religious and moral matters. See Laporte, *La doctrine de Port-Royal*, 2. 1. 110–1. In the final analysis, this was a profound moral intuition of theological and philosophical reasoning. Man is a totality and his moral character does not allow itself to be reduced to a particular level of his conscience. As Jansenist Pierre Nicole wrote, "*Les justes aiment Dieu durant le sommeil . . . et . . . les méchants aiment le monde pendant qu'ils dorment* [The righteous love God while they sleep . . . and . . . the wicked love the world while they sleep]" (*Instructions Théologiques et Morales*, 1:190; Edwards echoes this notion: "a man may be in the exercice of grace while he is asleep" (24, 377).

166. Saint Thomas Aquinas, *Summa Theologiæ*, 2–2. 156. 1. co.

167. Saint Thomas Aquinas, *Summa Theologiæ*, 1–2. 78. 2. co.

168. For a wonderful portrayal of the relations between the will, ignorance and sin, see Saint Thomas Aquinas, *Summa Theologiæ*, 1–2. 6. 8. co. In this regard, see the remarkable book by A. Kraus, *Der Begriff der Dummheit bei Thomas von Aquin*, as well as Parker, *The Devil in Calderon*, 14–15.

issue.[169] A favorite for preachers was the example of a drunkard who, though unable to understand the commandments of God, is "without excuse" because he is the author of his own diminished condition.[170] Edwards himself used this example and believed it was possible to conclude from a passage in Leviticus that individuals are responsible for the crimes they commit when they are drunk" (24, 253). However, a drunkard only represents a very specific case of voluntary ignorance and Edwards views this phenomenon more in the context of the Christian's neglect to examine and analyze his moral conduct and spiritual condition. In a discourse titled "The Necessity of Self-Examination," a text whose published version was edited by his son (IV, 379n.), Jonathan Edwards presented a popular, homiletic formulation of voluntary ignorance. Living in sin—he wrote—is a latent provocation against God and not having realized this, or not having understood our sinful condition, still does not excuse us. "Guilt is not incurred solely by leading lives that are considered sinful," but even by not examining our heart with sufficient diligence. Man always has sufficient light to discern evil but, as a sinner, his eyes are obscured and blinded by a "pernicious disposition" of his own doing (IV, 388–90).[171] Men have an inveterate tendency not to face their own failures, to hide from their sins that are right before their own eyes, to not consider fully or even at all what they ought to consider. As a result, they are ignorant of their sinful state, but nonetheless remain without excuse "because their ignorance is a willful, allowed ignorance (IV, 391)."[172]

Edwards reveals the conscious character of willful sins using supposedly psychological analyses, but his teaching isn't truly apologetic. Edwards the preacher tries to explain to his hearers about responsibility for apparently unconscious transgressions, whereas Edwards the theologian knows that someone is not guilty because he is responsible, but rather the contrary, that someone is responsible because he is guilty. Rather than teach that a person should not regard himself as guilty unless it can be proven that he consciously became so in one way or another, Edwards instead adopted the position that, because ignorance is guilt in religious and moral matters, it should be possible to show that it was a conscious choice. Moreover, all of this follows the affirmation of Christian theology itself that "outside of Christ, there is no salvation." Arminian thinking seeks to qualify this hard doctrine by trying to demonstrate that only those capable of knowing Christ

---

169. See Miller, *New England Mind*, 1:259–61.

170. Miller, *New England Mind*, 1:394.

171. See also, "sin greatly clouds their judgment" (18, 358). Edward Taylor speaks of "Sins Spectacles" (*Poems*, 206).

172. See also IV, 434: "Wicked men . . . industriously hide their eyes" (25, 619).

but who knowingly ignore him are unsaved, which is very different from the approach taken by orthodox Christianity. There is no salvation—only unremitted sins—outside of Christ. Sinners are guilty and therefore all who remain outside of Christ are guilty; but how could they be guilty without a personal contribution on their part? The authentic interpretation of revelation does not argue from law to fact, but from fact to law. A person should not be guilty because his ignorance was voluntary, but his ignorance must be voluntary since he is guilty. Based on Scripture, and apparently without any conceptual justification whatsoever, Edwards stated that an erroneous thought which denies the existence of God, or even simple ignorance of divine things, is mortal sin (18, 182–3).[173] Here again we encounter the doctrine on the will and freedom found in the *Enquiry*. An action is not free and voluntary by virtue of an antecedent free choice but because of a present effective action. The question is therefore not whether I voluntary chose the ignorance that dictates my volition, but whether I effectively want the volition that I accomplished in a state of ignorance.

The outcome of all this reflection on the voluntary character of ignorance in transgression was to moralize Calvinist teaching on responsibility for actions committed without full knowledge of the facts, but it had no effect whatsoever on the heart of Edwards's doctrine itself. The essence of the will is not defined by its cause but by its character,[174] and the quality of moral acts is not determined by their origin but by their nature (1, 337). This topic did not arouse any opposition to a form because all of these theorists believed in the indivisibility of the will, the indissociability of its essential factors, and the continuity of the volition's essence and its manifestations. What the critics call "the total visibility of the volition,"[175] or the profession of a certain continuity in man between noumenon and phenomenon,[176] refers particularly to thinking that views man as an integral totality in which his entire being is identified with his volition. The absolute rejection of any temporal succession gives the will the very color of being, although the ontology found in the *Enquiry* ignores all differences between appearance and reality. In a quasi-phenomenological reduction, Edwards referred to moral philosophy as "the thing itself" of the will and, envisioning that thing with its own appearance, thought it entirely legitimate to judge men according to

---

173. So too, "it is evident that a man may contract fearful guilt, and may undo himself to all eternity by that which he has no great sense of the badness of in the time of it" (24, 946).

174. J. Edwards, *Remarks on the Improvements Made in Theology by his Father, President Edwards*, in Edwards, *Works*, 1:482.

175. Carse, *Visibility of God*, 60.

176. Clebsch, *American Religious Thought*, 21.

their effective voluntary behavior. However, this moral philosophy, which paradoxically seeks only to be one of appearance, turns back on itself and becomes a judgment of the essence or *en soi* (in itself). If acts and exercises fully show the will and indeed are the will, then conversely an even inactive will can and must be construed as already engaged in exercises. Like Leibniz and Spinoza, Edwards thought that a criminal ought to be chastised for giving free rein to harmful behavior, regardless of his deeper motivation,[177] and that an evil heart ought to be condemned, even when there isn't an evil act (16, 318).

As previously said, Edwardsian doctrine can lead to either nominalism or moral realism. Nominalists only consider the effective use of the will, while realists will conversely say that only a taste or disposition can be morally evaluated. As we know, Jonathan Edwards and most of his leading disciples opted for realism and their line of argument is illustrated in a narrative by a belated Edwardsian. One day a Calvinist of nominalist persuasion named Moralist encountered a rattlesnake on the road. Pleading for its life, the snake stressed that it should only answer for its effective exercises and, because it hadn't yet bit anyone to death, it should be spared. Forgetting his own doctrine, Moralist called the reptile's reasoning "futile and fallacious" and said: "You cannot deny your deadly, poisonous nature, full of future acts just waiting for an occasion to take place." And he reminded the snake that, even if he hadn't harmed anybody, he wouldn't hesitate to poison anyone misfortunate enough to come too close to him. Ever a good nominalist, the snake protested that if his nature was evil, it was involuntary and that he did not deserve any blame: "my nature, such as it is, is not my work, and I wasn't consulted about it at all." Impatient, Moralist answered that he didn't care where the snake's nature came from, that it was enough for him to know that it was harmful and, to end the dispute, he pummeled the reptile with his stick.[178]

12. The sins of children

The parable of the Moralist and the snake is just a popular version of an old theological metaphor which, in order to designate a creature's perversion

---

177. Judges do not look for the reasons that led a man to have an evil intent, but concern themselves only with how evil it is (Leibniz, "Discourse on Metaphysics," 30). "Wicked men are no less to be feared and no less dangerous when they are necessarily wicked" (Spinoza, "Letters," 910 [letter 58]). This legal judgment is transposed to a radically different level by the theologian: "man, though he sins necessarily, nevertheless sins voluntarily" (Calvin, *Institutes*, 2. 4. 1).

178. *Gardiner Spring*, 1:146–50.

and dangerous character before and in the absence of any effective activity on its part, compared it to a wild animal. Such comparisons lead to that classic example of ill-will, moral responsibility, and no prior choice: the sinful condition of a newborn infant. Scripture compares natural man to the colt of a wild ass[179] and the epithet "wild" is eminently suitable for a young, unbaptized child. Ever since Augustine, "that severe father of little children," Pelagians of all stripes have become indignant about the teaching on the sinful condition of newborns and the possibility that they would be eternally damned. They believe that they can base their plea for the natural and invincible innocence of children on Scripture[180] and, to support their assumption of innocence, highlight their kindness, gentleness, and youth. However, what seems like innocence in children is not the purity of their soul but actually the weakness of their bodily organ,[181] and the fact that they have not yet committed mortal sin does not belie their corrupt nature. The theologian Zanchius wrote that "young wolves must be killed, even if they haven't yet ravaged flocks"[182] and, however young, a serpent is full of venom and must therefore be eliminated before it can use the venom against other living beings.[183] The children of men are a brood of vipers[184] and young vipers are harmful creatures!

Edwards himself didn't hesitate to designate young children as being "outside of Christ" and "young vipers" (4, 394) and in this he was following a tradition that viewed children as "men in miniature"[185] who, though perhaps to a lesser but nonetheless very real degree, were guilty of adult sins

179. Job 11:12; qtd. in 4, 394.

180. According to the Bible, the imagination of man's heart is evil from his youth (Gen 8:21). The children must be guilty because the wrath of Jehovah is being poured out on them (Jer 6:11). The context in which the little children are said to lack understanding is clearly pejorative (Ws 12:24; Ecc 10:16) and even the teaching of Saint Paul implies a certain inferiority on the part of the child, (Eph 4:14). Modern exegesis shows that, in using children as examples of moral and spiritual behavior, Christ wasn't affirming their innocence in any way, but was instead thinking of their situation in society at that time. For more on this topic, see the Kittel, *Theologisches Wörterbuch zum Neuen Testament*, 5:647ff.

181. Saint Augustine, *Confessions*, 1. 7.

182. "Beecher Against Calvinistic Infant Damnation," 517.

183. Perkins, *A Treatise Tending vnto a Declaration Whether a Man Be in the Estate of Damnation or in the Estate of Grace, Workes*, 1:382. See also, "An adder is hated not for the euill it hath done but for that poyson that is in it" (Lewis, *English Literature in Sixteenth Century*, 187). The comparison with the wolf and viper was used, among others, by T. Manton, in "Beecher Against Calvinistic Infant Damnation," 536–7, an author much studied by Edwards (20, 500–1; 21, 485; etc.).

184. Willard, *Divinity*, 212.

185. Emmons, *Conscience, Works*, 4:163.

and subject to the same chastisements as befall mature men.[186] Théodore de Bèze, an implacable guardian of Calvinist orthodoxy, taught that dead, unbaptized children have no hope of salvation[187] and the horrible saying that "hell is paved with the bones of infants"[188] was repeated in Calvinist circles in America. In *The Day of Doom*, a very popular poem by M. Wigglesworth, reprobate infants can be heard pleading for God's forgiveness because they themselves did nothing to share in Adam's transgression. Christ replies sternly that they were in the place of their ancestor, that they certainly acted like him and, as his posterity, would not escape the punishment for his sin.[189] Everyone sins as soon as he is able (3, 200)[190] and a 1702 sermon addressed to children declared that if you go to heaven, "it would be more in spite of the fact that you are children than because you are children."[191] It was said that the evil hidden in their hearts was only fully visible to God's scrutinizing gaze, although even human observers could see how children—even before they know how to talk—are full of egoism and obstinacy, dispositions found at the source of all sin.[192] Edwards had the reputation of be-

186. "They're children of wrath by nature, liable to eternal vengeance, the unquenchable flames of hell. . . . Truly it behoves them most seriously to consider how filthy, guilty, odious, abominable they are both by nature and practise. . . . Those who are not united to Christ by heart purifying faith are children of the devil, slaves to their own lusts, enemies to God and Christ, the subjects of guilt, having no pardon of sin nor title to glory, but are condemn'd by the law, and are every moment in danger of dropping into hell" (Wadsworth, "Nature of Early Piety," 11, 15).

187. "Nisi enim extra dei foedus ecclesi am salutem agnoscimus . . . et omnes omnino gentilium liberos a partu decedentes salvari, et maximi loco beneficii futurum iis, si ab obstetricibus suffocentur ab *labem*, et *reatum* naturali propagation in ipsos derivatum juste etiam a Deo reprobari" (Spanheim, *Opera*, 3:1173–74). Our attention was drawn to this passage by the translation of it presented by Warfield, *Studies in Theology*, 433.

188. "Beecher Against Calvinistic Infant Damnation," 43. Being in a Roman Catholic country, the favorite mealtime reading of seminarians from Louvain (Belgium) was a work on the damnation of unbaptized children. Sainte-Beuve, *Port-Royal*, 1:326n.

189. Wigglesworth, *Day of Doom*, 51–53. Kant said almost the same thing but without specifying that it was about children ("Conjectures on Human History," 8:123 [Academy pagination]).

190. See also N. W. Taylor, *Concio ad Clerum*, in Ahlstrom, *Theology in America*, 233.

191. Fleming, *Children and Puritanism*, 89–90.

192. Hopkins, *Systems of Doctrines, Works*, 1:224. In a text written very shortly after this treatise by Hopkins, Kant believed he was able to discern malignancy and a desire to dominate in the newborn's cry (see "Anthropology from a Pragmatic View," 7:268n. [Academy pagination]). T. Dwight, that famous president of Yale, declared with discouragement that, of the thousands of children and adolescents he had met, he never found one that was virtuous. Smith, *Changing Conceptions of Original Sin*, 68.

ing a second Gregory of Rimini, a "tormentor of children."[193] If he warned children in vivid and dramatic terms of the danger threatening them, it was to fulfill a sacred duty.[194] Jonathan Edwards was always interested in the pastoral care of children and adults. In a 1749 ordination sermon, he exhorted the new pastor "to show benevolent attention to little children from time to time," (25, 340) and spoke at length to the children in his farewell sermon to the congregation in Northampton (25, 483–84). S. Willard had already warned his readers about young people keeping bad company[195] but Edwards appreciated their sociable character and defended their prayer meetings in the face of criticism from wary adults (see 4, 407–8).[196] In his *Treatise Concerning Religious Affections*, he praised the wisdom and gentleness of children, cited them as an example that adults should emulate[197] and observed in *The Great Christian Doctrine of Original Sin Defended* that children are less inclined to evil than adults (3, 137). In a Miscellany from the thirties, he explained that children are not only as fitted for regeneration as adults but even have certain advantages over them (20, 75–76). Nothing afflicted this father of ten boys and girls more than the suffering and death of little ones. Living in an era of high infant mortality, Edwards remarked that divine chastisement seemed to affect children more frequently than adults, and that children suffered terribly and at a time of their life when they cannot reap any moral benefit from it (3, 211). He even went as far as to say that even if the sufferings of children were not wrought by experience but were invisible facts that only revelation could teach us, they would still not be discussed less than the mystery of the Trinity.[198] However, while Edwards's heart was afflicted by the suffering of children and his mind was

193. See
"And if they have been taught aright,
Small children carried bedwards,
Would shudder lest they meet that night,
The God of Mr. Edwards."
McGinley, *Times Three*, 19, in Manspeaker, *Jonathan Edwards*, 123.

194. Edwards shared Augustine's view regarding preaching to children: "Let him only spare the little ones so that he does not praise them harmfully and defend them cruelly; let him not say that they are in good health; let him permit them to come, not to Pelagius for praise, but to Christ for salvation" ("Marriage and Desire," 2. 60).

195. Willard. *Divinity*, 604.

196. Edwards, who as a child "built a booth . . . for a place of prayer," (16, 791) praised the marvelous work that God had done among children during the Great Awakening (4, 547). See also the famous account of the conversion of P. Bartlett, a four-year-old child (4, 199–205). For the negative implications of this emphasis on the religious autonomy of children, refer to Bushnell, *Christian Nurture*, 158–59.

197. See 2, 348–9, 360, 366.

198. See 20, 88; W, 1, 642.

perplexed by the spectacle of their pain, he also knew that these terrible sufferings were not confined to this life but, in some cases, would continue in the world to come.[199]

In an unedited sermon addressed to children, Edwards warned them that they were "in Danger every Moment of falling into Hell"[200] and, when bidding farewell to his parishioners in Northampton, he observed sadly that many of the congregation's children, "having no interest in Christ" and "still in an unconverted condition," were "in danger of going down to the pit of eternal misery" (25, 483). Lastly, in his most famous sermon at Enfield, Edwards repeatedly asked: "And you, children, who are unconverted, do you not know that you are going down to hell . . . ?" (22, 417). Some hold that Edwards only outlined the possibility of hell for children and did not advocate their effective damnation,[201] but we believe it is more truthful to admit that this "moral Newton, this second Paul" accepted the reality of their eternal chastisement.[202] To those who reproached him while recalling the gentleness of children, Edwards gave an Augustinian-style response. Children are only a paradigm of a kind of "negative virtue, innocence with respect to the exercises [and fruits] of sin, harmlessness as to the hurtful effects of it." The reason that children do not yet do evil is simply because they are not yet capable of performing genuinely moral actions (3, 423).

13. The moral meaning of a determined volition

The excursus on infant guilt provided a concrete example that highlighted Christian teaching on the will under bondage and the futility of seeking a liberty of indifference. This digression occurred against a backdrop of developments where we have seen Edwards use the subtle force of his logical argument to demonstrate the plausibility of a will subject to moral inability but nonetheless remaining accountable. Alongside these so-called *a priori* and logical arguments, and in the best tradition of Christian apologetics, Edwards deployed an *a posteriori* line of argument appealing to common

---

199. Thinking that the suffering of children because of Adam's sin ends with their death and annihilation "may sit easier on the imagination, than to conceive of their suffering eternal misery for it. But it does not all relieve one's *reason*" (3, 410). For the corruption and punishment of children, see the unpublished notes in Holbrook, "Introduction," 3, 27n.8.

200. Sermon on 2 Ki 2:23-24 in Fleming, *Children and Puritanism*, 100.

201. Beecher, "Future Punishment of Infants," 90. In a homily he preached at the funeral of his son, Emmons stated that he had no reason to believe that he was not in hell.

202. See 13, 169-70; Sermon on 2 Ki 2:23-24 in Fleming, *Children and Puritanism*, 99 et passim.

sense that exposed the absurd consequences of a moral doctrine which, by denying the compatibility of personal responsibility and moral inability, required a liberty of indifference in order to ethically evaluate behavior.

The great theme of Arminian theology is that the will is undetermined before it initially takes action. This theology teaches that the matter or content of an action still does not constitute morally good or evil behavior. The goodness or wickedness of an act is necessarily conditional on the liberty of its agent and such liberty means being able to choose among several volitions. In other words, an act is only good, i.e., accompanied by merit, if the agent was equally capable of committing an evil act and, conversely, an act is only evil, i.e., involves demerits, if a good act could have been performed in its stead. Edwards used the supreme example of God, who is inalterably good and absolutely free at all times, to demonstrate the absurdity of this position. It was certainly not without a sort of wicked pleasure that Jonathan Edwards based his position on the ideas of Locke, the oracle of his Arminian contemporaries, whose statement in the *Essay* Edwards quoted in the *Enquiry*: "The freedom of the Almighty hinders not his being determined by what is best"![203] Edwards quoted extensively from Locke and other rationalists such as S. Clarke and A. Baxter (1, 377n.1), but the native soil, the motherland, of his line of argument was clearly Calvinist theology. Without doubt, the goodness of God is inseparably linked to his divinity and therefore necessary, but it would border on absurdity and sacrilege to say "that little praise is due to God for a goodness to which he is forced."[204] God is inalterably predisposed to good but this disposition and determination still doesn't nullify his freedom in any way. Protagonists of a liberty of indifference think that the presence of a strong inclination or disposition towards good or evil cancels out the virtue or vice, respectively, of a behavior. Indeed, if such were the case, then Jesus would not be praised for his holy and righteous acts because he had a strong propensity towards good in his heart (1, 326)! Scripture unceasingly praises Jesus Christ for his obedience, gentleness, patience, and love but, according to the doctrine of a liberty of indifference, Christ—the most virtuous of men and the one with the greatest and most constant disposition towards good—would be less worthy of a heavenly reward than the least Christian and "no more worthy than a clock or mere machine, that is purely passive, and moved by natural necessity" (1, 291).

What is true in a paradigmatic way for the God-Man is also true for each one of us, and Edwards and his disciples devoted all of their ingenuity

---

203. Locke, *Essay*, 2. 21. 49 in 1, 377n. l.
204. Calvin, *Institutes*, 2. 3. 5.

to depicting the absurd and harmful consequences of a position that would make the merit or demerit of a volition dependent on its agent's ability to express a volition to the contrary.²⁰⁵ If taken to its ultimate consequences, this Arminian theory would ruin all moral motivation. If invincible motives towards good action remove freedom and therefore also virtue, then "the stronger the motives, the lesser the virtue, and the weaker the motives, the better it is, although it is best not to have any" (1, 337).²⁰⁶ Edwards always taught that the will's sense is not to be sought in what precedes it but in itself, and we now see the absurd consequences of the opposite position. If every firm disposition towards well-doing and every preponderant motive towards good is voided of moral value, then the determination towards moral good and, consequently, the good determination of the will, loses its meaning and the merit of a good will is to be sought in what precedes

---

205. We should ask the Arminians this question: "When the assassin plunges deep the fatal dagger, does he incur no guilt, unless he is equally inclined to spare his victim? When the Apostle Paul devoted his life to the service of Christ, was there no holiness in this, unless he had an equal inclination to continue his persecutions?" (Day, *Edwards's Inquiry on the Will*, 207). The answer is to be found in the works of Pierre Bayle, who wrote that, in paradise, "God is . . . served perfectly well, and yet the blessed do not enjoy free-will; they have no longer that fatal privilege of the power to commit sin" (*Historical and Critical Dictionary*, 4:112 ["Marcionites," note F; spelling in the English quote has been modified for contemporary readership as required]). Moreover, "being strongly persuaded that we are only obeying divine impulsions and directions in practicing virtue, far from diminishing the satisfaction of our conscience, only makes it more delicious. . . . A Calvinist who . . . in giving alms, persuades himself that God inspired that thought in him, and gave him the strength to act on it, is more content than a Stoic philosopher who assumes all the glory for an act of charity" (Translation of *Réponses aux questions d'un provincial*, *Œuvres diverses*, 3:659).

206. All of this recalls the philosophical sin of the seventeenth-century disputations, i.e., "a human act at variance with a reasonable nature and right reason" which, when commited by an ignorant man, "is not an offense to God . . . nor (a fault) worthy of eternal punishment" (*Péché. Dictionnaire de Théologie Catholique*, 12, 256). Such philosophism "did not want the greatest of crimes to be sins worthy of Hell, even though they were commited without any thought of God" (Arnauld, *Seconde Dénonciation de la Nouvelle Hérésie du Péché Philosophique*, *Œuvres*, 31:54). How could we not quote Pascal: "I see more people, beyond all comparison, justified by this ignorance and forgetfulness of God, than by grace and the sacraments! . . . I had always supposed that the less a man thought of God, the more he sinned; but, from what I see now, if one could only succeed in bringing himself not to think upon God at all, everything would be pure with him in all time coming. Away with your half-and-half sinners, who retain some sneaking affection for virtue! They will be damned every one of them, these semi-sinners. But commend me to your arrant sinners—hardened, unalloyed, out-and-out, thorough-bred sinners. Hell is no place for them; they have cheated the devil, purely by virtue of their devotion to his service" (*Provincial Letters*, 181–83)! Philosophy has retained this text to highlight the *aporia* of moral intention. In particular, see Hegel, *Elements of Philosophy of Right*, 171 [§140].

any determination, i.e., in the contingency itself (1, 459). However, seeking good (and evil) in a metaphysical sphere devoid of any inherent moral significance is not only absurd but also pernicious.

Throughout the *Enquiry* and then in abbreviated form in his last great letter to Erskine, Edwards soberly and brilliantly depicts the most pernicious consequences of Arminian doctrine. If a firm moral disposition that prejudges action is incompatible with freedom, i.e., excludes all moral responsibility, then even the very notion of virtue and vice is destroyed, all piety is trampled underfoot and sin becomes its own excuse. Virtue and vice are, respectively, our firm disposition towards good and evil. If the very firmness and constancy of a disposition are incompatible with moral responsibility because they exclude the idea of ever-shifting freedom, then inherent virtue and vice disappear (1, 325) and morality is reduced to a series of occasional, discontinuous actions. Moreover, if we care to push this self-destructive reasoning to its logical conclusion, all moral acts of any solidity and durability whatsoever consequently cease to merit any moral designation. With their instantaneous condition, good and evil are caught, in a manner of speaking, like a ball in flight and, at the very moment when they acquire a certain stability or when occasional, isolated acts become a disposition or take on moral character, they are suddenly emptied of all ethical meaning. To a certain extent, rejecting the notion of a moral disposition robs all ethical discourse of any purpose. If the propensity, disposition, and habit of the heart are opposed to true liberty and genuine responsibility, man would not show evidence of morality when exercising his inclinations. However, if habit is neither good nor evil, it cannot make its subsequent act good or evil, nor can that act in turn make its agent good or evil. After all, a tree doesn't become better because it is frequently visited by a swan or nightingale, nor does a rock become worse because rattlesnakes crawl over it more often (1, 327)!

We have just seen that Arminian doctrine destroys true morality and also wipes out all piety. The essence of Christian piety is throwing ourselves at the feet of Jesus Christ, declaring ourselves incapable of any good, and begging his forgiveness and grace. Those who excuse their moral inability do not think of themselves as guilty and consequently do not fall back on grace. The very meaning of conversion is to become radically dependent on the savior and find our salvation in his graciously imputed righteousness. However, if nothing externally imputed to us has any moral value for us, we no longer depend on God for our salvation but on ourselves and, in order to grant us salvation, God would therefore be dependent on us (1, 466–67).

Any attempt to excuse man because of his moral powerlessness is genuine blasphemy against the Lord because it amounts to forbidding him from commanding men to obey when they are unable to do so.[207] In this case, the justice of a command does not depend on its own content and the fact that it expresses the will of God, but is conditional on the subjective situation of the creature to whom it is addressed. The teaching that flows from this position is profane and—independently of its profanity—is also contrary to all morality because it destroys even the very notion of moral responsibility which Arminian thinking prizes more than anything else. "If merely that Inability that will excuse disobedience, which is implied in the opposition or defect of inclination, remaining after the command is exhibited, then wickedness always carries that in it which excuses it" (1, 309). Moreover, sin is not simply excused but acquitted in proportion to how strongly it is anchored in the heart. If an evil inclination absolves the transgressor of his responsibility, then the more he is possessed with covetousness, cruelty, and malice, the more excusable he is (1, 324). If man is wicked by nature and character, his neighbors must pardon him when he does them harm, precisely because he is predisposed to noxiousness (18, 540–1). Of course, a man whose heart is hardened is hardly capable of performing virtuous acts, but if he were to escape all censure because of his evil disposition, then all moral judgment would have to be thrown overboard and "sin's very strength becomes its excuse" (1, 468). Sinners certainly have a disposition towards sin, but if this disposition towards sin excuses those who commit sin, they are being excused precisely by what made them sin. In other words, sinners are to be acquitted of all guilt *as* sinners and because they *are* sinners (see 1, 137). Now the moral conscience of men is outraged by this paradox and they can no longer restrain themselves from asking this question, which is loaded with scathing irony: "Do moral agents become less blameworthy as they become worse?"[208] Without the least hesitation, the answer given is that, rather than being an attenuating circumstance, their moral disposition is an aggravating circumstance and that obstinate sinners are the guiltiest of all.

In the judgment of our common conscience, "the fact that a man's heart is firmly bent on wickedness does not make his wicked action less criminal . . . only more so." Some present the excuse of a bad disposition from childhood, but will the fact of having desired and practiced evil for a very long time, perhaps even from the start, excuse its author?[209] It is also said that the force of the evil inclination is such that it cannot be resisted, but

---

207. See Smalley: "God dependent on the self-determining power of every lawless creature is a perfect cipher," *The Works* 2, 225n.1.

208. Smalley, *Sinner's Inability*, 15.

209. Hopkins, *System of Doctrines, Works*, 1:231–33.

an irresistible tendency towards evil is but the expression of a wicked heart; and a man is to be condemned precisely in proportion to the wickedness of his heart (1, 362).

The irresistible strength of an evil inclination evokes cries of moral inability; but, to be precise, the moral inability to do good is the same thing as the moral inability to do evil, whereas the essence of sin is doing evil, is it not? Before their conversion, sinners are full of enmity towards God and consequently unable to love him, but is "an irrational hatred of God" an acceptable excuse for a lack of love towards Him (12, 306)? We ask this question—albeit to excuse them—and wonder why men cannot love God. Along with Emmons, Calvinist theology has a ready answer: "It is only because they hate God, that they cannot love Him."[210] Their inability to repent of their sins only serves to "express the extraordinary strength of their affection for sin." Periodically not obeying his parents is already a serious sin for a child, but becoming so obstinate that he no longer obeys them is entirely inexcusable. People ramble on about the sinner's inability to approach the savior. However, "if the impotence of the sinner to come to Christ provides an excuse for his lack of repentance and unbelief, it is because the aversion of his will to the Lord Jesus . . . is not culpable."[211]

Terms such as unbelief, aversion and obstinacy are scattered throughout the writings of the Edwardsians because the inability they describe is moral, i.e., voluntary. It can hardly be described as a thing or a fact, being more of an exercise, and not a heavy weight that hinders a particular movement, but more like a bodily exercise that gets a man accustomed to the habit and reflexes of a contrary movement. The character of the necessity commanding the sinner to transgress is not moral because the chaining of its elements would leave a certain amount of room for indetermination but rather because it is exercised in the moral sphere of the will. Its infallible determination does not deprive the will of its free character and, according to J. Bellamy in a work prefaced by Edwards himself, this is the reason why this habitual evil inclination is most free in the being who is most mired in sin, namely the devil. Bellamy chose the example of the devil to show in a striking way how moral impotence should not override the subject's responsibility,[212] and this example also highlights the realism of the will, which is the centerpiece—the *nervus probandi*—of Edwards's moral doctrine. We have just brought attention to the paradox where, if the Arminians are to be believed, there is an inverse relationship between the sinner's

---

210. Emmons, *Saints Desire to See the Beauty of the Lord, Works*, 6:322.
211. West, *Impotency of Sinners*, 34, 17, 20–21.
212. Bellamy, *True Religion Delineated, Works*, 1:154, 327.

obstinacy and the guilt incurred for his action. This absurdity is only the logical exacerbation of a position—a *conclusio ad absurdum*—which no Arminian would apparently have recognized as his own. After all, no sensible person would say that an individual becomes less evil by becoming worse! However, the situation is different with respect to another paradox that the Arminians will find harder to challenge. If this firm disposition, i.e., moral commitment, strips the volition of any moral significance by prejudicing our freedom to choose, then the will is being propulsed on its own surface and separated from the intimate core of its being. In that case, we are obliged to conclude that: "the more men's actions are from their heart, the less they are to be commended or condemned" (1, 466). If this is so, then we are detaching morality from a continuous subject and thereby depriving it of all metaphysical permanence.

Nominalism of the will is unacceptable from a purely moral standpoint. Popular Puritanism already knew "that they be not bad deeds that make a man bad, but he is already a bad man that doth bad deeds."[213] All of this Arminian rambling on free choice should not cause us to forget the simple and basic truth of all morality that "an evil will or a wicked disposition of the heart is wickedness in itself" (1, 467). The goodness or wickedness of a human action does not stem from a contingent, instantaneous choice but rather from the firm, permanent disposition of the soul. Realism of the will teaches that only a choice flowing from a virtuous principle can be virtuous and, consequently, "the natural virtue of the soul" precedes "the good act of choosing," just as "a fountain precedes the stream that gushes forth from it" (3, 224). The comparison with the fountain and stream shows that the relationship between initial disposition and moral behavior is not patterned in any way on the relationship between a thing present at the outset and its later effect. An effect may very well survive its cause, but a stream dries up as soon as its spring goes dry. The stream is more like an integral part of the spring than an independent effect that subsists by itself. The stream flows from the spring and the flow will end whenever the fountain dries up. The stream is only a manifestation of the spring, or rather its prolongation, and its waters are scarcely different from those of the spring itself.

14. Virtue and will

Through meandering dialectical arguments and conclusions that more often seem like paradoxes, Jonathan Edwards never ceases to defend the realism of the will and, consequently, a morality for the whole person. It's the quality

---

213. Bunyan, *Grace Abounding*, 220.

of the heart, the determined and constant character of the disposition that is the seat of moral judgment. Edwards's pulverization of the so-called liberty of indifference and refusal to persistently investigate choice kept his inquiry on the nature of the will from getting mired in a study of the circumstances surrounding the determination of the will and instead turned it towards the volition's effective present rather than its distant past. The object of moral judgment is man *hic et nunc*, a man who desires and acts now and who should be evaluated in terms of the quality of his voluntary commitment. However, it is important to note that confining the will to the present in no way reduces it to instantaneous volition. The volition is never separated from the will, because even though the will may indeed will in a moment, it is nevertheless not subject to succession in time. The Edwardsian will is an undivided, noumenal category and therefore capable of providing the speculative elements of a metaphysical deduction of liberty. Being free means being fully yourself and not subject to limitations in space or time. The will in the *Enquiry*—our good or evil heart—is always fully homogeneous within itself and fully present. The will is always wholly present and passes from moment to moment as a whole. If it changes from good to bad or from bad to good, it makes this change in its homogeneous whole and is the sole agent of this change. Entirely closed in on itself—or rather, entirely homogeneous—the will can only master itself and to the fullest extent of its own volitions. As formulated by Jonathan Edwards in terms of the whole will, the Calvinist doctrine of the will under bondage led to a more modern vision of an autonomous subject delivered from all determination by nature and time. It also tallied with the ancient doctrine of virtue as a *habitus*.

The Reformation is traditionally thought of as a profound reaction or violent revolt against pagan philosophy and its stranglehold on the proclamation of the Christian faith. The Reformation unquestionably rejected the domination of natural reasoning in theology and fiercely opposed every vague desire for moral autonomy. However, notwithstanding such diametrical opposition, there is an area where their content seems to converge: the doctrine of virtue and vice. Of course, the ancients never developed equivalents for the dogmas of original sin and justification by faith to explain the origin of vice and virtue and, in any event, they were less interested in the origins of moral disposition than in its effective operation. On the other hand, they believed firmly in the durable and permanent character of moral disposition. Ancient morality primarily viewed liberty as the absence of all physical (and political) constraints on a person's movements and was essentially ignorant of the very notion of a liberty of indifference. Ancient morality was not an ethic of intention but a morality of action—a *Sittlichkeit*—and believed action faithfully expressed moral disposition. According to the ancients, man sculpts a moral image of himself that is as firm and hard as stone or indeed metal. Calvinist doctrine also recognizes such firmness and immutability which, according to the Reformer of Geneva, originated in two divine acts. The first of these acts enclosed all men in transgression and the second—which only concerns the elect—sovereignly justifies some of them. The supreme accusation of Arminian thinkers against Calvinist theology is that it destroyed all human morality by considering some as predestined to transgression and others to holiness. In fact, the entire implicit theodicy in the *Enquiry* taught that this accusation is unfounded because the ultimate outcome of the doctrine of the will under bondage and its deliverance through irresistible grace is to fully restore all of morality's significance and seriousness. Natural man's actions are marked by anger (X, 138). They are evil because man himself is evil, whereas the acts of a converted sinner are good because he has been redeemed by grace.[214] The Reformers rejected the idea of a free will that is eternally new, virgin, and ready to rebound at any time, correct itself, and recommence its work; as Kierkegaard would later understand so well, such an idea risked compromising the seriousness of a moral decision and its irrevocable commitment. The Calvinist seeks to keep and even dramatize the firm, enduring character of moral good and evil, while confining morality inside the human subject and locating it in a homogeneous, undivided sphere. But the ancients themselves scarcely taught anything different. Totally ignorant of the artificial notion of a neutral, negative free will, they also located good and evil in the stable dispositions of the human subject and, perhaps not just from a material perspective, their ethics appear to be in continuity with those of the Reformers.[215]

Echoing the ancient doctrine of virtue and vice—with its *habitus*—and anticipating Kantian teaching on noumenal freedom, the Edwardsian interpretation went beyond the framework of an apology for Calvinism to become one of the great modern philosophies of the will. However, even though the doctrine of the *Enquiry* fundamentally approximated that of Kant, its arguments were deployed in a way largely reminiscent of Scholastic ratiocination and post-Cartesian rationalism. Edwards was still wrapped in the shell of a dogmatic dialectic and it is not the least of the paradoxes in the

---

214. Edwards expressly brought justifying grace and virtue together: infused grace. Socrates held that "virtue was not teachable or acquirable by nature or art, but the product of divine inspiration" (20, 250).

215. Recognizing the continuity of view between ancient philosophy and the Augustinian tradition—their common opposition to the liberty of indifference—Pascal addressed the representative of philosophism thus: "Look for no more support, then, father, from the prince of the philosophers [i.e., Aristotle], and no longer oppose yourselves to the prince of the theologians [i.e., Augustine]" (*Provincial Letters*, 192).

Enquiry that the incessant denunciation of efficient causality in the matter of the will makes outrageous use of the causal demonstration. Ever since his youth, Edwards had regarded the cause-effect relationship as a fundamental law of reality (6, 370–71) and he continually returned to it. However, Edwards's constant use of the causal demonstration might only have been a ruse to cover the reason why he made such self-destructive use of it. Once the desired conclusion has been reached and its role as an indispensable instrument for the mind has been fulfilled, causality loses all of its significance. Once a certain threshold has been crossed, we find ourselves in a place of efficient presence and immediacy, the universe of the will.

Indeed, you could say that the true greatness of this enterprise is to take analytical, critical reasoning to its ultimate limit, to that point where it gives way to "descriptive" reasoning that is faithful to common sense and experience. In descriptive reasoning, the appearance and the thing itself are further divided in moral terms: the essence is in its manifestation, the will is (in) the volition. Vigorously refusing the obsession of an "archeology of choice" conducting interminable digs, Edwards instead practiced a "geology of the will" whose first and essential presupposition is the transparent continuity of the layers that its light illuminates. Edwards's axiom affirms the complete homogeneity of the will and its volitions: the relationships that link the inmost depths of the heart to the rapid gestures provoked by a sudden emotion are no less direct than those between the fountain hidden in the rock and the stream hurtling down a wooded slope. In geology, a landscape surface study presupposes close continuity between open terrain and the hidden layers underneath; likewise in ethical matters, where you can expect solid continuity as a function of the moral will's inflexible and ever-renascent tension.

Edwards's predecessors and contemporaries used an old, formal dialectic and failed when faced with the formidable perplexities—*aporia*—raised by moral thinking. By skillfully handling this same dialectic, Jonathan Edwards would reach conclusions that made these *aporia* fade away. Freedom and necessity, i.e., moral necessity, are not incompatible but rather one and the same thing. Rather than lessening an agent's responsibility, the moral predisposition that makes it impossible to will something other than what we effectively desire actually reinforces it. The pursuit of a chimerical past intention that sprang from an evanescent liberty of indifference fades before the faithful description of the human subject's moral existence. The absurd outcomes that were a consequent, logical development of the doctrine of free will were abandoned in favor of conclusions confirming human experience and common sense. The heart's good disposition doesn't prohibit praise, nor does the strength of the sin excuse it. The wicked will and do evil acts and, conversely, willing and doing evil acts shows that they are wicked. Edwards remarked in *The Mind*: "Here we learn the propriety of the Scriptures calling the soul, the Heart, when considered with respect to the Will and the Affections" (6, 352). Scripture calls the entire moral agent the heart—and rightly so—because it essentially expresses that most common human experience, the indivisible unity of the moral subject. In his "grand inquiry" into the will (1, 141) Edwards likewise claimed that he was merely using reasoning to support the intuitions of the common man.

3

God and the Evil Will

1. The question of theodicy

As a result of his analyses and demonstrations concerning the will, Edwards plainly took a basic common sense position. Even though this theologian's philosophical journey ultimately coincided with the intuitions of natural reason, it is important to remember that his starting point was nevertheless a theme from positive theology, namely the will under bondage that arose as a consequence of original sin. Edwards used his brilliant philosophical dialectic to establish our will's determination towards evil but, unable to confine his analysis to the immanent operation of the will, he found it necessary to extend the scope of his inquiries to the human will's relationships with a transcendent reality, namely God. Even though original sin and the will under bondage might very well form the core of Calvinist thought, they remain incomprehensible whenever an attempt is made to treat them apart from other dogmas about God's will and actions with respect to the world. In a list of theological questions found among his papers, Edwards wondered about God's moral character and the divine decrees of predestination, and then asked "In what sense did He [God] introduce sin into the universe?" (W 3, 554). God is the creator and master of the universe, which he directs with sovereign freedom and whose history he has predetermined. The world is full of various evils, one of which is moral evil. While moral evil is certainly the work of the creature, the latter is only its secondary cause. God—the one who creates and predestines—remains its primary cause. According to Edwards, Adam's sin explained the sudden apparition of evil in the world. The first man apprehended his own "separate" good and thereafter was immediately opposed to the common good (3, 380–81). God united all men to their forefather by an arbitrary constitution so that they would also apprehend their own separate good. All men are therefore opposed to God, the sovereign good. However, if such is the case, doesn't this make the One "who has bound all men over to disobedience" the author of sin? In other words, "Is God, who is goodness and holiness itself, being made responsible for moral evil?" We would then be dealing with Calvin's "cruel God"[1] whose positive role in predeterminating towards evil would be incompatible with the moral properties that natural reason would necessarily attribute to divinity.[2] Edwards himself would be accused of having made God "the intentional and blameable Author of moral Evil"[3] and of professing dogmas more blasphemous than anything found in the writings of a Hobbes or a Spinoza.[4] However, it was precisely because he rejected "with horror" the idea that God might be the agent or author of evil[5] that Edwards continually wrestled with this mystery in his Miscellanies and addressed it in certain key chapters of the *Enquiry* and his treatise on original sin. Edwards saw John Taylor accuse the Calvinists of having made God "the author of a sinful corruption of [human] nature," (3, 380) and he intended to use every resource of his believing mind to refute this intolerable accusation.[6]

The Miscellanies have been portrayed as a work of theodicy.[7] However, a careful reading of Edwards's work shows that this great theologian never focused his attention on the development of a systematic apologetic for God.[8] A religious writer whose piety is anchored in his faith in the God-Savior of history scarcely feels the need to defend God's action in the world and Edwards, a subtle and rigorous metaphysician, was as deeply rooted in Biblical faith as Calvin and the Puritan preachers of the seventeenth century. It was more his disciples, the masters of the New Theology, who felt

---

1. Frank, *Geschichte der protestantischen Theologie*, 82.
2. Channing, *The Moral Argument against Calvinism, Works*, 461.
3. Dexter, *Literary Diary of Ezra Stiles*, 1:332.
4. Bledsoe, *Theodicy*, 106.
5. J. Edwards, *Remarks on the Improvements Made in Theology by his Father, President Edwards*, in Edwards, *Works*, 1:485.
6. Edwards's foundational thesis is that of Christian theology of all time: "evil is not from God. But . . . all good is from him" (24, 1167).
7. Whittemore, "Edwards and the Sixth Way," 73.
8. Even the *Enquiry* devotes only about fifteen pages to the question of whether God is the author of evil (1, 397–412).

obliged to justify "the wisdom of God in the permission of sin."[9] Edwards apparently thought that reading "A History of the Work of Redemption" provided a better theodicy than any metaphysical speculation. Nevertheless, as a speculative theologian, he couldn't avoid addressing the issue of God's relationship to evil and essentially developed two lines of reasoning, the first of which ultimately leads to the second. On the one hand, he wanted to demonstrate that the existence of evil is compatible with God and tried to qualify divine causality so that, while remaining positive, it could not be construed as actually producing evil. On the other hand, he asserted the created will's undivided responsibility for sin. Rather than trying to apportion divine and human responsibility for evil, Edwards, in the best tradition of Protestant orthodoxy, sought to show full causality on both parts. Like his great predecessors, he recognized that this approach was replete with formidable paradoxes.

2. Sin that glorifies God

The adversaries of Calvinism accused it of ruining the very notion of divinity by attributing the effective production of evil to God. The first and simplest response to this accusation is that sin *is not* incompatible with God. Regardless of its relationships to God, sin is only a finite reality and therefore cannot affect him. The best proof of this fact is the very existence of evil. If evil was incompatible with divine goodness, God would never have allowed it to appear![10] This argument, which allows for the *logical* possibility of the coexistence of God with evil in general, becomes inadequate and untenable once attention is focused on the sin that God permits. Sin and the good Lord are moral realities, and a moral reality can never simply be neutral; it always expresses itself in negative or positive terms. In other words, sin either takes from the glory of God or serves it. Calvinist theology clearly opts for the latter possibility and sings the praises of sins that serve to show the glory of God.[11] In a manner of speaking, this is a generalized form of the traditional doctrine of *felix culpa* favored particularly by religious writers in times when theologians, cornered by apologetics, were tempted by paradox or pushed by pique to be provocative.

---

9. *The Wisdom of God in the Permission of Sin* is the title of a series of sermons by Bellamy, *Works*, 2:7–117.

10. J. Edwards, *The Salvation of All Men Strictly Examined*, in Edwards, *Works*, 1:140.

11. Bellamy, *The Wisdom of God in the Permission of Sin*, *Works*, 2:12; Hopkins, *Two Sermons*, *Works*, 3:731.

While Christian thinkers have always taught that everything on earth and in heaven sings out the glory of God, reformed dogmaticians have made a special effort to include even those in hell in this choir. Moreover, their efforts are inspired by a traditional doctrine of natural theology. Speaking about God, Saint Thomas Aquinas, for example, said: "For he brought things into existence so that his goodness might be communicated to creatures and re-enacted through them. And because one single creature was not enough, he produced many and diverse, so that what was wanting in one expression of the divine goodness might be supplied by another."[12] Because the perfection of the universe as a receptacle of divine goodness requires difference and therefore inequality between creatures so that every degree of goodness is represented, there must be creatures of incorruptible goodness and others whose goodness can decrease or even cease. Now this "is precisely what evil is," namely, "a defection from good."[13] What we have here is a speculative proof of sin's quasi-necessary existence for the greatness of God, although the deduction is only indirect because what is required is diversity among creatures, with corruptibility and corruption only being consequences of the diversity itself. Jonathan Edwards stood in a tradition where moral evil as such is required to directly show the greatness of God (see 14, 167).

As the moral governor of his creatures (23, 345), God clothes himself with the attribute of justice, which requires that all receive their due, be it a reward for the good or punishment for the wicked. However, if punishment serves to demonstrate the glories of God's justice, it is likewise good logic for us to say that everything leading to punishment must also serve that purpose. Sin leads to punishment, *ergo* sin must serve to glorify God. Indeed, in Calvinism's predestined universe, transgression seems to differ only in a temporal sense, i.e., it precedes punishment; logically and metaphysically, they both have the same status. In other words, if punishment manifests the greatness of God, sin likewise merits and manifests it as well. Of course, we'll see a little later that Calvinism allows for a degree of asymmetry between election and reprobation that avoids having God will sin in the same manner as punishment,[14] although this asymmetry is missing in many statements that entirely lack nuance. The Reformer wrote that "the wicked were created for the day of evil simply because God willed to illustrate His own glory in them."[15] We read in the *Institutes* that "the reprobate . . . were adjudged to this depravity" and "were raised up . . . to show forth

---

12. Saint Thomas Aquinas, *Summa Theologiæ*, 1. 47. 1. co.
13. Saint Thomas Aquinas, *Summa Theologiæ*, 1. 48. 2. co.
14. See *infra*, p. 161ss.
15. Calvin, *Eternal Predestination of God*, 97.

his glory by their condemnation."[16] There hardly seems to be any difference between the fact of being given over to depravity and being destined to eternal damnation and, if this be so, we might then be tempted to say with Johnson that God subjects his creatures to inevitable misfortune "from a most selfish view of promoting his own glory, . . . and in effect, of necessitating their being sinful that they might be miserable."[17]

This is undoubtedly a superficial and even ill-intentioned reading because Calvinist theologians have unceasingly said and reiterated that if God *wills* sin, he does not will it in and for itself but only with a view to the good that would issue from its coming. But can we honestly fault uninformed readers for not discerning the subtle qualifications of these abrupt statements, especially when they suddenly read that sin is a great good because it consigns the sinner to hell and that it wouldn't be possible to manifest the greatest of God's perfections, namely his hatred of hell, if hell did not exist?[18] And what would he think of this statement by a Dutch dogmatician: "Sin should not be withdrawn from the providence of God. It falls under it as to start, progress and finish."[19] On the other side of the Atlantic, Willard remarked in the forty-third sermon of his immense dogmatic work: "so God is then *most Holy*, when He is giving of Men up to *Sin*."[20] Of course, these were secondary authors who excessively systematized the major paradoxes of Biblical religion[21] and yet, because they enable us to read and understand great writers, we begin our interpretation of Jonathan Edwards with Emmons, Bellamy, and Hopkins. Faced with skirmishes and endless attacks from a culture where the influence of the Enlightenment was disbanding and destroying its heritage of Calvinist dogmatics, the masters of the New Theology defied the proponents of a gentle and reasonable God who had to be at least as gentle as man.[22]

Bellamy, a severe man, set the tone: "the dark side of the divine government of the universe . . . is full of light, glory and goodness,"[23] and "the vindictive justice" that "arises wholly from love"[24] is "an amiable perfection

16. Calvin, *Institutes*, 3. 24. 14.
17. Schneider and Schneider, *Samuel Johnson*, 3:163.
18. According to French Calvinist Pierre Jurieu. Walker, *Decline of Hell*, 53.
19. Heppe, *Dogmatics*, 274.
20. Willard, *Divinity*, 134.
21. However, also see Leibniz, "and it would be a vice in the Author of things if he wished to change anything whatsoever in them" (*Theodicy*, 2. 125).
22. Shaftesbury, *Characteristics*, 1:29.
23. Bellamy, *An Essay on the Nature and Glory of the Gospel of Jesus Christ, Works*, 2:418.
24. Bellamy, *The Wisdom of God in the Permission of Sin, Works*, 2:102n.

in the Deity."[25] Vindictive justice shines with particular brightness in the punishment due for sin, which is why a "perfectly benevolent" man should desire moral evil![26] And when the Edwardsians weren't satisfied with logical arguments, they appealed to Scripture. We read in the Psalter that: "Surely the wrath of man shall praise thee" (Ps 76:11) and, according to traditional exegesis, this expression is said to dramatically affirm the pre-eminent role of sin in the manifestation of the glory of God. At the dawn of the nineteenth century, old Hopkins used this line as the epigraph of an important doctrinal sermon and explained that the Psalmist understood "wrath" to include the sins of which men are guilty. These sins "praise" God, i.e., honor and glorify him. They include all past, present, and future sins that, without exception, contribute to the glory and happiness of God and of his friends. Sins play their role faultlessly in this economy that manifests divine glory and there have never been sins in history that were not directed by the hand of God![27] Finally, we read in Emmons that: "All the wrath, all the malice, all the revenge, all the injustice and all the selfishness, as well as all the benevolence of mankind, must finally praise Him or serve to display the beauty and glory of His character.... At the great and last day, when all human hearts shall be unfolded and all human conduct displayed, the hand and counsel of God will appear in all, and shine the brighter by every act of disobedience and rebellion in His creatures. Their bad intentions will be a foil, to display the glory of God to best advantage."[28]

Until that day comes, we listen to his disciples. Edwards himself seemed far less inclined to speak of sin as glorifying God. He certainly supported the traditional position of *felix culpa*[29] and remarked that, without the possibility of sin, a very important divine perfection—the moral government of creation—could not be shown (20, 497). Elsewhere, he explained in a Miscellany that sin is necessary to show God's justice but paused on at least one occasion to qualify these developments: "Thus 'tis necessary that God's awful majesty, His authority and dreadful greatness, and justice and holiness [should be manifested]; and this could not be except sin and

---

25. This is the title of a chapter in Bellamy, *An Essay on the Nature and Glory of the Gospel of Jesus Christ*, Works, 2:413.

26. West, *Essay on Moral Agency*, 203.

27. Hopkins, *Two Sermons*, Works, 3:727–29; "it is the vileness and inexcusable criminalness of sin" that frequently serves the designs of God (Hopkins, *Sin through Divine Interposition an Advantage to the Universe*, Works, 2:515); compare with "Sin is the occasion of all good that comes to man" (Hopkins, *Sin through Divine Interposition an Advantage to the Universe*, Works, 2:502).

28. Emmons, *Human and Divine Agency Inseparably Connected*, Works, 4:377.

29. See 20, 50; 15, 592; etc.

punishment were decreed, or at least *might be* decreed" (13, 419-20).[30] Although Edwards's writings certainly do not lack occasional allusions to sin as an area where divine glory is revealed (see 18, 314-5), it was his attitude to the above-cited verse from Psalm 76 that perhaps best reveals his lack of enthusiasm for this kind of negative glorification of God. Hopkins quoted the entire verse which, in the tradition of the English Bible, reads as follows: "*The wrath of men shall praise thee and the remainder of wrath shall thou restrain.*"[31] While Hopkins quoted the entire verse and also commented on its second part, i.e., that God "restrains" certain sins,[32] he devoted two-thirds of his development to the first part of the verse, i.e., to the role in the praise of God that should be assigned to sin. Edwards treated this differently. He also quoted this verse in its entirety, but didn't utter a word about sin glorifying God and instead spent his entire development discussing how God "restrains" or allows sin (W 2, 520-1). In other words, though steeped in the holiness and unconditional goodness of the God of the Bible, this man for once preferred an attitude of theodicy to the defiant speculation that so often characterized the writings of his disciples!

In another context, however, Edwards insisted on the positive relationship between sin and the glory of God, although again in a somewhat reserved manner. Next to glory, wisdom is an essential attribute of the God of Scripture and the predetermination of sins relates to his divine wisdom. The adversaries of the great doctrines of grace don't care to hear about a divine predetermination to transgress, but what would we think of a theology which taught that God "made the noblest of his creatures without any special purpose?"[33] Edwards himself picked up and generalized this Calvinist argument by extending it to all evil. He said in a sermon that it would have been unworthy for an infinitely wise being to have created the world and then to have allowed events to occur by chance (19, 374).[34] Chance is

---

30. Italics mine. It is interesting to note that the words in italics were deleted from the published text of the Miscellanies (W, 2, 516). Jonathan Edwards the Younger wanted to erase any sign in his father's work of hesitation regarding a doctrine that the New Theology judged to be so important.

31. The New Jerusalem Bible translation of Psalm 76:10 reads: "Human anger serves only to praise you, the survivors of your anger will huddle around you."

32. Hopkins, *Two Sermons, Works*, 3:729, 731.

33. Calvin, *Institutes*, 3. 23. 7.

34. "The doctrine of men's being the determining cause of their own virtue, teaches them, not to do so much, as even the proud Pharisee did, who thanked God for making him to differ from other men in virtue" (W, 2, 549); compare with, "The virtuous actions of men . . . are not left to men's indifference, without divine efficacy, so as to be possible to fail" (W, 2, 557). "For if we have from God a certain free will, . . . but the good will comes from ourselves; then that which comes from ourselves is better

blind, so how could an event as important as the fall of man be left to such arbitrary arrangements?[35] The very glory of the Most High requires that good and evil enter the world in accordance with the judgment of infinite wisdom (1, 409). If such is the case, then sin is not merely compatible with God's moral perfections but they also require that he take an active part in its determination and production.

3. How might God will sin?

From the outset, mankind's religious and philosophical thinkers have been confronted with the issue of the origin of evil, and the development of the idea of an omnipotent, sovereign God who is good only appears to have made this issue even more inextricable. Thinkers in the Christian tradition asked, "*Si Deus est, unde malum* [If there be a God, whence cometh evil]" and the answers ranged from a blunt confession of Manichean beliefs to a negation of the very reality of evil itself. Saint Augustine had already formulated the essential elements of various Christian answers but, more than any other Christian theology, it was Calvinism that pushed the solution to this problem furthest, at least with respect to affirming God's positive role in the rise of evil. Obsessed with "the dread majesty of God"[36] and resorting to the Bible, Calvinist writers did not hesitate to "imitate the pagans of old, who ascribed to the gods the cause of their crimes, as if a divinity drove them to do evil."[37] The omnipotent God was the efficient cause of all things, and not merely the author of good but also of evil.[38] Did he not say by the mouth of Isaiah: "I form the light and create darkness: I make peace and create evil"?[39] Don't we read in Proverbs: "The LORD hath made all things

---

than that which comes from Him" (Saint Augustine, *De Peccatorum Meritis et Remissione*, 2. 18. 30).

35. See 19, 346. Could it be that machines function according to rational necessity and man's will in accordance with pure contingency? (6, 371)

36. Calvin, *Institutes*, 3. 20. 17.

37. Leibniz, *Theodicy*, 57 [indicating the page number; there are numbers for neither book nor paragraph in the preface].

38. Calvin said that from the will of God comes life and death, health and sickness, peace and war (*Institutes*, 1. 17. 3). More profoundly, Luther said this of King Saul: "das beyde geiste gottis seyn, der gute und der bosse [both spirits are God's, the good and the evil]" (*Die Sieben Busspsalmen, Erste Bearbeitung, Werke*, 1:218).

39. Isa 45:7 in Calvin, *Institutes*, 1. 17. 8; see also 1, 407n.6. For a contribution on the history of the interpretation of this text, see Veto, *Le fondement selon Schelling*, 464n.88.

for Himself: yea, even the wicked for the day of evil"[40] and, in the book of the prophet Amos, "Shall there be evil in a city, and the LORD hath not done it?"[41] Encouraged by the excessive formulations of an entire exegetical tradition, the latest master of New England Theology believed that he could answer Boethius (see 1, 407n.6): "There is but one true and satisfactory answer to be given to the question which has been agitated for ages, *Whence came evil?*—and that is, *it came from the great First Cause of all things.*"[42] As usual, Emmons had taken a profound intuition of Calvinist Christianity to its climax, but while he delighted in dispensing "ultraisms"[43] to his small village congregation in Franklin, Massachusetts, Jonathan Edwards—the most important Calvinist writer of his time—did not want to seek refuge in paradox and provocation.

Edwards was faced with the task that his Calvinist credo had assigned him: to show that God willed and ordained sin without actually approving or being the author of it. He first had to explain—in a coherent, mutually consistent way—why and then how God willed sin. God is goodness itself and, since he only wills what is good, any evil he might will can only be ordained for good.[44] But in what sense might evil be necessary for good? Ever since the Stoics and Augustine, people have brooded endlessly over the appalling notion that "evil enhances good." They talk of dissonances that reinforce overall harmony, of shadows that enhance the light,[45] of particular evils which—as "contraries"—maintain the peace and equilibrium of the universe,[46] and of faults that confer "a kind of beauty"[47] and "an agreeable sort of variety."[48] And the apologetic of the Age of Enlightenment pushed this thinking to a climax. Jenyns bent over backwards to show the eminent utility of immoral actions: "Thus, for instance, robbery may disperse useless hoards to the benefit of the public; adultery may bring heirs, and good humour too, into many families, where they would otherwise have been wanting." Moreover, this same Jenyns taught "that there is something in the abstract nature of pain conducive to pleasure; that the sufferings of

---

40. Prov 16:4 in Willard, *Divinity*, 157.

41. Amos 3:6, in Calvin, *Institutes*, 1. 18. 3; in Willard, *Divinity*, 106. Also see Malebranche, *De la recherche de la vérité*, *Œuvres*, 3:246.

42. Emmons, *Nature of Sin*, *Works*, 4:535.

43. Atwater, "Edwards and the New Divinity," 607.

44. See Calvin *Institutes*, 1. 18. 3.

45. Saint Augustine, "Literal Interpretation of Genesis," 5. 25.

46. Saint Augustine, *On Order*, 1. 7. 18.

47. Malebranche, *Recueil de toutes les réponses à Monsieur Arnauld III*, *Œuvres*, 8:765.

48. Berkeley, *Principles of Human Knowledge*, *Works*, 2:111.

individuals are absolutely necessary to universal happiness."[49] Before the celebrated earthquake in Lisbon—and even afterwards—people rarely dared to voice objections to these aberrations, and it wasn't a professional theologian but a great literary critic, Samuel Johnson, who mounted what was probably the deadliest attack on this docile acceptance of the suffering of others. Regarding the authors of theodicies, he wrote that "many a merry bout have these frolic beings at the vicissitudes of an ague, and good sport it is to see a man tumble with an epilepsy, and revive and tumble again, and all this he knows not why . . . they have more exquisite diversions, for we have no way of procuring any sport so brisk and so lasting, as the paroxyms of the gout and stone, which undoubtedly must make high mirth, especially if the play be a little diversified with the blunders and puzzles of the blind and deaf."[50]

Edwards was unable to completely detach himself from this apologetic, even though he took his examples almost exclusively from Scripture, i.e., in a field where that which might seem difficult for natural reason to accept gained plausibility when glimpsed from the perspective of the economy of salvation. Of course, in keeping with tradition, he repeated that "particular disproportions sometimes greatly add to the general beauty" (W 2, 552); that "the sense of good," otherwise "dull and flat," is "heightened" by the sense of evil (13, 421); that seeing the sins he commits leads man to humility and conviction, but he resorted particularly to examples of various crimes which, according to the narrative of Scripture, allowed God to show all the more the wonders of his mercy and grace to his elect. The sale into slavery of Joseph by his brothers, the revolt of Absalom against his father David and, finally, the crucifixion of Jesus Christ were hideous sins which God not only tolerated but willed (1, 399–400). And when he willed them, it was because the occurrence of a particular evil would bring good for all (see W 2, 546). Now, there is still the question of knowing how God willed evil. Being goodness itself, God could only will evil as good, from the point of view of both the object and subject of the volition. In other words, when willing evil, God does not will it as either evil or good, but rather wills evil as though he had not willed it.

---

49. Jenyns, *Nature and Origin of Evil*, 85; see also 67–68 in Holbrook, "Original Sin and the Enlightenment," in Cushman and Grislis, *Heritage of Christian Thought*, 148.

50. Johnson, *Works*, 6:65 in Willey, *Eighteenth-Century Background*, 53. Even after the 1775 Lisbon earthquake, young Immanuel Kant remarked that the shock which had destroyed the Portuguese capital had multiplied the number of healing springs at Teplitz (Bohemia) and consequently "the inhabitants of that town had good cause to sing *Te Deum laudamus*, while those in Lisbon began to sing in quite different tones" ("On the Causes of Earthquakes," 1:437 [Academy pagination]).

God can will evil but not as evil *per se*, and yet this does not mean that he wills the evil itself for the good that may come of it. Ever since Saint Paul, Christians have been slanderously accused of saying, "Let us do evil, that good may come." As for those who profess this doctrine, "their condemnation is just" (Rom. 3:8). We should not will evil for any good that may result from it (16, 243), because willing evil is a sin, and how can God sin? However, there is a way to will what *is* evil, without willing it *as* evil. For example, the fact that Pope Leo X sent out letters of indulgence greatly contributed to the popular religious explosion that led to the Reformation. Although the very fact of sending these letters was undoubtedly not a good thing in itself, i.e., from a moral and religious point of view, it nonetheless facilitated the occurrence of an event that was a source of religious or moral good. God did not will the event of sending the letters for itself, but he willed that these letters should be sent to provoke the faithful into reacting against corruption. At first glance, this position may seem rather simplistic. It seems to amount to having God will an evil event so that a good event comes of it. However, Edwards worked to develop a distinction that might be artificial, but which nonetheless avoids condemnation. He wrote: "It implies no contradiction to suppose that an act may be an evil act, and yet that it is a good thing that such an act should come to pass. A man may have been a bad man, and yet it may be a good thing that there has been such a man" (W 2, 520). Sin is certainly abominable, but it may be a good thing for the world that sin exists. Edwards tried to develop distinctions that would let him say that the same thing, when seen from two different angles, could legitimately be considered as being either good or evil. The thing itself might be evil but the fact that it came to pass might be good (W 2, 546). This line of reasoning makes a distinction between the event itself and the coming to pass of that event, which is to be understood in the total context of those things. It is this total context, representing the supreme interest of everything, which justifies the coming to pass of a thing that is bad in itself.[51] However, this distinction is extremely vulnerable because it doesn't involve any real metaphysical differentiation of terms. The thing itself is like the thing as seen from within and the event is like the thing as seen from without, starting from its role in the total configuration; and yet this total configuration is itself located within the same metaphysical space. At one time, it is situated in a corner of this space; at another, it is a meeting point for the relationships radiating towards all the other locations outside of this space.

Edwards believed that he had found the solution to this dilemma when he declared that "sin may be an evil thing, and yet that there should

---

51. In that regard, see Schlaeger, "Edwards' Theory of Perception," 204.

be such a disposal and permission, as that it should come to pass, may be a good thing" (1, 406). However, a little further on, he explained the real significance of the opposition between sin itself and the fact that sin must come to pass: "God may hate a thing as it is in itself . . . and yet that it may be His will that it come to pass, considering all consequences" (1, 407). The idea of "considering all (the) consequences" compromised the validity of the Edwardsian construction itself. Edwards rejected the popular idea of a God who willed evil so that good would come of it, and adopted the more subtle position of a divine will that did not will the evil thing in itself but acted in such a way that the evil thing came to pass. This appears to be what Channing called "a distinction without a difference." Edwards wrote: "It is in itself absolutely evil for any being to commit evil that good may come of it; but it would be no evil, but good, . . . to will that evil should come to pass, . . . or that more good would come to pass in that way than in any other" (W 2, 545). In this situation, the Edwardsian distinction appears to be simply one of a quantitative nature. If God wills a certain quality of evil to take place in order to allow the coming to pass of a greater quantity of good, then—as in Leibniz—the Deity becomes a sort of calculating mechanism in moral matters. Because good and evil are defined in quantitative terms, the fact that God wills any evil at all amounts to an admission that He wills evil.

The failure of this theodicy can be avoided by resorting to the traditional distinction according to which God is the cause of the *material* part of sin only and is therefore only the author of physical evil, whereas man has *formal* responsibility for sin and is therefore the sole agent of moral evil. Edwards himself leaned towards this double causality of the sinful act (see 2, 151) but was obliged to adopt a more radical position. God and his intelligent creatures don't divide the sphere of moral responsibility between them in terms of its physical and moral parts. Man is the cause of moral evil, but so also is God. According to a "phenomenological" theory of the will, willing occurs without reference to any external determination: "It is a wheel within a wheel, which has complete motion within itself while moved by the machinery without."[52] It remains to be seen how this machinery works, i.e., how God accomplishes his will and, more specifically, how God wills evil.

Medieval theologians wanted to acquit the Almighty of all direct responsibility for evil. God neither does nor wants evil, but only permits it. Steeped in the absolutely undivided efficacy of the divine will, Calvin revolted against this distinction between will and permission because he

---

52. The text is from Griffin, *Extent of the Atonement*, in Park, *The Atonement*, 265. Edwards himself was still only using Ezekiel's metaphor of two concentric wheels to illustrate the evolution of passing moments of cosmic and human history within the total providence of God (15, 373ff.).

was reluctant "to clear God's justice of every sinister mark by upholding a falsehood." Men find it unworthy and unreasonable that God determines the reprobate to evil and therefore "recourse is had to the evasion that this is done only by the permission, and not also by the will of God. He himself, however, openly declaring that he *does* this, repudiates the evasion."[53] With respect to damnation itself, some think that God should not be held responsible for it and say that "the wicked perish only by the permission, not by the will of God. But why"—the Reformer continued—"do we say that he permits, but just because he wills?"[54] Later dogmaticians also found the notion of an "idle permission"[55] of sin to be unworthy of God, but with the brilliant intuition of divine sovereignty fading, Protestant Scholastics ended up reintroducing this distinction with up to eight different cases of *permissio peccati* by God.[56] In the eighteenth century, when Christian theology was on the defensive and turned increasingly to theodicy, the notion of divine permission returned in force, and Jonathan Edwards was unable to avoid using it. Nevertheless, he did so more at the level of terminology and without calling the undivided intensity of God's will into question.

To answer attacks by Arminians claiming that Calvin's God is the author of evil, Edwards resorted to the distinction between producing and permitting a thing (1, 398). There is a great difference between the fact that God produces an intrinsically sinful act or the fact that He permits it, between not preventing it from coming to pass and the condition of being its "proper agent or actor by operation or positive efficiency" (1, 403).[57] God can permit sin, i.e., not hinder it or, alternatively, dispose events in such a manner that sin infallibly comes to pass. God also permits sin "for wise, holy and most excellent ends" and therefore, although very abhorrent to Edwards, we could keep the Arminian designation of the God of the Calvinists as "the author of sin" as it is only because he is the author of sin that he can be "the author of holiness" (1, 399). If God had to permit sin to occur in order to produce holiness, then he would permit it. A God who renounced bringing good to pass in order to hinder evil from happening would be, Luther said, *ridiculus*![58] It is not merely that God can permit sin

---

53. Calvin, *Institutes*, 1. 18. 1.
54. Calvin, *Institutes*, 3. 23. 8.
55. Heppe, *Dogmatics*, 90.
56. Heppe, *Dogmatics*, 275.
57. God is not the author of evil but the orderer of it (Heppe, *Dogmatics*, 275). See also, "God is not only the supremely beneficent Creator of good natures, but also the just Ruler of evil wills" (Saint Augustine, *City of God*, 11. 17).
58. Luther, *De Servo Arbitrio*, *Werke*, 18: 719. See also, "hoc est optare, ut Deus propter impios desinat esse Deus, dum eius virtutem et actionem optas cessare, scilicet,

but that he must permit it, and not just by simple omission but also by commission. If there is permission, it is effective (W 2, 533) and not just idle. Under pressure from the philosophico-theological *Weltanschauung* of his time, Jonathan Edwards was forced to adopt language foreign to orthodox Calvinism but, Calvinist that he was, he ultimately emptied it of its Pelagianizing significance.

The idea that God has an area of lesser intensity, a sort of periphery of his being where his will fades or weakens, is repugnant to those who are passionate about the absolute sovereignty of God's will. In reality, however, this is not just a question of God's blazing sovereignty: it has more to do with an acute intuition of the Deity as a willing being and one whose willing is *eo ipso* moral. Calvinists are frequently accused of having a theological view of God as a force of nature, a raw power, an unlimited well-spring, or a consuming fire. If this accusation is proven to be correct, their refusal to distinguish willing and permitting amounts to a rejection of the view that God has areas of lesser intensity or brilliance. But this position implies something deeper and even more specific. Calvin's sovereign God is personal. Master of nature and history, his will is the essence of his personality. The notion that God grants idle permission was rejected not just because of discomfort over a view of the Diety with limited effectiveness, but also because of a firm resolve to reject any theology that might concede any absence of homogeneity within God. God wills, and because God is God everywhere, his will is also everywhere. A distinction between willing and permitting equates to a lesser intensity in the will of God, i.e., to something in God and of God and yet less than God. We refuse to adopt a view of God with unequal personal structures because—unlike his finite moral subjects—God does not have levels of consciousness of varying intensity and because we want God to fully express himself in all his actions. However, the holiness of God does not allow us to affirm that God wills evil in the same way that he wills good and so, if we want to preserve the omnicausality of God's will, we are cornered into admitting that there are two types of wills in God.

---

ut desinat esse bonus, ne illi fiant peiores [this is to wish that God, for the sake of the wicked, would cease to be God; for this you really desire, when you desire his power and action to cease; that is, that he should cease to be good, lest the wicked should become worse]" (Luther, *De Servo Arbitrio*, *Werke*, 18:712). Later, Schelling remarked: "Thus if God had not revealed himself for the sake of evil, evil would have triumphed over the good and love.... Thus, in order that there be no evil, there would have to be no God himself" (*Investigations into Human Freedom*, 65–6). As Augustine had already stated, God "knew that it was more fitting to His omnipotent goodness to bring good out of evil than to permit [simply] no evil" ("Admonition and Grace," 10. 27).

4. Antecedent will and consequent will

Everything that occurs in the world happens because of God's will, and yet evil exists. On the other hand, we know that God forbids evil, which is against his will. How then does he will it? This contradiction can be addressed in a non-speculative way by saying that the divine will appears to will what it does not will,[59] or that "God wills . . . and does not will" sin.[60] As theological thinkers, however, we cannot be satisfied with merely stating this paradox, as fertile and deep as it may be, but should try to explain and resolve it in logical terms.

Descartes, a great champion of the sovereign will of God, struggled with the same difficulties as his Protestant contemporaries. He had to explain how God could simultaneously exhibit two seemingly contradictory wills: one in which God ordains or forbids certain acts, and another in which he puts us in circumstances where we contravene his ordinances and prohibitions. Descartes used the example of a king who prohibited duels, but put his subjects in situations where he was certain that some of them would fight. How do we reconcile these two seemingly contradictory exercises of his will? He wrote that "in the king . . . it is possible to distinguish two different types of volition, one according to which he willed that these gentlemen should fight, since he caused them to meet; and the other according to which he did not so will, since he forbade duels. In the same way the theologians make a distinction in God's willing: he has an absolute and independent will, according to which he wills all things to come about as they do, and another relative will . . . according to which he wants them to obey his laws."[61] The theologians to whom Descartes referred represented virtually the entire scholastic tradition which, under the influence of Saint John of Damascus, had distinguished an antecedent will and a consequent will in God. While both authentically divine, these two wills do not refer to the same objects.[62] This distinction was explained in more detail by Saint Thomas Aquinas, who cited this passage from Saint Paul: "in the sight of God our Savior, who desires all men to be saved," (1 Tim 2:4) and added that we nevertheless know very well that it will not be so and that men will be condemned. How do we explain this contradiction? While being one with itself, the will of God can be considered in two ways from the viewpoint of the things of this world. Everything, insofar as it is good, is willed by God,

---

59. Calvin, *Institutes*, 1. 18. 3.
60. Heppe, *Dogmatics*, 305.
61. Descartes, "To Elizabeth," 4:354.
62. Saint John of Damascus, "Orthodox Faith," 2. 29.

although it could happen that something considered good in itself might no longer be viewed as good when a particular feature or circumstance—a consequent consideration—is taken into account. "For a man to live is good and for him to die is bad, yet if you go on to qualify him as a murderer or public danger then that he should be put away is good and that he should remain at large is bad. Accordingly, we can speak of a justice that *antecedently* wishes every man to live, but [considering all the circumstances] *consequently* pronounces the capital sentence. So by analogy God antecedently wills all men to be saved, yet consequently wills some to be condemned."[63]

Developed by Scholastic thinkers, these definitions returned in force during the controversies at the time of the Counter-Reformation[64] and were given their most celebrated philosophical formulation by Leibniz. He wrote to Spanheim that we should distinguish "between the antecedent will, which always aims to produce good, and the consequent or resultant will, which arises out of the final clash [of all antecedent wills], and makes it so that the good willed antecedently is not always willed effectively and consequently, on account of stronger reasons that divert it."[65] Leibniz later redefined these terms in his *Theodicy*. The will consists in the inclination to do what seems good to the mind. "This will is called *antecedent* when it is detached, and considers each good separately in the capacity of a good. In this sense it may be said that God tends to all good." When willing in a way that is not detached, i.e., that does not set aside the circumstances, God does not will all good but rather the best. "God wills *antecedently* the good and *consequently* the best."[66] And it is the best that implies evil. In itself, good is a necessary object of God's will but, in fact, there is no such thing as a detached good. Later in his *Theodicy*, Leibniz nuanced his definition even further. The primitive antecedent will has as its object each good and each evil in itself. The mediate will "relates to combinations, as when one attaches a good to an evil: then the will will have some tendency towards this combination when the good exceeds the evil therein. But the *final and decisive will* results from consideration of all the goods and all the evils . . . it results from a total combination."[67] The effective realization of this good—itself the object of the antecedent will—is in a sense overshadowed and superceded by the good considered with respect to all circumstances. And Leibniz

---

63. Saint Thomas Aquinas, *Summa Theologiæ*, 1. 19. 6. arg. 1, ad. 1.

64. See Gilson, *La liberté chez Descartes et la théologie*, 393 and n. For Arnauld and Jansenism, see Laporte, *La doctrine de Port-Royal*, 2. 1. 251–53.

65. Leibniz, *Textes inédits*, 1:449.

66. Leibniz, *Theodicy*, 1. 22–23.

67. Leibniz, *Theodicy*, 2. 119.

concluded that "the consequent will," which "is all-encompassing and contains the final determination . . . is absolute and decretory."[68]

The notion that the consequent will is decretory was essential for Protestant dogmaticians because the discussion on the divine volition of sin raised the question of knowing how God could will by decree that things happen which were nonetheless forbidden by his precepts. Dogmaticians initially referred to the distinction between God's revealed will and his hidden or secret will. By his revealed will, God ordains good and forbids evil and, by his hidden will, acts in such a way that evil happens and good does not happen. This distinction is still unsatisfactory, however, because it doesn't always concur with the distinction between the inefficient volition of good and the efficient volition of evil and primarily because it is based on something external to God's essence, i.e., the ultimately contingent fact of his revealed or unrevealed will. The Scholastic distinction between God's declared will and his good pleasure was more profound and also more operational in nature. In the former, God declares what should be done and, in the latter, decrees what actually is done. However, even this definition can be awkward because it frequently happens that God's good pleasure is also his manifest will; after all, God doesn't only command those things to happen that he approves of in his commandments![69] The most valuable distinction, however, is that between God's preceptive and decretive will, where the former affects good and evil, i.e., an action's *moral* character, and the latter affects the action itself as an effective, existing event. God's perceptive will is legislative and therefore concerns what is *de jure,* whereas *de facto* matters only relate to God's decretive will. In his preceptive will, the Lord desires that all men be saved, but in his decretive will, he decides not to confer the gift of repentance and faith on all sinners so that they are effectively saved.[70]

68. Leibniz, *Causa Dei,* 24. *Schriften,* 6. 442.

69. Heppe, *Dogmatics,* 85–87.

70. Heppe, *Dogmatics,* 88–89. From the outset, all of these distinctions were vigorously criticized by the adversaries of Puritanism. Although he did not explicity refer to the distinction of the two seemingly contradictory wills of God, the great Richard Hooker thought that evil could only happen with God's permission and not by his "appointement, for it abhorreth from the nature of God, to be outwardly a sharpe and severe prohibitor, and under hand an author of sinne" (*Of the Laws of Ecclesiastical Polity, Works,* 4:136). Later, in the actual context of this distinction between the two wills of God, Jeremy Taylor had his Puritan opponent say: "It is true, O God, that Thou dost call us, but dost never intend we should come, that Thy open will is loving and plausible, but Thy secret will is cruel, decretory, and destructive to us whom Thou hast reprobated; that Thy open will is ineffective, but Thy secret will is only operative, and productive of a material event, and therefore although we are taught to say, Thou art just, and true in all Thy sayings; yet certainly it is not that justice which Thou hast commanded us to imitate and practise, it is not that sincerity which we can safely use to one

5. The asymmetry of divine causality with respect to good and evil

Jonathan Edwards, a faithful reader of Calvinist dogmaticians and an admirer of Turretin and Mastricht, had to have already encountered the doctrine of God's will (or wills) during his student days at Yale and complained in one of his very first Miscellanies that "the Arminians ridicule the distinction between the secret and revealed will of God" (13, 203). Writing in the *Inquiry* towards the end of his life, he counter-attacked once more and spoke indignantly of "the cavils of Arminians" concerning the supposed irrelevance of the Calvinist distinction between God's secret and revealed will or, more specifically, his disposing and preceptive will (1, 406-7). The Calvinist's problem is making it plausible to say "that things which are contrary to God's commands, are yet in a sense agreeable to His will" (13, 243). However, the co-existence of two wills isn't the fruit of idle theological speculation but rather the evidence that gets our attention every day. Readers of Scripture, we know that God's secret will was that Abraham should not sacrifice his son, yet God commanded him to do it. We also know that God willed to harden Pharaoh's heart, yet Pharaoh's hardness of heart was sinful and therefore contrary to the divine will. God also willed the crime of Absalom—who abused his father's wives—and Scripture plainly says that God willed that men would kill Christ (13, 204). At that time, young Edwards didn't resort to a speculative explanation of the two wills but, to demonstrate that they were genuinely real, was content to refer to the so-called facts, i.e., the narrative of Scripture. The cavils of the Arminians eventually obliged him to move beyond scriptural empiricism and develop a proper philosophical defense of traditional doctrine.

The Arminians held that it was absurd to attribute two wills to God since both have the same object, namely the sinful act. However, if studied very carefully, it becomes apparent that both divine wills do not have the same object but rather opposing ones. All willing is an inclination to something. God's revealed will or "will of command"—absolutely and simply considered—is his inclination to love virtue and the happiness of his creatures. However, the inclination of his "will of decree" is not as to a thing

---

another, and therefore either we men are not just when we think we are, or else Thou art not just who doest and speakest contrary things, or else there are contrary things which may be called justice" (*Ductor Dubitantium*, Works, 9:67-68 in Miller, *Errand into the Wilderness*, 95). Compare with, "which is much the same as to attribute to the Deity two distinct wills, whereof one is in direct contradiction to the other" (Milton, *On Christian Doctrine*, 1. 4; see also, the "double dealing" of the God of the Calvinists (Schneider and Schneider, *Samuel Johnson*, 3:163).

absolutely and simply, but with respect to the universality of things that have been, are and shall be. So God may incline to accept a thing which, absolutely considered, is inharmonious, i.e., contrary to the perceptive will of God, "for the promotion of universal harmony" (13, 323). Nothing could be more wrong than to suppose that both wills have the same object. In fact, their respective objects are the most opposite things in the world, namely good and evil. Let's take the example of that representative sin of mankind, the crucifixion of Christ. This was a horrible act in itself and, as such, opposed to the preceptive will of God. However, when we consider it in the light of "its glorious consequences," it appears praiseworthy in itself and as a possible object of God's "disposing" will (1, 407).

Edwards tried to answer the ancient question of how it is possible "that things which are contrary to God's commands, are yet in a sense agreeable to His will," but he didn't succeed in going beyond the traditional solutions of Scholastic Protestantism. To avoid positing areas of unequal intensity within God's will, he adopted the theory of a duality of wills, but distinguished what ultimately was only a quantitative difference between their objects. In any event, this attempt to safeguard the undivided intensity of God's will by positing two equally divine and efficient wills had its limits and especially its dangers. The finality of this distinction was to safeguard God's homogeneity from the dangers of dividing his will into two domains of differing luminosity and from conceding a composition of heterogeneous zones within the Deity. In practice, however, teaching two wills ended up aggravating the compartmentalization that Edwards had wanted to avoid at all costs. Hypostatizing "the elements" of the Deity meant heading towards a plainly Manichean duality of the Deity.

For Edwards himself, and especially in his treatises, this distinction of two wills played only a very modest role. He was more in the line of the prudent and disciplined Scholastics, who held that these two wills are essentially one in God. Such reticence didn't sit well with all Protestant theologians, not even the greatest among them. For example, Calvin said that God uses man's depravity so "that, by a guilty hand, he may accomplish his own good work,"[71] while Luther, quoting Isaiah 28:21—"to do His work, His strange work"[72]—taught that, by the same sacrament, God carried out his "own work" in the elect and his "strange work" in non-elect sinners.[73] This work

---

71. Calvin, *Institutes*, 2. 5. 14. In keeping with a long-standing rabbinical and Christian tradition, Saint Francis de Sales spoke of the work of God's "left hand" (*On the Love of God*, 9. 8).

72. Luther, *Von den Guten Werken*, Werke, 6:248.

73. Luther, *De Captivitate Babylonica Ecclesiae Praeludium*, Werke, 6:526.

"by a guilty hand"[74] would later play a significant role in Protestant-related religious thought, reaching its climax in *Grund* and *Nature de Dieu* from the Bohemian school.[75] More sober and empirical, and less inclined to speculation, Anglo-American Protestantism barely leaned towards hypostatization in the area of the works of God's disposing will[76] and Edwards himself never used the opposition of *opus alienum* and *opus proprium* to designate these two contrasting attributes of God.[77] However, he didn't ignore this notion and, after quickly defining and illustrating the traditional theological distinction between the two divine wills, Edwards quoted at length in a footnote from G. Turnbull, "an author who couldn't be suspected of being favorable" to Calvinists and one who, when discussing the problem of the divine causality of evil, had written: "the Lord *delighteth in goodness*, and as the Scripture speaks, *evil is his strange work*?"[78]

It is striking to see Jonathan Edwards quoting from a rationalistic writer of the Age of Enlightenment regarding a difficult notion of Lutheran orthodoxy for which he himself apparently did not want to take explicit responsibility.[79] It is well known that Edwards frequently employed his immense dialectical powers to demonstrate doctrines of Reformed theology; we have only to think of his series of arguments setting forth and defending God's effective permission of sin (W 2, 519–20)! However, he is averse to excessive speculation and taking liberties with Scripture, especially when there is a risk such speculation will go against his own original finalities. Edwards made use of the distinction between God's will and his mercy, but without hardening it into an ontological opposition (24, 304). On the other

74. Calvin, *Institutes*, 2. 5. 14.

75. The avatars of this notion in the context of transcendental philosophy are retraced in Veto, *Le fondement selon Schelling*.

76. However, see P. Sterry (compared to Edwards by Grosart, "Introduction," *Selections from the Unpublished Writings*, 12): "Hell is his *strange Work*. A work in which he *estrangeth* himself from himself; in which he goes to the vastest distance to bring forth a *Work* most unlike himself, in which he hides the Workman in the Horrors of the Work, and shows him, by *hiding* him so deep.... The Works of Wrath are the Strange works of Christ and God. This expression, His Strange Work signifies: a work with which he is not acquainted in His own Person, and Nature; a Work which is *uncouth* to Him, in which the Height of his Skill and Power delight not to put forth themselves; a work in which he is *descended* out of his own Form into some inferior Form of the Creature, and so became a Stranger to himself" (Sola Pinto, *Peter Sterry*, 160, 162). See also Shepard, "strange works" of the Holy Spirit, *The Parable of the Ten Virgins*, Works, 2:212.

77. The *opus alienum*, alien work, is mentioned by Edwardsian writer Stephen West, *Essay on Moral Agency*, 223.

78. Turnbull, *The Principles of Moral Philosophy*, 42, in 1, 407n.6.

79. However, see the quasi-furtive appearance of the "judgment is His strange work" formula in 20, 464.

hand, he didn't mention God's corrupt hand and avoided making the *opus alienum* his personal *theologoumenon*, perhaps fearing that the stratagems used to safeguard the undivided sovereignty of God's will might ultimately scuttle themselves and virtually divide God's actions according to his hypostatized attributes. Because anything tending towards metaphysical dualism was repugnant to Edwards's thinking, all that remained was for him to explore a new avenue for theodicy.

The doctrine of the two wills had to safeguard the absolute efficacy of the divine volition, but found itself being drawn towards a virtual partitioning of God according to his various attributes. It was therefore necessary to return to the idea of a single will of God while interpreting it in such a manner that it can be the cause of good and evil in distinct and even opposite ways. It's important to underline the qualifier—*opposite*—because otherwise we risk falling back on the anti-Calvinist distinction between willing and permitting.[80] The very logic of Reformed theology requires us to reject what, depending on its intensity, is ultimately a quantitative distinction between an active will and a semi-mobile, permissive will, a will of simple permission. Because God's own honor requires that his will be seen as the integral cause of good and evil, his willing of evil cannot be conceived of as equating to his willing of good, whether at a certain level of intensity or even none. The willing of evil should not be distinguished from the willing of good by degree but by kind.[81] This amounts to saying that it should be in an opposing direction.

Our religious conscience has an immediate, primitive intuition of the irreducible opposition of willing good and evil and—in an initial pre-speculative time period—quite simply refuses to ascribe the origin of evil to God in any way and without being concerned about attributing its rise to any particular place. The religious conscience operating in Christian piety can only experience our turning away from God and our communion with him as originating from two different sources, as otherwise we cannot think of them as truly opposite to one another.[82] Advocates of absolute divine sovereignty believe they have to insist on the divine origin of good and evil,

---

80. This distinction is nonetheless present in the *Book of Controversies* (see Ms. 273).

81. It is here that certain Edwardsians deviate, so to speak, from Jonathan Edwards and the great Christian tradition in general. For example, see Emmons: "There was the same kind, if not the same degree of necessity to create sinful, as to create holy beings," (*The Glory of God Illustrated*, Works, 4:254). For the physical influence of God upon sin in Edwards, see especially W, 2, 557–58.

82. Schleiermacher, *Der christliche Glaube*, 1. 63. 394–95 [numbers indicate volume, section, and page].

but find themselves victims of a glaring philosophical error. Good and evil are not entities belonging to the same ontological sphere but rather opposite moral realities, with each one forming a different metaphysical sphere. It's a fundamental view of Protestant theology that the flesh and the spirit do not represent the respective ends of the same scale of values, but are instead from two different universes. They are diametrically opposite realities that could not originate from the same source, and it is this great religious intuition that explains the Edwardsian critique of an identical volition for good and evil.

Edwards wrote that if some people say election is from God, then reprobation must also be from him. However, it is erroneous to believe that simply because one of these two opposites has its origin in a particular reality, that the other must also refer to it. If fresh water flows from a particular spring, that doesn't mean that it must also be a source of bitter water. It is absurd to proclaim that God, the source of all light, must also be the source of all darkness, or that the author of good must also accept blame for all evil. The evidence is rather quite to the contrary. If the sun is a source of light, then darkness certainly doesn't originate from it, but instead has some other cause.[83] Rather than proving an equally divine origin for disbelief, the divine origin of faith is actually a decisive counter-argument against it.

Although this line of argument clarifies the simple logic of the religious conscience, it is only the first rudimentary element of a development that ends by linking evil to God while still maintaining their irreducible opposition. Rather than simply being content to sharply reject any linking of good and evil, we devise a theory that emphasizes how evil is opposed to God, but also makes it come from him. Christian apologists are always pleased to appeal to images that safeguard the honor of God, and they use one to illustrate this strange type of causality where God, by the very fact of giving rise to evil, is actually pushing it furthest from himself. Calvin wrote that because men want their crimes to remain unpunished, they attribute their evil character to God himself. "And whence, I pray," the Reformer exclaimed, "the fœtid odour of a dead body, which has been uncoffined and

---

83. Compare with, "Sicut impossibile est contrarie inter se pugnantia, et detruentia se mutuo, causam efficientem formalemque esse posse sibi contrariorum: ut Lux non est causa tenebrarum, neque caliditas frigiditatis . . . ita impossibile est Deum, qui est Lux, Iustitia, Veritas, Sapientia, Bonitas, Vita, causam esse tenebrarum, peccati et mendacii, ignorantiae, coecitatis, malitiae et mortis [As it is impossible that things that are in direct repugnance to one another and are mutually destructive can be the efficient and formal cause of their contraries; as light is not the cause of darkness, nor heat of cold . . . so it is impossible for God, who is light, righteousness, truth, wisdom, goodness, life, to be the cause of darkness, sin and falsehood, ignorance, blindness, malice, and death]" (*Confessio Czengerina*, in Niemeyer, *Collectio*, 549).

putrefied by the sun's heat? All see that it is excited by the rays of the sun, but no man therefore says that the fœtid odour is in them."[84] Some 150 years later, S. Willard preached that God can bring about sin without tarnishing his holiness. "As the sun is not defiled by shining upon the most Dirty stinking Places, tho' they Stink the more for it's shining upon them."[85] Ever since Augustine, this religious intuition has been known by the term *nolonté de Dieu* (God's non-will or *noluntas*) or by what Luther called the divine *Unwille* (indignation, abhorrence), a notion that Christian preachers and dogmaticians have used to express the divine efficacy in the advent of evil, yet without making God the univocal and adequate cause of sin. In biblical terminology, the divine will is designated, "the wrath of God" which, especially since the Kaballah, Judeo-Christian speculators have tended to find at the origin of phenomena contrary to his preceptive will. Good comes from the love of God, which is a blessing; evil arises from his wrath, which is a cursing. The great Puritan poet, John Milton, wrote of those infernal regions as "a universe of death, which God by curse, created evil."[86] God does not create death in the manner that he directs and orders nature[87] because "God wills that which is evil, inasmuch as it is evil, by disallowing and forsaking it,"[88] and Edwards himself said that God created the wicked like he created the darkness—in a negative way—by withdrawing his light (24, 561). This profound intuition of the religious conscience that refuses to attribute the same kind of causality for evil as for good to God is at the origin of the grandiose Barthian doctrine of *Nichtiges*—the *leitmotiv* of all theodicies—which aimed to provide a divine causality for evil that would not make evil a proper work of God.

As we have already noted, Edwards wasn't inclined towards theological speculation on God's corrupt hand—the *opus alienum*—and he didn't use the theological image of creating by rejecting evil to explain God's willing production of evil. He contented himself with representing the divine causality of evil as something which shed additional light on the holiness of God and its absolute difference from evil. Edwards summarized his position on a magnificent page in the *Enquiry*:

84. Calvin, *Institutes*, 1. 17. 5.
85. Willard, *Divinity*, 184.
86. Milton, *Paradise Lost*, 2, 623–4, *Works*, 2. 1. 60.
87. Amesius, *Medulla Theologica*, 60–61.
88. Perkins, *A Golden Chaine or the Description of Theology*, *Workes*, 1:12. The good are resurrected by the virtue of Christ and the Holy Spirit, the wicked by the omnipotence of God (Heppe, *Dogmatics*, 701). God does not "govern" devils by his Spirit, he curbs them by his power (Calvin, *Catechismus Ecclesiae Genevensis*, *Opera*, 6, 18).

"As there is a vast difference between the sun's being the cause of the lightsomeness and warmth of the atmosphere, and brightness of gold and diamonds, by its presence and positive influence; and its being the occasion of darkness and frost in the night, by its motion, whereby it descends below the horizon. The motion of the sun is the occasion of the latter kind of events; but it is not the proper cause, efficient, or producer of them; though they are necessarily consequent on that motion under such circumstances: no more is any action of the Divine Being the cause of the evil of men's wills. If the sun were the proper *cause* of cold and darkness, it would be the *fountain* of these things, as it is the fountain of light and heat; and then something might be argued from the nature of cold and darkness, to a likeness of nature in the sun; and it might be justly inferred, that the sun itself is dark and cold, and that his beams are black and frosty. But from its being the cause no otherwise than by its departure, no such thing can be inferred, but the contrary: it may justly be argued that the sun is a bright and hot body, if cold and darkness are found to be the consequence of its withdrawment; and the more constantly and necessarily these effects are connected with and confined to its absence, the more strongly does it argue the sun to be the fountain of light and heat. So, inasmuch as sin is not the fruit of any positive agency or influence of the Most High, but, on the contrary, arises from the withholding of His action and energy, and, under certain circumstances, necessarily follows on the want of His influence; this is no argument that He is sinful, or His operation evil, or has anything of the nature of evil; but, on the contrary, that He, and His agency, are altogether good and holy, and that He is the fountain of all holiness. It would be strange arguing, indeed, because men never commit sin, but only when God leaves them *to themselves*, and necessarily sin when He does so, that therefore their sin is not *from themselves*, but from God; and so that God must be a sinful being: as strange as it would be to argue, because it is always dark when the sun is gone, and never dark when the sun is present, that therefore all darkness is from the sun, and that his disc and beams must needs be black" (1, 404).

The Edwardsian theodicy ends with this *reductio ad absurdum* and culminates in a positive manner. The essence of his argument, with respect to the cause of evil, was to find it in man abandoned by God and—secondarily and concomitantly—in God himself, because the primary aim of the argument was to acquit God of all responsibility for evil, and not so much to explain man's responsibility. The thematic exposition and development only appears in *The Great Christian Doctrine of Original Sin Defended*, where the theoretical foundation of man's responsibility for evil was laid.

6. The three moments of eternal condemnation

Ever since Augustine, Christianity's great thinkers haven't ceased to elaborate on the theme of "God" being the one "from whom to turn away is to fall" and "to whom to turn is to rise,"[89] enunciated more precisely by Calvin: "Man therefore falls, divine providence so ordaining, but he falls by his own fault."[90] This definition encompasses the various problematic situations faced by Christian dogmaticians struggling with notions of reprobation, hardening and damnation. Dogmaticians have to take account of God's positive interventions in the rise of evil which, more than anything, are also sovereign and seemingly arbitrary. God's relationship with evil is presented through a temporal reading grid. This is because—to use a Hegelian term— God appears in "religious representation" as having condemned man in the past, hardened his heart in the present and is pushing him towards hellish grief in the future. The positive character of this divine intervention is highlighted by this temporal refraction, which also reinforces its arbitrary appearance. The reprobatory decision, hardening decision and damning decision arise in an incomprehensible manner from the depths of God's will. The task that the dogmatician sets for himself is to announce the sovereignty of God's judgment while eliminating its arbitrary appearance. With Edwards, as with all of the great philosophical theologians, this operation is accomplished by portraying the essential immanence of evil in the human will that a transcendent decision appears to have imposed on it. This move in the direction of immanence was facilitated and supported by Edwardsian reflections on the doctrine of the indivisible will. Rejecting the archeological quest for a causal determination led to a position with a will that is always equal to itself. In other words, rather than presenting a relationship of priority or posteriority between the divine decision and the human one, a phenomenological or essentially Kantian reading of the will cancels its temporal refraction and leaves us with a will that is self-determined to evil

---

89. Saint Augustine, "Soliloquies," 1. 1. 3. Compare with, "the eye is sufficient in itself for not seeing, that is to say in darkness, but for seeing it is not sufficient in its own light" ("Proceedings of Pelagius," 3. 7). The stopping of our ears shows that hearing does not depend on us, although not hearing does ("Nature and Grace," 47. 55). A man may kill himself on his own, but cannot keep himself alive (*Enchiridion*, 30). All of this is summarized in a systematic, conceptual manner by Saint Thomas Aquinas (*Summa Theologiæ*, 2–2. 137. 4. 3).

90. Calvin, *Institutes*, 3. 23. 8.

at every instant. The initial reprobation, the hardening as the culmination of divine concourse with the present evil, and the damnation are no longer divine facts affecting the creature's will from the outside, or if they are, then only negatively. Evil done in the present and yet to be done in hell (the damned continue to sin!) is to be understood in terms of God's withdrawal, which is represented as refracting and taking place in time.

In his great sermon to the congregation in Enfield, Edwards said: "You have reason to wonder, that you are not already in Hell" (22, 416). The essence of the hellish condition is evil that rages without restraint, because men are presently full of evil, and the fact that they do not overflow with it at every moment is purely because the mercy of God retains and restrains them (see VI, 490). Edwards wrote about the presence of hellish principles in natural man (22, 407), and this wasn't simply a powerful image but the expression of an essential moment in his reflections. It was a profound intuition on the part of the Reformers that only the good and gracious will of God prevented the evil accumulated in natural men from overflowing, and this same vision is also found at the heart of Edwardsian preaching on judgment and damnation. It is not necessary to presuppose that God implanted a positive evil quality in man to explain the advent of original sin. Having the divine spiritual influence withdrawn from the heart and being left to themselves is enough for these natural principles to rise up in enmity and rebellion. At creation, two kinds of principles were implanted in man: natural principles that sufficed to take account of his human nature and superior divine principles that make him a "*virtuous, holy* and *spiritual man*" (3, 381n.5). As long as these natural principles of self-love and personal well-being acted under the government of superior principles, they were good and loyal servants, but with the withdrawal of these superior principles, they became independent and thereafter exercised unrestrained domination over the whole man. An appeal to an external, positive intervention isn't necessary to explain Adam's corruption; pointing to an immanent change produced by the disappearance of these superior principles, these "extraordinary gifts" of God, is sufficient.[91]

By virtue of the unity that God constituted between Adam and each of his descendants, men found themselves bereft of these supernatural principles and prey to the revolt of the natural principles that followed the withdrawal of the Spirit or rather—from the creature's perspective—the withdrawal itself. While they were not subordinated to the grace of regeneration, the natural principles—or, the flesh, as they are called in Scripture—continue in their rebellion. In other words, man never ceases to sin

---

91. See *infra*, p. 298.

(3, 38–9). Every natural man's homogeneous, undivided, evil will is such that he has enough of hell accumulated in him to find himself at any moment in the torments of the damned (22, 404–5).

The finality of this teaching on the withdrawal of the superior principles was to make man entirely responsible for evil. Immediately provoking the revolt of the flesh, without any intervening time delay whatsoever, this withdrawal seems like the undivided moment when the departure of the Spirit and the advent of the flesh, the negative causality of the Creator and the positive causality of the creature, are co-temporal. This co-temporality is an essential element of the evil will at every moment it is exercised, although human understanding cannot refrain from breaking this simultaneity—this co-temporality—in order to give preponderance to one of these two principles, even though they are in solidarity with one another. Our understanding is already inclined to characterize our sins as current and, depending on when they took place, to perceive them as posterior to the withdrawal of the divine principles, although the conceptual analysis might somewhat restrain this tendency and, within each evil volition, find the concave face of that essential and primitive event whose convex face is the withdrawal of the divine principles. On the other hand, simultaneity and organic solidarity appear to be definitively included when contemplating and explaining the dogmas of damnation and reprobation. Hell is represented as the consequence of the evil volition and reprobation as its antecedent, although in both cases the double divine and human causality upheld by Calvin[92]—with inspiration from Augustine[93]—and later by Edwards (W 2, 580) and the New Theology movement,[94] wasn't truly respected. The goal of the dogmaticians was, as far as possible, to remove the bark of representation from the essence of the objects of the Christian conscience by eliminating all representations of time delays from their portrayal of the relationships between divine and human decisions. The operation was to be carried out in two directions, but it proved easier to accomplish with the notion of damnation than that of reprobation. The fact that damnation involves clearly temporal moments—this present life, where the sinner "prepares" his damnation; the future life; and even moments in time, such as this world of earthly actions as "a local hell"[95] where the damned suffer—helped create a wealth of imagery. It was precisely this profusion of images that made it easier to relativize

---

92. Calvin, *Institutes*, 1. 18. 3–4.

93. Saint Augustine, "Grace and Free Will," 20. 41–43. .

94. Hopkins, *System of Doctrines, Works*, 1:134–35; Griffin, *Extent of the Atonement*, in Park, *The Atonement*, 264–65.

95. Milton, *The Doctrine and Discipline of Divorce, Works*, 3. 2. 441–42.

the representation and orient the analysis towards the will itself. This explains why damnation and hell have played such a huge role in Christian preaching in general, and in Edwardsian preaching in particular.[96] The situation is different for reprobation where representation, by the very fact of being projected into a sphere that is essentially foreign to it, defends itself by becoming hard and fixed. Wanting to explain the two causalities of evil, our finite mind finds itself lost in the world of the Lord, which it can only represent in terms of an infinitely distant past. The rarified atmosphere of this eternal past is precisely what precludes representation from using relativizing imagery in any way and prevents thinkers from getting beyond pure representation. The horrible decree of reprobation[97] forces dogmaticians to walk a narrow path between two precipices: the announcement of a brutal, divine arbitrariness and a Pelagianizing discourse on merit and demerit. The task is made almost impossible by the obligation to reconcile God's absolute sovereignty with his justice in a judgment passed on a yet uncreated creature whose very existence is solely dependent on God's good pleasure.

7. Double predestination

God's eternal decrees are the third doctrine addressed in the Savoy Declaration, immediately following the articles on the Scriptures and God.[98] For modern commentators, the central principle of Protestantism is neither justification by faith nor the primacy of Scripture but eternal predestination,[99] which Calvin didn't hesitate to put in parallel with the Holy Trinity.[100] Essential to his theology, no doctrine provoked more violent accusations against Calvin's heritage than predestination. Cudworth, a Cambridge Platonist, called predestination to salvation and damnation the "divine Fate immoral."[101] With his good Lutheran conscience, Hegel termed it "the most wretched contingency" of "the Calvinist view,"[102] and Baader, a Roman Catholic, faulted "this fatalistic predestination heresy" for the worst exaggerations of human passivity in the representation of the "opus

---

96. Of course, because it is a future state, we could also add that damnation might be the quintessential subject for a preventive, homiletical exhortation.
97. Calvin, *Institutes*, 3. 23. 7.
98. Walker, *Creeds and Platforms*, 370.
99. Warfield, *Studies in Theology*, 117 and n.
100. Calvin, *Institutes*, 3. 21. 4.
101. Cassirer, *Platonic Renaissance in England*, 79.
102. Hegel, *Philosophy of Religion*, 3:157.

operatum."[103] Unconditionally deciding man's happiness or damnation was "monstrous"[104] and made him a "plaything of divine caprice."[105] It was the doctrine of the eternal decrees that made it possible to accuse Calvinism of Hobbesian necessity and Stoic fatalism (1, 269). By the New Theology period, this teaching had become "hateful and frightful to many,"[106] but Edwards was already tormented during his adolescent years by this horrible doctrine according to which God elects whom he will to eternal life and rejects whom he will, abandoning them to eternal perdition and unending torture in hell (16, 792). Clearly, if predestination as an undivided whole was already the object of such violent criticism, what was said about predestination to evil *stricto sensu*, i.e., reprobation?

Anglicans, deists and "moderate Calvinists" raged against this horrendous doctrine, but of this immense number of denunciations, we are just going to consider one from a Catholic pen. Here is how it summarizes Calvin's doctrine on the reprobate: "God, from all eternity, predestined them to eternal damnation before ever foreseeing sin—even original sin—because that was His good pleasure; He plunged them into the original sin that the first man committed by necessity, giving them neither Savior nor means of salvation and, to torment them, carried out all manner of crimes that He imputed to them, and damned them, even though they were unable to save themselves, avoid the evil they committed or do the good they omitted to do." Because Calvin extended blasphemy as far as to say that God sent his Son to preach salvation to the reprobate in order to make them more criminal, he therefore "used the light of God's Word to blind those of the Reprobate to whom he communicated it." Again, according to Calvin, "God delivers men, bound hand and foot, over to Satan, obliging them to obey him. He takes away the knowledge of their duties and the ability to do good

---

103. Baader, *Der Morgenländische und Abendländische Katholicismus*, Werke, 10:136.

104. Kant, *Metaphysik L1, Ak.*, 28. 349. Through the doctrine of predestination "the concept of God would become a scandal and all morality would become a figment of the brain." Insofar as it implies reprobation, it "presupposes an *immoral* order" ("Philosophical Doctrine of Religion," 28:1115–16 [Academy pagination]). It "harms" the concept of freedom and makes a rational being into a machine. (*Metaphysik, Schriften*, 18. 484).

105. Baader, *Vorlesungen und Erläuterungen zu Jacob Böhme's Lehre*, Werke, 13:59–60. But the Calvinists themselves rejected this interpretation: "Calvin denied thirty times that he made God the author of sin, although he made every effort elsewhere to re-establish this detestable maxim *which all the Catholics attributed to him*" (Saint Vincent de Paul, *Correspondance, Entretiens, Documents*, 364 in Laporte, *La doctrine de Port-Royal*, 2. 1. 296n.31).

106. Hopkins, *Sin an Advantage to the Universe*, Works, 2:530.

from these wretches, unleashes Satan, the minister of His wrath, upon them and, by special inducement, requires him to lead men into crime; meanwhile, for His part, God determines their will, excites and confirms them in their evil designs, all to execute His judgments, i.e., on the sins to which He predestined them, and His Decree of Predestination to damnation, thereby glorifying His justice."[107]

The author of this diatribe was Jean-Baptiste du Chesne, a Jesuit who believed he had faithfully reproduced the literal doctrine of the *Institutes*, whereas the goal of the Protestant dogmaticians was precisely to show that this reading of the Reformer's teaching was fragmentary, truncated, and therefore radically wrong. The doctrine of predestination is a brilliant expression of the mysterious "conjunction of the love and wrath of God" that featured so prominently in Luther's meditations.[108] It's a "wonderful judgment of God whereby it comes to pass that some are born at Jerusalem, whence soon they pass to a better life, while Sodom, the gates of the lower regions, receives others at their birth."[109] The human mind is tortured by the mystery of the sovereign decision of God but, ever since Augustine, the truly pious could not have enough of the sweetness they tasted in contemplating the designs of Wisdom with respect to the creature.[110] Of course, predestination to salvation or damnation, because it is determined by God's good pleasure, is a "strange and hard" doctrine,[111] a veritable labyrinth where human understanding can go astray.[112] It is not for the human mind, left to itself, to search out the secret of reprobation[113] because Scripture admonishes us not to "seek for any cause beyond his will."[114] In short, if we approach it outside of mortal suffering and anguish, the mystery of predestination becomes a terrible abyss for us[115] since it is "one of the deep things of the cross."[116] However, for "godly persons," sovereignty is "an infinitely amiable part of

107. Chesne, *Le prédestianisme*, 352, 363, 393.
108. Luther, *In Oseam Prophetam*, 322.
109. Calvin, *Consensus Genevensis*, in Niemeyer, *Collectio*, 263.
110. Saint Augustine, *Confessions*, 9. 2.
111. Calvin, *Sermons sur L'épître aux Éphésiens*, *Opera* 51. 261.
112. Calvin, *Institutes*, 3. 21. 1.
113. Calvin, *Institutes*, 3. 21. 2. These are demons arguing: "Of Providence, Foreknowledge, Will and Fate, / Fixt Fate, free will, foreknowledge absolute" (Milton, *Paradise Lost*, bk. 2, ll.559–60, *Works*, 2. 1. 57.)
114. Calvin, *Institutes*, 3. 22. 11.
115. Luther, *Vorrede auf die Epistel Sankt Pauli zu den Römern*, *Die Deutsche Bibel*, *Werke*, 2. Abt. 7. 24.
116. Calvin, *Institutes*, 3. 2. 35.

God's moral character"[117] and predestination is "full of sweet, pleasant and unspeakable comfort."[118] For that reason, and in spite of all of the difficulties it presents, it should not be kept secret.[119] Jonathan Edwards himself considered the moment when he could view the sovereignty of God with love as a turning point in his own spiritual life (16, 792). He always thought that those who did not discern God's glory in his sovereign predestination didn't have "a correct understanding of God" (17, 282). The requirement to agree with reprobation, and even to love it, remains a *leitmotiv* of Calvinism and it returned in a disquieting and obsessive manner in the New Theology movement.[120] But what exactly should we understand by predestination and reprobation? Is reprobation an integral part of predestination and, if so, what is its relationship to election? Is their relationship one of parallelism or organic solidarity? In spite of frequent excesses of language and formulation, we think that the great theologians of the Reformed tradition are resolutely inclined towards an asymmetrical representation of reprobation and election and the presentation of reprobation as a simple shadow of election.[121] It is still the case in preaching—and not just at that level—that this asymmetry and disproportion aren't always highlighted and have sometimes even been questioned and repudiated.

The brilliant intuition of divine sovereignty led to affirmations that were seemingly unnuanced and unrestricted. Perkins declared that "God hath most justly decreed the wicked workes of the wicked,"[122] and he was only echoing the *Second Confession of Faith of the English Church at Amsterdam*: God "before of old, according to His just purpose ordained . . . both men and angels, to eternal condemnation."[123] The theologian knows that many are invited but few are elected, and this for the good reason that the death of Christ does not apply to those for whom he did not pray.[124] It is an aberration to say that the grace of Christ was effectively offered to

117. Bellamy, *True Religion Delineated, Works*, 1:94 n.

118. *The Thirty-Nine Articles of the Church of England*, in Schaff, *Creeds of Christendom*, 3:498.

119. Heppe, *Dogmatics*, 189.

120. For the faithful, being able to praise the reprobating love of God is "the most proper subject by which they try their Christian character" (Emmons, *Reprobation, Works*, 4:336), and "those who do really hate the doctrine of reprobation, deceive themselves when they think they love the doctrine of election" (Emmons, *Saints Desire God to Punish Sinners, Works*, 6:160). See also *infra*, p. 409–411.

121. Eusden, "Introduction," 27.

122. Perkins, *An Exposition of the Symbole, Workes*, 1:183.

123. Walker, *Creeds and Platforms*, 59–60.

124. Willard, *Divinity*, 282.

everyone.[125] Christ "offered Himself for those whom He knew the Father had given Him, but never by chance or accident—as some imagine that the grace of sacrifice has been scattered in the air, in order that he who would might snatch it for himself."[126] It was decided from all eternity that those who would not make a saving use of this grace—the reprobate—would be cast into the torments of hell. The meaning of the decree of reprobation is that "God . . . out of the mere good pleasure of His will . . . has resolved to leave fixed men, whom He does not elect, in the mass of corruption."[127] As Hopkins succinctly said: God, "who confers the means of salvation on the elect . . . refuses them . . . to the reprobate."[128] Edwards himself, fighting Arminianism whose "two rotten pillars" are the affirmations that God loves all men equally and gives each one the eternal grace in Jesus Christ for his redemption,[129] summarized the intolerant doctrine of orthodoxy as follows: "God hereby declares Himself the absolute disposer of the creature; He shows us how far His sovereignty and dominion extend, in eternally choosing some and passing by others, and leaving them to perish" (17, 282). Jonathan Edwards himself apparently professed double predestination in this sermon and considered it God's supreme self-glorification.[130]

In order to go beyond the rhetoric of preaching, we will now turn to theological definitions. The first kind of formulation defines predestination as the divine decree regarding man's eternal destiny and does so without making any distinction whatsoever between salvation and damnation. "Predestination," wrote Polanus, "is the decree of God by which, from eternity, He designated rational creatures to set limits, beyond this natural and temporal life, where they will be taken by means that were likewise pre-ordained from eternity."[131] Seventy years later, with his habitual simplicity, S. Willard summarized these definitions in a catechism sentence: "Predestination . . . is the decree of God, for the manifestation of His special glory, in the eternal state of men."[132] It is obviously almost natural to go from this definition, which speaks of the creature's eternal condition without mentioning the two possible ends, to an explicit expression of double

---

125. "Beecher Against Calvinistic Infant Damnation," 592.
126. Heppe, *Dogmatics*, 476.
127. Heppe, *Dogmatics*, 181.
128. S. Hopkins, *His Book*, in Ferm, *Colonial Pastor*, 102.
129. Owen, *Death of Death in Christ*, 35.
130. However, after stating his definition of this twin predestination, Edwards doesn't say a word about reprobation and only writes about election (17, 282–84).
131. Qtd. in Heppe, *Dogmatics*, 154.
132. Willard, *Divinity*, 253–54.

predestination. Predestination—wrote holy Perkins—"is the decree of God, by the which He hath ordained all men to a certaine and everlasting estate, that is, either to salvation or condemnation."[133] This great specialist on the order of *The Causes of Salvation and Damnation*, the author of a complicated diagram representing the multiple moments of the *golden armilla* of predestination,[134] didn't hesitate to specify further on that "the decree of reprobation is that part of predestination whereby God, according to the most free and just purpose of His will, has determined to reject certain men unto eternal destruction and misery."[135] Here, Perkins consummated the break with an ecclesiastical tradition which, since the Council of Orange, had only recognized negative reprobation, i.e., a predestination to damnation that only consisted of abandoning the sinner to his sin[136] and whose *leitmotiv* was the following expression by Prosper of Aquitaine: "Ac per hoc praedestinatio Dei, multis est causa standi, nemini est causa labendi [hence, God's predestination is for many the cause of perseverance, for none the cause of falling away]."[137] Perkins opted for positive reprobation, and the dogmatician of Puritan New England, S. Willard, followed his example.[138] However, positive reprobation or "predestination to death," as Augustine once let slip from his pen,[139] is only the product of what is in essence a very marginal current in ecclesiastical tradition[140] related to the actions of the sovereign, bountiful God, namely the mechanical parallelism of the action of material things. It was Isidore of Seville, a great scholar but mediocre theologian, who pronounced the fatal formula: "Gemina est praedestinatio, sive electorum ad requiem, sive reproborum ad mortem [Predestination is two-fold, being either that of the elect to repose or that of the reprobates

---

133. Perkins, *A Golden Chaine or the Description of Theology*, *Workes*, 1:16.

134. Perkins, *A Survey*, *Workes*, vol. 1, opposite p. 11.

135. Perkins, *A Golden Chaine or the Description of Theology*, *Workes*, 1:105.

136. See Scheeben, *Handbuch der Katholischen Dogmatik*, 272–3.

137. Saint Prosper of Aquitaine, *Responsiones ad Capitula Objectionum Vincentianarum*, PL 51. 184.

138. Willard, *Divinity*, 258.

139. Saint Augustine, *De Anima et eius Origine*, 4. 11. 16; see also *City of God*, 20. 24. For Augustine's vague inclination to profess double predestination, see *Letters*, 5:75–96 [letter 217]. We are greatly indebted to K. Barth for the references to this discussion, *Kirchliche Dogmatik*, 2. 2. 15–7.

140. However, the Council of Valence III (855) professed: "fidenter fatemur praedestinationem electorum ad vitam, et praedestinationem impiorum ad mortem [faithfully we confess the predestination of the elect to life, and the predestination of the impious to death]" (Denzinger, *Symboles et définitions de la foi catholique*, 232); (also *Enchiridion Symbolorum, Definitionum et Declarationum de Rebus Fidei et Morum*, 628)).

to death]."¹⁴¹ Two centuries later, Gottschalk would echo this Spanish thinker,¹⁴² and then, after the prudent distinctions and reservations of the Scholastics,¹⁴³ we suddenly find Calvin with this terrible definition: "By predestination we mean the eternal decree of God, by which . . . some are preordained to eternal life, others to eternal damnation."¹⁴⁴ And here, even more explicitly, is the two-fold decision: "since there could be no election without its opposite reprobation."¹⁴⁵ This fatal parallelism—"the *inseparable* connection between election and reprobation"¹⁴⁶—would haunt Reformed theology, and even if, by numerous dialectical subtleties, profound religious intuitions concerning the impossibility of attributing the eternal perdition of men to God's will—from the Arminians¹⁴⁷ until the Orthodoxy of Massachusetts—were successfully translated into a rejection of the symmetry involved in predestination, they never stopped uttering terrible platitudes about reprobation that "runs parallel with election."¹⁴⁸

Nevertheless, as K. Barth admirably explained it, election and reprobation are not in a symmetrical relationship.¹⁴⁹ Just as *Nichtiges* is only a shadow of being and good, reprobation is only a marginal and peripheral reality in the face of which election can flourish. Reprobation isn't an integral part of the divine decision and there is nothing in God's will that corresponds to it. In a way, it exists only where the external deployment of the Lord's saving will finds its bounds or limits.¹⁵⁰ There aren't two kinds of pages in the book of life, only pages on which the names of those called to life are inscribed; and reprobation only consists in not being inscribed in the book.¹⁵¹ This view of reprobation as not belonging to what is properly called predestination even finds expression at the level of ecclesiastical terminology. Already in Augustine, predestination was most frequently "ad gratiam [to grace]," and consequently "ad vitam [to life]." For Saint Thomas

---

141. Saint Isidore of Seville, *Sententiarum Libri Tres*, 2. 6. 1. PL 83. 606.

142. Hincmar, *De Praedestinatione Dei et Libero Arbitrio*, 1. 5. PL 125. 89.

143. For example, see Vignaux, *Justification et prédestination au XIVe siècle*.

144. Calvin, *Institutes*, 3. 21. 5. "God by his eternal and immutable counsel determined once and for all those whom it was his pleasure one day to admit to salvation, and those whom, on the other hand, it was his pleasure to doom to destruction" (*Institutes*, 3. 21. 7).

145. Calvin, *Institutes*, 3. 23. 1; *Consensus Genevensis*, in Niemeyer, *Collectio*, 231.

146. Emmons, *Saints Desire God to Punish Sinners, Works*, 6:160.

147. Barth, *Kirchliche Dogmatik*, 2. 2. 17.

148. Willard, *Divinity*, 266.

149. Barth, *Kirchliche Dogmatik*, 2. 2. 187; see especially 246–47.

150. Barth, *Kirchliche Dogmatik*, 2. 2. 184–86.

151. Barth, *Kirchliche Dogmatik*, 2. 2. 15.

Aquinas, predestination was of "a creature of intelligence, capable of eternal life," being "brought there, properly speaking, as sent by God," with "the idea of this sending" being that which "pre-exists in God";[152] and, in opposition to reprobation, is the part of providence that concerns those destined to eternal salvation.[153] The *Formula Concordiae* is even more explicit: "the *eternal election* or *predestination* of God, that is, the ordaining of God unto salvation, does not pertain both to the good and to the bad, but only to the children of God, who were elected and ordained to eternal life."[154]

In the Reformed tradition, with apparently only a few exceptions,[155] reprobation cannot be considered to be an integral part of predestination,[156] but in most cases, an attentive reading of the texts reveals a certain understanding of the asymmetrical, non-parallel character of election and reprobation. While insisting on the absolute sovereignty of God's decrees, the theologian tries to show that God decides "arbitrarily, but not without full knowledge of the facts"[157] and that his decrees are not based on "naked freedom."[158] Even Perkins, an advocate of positive reprobation, thought it important to remind his readers that God had not created man simply to damn him.[159] Of course, what matters is that the disproportion—the asymmetry of the two divine wills—was affirmed in classic manner by Scripture. "His anger," wrote the Psalmist, "lasts only a moment, but his favor lasts a lifetime" (Ps 30:11); and the prophet Isaiah spoke thus for Yahweh: "In a little wrath I hid my face from thee for a moment; but with everlasting kindness will I have mercy on thee" (Isa 54:8). This naïve opposition, represented by temporal categories, would be found at all levels of theology, starting with the elementary, formal level of a language distinction in its speculative

---

152. Saint Thomas Aquinas, *Summa Theologiæ*, 1. 23. 1. co.; see 3. 24. 1. The prophecy of predestination, contrary to that of foreknowledge, only concerns the elect. 2-2. 174. 1. co.

153. Saint Thomas Aquinas, *Summa Theologiæ*, 1. 23. 3. co.

154. *Symbolical Books*, 711.

155. Ritschl, *Dogmengeschichte des Protestantismus*, 275.

156. In a certain number of formularies—including that of the great anti-Arminian Synod of Dort—reprobation is presupposed but not mentioned. On the other hand, whenever it is mentioned explicitly, it always plays an essential role. In only one confession of faith—that of the English Congregation at Geneva (1556)—is reprobation defined before election. See Warfield, *Studies in Theology*, 223-25.

157. Willard, *Divinity*, 256; see also, "those whom he dooms to destruction are excluded from access to life by a just and blameless, but at the same time incomprehensible judgement" (Calvin, *Institutes*, 3. 21. 7).

158. *Confessio Fidei Ioannis Sigismundi Electoris Brandenburgiae*, in Niemeyer, *Collectio*, 650.

159. Ritschl, *Dogmengeschichte des Protestantismus*, 302.

finality. According to the Savoy Declaration, "Some men and angels are predestined to eternal life and others pre-ordained to eternal fire."[160] Because its intent is already speculative, the procedure used to look at material differences in the terms for reprobation and election is more significant. Firmly holding to divine sovereignty, the theologian wants to explain the disproportion between election and reprobation, starting from God himself but, in the end—and he doesn't ask for anything better from the beginning—he winds up having to assign the reasons for this disproportion to man. In a sample of unconditional declarations on divine sovereignty from the *Second Confession of Faith of the English Church at Amsterdam*, a vigorous insistence on the flawless parallelism of election and reprobation doesn't prevent the former from being defined as having been decided by God according to "the mere good pleasure of His will," and the latter "according to His just purpose."[161] The unexplained observation of the fact of election is contrasted with a finality in reprobation. A sovereignty of good pleasure is juxtaposed with justice that must be exacted. In other words, God's love and grace are, in a certain sense, opposed to his justice. Now, justice is something that is related to a standard, to objective facts. This objective fact is clearly sin, and relating reprobation to God's justice links reprobation with the universe of the evil will.

8. The selective love of God

Rational reasoning that obeys formal rules of logic turns in circles when faced with the disproportion, the asymmetry, of two acts of divine willing and, given that this sphere ultimately remains one of representation, poetry again proves best suited to penetrate it. In his majestic *God's Determinations [touching his Elect: and The Elects Combat in their Conversion, and Coming up to God in Christ together with the Comfortable Effects thereof]*, the metaphysical poet of Westfield, Edward Taylor, celebrates the selecting love of God in his decrees:

> Almighty makes a mighty sumptuous feast:
> Doth make the Sinfull Sons of men his guests.
> But yet in speciall Grace He hath to some, . . .
> He sends a Royall Coach . . .
> To fetch them in, and names them name by name. . . .
> The Coach . . .

---

160. Walker, *Creeds and Platforms*, 372. This is a quasi-literal echo of Calvin, *Articuli de Praedestinatione*, Opera, 9, 713–14.

161. Walker, *Creeds and Platforms*, 60.

> All mankinde splits in a Dicotomy,
> For all ride to the feast that favour finde,
> The rest do slite the Call and stay behinde.[162]

Apparently everyone is invited, but only certain specific people get to the banquet, those whom the Host has brought to himself. The effective election of some sinners implies the abandonment of others, although in such a way that the latter explicitly oppose the Host. The Host's relationships with the called differ, depending on whether it is a matter of election or reprobation. Saint Thomas Aquinas had already noted that, from the point of view of causality, reprobation and predestination (i.e., election) are not realities of the same order. Election is the cause of grace in this life and glory in the next, whereas reprobation only causes damnation in the next world. On the other hand, the sins committed here below come from the free-will (of the person) that God abandons to himself.[163] In spite of his inclination towards *gemina praedestinatio* and notwithstanding a great number of exceptions, Calvin himself doesn't seem to admit that the same analytical relationship connecting election to sanctification and salvation can be applied to the divine causality in damnation.[164] But it was only much later dogmaticians who found adequate formulations for this elementary biblical intuition of the Calvinist faith: "Salvation is from God, perdition is from us [Et ex Deo salus, e nobis perditio est]."[165]

According to Keckermann's rigorous summary, reprobation has two moments: (a) a first act where, by virtue of his absolute will, God decides to abandon certain men to themselves, and (b) a second act whose purpose is to condemn certain men and which implies consideration of sin. We can say that we are saved because of election but not that we are condemned because of reprobation. Election is the positive principle of salvation but reprobation—original sin, as in Edwards—only consists of removing or withdrawing the positive principle.[166] Or again, there exists a negative rep-

---

162. Taylor, *Poems*, 399–400.

163. Saint Thomas Aquinas, *Summa Theologiæ*, 1. 23. 3. ad. 2–3; see also Laporte, *La doctrine de Port-Royal*, 2. 1. 301.

164. In this regard, see the subtle interpretation by P. Jacobs of the isolated role played by the doctrine of reprobation in *Prädestination und Verantwortlichkeit*, 154ff. For a very helpful look at this entire issue, read the insightful developments in Vincent, *L'herméneutique du discours théologique*.

165. Hos 13:9 in *Ecclesiarum per Helvetiam Confessio Fidei*, (1536), in Niemeyer, *Collectio*, 117.

166. Heppe, *Dogmatics*, 181. For a simple, enlightening portrayal of the negativity of reprobation and its assymetrical relationship to election, see Amesius, *Medulla Theologica*, 114–16, 200.

robation and a positive reprobation[167] that correspond respectively to the divine abandonment of the sinner and the human accomplishment of sin. According to the *Lambeth Articles*, "all men are not drawn by the Father, that they may come to the Son,"[168] which essentially recalls the Augustinian position. The reprobate are those who have not been singled out but left in the mass of the lost.[169] Those whom God leaves unelected—and here we have an echo of Calvin—he reprobates,[170] i.e., abandons to their own wickedness and obstinacy.[171] Without a doubt, theologians insist on the fact that the creature's sin is not a cause but only a "condition of the determination of the will" of God.[172] In the end, and regardless of all protests, the Calvinist dogma ends up being close to a simple permission or a negative causality inasmuch as it seeks to coordinate the negative and positive moments of reprobation rather than making the latter asymmetrically subservient to the former.[173] Kant's position was the logical result of these developments. This philosopher wrote that as long as the author of this world is represented anthropomorphically, foreknowledge also implies predetermination, the unconditioned decree of God, which is "the *salto mortale* of human reason." However, when we jump to the intelligible order of the laws of freedom where time disappears, we are left with knowledge that sees everything and freedoms that are determined in an inexplicable manner and according to opposing principles.[174]

In spite of his refusal to concede unqualified foreknowledge (see W 2, 521) and his remarkable dialectical efforts to represent divine sovereignty in "the decree of reprobation" as something more than a mere expectation of failure, the theme of Edwards's reflection is still just a well-developed version of a negative asymmetric causality that abandons the reprobate to their sins. The author of the *Enquiry* "has presented the dogma of predestination in a form far less dishonorable to God . . . than that in which Calvin has stated it";[175] but, as noted by an eighteenth-century critic unaware of the Miscellanies, Jonathan Edwards "keeps his notion of Reprobation somewhat hidden behind the curtain, which makes the more

167. Heppe, *Dogmatics*, 181–82.
168. *The Lambeth Articles*, in Schaff, *Creeds of Christendom*, 3:524.
169. Saint Augustine, "Admonition and Grace," 7. 12.
170. Calvin, *Institutes*, 3. 23. 1.
171. *Canones Synodi Dordrechtanae*, in Schaff, *Creeds of Christendom*, 3:552.
172. Heppe, *Dogmatik*, 147.
173. See Heppe, *Dogmatics*, 181.
174. Kant, "Religion within Boundaries of Reason," 6:121, n.
175. Channing, "Edwards and the Revivalists," 381.

dangerous, and more likely to deceive common readers."[176] Edwards refused to consider the glorification of God's vindictive justice as an absolute end of reprobation (18, 315), and here again remains faithful to the thesis of a withdrawal of grace that amounts to a negative causality. Like R. Hooker, Edwards knew that "sin is no plant of God's setting"[177] and explained, in a previously mentioned note on *Proverbs*, that God, in the same negative way that he created the darkness by withdrawing his light, likewise created the reprobate by withdrawing his grace (24, 561). Withdrawal exposes or uncovers sin, so to speak, and it is in this sense that the Miscellanies present reprobation almost in terms of an explanation of the reprobate's own imminent condition. Reprobation is neither arbitrary nor the consequence of a subjective choice on God's part, because "what sense is it to say, that a creditor chooses out those out of his debtors to be free from debt that owe him nothing?" Why would he bestow eternal life "upon those who have a right to damnation" (13, 234)? The abrupt and "parallelist" formulation of this Miscellany from Edwards's youth was surpassed by a major text written at the beginning of the 1730s in which Edwards gives a remarkable summary of his doctrine. He wrote that there is an essential difference between election and reprobation. Election is entirely independent of any divine foresight of faith and good works. It essentially serves to communicate God's happiness to the creature and glorify his divine grace, neither of which necessarily supposes faith and good works. It is only the arbitrary appointment of God's wisdom, wherein he will bring men to partake of his grace. Reprobation is different. The decree of reprobation undoubtedly implies the glorification of God's vindictive justice and, because this presupposes sin to be avenged, it therefore follows that the existence of sin is presupposed in the decree of reprobation (18, 282-3). More specifically, in presupposing sin and the glorification of God's vindictive justice as its grounds, this decree presupposes sin as antecedent to glorification. Vindictive justice is but a means, not an ultimate end in itself. It is not a divine attribute. The existence and sin of the reprobate have been wrongly seen as posterior to the glorification of God's vindictive justice and even solely for that purpose. Given that, in the conceptual order, glorification can only follow the sins of the reprobate, the first ground of the decree of reprobation is therefore "the sin of the reprobate" (18, 315).[178]

176. Smith, *Fall of Angels and Men*, 41.

177. Hooker, *Of the Laws of Ecclesiastical Polity, Works*, 4:142.

178. Edwards deployed his doctrine from his asymmetrical conception of these two predestinations. Of course, God has "determined from all eternity the number and persons of those that shall perform the condition of the covenant of grace" ("Controversies" notebook, *Ms.*, 275), but salvation remains a free gift and therefore damnation,

Based on this distinction, and in a subtle, profound way, Edwards developed parallels between election and reprobation, although without subjecting the will of God to narrow requirements for symmetry between mercy and justice. He wrote that God's decree of eternal damnation of the reprobate does not precede their existence and fall, whereas his decree of the eternal glory of the elect precedes the existence and faith of the creatures to whom it applies. God's glorification of his love and communication of his goodness are ultimate ends and, as such, precede the very being of the creature and do not presuppose it. However, the situation changes radically when the will to glorify no longer concerns the elect in general but rather the elect as creatures subject to misery and sin. In this case, because the glorification of grace is accomplished through fallen creatures, it is no longer considered an ultimate end or unconditional act but simply a means to that ultimate end. An absolute, unlimited reality—the glorification of God and the communication of his divine goodness—becomes particular in the form of a decree (18, 316–7).

According to dogmaticians, a decree is "a specification and resolution of the eternal counsel of God regarding things coming into existence in time."[179] God's will in glorifying his love and communicating his grace must be considered as prior to any relationship to the creation and fall and, insofar as it concerns a certain number of creatures (subject to sin), should be represented as posterior to any foresight of the creation and fall (see 18, 316–17). Reprobation, on the other hand, has no part in the original condition of election. It only arises at the actual moment of election, i.e., of "distinction or discrimination," and does not presuppose the foresight of a determination in the creature. More precisely, these decrees of election and reprobation must be looked upon as beginning at the moment when, by abolishing the common state of the creatures, the divine will preceded to make a distinction,[180] i.e., in the call to life (18, 318). In a broad sense and as an exercise of God's antecedent will, predestination is therefore election, the call of all to salvation. On the other hand, in a more precise sense and insofar as it expresses God's consequent will, predestination is election and

---

the debt of unbelief, is a merited punishment (18, 244). Though giving an interest in Christ is evermore an act of mere sovereignty, yet denying an interest in Christ may be a judicial act (18, 321). Men may be the means of their reprobation, but not of their salvation (*Bl.*, 211); forgiveness is not due to our merits, but the denial of forgiveness is caused by our demerit (18, 223). In short, we are not accepted because we are worthy, yet are rejected because we are unworthy (18, 243). God freely bestows happiness on the saints, but inflicts torments on sinners in an immanent manner (19, 790).

179. Heppe, *Dogmatics*, 137.

180. Set before the selective love of God is "the corrupt mass of mankind . . . wherein both vessels of honor and dishonor lay undistinguished" (24, 1023).

reprobation. God's primary, unconditional will is his saving will, whereas his secondary will allows for perdition. Reprobation always relates to this secondary, sin-conditional will, although "the decree of the permission of sin is prior to all other things in the decree of reprobation" (18, 321).

9. Hardening of the heart

The horrible decree of reprobation fills the heart with indignation because it concerns and strikes a yet uncreated being who, to all appearances, never intervened in any way in his "predestination to death." Moreover, eternal condemnation inspires horror because it inflicts infinite suffering on the creature without any possibility of expiation. For its part, hardening is the supreme example of representing God as the effective author of the present moral evil. By hardening the hearts of sinners, God pushes them to sin, thereby seeming to actually cause moral evil, and "the carnal mind can scarcely comprehend how, when acting by their means, he contracts no taint from their impurity."[181] In the context of divine sovereignty, which the Calvinist tradition professes with particular emphasis and one where God claims responsibility for "all the *Evils* that do befall the Children of Men,"[182] the issue of divine responsibility seems starkest and most concentrated in ecclesial teaching on the hardening of the heart. In reprobation, there is a time gap between God's eternal counsel and man's sinful will. This gap is also found in the doctrine of hell, along with the issue of physical and moral punishment. On the other hand, hardening does not include anything likely to divert the mind from the divinity's positive role in the human will's determination towards evil. God hardened Pharaoh's heart and Pharaoh increasingly hardened himself in sin. The mystery of divine causality in sin is virtually laid bare for us here: nothing comes between God who hardens and the man whose heart hardens itself. The Apostle Paul succinctly stated that "God has mercy on whom He wants to have mercy, and He hardens whom He wants to harden" (Rom. 9:18), and the dogmatician has to explain and interpret this verse without softening it.

Of course, in the Edwardsians's theology of paradox and provocation, there is an obsessive insistence on complete causality without any intermixing of God and hardening. Bellamy wrote that "God, the infinitely wise superintendent, calmly looks on, and lets him [i.e., Pharaoh] take his course."[183] God was not content to leave Pharaoh to himself—and now we

---

181. Calvin, *Institutes*, 1. 18. 1.
182. Willard, *Divinity*, 106.
183. Bellamy, *The Wisdom of God in the Permission of Sin, Works*, 2:16.

hear N. Emmons—"But God knew that no external means or motives would be sufficient, of themselves, to form his moral character." The divine will "determined, therefore, to operate on his heart itself and cause him to put forth certain evil exercises." Emmons punctuated his catalogue of the crimes of Pharaoh, "this dark prototype of all the rejected,"[184] with the phrase, "God stood by him and moved him."[185] Emmons evidently took morbid pleasure in provoking the religious and moral sensibilities of his contemporaries, but hadn't Calvin himself expressed something similar? It's an "inadmissible" conjecture, he wrote, to think that God merely "desert[s]" those hardened in sin. It is not a matter of bare "permission" because the Almighty is active in hardening, and his will is its primary cause.[186] Moreover, "not those were blinded, who so deserved by their wickedness, but who were rejected by God before the foundation of the world."[187] And God had not only affirmed that Pharaoh's fury "had been foreseen by Him . . . but that He had also thus designedly ordained it, and indeed for this end,—that He might exhibit a more illustrious evidence of His own power."[188] Commenting on the story of Pharaoh, Calvin echoes a verse of the *Second Epistle to the Thessalonians*: "to those who are perishing," God sends a delusion to lead them astray.[189] "God," the Reformer wrote, "blinds the minds of men, and smites them with giddiness, intoxicates them with the spirit of stupor . . . and hardens their hearts," and "is said to have given men over to a reprobate mind" and cast them into base desires.[190]

As with reprobation and also with hardening, and using language that frequently becomes overly rigid and unnuanced, Calvin never ceases to be inspired by Augustine.[191] None of the great writers of the Christian tradition expressed the terrible dilemma of hardening with more richness and depth. In his great texts on anti-Pelagian controversies, Augustine abandoned the

---

184. Barth, *Kirchliche Dogmatik*, 2. 2. 243. Edwards called Satan the "spiritual Pharaoh" (15, 96, 237). This expression seems to have originated with Saint Ambrose, *Hexameron*, 1. 4. 14.

185. Park, *Memoir of Nathanael Emmons*, 409–10.

186. Calvin, *Institutes*, 1. 18. 2.

187. Calvin, *Commentarius in Epistolam Pauli ad Romanos*, *Opera*, 49, 216.

188. Calvin, *Commentarius in Epistolam Pauli ad Romanos*, *Opera*, 49, 183.

189. 2 Thess 2:11 in Calvin, *Institutes*, 2. 4. 5; see Heppe, *Dogmatik*, 222n.

190. Calvin, *Institutes*, 1. 18. 2.

191. "Further, Augustine is so much at one with me that, if I wished to write a confession of my faith, it would abundantly satisfy me to quote wholesale from his writings" (Calvin, *Eternal Predestination of God*, 63). Pascal thought otherwise: "Calvin n'a aucune conformité avec saint Augustin, et en diffère en toutes choses depuis le commencement jusqu'à la fin [Calvin has no conformity with Saint Augustine and differs from him in every way from start to finish]" (*Écrits sur la grâce*, *Œuvres*, 319).

thesis of an inherent reality in man that provoked a predetermination to hardening on the basis of a foreseen demerit[192] and advocated instead in favor of a divine decision without any contribution on the creature's part. God hardens whomever he wills and because he so wills. However, this great theologian's religious understanding didn't allow him to content himself with this unilateral explanation, and he produced numerous developments in which divine and human causality are affirmed in a profound and mysterious reciprocity. God—he wrote—does as he pleases with the human will, inclining it either towards good or towards evil. However, even though God inclines the wicked man's heart towards sin, sinners are still held accountable for evil.[193] God stirs up animosity in the sinner's heart and yet the latter gives himself freely over to it. The sinner plunges into evil and God works this terrible mystery of hardening, which should be considered a punishment for man's wickedness. Augustine concluded: "God . . . hardened . . . the heart of Pharao" and yet "Pharao . . . hardended his own heart," i.e., "God, by His judgments, Pharao, by his free will."[194] This insistence on double causality implies a strong emphasis on its negative aspect, that of being abandoned by God. "God does not harden by imparting malice . . . but by not imparting mercy,"[195] so that nothing "is imposed by God whereby a

---

192. For his initial position, see *De Diversis Quaestionibus LXXXIII*, 94, 4–5.

193. Augustine's doctrine has been admirably "summarized" by Bossuet. The Scriptures do not represent God's will as a sort of energy that propels a hardened person's action. God inclines this action in a given direction. We recognize that "a will that is *already evil* because of its own dissoluteness and going downhill . . . and is not becoming more evil by focusing on one object rather than another, could also be led to an object by a secret operation of God who, without having any part whatsoever in causing evil or influencing the degree of evil involved, is free to vary these movements." If we say that "God pushes to evil," this should not be understood as "a positive impetus causing a wrong move, but like water that is inclined to fall when a dike is raised and its course in one direction rather than another is determined by the opening left for it, while the rest is kept closed off. . . . Without pushing men to either general or particular evil, God turns a will that is already evil—and bent on evil—*towards one evil rather than another* . . . which is not in the least . . . to push it to evil but, on the contrary, by restraining it on one side, He allows it to fall on the other side under its own weight" (*Défense de la tradition et des Saints Pères*, 411–12).

194. Saint Augustine, "Grace and Free Will," 20. 41–23. 45. Later Protestant exegesis showed that the book of Exodus itself presents two series of statements, one which says that Pharaoh hardened his own heart and another which says that God hardened Pharaoh's heart. The first series of statements (7:13, 22; 8:15, 32) precedes the second (9:12; 10:20, 27) (Müller, *Christian Doctrine of Sin*, 2:413).

195. Saint Augustine, *Letters*, 4:310 [letter 194]; God should simply be represented as "not bestowing on him [i.e., Pharaoh] the grace which would have brought about his change of heart" (Descartes, "Replies to Second Set of Objections," 7:143 [Adam and Tannery pagination]).

man is made worse"—i.e., made to sin—"but only that he provides nothing whereby a man is made better."[196] Hardening should not be presented as a mere decree but as an act of justice: "God . . . does not forsake him [i.e., man] (if he is not forsaken [by him])."[197]

Although it is generally felt that Augustine's brilliant vision of divine sovereignty was diluted in or drained out of medieval thought, the essential core of Augustine's teaching was picked up again by the Scholastics and, for example, by Thomas Aquinas, who insisted on the role of the human will but was anything but silent about God's part in hardening. Aquinas wrote that, on the one hand, God is not the cause of the movement of the human mind in cleaving to evil; on the other hand, he is the cause of the withdrawal of grace that leaves the sinner blind. Unlike the sun, which fails to light the interior of a house whose window-shutters are closed, if God does not shine the rays of his grace into the souls of those in whom he finds an obstacle, it is because God "by his own choice . . . withholds the light of grace." "In this way," the Angelic Doctor concluded, "God is the cause of spiritual blindness and hardness of heart." God is therefore the cause of hardening. However, hardening must not be taken for a gratuitous curse emanating from the divine will. That the sinner is unable to break free of evil is rather the consequence and not the cause of the evil into which the sinner plunges ever deeper, and hardening is a demeritorious punishment of the inveterate sinner.[198]

The position of Saint Thomas Aquinas expresses the essential intuition of Christian theology on this subject. Augustine had already said that the evil in which a man is engaged invariably tends to progress and grow, and such later sins as may arise are to be viewed as punishment for previous ones.[199] By resisting the Holy Spirit, men make themselves incapable of welcoming grace and "by reason of their crimes going before, they did owe to themselves a kind of penalty; which so punisheth them, that now they continually incur further guiltiness, and make themselves daily more punishable."[200] God does not hinder the sinner from sinking into evil,[201]

---

196. Saint Augustine, "To Simplician," 1. 2. 15.

197. Saint Augustine, "Nature and Grace," 26. 29.

198. Saint Thomas Aquinas, *Summa Theologiæ*, 1–2. 79. 3. co., ad. 1, 3.

199. Saint Augustine, "Grace and Free Will," 20. 41; "this is the punishment of iniquity, as well as being itself iniquity" ("Nature and Grace," 22. 24).

200. Hooker, *Of the Laws of Ecclesiastical Polity*, Works, 4:160. See also, "the will / and high permission of all-ruling Heaven / Left him at large to his own dark designs, / That with reiterated crimes he might / Heap on himself damnation" (Milton, *Paradise Lost*, bk. 1, ll. 211–15, Works, 2. 1. 16).

201. "What if the malice of the greatest part do come so near diabolical iniquity,

and because it is not the Lord's intent to annihilate him, the sinner remains subject to the almighty agency of God. To the extent that it is physically and ontologically subject to God, hardening formally remains the work of man. Luther wrote: "Although God did not make sin, yet, He ceases not to form and multiply that nature, which . . . is defiled by sin." His action is compared to that of a good carpenter who "would cut badly with a saw-edged or broken-edged axe." Hence it is, that the wicked man cannot but always err and sin; because, being carried along by the motion of the Divine Omnipotence, he is not permitted to remain motionless, but must will, desire, and act according to his nature. Because his nature has become wicked, "he must continue of necessity to sin."[202] Hardening is frequently portrayed as abandonment to Satan. Indeed, the hardened person no longer really needs the assistance of the devil: "our corrupted hearts are the factories of the devil, which may be at work without his presence; for when that circumventing spirit hath drawn malice, envy, and all unrighteousness unto well rooted habits in his disciples, iniquity then goes on upon its own legs; and if the gate of hell were shut up for a time, vice would still be fertile and produce the fruits of hell."[203] This insistence on the natural aspect of self-propagating sin is especially strong among Arminians, many of whom were actually Anglicans (9, 431–32), and even orthodox Calvinism, which loudly proclaims God's sovereign role, devotes a good portion of its time to portraying hardening not as "a kind of anti-grace"[204] but as a "merited punishment."[205]

that it overmatcheth the highest measure of divine grace, which the laws of the providence of God have assigned unto men on earth?" (Hooker, *Of the Laws of Ecclesiastical Polity*, *Works*, 4:159–60).

202. Luther, *De Servo Arbitrio*, *Werke*, 18:708–10.
203. Browne, *Christian Morals*, *Works*, 1:109.
204. Leibniz, *Theodicy*, 1. 99.
205. Wollebius, "Deus eos solum indurat, qui se ipsos indurant [God only hardens those who harden themselves]" (Heppe, *Dogmatik*, 222); "As for those wicked and ungodly men, whom God . . . for former sins, doth blinde and harden, from them he not onely withholdeth his grace, but sometimes . . . gives them over to their own lusts . . . whereby it comes to pass that they harden themselves" (Walker, *Creeds and Platforms*, 373). This naturalization of hardening reached its climax with Milton, who found truths of natural reason in it that were known and professed by the great writers of classical antiquity. The ancients knew that the punishment was greatest when "God Himself throws a man furthest from him," which he did "when he blinden'd, harden'd, and stirr'd up his offenders to finish, and pile up their disperate work since they had undertak'n it." The most appropriate punishment for this crime isn't relegation to a "local Hell," but to "punish sine with sinne." Milton paraphrased Cicero, "God cannot punish a man more . . . than still making him more sinful" (*The Doctrine and Discipline of Divorce*, *Works*, 3. 2. 441–42). Elsewhere, Milton concluded his discussion with a line from Homer, "they perish'd self-destroy'd [/] By their own fault." (*Odyssey*, 1. 9–10 in *On Christian Doctrine*, 1. 4).

We might disenchantedly observe that the reaffirmation of this paradox is a rather meager outcome for thirteen centuries of ecclesial reflection and, especially with the double causality (divine and human) of moral evil in hardening presented in such a clear, bare and concentrated manner, there were expectations that it might lead to conclusions that would go beyond the theses on reprobation. Indeed, as already noted, it is precisely the purity and bareness of the configuration of these two wills that condemn this reflection to such a limited outcome. Whenever reason becomes ensnared in a rich crop of imagery—as happens in the case of hell—or is applied to a situation where the representation hardens into a concept—as happens in reprobation—dogmaticians find themselves almost obliged to carve a path through these images. On the other hand, they are spared this effort if the concept's external representation leaves its inner core visible and if the initial paradox can be clarified and reaffirmed without resorting to excessive rambling. This fact may explain why so few passages in Edwards's body of work deal explicitly with hardening.

While hardening is essentially understood in terms of the doctrine on the self-determining evil will and is even its true paradigm, Jonathan Edwards did not feel obliged to explain it in detail or provide elaborate definitions.[206] He undoubtedly did not think that God's abandonment of men to the blindness of their minds was only a phenomenon of a bygone past. He knew for a fact that the divine judgment continued to strike a large number of his contemporaries. He was conscious of the misery of those "reserved, and sealed over to the blackness of darkness for ever" (II, 418).[207] However, in the *Enquiry*, where he defined and illustrated the will's process of self-determination to evil in profuse detail, Jonathan Edwards considered it "needless to stand particularly to inquire what God's *giving men up to their own hearts' lusts* signifies" (1, 296). In a Miscellany from his youth and in keeping with tradition, Edwards recalled that "God willed that Pharaoh's heart should be hardened, and yet that the hardness of his heart was his sin" (13, 204), although he later stressed the fact that God's hardening of the heart is not to be understood as a positive intervention or act. God hardens men in two ways. On the one hand, "by withholding the influences of his Spirit, without which their hearts will . . . grow harder and harder" and, on the other hand, "by ordering those things in his Providence which, through the abuse of their corruption, become the occasion of their hardening" (X, 201–2). This negative view of hardening is better understood in

---

206. See Gerstner, *Steps to Salvation*, 46–47.

207. For the torments of those who, during the Great Awakening, believed that they were abandoned to "judicial hardness," see 4, 161.

its epistemological context. In his *Treatise Concerning Religious Affections,* Edwards states: "God's leaving men to the power of the sin and corruption of the heart is often expressed by God's hardening their hearts." And a little further down, he defines a hard heart as an "unaffected heart." Scripture understands a hard heart to mean "a heart destitute of pious affections," and Edwards added that "divines are generally agreed, that sin radically and fundamentally consists in what is negative, or privative" (2, 117–8). Indeed, the negativity and privation in this great treatise on "experimental religion" is not mere Procline tradition but has its own meaning and positive content. Rather than speak of a heart dominated by evil affections, Edwards prefers the term "unaffected heart." An unaffected heart is—in its natural, fallen state—the heart of a fallen creature whose corrupt will continually confirms the creature's immanent self-determination towards evil at every moment.

10. Preaching on hell

In America's cultural memory, Jonathan Edwards is remembered as a hellfire preacher.[208] He is known as the ideologist of the Great Awakening. And wasn't the Great Awakening a moment in American history when the exaltation of the masses was expressed in morbid demonstrations of collective hysteria? Edwards is severely criticized for provoking terror in his hearers and for pushing unbalanced and confused multitudes into irrational piety.[209] In fact, Jonathan Edwards didn't usher in this form of preaching, nor did he practice it in an exaggerated way. In his mouth, such preaching was simply a well-controlled instrument of his overall pastoral ministry and highly articulate dogmatic.[210] Hellfire preaching is a very ancient evangelization technique. It began with Jesus Christ[211] and its great practitioners never give themselves lightheartedly to it. Even though many preachers treated the subject of hell with a kind of morbid delight, and even if it was thought that God's own power and honor virtually implied its existence,[212] Christian homiletics never professed it with indifference or complacency.

---

208. See *supra*, p. xx.

209. The great American historian, Brooks Adams, has only one sentence on Edwards: "Jonathan Edwards frightened people into convulsions by his preaching." *Emancipation of Massachusetts,* 259.

210. In fact, contrary to Puritan tradition, Edwards didn't write about hell in his major theoretical works and only addresses it in his sermons.

211. "Of all preachers that we read of in Scripture, none was so frequent in warning the people to avoid Hell, as Jesus Christ" (Loring, *Miseries of Hell,* 1, in Fiering, *Moral Thought and British Context,* 206n.15).

212. See Hopkins, *The True State and Character of the Unregenerate, Works,* 2:481.

Augustine had already written to Evodius: "For, if we say that all of those who were found there [i.e., in hell] were set free [by Jesus Christ] without exception, it would be a cause of gratification—if we could prove it."[213] Much closer to Edwards, Increase Mather appears to testify to the difficult situation in which the Puritan pastor found himself: "*Knowing the Terror of the Lord*, I seek to perswade you by those Arguments; nevertheless I take no pleasure to tell you thereof."[214] The problem, as S. Stoddard noted with hard irony, is that "There is a great deal of Light in Hell-Fire,"[215] and what is the Christian preacher's vocation, if not to illuminate the minds and hearts of his hearers?[216]

In comparison to the texts of some of his predecessors and contemporaries, Edwards's sermons are more striking for their moderation.[217] He warned against those who constantly have the devil and hell on their lips (4, 419), especially because he knew that those most ready to preach damnation thought it was only the lot of others (2, 311)![218] Nonetheless, Edwards underlined that such preaching was both legitimate and necessary. If there is a hell of infinitely horrible torments to which—for want of a clear sense of its terrors—a majority of the inhabitants in Christian countries go, (4, 246–7)[219] then why shouldn't those called to be concerned about and to

---

213. Saint Augustine, *Letters*, 3:383 [letter 164].

214. Mather added, "But now that I am speaking to you of the pardoning grace of God, me-thinks I am in my element" (Niebuhr, *Kingdom of God in America*, 95).

215. Stoddard, *Fear of Hell*, 7. "Men need to be terrified . . . that they might be converted," (*Defects of Preachers Reproved*, in Trefz, "Satan in Puritan Preaching," 72).

216. The preachers of the Great Awakening opposed those pastors who "strengthen Men's carnal security" and "have not the Courage, or Honesty, to thrust the Nail of Terror into sleeping Souls" (G. Tennent, *The Danger of an Unconverted Ministry*, in Heimert and Miller, *Great Awakening*, 78).

217. For example, see T. M. Davis and V. L. Davis, "Taylor on Day of Judgment," 541–47. Three weeks prior to the sermon in Enfield, Charles Chauncy himself had preached in terms that were very similar to Edwards: "There is nothing betwixt you and the place of blackness of darkness, but a poor frail uncertain life. You hang, as it were, over the bottomless pit, by the slender thread of life, and the moment that snaps asunder, you sink down into perdition" (Gaustad, *Great Awakening in New England*, 86).

218. As Simone Weil said, "L'acceptation de l'enfer par respect pour la volonté de Dieu est bonne quand une âme se sent au bord de la damnation; mauvaise quand elle se sent à portée du salut, car alors on accepte l'enfer pour les autres [The acceptance of hell out of respect for the will of God is good when the soul feels itself on the brink of damnation, evil when it feels itself on the brink of salvation, for then one accepts hell for others]" (*Cahiers*, 153).

219. Ever since Augustine, the tradition in which Edwards stands has taught that the number of the damned far exceeds that of the saved, ("Admonition and Grace," 10. 28). "Il n'y a pas vingt personnes sur mille qui iraient au ciel [There aren't twenty people in a thousand who will go to heaven]" (Malebranche, *Recueil de toutes les*

care for souls not do everything in their power to alert them to this punishment? "If I am in danger of going to Hell," wrote Edwards, "I should be glad to know as much as possibly I can of the dreadfulness of it." Some say it is unreasonable "to frighten people into Heaven. But I think it is reasonable to try to frighten people away from Hell" (4, 246–47).[220] Pastors are accused of sowing terror in their hearers, but man's natural condition can only be portrayed in frightening terms. Of course, it is not enough to inspire terror; the good news also needs to be preached to men likely to repent, although they will only find their consolation and salvation in Christ after they abandon their present natural condition (4, 391). In hell, the damned would do anything to be delivered from their torments, although by then it will be too late. If a preacher believes he needs to continually return to the subject of damnation, it's because sinners can only profit from offers of mercy and turn in repentance during their earthly life here below (VII, 479).[221]

Among numerous great sermons by Edwards, none is more famous than *Sinners in the Hands of an Angry God*. In fact, it's his most renowned work and Edwards is cited more often as the author of "the archetypal revival

---

réponses à Monsieur Arnauld, Œuvres, 7. 534); Calvin stated that of a hundred people, only twenty will hear a sermon with "the prompt obedience of faith" (Calvin, *Institutes*, 3. 24. 12). Edwards mentioned Shepard's *The Sincere Convert, Works*, 1:55 in his reflections on the number of the saved (18, 63–65). He quoted Virgil—"A few abide in happy lands" (20, 456)—and Solomon—who found only "one man among a thousand" (3, 161–62)—and concluded that, "yet there are but few who do not go to Hell" (V, 449; 3, 203; etc.). However, with the advent of the millennium, the situation will change: the number of the regenerate will be so vast that, in the end, the percentage of the damned will be of little importance (5, 442). Targeted by growing attacks against the doctrine of hell, many of the Edwardsians took a more "optimistic" view. Hopkins thought that the number of the elect would be a thousand times greater than the number of the damned (Foster, *History of New England Theology*, 198), and a century later, the last of the Edwardsians, E. A. Park, stated: "Hell in the universe will occupy no greater place in comparison than the state's prison in the commonwealth" (Foster, *History of New England Theology*, 535). We should also recall Bellamy's fanciful calculations, where he multiplied the number of elect angels (two times greater than the fallen angels) by their proportionable degree of happiness and holiness since the fall (100 times greater) and, accounting for the misery of the fallen angels (100 times greater), succeeded in posting a clear gain of 9,600,000,000 degrees of happiness (*The Wisdom of God in the Permission of Sin, Works*, 2:67n.). Bellamy remarked that, if the same calculation was applied to men, it would result in an even greater degree of happiness (*The Wisdom of God in the Permission of Sin, Works*, 2:97n).

220. "The more we bring sinners into the light, while they are miserable, and the light is terrible to them, the more likely it is that by and by the light will be joyful to them" (4, 390).

221. Indeed, it would be better for a man "given up to sin" to spend his time in hell than on earth where he would only continue to prepare and aggravate his damnation (19, 119).

sermon"²²² than of his great *Enquiry*. Perhaps the finest piece of his immense homiletic work, and notwithstanding the absence of elaborate rhetoric or extravagant imagery, this sermon has wielded extraordinary influence.²²³

The homily's epigraph is "Their feet shall slide in due time," a line taken from Deuteronomy 32:35 that threatens the vengeance of God on the impious Israelites, who were nonetheless living under a visible dispensation of Yahweh. The essence the sermon is that every unconverted man is continually at risk of sudden, unexpected destruction. Because of their depraved nature, men are ready for the pit at any moment—to be left to fall into hell, as they are inclined of their own weight—and they are only preserved by the good, sovereign pleasure of an angry God.²²⁴ "The wrath of God burns against them, their condemnation does not slumber; the pit is prepared, the fire is made ready, the furnace is now hot, ready to receive them; the flames do now rage and glow. The glittering sword is whet, and held over them . . . The old serpent is gaping for them . . . and the flames . . . would fain laid hold on them, and swallow them up." Unconverted men "walk over the pit . . . on a rotten covering" (22, 406–7)²²⁵ The hand of God holds them like a spider over the fire but the moment will come when it will let the insect fall into the flames.²²⁶ This abandonment has been prepared long beforehand by God "because the wrath of God is like great waters that are dammed for the present; they increase more and more, and rise higher and higher, til an outlet is given. . . . The bow of God's wrath is bent, and the arrow made ready on the string, and justice bends the arrow at your heart, and strains the bow, and it is nothing but the mere pleasure of God, and that of an angry God . . . that keeps the arrow one moment from being made drunk with your blood" (22, 410–11). However, it is not only the wrath of God that is unleashed against the sinner: the entire creation, which he abuses

---

222. Slotkin, *Regeneration through Violence*, 103.

223. Already published eight times in America prior to 1800 (Fiering, *Edwards's Moral Thought*, 201n.3), this text was characterized in 1922 as only being inferior to the Sermon on the Mount (Lesser, *Jonathan Edwards*, 141).

224. The essence of this 1741 theme was already present in the first known sermon by Edwards (10, 288).

225. For the origin of this imagery, see Erdt, *Sense of the Heart*, 69.

226. This is the text that "inspired" J. L. Borges, "Jonathan Edwards (1703–1758)"

Piensa feliz que el mundo es un eterno	Happily he thinks the world is an eternal
Instrumento de ira y que et ansiado	instrument of ire and the long-awaited
Cielo paraunos pocos fue creado	Heaven was created for a few good men
Y casi para todos et infierno.	and Hell for almost everybody else.
En et centro puntual de la marana	In the central point of this tangled web
Hay otro prisioniero, Dios, la Arana.	lies the spider: God, another prisoner.
(*Obra Poetica*, 223.)	(*Poetic Works*, 223.)

and diverts from its purposes, revolts against him. In fact, there is nothing but air without resistance or consistency—thin air—between the sinner and hell. In any event, outside and independently of God's wrath and creation's revolt, the sinner is headed for disaster by virtue of his own corruption. It is "your wickedness makes you as it were heavy as lead, and to tend downwards with great weight and pressure towards hell; and if God should let you go, you would immediately sink and swiftly descend and plunge into the bottomless gulf" (22, 410). Of course, natural men have always believed they can trust in their own efforts to escape destruction, but they delude themselves (22, 410) and it would be a wonder, if there are some that are now present should not be in hell in a very short time, even before the year is out (22, 416). There you will be crushed by a merciless force. You will undergo torments that you will not be able to bear, and yet you will continue to be subjected to them indefinitely (22, 413–14). You now find yourself at an exceptional moment in time. God is assembling his elect—it's the Great Awakening—and is giving you an unexpected opportunity to join with him, but those of you who harden your heart to his call will find yourselves in a grievous situation (22, 417–18). This is the sermon, the fruit of Edwards's "monstrous error" to profess eternal damnation;[227] the sermon which, on the bicentenary of his birth, the theologians of his own denomination "neither wanted to hear nor recall";[228] the classic example of that preaching for which New England has never forgiven Jonathan Edwards![229]

---

227. Channing, "Edwards and the Revivalists," 379.

228. Kingman, *Jonathan Edwards*, 20. This sermon, said a participant at the Edwards family reunion in Stockbridge, goes still farther beyond "what an age like ours, of tender benevolence, with no strong-backed sense of justice, could endure" (T. Woolsey, "Commemorative Discourse," in Woodbridge, *Memorial Volume*, 77).

229. Parrington, *Currents in American Thought*, 1:159. For the reactions of the Enfield congregation, see Tracy, *Great Awakening*, 216. Although this sermon has become the most famous of the Edwardsian texts, Edwards himself—moreover very discouraged by the poor results of his preaching (Gerstner, *Edwards on Heaven and Hell*, 51–52 and n.2)—considered *The Justice of God in the Damnation of Sinners* (19, 339–76) to be by "far the most powerful and effectual of his discourses" (*Dw.*, I, 142). It was this sermon, whose importance was recognized by P. Miller (*Jonathan Edwards*, 3ff.) that scandalized the author of an old review: "doctrines of this complexion totally destroy all general distinctions and had this sermon been preached in the chapel of a prison filled with the most abondoned miscreants that were ever sentenced to the gallows by a court of justice, the preacher could not have stigmatized and vilified them more than he has, as we would charitably hope, a congregation of well-disposed Christians" ("Monthly Catalogue," 245).

11. Infinite punishment

At a certain point, the critics ceased to engage in violent diatribe and a more attentive, less passionate and less prejudicial reading of the text showed that, in actual fact, Edwards didn't preach hellfire but rather the mercy of God that keeps us from falling into the flames.[230] Even though the sermon clearly emphasizes "the mere pleasure of God, and that of an angry God, without any promise or obligation at all" (22, 409), the core of its argument is that hellfire is nothing other than our own evil and that God's will is to be understood in terms of unfathomable mercy. Augustine was undoubtedly able to declare, in a peremptory manner, that God is good and just and therefore can deliver a man without merit but cannot damn a man without demerit.[231] However, the sentiment of orthodox Protestantism was expressed in this statement by Luther: "Hic est fidei summus gradus, credere illum esse clementem, qui tam paucos saluat, tam multos damnat, credere iustum, qui sua voluntate nos necessario damnabilis fecit [This is the highest degree of faith—to believe that he is merciful, who saves so few and damns so many; to believe him just, who according to his own will, makes us necessarily damnable]."[232] In New England, S. Willard quoted the *Epistle to the Hebrews*: "Vengeance is mine,"[233] which, in our context, signifies that "the principal efficient cause" of hellss torments is "God Himself."[234] And do we not read this from the pen of the "gentle Mr. Shepard": "I tell thee, Christ is so far from saving thee, that He is thine enemy"?[235] Puritan preachers—and not only they—always took pleasure in celebrating God's vindictive glory, and the Edwardsians didn't fail to add to the celebration. "The punishment is inflicted," said Emmons, loudly and clearly," because God does not pursue the good of the creature but His own good."[236] Nevertheless, "the whole dark side of things"—and now we hear Bellamy—"is full of light, glory, and

---

230. Cady, "Artistry of Edwards," 69. In 1903, it was noted: "The brittle thread is mentioned once, but three times the hearer is told that God's hand prevents the fall into perdition" (Anderson, "Preaching Power of Edwards," 464).

231. Saint Augustine, *Against Julian*, 3. 18. 35. "Being just, He will indeed render evil for evil; being good, He will render good for evil; being both good and just, He will render good for good. This only He will not do, namely, render evil for good, seeing that He is not unjust." ("Grace and Free Will," 23. 45).

232. Luther, *De Servo Arbitrio*, Werke, 18. 633.

233. Heb. 10:30 in Willard, *Divinity*, 202.

234. Willard, *Divinity*, 241.

235. Shepard, *The Sincere Convert*, Works, 1:45.

236. Emmons, *The Deceitfulness of the Human Heart*, Works, 5:553, 576; see also Bellamy, *The Great Evil of Sin, as Committed Against God: A Sermon*, Works, 3:517 n.z.

beauty,"[237] and nothing propagates God's glory as much or is as agreeable as God's victory in damnation.[238] As for Edwards himself, he hardly falls into such pathetic excesses. In Enfield, he spoke of "the floods of God's vengeance" (22, 411) but, as we shall see, he understood it in terms of the great biblical asymmetry: "You are destroyed, O Israel, because you are against me, against your helper" (Hos 13:9). In another sermon, he spoke of God's presence with the damned. God knows the sufferings of the damned. He is present with them because "He is where every devil is." Moreover, he makes his wrath enter into them; he is a consuming fire to them. But how can this presence and efficacy of God be defined? God is present in hell according to his knowledge and his essence (VII, 421). In other words, in the millennial tradition of Christian teaching, Edwards, while announcing divine causality in damnation, refuses to portray it in terms of an immediate link between God and hell or, if he does allow for a direct link, it is on an ontological level and not with reference to a merciful and free God.

Edwards, a speculative theologian, wanted to explain the justice of eternal damnation. He liked to address it in the context of the Last Judgment because judgment clarifies and brings an immanent situation to view. Judgment means that God presents wicked reprobates with their sins and their justice to his elect saints "so that they know the reason of the sentence given, and their consciences are made to testify to the justice of it" (IV, 447). The Last Judgment therefore doesn't appear as the sovereign and exclusive fact of God's will but instead as something that makes an immanent fact explicit. Edwards was attracted to this presentation of the doctrine of damnation because the notion of justice translates metaphysical relationships particularly well in anthropological and moral terms. And yet Edwards, who preached that God is free and sovereign and also "wholly arbitrary" in both election and reprobation (*Bl.* 216), could only adopt this overly immanentist conception by formulating it in terms of the doctrine on the self-determinating will's radical evil. This enabled him to confine immanence to God and consider it under the aspect of his vindictive justice while safeguarding God's transcendence with respect to his mercy. Within this ontological and immanentist interpretation, Edwards was faced with two possible options. He could choose the option of homogeneous immanentism by—at least temporarily—setting aside God's moral attributes and teaching like Leibniz that "sins must carry their penalty with them by the order of nature, and even

---

237. Bellamy, *An Essay on the Nature and Glory of the Gospel of Jesus Christ, Works,* 2:418.

238. West, *Essay on Moral Agency,* 215, 193.

in virtue of the mechanical structure of things."[239] Alternatively, he could choose the more difficult, more promising and more dangerous option that was not content to portray God's justice as the homogeneous explanation for the consequences of sin, but rather as a result of the mutual relationships between God's mercy and His wrath. Edwards barely touched upon this second option, even though it was implied and perhaps even required by his various pronouncements on the essential solidarity between understanding the odiousness of sin and discerning the holy glory of God.

Speaking of unconverted sinners, Edwards said: "If they will not be willing subjects to the golden sceptre, and will not yield to the attractives of His love, they shall be subject to the force of the iron rod, whether they will or no" (VII, 452). The preacher portrays the action of these two divine attributes as sequential, but the relationship is essentially simultaneous or, more precisely, outside of time because justice and mercy express the same love and their action is but a function of the response to this love. The Edwardsians's obsessive insistence on damnation stemming from the very love of God and on the fact that cursing the sinner is simply loving God[240] expresses a basic intuition of the religious conscience in a troubling manner. If God is love, then all of his actions, including damnation, must flow from love. "God," wrote N. Emmons, "always did and always will love Judas with the love of benevolence; but never did, and never will love him with the love of complacence!"[241] God loves the saints with gentleness, but his anger

---

239. Leibniz, "Monadology," 89.

240. Bellamy, *An Essay on the Nature and Glory of the Gospel of Jesus Christ*, Works, 2:416.

241. Emmons, *The Plea of Sinners against Endless Punishment*, Works, 5:595.

burns where he "meets with" sinners.[242] "The Holiness of God is a glass in which all ungodly Men may read their doom."[243]

Edwards himself didn't really make use of this dialectic of wrath and love[244] and preferred to keep the representation of justice and mercy in terms of a time difference. Clothed with gentleness and compassion, Christ calls the saints to himself but, in accordance with his terrible attributes, repels the wicked, or rather, the latter recoil by themselves. "The reprobate world . . . sinks of itself, flees away and breaks in pieces as it were, by beholding the manifestation of His awful majesty and wrath, and the shining forth of the infinitely pure and powerful holiness and justice and wrath does as it were of itself set all on fire" (20, 23). The desperate flight of the iniquitous from the resplendent glory of God's wrath is but a vivid impression of that immanent movement where the sinner's wickedness unfolds. Hardly the outcome of an arbitrary decision of God's will, it is as if the punishment is required by order of nature. Referring to a famous verse in the *Epistle to the Romans*, Edwards commented that "creation groans" because of the sinner (VI, 541).[245] He tells the sinner that "the sun does not willingly shine upon you to give you light to serve sin and Satan; the earth does not willingly yield her increase to satisfy your lusts; nor is it willingly a stage for your wickedness to be acted upon; the air does not willingly serve you for breath

---

242. P. Sterry, "If He (i.e. God) meet with any pure and sweet Spirit, like Himself; He closeth with it, in all manner of gentleness, and softness, as *Two Flames* embrace one another. But where He meets with opposition He rageth. He burns upon dark, unclear, untractable Hearts, as *Fire* in the Ironworks; till He hath poured them Forth into the Temper, and Mold of His Spirit, and Image" (in Walker, *Decline of Hell*, 113–4). Stated more succinctly, "Such as men themselves are, such will God Himself seem to be" (Smith, *Select Discourses*, 8). This entire matter is aptly summarized by the traditional exegesis of Ps 18:27: he is good to the good, but evil to the wicked. Malebranche, *Traité de l'amour de Dieu, Œuvres*, 14:24. "l'amour agit de deux manières différentes. Il tourmente les pécheurs . . . et il réjouit les bons [love acts in two different ways. It torments sinners . . . and delights the good]" (Saint Isaac the Syrian, *Discours ascétiques*, 415). "Sa justice contre les méchants et son amour pour les bons ne sont que la même chose: c'est la même bonté qui s'unit avec tout ce qui est bon, et qui est incompatible avec tout ce qui est mauvais [his justice against the wicked and his love towards the righteous are the same thing; it is the same quality that unites him to everything that is good, and is incompatible with everything that is evil]" (Fénelon, *Lettres et opuscules spirituelles*, 696). Or again, "even the most dissolute and false life still remains and moves within God . . . But it [this life] perceives him as consuming fury" (Schelling, *Investigations into Human Freedom*, 66). For this theme from speculative theology in a Lutheran tradition, see Veto, *Le fondement selon Schelling*, 463–65.

243. Willard, *Divinity*, 74.

244. However, see 22, 484–85. Edwards constantly built upon the major theme of how God is present in hell by his wrath (8, 390; 22, 486, etc.).

245. For the consequences of the fall on nature, see *supra*, p.70 n.41.

to maintain the flame of life in your vitals, while you spend your life in the service of God's enemies. You are a burden to nature and it would immediately reject you were it not for the restraining hand of God" (22, 410). The bowels of the earth no longer want to hold the exposed sinner and he has no hope of being able to slip away on Judgment Day (VII, 454-5). In a manner of speaking, the evil of the transgression spills into the evil of punishment and the requirements of God's vindictive justice are written into the very nature of things.[246] The punishment should be proportionable to the demerit (VII, 469), even if it can never be absolutely adequate.[247] There should be agreement and an "exact mutual answerableness" between the transgression and the sanction (19, 337). That is why the Gospel requires of the sinner that "his sins must be fully balanced and recompensed, and satisfaction obtained" (VII, 453). It is by virtue of this strict proportionality that the punishment of the damned should be eternal.

The most important objection against the biblical and ecclesial teaching on eternal punishment concerns its infinite duration and, since Augustine, the hypothesis of a "medicinal" role in serving sentences periodically reappears in Christian theology.[248] Edwards himself never appeared to waver in his conviction on the eternal nature of hell's sentences,[249] and he used all the extraordinary ingenuity of his dialetic to make this doctrine plausible and to show its validity and coherence (23, 391-2). All of the arguments and proofs for the infinite nature of such punishment are based on the conviction that the punishment must be infinite because the offense is also infinite. This is axiomatic for Edwards and he ascribes any questioning or denial of it to the corruption of the human mind and heart.

In a 1739 sermon, we read that men object to the doctrine of eternal punishment for two reasons. On the one hand, it is contrary to their depraved inclination and, on the other hand, they don't see the correspondence and proportionality between the punishment and the demerit (VII, 469). Ecclesial teaching is said to be against the requirements of good sense, but if this is so, it is simply because we are blind to the enormous evil of sin. Because our horror of transgression has been dulled, we cannot accept that punishment is infinite. We think that an eternal sentence is contrary to good sense,

---

246. The sinful being's end is realized only by his ruin (VI, 544).

247. See Colwell, "Glory of God's Justice and Grace," 301.

248. For a "liberal" critique of the doctrine of eternal damnation by contemporaries of Edwards, see Jones, *Shattered Synthesis*, 150, 170; Haroutunian, *Piety Versus Moralism* 135-7, etc.

249. In the strict, metaphysical sense of that term, the punishment of the damned is only infinite in God's idea (13, 226), yet this in no way changes the fact that the punishment never ceases.

but this amounts to equating a state of mind based on a corrupt disposition with good sense itself (MO 395). If pity for the creature punished moves us to formulate objections against the author of his being, it's because of "a want of a sense of the horrible evil of sin" (20, 107).[250] Man's corrupt mind doesn't want to be reconciled with the "never-expiring infelicity" of the sinful creature,[251] whereas a mind illuminated by the Bible will understand that "the least sin deserves total and eternal destruction" (X, 299). We have already seen that the *nervus probandi*—the crux—of Edwards's argument is very simple and he constantly returns to it: an offense against an infinite being is infinitely heinous and, as such, has infinite demerit (19, 162).[252] In 1723, this position was also enunciated in Miscellany nn that Edwards the student was going to incorporate into his Master's thesis—written in Latin (14, 57–58)—a position that he would never change, even as he developed it further. In a previously mentioned sermon on Rom. 2:8–9, Edwards hammered home these parallels: "This punishment, as dreadful as it is, is not more so than the Being is great and glorious against whom you have sinned. . . . The wrath of God that you have heard of, dreadful as it is, is not more dreadful than that Majesty which you have despised and trampled on is awful . . . for men do not hate misery more than God hates sin. As great as this wrath is, it is not greater than that love of God which you have slighted and rejected" (X, 306–7). If the obligation to love, honor and obey God is infinite, a violation of that obligation must likewise entail infinite consequences (VII, 467).[253]

---

250. Man's "devilish disposition" prevents him from seeing the "horridness" of sin (18, 71).

251. Willard, *Divinity*, 233.

252. However, the infinitely hateful character of every sin does not abolish the distinction between sins. Of course, all sins have the same aggravation with respect to the dignity of their object, yet some sins may be more heinous than others in other respects: "as if we should suppose a cylinder infinitely long, it can't be greater in that respect, viz. with respect to the length of it; but yet it may be doubled, and trebled, and made a thousand-fold more, by the increase of other dimensions" (19, 163). Although all sins are equally infinite in terms of God's "aversion" to them, they may differ in terms of their particular "conversion" to the creature. The diversity of infinite punishments is based on this distinction (19, 163–64).

253. See also 22, 484. The sinner's guilt is qualified in terms of the infinite object of the obligation violated (2, 326). On the other hand, the righteousness of the saints is not judged in terms of its infinite object (i.e., God) but in terms of its finite subject (i.e., man). See 19, 162; 20, 554, and the subtle developments of Jonathan Edwards the Younger, "Liberty and Necessity," in Edwards, *Works*, 1:459–61.

12. Hellfire and the wrath of God

Over and above all quantitative or temporal considerations, the infinity of the infernal state shows the fulfillment or perfect realization of a state of separation from God.[254] Sin is like poison whose spread in the body can be momentarily stopped, but when the agent preventing it from spreading is withdrawn, the poison resumes its work. "Natural men," wrote Edwards, "have as it were the seeds of Hell in their own hearts." These "will at length breed the torments of Hell in them, and that necessarily, and of their own tendency" (X, 127).[255] There is a continuity of essence between the natural man's life on earth and his condition in hell, whose realization is only delayed by the power of God. Indeed, the wicked are even now subject to the same wrath that the torments of hell will later express: their corruption is like "fire contained" by God's good pleasure which, "if it was let loose, would set all of nature on fire" (22, 407).

Latent and burning covertly in this life, this same fire burns openly as great flames in the next. This identity over time presages a deeper affinity or unity between God's fire and man's fire. Edwards said that the wicked would be tortured in hell by the fire of God's curse and the fire of their own wickedness (V, 314), but don't these two fires have a hidden unity? The damned are incandescent, completely possessed by fire. They are like worms or spiders which, when thrown into the fire, "have retained their shape after [being] burned to a coal, and looked white with the fierceness of the heat" (13, 550). When a spider falls into the fire, "the fire takes possession of it, and at once it becomes full of fire." It *is* the fire (VII, 464).[256] The exterior fire is then the interior fire and the wrath of God is no longer just "the bellows of Hell"[257] but is now plainly identified with the fire of punishment.[258] Moreover, because the rupture between the creature's sense and spirit is healed in this infernal state—at least after the Last Judgment—the metaphysico-logical

---

254. Given the metaphysical logic of the radical opposition of good and evil—which does not allow for any intermediate moment or step—there cannot be any "middle place" between "the house of God in Heaven" and "the habitation of devils" (19, 744), a "middle state" between two eternal conditions (*Bl.*, 43). Hell is "a state of perfect separation from God and eternal removal from all His goodness" (*Bl.*, 40).

255. "sin has Hell in it" (19, 269).

256. It's the "negative transfiguration" of the infernal condition, Scheeben, *Die Mysterien des Christentums*, 587–89; see the "dark transfiguration" of the soul whose evil will was thwarted, Hawthorne, *The Scarlet Letter, Works*, 1:194.

257. Winslow, *Meetinghouse Hill*, 113.

258. In hell, "tis the infinite almighty God Himself that shall become the fire of the furnace exerting His infinite perfection that way" (Sermon on Job 41:9f. in Gerstner, *Edwards on Heaven and Hell*, 56).

fire of punishment can be viewed as one with the fire of the hardened will and the combustion of the spirit's "reason to be angry [rational rage]."[259] If this is so, then the wrath of God can be paired with the creature's hardened, evil will. This hypothesis is most certainly pantheistic and injurious to God's absolute goodness and purity. Paradoxically, it seems to be the last hidden metaphysical resort of the doctrine of absolute sovereignty, especially in the extreme form of it professed by the Edwardsians. Their insistence on God's absolute sovereignty and unlimited omnicausality deprives the creature of all autonomy and reduces it to nothing, so that to be master of everything, God ceases to be master and lord. In other words, the reluctance of the religious conscience to extend divine sovereignty to the causality of evil has a metaphysical function. It alone can safeguard divine transcendence, because it alone can designate and delineate those spheres that should never be included in God's world or fused into the divine. The autarky of evil remains a *sine qua non*—an indispensible condition—of God's transcendence and sovereignty: to be sovereign requires limitations.

Interpreted in ontological terms, Edwardsian immanentism takes a pantheistic direction because, in the last analysis, the ontology virtually abolishes the difference between good and evil. As a theologian and metaphysician, Edwards knew for a fact that nothing justifies erasing this difference and that the only reasonable outcome of immanentism is to resolutely reaffirm double causality, to "confess a hundred times" with Calvin that "God is the author" of the "destruction" of the damned, but that "they are drawn spontaneously by their own nature" to it.[260] The essence of the Edwardsian doctrine of damnation accordingly consists of an immanentist description of the evil will and, while the great sermon of Enfield puts more stress on the state before hell than on hell itself, from a conceptual point of view there is hardly any difference between the suppressed fire in this life and the blazing fire in the next. The condition of the evil will is also magnificently portrayed. The evil will falls by itself and inevitably so. "As he that stands or walks on slippery ground, needs nothing but his own weight to throw him down" (22, 404). The sinner who hangs "over the pit of eternal misery ... must necessarily drop into it" if left to his own strength (VI, 490), because—left to itself—even the angelic nature would not fail to sink into evil (13, 487). Just as a lead weight tends downwards, so the sinner tends towards evil and, if let go, "would immediately sink and swiftly descend and plunge into the bottomless gulf" (22, 410). While the sinner lives on Earth, God slows down and hampers the effective, external fulfillment of this fall,

---

259. Leibniz, *Confessio Philosophi*, 93.
260. Calvin, *Institutes*, 3. 23. 3.

but his wicked will continues to sink inward and plunge itself "deeper and deeper in debt" (VII, 450). This fall, this inward sinkage of the will, takes free rein in the next world where, even if no new transgressions are added, "of its nature an irreparable sin should endure forever, and therefore an everlasting punishment is its due."[261] Orthodox Calvinism thinks that the damned sinner in hell is odious to God and "even now"[262] continues to sin, and Edwards would agree with Leibniz "that no one is damned unless he wills it but also that no one remains damned unless he continues to damn himself. The damned are never damned absolutely; they are always worthy of damnation."[263] Instead of humbling them and causing them to repent, their punishment will "stir up their hatred to God" (13, 353) so that, "by constantly renewed acts of hatred and bitterness," they become the cause of their own torment and continue procuring that same sinful disposition for themselves that they had at the moment of their death (13, 366).[264]

The condemned sinner—Edwards explained—persists in his sin. He exercises his hardened, evil will and even aggravates his guilt. The logical modalities of this aggravating persistence in ill will are subtly analyzed in the Miscellanies (23, 391-2), but the essence of Edwards's reflection on the infernal state is summarized in a sermon which, like that of Enfield, was preached during that notable year of 1741. In hell—Edwards taught—"there will be that sinking of heart, of which we now cannot conceive." We often see how the body jolts in torment and how it resists, but when the body experiences pains so extreme that it cannot bear them, it sinks down and dies. The soul will also sink in hell, yet remain capable of perception. Exposed to vastly disproportionate pain, the soul will only be capable of continuing to sink endlessly, without struggle or hope. "This is dying in the highest sense of the word. This is to die sensibly, to die and know it. . . . This is to be undone. . . . This sinking of the soul under an infinite weight, which it cannot bear, is the gloom of Hell" (VII, 458-9). The creature founders and sinks. It cannot stop itself from foundering and sinking and it founders and sinks of its own accord. We might be tempted to see Edwards's vision as purely allegorical, but in spite of the fact that preaching the "dreadfulness of the punishment" should primarily serve as a means to teach the common man, (13, 283)[265] Jonathan Edwards concluded that "the similitudes

261. Saint Thomas Aquinas, *Summa Theologiæ*, 1-2. 87. 4 ad. 3; see also 2-2. 13. 4. co., ad. 3.

262. Willard, *Divinity*, 244.

263. Leibniz, *Confessio Philosophi*, 93.

264. See also 13, 353.

265. For the finalities of preaching on eternal punishments, see the admirable text that ends Book 3 of the *Institutes* (3. 25. 12).

that are used in Scripture . . . don't go beyond the truth." God does not use "uncertain metaphors"[266] or rather "that metaphor of fire will probably be no *metaphor* after the Resurrection" (14, 313); nor do preachers exaggerate when describing torments (VII, 453). Of course, no one knows precisely to what degree those who leave this world in a state of mortal sin are going to be tortured—it's not essential for man in this life to know this (18, 91)[267]—but Edwards nonetheless conjectures that the senses of the damned will be "immensely increased" so that they will experience sensations to an extreme degree (20, 168). God wants to increase the capacity of the damned to become miserable but does not give them added strength to endure their suffering. Unable to bear their torments, the damned flounder and sink without end; such is the gloomy darkness of hell!

Edwards is certainly in agreement with Coccejus: punishment by mere loss of felicity, without a sense of pain, is nothing but a fable,[268] but the essence of his reflection remains the axiom that the wrath of God "is a fire of your own kindling" (X, 305). While the image that posterity has retained from Edwardsian preaching is especially one of an angry God casting sinners into the flames of hell, Edwards himself thought that damnation is certainly a punishment from God, but the infernal state is the culmination or, rather, the perfect manifestation of the autonomous evil will, which is fulfilled in an immanent way.

266. Sermon on Job 16:24 in Kimnach, "Literary Techniques of Edwards," 331. See also "Let not the sinner imagine that these things are bedbugs," *Sermon on Job 41:9f,* in Gerstner, *Edwards on Heaven and Hell,* 57.

267. See also Amesius, *Medulla Theologica,* 72; "the torments of Hell will never be understood . . . till experienced" (Willard, *Divinity,* 240).

268. Heppe, *Dogmatics,* 711.

4

THE EVIL IN GOOD

1. Good will and justification

HELL IS THE ULTIMATE form and degree of the evil will. Damnation is the evil will sinking and plunging deeper into itself. Here, the evil will is quantitatively and qualitatively at its maximum point. The evil will reaches and achieves its greatest intensity to the extent that it is reduced to itself and, stripped of every contingent element, burns in its own devouring purity. However, even though the state of damnation is the ultimate form of the evil will, its relationship to the hardening that precedes it is one in which evil increases only by degree and not by nature. Hardened individuals have a will that is as vicious and as completely enclosed by evil as that of the damned but, because of restraining grace (and the physical and material components of earthly life), this evil will is kept encapsulated, hidden, arrested and paralyzed. In essence, however, there is no difference between the will of the hardened and the damned for the very reason that the nature of every evil will is the same. The essential indivisibility of evil wasn't adequately described until Kant's practical philosophy, although the religious vision of the Reformation was so allergic to any relativization of sin that it rejected any gradual conception of it. Venial sins, we know, are only so because God does not want to count them as mortal sins.[1] However, since each and every sin is intrinsically mortal, every evil volition is completely and implacably evil. More precisely, my evil will is totally evil, independently of its specification or degree.

1. See *supra*, p. 72.

If this is so, theologians must go beyond any "order in time" consideration of the evil will, just as they felt obliged to go beyond moral casuistry. In casuistry, a reasoned catalog of sins is constituted which clarifies and classifies sins according to the relative seriousness of the transgression involved. A type of imaginary moral space is established in which an infinite multiplicity of evil volitions of varying intensity coexist. While this process eventually culminates in a detailed description of the world of the evil will, merely establishing an inventory of moral entities necessarily limits it to an external approach. Order in time investigations of the evil will, which proceed from reprobation to hardening and from hardening to damnation, will likewise lead to what is ultimately a quantitative interpretation of evil. For example, if it was decreed in casuistry that the vice of gluttony was less serious than assassination, then we might conjecture that the will of a damned individual burns more intensely than that of a hardened one and that it will burn even more after the Final Judgment (20, 218). Rather than attempting to describe the evil will in terms of an immanent (i.e., essential) distinction, casuistry and order in time considerations of the evil will are based on the inessential determination of number and quantity.[2] The undivided radicality of the evil will does not mean that all of these volitions are equal in value. Understanding this requires an analysis of the evil will itself that is moral in nature yet subject to what, properly speaking, are theological notions. Rather than taking a qualitative, purely content-oriented approach, the analysis of the will should be conducted according to its form. This would help show that the will is ultimately not defined in terms of its hypostatized instances or a progression in time, but according to the ordination of its intention. The irreducible opposition of the evil will's material multiplicity of manifestations and the homogeneous unity of its essence can only be surmounted by a formal vision in which the will is differentiated by its indivisible essence. This means undertaking an analysis of the order of intention and, additionally and more generally, of the total moral agent or subject.

Beginning with the Gospel, Christianity has taught that man's happiness is essentially a matter of his good will (Lk 2:14). Augustine wrote: "It is precisely the will by which one sins and lives rightly."[3] To be good, the will must conform to the will of God. This is why—and now we hear Saint Thomas Aquinas quoting a gloss—"his heart is upright who wills what God wills."[4] However, a *leitmotiv* of Reformation teaching was that the Scholastics did not adequately emphasize the primacy of the will and heart. More

2. See Hegel, *Phänomenologie des Geistes*, 162.
3. Saint Augustine, *Retractions*, 1. 8. 4.
4. Saint Thomas Aquinas, *Summa Theologiæ*, 1–2. 19. 10. s. c.

precisely, the emphasis on the primacy and sovereignty of the intention had yet to be expressed and formulated in a substantial way, i.e., as a doctrine on the will and agency of the total subject. Saint Thomas Aquinas certainly said that the goodness of the will depends on the goodness of the end of our intention, that our will is as evil as our intention is evil[5] and that, as long as we will good, no circumstance can make our will evil.[6] However, the *Summa Theologiæ* was also meant to be a moral encyclopedia and, as such, it continually addresses the morality of the intention using a doctrine of moral acts in which the regime of the total subject does not seem to be the only criterion determining the universe of his acts.

Saint Thomas Aquinas wrote that there are acts, such as giving alms to a poor person, that are under a species of good, i.e., good *per se* and in themselves, because they are in accord with the rational order. Other acts that oppose this order, such as stealing, are evil.[7] Sins are more or less serious, depending on the greater or lesser degree to which they transgress this order. Murder, for example, is a more serious sin than theft.[8] This classification obviously isn't based on mere external criteria, but is rather a function of formal preoccupations, one of which is the relationship between the end of a particular act and the universal order.[9] However, simply treating moral acts as entities determined by a substantial form to which their objects are accidentally added—objects from which their species is derived[10]—can seem damaging to a morality based on an invisible will, on the total subject. After discussing the gravity of sins in the light of their subject's condition and proposing quite diverse solutions for various cases,[11] Saint Thomas Aquinas concluded by quoting the opinion of some who would go as far

---

5. Saint Thomas Aquinas, *Summa Theologiæ*, 1–2. 19. 7. s. c.; 19. 8. ad. 3.

6. Saint Thomas Aquinas, *Summa Theologiæ*, 1–2. 19. 2. ad. 2; Augustine had already taught—perhaps even more vigorously—the efficacy of the will, in and by itself: "ut nihil enim tam facile est bonae voluntati, quam ipsa sibi: et haec sufficit Deo [For to a good will nothing is so easy, as this good will to itself, and this is enough for God]" (*Sermo*, 70. 3). For good and bad intentions that already count as actions, see *Expositions on Psalms*, 84. 3.

7. Saint Thomas Aquinas, *Summa Theologiæ*, 1–2. 18. 8. co.

8. Saint Thomas Aquinas, *Summa Theologiæ*, 1–2. 73. 3. co.

9. For this, see the developments by Gilson, *Spirit of Mediaeval Philosophy*, 304–44.

10. See Saint Thomas Aquinas, *Summa Theologiæ*, 1–2. 18. 2. co.; 3. co.

11. The sins of believers are generally more serious (*Summa Theologiæ*, 2–2. 10. 3. ad. 3). However, for example, if a member of the clergy commits a sin—provided it is not against the vow he took—his sin "is absorbed, so to speak, by the numerous good works he performs" and he is more easily pardoned for it (*Summa Theologiæ*, 2–2. 186. 10. co.).

as to say that "for the perfect every lie is a mortal sin." Saint Thomas Aquinas rejected this opinion because he thought that no circumstance causes a sin to be infinitely more grievous unless it changes the sin's species. As a circumstance, the subject does not change a sin's species, unless something additional is added, i.e., something not from that subject *stricto sensu*.[12] Although the Angelic Doctor certainly didn't deny that the subject had a role in determining the quality of its action, he nevertheless viewed it as just a circumstance, i.e., an accident of the moral act, the "perfect, elect and justified" condition of its author. Being elect and justified radically changes the subject's ordination with respect to the savior God, who is the sovereign good, but this should nevertheless not change the character of his act.

Of course, this vision is but one of the key thrusts of classic Christian theology. The Augustinian doctrine on the virtue of pagans went in a different direction. While Saint Thomas Aquinas refused to consider the least sin of the elect as infinitely grievous because it was committed against accrued light and grace, Saint Augustine taught that the best acts of pagans or, more generally, the non-elect, were but "latent vices."[13] Augustine based his doctrine on this essential intuition of total subject morality: no act is evil in itself and only the person doing it makes it evil.[14] Likewise, no thing—not even that moral thing, a human act—is good in itself. It only becomes good when its end is ordained by God.[15] Without true religion, true worship, there is no authentic virtue: conjugal chastity itself is truly a good only because of faith in God, the sovereign good.[16] Augustine made great efforts to explain his paradoxical teaching on the "splendid results [vices]," the only outwardly virtuous character of the ancients. The Romans certainly demonstrated tremendous manly courage, but the motive behind their exploits was only a corrupt desire for praise.[17] In other words, "when human beings do without faith actions" that seem to conquer sin, "they do not avoid sins;

---

12. Saint Thomas Aquinas, *Summa Theologiæ*, 2–2. 110. 4. ad. 5. On the other hand, in the case of unbelievers, it does not follow that they sin in everything they do (*Summa Theologiæ*, 2–2. 10. 4. co.). This is moreover how Arnauld interpreted the Augustinian tradition; see Laporte, *La doctrine de Port-Royal*, 2. 1, 150n.312.

13. Among modern works on Augustine, we only know of one devoted to this difficult subject: Wang Tch'ang Tche, *Saint Augustin et les vertus des païens*.

14. "We should not blame . . . silver and gold because of greedy men . . . or the feminine form because of fornicators" (Saint Augustine, *Free Choice of the Will*, 1. 15. 33). Even hell-fire is good in itself (*City of God*, 12. 4)!

15. See Saint Augustine, *Expositions on Psalms*, 32. 4.

16. Saint Augustine, "Marriage and Desire," 1. 4.

17. Saint Augustine, *City of God*, 5. 13.

rather certain sins prevail over other sins."[18] Focusing his entire attention on faith as the essential criterion for the proper ordination of the will,[19] Augustine refers to a deep level of subjectivity as the place where the goodness or viciousness of an action is decided. This vision of action with the criterion of "true faith" inspired the Reformation's huge theological attempt to present a comprehensive evaluation of man's relationship to God that integrated all partial criteria into a vision that was determined and unified by faith. It was a matter of going beyond both the objective, ontological viewpoint and the subjective, psychological intention. The doctrine of the inherent and immanent goodness and wickedness of moral acts was understood from the standpoint of an objective ordination of the act with respect to the order whose guarantor and end is the sovereign good. The doctrine of intention was based on the exclusive consideration of the subjective will, which is always under the subject's control and therefore essentially periodic and temporary. On the other hand, the Augustinian insistence on faith as the exclusive criterion unified these two viewpoints by going beyond them. Its "true faith" is a permanent condition—an objective, stable situation—that directs the individual with respect to the sovereign good as redeemer and savior. Faith nonetheless remains a subjective factor, because it is anchored in the subject's heart.

Taking faith alone as its starting point, Reformation theology was able to go beyond the doctrine of moral acts and a pure morality of intention. Calvin thought it best "not to dwell on single virtues and vices"[20] and did not include even a rough draft of systematic ethics or an attempted outline of morality in his entire body of work. The Reformer knew that man must obey the law of the Lord and that the Lord is not a "human lawgiver." Human lawgivers only judge intentions expressed by "outward acts," whereas God searches out "secret thoughts."[21] However, these secret thoughts should not be understood as periodic and temporary acts, but rather as an expression

---

18. Saint Augustine, "Marriage and Desire," 1. 4.

19. Saint Augustine, "Answer to Letters of the Pelagians," 3. 14. For the patristic background to this expression, see Araud, "Quidquid non est ex fide peccatum est," 127–45.

20. Calvin, *Institutes*, 3. 14. 2.

21. Calvin, *Institutes*, 2. 8. 6. As a Spirit, God didn't merely give civil laws; "he has given us a rule, not only for our hands and feet, but also for our affections and thoughts," (Calvin, *Sermons on Deuteronomy*, 5:17). "God . . . is not an earthly legislator, who only forbids the outward act, and yet allows us to have evil affections: because God does not want eyeservice, and He not only forbade the act, when marriage is actually violated or broken up, but He also forbade all evil cupidity and affections" (Calvin, *Sermons on Deuteronomy*, 5:18). For the "good, orderly intention" that makes an "outwardly performed duty" praiseworthy, see Vincent, *L'herméneutique du discours théologique*, 382.

of the individual's basic orientation with respect to God, which is a firm and stable condition of his entire being. Like Augustine, Calvin thought that those who did not have true religion "not only deserve no reward but rather punishment, because by the pollution of their hearts they defile God's good works." They can, of course, exercise civic virtue and appear to do good works but, in fact, "they are kept from acting ill, not by a sincere love of goodness, but merely by ambition or self-love, or some other sinister affection."[22] Despite any ultimate appearance to the contrary, if a moral agent is not fully and enduringly directed towards God, all of his "works . . . are so far from being riteousness in the sight of the Lord that he regards them as sins," because the "works are not pleasing to God unless the person" doing them "has found favour in his sight."[23] Here Calvin is powerfully echoing Luther's great proclamations. The righteousness of the just is not from works; his works come from his righteousness.[24] Just as trees precede their fruit, a person must first be pious or evil before he can do good or evil deeds. It is not deeds that make the person good or evil; but the person who makes the deeds good or evil.[25] This elementary intuition of the Reformation is expressed with great simplicity in one of the very first Protestant texts in English, W. Tyndale's commentary on the *First Epistle of John*: "the bishop of Rome . . . saith that the works do make the man righteous; and Christ's doctrine saith that the man makes the works righteous. A righteous man springeth out of righteous works, saith the bishop of Rome's doctrine; righteous works spring out of a righteous man, . . . saith Christ's doctrine."[26]

The teaching on justification by faith alone, the doctrine of *sola fides*, remains the powerful *leitmotiv*, the material principle of Protestant preaching. Not wanting to stop at every individual vice and virtue and also refusing to give primacy to subjective and unstable intention,[27] the doctrine of

22. Calvin, *Institutes*, 3. 14. 3.

23. Calvin, *Institutes*, 3. 14. 8. But Saint Thomas Aquinas said something very similar to this: "Clearly they cannot do the good works which are of grace, that is meritorious works" (*Summa Theologiæ*, 2–2. 10. 4 co).

24. "Non ex operibus erat iustitia, sed opera eius erunt ex iustitiae [righteousness does not stem from works, but works from righteousness]" (Luther, *Dictata super Psalterium, Werke*, 4:3).

25. Luther, *Von der Freiheit eines Christenmenschen, Werke*, 7:32; see also, "Menschen richten die person nach den wercken, Gott richtet die werck nach der person [While men judge individuals by their works, God judges the works by the individual]" (*Kirchenpostille, Werke*, 10. 1. 1. 339).

26. Tyndale, "Fyrste Epistle of Seynt Jhon," 123.

27. Indeed, Luther wrote, "The whole difference, however, lies in the opinion, the intent, the conscience, the purpose, the motive, etc." (*Lectures on Galatians (1519), Luther's Works*, 27:329); for "opinions" as a "source of morals," see *Operationes in Psalmos*,

justification separated man's actions and being into two separate, opposing regions. *Before* he is reconciled to God, everything a man thinks, says and does "is cursed."[28] After justification, the Christian lives under the glorious freedom of the children of God and his works are acceptable to him. It's the acceptance of the person, Calvin said, that makes his works acceptable and this insistence on the person is also the essential moral message of the Edwardsian doctrine of justification.

"Justification by Faith Alone" was one of *Five Discourses on Important Subjects* that the parishioners of Northampton wanted published (19, 790). The longest and most important of these five discourses, it was the only truly theological treatise that Edwards completed and published in his lifetime.[29] The central theme of the treatise was the absolutely gratuitous character of justification, which this young theologian developed and analyzed in minute and great detail. Countering Arminian attempts to reintroduce a works righteousness into the new world of evangelical dispensationalism, Edwards firmly stated: "According to the tenor of the first covenant, the person was to be accepted and rewarded, only for the work's sake; but by the covenant of grace, the work is accepted and rewarded, only for the person's sake" (19, 214). The person is a constantly recurring term in the discourse[30] and even if the writer—like all Reformed dogmaticians—hadn't yet managed to get beyond the residual notion of acts that are intrinsically good or bad in themselves,[31] he tried to qualify them in terms of their agent's plan of salvation. Young Edwards wrote that our actions—"even the holy acts themselves, and the gracious exercises of the godly"—are "defective," because sin remains in the unjustified man's heart and corrupts the way in which his works are performed. None of our works, nothing of ourselves, is acceptable

---

Werke, 5:28. However, this is more of a radicalization at the word level that still ought not to call into question the teaching regarding the total, durable condition of the subject as that which determines the value of his actions.

28. Calvin, *Institutes*, 3. 14. 4.

29. "Mr. Edwards's excellent discourse on Justification by Faith alone," (Bellamy, *True Religion Delineated*, Works, 1:103n) was still regarded, in 1829, "as the common Text-book of students in Theology" (*Dw.*, I, 141); and again, "one of the most successful efforts of his genius" (Wynne, *Eminent Men of America*, (New York, 1850), 146). However, towards the end of the nineteenth century, A. V. G. Allen regarded this work as "almost like a relic of an earlier theology, something intruded into an uncongenial sphere" (*Jonathan Edwards*, 93).

30. See 19, 150, 163, 214, etc.

31. For example, see the *Leiden Synopsis*: the action of the unjustified "*etiamsi feratur in bonum, et, si actum ipsum spectes, in et per se sit bona, attamen, quia non fit bene, peccatum redditur* [although directed towards good and, if you look at the act itself, good in and for itself, *yet because not well done, is turned into sin*]" (Heppe, *Dogmatik*, 293).

as long as we are not in Jesus Christ (19, 212–13), since it is "being in Christ" that procures the fruits of acceptance for us (19, 156) and because it is man, approved of God as a "proper subject" of pardon, that makes his works "approvable" (19, 154). However, once in Christ, the personal guilt and odious pollution that stain even our good works are taken away. Their relation to Christ "adds a positive value" to the good works of the justified because the value and dignity that God sets on their person could only but reflect on their works (19, 214). God does not reward an elect, justified man for the excellency of his obedience absolutely considered, but because of "his standing in so near and honorable a relation to God" (19, 216). Objectively speaking, of course, there might be good in man prior to his justification, yet this goodness is very justly looked upon as nothing until after justification (19, 164–5). Edwardsian preaching vaunted the superiority of an evangelical morality that avoided being spread among a multiplicity of individual works and instead derived the good and evil of humans and their actions from the stable state of the whole man. However, in the eyes of its Arminian detractors, justification by faith alone did not convey a pure, autonomous morality of the person but instead seemed more like an expression of heteronomy because—as we remember—justification is free. It is not merited. It is imputed to us by God and only bears fruit "if we are in Him" (18, 341).

We previously quoted Tyndale, but not in entirety. Let us now hear all of what he taught: "A righteous man springeth out of righteous works, saith the bishop of Rome's doctrine; righteous works spring out of a righteous man, *and a righteous man springeth out of Christ,* saith Christ's doctrine."[32] Of course, a good tree must come before good fruit, but this tree is only good because of something other than itself. To paraphrase Edwards, a person determines his "performance" (19, 217), and yet he is only who he is by virtue of his free acceptance by God in and through Jesus Christ. The works are not valued in themselves but in terms of their acts, and they are accounted good if their author is not "in himself" but "in Christ." The forensic justification in and through Jesus Christ doesn't seem capable of overcoming a radical metaphysical duality. In himself man remains evil, a sinner, and as one who is merely covered by the mantle of justification.[33] He is not good, and his works are only good "in God's sight" (19, 213) and not in themselves.[34] While justification remains forensic, and while we do not confess with Kant

32. Tyndale, "Fyrste Epistle of Seynt Jhon," 123.

33. Augustine wrote, "sin has been . . . covered" ("Marriage and Desire," 2. 58). Calvin called marriage a covering for the "unruliness of the flesh . . . [which] is to be condemned of itself" (*Sermons on Deuteronomy*, 5:18).

34. According to Charnier (a Huguenot), Saint Laurent deserved to suffer the torments of fire in hell for Jesus Christ (Laporte, *La doctrine de Port-Royal*, 2. 1. 170).

that grace is only a supersensible principle intrinsic to human nature[35] and that satisfaction by the savior's merits and the moral transformation of life are only two sides of the same "practical idea,"[36] it would seem that complete heteronomy has to persist between the natural and legal moral order and the evangelical order of the justified state. Although the justified are undoubtedly also sanctified, they continue to commit serious sins, and the universe of intrinsically good and evil moral beings continues to be juxtaposed with those who are impious and reprobate or those who are holy and acceptable to God.

This duality and heteronomy is also present in Edwards's work, but we think that, more than anyone else in his tradition, Jonathan Edwards continued to attenuate and defuse it. Dogmaticians say that justification in and through Jesus Christ cannot be accepted as a principle of man's moral behavior, because even if the justified person is sanctified and does good—and here we set aside his future sins—it is Jesus Christ and not the justified person himself who is the source of his sanctification and changed intentions. The justified person himself can *now* will good, but his willing of good does not have any authentic worth or value in itself because it results from divine intervention, i.e., from an external efficient cause. The Edwardsian doctrine of the will, which rejected all archeological ambitions and sought to be pure phenomenology, can be of great assistance in this area. Edwardsian thought does not seek a distant antecedent. It is content to analyze the effective present. An act does not become good or bad because of something that precedes it, but is what it is in itself. When judging the will or actions, we should not look for a past cause but rather its present deployment. It certainly remains true, from a purely dogmatic perspective, that the goodness of an act continues to be dispensed to it by justifying grace although, within the scope of Edwardsian thought, this will would only be considered good. The same goes for the will of natural man. It is certainly determined to sin by Adam's distant transgression, yet this causal determination does not call into question the fact that the will itself is evil.

That we are powerlessly subject to the effective causality of our ancestor's original sin does not in any way change the fact that we are fully accountable for the sins we now commit. Thanks to his phenomenological doctrine, Jonathan Edwards was able to propose a credible metaphysical reading of the doctrine of forensic justification. However, in doing so—and this question was already raised during the thematic discussion of the will—was he not compromising the volition's truly *moral* character, i.e., its

---

35. Kant, "Conflict of Faculties," 7:43 [Academy pagination].
36. Kant, "Religion within Boundaries of Reason," 6:119.

determination by a sovereignly autonomous intuition? Does this great effort to limit ourselves to the will's present moment only not impel us into a more ontological than ethical reading of the will? The refusal to look for root causes reduces the will, in a manner of speaking, to its own epidermis. It is henceforth only a surface without depth and consequently without anteriority. In this case, is it anything other than a material cut or isolated sliver of the natural or justified state? Refusing to consider any external efficient causality is ultimately misinterpreted as a refusal of all causal backtracking or searching for even the most immanent of root causes. Ceasing to be an active and *a priori* relationship of its moments, the will seems more like a series of peelings disassociated from a core or a series of soulless moments. As this leads to exterior homogeneity, to a series of volitions that are void of any immanent mediation, are we not in danger of the very extrinsicality that the doctrine of justification by faith specifically seeks to avoid? In other words, if the position of two diametrically opposed states of being and acting—the state of those justified by faith and the natural state determined as a consequence of original sin—doesn't favor an ontology or even an actual physics of the will, shouldn't we therefore appreciate the concerns that motivated the refusal by Thomas Aquinas to support the idea of an integral qualification of moral action based on his agent's situation with respect to the Savior-God? Edwardsian reflection on the will made it possible to resolve this problem situation and it was forensic justification in particular that gave this resolution its true clarity.

2. Moral sincerity

As we know, Jonathan Edwards's main preoccupation always was to oppose Arminian efforts to re-establish the doctrine of justification by works in theology. The specificity or essential moment of the Arminian position is less about the effective highlighting of good works performed after all, orthodox preaching also strongly emphasizes the presence of good works as outward signs of justification—and more about its teaching on the ethical-religious significance of the sincerity of the effort. Arminians prize this more than any personal freedom or initiative and believe that if a person makes a sincere effort, God will not fail to take it into account and grant that person salvation. Arminians believe that God, who tests hearts and minds, will fully appreciate natural man's genuine effort and sincere desire to avoid sin and therefore cannot nor will not ask man for more than he is actually capable of doing. Destroyer of the so-called moral powerlessness that was supposed to calm the conscience and allow the sinner to be acquitted, Edwards could only challenge the theory that partial, incomplete, yet sincere faith and obedience would oblige God to accept the sinner and his works. He then proceeded to make a devastating critique of moral sincerity, which he viewed as simply a material notion of the will that ultimately designated only its physical acceptance.

This entire discussion was anticipated by Augustine's famous distinction between *facultas* and *voluntas*, that is between power and the will. God does not look at the *facultas* of our volition but judges us according to what is, properly speaking, the will in willing, its quality and direction.[37] Arminians ignore this distinction and sink ever deeper into their inveterate Pelagianism. They never cease to affirm and reaffirm that God must save all of those who sincerely desire salvation (1, 316) because they consider sincerity itself to be a moral virtue. However, this position is the result of confusion over terms where reality of will is mistaken for a will that wills good for good. "The devils," wrote Edwards, "that possessed the Gadarene were doubtless really afraid Christ was going to torment 'em, and were sincerely willing to avoid it" (23, 52). In the same way, we may sincerely desire to eat when hungry or be sincere when joining a crew of pirates or a gang of thieves. We can be sincerely virtuous or sincerely vicious and can even sincerely will acts that are indifferent from a moral perspective (1, 315).

Arminians are convinced of the justifying virtue of sincerity, provided it is "real," "virtuous" and "great" (1, 315). A closer examination of these three adjectives will show that their sincerity is merely a material notion specifically based on the physical view of the will that they loudly attribute to Calvinists. The reality of the sincerity is considered a sign of its authenticity. A desire for salvation marked by real sincerity is an infallible expression of an authentic desire to be saved, but does this authenticity already imply a positive moral and religious qualification of the desire? Natural men most sincerely desire to be delivered from the punishment of damnation and go to paradise, yet this has nothing to do with the goodness or viciousness of their will, but simply with the fact that it wills, with the very fact that there is a will, and that the will is exercised. In this case, to will sincerely means to truly or really will and not just to simulate or pretend to will. "Sincerity signifies no more than reality of disposition and will to endeavor for some

---

37. "for God takes account not of power, but of will" (Saint Augustine, *Expositions on Psalms*, 84. 3). This distinction would survive until Kant, "moral goodness consists in the perfection of the will, not the capacities," i.e. the "powers to carry out everything willed" ("Moral Philosophy: Collins's Notes," 27:266 [Academy pagination]); "potestas: arbitrium [power: will]" (*Metaphysik*, *Ak.*, 17. 589). It was in this context Emmons wrote that justifying grace "does not give you any new power, but only a new choice" (*The Nature and Effect of Divine Teaching*, Works, 6:82). This opposition is portrayed and described by Veto, *La naissance de la volonté*, 39–40 *et passim*.

end" and this "without any consideration of the nature of the principle or aim, whence this real will and true endeavor arises" (1, 316; 21, 306–7). The real character of the sincerity denotes the mere fact of the will, but this is only taken here in a purely material sense, i.e., one of power or psychological faculty.

In addition to using the adjective "real" as a mere paraphrase of "reality of will," the Arminians also emphasize the vigorous ("hearty") character of the will. The term "vigorous" has the particular virtue of testifying to a person's strong commitment, one that involves the whole man. However, we shouldn't forget that even an involvement desired with all of our being isn't necessarily good.[38] The devils who implored Jesus not to torment them were certainly very hearty in their desire to be spared from punishment, but did that make their desire proper and good (1, 315)? A man might help and assist his neighbor's sick spouse and "heartily and earnestly desire" her recovery, and yet his involvement, actions and aspirations might not spring from a good intention. Having previously lived in adultery with her, he earnestly and heartily desires to resume the liaison interrupted by illness (1, 317).

This subjective and—because of the intimacy and immanence of human action—seemingly moral character ultimately reveals itself in its purely material, quantitative truth. Arminians believe that, in order to be justified, a person must have a certain amount or degree of good will, even if the quantity or degree only employs purely subjective criteria based on the person's own physical and psychological make-up or the external circumstances of his life. Arminians say that if the sinner has done all that he can, God is obliged to accept and save him. Having done everything that he can do means having done enough in terms of his own strengths and light. Man's will is accordingly represented as a moral force and—like every force and faculty—each will has its very own quantity. Each man's moral force differs in intensity and strength and the justifying virtue of his sincerity can be measured in terms of his faculty of the will. According to the "Arminian system," what needs to be determined is "how great a degree of this sort of sincerity . . . a man must have" in order to be entitled to inherit "the promise." It must be possible to declare "how often and how great a part of the time of man's life he must exercise this sincerity" (21, 306–7). It is clear that all men fail in part of their duty, but could we not say that the saved must "do more than half their duty, though they sincerely neglect the rest?"

---

38. As Leibniz said, a conviction is not necessarily right because it is strong (*New Essays*, 4. 19. 9).

(21, 308).[39] This entire quantitative point of view is absurd, because the only kind of sincerity that can truly qualify us to inherit the promises of Jesus Christ does not depend "on any particular degree of sincerity to be found on the difficult and unteachable rules of mathematical calculation" but on the nature of the sincerity itself (21, 308).

The physical reality of will hidden in the expression "the reality of the sincerity," the subjective ardor which the adjective "vigorous" is designed to translate and the "greatness" intended to imply a sufficient quantity of volition still only convey a material view of the will and should not be read as numbers on its moral goodness. If men do what they can but not from a virtuous disposition of their heart, their action has no moral value and "no more positive moral goodness" than a windmill's best efforts (1, 318). Gracious sincerity is not a matter of some sort of general, indifferent willingness, but of a "good willingness" (23, 50). What is needed is not "the reality of the will" but its "goodness" (21, 306). As a physical power or *facultas,* the will doesn't yet have any moral qualification and is only morally determined by the *voluntas,* i.e., our good or evil will.

Edwards developed his "demonstration" by proposing a distinction between two kinds of sincerity. The first of these is the one blindly extolled by Arminians. It simply denotes the fact of actually (i.e., really) willing the thing in question. There is, however, another kind of sincerity, the only virtuous one. Edwards wrote that sincerity is virtuous when "in the performance of those particular acts that are the matter of virtue . . . there be not only the matter, but the form and essence of virtue, consisting in the aim that governs the act, and the principle exercised in it . . . not only the reality of the act, that is as it were the *body* of the duty; but also the soul, which should properly belong to such a body." To be sincerely virtuous, a man must not be content to only desire the substance of virtue but must also desire what is prescribed to be virtuous (1, 317).[40] "In this sense," Edwards concluded, "a man is said to be sincere, when he acts with a *pure intention*; not from sinister views, or by-ends. He not only in reality desires and seeks the thing to be done . . .[41] but he wills the thing directly and properly, as neither forced nor bribed; the virtue of the thing is properly the object of the will" (1, 317). "His choice is free. . . . He seeks it as virtue and chooses it

---

39. Let's also recall those ships—human nature partially capable of good actions that are only partially polluted—which only founder and sink after having crossed a great part of the ocean.

40. Expressed in the purely religious language of preaching, what is required is "not to do what God requires only, but because God requires it" (Hooker, *Writings in England and Holland*, 200).

41. The *Enquiry* specifies "for some end or other" (1, 317).

for its own [sake], as delighting in virtue" (23, 55). Starting from a so-called morality of slavery to the absolute heteronomy of forensic justification, Edwards ends up with a brilliant reformulation of the purest ethic of intention. If natural man's sincerity is unacceptable to God, it is only insofar as it is not motivated by a virtuous intention and remains a reality devoid of any moral value.[42]

3. Love of God and self-love

Based on this analysis of moral sincerity which, in its purely natural acceptance, Edwards did not hesitate to compare to the faith of the devil (VII, 231), the most outrageous pronouncements on the pernicious character of the good works and religious exercises of the unjustified could be interpreted in purely moral terms. This ethical rereading, which the Miscellanies also outline in theological terms, gets its metaphysical framework from the lucid developments of the posthumous treatise on *The Nature of True Virtue*. Stripped of its traditional dogmatic formulation, the radical distinction between virtuous sincerity and mere natural sincerity was demonstrated using the double doctrine of theonomic and autonomic love. There are essentially only two types of love: love of benevolence and love of complacence. These two loves can be explained in two ways. Firstly, in terms of the opposition between a love whose object is God and what belongs to God, and a love whose object is something other than God. Secondly, in terms of a love that loves its object for the object itself and a love that only loves its object out of self-love.

Let us now conduct a quick review of the Edwardsian theses. A general love of benevolence is the most excellent moral virtue and, of course, designates the most perfect virtue that exists. The most perfect virtue is the one that most perfectly relates to its object and that object is God or Being in general. Since God is "the head of the universal system of existence . . . the foundation and fountain of all being" (8, 551), love, i.e., the good will exercised towards him, embraces all of the beings created by him. The essence of true virtue is therefore a "supreme love to God" (8, 554) which necessarily implies love for all of the beings that God loves. A will that does not tend towards God himself differs from this love, is opposed to it and has something other than God as its proper object. Whether it be a matter of affection towards a single being, an entire nation, humanity itself or even the sum total of all perceptive beings in the universe, this love will not be virtuous in that it excludes Being in general (8, 555). This distinction between

---

42. See Veto, *La naissance de la volonté*, 163–64.

two loves based on their objects is an expression of what could be termed theonomic morality. It describes a will whose object is God, and everything that flows from God, as virtuous and designates affection towards anything less than God as vice. Moreover, theonomic morality is not satisfied with what might be termed mere descriptive or objective criteria, but adds depth to its requirements by defining the will as having God himself as its object of intention.

It is not enough to love God; we must also love him for himself (8, 182). Nor it is enough to love finite things because they come from him, i.e., simply because of their ontological dependence on God. As far as possible, we must love them in the same manner as he loves them. In other words, it is not enough to will and love things as effects of God's will, but we must also primarily love them as ends of his will (8, 559). The essence of theonomic morality is that if God is the necessary object of the virtuous will, he is not to be regarded as a mere object. God does not want to be desired and loved from the perspective of, or because of, the aims of the one who loves him, but in and for himself. The first object of a virtuous benevolence—wrote Edwards—is Being in general, whereas the object of the ultimate propensity of this benevolence is the highest good of Being in general, as well as the good of every individual being insofar as it relates to the highest good of Being in general (8, 545). At this point we see a radicalization of the theonomy, although this is also the precise point where, in a manner of speaking, theonomy transposes itself into autonomy. If Being in general is the object of a virtuous benevolence, then virtue would ultimately only desire the good of Being: a being is not conceived of by itself, apart from its good, for the good reason that every thing essentially exists with a tendency towards good that is identical to its being. In other words, true benevolence can only be expressed in terms of an essential orientation towards the good of the thing to which it is directed. This transcends all objective and material morality and inevitably takes us towards a formal morality where the will is not defined in terms of what it wills but in terms of the end for which it wills. At this point, it's as if we are transported to the ground of that secondary distinction which this most adequate formulation of benevolence presents.

Since the Scholastics, a traditional distinction had been made between love of benevolence and love of complacence although, under Edwards's pen, this old distinction was used to formalize the extreme opposition of pure love and self-love. Towards the beginning of the treatise on true virtue, we read that love of benevolence is "that affection or propensity of the heart to any being, which causes it to incline to its well-being or disposes it to desire and take pleasure in its happiness." On the other hand, love of complacence is "no other than delight . . . in the person or being beloved for his beauty" (8, 543). Love of benevolence is that pure and selfless love that only inclines to the good of its object, whereas love of complacence is the natural attitude that rejoices and delights in the beauty of its object. Love of complacence seeks and finds its joy in the qualities of the object that please, attract and might somehow ultimately be useful to it. In opposition to the distinction that enabled the development of a theonomic morality, we now have a second distinction that enabled the development of an autonomic morality, or rather, helped a theonomic vision of morality mature into an autonomic vision of morality. We transcend the essentially material notion of a will with the greatest Being as its object in favor of an entirely formal notion of a will that wills its object for itself. However, even this formulation isn't precise, because theonomy is not a moment that autonomy must transcend; rather, it is more a matter of theonomy and autonomy coinciding at their greatest moment. Theonomic morality teaches that only God—in and for himself—can be the object of true virtue, while autonomic morality reformulates this teaching by showing that only God can be willed for himself. True autonomy is theonomy, because no being other than God is able to be willed on its own terms.

Only God can be willed in himself, because it is only in him that the will can truly find a conclusion, whereas all other things—be it another person, his family or all of humanity—can only appear to be willed in themselves because the will does not find its conclusion in them, cannot rest in what is less than absolute and is condemned to revert and return to itself. Inside the love of anything other than God or, more precisely, the love of things unrelated to God, Jonathan Edwards found self-love.

It's in the fourth chapter of his treatise on true virtue that Edwards explains his definitive teaching on self-love. In its most general sense, self-love is "a man's love of his own happiness." However, Edwards continued, the expression "his own" is ambiguous. His own happiness may denote all the happiness or pleasure of which man is capable, without distinction and without any particular or separate consideration. And so self-love can be understood in two ways (8, 575–76). First of all, there is that very general love that has to do with any pleasure, delight or happiness that a man can experience. Self-love is therefore merely the fact of liking what pleases us or of loving what we love. In this case, it is legitimate to say that all love resolves in self-love since it is absolutely clear "that whatever a man loves, his love may be resolved into his loving what he loves . . . If by self-love is meant nothing else but a man's loving what is grateful or pleasing to him, and being averse to what is disagreeable . . . this is calling *that* 'self-love' which is only a general capacity of loving, or hating." Indeed, Edwards continued, this is "the same thing as a man's having a faculty of will" (8, 575). In this sense, self-love is simply that natural faculty, that quasi-physical power of the will that constitutes our being and is identical with the "moral sincerity" defined as "reality of disposition and will to endeavor for some end, only provided such end be innocent," such as serving our self-preservation (21, 306). Vigorous sincerity has been reduced to the will itself (1, 316) and now finds itself subsumed under the general faculty of natural self-love. This self-love is simply man's own inclination to pursue what is agreeable and useful to him, whether it is his own private good, the good of his neighbors or the glory of God (8, 576). In other words, because self-love—a necessary and natural faculty—is both necessary and natural, it can have anything as its object, including realities that evidently do not pertain to its own natural universe.

There is, however, a second accepted meaning for self-love, which is actually the most commonly recognized one. According to this sense, self-love is a man's pursuing the advancement of his own proper and separate good as distinct from the general good. And this separate good will ultimately appear to be opposed to the universal good, because every individual good eventually reveals itself as a private good, i.e., where "private" denotes the world of self as opposed to the good of Being in general.

At the source of our egotistical, vicious love, we find the individual pleasures and pains that are originally our own and which we experienced independently of others (18, 577). This is the only sense in which our own proper love of this separate good is not vicious. However, purely private and separate affections only represent a very narrow sphere of a man's aspirations and delights, and because they are quasi-inevitably linked to objects, they fatally choose objects that excite affections towards others, namely God and our neighbor. At this point, the purported neutrality and moral indifference of natural self-love disappear and the option for a separate good shows itself to be in opposition to Being in general.

Private affection that detaches itself from the love of Being in general not only separates a person from the "system of existence" in general (see 8, 551) but also necessarily puts him in opposition to it. Someone who abandons himself to private affections inevitably sets an end—a particular object—above Being in general and consequently finds himself in "explicit opposition" to it. By setting his object above Being in general, a person subordinates the universal to the individual. Edwards concluded that affection with regard to individual realities without any consideration of Being in general not only produces opposition to the supreme object of virtue as its effect and consequence but itself constitutes opposition to that object (8, 555). Any will that wills a particular object without considering Being in general reveals itself to be evil, because the particular should not be conceivable apart from, or as mere otherness to, the universal Supreme Being. If this is so, it is because the particular in the metaphysical context of Edwardsian reflection doesn't seem to be a dispersed and purely material category, but rather a formal category opposed to sovereign good and to Being in general.

At this point, all that remains is to draw the proper metaphysical consequences of these developments. Firstly, if the particular ends up by reducing itself to its own good, or rather, if we can express and represent the domain of the particular as that of the self, we will have taken a decisive step towards understanding how the first Edwardsian distinction of virtue necessarily leads to the second one. The first distinction—let's recall—says that love is vicious when it gives itself to something other than God and has its conclusion in a particular reality. In contrast, the second definition states that love is vicious because it does not desire its object in and for itself but for self. However, since all particular good shows itself to be the object of private affection and consequently opposed to general benevolence, it should therefore be understood that no particular thing can be willed for itself but only in terms of the interests of the person who wills it. There is ultimately only a love of complacence towards particular objects, because these objects can only be willed in an egotistical way. In other words, this will or love is, in Kantian terms, pathological. A second consequence of these reflections is to provide a new demonstration of the doctrine of the evil will at the most general level. Because it is practically impossible for the will to confine itself to the private sphere—hermetically separate from the world of others around it—natural self-love is condemned to degrade into vicious self-love, which effectively amounts to saying that the will is always evil. Edwards could compare natural man's moral sincerity to the faith of devils because it is simply a synonym for natural man's will and its fundamental desire to persevere in its being, which always implies opposition to the Sovereign Good. This is why, as R. Baxter said, "It is self that the Scripture principally speaks against."[43]

If this is so, then this Reformed theologian, who liked to think that he had transcended the anti-materialism that Christianity inherited from the ancients, more specifically from the various branches of the Platonic tradition, seems to have taken this same condemnation of the individual to a higher level. Of course, this is not about an individual at the purely ontological level, but about the individual in terms of a metaphysic of self. The self, which is what the Gospel denounces, penetrates to the inmost depths of each of our thoughts and actions. But is there an action that wills good for good? Let's set aside clearly vicious behavior, along with anything that is violent, coarse or blasphemous, and look at seemingly virtuous volitions

---

43. Bercovitch, *Puritan Origins*, 17.

and actions. After all, one of the essential issues of Edwardsian reflection concerns "the distinguishing notes of that virtue and holiness, that is acceptable in the sight of God" (2, 84).

A volition or action is considered good when performed for the good of another being. An affection or dilection can be termed "authentically good" or be considered "truly charitable" when directed towards others for their sake. But can we really will in this way?[44] Edwards answers this question, both by refuting the common cynicism that rejected any sincere and gracious love for God (or our neighbor) and by opposing Arminian naturalism, which believes it can assert the innate ability of the unjustified to have pure love for others on the grounds that the good we feel and the pleasure we experience through and in another person do not precede our inclination towards that person but are instead conditioned by it.

Let's consider the case of love of God. A man may indeed experience pleasure and satisfaction in the goodness and glory of God, but in order to be capable of rejoicing in goodness that is foreign to him because it belongs solely to God, he first has to unite his will to God, i.e., to love him (2, 240–41). On the contrary—and this is the crux of the current discussion—an unjustified man, as a slave to sin, can never have such an inclination and therefore remains absolutely incapable of experiencing altruistic love or of having a will that is good in itself. In Miscellany 530, dating from the beginning of the 1730s, being a text that briefly anticipated his doctrine of maturity, Jonathan Edwards distinguishes between simple self-love and compounded self-love. Simple self-love is what arises simply and necessarily from the nature of a perceiving, willing being and does not have any moral qualification hidden within it. Compounded love also arises from the very depths of a willing and perceiving being's natural nature, whereby he takes his own pleasure or delight, although he is also subject to a second principle that determines the exercise of his natural movement. This second principle unites the person with another and causes the good of another to be his own good (18, 75). Self-love is truly good when its second constituent principle is the good of another person for its own sake. On the other hand, self-love is vicious when this second principle is merely a person's own good. In the first case, we are dealing with a spiritual man who loves others "as of God, or in God, or some way related to Him." In the second case, we encounter a natural man who may love others, but only in "some way or other as appendages

---

44. A certain critique of this doctrine finds its characteristic expression in a text by William Hart: benevolent love of being in general for himself is "much such a foundation to virtue as the Indian's tortoise was to the earth; which he said, bore it upon its back. When he was ask'd what the tortoise stood upon, he cry'd out with surprise 'me don't know!'" (*Remarks on True Virtue*, 22).

or appurtenances to himself" (18, 533). A natural man's good works and pious exercises remain unacceptable to God because they are born of affection that very quickly turns back on itself. Man's sincerity is virtuous—let's recall—because he wills an action "directly and properly, as neither forced nor bribed!" However, it is precisely in the natural condition that dominates the self that natural man is unable to love in this way. The essence of natural self-love, common to men and devils, is "to desire pleasure and be averse to pain," so naturally our works can only be performed to obtain some gain or escape some evil (13, 283).[45]

Of course, some might counter that there are men who respect and love virtue without having any hope of benefiting from its fruits, but this passion for good without any evident personal benefit "is no more unaccountable than that they should love that sweet fruit and pleasant food, the sweetness of which they are sensible of, though they as yet receive no benefit of it." (18, 532). Moralists go to great lengths to explain and uncover the reasons why self-love excites a natural, selfless sympathy in man towards virtue or nobility of character, but is it not really strange that men would quasi-instinctively approve of a character which, by its nature, fits well with self-love and is known by experience to tend to the benefit and pleasure of men, his neighbors? On the contrary, we could also cite the case of a child who often heard about the rattlesnake's deadly, dangerous nature and consequently developed such a deep aversion to this reptile that even a picture of that animal would be enough to evoke his disgust. This same reason—natural self-love—is what gives a child pleasure when he sees an image of a bird whose sweet singing frequently delighted him in the past. The child is not afraid of being bitten by the picture of the snake, nor does he expect to hear the image of the bird sing. However, the fact that he experiences dislike or approval respectively is explained by the awakening of his natural feelings of delight and approval, which are conveyed by a familiar association between terrible or pleasant ideas and the strength and characteristics of the snake and bird (8, 585). In the same manner, we can explain that this child may hate the general character of wicked and malicious men and, conversely, love a mild and loving character. As if by intuition, he senses that, in the first instance, he is dealing with a being that is dangerous to humans and, in the second, with one favorable to them; and this is enough to determine his feelings. Here we hardly see any selfless inclination with respect to vice, but rather a dissimulated and yet very real form of natural self-love. After all, don't we see that men most vigorously approve of those virtues that best

---

45. In hell, there will be "as strong a desire after happiness then as now, and as great an aversion to misery" (25, 219).

suit the interests of their particular situation and conditions? Members of the lower classes and those of modest means feel a particular passion for the great of this world when they discern condescension and power in them. The poor admire and are fond of the generous, and those of the weaker sex "who especially need assistance and protection, will peculiarly esteem and applaud fortitude" in those of the other sex (8, 586). Certain vices become odious in themselves because of a habitual connection with the despised in society, because self-love and self-esteem are averse to perhaps nothing else more than contempt for others and the same kind of association with praise and consideration gives rise to a quasi-instinctive esteem and affection in men for certain virtues.[46] And the missionary to the Indians in Stockbridge concludes his explanation by noting that this sort of disapproval and aversion for vice, born of self-love and the association of ideas, is made virtually invincible by education, as known by those acquainted with "American savages and their children" (8, 588). It was association of ideas and education and, consequently, external methods and procedures rather than moral considerations that accounted for the seemingly selfless inclination to virtue and seemingly selfless disinclination to vice.[47]

4. Mercenary love

Notwithstanding their objective goodness or even their heroism, the good feelings of compassion and self-sacrifice that we show to our neighbors—and, more especially, to those close to us—still do not mean that true virtue is present. The affection we feel for those close to us is as infallibly obedient to self-love as the fall of a physical body is to the law of gravity. No additional principle needs to be involved to turn our self-love towards those close to us; love for those connected to us or dear to us is only a natural extension of our own self-love. Self-love naturally tends towards anything that pleases or is useful to us, and is exercised as infallibly towards those who love us (8, 578–9). This is also why Christ was able to say that there is no merit in loving one's friends; pagans, i.e., natural men, do as much! Ever since Augustine, theologians haven't ceased to assert that, to be virtuous, our affection for another person should not be motivated by the pleasure which that other person might be able to procure for us, but by the good of

---

46. The "voice of conscience" is also explained naturally by the unease provoked in situations where individuals are in conflict with themselves. Here also, they do not transcend the natural and its egotistical motives (8, 589–90).

47. For the purely natural character of faith and of knowledge through education, see 19, 102.

that other person. We ought not to love and appreciate men as we hear gluttons say: "'I love thrushes.' Do you ask why? That he may slay and consume them. And he says that he loves, and he loves for this purpose, that they may not exist . . . And whatever we love for eating, we love for this purpose that they may be consumed and we may be refreshed."[48] This is the "cannibal love" of which a certain Simone Weil speaks—a love that crushes and devours its object—[49]and one of which the ardent affections of natural men are but so many variations.

Cannibal finality corrupts the affections of natural men, although this devouring love is not only directed towards our neighbor but is also hidden at the base of our religious affections. Christian preachers unceasingly decry a mercenary love for God, which can nevertheless lead to the severest of mortifications, to the greatest sacrifices and even to death. Someone may experience pain, suffer, and die for God without truly loving him in a truly virtuous way. As T. Shepard wrote: "A man, though carnal, will die for his religion, and that with some cheerfulness."[50] Edwards himself essentially reiterated this when he explained that no pious exercise would be pleasing to God if its end wasn't in God himself, his good, and his glory. Without virtuous sincerity, "let what may be done and suffered . . . it is all but an offering to some idol" (8, 181), and that idol, in the final analysis, is the self (8, 265). God has no need of my works, be they the most religious, and will only approve of them if they are performed with good intention. If not, they will fall back, so to speak, on their author or, rather, will never succeed in breaking away, emerging and coming out of their own egotistical sphere. Perfect virtue springs from our love of God and seeks his glory.[51] As Edwards magnificently wrote: "They whose affection to God is founded first on His profitableness to them, their affection begins at the wrong end; they regard God only for the utmost limit of the stream of divine good, where it touches them, and reaches their interest; and have no respect to that infinite glory of God's nature, . . . the first fountain of all loveliness of every kind." (2, 243).

Unjustified men may well feel love and overflowing affection for God, but it is towards a God made to suit their inclination and to fulfill their desires. Some think that the mercy of God isn't free and gracious, but is necessarily extended and exercised according to their morality and merit. These same people have no sense of the heinousness of their sin or the seriousness

---

48. Saint Augustine, "On the First Epistle of John," 8. 5.
49. For this, see Veto, *Religious Metaphysics of Simone Weil*, 61.
50. Shepard, *The Parable of the Ten Virgins, Works*, 2:286.
51. Heppe, *Dogmatics*, 364.

of their state. Having fashioned a God to suit themselves, they won't fail to love him sincerely. Men who believe that they are chosen, adopted, and saved by God think of him as amiable, but their judgment is conditioned by the conviction "that God has forgiven them . . . and loves them above most in the world, and has engaged to improve all His infinite power and wisdom in preferring, dignifying and exalting them." It's easy for them to own Jesus Christ to be a lovely person, that He, though Lord of the universe . . . is captivated with love to them . . . and loved 'em from eternity, and died for 'em, and will make 'em reign . . . in heaven" (2, 244–45). Those who profess this perverted religion fill the world with their lively protests that they love Jesus Christ. They undoubtedly love him, in their own way, of course, but—rather unfortunately for them—their affection remains unacceptable in God's eyes. These false confessors of the faith throw themselves down before Christ, declaring him to be their only Savior, yet their acceptance and faith are still stained by corruption. "Such persons as these, instead of embracing Christ as their *Savior from sin*, they trust in him as the *Savior of their sins*: instead of flying to Him as their refuge from their spiritual enemies, they make use of him as the defense of their spiritual enemies, from God, and to strengthen them against him. They make Christ the minister of sin, and great officer and vicegerent of the devil, to strengthen his interest, and make him above all things in the world strong against JEHOVA . . . They trust in Christ to preserve to 'em the quiet enjoyment of their sins, and to be their shield to defend 'em from God's displeasure" (2, 358)[52]

Those who love and venerate God out of self-love, who are "bribed" by the benefits they expect to get from Jesus Christ, reverse the order and structure of virtuous affection. The affections of the saints begin with God, whereas the affections of the hypocrite come from himself. The love of true saints has God as its foundation; in counterfeit affections, man is at the base and God is only a superstructure.[53] When speaking of their religious experiences, saints relate what they have felt and experienced, i.e., they present

---

52. Here Edwards takes his inspiration from remarkable developments by Shepard, who refers back to the Augustinian opposition between *Christum assequi* [to have Christ] and *sequi Christum* [to follow Christ] (*The Sound Believer, Works*, 1:214). Elsewhere, he wrote, "a man is sometimes content to forsake all for Christ, that he may make a booty of Christ." However, "when men's expenses for Christ exceed their receipts from Christ, they cease spending" (Shepard, *The Parable of the Ten Virgins, Works*, 2:285–86).

53. See 2, 247; see also 2, 249, where Edwards notes the saints rejoice in Jesus Christ, hypocrites in themselves. Guillaume de Saint-Thierry said of Christ, "Locus tuus pater tuus," (*La contemplation de Dieu*, 124). For this, see Potterie, *La vérité dans saint Jean*, 932 and n.73. On the other hand, "the place of Judas was *locus* suus" (Hooker, *Of the Laws of Ecclesiastical Polity, Works*, 4:146).

and praise the object of their discovery, while hypocrites dwell on their own experiences. "A true saint ... has his mind too much captivated and engaged by what he views without himself, and his own attainments." The joy that floods his heart does not come from considering his own state but "from the divine and supreme beauty of what is the object of his direct view, without himself" (2, 251–53). In contrast, hypocrites and, more generally, all natural men are incapable of turning their gaze outward and directly viewing this exterior. Captivated with themselves, in the sphere of self, they are incapable of relating to others without referring back to themselves or, rather, their ultimate involvement with others is always mediated by a stronger commitment to themselves.

The referral to self found in religious exercises performed for a benefit is also a structural, essential moment of works motivated by fear: "the mercenary hope of heaven" has "the servile fear of Hell" as its counterpart. In a period that was still profoundly marked by an obsessive fear of hell, Jonathan Edwards continued to warn against the illusions of those who held that works done out of fear of punishment would be acceptable to God. Edwards is part of a preaching tradition—extending back more than one thousand years—that distinguishes between a chaste fear and a servile fear of God, one in which the fear of hell could only be a particularly repugnant modality of servile fear.[54] "Whoso fears punishment," wrote Augustine, "wishes, if it were possible, to do what pleases him and not to have what he fears. God forbids adultery, you have coveted another's wife, you do not go in unto her, you do not do so, opportunity is given you. . . . Why do you not do it? Because if you do, you will be cast into hell fire. It is the fire you fear. O if you loved chastity, you would not do it, even though you might be altogether unpunished!"[55] Indeed, because it motivates moral behavior towards our neighbor or the periodic and regular performance of religious duties, servile fear is not entirely useless. It can keep man from evil actions and, just as a needle introduces a thread, servile fear can prepare the way for a chaste

---

54. The source of this distinction is Saint Augustine: Mausbach, *Die Ethik des heiligen Augustin*, 1:184–90; see also the Venerable Bede, *In Lucae Evangelium Expositio*, PL 92, 523–4; Pierre Lombard, *Sentences*, 2. 34. 4; Saint Thomas Aquinas, *Summa Theologiæ*, 2–2. 19. 2. co. For Luther, see the references in Köstlin, *Theology of Luther*, 470–1; Calvin, *Institutes*, 3. 2. 27. The distinction between these two fears is even found at the heart of Kantian morality: "So God must be regarded as a moral or pragmatic legislator. In the first case, we obey Him as children by virtue of moral intention; in the second, as subjects by virtue of pragmatic design" (*Moralphilosophie, Rechtsphilosophie und Religionsphilosophie*, *Ak.*, 19. 249). See also "*slavish* and mercenary faith" in "Religion within Boundaries of Reason," 6:115.

55. Saint Augustine, *Sermo*, 145. 3.

fear.[56] Nonetheless, it remains an inferior and even pernicious form of religious affection and, especially since the Reformation, one that is treated with great severity. Luther compared the self-reproaches of an unjustified man to the remorse that seizes a criminal when he is led to the gallows,[57] while Calvin said that repentance motivated only by terror when faced with the God's wrath was only a "threshold to hell."[58] Closer to Edwards, S. Stoddard said of the Christian that he "is frightened into reformation: he don't know how to bear the flames of hell; he would be as bad as the worst, but that he dare not."[59] A successor of Edwards at Princeton, Samuel Davies,

---

56. Saint Augustine, "On the First Epistle of John," 9. 4.

57. Luther, *Grund und Ursach Aller Artikel D. Martin Luthers, so durch Römische Bull Unrechtlich Verdammt sind, Werke*, 7:355. Conversely, all the good works of those who do not believe in Christ and do not have the Holy Spirit can only come from servile fear: "ob er gleich etwas thut, das an ihm selb nicht bös, sonder gut ist, das thut er wie ein Knecht, allein aus Forcht, und nicht aus einem rechten, herzlichen Gehorsam [and if perchance he performs some work not evil in itself, and proper, he does this in slavish fear and not from true, earnest obedience (to God's Word)]," (*Hauspostille, Werke*, 52:291–92).

58. Calvin, *Institutes*, 3. 3. 4. According to Jansenius, righteousness born of fear is our own work and doesn't justify the soul because it doesn't transform it: a wolf is always a wolf, even if the barking of a dog prevents it from doing evil (*Augustinus*, 3. 5. 25, 236). Quesnel went even further: "Qui ne s'abstient du mal que par la crainte du châtiment, le commet dans son cœur, et est déjà coupable devant Dieu [He who abstains from evil only through fear of punishment, commits it in his heart, and is already guilty before God]. Voire, la crainte des peines éternelles rend semblable aux bêtes : elle est un effet de la cupidité et elle n'est point une grâce de Jésus-Christ [Indeed, fear of eternal punishment makes men like beasts: it is an effect of cupidity and not a grace of Jesus Christ]" (*Unigenitus, Dictionnaire de Théologie Catholique*, 15, 2104). Let's also recall Nicolas Boileau-Despréaux:

> On entendit prêcher dans l'école chrétienne
> Que sous le joug du vice un pécheur abattu
> Pouvait sans aimer Dieu ni même la vertu
> Par la seule frayeur au Sacrement unie,
> Admis au ciel, jouir de la gloire infinie. (*Satire XII, Œuvres complètes*, 128)

All of this is expressed in a much more balanced way by *Caritée*, (J.-P. Camus), who carries a pitcher of water in her right hand and, in the other, a burning torch: "Avec ce flambeau, disait-elle, je désire mettre le feu au paradis et le réduire tellement en cendres qu'il n'en soit plus parlé ; et, répandant cette eau sur les flammes de l'enfer, je prétends les éteindre ; afin que désormais Dieu soit aimé et servi pour l'amour de lui-même [With this torch, she said, I want to set fire to paradise and reduce it to such ashes that there will be no more mention of it; and, by spreading this water on the flames of hell, I intend to extinguish them so that God will henceforth be loved and served out of love for himself]," (Brémond, *Sentiment religieux en France*, 11:201). Compare with 207–8.

59. White, "Stoddard's Theories of Persuasion," 251.

uses this similar, stone-throwing formulation: "It is not sin they hate, but Hell."[60]

The true finality of natural man's religion is to escape the rigors of judgment and "the very devils themselves, notwithstanding all the devilishness of their temper, would wish for a holy heart, if by that means they could get out of Hell" (1, 313). In criticizing and condemning a fear of sin that is only our natural tendency to flee sin, Edwards finds a theoretical project for his reflections. The fear of hell incites men to perform actions that please God and to particularly avoid actions that displease him. What is very serious here is that, unlike a truly pious man who fears and abhors divine displeasure in itself, the sinner merely wants to avoid the consequences of that displeasure. For saints, the end of their action is an external or, rather, a transcendent God on whom they directly set their sights, without any reference back to themselves, while the finality of natural action is to seek the gifts of God and avoid his punishments. Even though Edwardsian preaching frequently contained exhortations to do everything possible to avoid the flames of hell and was lavish with descriptions of the wonders of paradise, at a certain deeper, more speculative and more dogmatic level, it ran counter to moral philosophies with retribution beyond the grave as an essential moment. Edwardsian theology considered a man's religion to be a counterfeit of true piety if he wouldn't serve God if heaven and hell no longer existed.[61]

---

60. Sweet, *Revivalism in America*, 68. Natural men turn from sin like "a thief going to the gallows" (25, 651n.5).

61. Bellamy, *True Religion Delineated*, *Works*, 1:140. This requirement for a disinterested love of God can lead to formulations where heaven and hell are reduced to mere symbolic places, and figures of the creature's moral state. Sir Thomas Browne wrote, "every Devil is an Hell unto himself; he holds enough of torture in his own *ubi*, and needs not the misery of circumference to afflict him" (*Religio Medici*, *Works*, 1:64). For B. Whichcote, "Heaven is first a temper and then a place," (*Aphorisms*, in Inge, *Platonic Tradition*, 51). J. Smith thought that "Hell is rather a nature than a place" (*Select Discourses*, 446). These are Anglican voices, although this vision isn't missing in the Puritan tradition, which reformulates it in accordance with its own theocentrism: heaven and hell are not figures of our own spiritual state but denote the presence or absence of God. As Massachusetts was being established, one poetess wrote, "Yea, oft have I thought were it hell itself, and could there find the love of God toward mee, it would be a Heaven ... in truth, it is the absence and presence of God that makes heaven or hell" (*Works of Anne Bradstreet*, 8). Or again: "His own Heaven to himself, in the *Depths* of *Hell* beneath," (Sola Pinto, *Peter Sterry*, 95). But the most striking texts are those of Milton: Satan declaims, "The mind is its own place, and in itself / Can make a Heav'n of Hell, a Hell of Heav'n," (*Paradise Lost*, bk. 1, ll. 254–55, *Works*, 2:1, 17). And elsewhere: "all good to me becomes / Bane, and in Heav'n much worse would be my state," (*Paradise Lost*, bk.9, ll.122–23, *Works*, 2:2, 264). This is why "Our Savior" will say to the Devil:

"the happy place Imparts thee no happiness, no joy,
Rather inflames thy torment, representing

The formalism of Edwardsian moral piety rejects actions lacking "intrinsic direct loveliness" (13, 247). The radical theonomy of this reflection refuses to support a love towards God which does not act "freely" but "wholly for by-ends, and from sinister and mercenary views . . . induced by regard to things foreign" (W 2, 553).[62]

5. Sinners in Zion

The actual explanation in *The Port-Royal Logic* begins with basic definitions of the mind's main operations, one of which is reasoning. "Reasoning," wrote

---

Lost bliss, to thee no more communicable,
So never more in Hell, than when in Heaven." (*Paradise Regained*, bk. 1, ll.416–20, *Works* 2:2, 420)

Conversely, as Saint Thomas Aquinas said, "the [good] thief [who] descended locally with Christ into hell . . . was in paradise, because there he rejoiced in the divinity of Christ" (*Summa Theologiæ*, 3. 52. 4. ad. 3). See also this text of the French School: "O cœur de Jésus-Christ, il ne faut pas que vous seul pour faire mon paradis. Et si je l'avais au milieu des enfers, je convertirais les enfers en un vrai paradis. . . . Et dans les enfers même, je n'y vois guère autre chose pour tout enfer, sinon que l'on n'y trouve point le cœur de Jésus-Christ [O heart of Jesus Christ, you are all I need to have my paradise. And if I had it in the middle of hell, I would convert hell into a true paradise. . . . And even in hell itself, I would scarcely see another thing in all of hell, if the heart of Jesus Christ were not found there . . .]" (J.-B. Nouilleau in Brémond, *Sentiment religieux en France*, 7:259). The source of this *theologoumenon* is the formula of an ecclesial text on Christ: "ad inferna descendens et a Patris gremio non recedens [descending into hell and not leaving the bosom of the Father]," (Denzinger, *Symboles et définitions de la foi catholique*, 135); see also *Enchiridion*, 369. See also a contemporary interpretation: "Jesus himself is 'heaven,'" (Ratzinger, *Jesus of Nazareth*, 150). We find this same theme transposed into philosophy: "L'homme qui est vertueux est au ciel [The virtuous man is in heaven]," (Kant, *Metaphysik 51, Ak.*, 18, 592). This insistance on the moral and religious essence of otherworldly reality wasn't so strange for Edwards, for whom hell simply made our own moral state explicit, see *supra*, p. 185. However, with the sole exception of a passage from his youth in which Edwards—anticipating the victory on the cross—regarded the hades of the patriarchs as a metaphor or symbol (13, 229), he never fails to invoke the physical dimension of the next world. We have only found one allusion to a "moralized" conception of hell in the entire Edwardsian tradition. J. Bellamy had Satan declare that God could have vacated and set aside the law for himself and for man, and therefore, "my exclusion from heaven was an arbitrary act; if arbitrary, then tyrannical. And what care I for the wrath of an angry tyrant? Hell will be no longer hell to me" (*An Essay on the Nature and Glory of the Gospel of Jesus Christ, Works*, 2:342). The homiletic work of young Edwards provides examples of analogous considerations. Atheists have "actually felt" hell before their death (10, 370). Conversely, a loving soul "is like a little heaven upon earth" (10, 617).

62. This condemnation of any consideration that was not motivated by the love of God for God led Edwards, and especially the Edwardsians, to ask if such a radical rejection of any servile fear, and of hell in particular, which implied acceptance of, and even a desire for, one's own damnation, was indeed the will of God. See *infra*, p. 403ss.

Arnauld and Nicole, "is that operation of the mind through which it forms one judgment from many others; as when, for instance, having judged that true virtue ought to be referred to God, and that the virtue of the heathens was not referred to him, we thence conclude that the virtue of the heathens was not true virtue."[63] Uninformed readers might think it more appropriate to have more general or neutral examples in a treatise on logic; in fact, the authors' choice is deliberate. Ever since Augustine said *"Tota infidelium vita peccatum est* [the unbeliever's whole life is a sin],"[64] theologians haven't stopped commenting on and explaining the sense and scope of this statement, which has become an important component of Christian reflection. The primary justification for this definition is undoubtedly its reference to passages of Scripture, although theologians have always tried to round out this explanation with a sort of philosophical reflection in which pagan or unjustified man becomes synonymous with egotistical or evil man. This task was accomplished with dazzling clarity in Edwards's dissertation on *The Nature of True Virtue*, which explained Augustinian Christianity's dogmatic teaching in purely metaphysical terms, stripped of any positive theological formulations.[65] Thanks to this treatise, all of the apparent paradoxes concerning the virtue of heathens,[66] natural man's moral sincerity and, more generally speaking, the works of the unregenerate, were explained by a development in which love of God for God himself was shown to be the only possible form of selfless love and in which relentless analysis exposed a hope of gain and a fear of punishment as the innermost motivations of seemingly perfect and praiseworthy moral and religious actions.

Calvinist preaching recognizes and admires the good works "of civil men" and, if it refuses to consider them good in and of themselves, it is

63. Arnauld and Nicole, *Logic, or Art of Thinking*, 25. Elsewhere, Arnauld presents upwards of six demonstrations of this thesis, *Difficultés proposées à M. Steyaert, Œuvres,* 9:330–46.

64. Saint Prosper of Aquitaine, *Liber Sententiarum ex Operibus Sancti Augustino Delibatarum*, 106. *Opera*, PL 51. 441.

65. The posthumous treatise which F. H. Foster regarded as "Edwards' principal contribution to religious thought," (*History of New England Theology*, 91), remains the least understood of his works. This "commentary on Hutcheson" (Aldridge, "Edwards and Hutcheson," 35) had an unfortunate influence on theology in America (Miller, *Jonathan Edwards*, 242). Even associated by R. Hall with atheism (note by W. Hamilton 2. 67–72), this "pious blasphemer" (Lesser, *Jonathan Edwards*, xxxv) professes notions of virtue that are "wrong, imaginary, and fatally destructive of the foundations of morality and true religion" (Hart to Hopkins, in Park, *Samuel Hopkins*, 196, in Hopkins, *Works*, vol. 1).

66. Edwards approved of Augustine's view that the virtues of pagans were "splendid sins" by citing Gale, *Court of the Gentiles*, 2. 316n.6, as he refers to the *opus alienum* in a citation from Turnbull, see *supra*, p. 146.

because what matters in moral action is "not only the doing of the thing, but the heart with which it is done."[67] Nothing is good or evil in itself if we set circumstances aside (13, 200) and the essential circumstance is the heart. "Works done by unregenerate men," we read in the Savoy Declaration "although for the matter of them they may be things which God commands . . . yet because they proceed not from a heart purified by faith . . . nor [are done] to a right end . . . are therefore sinful."[68] This position, repeated even more forcefully in New Theology, is here stated by Joseph Bellamy: "the very best religious Performances of all unregenerate Man are, complexly considered, sinful, and so odious in the Sight of God. They may do many Things *materially* Good, but the *Principle, End* and *Manner* of them are such, as that, *complexly considered*, what they do is *Sin* in the Sight of God."[69] Lastly, as usual, Nathanael Emmons proposed a brutal formulation of the teaching concerning the unregenerate: "Their apparent goodness is the essence of moral evil. Their partial love is general malevolence, and their best deeds are an abomination to the Lord."[70] The implacable logic of the total subject ethic conveyed by forensic justification theology rejected all material consideration of good works and made this explicit with the maxim: "Only evil can come from evil."[71] The outcome of this is that any apparent good stemming from evil only seems good but actually is evil.[72] We can understand why writers with a penchant for paradox and a taste for provocation even said that it was possible for acts to be materially identical and yet radically opposite in terms of the subject's state.[73]

---

67. Willard, *Divinity*, 213.

68. Walker, *Creeds and Platforms*, 384. Calvin invoked Horace and Ovid to show that even the gods of antiquity refused the tribute of the wicked. Wencelius, *L'esthétique de Calvin*, 387.

69. Bellamy, *True Religion Delineated*, Works, 1:222.

70. Emmons, *Selfishness: The Essence of Moral Depravity*, Works, 4:547.

71. This is why "all human righteousness," all combat against sin that comes from our corrupt human nature, "is not righteousness but hypocrisy" (Luther, *Ad Romanos*, Werke, 56:395).

72. Human goodness before justification is as nothing or even something hateful (19, 165); compare with "the prayer which is not made through Christ, not only cannot blot out sin, but is itself turned into sin" (Saint Augustine, *Expositions on Psalms*, 109, 9). Compare also with the Kantian view that actions arising from the "*perversity* of the human heart" can only be "legally" good ("Religion within Boundaries of Reason," 6:30).

73. See also R. Sibbes, "What another man doth only civilly, a gracious man will do holily" (*The Bruised Reed and Smoking Flax*, Works, 1:61). Sinners in Zion can perform "materially good" works (14, 259), yet they only spring from "counterfeit graces" by which "the Devil apes God" (19, 127 and n.4).

These are seemingly marginal theses, morbid outgrowths of an Augustinianism that succumbed to the temptation to excessively systematize the great Christian paradoxes of sin and grace. Jansenists and Calvinists attributed these paradoxes to a truly pernicious knowledge of the Christian mysteries,[74] to the fact that even the Devil cannot sin or—to a far greater extent—as viciously as Christians living under the dispensation of grace.[75] In short, it would have been better for many of us if Christ had not come on Earth (X, 284) because the grace of God can be dangerous (15, 368)! In reality, however, a base of profound meaning and real truth underlay even the most extreme formulations and most shocking affirmations: that of a subject ethic pushed to its ultimate consequences. While averse to the excesses that would make his disciples famous, Jonathan Edwards himself said that a person who sincerely performed only the body or material part of virtue but not its form and soul remained "a vile hypocrite" (1, 317), that "the sinners in Zion" will be lower in hell than those who do not profess the Gospel or practice the sacraments because they are not members of the visible church (22, 268). Edwards doesn't specify which particular transgressions justify this severe condemnation. He contented himself with commenting that God would pronounce his judgment based on the moral subject's state with respect to the grace of Jesus Christ and that hypocrites abuse that grace. Beginning with the Gospels, preachers have constantly returned to the serious situation of those who, though they live under the administration of God's grace and in the light of the Redemption, only profess their faith verbally and, in particular, only perform their moral and religious works in an outward manner, without any true submission to Jesus Christ as their Savior. We know that the judgment of Tyre and Sidon will be more tolerable than that of the holy city of Jerusalem and that the Pharisees are guiltier before God than the publicans and prostitutes. This *leitmotiv* of Christian preaching, which was particularly enduring in the Augustinian tradition, became even more so in the Reformation world. Calvin said that God "rises with greater severely against hypocrites, and doubles their punishment,"[76]

---

74. Unigenitus, Dictionnaire de Théologie Catholique, 15, 2080.

75. Hopkins, *The True State and Character of the Unregenerate*, Works, 3:306. This is why Arnauld said ironically, "au lieu que nous devons sans cesse prier Dieu, afin qu'il nous donne sa Grâce, nous le devons prier, au contraire, qu'il ne nous donne jamais celle-ci [rather than having to pray unceasingly that God would grant us his grace, we should instead pray that he never gives it to us]" (*Première apologie pour M. Jansénius*, Œuvres, 16:118).

76. Calvin, *Institutes*, 3. 3. 25.

and there is a true consensus in Puritan rhetoric that "that man's sin that lives under the Gospel is the greatest sin of all."[77]

This discourse on the aggravation of sin and the doubling of the sanction it deserves reveals an ethical vision where the value of an action is essentially determined according to the total state of the willing subject. The act is not defined by its material part—absent the general context, which is the subject's ordination with respect to justifying grace—but its ordination towards grace is instead evaluated specifically in terms of that essential circumstance of morality known as the heart.[78] It was this vision that made Luther—and others after him—say that a justified person's transgression did not, in a manner of speaking, count as sin. This also inspired Calvin's teaching that God preferred the "feeble and slender . . . faith" of his elect to all the light of the reprobate.[79] It was also this theological logic that made Edwards conjecture that God would more gloriously reward the "the little weak love, and poor and exceeding imperfect obedience of believers in Christ," than he would have done Adam's perfect obedience (19, 214).[80] In this logic of free, forensic justification, an action's imperfection and evil are wiped away or at least set aside so that, in a certain way, the evil committed by the justified person is transposed into good. But how are we to reconcile this teaching with the denunciation of the sinners in Zion, those hypocrites who aggravate their sin and incur guilt for their entire act by their very proximity to the Gospel? Now, this contradiction is only apparent because, in the latter instance, the same total subject ethic explains the remission of the justified subject's sins and the condemnation aggravated by the deficiencies of the hypocrites, not to mention the condemnation of their good works. The sins of the elect are only material. In terms of form, their sins are subsumed under the justified state of their author. The lesser deficiencies and good works of the hypocrites are minor imperfections and material goodness respectively, although it is the general evil orientation of their agent that gives them a final moral determination.

Hypocrites, the sinners in Zion, "are worse, and more provoking enemies to God, than the very heathen, who never sinned against gospel light and mercy" (12, 420). Because the hypocrite is a man who finds himself in a situation that is extremely favorable for virtue, doing evil while having everything needed to do good only doubles the seriousness of their wrongdoing.

---

77. Hooker, *Writings in England and Holland*, 216.

78. See *supra*, p. 102ss.

79. Calvin, *Institutes*, 3. 2. 12.

80. The saints enjoy greater happiness than our first parents did in their innocence (22, 235).

Edwards initially uses an ancient saying to explain the hypocrite's particular situation: opposites highlight and reinforce each other. Good and evil, pleasure and pain, happiness and misery continually reinforce the sense of each other (V, 355). A vigorous perception of good depends largely on an awareness of its opposite—evil—and we could even say that "happiness receives all its relish from a sense of the contrary; if it were not for this, joy would be dull and flat" (13, 286). All of these maxims might seem to be nothing more than rather banal wisdom offering its services a little too easily to doubtful theodicies. However, it should be recalled that, on the one hand, the motto of the development is this great sentence: "The light of God's beauty... truly shows the soul its own deformity" (25, 637) and that, on the other hand, Edwards developed his theses within the context of the *theologoumenon* of *felix culpa*, that happy fault, and out of a continuous meditation on the Christian mysteries.

Our experience of evil deepens our experience of good (20, 506) because true purity should not be understood as empty innocence but rather as a victory won over evil.[81] However—and this is where Edwards resolutely transcended the platitudes of the wisdom of the nations—the opposite phenomenon is equally possible. The appearance of good might favor the advent of evil, aggravate evil or even provoke it. On a purely natural level, and within the context of the beauty and proportion of physical things, Edwards remarked that "the nearer the relation and the stricter the connection, so much the greater and more disgustful is the deformity" (8, 568). Nothing is easier than to harm what is perfect, precisely because of its perfection. And this also holds true in the spiritual and moral domain. Someone who occupies high ground risks more than someone crouching in a hollow. This is why the fall of hypocrites is so serious (11, 107).[82] And we also need to understand that their exalted position not only makes their fall more violent and dangerous but even easier and, in a certain sense, even provokes it. In the spiritual and moral domain, if you do not progress, you relapse (22, 528);[83] and the higher you are, the steeper and more precipitous the slope becomes.

81. Milton, *Aeropagitica*, Works, 4:310. "Truth never gets up into her throne with that advantage as when her enemy (the opposite error) is made her foot-stoole," (T. Goodwin, *Imputatio Fidei*, in Haller, *Rise of Puritanism*, 201).

82. This is the context in which this strange sentence has to be placed: "Hence learn that Satan before his fall was the Messiah or Christ or anointed" (18, 298).

83. This is a classic theme of moral thought. "Quia enim non proficit in via Dei, deficit [For he that does not go forward in God's way goes backward]" Luther, *Epistola ad Romanos*, Werke, 56:239. Luther referred in this text to what Saint Bernard had previously said: "if you try to stand still [on God's path] you cannot but fall [back]" "Letter XXVIII," 120. "All the masters of the spiritual life agree in this maxim, that not

Of course, at the source of this vision of a state aggravated by the advent of the light is the Pauline teaching on the Law that provokes transgressions, which would be picked up in turn by great Christian theologians. The Law is like a dyke, wrote Augustine. It certainly protects against the assaults of sin, but when overwhelmed, unleashes an even greater outburst.[84] Precisely because it is resisted by the Law, covetousness becomes even more virulent,[85] while sin doubles[86] and perpetuates itself even more vigorously and in a more pernicious way after the commandment.[87] Calvin wrote that love of the Law becomes a cause of the aggravation of sin because "the person who before simply overstepped the bounds of righteousness . . . becomes . . . a despiser of divine power and authority, by which he was made acquainted with the will of the Lord of Hosts."[88] Of course, the Law does not call the transgression as law and yet the incitement to sin that emanates from it is no less immanent. The Law only increases sin accidentally, i.e., not by itself but by virtue of how it is received by men and according to their attitude. The doctrine of God may be a cause of blindness, although it is not so because of its nature,[89] but only accidentally. "It is like the dimsighted going out in the sunshine. It only makes their eyes weaker still. Yet the fault lies, not in the sun, but in their eyes. When the Word of God blinds and hardens the reprobate, it is through their own native depravity; so far as the Word is concerned, it is accidental."[90] Puritan preachers interpreted this pernicious, accidental efficacy in terms of the Pauline anthropology. The second use of the law, wrote W. Perkins, "is accidentally to effect and augment sin by reason of the flesh, which causeth man to decline from that which is commanded and ever to incline to that which is prohibited."[91] Edwards himself

---

to advance is to fall back" (L. Lallemant, *Spiritual Doctrine*, 67). As for virtue, "if it is not rising, it is unavoidably sinking" (Kant, "Metaphysics of Morals," 6:409 [Academy pagination]); see "Whoever does not want to go onward, sinks back" (Schelling, *Clara*, 26, etc.). All of this also has patristic antecedents: "stopping in the race of virtue marks the beginning of the race of evil" (Saint Gregory of Nyssa, *Life of Moses*, 30).

84. Saint Augustine, "Spirit and Letter," 6.

85. Saint Augustine, "To Simplician," 1. 1. 3.

86. Saint Augustine, *De Diversis Quaestionibus LXXXIII*, 66, 1.

87. Saint Augustine, "To Simplician," 1. 1. 4.

88. Calvin, *Commentarius in Epistolam Pauli ad Romanos*, *Opera*, 41, 102; compare with "Proper effect of God's Word to make a man better, an accidental to make him worse" (6, 350n.6).

89. Calvin, *Commentary on Corinthians*, 2:192. For an original definition of a thing that is good in itself but which the mind apprehends and then considers to be evil, see Saint Thomas Aquinas, *Summa Theologiæ*, 1–2. 19. 5. co., who refers back to Aristotle.

90. Calvin, *Harmony of the Gospels*, 2:67.

91. Perkins, *A Golden Chaine or the Description of Theology*, *Workes*, 1:69.

occasionally echoed this explanation in more psychological terms (17, 159), but the core of his teaching is an emphasis on the particularly odious character of sin committed with full knowledge of the facts (14, 363) and, as it were, in proximity to the work of the Savior-God. Edwards and the authors of the *Half-Way Covenant* knew that "it is an high favor to have a place . . . in the house of God . . . but it is a Dreadful place"[92] because those who are so close to the Lord will be judged even more severely. The converted are under infinitely more "solemn" and strict "obligations" than natural men (*Dw.*, I, 150), the sins of Jerusalem are more serious than those of Sodom (IV, 438), and apostates bring more dishonor to religion than the heathens themselves.[93] His domestic adversaries, Edwards remarked, are the most hateful enemies of Christ. They are guiltier than those who plainly refuse the sacraments. "Gospel sinners" practice the sacraments while continuing to engage in transgressions. We might say that they came "into His presence on purpose to affront Him" (IV, 432).

They are Gospel sinners, because if love of the Law so aggravated the situation of transgressors, how could the proclamation of the Gospel and promulgation of its reign not have exasperated the situation of God's enemies even more? Legal hypocrites accept the moral and ceremonial order and yet do not cease transgressing; Gospel hypocrites make themselves even guiltier because they announce that they have accepted the Gospel and often believe sincerely in their profession of faith. They confess faith in Jesus Christ but, at bottom of their hearts, are more or less consciously opposed to the Gospel. The increased seriousness of this opposition—this transgression against the Gospel administration—is a function of objective and subjective

92. Walker, *Creeds and Platforms*, 311.

93. "the sin of such who lived in the rejection of a Savior, even in the very house of God, in the midst of gospel light . . . was peculiarly aggravated" (12, 249). Edwards stressed, "Those people are like to sink the deepest into hell hereafter, that go to hell from under the care of the most faithful ministers" (25, 75). Many who argue over the salary of an excellent minister "pay so much money for the better place in hell and are at great expense for double damnation" (*Salv.*, 145). Sins committed on the Sabbath become "the more exceedingly sinful" (17, 247), while the Great Awakening itself had caused the spiritual state of some people to worsen (19, 294–95). The Enfield congregation was as guilty as the wicked Israelites, who nonetheless lived "under means of grace" (22, 404), and many parishoners in Northampton, that town with so much of the presence of God and where he performed his marvelous works, "must not expect an ordinary place in hell" (19, 407). In short, sinners in Zion and hypocrites are more odious to God "than the most impure beast in Sodom, that makes no pretense to religion" (2, 318), just as the rejection of Christ by the Jews was "more heinous" than idolatry itself (24, 302). The guilt of those who live "under the gospel" is "aggravated" (14, 361). If the sanctified Christian can have spiritual experiences and joys that are superior to those enjoyed by innocent Adam, then in order to attain perfection, he must love God "in an unspeakably higher degree" (20, 153).

factors. And the Gospel sinner's state is more serious because, on the one hand, the correlate—the end of his opposition—is the greatest, most holy Being and, on the other hand, he utters his refusal of the light from the very core of his being.[94]

6. Sinning against the Spirit

The odiousness of a transgression, as we well know, is directly proportionate to the holiness of the being against whom it is perpetrated,[95] while the

---

94. Legal hypocrisy can have two senses: (1) Reminiscent of the Pharisees, this is strict external or internal obedience to various religious rules and obligations. (2) However, in the context of the controversy with the Arminians, "legal hypocrite" referred to Christians who based all of their religion and morality on the (new) law of moral sincerity, whereas "evangelical hypocrite" referred to those whose faith and joy were based on the discovery of a fictitious pardon of their sins and an imaginary love of God rather than an apprehension of the infinite excellence of the divine nature (Bellamy, *True Religion Delineated*, *Works*, 1:126). The notion of hypocrisy is specifically Christian. For the ancients, intentions were secret and it was impossible, for example, to distinguish an individual who did not want to do good from one who wanted to do good but lacked the means to do it (Aristotle, *Nicomachean Ethics*, 1178a [Bekker pagination]). On the contrary, for the Christian, "all intentions are manifest because they are so to God" (E. Gilson, *Spirit of Mediaeval Philosophy*, 476n.4). Jesus based his denunciation of hypocrites on the transparency of their evil intention to God. From a theoretical point of view, Christian theology defines hypocrisy as the dissimulation in one "of a virtuous intent that he does not have" (Saint Thomas Aquinas, *Summa Theologiæ*, 2–2, 111, 2 ad. 1). Hypocrisy is therefore not understood as contrary to a particular virtue but rather to that of truth or truthfulness itself (Saint Thomas Aquinas, *Summa Theologiæ*, 2–2, 111, 2 ad. 1). More recently, Hegel thought that, for an action committed in bad conscience to become hypocritical, it was necessary to add a formal determination of lying, which is the fact of affirming before others that something evil is good (*Elements of Philosophy of Right*, 170–71 [§ 140]). It is difficult to effectively discern hypocrisy because hypocrites "not only . . . impose upon [other] men . . . a false semblance" but even deceive "themselves" (Calvin, *Institutes*, 3. 2. 10). We will therefore consider some distinctions and descriptions. For example, J. Cotton identified two types of hypocrites: washed swine, the grosser kind of hypocrites, and goats. The goats "are clean Beasts such as chew the cudd; meditate upon Ordinances . . . they live both in a general, and particular calling. . . . And they are full of Ambition; . . . they attend upon their own ends, and will outshoot God in his own bow" (*New Covenant*, in Miller and Johnson, *Puritans*, 1:315). While masters of experimental theology may analyze the phenomenon of hypocrisy insightfully and in depth, it is perhaps poets who portray it best. The hypocrite delights to fish in "Holy-Waters" but "selfe is all thine aim; not God thine end" (Taylor, *Poems*, 412). Edwards himself remained very circumspect in his theoretical statements. He basically considered any relationship with God that did not come from the heart to be hypocritical (VI, 545). On the other hand, he provided marvelous descriptions of the way in which the religious and moral practice of hypocrites becomes weak and cold (VII, 430–31).

95. See *supra*, p. 71.

gravity of a violation depends on the importance of the precept it offends. Luther violently denounced the celebration of the Eucharist by unworthy priests because "the nobler the sacrament, the greater the damage caused by its abuse,"[96] and if the Gospel sinner's transgression is so great, it is because he is sinning against the mercy of God who gave and delivered up his own Son for us (22, 279). The proper offence of the sinner in Zion is scoffing at and refusing the word of God and, in times when the Spirit is especially at work, it is because of this that infidelity and apostasy are virtually unpardonable (see 19, 294–5). Indeed, the supreme sin of hypocrites is their sin against the Spirit, which is unforgivable insofar as it is perpetrated against the gracious and merciful function of the Deity itself. According to the teaching of Protestant theology—and here we see a genuine consensus from the orthodoxy of the seventeenth century to Hegel—Christ's statement in the Gospel according to Matthew wasn't so much about an offense against a particular person of the Deity as it was about opposition to that most divine of God's activities. For Polanus, the Sin against the Spirit does not represent an offence against the divine essence—by virtue of the fact that the Holy Spirit is God—nor against the person of the Spirit, but against the Spirit as the believer's source of illumination and sanctification. It is the supreme sin because it opposes the Holy Spirit's proper function, which is to illuminate minds, engender faith and consecrate the whole man to God.[97] And this sin is unpardonable—said Hegel—because it opposes the Spirit, i.e., the only power who knows how to efface all that has come to pass and, consequently, to remit sins.[98]

Saint Thomas Aquinas himself defined the unpardonable sin as hatred of God himself,[99] while for Calvin it did not concern "one particular lapse or two" but rather a "universal revolt" against God.[100] For his part, Edwards frequently returned to the gravest of all sins, the sin against the Spirit. While he certainly thought that even a partially complete description was nowhere to be found in Scripture (24, 903), he believed that, in a more general sense, this sin designates any offence against divine things *per se* (see 13, 518) and, in a stricter, more precise sense, it could be defined as an offence against

---

96. Luther, *Ein Sermon von dem Hochwürdigen Sakrament des Heiligen Wahren Leichnams Christi*, Werke, 2:751.

97. Heppe, *Dogmatics*, 354.

98. Hegel, *Phänomenologie des Geistes*, Gesammelte Werke, 9:360–61.

99. Saint Thomas Aquinas, *Summa Theologiæ*, 2–2. 34. 2. co., ad. 1. As for the Puritans, they were not unanimous in professing this traditional view. For example, see Baxter, "There are Haters of God of a lower Rank," *The Unreasonableness of Infidelity*, *Practical Works*, 2:300.

100. Calvin, *Institutes*, 3. 3. 23.

God and the "very loveliness" of God (13, 429). The sin against the Spirit—we read in the great Miscellany 706—is "a sin of the most heinous kind with regard to the object against whom it is committed" because it is "a sin committed primarily and most directly against God." This is not a transgression against the presence of the Holy Spirit alone, because a person who revolts against the Holy Spirit—both against himself and his work and office—turns against the whole Trinity. On the one hand, the Holy Spirit is the ultimate end and proper good of all the operations of the other two persons and, on the other hand, acts in their name and represents the very essence of their Being and action. Since all of God's operations, and especially the sanctification of believers, are consummated in the Holy Spirit, it follows that opposing the Spirit is to oppose the entire Godhead. Reproaching God without distinguishing a person or reproaching both the Father and the Son is a lesser offence, because what is being maligned, vilified, attacked, and blasphemed by the sin against the Spirit is the very excellence, beauty and goodness of the whole Divine Being (18, 322–4).

This is an attempt to explain the sin against the Spirit in objective terms, i.e., in terms of the excellence of the reality offended. However, Jonathan Edwards did not forget that theologians have always stressed this sin's subjective factors, i.e., the transgressing subject's specific state. Calvin, for example, centers his description almost exclusively on such subjective moments. The sin against the Spirit is nothing other than the offence which "proceeding from desparate fury cannot be ascribed to infirmity,"[101] because it is the work of "willful apostates who . . . fall away from faith in the Gospel." And the Apostle, notes the Reformer, expressly adds the word "willingly," to characterize the apostasy of those who "with deliberate impiety" have choked "the light of the Spirit."[102] Notwithstanding his seemingly objectivistic descriptions of the elements that constitute the unpardonable sin, Edwards's developments demonstrate such a highly formal vision of the unpardonable sin that those same descriptions made it possible to translate the objectivistic versions of this doctrine into a morality of the total subject.

In Miscellany 706, Edwards explains that the sin against the Spirit is the most odious of transgressions because of its object. He states through the Miscellany that this object is God, not "undistinguishedly" but in his Spirit who, in turn, is to be understood not just in a purely ontological sense

---

101. Calvin, *Institutes*, 3. 3. 21. Saint Augustine linked the unpardonable sin to final impenitence (*Retractions*, 1. 18. 7). For Saint Thomas Aquinas, it was deliberate sin as such (*Summa Theologiæ*, 2–2. 34. 2. ad. 1). For Luther, it amounted to turning against divine truth and the Holy Spirit "mit offenen augen und auffgerechten hals [with open eyes and stiff necks]" (*Von der Sunde widder den Heiligen Geist, Werke*, 28:15).

102. Calvin, *Institutes*, 3. 3. 21, 23.

as a particular person of the Godhead but in terms of his work of illumination and sanctification (18, 327). Elsewhere, Edwards also states that "it is a sin of the highest kind, as 'tis committed against the greatest and most glorious objective light . . . the glorious light of the Gospel" (18, 324). This objective light of the Spirit radiates through the Gospel, and is fittingly termed "objective" because it illuminates man's mind and conscience. The aim and illuminating work of the Spirit is not only to put the minds and hearts of believers in the presence of this light, but we should rather say that this illuminating work is nothing other than communicating the light to our mind. The objective and external mind is *eo ipso* subjective and internal, and it is consequently understood that the transgression against the Spirit's illuminating work is not merely an offence against an external reality—even though it be the greatest and most holy—but is also an immanent, moral state of the subject. Opposition to this external light, which turns into "blackness of darkness" (22, 279), extends to violating the subject's own conscience, so that the sin against the Spirit should not be considered as the supreme instance of a universal casuistry but as an abbreviated expression of the will's deviant state.

A more detailed analysis of the Edwardsian developments reinforces and illustrates this formal vision and conception stemming from a morality of the total subject. Edwards who, as we recall, defined an act's moral character with respect to its circumstances (13, 200), remarked that the sin against the Spirit is the highest kind of sin against God by virtue of the agent's circumstances and also emphasized the fact that it was not merely opposition to external, objective light but also to "the plain dictates and clear light of conscience" (18, 324). A vicious soul undoubtedly has subtle ways to act against its own conscience without it being absolutely plain and clear. A man may have sufficient light to note a given situation but a vicious opposition of his mind could "keep him from owning it." He may be "inwardly sensible" of a thing but "he does as it were willfully stop the mouth of his understanding" (13, 519). Because this tortuous malice concludes a kind of alliance with the superficial levels of the conscience, a man can resist the divine calls which nonetheless echo in the innermost recesses of his heart (18, 324–25). The outcome of this Edwardsian emphasis on opposition to the inward operations of the mind and to the voice of one's own conscience was to illustrate traditional teaching: a man sins against the Spirit "from [a] full will, from a settled malice, with a rational, deliberate, full design" (13, 450). This is a sin of the most inexcusable sort because it is the most willful. It is not committed out of fear or expectation of profit, i.e., for anything other than itself.[103] It is so deliberate and willful that it happens almost without external motivation and, so to speak, spontaneously (L. *sponte*) by itself (18, 324).

Edwards repeatedly stated the unpardonable sin's deep-rootedness in the subject's inmost core and its radically immanent character proper to man, yet considered it essential that this sin, which is never mere omission but true commission, be completed in and by outward acts (18, 322–23). In fact, this essential element of exteriority is not, at first glance, opposed to the action's profoundly inward and intimate character. The visible and outward condition of the misconduct and evil will only serves to illustrate the explicit and deliberate character of the moral intention. A deliberate volition is not a vague desire but an act of the will carried to its external end. This same essential exteriority of the unpardonable sin shows that its author belongs to the visible church.[104] Those who voluntarily entered into a covenant with God and believe they accepted Jesus Christ as their Savior are in very close proximity to the "objective light," which only serves to aggravate their lapse. That is why those who hold an exalted position in the visible church, as was the case with the Pharisees, are especially susceptible to this supreme transgression (18, 325). When meditating on the Revival, Edwards thought he could say that "no sort of men in the world will be so low in Hell, as ungodly ministers" (4, 507). After all, they best fit the definition of sinners in Zion![105]

---

103. This is rebellion "for the sake of rebelling" (13, 525). Here Edwards is echoing Calvin (*Institutes*, 3. 3. 22) and dogmaticians (Heppe, *Dogmatics*, 357–58).

104. See Heppe, *Dogmatics*, 355.

105. The aggravation of the sinner in Zion's situation is understood from the general principle that his proximity to a superior reality makes what is already odious in himself even more so. The filthiness of a toad is more abominable for being joined with life—which is in itself excellent—than the same filthiness would be in lifeless matter. That is why the Church of Rome is, compared to Muslims and pagans, as a viper to "lifeless ... matter of the same shape" (13, 186). This is the principle which explains why "a very great part of those that sit under the Gospel, do so abuse it that it only proves an occasion of their far more aggravated damnation" (4, 393). Ever since the life and death of Christ, i.e., since the time of probation has passed, the sins of the believers have been aggravated (13, 309) and, without the redemption, the transgressions of the reprobate would have been less culpable (V, 368). Speaking of those in an unregenerate state who give themselves over to religious exercises, Edwards said that the practice of the sacraments and preaching, which are "spiritual privileges," becomes a curse for them. It would have been better for these men to have died as quickly as possible. It would have been better for them to live in hell than on Earth and, when dead, they will wish they had never enjoyed the light of the Gospel: "They will wish that Christ had never come into the world to die for sinners so as to give men any opportunity to be saved. They will wish that God had cast off fallen man as He did the fallen angels and never had made him the offer of a Savior" (X, 132). Those who now live "under the full blaze of gospel light" are more guilty than if Christ had not come, and even more guilty than

7. Common graces

Rather than going against the logic of a morality of the total subject, the analysis of the unpardonable sin against the Spirit showed that the aggravation of this offence because its author is under the Gospel administration is actually a brilliant illustration of it. Because sinners in Zion sin against greater light and the clarity of their own conscience, their sinful state is radicalized.[106] However, Puritan preachers did not content themselves with merely warning Christians about the greater seriousness of their sins and their added risk of lapsing. They not only taught that the sins of Christians arouse God's wrath more than those of heathens (see IV, 438), but were not reluctant to conjecture that Christians could do evil insofar as they intended to do good. If we are to believe Leibniz, the teaching that the virtues of pagans are splendid vices is only "a sally of St. Augustine's which has no foundation in holy Scripture" itself,[107] but the Puritans went even further than Augustine. They did not stop quoting the Bible passages which say that the prayers of the ungodly are an abomination to the Lord and, of course, understood these ungodly to be Christians or, more precisely, Gospel hypocrites. "For whatsoever is not of faith is sin," exclaimed the Apostle Paul[108] and, once it became a centerpiece of the theology of grace, this expression became a particular favorite to apply to the religious exercises of the sinners in Zion. The Scriptures charge that all men are sinners,[109] but we could also

those who opposed him during his lifetime (Hopkins, *The True State and Character of the Unregenerate*, Works, 3:308; see also *supra*, p. 221 n.93). Without the redemption, they never could have had opportunity to commit "such amazingly aggravated crimes" as they do now and of which the devils themselves are incapable (Hopkins, *The True State and Character of the Unregenerate*, Works, 3:306). This entire theologoical view is summarized by this reminder in Prov 15:8, "The sacrifice of the wicked is an abomination to the Lord" (Calvin, *Institutes*, 3. 14. 8; see 10, 379; 19, 529; 24, 251, etc.).

106. See 12, 219–20. If we are to believe Descartes, this is similar to opposing our own conscience, which makes us guilty of believing without the illumination of grace: "Let us take the case of an infidel who is destitute of all supernatural grace and has no knowledge of the doctrines which we Christians believe to have been revealed to us by God. If, despite the fact that these doctrines are obscure to him, he is induced to embrace them by fallacious arguments, I make bold to assert that he will not on that account be a true believer, but will instead be committing a sin by not using his reason correctly" ("Replies to Second Set of Objections," 7:148). As F. Alquié observed, for Descartes, "croire sans avoir la grâce, c'est pécher contre la raison [To believe without having grace is to sin against reason]" (Descartes, *Œuvres Philosophiques*, 2:574n.2).

107. Leibniz, *Theodicy*, 3. 259.

108. Romans 14:23 in 10, 487.

109. P. Melanchthon, "Evangelium arguit omnes homines, quod sint sub peccato [For the Gospel convicts all men that they are under sin]" (qtd. in Barth, *Kirchliche Dogmatik*, 4. 1. 439).

add that many are hypocrites who immerse themselves in religious practices that double their guilt. Acting against the light aggravates the lapse of which we are guilty and destroys all the true goodness and value of our will and action. If the Reformation succeeded in partly clarifying the essential moral inspiration of Christianity, it was in making the principle even clearer that we cannot do good if our intention is evil. However, later on and especially since Calvin, it has been understood that it is not enough to teach the impossibility of doing good with an intention that is not good in itself or the sterility of works born of an unregenerate heart; we also need to envisage a situation where good, so to speak, becomes evil in direct proportion to its "good" character. Certainly, nothing is nobler for a Christian than performing religious acts. Nonetheless, praying, attending the sacraments and studying the Scriptures only increases the sin of a person engaging in these exercises if his act is not in radical conformity with the Gospel or with a total submission of his heart to God. In this context, works of piety become snares of the Devil; therefore, you need to pray for the ability to repent of your repentance and beg pardon for your prayers because[110]—and this is an essential theme of all Protestant theology—religion itself becomes the leading place for those sins that are the most dangerous for the Christian.[111]

However, before discussing prayer that is an abomination to God, we need to explain the possibility of Gospel hypocrisy itself, i.e., the fact that, even under grace, a person can commit unremitted, unpardoned sins. Hebrews sets the unforgivable sin—the supreme sin of hypocrites—in the context of apostasy and only attributes it to people who have already accepted the Gospel. For their part, dogmaticians teach that only those who have already tasted the heavenly gift and become partakers of the Holy Spirit can sin against the Spirit.[112] Moreover, we know that, in orthodox Calvinism, justification is not only immediate and total but also irrevocable. In other words, any qualification or limitation on justifying grace is rejected. It is irresistible. It justifies the faithful irrevocably and provides the gift of final perseverance. If this is so, then a very simple explanation for Gospel hypocrisy, i.e., the Christian's infidelity, can be proposed. The grace enjoyed was not justifying and did not grant a spirit of adoption and regeneration. It was not truly redeeming grace but only a gift of the Spirit "common to the

---

110. Hooker, *Soules Humiliation*, 186.

111. Compare with "das Evangelium keine argeren Feinde hat, denn was hochverständige, vernünftige, weise, tugendsame, heilige Leute vor der Welt sind [the Gospel has no worse enemy than what highly intelligent, sensible, wise, virtuous, holy people are to the world]" (Luther, *Hauspostille, Werke*, 52:71).

112. Heppe, *Dogmatics*, 355. For the new birth by the Spirit as a necessary condition of the sin against the Spirit, see Müller, *Christian Doctrine of Sin*, 2:423–24.

elect and the reprobate." Mastricht, whom Edwards had studied at length, defined the apostasy of the hypocrite as being from the truth and "common gifts of the Holy Spirit."[113] Edwards himself conjectured that the Pharisees had succumbed to the unpardonable sin after having had much of "the common influences of the Spirit" (24, 903).

In the simple and colorful language of S. Willard, "common mercy," i.e., common grace, "only visits the prisoner and gives him some supports, but leaves him there; whereas Grace opens his prison, and brings him out of it, and ceaseth not till it hath possessed him of eternal life."[114] What Willard expressed in everyday language—the question of common grace or rather the difference between common grace and saving grace—is an essential issue in the reflections of Jonathan Edwards. Nothing provoked the Edwardsian controversy more than this Arminian thesis: God could not ultimately refuse saving grace to those who had sincerely tried to apply the common grace imparted to them.[115] For Arminians, there is therefore a kind of continuity and even affinity between these two graces while Calvinists ascribe the source of all heresies to this very absence of a distinction between common grace, and saving grace.[116]

The issue of the difference between these two types of grace has continued to cause controversy throughout the entire history of Christianity, beginning with the confusion and bewilderment felt by Christians in Antiquity on seeing the troubling spectacle of infidelity of many of their brethren. They were confused and scandalized by the relapse into sin and apostasy of their coreligionists and did not understand the seeming sterility of grace. It was Augustine who recognized and developed this issue in theology by reframing it as a radical refusal to recognize the presence of saving grace, in those without evidence of final perseverance. Augustine quoted Saint John: "For if they had been of us, they would have continued with us" (1 John 2:19). Augustine wrote that the non-persevering are not numbered among the predestinated. Their apostasy proves that they were not

---

113. Heppe, *Dogmatics*, 355. This is "wild and common knowledge," as opposed to the "gracious and sanctifying garden knowledge" of true saints (Hooker, *Saints Dignitie and Dutie*, 206).

114. Willard, *Divinity*, 271–2.

115. Compare with, "I can't suppose, that any one . . . Who at all times, faithfully improves the *common Grace* he has, *that* is to *say,* is diligent in attending on the appointed Means of Grace with a desire to profit thereby; . . . and in a work, who walks up to his Light, to the utmost of his Power, shall perish for want of special and saving Grace," (Phillips, *Orthodox Christian*, 74 in W. Walker, "Jonathan Edwards," in Levin, *Jonathan Edwards*, 96).

116. Jones, *Shattered Synthesis*, 25. See also, "many will finally perish for their confounding common and saving knowledge," (Parsons, *Sixty Sermons*, 2:422.

truly children of God, even though they might have appeared otherwise.[117] Non-perseverance shows that, in spite of its seeming intensity and sincerity, faith may only be a temporary gift, "a hedge faith, a bramble faith."[118] Grace, in the soul is "like a spark of fire, which has been lighted upon an icy pavement, and is blown upon by all the winds of heaven,"[119] which sweep away and extinguish it (12, 308). Faith does not arise here from a spirit of regeneration and adoption, but is only a superficial and purely intellectual phenomenon.[120] The troubling truth, and here it is Calvin speaking, is that "the reprobate are sometimes affected in a way similar to the elect." They are given "a temporary faith" not because "they truly perceive the power of spiritual grace," but because "the Lord, the better to convict them, and leave them without excuse, instils into their minds such a sense of his goodness."[121] As for the elect, God "effectively seals in them the grace of his adoption.... But in this there is nothing to prevent an inferior operation of the Spirit from taking its course in the reprobate." They are not partakers of the same regeneration as the elect "but ... seem to have a principle of faith in common with them."[122]

Calvin dramatically describes this situation in which God "only gives them [the reprobate] a manifestation of his present mercy" by temporarily pardoning them.[123] The virtue of men is only "smoke."[124] They live "for a time

---

117. Saint Augustine, "Admonition and Grace," 8. 19–9. 22. To prove that final perseverance is a work of grace alone and cannot be conjectured or deduced in advance, Augustine told the story of a widower who, after living a chaste life in an exemplary manner for a very long time, ended up taking a concubine at 84 years of age (*Against Julian*, 3. 11. 22).

118. Shepard, *The Sound Believer*, Works, 1:198, in 2, 366n.2.

119. Sainte-Beuve, *Port-Royal*, 1:378.

120. Heppe, *Dogmatik*, 423.

121. Calvin, *Institutes*, 3. 2. 11. This thought was considered particularly blasphemous by Catholic controverters (Möhler, *Symbolik oder Darstellung der Dogmatischen Gegensätze der Katholiken und Protestanten*, 3:122–23).

122. Calvin, *Institutes*, 3. 2. 11.

123. Calvin, *Institutes*, 3. 2. 11. Jansenius spoke of soft attitudes towards good and vague desires. These are but inefficacious "little graces" (Laporte, *La doctrine de Port-Royal*, 2. 1. 404, 408). "Temporary believers" are hypocrites (Walker, *Creeds and Platforms*, 385n.) whose faith lacks proper finality (Heppe, *Dogmatik*, 422).

124. Calvin, *Quatre Sermons*, Opera, 8, 396–97.

... well and faithfully,"[125] they have, so to speak, "sober fits,"[126] but their state can still only be seen in light of Saint John. Notwithstanding any evidence to the contrary, Edwards himself was firmly convinced that hypocrites are not imbued with a true spirit of prayer (VII, 433) and never perform good works (18, 498): if they fall away after having shown external evidence of new birth, fervent piety and virtue, it is "a sign they never were risen with Christ" (2, 391).[127] As N. Emmons said with his habitual bluntness: "the finally impenitent never had one right affection, nor one good intention."[128] Now, if a fall from good works and fervent religious exercises, and especially a final impenitence, is striking evidence of false conversion, how can this essential judgment be made while the hypocrite is still zealously practicing his faith? What should we do when we encounter this troubling imitation of goodness and these devious ways the Devil mimics God? How should we act—or rather react—when faced with the similarity between the state of the justified and that of those who enjoy only the effects of "the lowest operations of God"? The works of common grace, and those of saving grace, are often quasi-identical because, after all, "nothing is so like charity as greed"![129]

S. Stoddard had already taught that common graces are a kind of image of authentic saving graces, i.e., their types.[130] T. Shepard spoke of "shadows,"[131] and Edwards pointed to common ground in Christian spirituality when he remarked that "false spirits . . . mimic the operations of the Spirit of God" (2, 141). The reprobate, wrote Calvin, "have signs of calling similar to those given to the elect."[132] Perkins warned his readers of "the similitude and affinity between the temporary professor of the Gospel and the

---

125. Saint Augustine, "Admonition and Grace," 13. 40. The state of the unregenerate who nonetheless live as "civil men" can be viewed as a sort of parallel extending over their entire life of temporary faith. Grace restrains their wickedness and even imposes seemingly good behavior on them. They are like "wolves chained up, tame devils, swine in a fair meadow," (Shepard, *The Sincere Convert*, Works, 1:57).

126. Smith, *Select Discourses*, 14.

127. They only had a "temporary regard for Christ," (*Book of Controversies, Ms.*, 111) a "common temporary faith" (8, 359).

128. Emmons, *The Nature, Extent and Influence of the Moral Depravity of Sinners*, Works, 4:527.

129. Pascal, *Pensées*, 615.

130. Stoddard, *Guide to Christ*, 31–2. For a "foolish and maladjusted imitation" and for Satan as the "inverted figure of the hermeneutical Jesus," see the admirable developments of Vincent, *L'herméneutique du discours théologique*, 384–5, 918.

131. Shepard, *The Parable of the Ten Virgins*, Works, 2:282.

132. Calvin, *Institutes*, 3. 24. 7.

true professor of the same"[133] and Shepard said that "whatever is in a godly man, the likeness and similitude of it is for a time in an hypocrite."[134] The extreme similarity between the outward manifestations of these two administrations of grace, disallows any hope of making concrete and empirical distinctions and definitions. Neither the intensity or vigor of religious feelings, nor their truly inward character, nor the fact that they are accompanied by the extraordinary gifts of the Spirit, miracles, visions, or prophecies allow us to conclude that saving grace, is present. As already seen in the case of moral sincerity, the vigor and intensity of feelings are ultimately only material criteria, while extraordinary gifts—which only express the bends and changes in the natural operations of the mind and body—may very well only come from the world of nature. Strength of feeling and extraordinary phenomena are evidence of an astonishing intensification of our moral and religious affections, which may indeed cause feelings of greater piety, although they only elaborate on and embellish given mental content. They are still not evidence of an irruption of transcendence[135] or, as the *Treatise on the Religious Affections* put it, they did not arise by virtue of the "new simple idea"[136] of grace.

The reprobate may have charismata which far exceed the usual gifts of nature.[137] "Common graces," wrote J. Cotton, "many times chokes all the hypocrites within the bosom of the church . . . they prayed to God . . . they prophesied . . . and they were able to cast out devils," and yet they remained "workers of iniquity."[138] Extraordinary gifts are common to the elect and the ungodly (8, 153). For example, miraculous healings come—without a shadow of a doubt—from the Holy Spirit but are only images of the Spirit's work of sanctification in souls (18, 236). We could say that God throws extraordinary gifts "to pigs and dogs," as he did in the case of Balaam, Saul, and Judah. As the purely spiritual influences that do the work of sanctification,

---

133. Perkins, *A Treatise Tending unto a Declaration, Workes*, 1:380.

134. Shepard, *The Parable of the Ten Virgins, Works*, 2:363. This position is not proper to Protestant preaching. According to D. Soto, there is no moral act where the likeness of its substance may be found in a man who lacks grace (*Grâce, Dictionnaire de Théologie Catholique*, 6, 1585). Saint John of the Cross drew from a very ancient source when he recalled the similarity of the miracles performed by Moses and Pharaoh's magicians, respectively ("Dark Night," 2. 23. 7).

135. Unlike the gifts of salvific (i.e., saving) faith, the benefits of common grace are bestowed according to the fixed laws of the succession of events and are "statedly connected with preceding things in the creature, so that they are in a sense dependent on the creature" (13, 523–24).

136. See *infra*, p. 308ss.

137. Heppe, *Dogmatics*, 185.

138. Cotton, *Christ the Fountaine of Life* in Miller and Johnson, *Puritans*, 1:332.

God reserves them for the elect. He gives them saving grace and "to have grace in the heart is an higher privilege than the blessed Virgin herself had, in having the body of the Second Person in the Trinity conceived in her womb, by the power of the Highest overshadowing her" (4, 279). In the latter case, even the begetting of Jesus Christ is but the exercise of a natural power of the Spirit. While it's certainly an operation of the Spirit that confers common grace on men, this operation still falls under the relationships that God maintains with nature.

Aside from extraordinary gifts, i.e., various physiological and psychological phenomena,[139] "common illuminations" also include "an ideal apprehension of the things of religion with respect to what is natural in them" (18, 465). In other words, theoretical or speculative knowledge (18, 463), as well as sensible and therefore existential knowledge or experience of the wonders of religion, also come under common grace. Having witnessed the lively religious emotions of the Great Awakening, Jonathan Edwards knew all too well that the Spirit can not only cause his common influences to be felt externally but also internally, and not just in the understanding of men but also in their affections (see 4, 379). When addressing this issue, Edwards benefited greatly from T. Shepard's remarkable descriptions on the operations of common grace. With verve and insight, Shepard described this world of "fruitless graces"[140] that only offer the Christian "a dry and common Christ."[141] The Spirit may very well perform works in men's hearts which, though internal, nonetheless remain common operations.[142] He may water the soul with spiritual and yet common mercies, and may communicate genuine inner and yet common knowledge of the Gospel to men. Notwithstanding the strength and vigor of these experiences, they are "dead graces"[143] and, generally speaking, we could define common graces as "lifeless knowledge."[144] This is close to the Calvinist doctrine of purely historical and notional grace,[145] while the uniqueness of Sheperd's descriptions is their amazing insightfulness in discerning the absence of genuine saving grace,

---

139. Compare with "such childish things . . . as the miraculous gifts of the Spirit" (15, 278), "faith of miracles" (20, 524).

140. Shepard, *The Parable of the Ten Virgins*, Works, 2:277.

141. Shepard, *The Sound Believer*, Works, 1:208.

142. Shepard, *The Sincere Convert*, Works, 1:61.

143. Shepard, *The Sound Believer*, Works, 1:136, 218, 241–42.

144. Shepard, *The Parable of the Ten Virgins*, Works, 2:473.

145. Regarding the convergence between common grace and morality: "The legal moralist is not only a stranger to, but an enemy of this faith. He acknowledgeth not her faith but one that is Historical, and is contained in the assent given to the articles of religion" (Willard, *Morality Not to be Relied on for Life*).

even in the midst of vigorous and powerful religious emotions, and therefore in the world of "experimental religion" itself.

Shepard wrote that the Spirit can flood the hypocrite's soul with "awakening grace," thereby giving him spiritual prosperity and refreshment for a moment. This grace is not obtained by imitation, education or moral persuasion; it is inculcated by the physical operations of the Spirit. This grace illuminates the unjustified, giving them admirable experiences and affections but not regenerating them.[146] Some may believe that, if overflowing religious affections might very well not be genuine signs of saving grace, then humility and a sincere recognition of spiritual poverty should, on the other hand, be evidence of a person's justified state. Shepard thought nothing of the sort, because hypocrites can be taken in by others and they themselves may even mistake the mere discovery of their moral misery for the evangelical spirit of poverty. While humility is usually a sign of true religious feelings, seeing and observing corruption in the heart and subsequently being somewhat affected by this discovery in no way proves the presence of a true spirit of poverty. The realization that we are nothing, that all we have is impure, comes only from a simple understanding of our effective situation. This is mere theoretical and external knowledge which the devils themselves possess to even the highest degree.[147] It's an unhealthy illusion to think that true sanctification means not being able to discover any trace of evil in ourselves or that true purity is not being able to observe anything in ourselves but impurity. Poverty of spirit is a grace peculiar to those to whom the kingdom of heaven belongs, while not having grace in themselves is the common situation of all those excluded from the kingdom. If merely noting the absence of grace was a sign of true poverty of spirit, then the relatively common gift of a kind of clairvoyance with respect to our spiritual state would become a special grace and our state—devoid of grace—would itself become a principle of the special grace of adoption, regeneration and salvation.[148] This discovery might provoke sadness, a despondent spirit and terror but yet, in itself, does not lead to the healing of our condition. Nor is having a kind of humility—whether theoretical or at the level of their feelings—any guarantee of sanctification for hypocrites[149] because sanctification never concerns a mere refinement or change of their natural state

---

146. Shepard, *The Parable of the Ten Virgins*, Works, 2:452.

147. Shepard, *The Parable of the Ten Virgins*, Works, 2:458–59.

148. Shepard, *The Parable of the Ten Virgins*, Works, 2:462–63.

149. The truly poor in spirit "did not only see a want, but feel a need of bread; I die without it" (Ps 40:9, 10 in Shepard, *The Parable of the Ten Virgins*, Works, 2:464. For an in-depth analysis of humility and conviction, see 2, 331–32.

but rather a radical transformation of it. It is not a material change, however powerful it may be, but a formal and necessary existential change.

Nourished by Shepard's teaching, the Edwardsian developments essentially affirmed that—in his common operations—the Holy Spirit does not infuse any new supernatural principles into the soul but is content to simply assist and reinforce natural principles and forces. The light that the Holy Spirit communicates is not essentially different from what the soul could have obtained in and of itself, but is simply stronger and more intense. In these operations, the Spirit acts only as "an extrinsic occasional agent," does not unite himself to man, does not communicate with man according to his nature, nor live in him (17, 411). Common operations certainly originate from the Spirit of God, but still do not partake of his divinity (21, 180). After all, the movement over the waters at the beginning of creation was also an operation of the Spirit (21, 192)! Common operations are gifts and not virtues of the Spirit (2, 199). Common grace doesn't bestow anything above nature upon those who receive it because it doesn't impart grace (17, 410)! This expression is taken from a sermon and, as such, is less terminologically precise. Nonetheless, it is still very characteristic of a theology in which the common operations of the Spirit are only related to grace in a very general sense of that term and, in the religious sphere, are ultimately only manifestations of the general assistance that God provides to all his creatures.

8. The prayers of hypocrites

Throughout all of these definitions and descriptions, Edwards unceasingly underlined the essentially *natural* character of the Spirit's common works. He frequently compared them with moral sincerity,[150] i.e., the insufficient efforts of an unjustified person in purely religious matters. In the great Augustinian and Calvinist tradition, works of common grace are compared to the "civil ornaments" that are the virtues of the unregenerate.[151] These works only relate to the general grace[152] that underlies the general calling sparked by the outward preaching of the Gospel[153] and serve more to restrain evil in the unregenerate than lead them towards sanctification. Common grace will be withdrawn from souls at death (8, 367), although even now it only

---

150. See 12, 222, 230; "gracious charity" vs. "moral bounty" in 17, 384.
151. Willard, *Divinity*, 239, also see 9.
152. Calvin, *Institutes*, 2. 2. 17.
153. Calvin, *Institutes*, 3. 24. 8.

properly represents man's fallen state.[154] In spite of any appearances to the contrary, the external manifestations of common grace do not represent anything radically new in terms of the possibilities of man's fallen nature because, in Edwardsian Calvinism—and this is essential—common grace not only differs from saving grace in degree but also in kind and nature (20, 327–8).[155] The new religious affections that can arise under the influence of common grace are "nothing but nature extraordinarily acted" (2, 209) and have no continuity with truly gracious affections. There can be no intermediate or middle way between being and nothingness, life and death, Christ and Satan (12, 393).

The internal logic of this theology seeks to rigorously separate these two types of grace but doesn't merely note and demonstrate differences; it also implies that they be declared in radical opposition to one another. This requirement had already been perfectly understood before Edwards by a man named S. Stoddard. As a theologian influenced by the Augustinian doctrine that the virtues of pagans are hidden vices, this predecessor (and grandfather) of Edwards in Northampton said: "There is an opposition between saving grace and common grace . . . common graces are lusts, and do oppose saving grace." Consequently, "the man that hath but common grace . . . sets himself against that way of salvation which God prescribes." Edwards quoted this passage in his great polemic text against S. Williams to justify his refusal to admit any to communion who could not testify to a conversion experience.[156] He not only felt that common grace lacked any spiritual experience (2, 204) and was therefore powerless to nourish true piety, but also thought it might even be positively harmful to true piety and could aggravate the guilt of those performing their religious exercises. He believed that this aggravation is in direct proportion to the strength and richness of common affections and convictions. Sinners living under the administration of the means of grace are habitually more hardened in sin

---

154. Common grace—from which natural and common religious affections arise (see 2, 217)—is used, in a broader sense, as a synonym for moral piety (12, 222) and the common influences of the Spirit are portrayed as falling under the universe of "restraining grace" (V, 308–10). Elsewhere, common religion—though associated with moral sincerity—regains its religious specificity and is condemned for its "transient and vanishing" quality (12, 415). Whether it refers to moral works or piety, the adjective "common" ultimately connotes the unregenerate sphere.

155. Compare with, "saving faith differs from all common faith in its nature, kind and essence" (W 2, 632), and the difference isn't simply gradual (25, 500–501). It is the Devil who "makes Civility to pass for Grace," (Taylor, *Poems*, 443).

156. Stoddard, *Concerning Conversion*, 9, in 12, 403, see 12, 397, etc. See also 21, 154.

than pagans,[157] while some individuals under the ecclesial administration of the means of grace are not only dead but are, so to speak, "doubly so."[158] Just as the advent of the visible church, on a historical and community level, aggravated the world's opposition to the light, so receiving the fruits of common grace stirred up the hypocrite's hostility to God and divine things.

The guilty character of religious exercises can be understood either from the viewpoint of their agent or of God. We could say along with Calvin that it is "a perverse mode of prayer"[159] or that the preaching of the word itself could harden even more.[160] Edwards, and especially his disciples, returned unceasingly to this theme. In a note on Leviticus 10:1, which tells of fire "coming out from the Lord" to consume the priests Nadab and Abihu for having "offered strange fire before the Lord," Edwards used a remarkable series of contrasting adjectives. He successively rendered "holy" fire as "profane," "common," and "strange" fire (24, 252–53). In this context, "strange" has affinities with the *opus alienum*, the "strange work" of God, which does not depend on God Himself in this world created by him and is ultimately evil.[161] Consequently, "common" is not only "profane," i.e., not simply what is not holy *stricto sensu* but in fact evil and therefore sinful. Ergo, the fact of having offered a sacrifice to God—of having performed a religious act that could not please him—had very justly provoked the destruction of its authors. It is within this universe of thought—one in which the flames of an irregular sacrifice can burst back upon the very people offering them—that the Edwardsian *theologoumenon* and the positions stemming from it need to be understood.

Edwards wanted to re-establish a personal experience of conversion as a basic criterion for receiving the body of the Lord because, like the poet, he believed that anyone partaking of the sacrament without being reconciled with the Lord tears "the sign" from what it signifies.[162] Of course, the New Theology brought the "sallies of Saint Augustine" to an intense climax. N. Emmons said that the piety of an unregenerate person is positively evil.[163] S. Hopkins warned his readers that it would be better for an unregen-

---

157. Sermon on Matt. 11:21 in Gerstner, *Steps to Salvation*, 46.

158. Gerstner, *Steps to Salvation*, 55.

159. Calvin, *Institutes*, 3. 5. 10; compare with 12, 301.

160. Calvin, *Institutes*, 3. 24. 12.

161. See *supra*, p. 145ss.

162. Taylor, *Poems*, 275. Citing E. Taylor in this context is essential because he was vigorously opposed to Stoddard's lax practice of admitting all Christians to the Lord's Supper, a practice that Edwards would later abolish. For the Taylor-Stoddard controversy, see the more recent *Edward Taylor vs. Solomon Stoddard*.

163. Emmons, *Giving the Heart to God a Reasonable Duty*, Works, 5:171.

erate man to kill his parents than to pray earnestly for converting grace.[164] Edwards himself had already explained that, regardless of what they might do, the wicked can only perform and accomplish evil. They think that they can lessen their guilt by praying and doing pious readings but, in reality, they only add to their sin (VI, 517). In his time and in a more psychological vein, Calvin had outlined the torments of the reprobate when they invoke the mercy of God,[165] whereas Jonathan Edwards and the Edwardsians always emphasized the objective dangers concerning salvation that threaten the prayers of hypocrites. Unregenerate sinners—hypocrites—may, after a "false conversion" (VII, 434), devote themselves to works of piety, exalt the wonders of the Lord and celebrate his redeeming grace. In reality, however, they are only sinking themselves deeper into evil. Just as someone can reason correctly[166] but goes further astray by starting from a false premise, a person who acts piously and partakes in the sacraments while in an unregenerate state aggravates his sin. Hypocrites perform religious exercises which, in the final analysis, are carried by "the energy of their own self-love" (2, 217n.6). They believe they are getting ever nearer to God yet, in reality, are getting further way from him (19, 519) and becoming more hypocritical. If this is so, why pray? Ever since Saint Jerome, it had been repeatedly said that it would be better to sin openly than to fake holiness,[167] but what reason and justification can be given for the religious obligations of the unregenerate?

In most cases, an empirical answer is given without resolving the theoretical problem. According to the Savoy Declaration, works done by unregenerate men "cannot please God . . . and yet their neglect of them is more sinful, and displeasing to God."[168] As J. Cotton said, "Hypocrites give God part of his due, the outward man, but the profane person giveth God neither outward nor inward man."[169] Undoubtedly, good works that originate from

164. Dexter, *Literary Diary of Ezra Stiles*, 2:115. C. G. Finney appears to have demonstrated some progress with respect to this position, because he only taught the *moral equivalence* of parricide and helping the poor out of mere benevolence, or of becoming a pirate and preaching the Gospel if it did not originate from a "regenerated" nature (Hodge, *Systematic Theology*, 3:10).

165. "The names of conversion and prayer are improperly given to that blind torment by which the reprobate are distracted when they see that they must seek God if they would find a remedy for their calamities, and yet they shun to approach him" (Calvin, *Institutes*, 3. 3. 24).

166. Malebranche, *Méditations chrétiennes et métaphysiques*, *Œuvres*, 10:101.

167. Saint Jerome, "levius malum est aperte peccare, quam simulare et fingere sanctitatem [of the two evils, it is less to sin openly than to simulate and feign holiness]" (*Commentariorum in Isaiam Libri Octo et Decem*, PL 24. 240).

168. Walker, *Creeds and Platforms*, 384.

169. Miller, *Orthodoxy in Massachusetts*, 199.

an evil heart are ultimately corrupt, yet "it is less sin to do them than to omit them; therefore, if thou wilt go to Hell, go in the fairest path thou canst in thither."[170] Speaking of the "negative moral goodness in sensibility of conscience" of the unregenerate (8, 615), Edwards said that even though their works gave no absolute assurance of heaven, it is certain "they shall escape an exceeding Intolerable addition to their Eternal misery."[171]

These rather empirical considerations had their conceptual culmination in New Theology. Hopkins remarked that if a sinner pretends not to want to perform religious duties for fear of incurring greater guilt, then he should be asked if it is the only sin he fears and, if it troubles him that much, why does he so blithely continue in his other sins?[172] Unregenerate men have to perform their religious duties, which aggravate their guilt, and yet their guilt is not for resorting to the means of grace because it existed prior to their sinful state. Let's take the example of two sons who, hating their father, decide to leave him and run away. The father commands them to return and listen to him. One refuses to comply with the command and the other obeys, yet ends up adding to his sins. He returns and hears his father's words but refuses to submit to him. At first, he was simply obeying his father, yet the eventual outcome of this particular act of obedience was to aggravate the evil of his rebellion, his former, deep sin. In a manner of speaking, resorting to the means of grace was not only an opportunity to aggravate evil but also his deep-rooted corruption.[173] The religious exercises of the unregenerate certainly increase sin, although not in themselves or as such but rather accidently. And to those who might still not be convinced of the soundness of this distinction, S. Hopkins made this invincible argument: if the unregenerate could pray in a profitable way, i.e., in accordance with God's will, then God would set aside his own will, which was precisely not to justify, regenerate and sanctify them![174] With this argument, we find ourselves faced with the second formulation of the danger of a natural man's religious acts, namely the one which puts him at risk of a positive divine

---

170. Shepard, *The Sincere Convert*, Works, 1:32. A century later, E. Stiles thought "that if predestined to misery yet that misery would be less, the less I sinned and the more earnestly I sought the divine Favour. From this Time I more vigorously resolved to refrain from Sin, if not to obtain Heaven of which I saw no prospect, yet to mitigate and lessen the Torments of Damnation" (Morgan, *Gentle Puritan*, 62).

171. *Sermon on Matt. 5:22*, in Gerstner, *Steps to Salvation*, 69.

172. Hopkins, *The True State and Character of the Unregenerate*, Works, 3:409–10.

173. Hopkins, *An Inquiry Concerning the Promises of the Gospel*, Works, 3:272–73.; compare with the explanation of the unregenerate's desire for grace in 13, 320–21.

174. Hopkins, *The True State and Character of the Unregenerate*, Works, 3:426.

intervention leading to the aggravation of the unregenerate man's spiritual state.

Jansenius taught that the grace of the Jews was prevenient grace because it caused them to sin even more,[175] and Malebranche, for example, did not hesitate to speak of a "misleading reward . . . which fattens the victim for the sacrifice."[176] Edwards himself thought that impenitent sinners become worse as a result of the gracious calls and counsels of the word of God (15, 379) and that the very light of the Gospel and the means of grace, the sacraments, become like a curse to them (X, 137). With his usual extremism, Emmons explained that it was worse to fall into the hands of a holy God than an unholy God because his benevolent love makes the unregenerate suffer.[177] Lastly, how could we forget the passage of that great, belated Calvinist, N. Hawthorne, on the sight of sacred objects that "bewildered the wretched man with everlasting errour, and the blessed Cross itself was stamped as a seal upon his heart, so that it should never open to receive conviction"?[178]

It should be understood, however, that these are not excesses of preaching rhetoric but rather a formulation—albeit a colorful one—based on solid doctrinal reflection and in which the divine opposition that aggravates the state of the unregenerate can also be read in terms of the latter's obstinate and perverted resistance. The unregenerate and hypocrites fight the operations of grace with every means, not the least of which is subtle lies to themselves. What is especially pernicious is that their sinful nature nourishes this enmity to holy things because of their very holiness (X, 406).[179] The devils hate God for his moral beauty (25, 634)[180] and even the very joys of paradise would only nauseate the fleshly nature (VI, 541).

---

175. Jansenius, *Augustinus*, 3. 8. 119–20.

176. Malebranche, *Conversations chrétiennes*, *Œuvres*, 4:42.

177. Emmons, *The Moral Rectitude of God*, *Works*, 4:232; compare with "the God of Love is harder than the God of Law," (Kierkegaard, *Journal* 5, 121).

178. Hawthorne, *The Marble Faun*, *Works*, 4:33. For the sense of conviction, see *infra*, p. 279ss.

179. Compare with VII, 402; X, 130–31; etc. Natural men have a practical "disposition" to deny God, so that "it would suit them" if he did not exist (17, 48). They are "prejudiced against His being" (17, 54), but particularly hate God for his holiness (18, 309): "for holiness is the very thing that the corrupt nature of man is at direct enmity against" (19, 140).

180. The Devil mortally hates the history and doctrine of redemption (4, 250); "he is enraged against the Bible . . . Every text is a dart to torment the old serpent" (4, 254); compare with Saint Thomas Aquinas, the Devil suffers because of God's excellency (*Summa Theologiæ*, 1. 63. 3. co.).

The fallen nature's deep repugnance for grace is portrayed as a constraint upon God by the reprobate who prevents him from extending mercy. "The unbelieving," wrote Calvin, "draw back from His hand and, as far as they can, impede His work," not permitting Him to display His power.[181] God confers his gifts on us so that we may glorify him in them, but we profane them and then "God therefore, as it were, transfigures Himself, so as to reprove His own gifts" and his love changes to anger.[182] It is in this situation when "the brightness of the Divine countenance . . . is a kind of labyrinth,—a labyrinth to us inextricable,"[183] that the Lamb will appear like a roaring lion and the sweet word of the Gospel will become a torment for us.[184] Undoubtedly, the word "will exquisitely torture, and become an executioner of men in Hell,"[185] but even now the unregenerate can cry out with J. Parsons that "it is an awful thing to be left to the gospel in word only," without the "saving influences" of the Spirit.[186] More precisely, if an encounter with the Gospel in the absence of the regenerating and sanctifying Spirit is a terrible torment, then the same experience in the presence of the Spirit is the greatest good. This amounts to saying that, depending on the state of the person receiving them, certain spiritual realities can have two types of effects that are diametrically opposite to one another. Calvinist preachers constantly repeated that if the announcement of God's word was an odor of life for the justified, then it was an odor of death for the unregenerate.[187] For the Israelites, it was a means of salvation; for the Egyptians, a sword that destroyed them (15, 368).[188] Now—and this is essential—this opposite efficacy of the same spiritual reality is neither the result of a fortuitous accident nor an immediate act of God, but depends on the state of the creature affected by the divine action.

---

181. Calvin, *Harmony of the Gospels*, 1:30.

182. Calvin, *Praelectiones in Ezechielis Prophetae, Opera*, 40, 348.

183. Calvin, *Institutes*, 1. 6. 3.

184. Bunyan, *Grace Abounding*, 58; compare with "dreadful scriptures" (Bunyan, *Grace Abounding*, 74). For the Torah as a deadly potion, see Strack and Billerbeck, *Kommentar zum neuen Testament aus Talmud und Midrasch*, 498.

185. Goodwin, *Of Gospel Holiness in the Heart and Life, Works*, 7:304.

186. Parsons, *Sixty Sermons*, 444.

187. Calvin, *Commentary on Corinthians*, 2:160–61; compare with 15, 350.

188. "the same that is the refreshing light of Israel is the consuming fire of the sinner" (Isa 10:17 in 20, 182). Compare with "that pillar of fire and of a cloud that parted between the Israelites and the Egyptians, giving a clear and comfortable light to those that are under the manuduction and guidance thereof, but being full of darkness and obscurity to those that rebel against it" (Smith, *Select Discourses*, 286).

Speaking of God, the Psalmist wrote that "with the pure Thou dost show Thyself pure, and with the crooked Thou dost show Thyself perverse," (Ps 18:27) and the Christian tradition understands very well that this is not a statement about the nature of God but rather a formulation of an anthropological order.[189] God shows himself pure to the pure because they are pure, and perverse to the crooked because they are evil. Christ's descent into hell—wrote Saint Thomas Aquinas—confounded the wicked and edified the good;[190] but if it edified the good, it was because they were already good and therefore edifiable, and if it confounded the wicked, it was because they could only sink themselves further into evil by opposing grace. Later, the great Malebranche taught that the light of God issues forth a flame that consumes demons, and that it is so harmful to them because the very beauty of order wounds their corrupt mind and provokes horror in them.[191] Demons—fallen angels—"are in the luminous substance of God," which now appears to burn in them.[192] In his farewell sermon to the congregation in Northampton that had dismissed him, Jonathan Edwards said with sadness that the word he had preached to them might only have been "a savor of death unto death" that had hardened them all the more (25, 475–7). Well, if God's word is only an odor of death for those who hear it and Christ's body a deadly poison,[193] it is because they have not been perceived and received in an appropriate manner. Let's revisit that brutal image of a rotting, decomposing corpse: "the heat of the sun, which gives health to a living and animated body, draws forth stench from a corpse."[194] Augustine had already resorted to the image of an unhealthy palate giving a bad taste to savory meals,[195] and Calvin explained that "just as corporeal food, when received into a stomach subject to morbid humors, becomes itself vitiated and corrupted, and rather hurts than nourishes, so this spiritual food also, if given to a soul polluted with malice and wickedness, plunges it into greater ruin."[196] It is always an evil or pernicious use of the means of salvation which, when perverted, turn against the person using them.[197]

189. See *supra*, p. 181 n.242.
190. Saint Thomas Aquinas, *Summa Theologiæ*, 3. 52. 6. ad. 1.
191. Malebranche, *Traité de morale*, *Œuvres*, 11:105.
192. Malebranche, *Entretiens sur la mort*, *Œuvres*, 13:401.
193. Calvin, *Institutes*, 4. 17. 40.
194. Calvin, *Consensus Tigurinus*, in Niemeyer, *Collectio*, 209–10; Calvin, *Opera*, 9, 25.
195. Saint Augustine, *Confessions*, 7. 16.
196. Calvin, *Institutes*, 4. 17. 40.
197. Compare with "Whoever contemplates the grace of God with a satisfaction and sort of pleasure of ownership, turns it into poison" (Fénelon, *Lettres et opuscules*

Diverted from their proper end—salvation—the means of grace become instruments of perdition. In that regard, Milton wrote that "those means, which are of saving knowledge to others, he [the reprobate] makes to them an occasion of greater sin."[198] The Savoy Declaration expresses this same idea with greater precision and emphasizes human causality. Speaking of obstinate sinners, the Declaration states that "the means God uses to soften some, the wicked and ungodly use to harden themselves," a definition the Saybrook Platform rewords in a very meaningful way: "they harden themselves, even under those means which God uses for the softening of others"![199] In and beyond the colorful language of preaching, the dogmaticians were trying to specify that it is not so much God who makes the means of salvation an opportunity for the hardened to fall, but it is rather the hardened themselves who pervert the means which fully profit the regenerate.

The aggravation of sin in proximity to the light is not to be reckoned an actively mutual distancing of God and man. Christ, said Edwards, is unchangeable and always remains the same; it is the sinners in Zion who continually add to their sins (X, 489–50). As with hardening and hell, the descent of the Gospel sinner is also heard in this expression of Calvin: "in the same work, even as God does good according to His goodness, man does evil according to his malice."[200] This is the deep meaning underlying that great exclamation by Edwards: "God is love, but He is also wrath!"[201] And again, we recall with Hopkins that unbelievers who avail of the means of salvation aggravate their state, although this aggravation is not due to the means themselves but to their own wickedness!

At the core of this theological vision—dominated by the doctrines of irresistible grace and reprobation—is a constant and vigorous reaffirmation of man's total and undivided responsibility for aggravating his state through religious exercises, although an unwavering profession of forensic justification does not prevent the Calvinist from resorting to ideas from heterodox sources. There is the traditional, well-known argument reformulated by

---

spirituelles, 619).

198. Milton, *The Doctrine and Discipline of Divorce*, Works, 3. 2. 441.

199. Walker, *Creeds and Platforms*, 373 and n.6.

200. Calvin, *Epistre.Contre un Certain Cordelier*, Opera, 7, 353.

201. Sermon on Ex 9:12 in Gerstner, *Edwards on Heaven and Hell*, preface. See also: "God is a consuming fire, as well as the Lord God, gracious and merciful" (10, 445). He is present in the just as "a helper and protector," in reprobates as "terror and torment" (*Bl.*, 113). The sacrifice of Christ is offered in the "twofold flame" of God's wrath and of his "own love to God" (18, 490). That "eternal flame that the bodies of the wicked are to be tormented in" and the "eternal light with which his countenance shall shine" both show God's glory (20, 171).

Leibniz which compares men—moral subjects—to boats and the grace of God to the current that carries them along. The same current moves the boats, so their progress at different speeds is purely a function of their particular build and cargo.[202] This image appears in *God's Determinations*, that great Calvinist poem in which E. Taylor has Soul say: "I swim in Mercy: but my sins are sayles That waft my barke to Hell by Graces Gales."[203] The action of grace captured by sin quickly sends man to perdition! The same idea is expressed somewhat more explicitly by T. Goodwin: "in carnal hearts all influences from heaven and means outward administered, do but nourish self ... a poisoned plant turns the rain into poison. The thorns did not only overtop, outgrow, and choke the gifts and graces given, but did convert and turn the actings of those gifts into thorns."[204] The grace that falls on shallow, thirsty soil—and this is not a heterodox teaching—can only produce bad fruit.

---

202. Leibniz, *Theodicy*, 1. 30.
203. Taylor, *Poems*, 434.
204. Goodwin, *Of Gospel Holiness in the Heart and Life, Works*, 7:299.

5

SPIRITUAL IDEA AND NATURAL KNOWLEDGE

1. The notion of idea

WE HAVE SAID THAT Edwardsian thought dealt with three major metaphysical topics: Being, the will, and knowledge. In a way, the study of Being introduced this system and delineated the issues involved. However, it was the study on the will that helped us understand the *sui generis* originality of this thought: first and foremost, by setting forth the doctrine of the will itself and then, to a lesser degree, by analyzing and describing the will's various levels of engagement and operation.

Throughout this study, the will has been understood as evil will, fallen will and the will under bondage. This also made it possible to define the contents of a doctrine of evil and begin to describe the human condition as it is, i.e., its effective reality. It now remains for us to repeat the same procedure for knowledge.

We will begin by describing the essence and operation of knowing and then analyze the levels and moments of its exercise. However, there is an important difference between this study of knowledge and the one on the will. In the domain of the will, only descriptions of its fallen state were given, whereas in this discussion on knowledge, the description of natural man's knowledge will be followed by a detailed development on the justified man's knowledge, i.e., that of a person penetrated and transformed by saving grace. This is not at all a question of favoring the mind at the expense of the will or of making understanding superior to volition. In any event, with respect to their effective existence, the will and the mind are inseparable. The activity of the will implies the exercise of the mind, which presents it with its object; and the apprehension where the mind unites with its object is only conceivable if a movement of the will is deployed, which is why knowing is essentially of a moral order.[1] We were accordingly led to portray the natural, fallen state in terms of willing and—to take account of the phenomenological structure of these two faculties as different aspects of the human spirit—we will treat the justified state within the context of knowing. The will emanating from our subjectivity expresses who we are *vis-à-vis* an exterior to be influenced and dominated, whereas in knowledge we submit to the real exterior. From the Edwardsian theological perspective, what emanates from man can only express his egoism; conversely, whatever he turns outward will eventually submit to this external reality, which is ultimately founded upon God. However, this does not mean that we turn to God with our mind and turn away from him with our will. It is simply a question of studying our deviant subjectivity—wrapped up in itself—with a particular focus on the will. On the contrary, the action of the creature reintegrated with normality is best understood by describing the mind, whose proper finality is to adopt the contours of its object and assimilate itself with it. In this study of knowledge, we first conduct an analysis of its essential moments and then proceed to describe how it optimally assimilates with its object. With the light at this summit, we will then see the lower levels of knowledge, those diverse forms of external, abstract knowledge that are proper to man's natural state. The study on conversion will allow us to consider the rupture where the spirit tears away from itself, thereby gaining access to higher knowledge that enables it to see things as they really are. The proper object of this sufficient knowledge is the holy beauty of divine things and—in its ultimate moment, i.e., its end—Edwardsian thought foresaw the possibility of a reflection on the conceptual articulation of God's holy beauty in the mysteries that form the content of the Christian faith.[2].

Because Edwards had always worked on epistemological themes from within a theological context and with a theological finality, it is quite appropriate to describe his theory of knowledge using his developments on a theological theme, namely the state of Jesus Christ, who descended into hell. Orthodox Protestantism has never ceased to meditate on the theme of Christ exposed to wrath because of the sins of men. Since Christ came into the world to expiate our sins and satisfy the terrible requirements of divine ire, any somewhat systematic reflection cannot avoid the question of the

---

1. Hopkins, *System of Doctrines, Works*, 1:400.
2. See *infra*, chapters 7 and 8.

relationship between the supreme ordeal of Jesus Christ and the infernal suffering of the damned. An ancient theologomenon—*descensus ad infernum*, that descent into hell—has been the particular focus of this inquiry, although it is often not interpreted in a realistically physical or topographical sense. Calvin taught that the abandonment on the cross can be considered "the commencement" of Christ's descent into hell,[3] although this should not be taken in a physical sense. Christ indeed endured the pangs of hell, yet he had already endured them on the cross. To experience the full measure of God's wrath, "it was necessary that he should engage, as it were, at close quarters with the powers of hell and the horrors of eternal death." Not only was Christ's body given as the price of our redemption; but he also paid "a greater and more excellent price—that he bore in his soul the tortures of condemned and ruined man."[4] Calvinist dogmaticians accordingly profess that Christ truly "experienced the sufferings of Hell in His death,"[5] yet how are we to understand and interpret this statement? We might be content to declare in a popular catechism that "he felt also the pangs of Hell,"[6] but at a strictly theological level, hasten to clarify that "although He did not experience eternal death with respect to damnation, nevertheless, in terms of their intensity and quality, He felt the torments of the damned."[7] Yet, how do we explain this compassion of Jesus Christ up close and in detail? And how do we have him partake in the sufferings of the damned without detracting from his immaculate and uninterrupted holiness? After many attempts by his predecessors, Jonathan Edwards encountered this issue himself and proposed his solution to it in terms of his own philosophy.

He wrote that the punishment of sin and the infinite displeasure of God are essential elements of infernal suffering. Because Christ was not personally hated by God, he could not be tormented directly by God's divine displeasure and only experienced infernal sufferings though the sensation swelling from his very vivid apprehension of horror at the sins of the reprobate and by his compassion at the pains of their punishment. Christ surely had a very vivid and clear vision of God's anger towards the damned and the heinous character of their transgressions. "Dismal views" and "gloomy ideas" provoked by sin swallowed up his mind and it was as if he was penetrated by a great and dreadful sense and sight of the "odiousness of that sin." Edwards wrote that, as a result, Christ suffered more than the damned

---

3. Calvin, *Institutes*, 2. 16. 12.
4. Calvin, *Institutes*, 2. 16. 10.
5. Heppe, *Dogmatics*, 465.
6. Perkins, *The Foundation of Christian Religion, Workes*, 1:5.
7. Heppe, *Dogmatics*, 466.

because they don't see how heinous sin is in itself. Now concerning what are properly termed the sufferings of the damned, Christ experienced them by the simple fact of having understood them perfectly. Human nature is such that "a great and clear and full idea of suffering . . . brings suffering, as appears from the nature of all spiritual ideas: they are repetitions . . . of the thing itself; they are ideas of [it]." And therefore if Christ had had a perfectly clear and full idea of what the damned suffer, "the suffering He would have had in the mere presence of that idea would have been perfectly equal" to their suffering (20, 329–30).[8]

This late Miscellany contains the essential points of the Edwardsian epistemology in an abridged form: an ambiguous use of the term "idea," in close proximity to "vision" and "sense," and the particular notion of a spiritual idea as a repetition or a kind of existential double of its reality.

The origin of the Edwardsian notion of an idea is found in Locke's *Essay Concerning Human Understanding* that the Yale student had read with the delight of a "greedy miser."[9] To the young Edwards, who had been taught philosophy from the manuals of Scholastic Protestantism, Locke's empiricism seemed truly liberating, like a breath of fresh air.[10] Edwards quickly assimilated the lesson of the *Essay*, although the conclusions he would draw from it took a very different direction from the profound trends of Lockean thought.[11] The Age of Enlightenment venerated Locke as the author of an epistemology that liberated thought from the restrictions of speculation and, under the pen of this American philosopher, the empiricism of the *Essay* would serve to renew the metaphysical interpretation of Calvinist teaching on the action of free grace and the consequent development of a profoundly orthodox doctrine of religious knowledge.

According to Locke, all knowledge is founded on ideas, of which we possess two types: simple and complex.[12] Simple ideas are indivisible atoms of knowledge, its primitive elements;[13] on the other hand, complex

---

8. In this Miscellany, Edwards "gave an analysis of the mental pains of the Redeemer, which is of unsurpassed interest" (E. A. Park, "The Rise of the Edwardean Theory of the Atonement: An Introductory Essay," in Park, *The Atonement*, xxv).

9. Hopkins, *Life* 6; compare with W. Anderson, Editor's "Introduction," 6, 24–26.

10. Locke's influence on Edwards has been amply discussed in secondary works, of which the most important is Miller, *Jonathan Edwards*. See also the excellent book by Fiering, *Edwards's Moral Thought* and Laurence, "Religious Experience in Edwards."

11. Compare with L. Howard, "Edwards seems to have been constitutionally incapable of following for long in Locke's footsteps" (*"The Mind" of Edwards*, 67) and also L. Stephen, "The disciple owed to his master not a body of doctrine but the impulse to intellectual activity," ("Jonathan Edwards," 221).

12. Locke, *Essay*, 2. 2. 1.

13. Locke, *Essay*, 2. 2. 2.

ideas are only assemblies or compounds of simple ideas.[14] As regards their origin, simple ideas only come to us from experience, whereas the mind develops complex ideas from the simple ideas it has previously received and stored within itself. The understanding can produce new complex ideas at will "but it is not in the power of the most exalted wit or enlarged understanding ... to invent or frame one new simple idea in the mind."[15] No one can imagine the idea of an odor that he has never smelled before, nor the taste of a pineapple if he himself has never eaten this exquisite fruit.[16] But what exactly did Locke understand by "idea? According to the definition in the *Essay*, "whatsoever the mind perceives in itself or is the immediate object of perception, thought or understanding" is called an idea.[17] In other words, mental content—any sensation or thought—can be labeled an idea. Whether the mental content comes to us by touch or vision[18] or is given to us as a thought,[19] the simple fact that it immediately comes to our minds is enough for it to be called an idea. However—and this complicates the situation—the Lockean description of this immediately perceived mental reality remains rather ambiguous. For Locke, an idea—as a commentator once said—"is at once the apprehension of a content and the content apprehended."[20] In other words, an idea doesn't simply mean the content of the mental act, but also the mental act itself. Edwards would inherit this ambiguity, which enabled him to transpose and metamorphose the Lockean doctrine of knowledge by experience into a theory of spiritual knowledge.

It was in *Mind* that Edwards first introduced his doctrine on ideas as a theme, although he returned to it frequently in certain Miscellanies that were among his most important writings and used it in an innovative and profitable way in his great *Treatise Concerning Religious Affections*. In a long Miscellany on the Trinity, Edwards defined an idea as "the immediate object of the mind's intuition" and he added that "the soul receives nothing but ideas" (13, 258). It was extremely rare that Edwards presented a real definition of an idea and he preferred to use the term in association or juxtaposition with one or more synonyms. In most cases, these synonyms were less related to mental content than to a mental act. We certainly find synonyms related to content, beginning with that of an image (2, 211). In

14. Locke, *Essay*, 2. 12. 1.
15. Locke, *Essay*, 2. 2. 2.
16. Locke, *Essay*, 3. 4. 11.
17. Locke, *Essay*, 2. 8. 8.
18. Locke, *Essay*, 3. 4. 10.
19. Locke, *Essay*, 1. 1. 8.
20. Gibson, *Locke's Theory of Knowledge*, 19 in Aaron, *John Locke*, 100n.1.

an expression that has every appearance of a definition, Edwards even said that "ideas are images of things (13, 258)."[21] Elsewhere, when referring to "the seal . . . of the Spirit of God on the heart" of the children of God, he noted that "natural men . . . can have no manner of notion or idea of it" (2, 238) unless "the species or ideas" are received "by the phantasy" (2, 288). Another text speaks of "thought or idea" (21, 120), but the objective connotation may go as far as to make it an equivalent of "knowledge" (2, 228) or "understanding" (21, 114) and, when speaking of the Trinity, Edwards did not hesitate to say that "God's knowledge, or reason of wisdom, is the same with God's idea" (13, 260). However, connotations that are objective or that arise exclusively from the order of content are fewer in number than connotations with ambivalence, at the level of verbal expression, between the objective element (the content) and the subjective element (the mental act). The term used here as a synonym for idea could equally be used to characterize the act of perception and what that act contains. He who does not see the beauty of God's holiness "is destitute of any idea or conception of all gracious exercises of soul" (2, 275). Earlier in the same treatise, Edwards wrote that all gracious exercises "arise from some apprehension, idea or sensation of the mind" (2, 207–8) and he finished by juxtaposing "perception or idea."[22] However, whether it is a question of conception or sensation, apprehension or perception, ambivalence prevails between the subjective and objective, the content and the act.

Lastly, there is a third group of expressions in which the meaning of "mental act" really seems to predominate. Here idea appears as the equivalent of "taste" (6, 360) or "delight" (2, 208). Or again, recalling the above-mentioned text, Christ's sufferings "consisted in the great and dreadful sense and idea" he had of what "an odious and dreadful thing sin was" (20, 332–33). And the profoundly subjective and active element of the expression "sense" becomes even more profound. In *A Faithful Narrative of the Surprising Work of God*, Edwards described the difficulties of those who, after having enjoyed exercises of grace, cannot recover "a sense or idea" of that which was sweetest and best in their experiences (4, 187) and, finding themselves "in a dull frame, they can't recall the idea, and inward sense" they had beforehand of the relish and divine excellency of exercises of grace (4, 180). And, lastly, we can mention the passage, in a development on the Trinity, where Edwards identifies the idea a person has of himself with the

---

21. For the "image" in Edwards, see Colacurcio, "Glory of God in Edwards," 153–55.

22. See 21, 113; 6, 375; etc.

happiness and joy he experiences in the relationship and communion he has with himself (18, 260)!

Jonathan Edwards never overcame the ambiguity in his notion of idea—at least with respect to terminology—although a preponderance of subjective meanings related to the realm of the mental act was ultimately recognized and the Miscellanies developed the distinction between external and spiritual ideas where the latter, while not exactly the same as the container-content duality, nonetheless emphasized its essential implications.

Locke had also led the way here by distinguishing between two types of ideas. Ideas come from experience, of which there are two kinds: internal experience and external experience. External experience takes us into the sensory world of "sensible objects," and it is how "we come by those ideas we have of yellow, white, heat, cold, soft, hard, bitter, sweet." In short, we get our sensations from external experience.[23] The other source of ideas is our perception of the operations of our own minds. These operations, which our "internal sense" makes apparent to us, are subsumed under the generic category of reflection.[24] This distinction between sensation and reflection, i.e., between the ideas that represent the sensory world and those that reproduce the mental world, inspired the Edwardsian developments that would lead to the *Treatise Concerning Religious Affections*.

In the context of a discussion on the truly gracious character of spiritual experiences, Edwards remarked that a sudden apparition of the image of Christ hung on the cross with blood flowing from his wounds, of heaven with its radiating rows of saints, or indeed the hearing of the encouraging words of Scripture might only be illusions or even diabolical deceits because their origin is not truly spiritual but merely corporal. These imaginary visions and auditions do not have any organic relationship with the merciful grace of a new birth, but rather continue to arise only from the world of the five senses. They are merely external things and the ideas we get in this way are likewise merely "external" (2, 209) and "sensible" (18, 454). In juxtaposition to such sense-derived ideas, we have "reflection, abstraction, reasoning, etc. and those thoughts and inward motions which are the fruits of these acts of the mind" (2, 289). Like Locke, Edwards also understood "ideas of reflection to be "ideas of the acts of the mind" (13, 353), although with a notable shift in meaning that would ultimately change the metaphysico-theological impact of Lockean empiricism in a profound way.

For the author of the *Essay*, sensations and reflections had to do with the realm of simple ideas, i.e., those the mind passively receives through

---

23. Locke, *Essay*, 2. 1. 3.
24. Locke, *Essay*, 2. 1. 4.

experience. Whether the material world or the intellectual world, the power of the mind is the same: it cannot produce or determine its content, but can only combine, juxtapose, or separate. In other words, the only power the mind has is to combine simple ideas into complex ideas, such as "beauty, gratitude, a man, an army, the universe."[25] While the mind possesses the faculty to combine what it receives by experience, it cannot independently procure "the materials of all its compositions."[26] It exercises real power over complex ideas only, but has no power over simple ideas.

In his first works, Edwards took liberties with the terminology in the *Essay* but was nonetheless broadly inspired by its spirit.[27] In fact, this young thinker was rather hesitant in his developments. He first used ideas in a generic sense to designate all mental acts, but immediately afterwards said that, properly speaking, love and comprehension, pleasure and pain are not ideas. Ideas, *stricto sensu*, are only what the mind receives passively. Now, mental operations are acts (6, 384).[28] Only mental facts that originate from sensations can legitimately be termed ideas, which is why ideas are merely one category, among others, in the world of the conscience (6, 343). We now understand why, in an important Miscellany, Edwards not only limited what could be termed a simple idea but even appeared to exclude the *Essay*'s second group of simple ideas, namely ideas of reflection, from this notion. Indeed, he remarked that if we diligently attend to our own minds, we would find that ideas of reflection—more correctly, mental ideas—are not properly ideas (13, 353–4). In the strict sense of that term, only sensations are apparently ideas. However, the Edwardsian position is only negative and limited on a terminological level, given that the specific reason for this momentary refusal to designate what are not properly representations of mental acts as ideas is their need to be better represented. That ideas of mental acts are not mental acts—in the proper sense of that term—is because they are not simple representations but rather repetitions of those acts. The only way to have an idea of an idea, Edwards declared, is to repeat that same idea (13, 353). In most cases, to allow our mental operations to take place quickly, we are content to represent general notions and spiritual realities as simple signs, but the moment we want to get a faithful and adequate understanding of them, we are obliged to represent them in their entirety. With respect to "the ideas, acts, and exercises of minds . . . there is no actual idea

25. Locke, *Essay*, 2. 12. 1.

26. Locke, *Essay*, 2. 12. 2.

27. For a sense of how Edwards developed his notion of an idea, see the excellent remarks by E. F. Flower and M. G. Murphey in *History of Philosophy in America*, 1:159ff.

28. For ideas as acts, see Flower and Murphey, *History of Philosophy in America*, 1:161.

of those things, but what consists in the actual existence of the same things ... in our own minds" (18, 455). This repetition, or reproduction, of mental reality, which can vary from the very faint to the very lively, is what Jonathan Edwards called a spiritual idea (13, 354). His provisional refusal to use the designation of idea for the reproduction of a mental reality only served to draw attention to the spiritual exercise of the mind's own perfect power of presentation. When the spiritual idea is "perfect," then the thing of which it is the idea is fully present in the mind, and this total presence—a *sine qua non* condition of spiritual conscience—is not obtained at will (13, 463).

2. Spiritual idea

The notion of a spiritual idea, which was even briefly denied the designation of idea, continued to take its revenge and ended up absorbing all the metaphysically significant elements of that notion. It ultimately enabled Edwards to develop a theory of spiritual knowledge based on infused grace. Edwards made a claim for absolutely adequate knowledge of external reality and situated its presence in the mind. This vision can only be understood from the standpoint of his idealistic doctrine, namely that the things of the material world are truly nothing and only the intellectual sphere, the operations of our minds, are real in the proper sense of that term. First of all, we need to understand that precisely because all authentic existence, *stricto sensu*, of the things of this world is only mental (6, 341), that they can—or rather can only—be fully represented by the mind which thinks them. That one thing might be exactly like another still does not make it the proper image of that other thing. The proper image of a thing is ultimately not its physical or metaphysical double but its ideal representation in a mind. The only perfect image of the Father is the Son, the idea that God has of himself (13, 268), "His own perfect substantial idea" (15, 319) and not that of some other god outside of himself. It was to preserve this perfect representative faculty of the mind that Edwards was led to assert its complete passivity. For me to fully know a thing, it must be present in my mind as it is in itself, without any (modifying) contribution on my part. Ideas of things are but the repetitions of those very things (6, 383). Or again, an "absolutely perfect idea of a thing is the very thing" (13, 258), and seeing the perfect idea of a thing is to all intents and purposes the same as seeing the thing itself (13, 368). If a man "had a perfect reflex ... of every thought," he would "indeed be double; he would be twice at once: the idea he has of himself would be himself again" (21, 116).[29] Moreover, if one mind was so made by God that it

---

29. "Duplicity" [i.e. having an idea of oneself] is a necessary precondition for true

necessarily perceived all the ideas of another, these two minds would effectively be "the same individual person" (18, 427). While it was his concern to preserve the perfectly receptive and passive character of the mind that led Edwards to momentarily limit the scope of idea to simple sensation, he quickly overcame his hesitations in order to resolutely follow the path that would take him to his final position. Idea for Edwards would always mean a simple idea, although once he returned to ideas of reflection as his second original component, simple idea would expand to also include what Locke considered a complex idea.

It was ultimately his definitive formulation of a simple idea that enabled Edwards to gradually smooth over the differences between a simple idea and a complex one. At first, he maintained a distinction between a simple spiritual idea and a complex one. The former consisted in "mental motions, energies and operations . . . that are got only by the internal feeling and sense of the mind." Complex spiritual ideas, e.g., about benevolence or God, can include or be derived from a certain number of simple ideas (13, 286–87). According to the Lockean doctrine, the mind is sovereign in its evocation of these complex ideas, whereas the Edwardsian reflections denied that it had this power (*ibid.*) and instead emphasized the essential continuity between a simple spiritual idea and a complex one. There might be a difference of intensity, or of clarity and immediacy, in the repetition of the idea of spiritual reality, but as long as it is a matter of spiritual ideas, the repetition alone is sufficient to represent a thing whose most "perfect" form is a certain presence of the thing itself (13, 354). Edwards never ceased saying that this presentifying repetition was not in the mind's power.

In his late Miscellany on Christ's sufferings, Edwards no longer made any distinction between the simple and the complex. He initially began with the undivided notion of a spiritual idea whose nature is to be a repetition of the thing of which it is the idea (20, 331). However, starting with Miscellany 123, we see the differences between simple and complex ideas begin to disappear, with a complex idea appearing more like a reality *sui generis*. A complex idea of benevolence is "a certain sweet motion of the mind" that consists chiefly of some simple ideas, but nowhere does it say that our mind organizes and develops a complex idea from simple ones (13, 286).[30] The

---

self-awareness: "if there is no duplicity, it will follow that Jehovah thinks of Himself no more than a stone" (13, 262). A notion from classical logic (Crusius, *Weg zur Gewißheit und Zuverlässigkeit der menschlichen Erkenntnis*, §§. 242–43 in Leibniz, *Confessio Philosophi*, 126), "duplicity" would play a central role in Schelling's metaphysics, *Contribution à l'histoire de la philosophie moderne*, 120.

30. In Miscellany 123, Edwards initially wrote that people don't have a complex idea of benevolence because they lack the simple ideas that constitute it. However, a

simple spiritual ideas that make up that "sweet harmony" we call benevolence do not precede the latter but rather seem to depend on it. The idea of benevolence is hardly a composition of previously received ideas, but is instead to be thought of as a global perception (see 13, 286-7). In other words, when deprived of the simple ideas that constitute true benevolence, I cannot conceive of it; and I am deprived of these simple ideas for the very reason that I do not have a benevolent disposition.

The cause of this state of affairs—its "formal" cause—was the quasi-coincidence of the idea's "container" and "content" elements. Edwards, as we noted, seemed to foster confusion between an idea's subjective and objective components, although this confusion had a lofty end: the development of the notion of a spiritual idea is like a key to decode the ultimate mental fact where we cannot conceive of the notional content in abstraction from the way in which the mind receives and formulates it. The introduction of this new notion of an idea occurred in the *Treatise Concerning Religious Affections*. We will discuss this essential portion of Edwardsian reflection later—because this religious epistemology is like the central knot of his metaphysic of the regenerated state—but for now we can give at least a brief overview of it.

In those gracious exercises that are wrought in the regenerated heart through the saving influences of the Spirit of God, there is a new, inward perception or sensation, something entirely new that we cannot produce ourselves by "exalting, varying or compounding" the type of perception which our mind had before. Grace is a new principle of knowledge and the sense, action or perception it engenders "is what some metaphysicians call a new *simple idea*" (2, 205). While now including John Locke with "some metaphysicians," Edwards is nonetheless very conscious of the changes he has made to the master's doctrine.[31] The content of this new perception is "the beauty of God's holiness" which, for Locke, would only have been a highly complex (and rather abstract) idea. Edwards felt able to use the term "simple idea" to designate such an apparently complex idea because he believed that he had solved the thorny problem of the metaphysical difference between simple and complex in the domain of knowing. After

little further on, he seemed to think that what they lack are not the simple ideas that constitute a complex idea, but rather the complex idea itself: "the wicked man sees not the amiableness of holiness, for he has not that idea that is expressed by the name of holiness" (13, 287). This shift from the Lockean position can be observed in this Miscellany by the way Edwards develops the idea of benevolence in strict analogy with that of a rainbow, while the *Essay* gives precedence to the simple ideas that constitute the complex idea of a rainbow—see Locke, *Essay*, 3. 4. 13.

31. In *A Treatise Concerning Religious Affections*, (1746), Edwards only mentions Locke's name once and without reference to any specific doctrine (2, 299).

a quarter century of reflection, he finally understood that—at least at its highest level—the container-content distinction doesn't really exist. This equivalence of the subjective and the objective has major epistemological consequences. In his magnificent essay on "The Rhetoric of Sensation," P. Miller very pertinently remarked that, as penned by Edwards, an idea became a principle of organization and perception not only for the intellectual man but also for the passionate man, for the loving and desiring man, indeed for the whole man. An idea was no longer a simple reality of an intellectual order but also an "emotion"[32] and, consequently, an undivided reality *sui generis*. It is not just a factor or moment of experience, but rather "a unit of experience."[33] From a strictly epistemological point of view, this fact meant that an idea not only designated what was conceived but also the manner in which it was conceived. Again, we could say that, on a purely objective level, the conceiver's feelings form part of the idea itself. However, it must be understood that Edwardsian teaching on the notion of an idea was not only concerned with the theoretical sphere of epistemology but also extended to what Kant called the practical domain. Edwards perfectly understood the futility of attempts to separate the objective pole and subjective pole, the notional content and the mind that conceives it, but he never wanted to limit feelings to its elementary, psychologically superficial sense. Of course, the simplest and most obvious distinctions in the way the mind perceives content concern the faded or vivid, transitory or permanent, and intuitive or discursive character of apprehension, although Edwards broadened this range of distinctions, especially by grounding psychological and epistemological distinctions on a religious and moral level. In this sense, and independently of any affinity with Berkeleyism, Edwardsian thought is a form of idealism (even beyond the issues in *The Mind*), which implies "the primacy of the practical" in a more general or, if you will, a more formal sense. Knowledge is only determined from the standpoint of the subject or, more precisely, from the subject's essential, stable, basic state, which is of a religious and moral order.

The vividness of our representations is an essential element of a spiritual idea, and this vividness—their clear or faded character—is a function of our affections. When we represent the love that another man vows to a woman about whom we are unconcerned, we scarcely have any proper idea of his feelings, and so we try to represent them in terms of their effects and concomitant circumstances, i.e., in an indirect manner (13, 354). We

---

32. Miller, *Errand into the Wilderness*, 179–80. We once again note that, in Miscellany 123, simple ideas are equated with "energies" (13, 286; see also 21, 113).

33. Miller, *Errand into the Wilderness*, 181.

can only have a genuine idea of the feelings of others by experiencing these feelings ourselves and putting ourselves in the place of others (8, 591). In the case of the woman about whom we are unconcerned, we have no inducement to put ourselves in the place of the man who loves her passionately and therefore do not get a real idea of his love. Our indifference towards this person, our absence of loving affection for her, equates to a kind of neutrality. Moral neutrality, i.e., non-engagement with an external reality, also indicates non-engagement with respect to the representation claiming a presentifying repetition, which is why there is a direct link between love and knowledge. However, before dealing with the complex epistemologico-metaphysical implications of the subject's ethnico-religious state, we need to determine its strictly epistemological premises.

3. Sensible knowledge

A veritable summary of Edwardsian efforts in the area of epistemology, with an ethnico-religious finality, is given in Miscellany 782, a marvelous text that nonetheless remained unpublished for more than two centuries[34] and one which, for the density of its thought, the clarity of its descriptions and the richness of its speculative implications, might never have been surpassed by any other work of his later years. Edwards profoundly remarked that everything we know, in one way or another, concerns the will and heart of spiritual beings and that it is only insofar as it relates to the will that our knowledge of a thing matters to us. In other words, the objects of knowledge should be studied in terms of their relationship to the happiness and misfortune and the good and evil of spiritual beings (18, 459–60). If cognitive objects are distinguished by the way they affect the interests of spiritual beings, the knowledge of these beings does not form a homogeneous sphere but must be characterized in terms of their object's importance with respect to the knowing subject.

First of all, Edwards identified two types of knowing: mere cogitation and direct apprehension. In mere cogitation, the mind does not require the effective presence of an idea of things and is content with reading things indirectly through their signs. Conversely, there is immediate apprehension whenever the mind forms a direct idea of a thing. The objects of this direct, immediate apprehension are divided into two groups. On the one hand, we have the things that pertain merely to our theoretical understanding and its related operations, such as judging or speculation. On the other hand, ideal

---

34. The first transcription of this Miscellany—written circa 1732—dates from 1948 (Miller, "Sense of the Heart," 123–45).

apprehension appertains to everything that has to do with the faculty we call "the heart." When we have things of the heart or will in our mind, we say that we have "a sense" of them because they essentially consist of sensations of pleasure or pain, agreeableness or disagreeableness (18, 458–59). However, this primary distinction between cogitation and apprehension must be complemented or superseded by what might be "the most important" distinction in epistemology, which juxtaposes speculative knowledge and sensible knowledge and is also called "the sense of the heart." Speculative knowledge *stricto sensu* does not fully correlate with simple cogitation because it not only covers all indirect knowledge acquired through signs but also includes the ideal view, i.e., the direct apprehension of all things that only concern the intelligence and are not related to the will. In other words, speculative knowledge is defined in terms of the origin of its objects from theoretical intelligence and without regard to the way in which they are conceived. In contrast, sensible knowledge, which is simply known as "the sense of the heart," only concerns things that relate to the heart and only insofar as the heart directly apprehends them. This "sense of the heart includes all ideal apprehension of beauty and deformity," wrote Edwards, "all ideas of delight or comfort . . . all ideal views of dignity or excellency of any kind, and also all ideas of terrible greatness or awful majesty, meanness or contemptibleness, value and importance." In fact, what we call "sensible knowledge" only involves feelings of pleasure or pain, i.e., knowledge concerning the heart and the will and therefore ultimately related to good and evil (18, 455).

At this level—one where the sensible and moral are not yet differentiated—it's obvious that good and evil do not yet have a truly determined sense. We might well ask if this knowledge is truly objective, merely a simple perception of pleasure or pain or, at best, knowledge that has been modified, weakened or deformed by a subjective apprehension of good and evil. The Edwardsian response, which we will examine later in more detail, was that sensible knowledge of a thing's goodness or evil involves apprehending an entire web of content and that, rather than being contaminated by subjective interest, such apprehension is clarified and deepened by the existential engagement of the subject, who discerns the web of relationships between these things with incomparable insight.

Sensible knowledge, Miscellany 782 continued, is not confined to an ideal apprehension of the goodness or evil of a thing, i.e., what we understand by "having a sense of them," but also involves the apprehension of other realities related to the thing perceived as good or evil, agreeable or disagreeable. For instance, some men are said to have a sense of the dreadfulness of God's displeasure and, consequently, sensible knowledge of the pain God is supposed to feel and also a sense of the displeasure of God's heart. However, having this sense of the terribleness of God's displeasure implies more than simply understanding the misery and pain of the damned and having a sense of God's heart; it also implies an ideal apprehension of the Being of God, of his greatness and of the greatness of his power (see 18, 460). A sensible knowledge of a thing's goodness or evil extends our apprehension over an entire web of realities related to the thing in question and the knowledge of it that we obtain is ideal, i.e., direct. In other words, because of immediate apprehension relating to the will, we get immediate knowledge, the spiritual idea of realities that are not voluntary. And we could also add that the ideal knowledge obtained in this manner, which has an organic relationship to sensible knowledge, ends up becoming sensible itself. Truth lets us consider the "cordial" knowledge of religious contents, which are only conceptual or, as Edward said, notional.

Sensible knowledge of a thing provokes a veritable avalanche of perceptions and entails ideal apprehensions of other things. In short, one idea leads to another. Here we are dealing with a phenomenon that can be considered from either a subjective or an objective standpoint. From a subjective viewpoint, we get the impression of a light flooding the cognitive landscape, filling the gaps between ideas and linking them with one another in a way that makes the world fully intelligible (13, 469). Conversely, from an objective viewpoint, we become aware of relationships between ideas that have always existed but were previously unknown to us, which ultimately leads to a situation where all ideas interconnect to form a complete configuration (see 13, 338). In fact, these two viewpoints could very well be united because light in Edwardsian idealism is nothing but the subjective translation of the immanent links between ideas. The mind's profound engagement with sensible knowledge makes the ideas of which it "has a sense" appear clearer and livelier and, as a result, their relationships with other ideas are necessarily more apparent. We not only find more ideas, but can also discern them more clearly (see 18, 459-60). Unlike mere ratiocination—which only leads to abstract, weak and fragmentary knowledge—sensible knowledge makes things appear real because the powerful light it casts on them reveals their various mutual relationships to us. The highly complex idea of religion, for example, is based on the mutual agreement of simple ideas, which itself consists of "ten thousand little relationships and mutual agreements" (13, 388).[35] We don't initially acquire these simple ideas all at once; rather, by virtue of the mind's engagement in sensible knowledge, "attentive

---

35. For the profound and complex metaphysico-theological implications of these biblical allusions to "ten thousand," see 1 Samuel 18:7 and Song of Solomon 5:10; M. Veto, "Beauté et Compossibilité: l'Epistémologie Théologique de Jonathan Edwards," in Veto, *Philosophie et religion*, 157-8, and 22, 171; 22, 397; 19, 440; etc.

reflection" (see 18, 456) instead causes them to progressively appear on the horizon. Let's not forget that an archetypal spiritual idea is complex and is more about acquiring a global perception than a laborious composition of elements. And this globalizing perception is true knowledge inasmuch as the power of the vision is a function of the immanent unity of what it sees.

In what follows, we will see that true knowledge is spiritual knowledge. The "new simple idea" of grace grasps the beauty of God's holiness and the hideous deformity of sin as they really are. The basis for this claim to great objectivity is that the mind's existential passion for reality compels it to disappropriate itself: the container becomes nothing, the content becomes everything. In other words, the mind can only adequately grasp the real when it purifies itself from every purely subjective element and, like the good butcher of Phaedra, begins to follow the immanent articulation of the world. Paradoxically, it is only powerful (external) engagement that can guarantee the mind's true objectivity by allowing it to go outside of itself and begin to listen to reality. This engagement is moreover the true opposite of a certain complacency with respect to its own feelings and Edwards, especially in his *Treatise Concerning Religious Affections*, never stops fighting the tendency to focus on his own spiritual experience rather than its transcendent term. Hypocrites, let's recall, spend their time holding forth on their experiences and the feelings that accompany them! In contrast, the regenerate man "has his mind too much captivated and engaged by what he views without himself, to stand at that time to view himself, and his own attainments." Instead, he scarcely stops to take his eye off the ravishing object of his contemplation, which is the object of his "direct view" inasmuch as it is "without himself" (2, 252–53). A direct view remains focused on its external object, without engaging in introspection. In consequence, it doesn't distort our vision by directing it in accordance with its own subjective point of view. A view is said to be direct when there isn't any deviation—more specifically, any subjective deviation—from its object and it is very significant that Edwards quoted a text by J. Owen in which "direct" and "intuitive" are synonymous (2, 250n.7).

In all great philosophy—whether it be Kant's archetypal intellect or Schelling's intellectual intuition—"intuition" and "intuitive" are never used to denote a subjective mode of reality but rather a repetition or reproduction of that particular reality's immanent structure. True spiritual ideas originate from intuitive knowledge that does not leave any room for self. It was therefore no accident that Edwards used the term "intuitive" in a context of pure self-disappropriation and of absolute submission to external reality. According to *The Mind*, when a prophet is inspired "immediately," he has "intuitive knowledge. He gets such brilliant ideas and has such "perfect agreement with the excellencies of the divine nature" that "the Deity appears" in his knowledge. Being fully submissive to divine inspiration, the prophet's mind is completely emptied of self; this is why the ideas that spring up before him are so clear and have such harmony that he perceives "all the Deity" (6, 346 § 20), i.e., the complete web of simple ideas that form the "highly complex idea" of God (see 13, 177). Those who speak about intuition emphasize its direct aspect, the immediacy of its act and—like Locke—the irresistible power that imposes this knowledge on the mind.[36] Edwards himself identified intuitive knowledge with immediate sensation[37] but, beginning with this note on prophetic inspiration, went far beyond the traditional position because he presented this direct grasp of reality as the deployment of the web of its moments. Whether it's a matter of empirical or superior, moral or religious use, intuition has always been conceived of as a faithful grasp of realities represented as so many undividable units. For Edwards, intuitions intimate, undivided and existential knowledge hinted at this claim to portray reality in terms of its immanent structures.[38]

4. Historical and notional knowledge

The Edwardsian epistemology culminates, in the doctrine of spiritual ideas, with a teaching concerning presentifying knowledge which, in a manner of speaking, assimilates with its object. Now, this immediate presence, this assimilation with its object, is peculiar to sensible knowledge, which distinguishes itself from speculation by its subject's higher level of engagement. Conversely, the adequate, authentic knowledge of spiritual realities is sensible, although sensible knowledge is still not *eo ipso* spiritual. The sensible character of knowledge is determined by the cognitive subject's vigorous engagement; however, taken by itself, the engagement is still only a neutral category. The power and strength with which the subject applies itself to the object and seizes it is an issue, although power and strength are only quantitative, material categories and can be used for very different and even opposing ends.[39] Now, what matters most is the end of the engagement

36. Locke, *Essay*, 4. 2. 1.
37. 6, 346 § 19; see "immediate and intuitive" knowledge in 18, 427.
38. For intuitive knowledge in Edwards, see *infra*, p. 381 n.39.
39. See teaching by Edwards on "sincerity," *supra*, p. 197 ss. Compare with Saint-Cyran, Dieu n'aime pas "davantage la douceur d'un agneau que la fierté et la violence d'un lion [God does not love the gentleness of a lamb more than the pride and violence of a lion]" (Orcibal, *Les Origines du Jansénisme*, 407. "Dieu veut . . . la solitude de tout le créé, aussi bien du plus spirituel, que du grossier et du profane [God wants . . . the

and, in a theory of knowledge where knowing is a function of the subject's moral state, knowledge can be directed to either good or evil. Edwards, who scarcely believed in *adiaphora*, would not fail to demonstrate the impossibility of neutral knowledge vigorously determining to set its gaze on the world without first opting for either good or evil.

In this Calvinist-inspired metaphysic, the mind, i.e., knowledge, is always engaged—if not for good, then for evil. What purports to be "nonengaged knowledge" is commonly called "speculative knowledge," which is what that great Miscellany 782 understands as knowledge by signs and therefore indirect and mediate knowledge of any intelligently ordered reality. Man cannot do without knowledge by signs because of a certain inability of his mind to set its presentifying gaze on ideas. Incapable of grasping and immediately apprehending reality, the mind uses substitute signs to represent realities without needing to imagine or invoke the realities themselves. The use of signs condemns the mind to a view of reality formed only of evanescent and vague representations without true clarity or distinction. This weaker, more abstract way of knowing can be extended to any aspect of reality, although the mind is particularly inclined to resort to signs to represent "spiritual ideas" (18, 456). There is an inverse relationship between the degree to which an idea belongs to the natural sphere of the mind and the inclination of the intelligence to represent it in the form of a sign. In reality, so-called ideas of external or sensible things are far less external than sensible; and an individual is not obliged to make any special effort to invoke them, because they only arise in close dependence on the body (see 2, 286–88) and belong to the individual's own innate sphere. It is not the same case for spiritual ideas, which are "a kind of things that we are mainly concerned with" (18, 456). They can only be presented when given special "attention" (*ibid.*), i.e., a faculty which, for many Christian thinkers, was seriously affected by the consequences of original sin.[40] By reason of the great subjection of the soul in its fallen state to external senses, it finds itself in a veritable state of "alienation of the inclinations and natural dispositions of the soul from those things as they are" (18, 461). Only an infusion of "the new simple idea of grace" will enable the soul to overcome this alienation and, until then, it can only develop mediate, indirect knowledge based on the signs of these realities (see 18, 455–57).

Edwards distinguished two categories of signs in the sphere of the mediate knowledge of spiritual ideas and, consequently, of religious and moral

---

solitude of the entire creature, from the most spiritual to the vulgar and profane]" (Guilloré, *Le progrès de la vie spirituelle*, 523).

40. See Malebranche, *De la recherche de la vérité*, 1. 12. 3, *Œuvres*, 1:136.

knowledge. The signs the mind employs can be either the ideas or names used for the things represented or some sensible images, concomitants or consequences of those things (18, 456). The first type of sign can be understood as providing the content of what is traditionally called knowledge or a faith that is merely doctrinal or literal; the second, that of knowledge or historic faith. In the first instance, we are dealing with conceptual knowledge only; in the second, with imagery; and these two types of knowledge—or rather non-knowledge—ultimately meet up in the developments of Protestant-inspired theology and philosophy, of which Edwardsian thought is a notable example.

As for historic faith, the Reformers thought that it was "nothing more . . . than a certain common assent to the Gospel History,"[41] knowledge that treats the content of the Gospel "in the same way in which they believe the records of past events, or events which they have actually witnessed."[42] It was this characteristic—that of being limited to images, i.e., to the senses or, more precisely, the empirical—that Edwards himself denounced as knowledge "obtained by hearsay" (17, 414). While the crudely empirical, image-based nature of this type of knowledge greatly contributed to the theologian's derogatory judgment, it was less a matter here of objecting to images or the empirical than of highlighting the superficial, non-engaged way the mind acquired knowledge. Thomas Shepard, who had the strongest influence on Edwards's religious epistemology, wrote of knowing Jesus Christ "by tradition and report" as the lowest degree of religious knowledge[43] and this, moreover, for two convergent reasons. On the one hand, the mind receives its contents passively, without exerting any effort of its own and, on the other hand, the contents it receives aren't presented in any immanent order or with any immanent connection between them. Edwards himself characterized this type of faith as one acquired by tradition and education (19, 102); and by education he understood a method of knowing which, from without, strengthened the quasi-instinctive association of certain contents that otherwise would not share any immanent affinity (see 8, 588).

In contrast to knowledge built on evidence, i.e., acquired from some immediate realization or internal apprehension, knowledge acquired by education only comes to us through the testimonies of others. In his apologetical writings on Revelation, Edwards showed that he knew how to judge the epistemological value of opinions and did not condemn the fact that our

---

41. Calvin, *Institutes*, 3. 2. 1.
42. Calvin, *Institutes*, 3. 2. 9.
43. Shepard, *The Parable of the Ten Virgins, Works*, 2:121.

knowledge had its origin in human intersubjectivity. Rather, what he deplored was the absence of true presentifying continuity between the knowing subject and the mental content that others passed on to him. In fact, the truth and excellence of its content is still not sufficient to authenticate a particular belief. The facts of the Gospel are undoubtedly of greater worth than, for example, the beliefs of Muslims. Nonetheless, "though the thing believed happens to be true; yet the belief of it is not owing to this truth, but to education" (2, 295). When the articles of our faith are handed down to us by the tradition of our fathers or by the profession of faith of our neighbors, our faith can remain undetermined and ineffective (19, 102). In both cases, if it hasn't involved personal effort, such conviction does not, as Calvin said, "have a fixed seat" solidly in the heart.[44]

The Reformer himself seemed to emphasize the sensible or pictorial character of all historic faith, whereas dogmatics—which came later and was what Edwards had studied—primarily emphasized the non-existential, non-engaged character of historic faith, without necessarily considering whether it was merely pictorial or already adhering rigorously to this concept. The German dogmatician Wyttenbach proposed the following definition: "If anyone gives assent to the truths necessary to be apprehended merely *as matters which he does not greatly long to have for his own and which do not interest him*, i.e. without emotion, it is called *fides historica*."[45] Historic faith appears free of its original image connotation and is portrayed as a weaker adherence by the subject to the objects of his belief. A development that began with seventeenth-century dogmaticians bore fruit in Protestant-inspired philosophy when its pejorative judgment of purely historic faith was transposed into a critique of a moral and metaphysical order. This generalization, and a sort of secularization of these dogmatic themes, occurred especially in German idealism, a philosophy with strong theological foundations.

Hegel, who considered himself the savior of Protestant dogmatics, brought historic knowledge in general back to a simple indication based exclusively on the testimony of others, i.e., knowledge that has not been learned in and for itself.[46] A person who only has historic knowledge is like the manager of a business firm who handles someone else's goods without owning any merchandise himself.[47] The purely historic element in theology

---

44. Calvin, *Institutes*, 3. 2. 10; compare with the notion that true Christian faith is not content with a simple historical knowledge but takes its seat in the heart of man (*Institutes*, 3. 2. 6).

45. Heppe, *Dogmatics*, 529.

46. Hegel, *Lectures on Proofs of God*, 47, 82–83.

47. Hegel, *Lectures on Philosophy of Religion*, 1:128.

is relegated to mere contingency and ascribed to "sentiment."[48] In Hegelian terminology, such empirical knowledge is simply "immediate knowledge." It hasn't passed through the crucible of mediation, nor is it integrated with the immanent action of the knowing mind but, despite appearances, remains a foreign body within the subject. Hegel himself went so far as to liken immediate knowledge to immorality and idolatry,[49] but it was Kant, in particular, who drew out the philosophical implications of Protestant teaching about faith that is purely historical. Historical knowledge is *cognitio ex datis* (knowledge from facts) and all knowledge "is still historical for him who possesses it if he cognizes it only to the degree and extent that it has been given to him from elsewhere." In itself, a cognition may be philosophical, i.e., based on principles, and yet, from a subjective point of view, remains merely historical because it has only been adopted from an "alien reason" rather than arising from the efforts of our own reason.[50] The heteronomy proper to mere historically based faith results in a religion expressed in outward ceremonies. Such faith is only empirical[51] and, because it doesn't have internal validity for everyone,[52] is marked by contingency.[53] Kant contrasts "dead ... historical faith" with genuine, "saving faith."[54] Grounded on the autonomous subject's genuine intent, the latter is expressed as a radical, outward transformation and is essentially practical; historic faith, in contrast, is only mercenary and servile. Historic faith carries out acts induced only by fear or covetousness—acts which an evil man also can perform.[55] Kant

48. Hegel, *Philosophy of Religion*, 1:466. For the distinction between "unphilosophisch" and "historisch," see *Vorlesungen über Rechtsphilosophie*, 81.

49. Hegel, *Enzyklopädie der philosophischen Wissenschaften im Grundrisse, Gesammelte Werke*, 20:114. With his speculative identification of the formal and the immediate, Hegel here seems to ratify the distinction that theologians have made between historic and doctrinal faith.

50. Kant, *Critique of Pure Reason*, A836–7/B864–65 [pagination of first and second editions is used for this text]); compare with "Ein kind lernt allgemeine Moral im catechismus historisch [A child learns general morality historically in the catechism]" (*Logik Philippi, Ak.*, 343); "subjectiv-historisch [subjective-historical]" (also *Ak.*, 9. 25).

51. Kant, "Religion within Boundaries of Reason," 6:119.

52. Kant, "Religion within Boundaries of Reason," 6:43n. What is necessarily valid for all can be immediately understood by each and every one. This is why that which is "simply taught and transmitted historically" is contrasted with what is "immediately understood" (*Metaphysik., Ak.*, 18. 434).

53. Kant, "Religion within Boundaries of Reason," 6:115.

54. Kant, "Religion within Boundaries of Reason," 6:111.

55. Kant, "Religion within Boundaries of Reason," 6:115–6; see also *supra*, p. 211 ss. The historical understanding of the Gospel facts is opposed to moral faith (*Correspondence*, 10:178–80 [Academy pagination]) when it is only a means and not an end (*Metaphysik, Ak.*, 18. 486). For this entire topic, see also M. Veto, "Le Témoignage de

was only clarifying an essential insight of the Reformation which saw an indifferent attitude and beliefs not made one's own[56] as signs of a radically insufficient faith. The religious epistemology of Jonathan Edwards is merely a faithful expression of the same vision.

At the root of all these developments concerning *fides historica* was the Calvinist refusal to accept a common assent to the Gospel history as genuine faith. Without a doubt, *sola scriptura* remains the formal principle of Protestantism, but it also needs to be understood that "even the gospel is not always *spirit*"![57] There is certainly a bit of a difference between belief in a crude spirit on the basis of mere hearsay and faith based on a scholarly exegesis of Scripture, although a cognition based on a simple letter is never truly more than a product of the imagination.[58] Of course, we could develop, systematize and draw general conclusions from literal faith but, in the end, it will always remain the same: a cognition based on an entirely external assimilation of contents. Historical or literal faith was essentially criticized for the contingent way in which it was acquired: the believing subject's mind had not ensured that a truly immanent connection between the contents themselves actually existed.

It was thought possible to compensate for these serious deficiencies of history and letter by elevating faith to the level of reason and speculation. The image would then be purified into a concept and the testimony of others replaced by operations deployed by our mind. However, even the notional and doctrinal knowledge that only concerns "the *Grammatical* and *Logical* meaning of Gospel *Theorems*"[59] could not be radically differentiated from belief based on hearsay. Of course, historical faith obtained by tradition and education is merely a simple persuasion based on "the opinion of others" and can be overcome by a cognition based on reason and demonstration, i.e., knowledge that is the culmination of efforts by our own mind. And yet, even this cognition is very imperfect, because it only achieves its results by mere ratiocination (2, 295). In a great sermon entitled *A Divine and Spiritual Light*, Edwards associated the evidence of faith based only on history with faith based on the reasonings of learned men (17, 423) and used the attributive adjectives "historical" and "doctrinal" as synonyms for them (12, 210).[60] Made without any particular explanation, this association

---

l'Esprit selon Hegel," in Veto, *Philosophie et religion*, 170–71.
  56. See Barth, *Kirchliche Dogmatik*, 4. 1. 855.
  57. Calvin, *Commentary on Corinthians*, 2:173.
  58. See Shepard, *The Parable of the Ten Virgins, Works*, 2:121–2, 312, etc.
  59. Miller, *New England Mind*, 1:292.
  60. See "a bare dogmatic or historical faith" (Miller, *New England Mind*, 2:236).

was not fortuitous, however, because the fact that someone reduces a rich abundance of images to the order of a concept and performs operations in which faith is articulated is still not true adherence or an effective commitment of the mind to the mysteries of religion, to the truths of Jesus Christ. Edwards, as we know, showed immense respect for the power of reason in its own domain, which included theology and religion,[61] but did not refrain from comparing natural reason in spiritual matters to mere opinion (25, 91) and even to dreaming (MO, 394).[62]

Following those Puritan theologians who denounced belief acquired by rational persuasions but unable to carry over the will effectually to God in Jesus Christ[63] and for whom true knowledge was not literal or speculative, but inward, transforming the mind,[64] Jonathan Edwards portrayed speculative faith as an ephemeral, evanescent cogitation incapable of effectually accessing spiritual realities. Doctrinal knowledge might invoke its intellectual pedigree but, in Edwards's eyes, it was known much less for the clarity and rigor characteristic of reasoning than for its powerlessness to reach what is real. In a preparatory notebook for the *Treatise Concerning Religious Affections*, we read that a man who is not truly godly is no more capable of grasping the essence of piety than a blind man can conceive of color: "Though he may have an idea of effect, circumstances . . . yet that which is as it were the nucleus, the kernel, the spiritual part, he can have no manner of idea of."[65] In notional knowledge, it is as if the mind is condemned to only glimpse spiritual realities from without, to circle around them, to only make out and contemplate their contours. This powerlessness to reach the true nucleus of a reality can be expressed using the metaphor of grasping only its shadow. In the words of the Apostle Paul, someone who doesn't see the moral beauty of God's holiness has but "the form of knowledge" (2, 274). Lacking benevolence to Being in general, an egotistical man does not see God as part of

---

61. Young Edwards made this resolution: "Resolved, when I think of any theorem in divinity to be solved, immediately to do what I can towards solving it" (16, 754). He defended reasoning in theology (19, 795–6) and the spiritual life (2, 213n.2). It is "a glorious argument of the divinity of the holy Scriptures" that their doctrines appear to be "exactly agreeable" to certain, natural dictates of reason (1, 439). Contrary to Locke, who was wary of any dogmatic construction, Edwards affirmed that "the only way we know what He is, is by speculation. He is a speculative Being in that sense." He observed that "one great reason why speculative points are thought of so little importance" is because "modern religion consists so little in respect to the Divine Being, and almost wholly in benevolence to men" (MO, 397).

62. See waking = real (13, 338). See also 14, 74, 202, etc.

63. Baxter, *Practical Works*, 20:30, in Nuttall, *Puritan Faith and Experience*, 135.

64. Cromwell, *Letters and Speeches*, in Nuttall, *Puritan Faith and Experience*, 136.

65. *Ms.* "Affections Notebook," No. 7 (online WJE Vol. 37).

the "system of real existence," but merely as a kind of "shadowy, imaginary being" (8, 611). According to a comment in a late Miscellany, having the things of religion subject to the hold of reason makes the teaching "appear with dim evidence, like a shadow, or the ideas of a dream" (MO, 394). The lesson that the treatises, Miscellanies and sermons proclaim is that speculative knowledge can access the notional understanding of the truth of a thing, yet this is still not "real" understanding (V, 298). Or perhaps, to paraphrase Emmons, we might say that, at this level of knowledge, men have at most the power of describing the things of God but not yet of presenting them.[66]

This critique of mere doctrinal or notional faith also represents the fulfillment of Edwardsian idealism. In the metaphysic of *The Mind*, material things were taken as mere shadows, although we also see that this shadowy state can equally be the privilege of intellectual things inasmuch as they are only the contingent contents of the understanding rather than immanent moments arising from it. In contrast to spiritual ideas with a shared state of mind that reflects the univocity and homogeneity of its contents, the effects of abstract, speculative knowledge are but the pale, immobile shadows of notional faith or the mobile, agitated shadows of historic faith. However, Edwardsian idealism not only devalued speculative knowledge, but went even deeper by closely analyzing the apparent non-commitment that produced these shadows. Edwards ultimately showed that this non-commitment was merely the deceptive mask of an effective commitment to evil. There are "two competitors for the kingdom of this world, Christ and Satan" (13, 393), and we follow either one or the other.

Edwards emphasized the unreality and powerlessness of purely doctrinal knowledge, but inflected his denunciation of unreality in the direction of illusion. For example, don't we read in *Some Thoughts Concerning the Revival* that, during the great religious events of their history, Christians were over-inclined "to lay weight on those things that were very notional and chimerical" (4, 319)? The epithet "chimerical" certainly connotes the essential unreality and insufficiency of mere doctrinal knowledge, but it also refers back to vanity, and vanity is more than a state of simple unreality (23, 83)[67]. At first sight, this denunciation of the non-existential, powerless character of notional faith concerns the absence of any profound commitment. A somewhat closer reading of the Edwardsian texts, however, shows that it's not about a simple lack of vigor and strength but rather a practical transgression, i.e., a refusal to commit to the reality that is the unique required end of all human effort. During the controversy in Northampton

---

66. Emmons, *The Nature and Effect of Divine Teaching*, Works, 6:74.

67. For a comparison of speculative knowledge and vanity, see 24, 606.

over the qualifications required for admission to communion, Edwards remarked that merely declaring "right speculative notions" of God and only manifesting a doctrinal knowledge of the things of religion doesn't necessarily mean that a person truly belongs to God or has "a supreme respect of heart towards God" (12, 219). Only the faithful who are united to the Lord by a real attachment should partake of the sacrament because the profession "of only a historical or doctrinal faith" does not in any way imply that we have committed ourselves to submit to him as "our King" (12, 210).

5. The Devil's faith

Faith that is only historical or speculative shares the apparently neutral state of nature, although the effective nature of our fallen state—burdened with corruption—is hardly neutral. Speculative knowledge is undoubtedly "a natural good" (2, 255) and is indeed directly equated with "natural knowledge" (18, 463). We know that the light from what is natural is not only weak but also a "contrary light," i.e., to the Spirit.[68] The natural knowledge of God—and now we hear Calvin speaking—is not peculiar to "philosophers" but is common "to all nations, and to all ranks of men. There were indeed none who sought not to form some ideas of the majesty of God, and to make him such a God as they could conceive Him to be according to their own reason. This presumption," the Reformer continued, "I hold is not learned in the schools, but is innate, and comes with us, so to speak, from the womb."[69] Our "extravagant,"[70] vagabond[71] speculations are not only "idle,"[72] but also and especially "frivolous."[73] They do not result from a simple, theoretical occupation or a neutral, innocent pastime, but are rather the fruit of a corrupt mind.

Insufficient, frivolous faith—"human and useless" faith, according to Pascal[74]—is not a degree below the real faith of the regenerate but actually its opposite. The difference between a boat capable of crossing an entire ocean and one that can only go a major part of the way is not one of degree but of

---

68. Hopkins, *System of Doctrines*, *Works*, 1:400; compare with, "not a mere absence of light, but a malignant opposition to the light" (Hopkins, *System of Doctrines*, *Works*, 1:419). In Scripture, a "natural" man is an "ungodly" man (2, 197).
69. Calvin, *Commentarius in Epistolam Pauli ad Romanos*, *Opera*, 49, 25.
70. Calvin, *Sermons sur le Livre de Job*, *Opera*, 35, 478–80.
71. See Calvin, *Institutes*, 1. 5. 14.
72. Calvin, *Commentary on John 11–21*, 84.
73. Calvin, *Contre la Secte Phantastique et Furieuse des Libertins*, *Opera*, 7, 164–65.
74. See Pascal, *Pensées*, 110.

nature: the first boat will arrive safely in port while the second will founder and sink during the voyage!⁷⁵ It is from this very Augustinian realization about the impossibility of any middle way, any intermediate stage between the natural state of the children of wrath and the gracious state of filial adoption that theological epistemology seeks to develop its distinctions. Mere literal knowledge remains "dead" and "carnal"⁷⁶ and a traditional faith is like that of Herod⁷⁷ because it is still only an "assent" by which "any despiser of God may receive what is delivered by Scripture"⁷⁸ and, as Kant said, a faith which even "an evil human being can perform" without changing his moral intention.⁷⁹ The tone of denunciation rose and the descriptions of an epistemological order gave way to analyses based on the doctrine of grace. Some of these analyses contrasted historical and justifying faith,⁸⁰ while the others identified it with temporary faith.⁸¹ Finally, there was yet one more higher qualification, the supreme qualification of fallen doctrinal-historical knowledge in which epistemological preoccupations would resurface in the form of a figure drawn from the history of salvation.

Ever since Augustine, Christian preaching connected "the faith of demons" mentioned in *The Letter of James* with that of "evil" Christians,⁸² and Calvinist theology made this connection explicit by applying it to historic faith⁸³ and doctrinal faith,⁸⁴ respectively. Edwards followed this tradition when he referred to the Devil as a paradigm for this knowledge of God, without the real "inclination" (2, 272), hidden in a perverted mind. Beginning in 1739, he remarked that mere speculative faith is no better faith than the devils have (8, 139), although it would be in his great sermon in Newark—*True Grace Distinguished from the Experience of Devils*—that Edwards, with

75. See *supra*, p. 74.

76. Shepard, *The Parable of the Ten Virgins*, Works, 2:122. Compare with, "the cold and faint knowledge of sin" (Calvin, *Commentaries on First Book of Moses*, 159).

77. Shepard, *The Parable of the Ten Virgins*, Works, 2:311; compare with, "Herodisch heylickeyt [Herodian holiness]" (Luther, *Kirchenpostille, Werke*, 10. 1. 1. 631).

78. Calvin, *Institutes*, 3. 2. 8.

79. Kant, "Religion within Boundaries of Reason," 6:115–16.

80. White, *Tree of Life*, vii in Nuttall, *Puritan Faith and Experience*, 135n.1.

81. Miller, *New England Mind*, 2:77.

82. Beumer, "Et daemones crededunt (Iac. 2, 19)," 232–33. For the Jansenist position, which stopped short of any explicit identification of human faith with the faith of devils, Russier, *La foi selon Pascal*, 1:364–5. Another text from James 3:14—"earthly, sensuous, devilish... wisdom"—is also used by Saint Augustine ("Grace and Free Will," 24. 46). See also "*devilish*... wisdom" (Saint Thomas Aquinas, *Summa Theologiæ*, 2-2. 45. 1. ad. 1). See also Kraus, *Der Begriff der Dummheit bei Thomas von Aquin*, 60.

83. Heppe, *Dogmatics*, 528.

84. Shepard, *The Sound Believer*, Works, 1:192.

remarkable brilliance and theological imagination, expounded the theme of the rigorously vicious character of the unregenerate's theoretical knowledge of the things of God. This Christian thinker sometimes appears to be very generous with respect to the scope of natural man's religious knowledge.[85] However, we begin to question the extent of this generosity on reading that even the damned will see that Christ is a divine person (2, 310)[86] or that even the Devil's relationships with sorcerers tend to convince the latter of the truth of certain religious beliefs (2, 310)![87] Contrary to certain crude

85. See, for example, 23, 84. In the last years of his life, Edwards made preparations for a major work that would draw on writers of antiquity—whom he knew second-hand—to prove a kind of universal, natural knowledge of Christianity's essential doctrines (20, 241; 20, 246-8; 23, 636; etc.), including justification by faith. Edwards quoted Gale's observation that Plato "seems to disown any free-will to true good" (3, 432-3; see also *supra*, p. 109. 2). His mention that Socrates was only a midwife and quoting of Seneca's proclamation that "it is God who comes to man" attests to pagan philosophy's intuition of the teaching on "infused grace" (20, 251, 365). For the religious truths in ancient philosophies, see 1, 372. Of course, Edwards believed that he could discern biblical origins for many religious and philosophical doctrines of the ancients: the *Odyssey* got its moral notions from Moses (24, 293); Greek thinkers were able to find the theme of four ages in Daniel (24, 760), etc. Transcending all "historical" conjecture was the key notion that Christ had not merely come to enlighten the Jews but all men (24, 923)!

86. Tradition—from Saint Thomas Aquinas (*Summa Theologiæ*, 3. 44. 1. ad. 2) to Milton (*Paradise Regained*, 4, ll. 517-20, *Works*, 2. 2. 477)—teaches that the Devil could only speculate about the divinity of Jesus Christ. For more on this topic, see Pope, *Paradise Regained*, 31-33.

87. Edwards is accordingly heir to a tradition which, without going as far as equating "Mahomet's soldiers, thieves and heretics, and likewise logicians," (Pascal, *Pensées*, 794) adopted an extremely negative position regarding the role of natural reason in the knowledge of God. After all, Calvin had written that we aren't naturally more precious or excellent than elephants (*Sermons sur le Livre de Job, Opera*, 35, 446). This expression carries weight if we recall that, according to Pliny the Elder, man shares the (natural) moral virtue of piety with elephants (*Natural History*, 8. 1, cited by P. Bayle, *Historical and Critical Dictionary*, 4:904 ["Rorarius," note D]). Contrary to those Scholastic theologians who called God simply the "object" of religion (*Institutes*, 3. 2. 1), i.e., that he is knowable by the inquiries of fallen reason, the Reformer knew that our reason is naturally idolatrous (*Institutes*, 1. 7. 11) and that "no one under the guidance of mere nature ever made such proficiency as to know God" (*Commentary on Corinthians*, 1:86). Edwards denounced the dangers of theological naturalism regarding the deism of his day. He did not believe in that "dark and degenerate nature, by the imaginary light of which deists suppose the right idea of God may be easily and universally discovered" (23, 446). He discussed in detail the absurdity of a natural knowledge of God, without the help of revelation (23, 43-44). Only Scripture, and not natural light, could prove that there was only one God, and the work of creation was as mysterious as that of redemption. Emmons, *The True God is to be Worshipped as Existing in Three Persons; A Personal Distinction in the Godhead, Works*, 4:129, 125; the existence of God is as incomprehensible for natural reason as the incarnation (Hopkins, *System of Doctrines, Works*, 1:280) and, instead of simply highlighting its insufficiencies, he set deism in opposition to the Gospel (4, 503). Deists are worse than pagans (23, 244-45); and Edwards

representations, the intelligence of devils is not weak but indeed sharp and strong. The Devil—wrote Edwards—has a high degree of speculative knowledge in theological matters. After all, wasn't he educated in the best theological school of all, i.e., "the heaven of heavens"? The Devil has precise and extensive knowledge of God's nature and attributes and, having been an attentive spectator at the creation of the world, knows God's works perfectly. He also has remarkable knowledge of the other world; of Jesus Christ, the savior of men, and of the great moments of his saving work. A keen expert on the Scriptures, he is an informed exegete. A knowledgeable theologian, he is very orthodox in his beliefs. The Devil is neither a Deist, a Socinian, a Pelagian nor an Antinomian: his articles of faith are solid (25, 614–15).[88] And Edwards concluded that no natural man had the same superlative degree of speculative knowledge as the Devil (25, 629)![89]

6. Imagination and speculative knowledge

As a paradigm of speculative knowledge in religious matters, the Devil illustrates the abstract, non-existential character of this kind of knowledge in a particularly striking manner. Between the common credulity of the simple to what was narrated in the Gospel and the subtle exegesis and doctrine of the Devil lies a whole range of knowledge that remains, so to speak, confined to the head and does not reach the heart. All of this only showed the so-called neutrality of this knowledge, but Edwards also wanted to explain its chimerical character in epistemology. He therefore drew a comparison between imagination and speculative knowledge in religious matters. Heir to a long tradition where imagination was denounced as "the capricious woman of the house" or questionable *eikasia*, Edwards also found himself at the center of violent controversies which religious enthusiasm had stirred up. His reading of the imagination should be understood within the context of his observations about the unhealthy concomitants of the Great Awakening.

---

reproached them for public infidelities (2, 411–12) and for being blasphemers (9, 475); compare with, "hypocrites ... heretics, deists" (9, 497). For a comparison of deism and Arminianism-Pelagianism, see 3, 375–76. Later, Emmons wrote that the Devil leads men from lying to cheating, from cheating to stealing and from stealing to murder even as he leads them from Arminianism to Arianism, from Arianism to Socianism, from Socianism to Deism, and from Deism to Atheism (*The Scriptural Account of the Devil ought to be Believed, Works*, 4:441).

88 For the Devil as an exegete of Scripture, see 19, 124.
89 For the "great subtlety" of the Devil, see 2, 141.

Edwards picked up and explained afresh the very ancient paradox that our imagination is the faculty that gives us our most intimate and vivid knowledge and yet, at the same time, is also the one that hinders us from having an adequate comprehension of our world. In one of his very first texts, he brought up the power of the imagination, "the source of opinions that take us as soon as we are born," that are "beat into us," that "grow up with us," and then "grow into us" (6, 196). Later, the imagination is described—very traditionally—as the faculty that enables the mind to have an image of some external thing when that thing is not present in reality (2, 211), i.e., like a cognition where the mind remains separate and distinct from its object. Edwards deals with the imagination very quickly because he is only interested in it insofar as the great difference between "the imaginary" and "the spiritual" (4, 189) can illustrate his theological thesis of a radical difference between natural cognition and regenerated cognition. "External and sensible objects" are what Edwards called the contents that our mind receives from the senses (2, 213-14). Ideas come from seeing, hearing and touching, and we ordinarily get them from physical things that are effectually present with us. We are therefore dealing with new sensations and perceptions. However, a powerful mental commotion might happen to influence our "animal spirits" so that these external and sensible ideas are presented to our understanding, even when the realities that normally occasion their coming are clearly absent. In this case, we are dealing with the imagination (2, 210-11). The essential characteristic of "sensible" ideas that originate from our imagination is the fact that they are external, i.e., they concern things outside of ourselves and, in particular, are not the fruit of a genuine assimilation or conformation of the mind to the things which those ideas represent. Colors, figures, sounds, and odors do not portray external realities as they actually are in themselves but only in terms of our sense organs. Unlike the spiritual idea of benevolence—which conceives of only a mind that became benevolent itself—external, sensible ideas are not the fruit of a modification proper to the perceiving mind itself, but simply result from its natural exercise.

As a pastor in Northampton during the troubled period of the Great Awakening, Edwards met and observed people who claimed to have had religious visions and auditions. Some saw Christ hung on the cross, with blood flowing abundantly from his wounds. Others had their attention forcefully drawn to certain passages in Scripture, while yet others heard supernatural words announcing unknown events in the future or revealing their own spiritual state or that of their neighbor. Edwards did not entirely reject these visions, auditions or specific revelations, although he subjected them to severe criticism, which relativized their significance.

First of all—and now we hear the theologian of the Great Awakening—nothing warranted setting aside the possibility of vigorous natural effects concomitant to religious experiences which, in turn, exert great pressure on the human psyche. The joy and terror felt, the acts and cries perceived and Scripture passages that seemed to have a different significance than in the past are legitimate and normal consequences of ineffable experiences and, in themselves, are neither harmful nor very important (2, 207).[90] Of course, since these extraordinary phenomena are more often the result of an overheated imagination, we have to be wary of them. Visions and auditions may very well stem from the machinations of the Devil who—and this is a consensus among theologians—is incapable of acting directly on the mind and can only influence man's body or, more precisely, what links body and soul, i.e., the imagination (2, 288–90). Once we have duly considered the natural or diabolic element of extraordinary religious phenomena, we cannot exclude the possibility that they are genuinely divine in origin. God is quite able to communicate, and may indeed communicate, knowledge and information to minds in a natural state, and even the reprobate may have spiritual illuminations.[91] God can inspire an unregenerate person but what matters is that such inspirations, even if they concern divine things, are not properly of a spiritual order. Let's remember reading what Edwards wrote about the movement of the Spirit over the waters at the dawn of creation or the presence of the Second Person of the Trinity in the womb of the Virgin Mary: that these were simply exercises of God's natural, physical power.[92] These statements are now clarified by epistemological considerations.

The essence of Edwardsian doctrine is that—analogous to the difference between a physical and a spiritual presence of God—a distinction needs to be made between the natural and supernatural ways that the mind receives ideas or, more precisely, between natural-external ideas and spiritual ideas. All knowledge is characterized in terms of its constituent ideas. Now, from extraordinary visions and auditions we only get sensible ideas, i.e., from the five external senses that we share in common with brute beasts (2, 213). Moreover, these external ideas not only share animal sensations, but they are also not distinct in any way from ideas proper to unregenerate minds. A man might claim to have a moving view of Jesus Christ on the cross, bleeding profusely from all his wounds. But didn't those who hated Christ with all their heart and crucified him not also see him hung on the cross? Another might be fascinated by a dazzling vision of God's glory and

---

90. See also Torrance, *Calvin's Doctrine of Man*, 9–10.
91. Heppe, *Dogmatics*, 185.
92. See *supra*, p. 233.

yet, on the Day of Judgment, won't the reprobate see the glory of the Just Judge with incomparable clarity (2, 214)? The fact that our religious experiences affect us directly, or are received in an immediate manner, often leads us to conclude that they are supernatural in character. Could the particular way in which ideas are imposed on our minds determine their proper nature? Edwards emphasized the important principle that what mattered wasn't the order in which religious ideas were presented but their intimate nature, and that, at a psychological level, a change in this order would not affect our ideas themselves in any way (2, 159).[93] Imagine that, in a jest, a very poor man living in a humble cottage was transported to a magnificent palace. He was arrayed in princely robes and seated on a throne, with peers and nobles bowing before him. Dazzled, he imagined that he was a glorious monarch, but the nature of the ideas that filled his mind and the contents of his thoughts and sensations did not change; their character remained the same as it was before he was transported to the palace. His habitual ideas were not replaced by other ones; rather, this was no more than "newly exalting, varying and compounding" his ideas and "only extraordinarily raising and exciting natural principles" (2, 209–10). Because of vigorous commotions, we might receive sensible, external ideas in an unusual way and yet—as Edwards remarked—this does not make them any better (2, 214). From a strictly epistemological point of view, extraordinary religious phenomena are described in terms of the same external ideas that constitute any sort of imagination. Edwards, however, went further and showed us that, like our imagination, although in a much sharper way, mere neutral imaginings, visions and auditions are cut off from the external world.

When under the influence of powerful religious emotions, people often believe they hear a mysterious voice. "Fear not, . . . for it is your Father's good pleasure to give you the kingdom!" Delighted by these words, and overcome with pleasure and hope, they discover the promises of Scripture to be excellent, in a new and greater way, but such fervent appreciation of Scripture occurs especially when they consider these promises to be addressed to them (2, 219–21). An analysis of this situation helps understand the moral roots of any assessment of immediate experiences *per se*. The passion felt when we believe the promises of salvation are addressed to us personally makes ideas appear to come to us immediately, but this immediacy is the opposite of what characterizes the relationship of spiritual ideas to the mind that perceives them. Those who believe they have received a promise of salvation earnestly praise the dazzling glory of God and the marvelous bliss of paradise, yet their perceptions in no way reflect the goodness

---

93. See also 2, 214–15; 2, 223; 7, 511; etc.

and excellence of these supreme realities in themselves. That we perceive them as such is simply because—as unregenerate creatures and therefore separated and alienated from God[94]—we believe that we ourselves will one day be able to enjoy that glory and bliss. This new perception of ideas of spiritual things is only a callow fiction because we remain separate from the things which those ideas represent. The ideas of our imagination are indeed so rooted in our mind that they are said to be "incorporated" with it (6, 196). However, this is precisely because we only perceive what is in reality no part of the things which those ideas represent, i.e., we are under an illusion that they belong to us when they are actually completely foreign to us. Imagination is really an ability to visualize things when they are absent (2, 213–14). It therefore only gives us a fictitious immediacy and, in the case of imaginings of a religious nature, the moral or rather the immoral root of this immediacy is clear. As the result of an error provoked by egoism, the mind believes it has accessed certain realities when, in actual fact, it only has a kind of reflection of something that truly does not belong to those realities but which the mind itself has produced. Thus the mind is under a deception and at the root of this deception we find mercenary love, self-love dreaming of the ultimate prize.

The Edwardsian argument was founded on the dialectic understanding that underlies the notion of imagination. By virtue of this faculty, the most intimate and immediate are precisely the most distant and external, and it was with this very dialectic that Edwards would integrate religious imagination with notional, doctrinal knowledge. After considering the sick imaginations of deluded minds partial to spiritual experiences and avid for personal promises and spiritual benefits, we are left with the issue of supernatural communications that actually come from God and announce truths. Edwards thought that communication—and, consequently, divine inspiration—is not so high an honor and privilege as some might think (23, 84). We have merely to think of Balaam—a pagan soothsayer—or King Saul—a hardened sinner—who nonetheless prophesied and even prophesied the truth (2, 206)! These men announced events that directly concerned the history of salvation, but the ideas they received were nonetheless of a natural order and not in any way from minds conformed to divine things.[95] For example, God might want to directly (i.e., immediately) reveal their assignment, and sometimes actually does so to certain men, but in making his will clear, God is still not communicating anything to their minds in a truly

---

94. See *supra*, p. 261.

95. Compare with, "If a man has anything revealed to him from God . . . 'tis . . . but dross and dung in comparison of the excellency of that gracious leading that the saints have" (4, 436).

spiritual manner (2, 279).⁹⁶ As with knowledge about the nature or works of God, knowledge about his will is, in itself, also nothing more than a sort of "doctrinal knowledge."⁹⁷

This definition is found amongst the analyses and descriptions of the *Treatise Concerning Religious Affections*, although that masterpiece of epistemological conciseness—the great Miscellany 782 on the sense of the heart—had already anticipated and summed up these developments in a striking way: "The extraordinary influence of the Spirit of God in inspiration, imparts speculative knowledge" (18, 462). From the visions and auditions of enthusiasts to the placid inspiration of heathen philosophers (23, 84), we continue to deal with speculative knowledge (see 8, 151–52). This kind of knowledge includes every imaginary view of God and Jesus Christ, every claimed witness of the Spirit, every immediate revelation of hidden things and every application of the words of Scripture to specific questions or the spiritual state of a given individual, along with any allegorical or mystical interpretation of the meaning of Scripture. According to Edwards, each of these cases involves "impressions on the imagination" and "impressions in the head" (2, 286). He accordingly grouped the extravagances of the enthusiasts, the unhealthy excesses of the compulsively lying imagination's allegorical reading of Scripture (18, 458)⁹⁸ and supernatural communications together, subsuming them all under the heading of "impressions in the head." Here Edwards echoes his great Miscellany 782 in which anything based solely on the understanding, including "direct, ideal . . . apprehension," is ascribed to the head, while everything related to the will, pleasure or pain, or to what is good or vile, is ascribed to the heart.⁹⁹

The enlargement or rather the explicitation of the notion of "head" to include the mirages of the imagination almost amounts to an ultimate unification of all religious apprehension inasmuch as it denotes the reception of contents. Edwards, let's remember, used the terms "doctrinal" and

---

96. Compare with, "not only reprobate sinners, but also the Divells, and Fallen Angels have received of great knowledge in the Mysteries of the will of God," (Taylor, *Christographia*, 369).

97. Compare with "an imagination that some have of speculative knowledge received from the Spirit of God in those that have no real inspiration, is that wherein ENTHUSIASM consists" (18, 462).

98. In 1734, with reference to religious truths, Edwards contrasted "the notion of them in our heads" with "the divine excellency of them in our hearts" (17, 416; see also 2, 120). For imagination vs. heart, see 12, 310; 17, 412–13, etc. For mouth vs. heart, see 22, 221.

99. Extraordinary gifts "are something adventitious . . . excellent things," but are like beautiful "garments" that do not alter the nature of the man who wears them (8, 158).

"historical" interchangeably.[100] Consequently, any image or concept—be it from an external source or from reasoning—i.e., every apprehension of religious content as content, is ultimately of the same order. An analysis of the imagination enabled Edwards to go even further in the direction of this generalization or formalization. The assimilation of the historical with the doctrinal is possible because contents of empirical or rational origin and character are of the same order. In other words, although they differ greatly in exactness and rationality, these contents stand in metaphysical continuity. However, the inclusion of imagination within the confines of the head means that not only the exact and less exact, but also the exact and inexact—or rather, the true and the false—can arise indifferently from the same sort of cogitation. Historical knowledge proceeds by hearsay and provides the understanding with information that is less precise and harder to verify than what reasoning presents in doctrinal knowledge. However, when we switch to the imagination, the situation changes radically because we are then accessing content that might quite simply be false. I believe that I heard these words spoken to me: "Fear not . . . for it is your Father's good pleasure to give you the kingdom!" Now, this is just an illusion, because I am and remain unregenerate and the Father is not giving me the kingdom. The assimilation of this sort of inspiration with apprehensions of a historical or notional order, and their common subsumption under the head, is made possible when particular revelations of immediate imaginations are brought together. Balaam uttered words of truth, while those of "the promise" were never actually addressed to me; however, assimilating both into the sphere of the head opens up new perspectives in religious epistemology. The rapprochement of false and true within the specific sphere of the Spirit's extraordinary gifts facilitated a generalized rapprochement of all cogitation, defined solely in terms of its contents. Whether images or concepts, whether true or false, religious contents as contents fall into the category of knowledge "in the head" for both the elect and the reprobate, for David as well as for Saul. After demonstrating that the authenticity of knowledge does not depend on the intensity of the act of knowing, we see that knowledge is not contingent on the exactness of its contents nor even their factual truthfulness.[101]

---

100. See *supra*, p. 261.

101. A 1744 sermon expanded the notion of "the head" even further and extended it to the entire realm of the unregenerate. In contrast to the "true piety" of the "heart," the things of the "head" consist in "speculative knowledge or opinions . . . outward morality . . . forms of religion" (25, 91). In other words—besides notional or natural knowledge—"the head" includes purely natural virtue and the piety nourished by mere common graces.

7. Awakened knowledge and conviction

Edwards's great sermon in Newark, which describes the Devil's highest theological accomplishments, distinguishes—even in its title—between "true grace" and "the experience of devils" and quotes this famous verse from the Epistle of James: "You believe that God is one; you do well. Even the demons believe—and shudder" (25, 608). The opposite of the true faith of the regenerate is not a mere theoretical, notional apprehension but knowledge that is rich in real-life experience; that involves deep emotions, such as fear and terror, and that is also designated explicitly in terms of faith. Kant described mere doctrinal faith as "unstable"[102] and Calvin wrote of some—even the reprobate—having "a slight knowledge" of the Gospel;[103] but the real opposite of justifying faith is solid assent or firm belief—in short, a committed attitude of involvement in sin and transgression. In his great Miscellany 782, Edwards might ultimately have been too hasty when he wrote that "perhaps this distinction of the kinds of our knowledge into speculative and sensible . . . will be found the most important of all" (18, 460). Implied by the developments in this same Miscellany, though only understood in terms of an epistemology incorporating religious data within itself, the fundamental distinction actually lies within the domain of the sensible itself, i.e., between mere natural knowledge of good and evil and a spiritual understanding of the same (see 17, 410–1).

Unlike later literary representations, the Devil of Calvinist dogmatics is neither an intellectual devoted to doubt, nor a "philosopher," but rather a fallen angel who is "orthodox in his faith" (25, 617). His knowledge in fundamental areas is not only theoretical but also practical in nature;[104] his revolt is neither a game without consequences, nor mere rational doubt, but violent and hateful opposition towards a reality that is the object of his strongest beliefs. Doctrinal or historical faith has been portrayed as being one of the consistent "impressions in the head" which even natural men may experience and one which, notwithstanding its frequently chimerical or frivolous character, is only contingent on our moral (i.e., natural) state. On the other hand, given the terror and remorse of the Devil and the reprobate, we might think that we are dealing with faith proper to the regenerate. We might even be tempted, like Hopkins, to recognize three types of religious knowledge: speculative, awakened and regenerate.[105] This position

---

102. Kant, *Critique of Pure Reason*, A827/B855.

103. Calvin, *Institutes*, 3. 2. 12.

104. Althaus, *Die Prinzipien der Deutschen Reformierten Dogmatik im Zeitalter der Aristotelischen Scholastik*, 35.

105. Hopkins, *Two Sermons, Works*, 3:528.

would not truly do justice to the subtlety of the Edwardsian distinctions, given that it resorts indiscriminately to epistemological and religious-moral criteria, although without in any manner interlinking them.

Edwards defined speculative knowledge in purely epistemological terms. Speculative knowledge designated all knowledge of a theoretical, notional order, without regard to its subject's spiritual state. The epistemological characterization of awakened knowledge was not the same and only dealt very superficially with a religious and moral criteriology. The spiritual literature and preaching of the Puritans described the awakened state as consisting in strong emotions of remorse and joy, fear and hope. However—and this is essential—such notions were not applied generally but only to minds impressed by the importance of religious things, the greatness of God and the misery of their own sins, though still not yet regenerated. Awakened knowledge is defined as an engaged apprehension, with natural man *per se* as the subject. At first glance, of course, awakened faith seems to be portrayed (and rejected) in subjective terms. If doctrinal faith is merely theoretical, contemplative knowledge without any inclination towards its object (see 2, 272), awakened faith is existential and emotional in nature. Neither the absence nor the presence of inclination is sufficient to determine the religious significance of faith. Psychologically speaking, the subject's attitude therefore does not have any real impact in this domain. On the other hand, the discussion on doctrinal faith demonstrated that neither is notional knowledge *per se* of any consequence in this domain.[106] However, if the knowing subject and the known object, i.e., the religious notion, are of no importance when it comes to determining the difference between true and counterfeit faith, shouldn't we forego the use of all immanent, objective criteria to explain the different types of religious knowledge? Now—and this is the core of these Edwardsian developments—the true object of faith is not the religious notion itself but the spiritual reality to which it refers. Once that is understood, it becomes possible to move towards an explanation, in immanent and objective terms, of the distinction between regenerated knowledge and unregenerated knowledge. Then and only then will it also become apparent that epistemological and religious-moral criteria, which seem to be of two different orders, can be unified and that moral-religious data can be adequately explained in metaphysico-epistemological terms. Studying the awakened state in which natural man undergoes conviction helps decipher the complex lines of interdependence between the epistemic and the moral-religious.

106. People can be "zealous … even of the ordinances of God, from no better principles than the Papists and the heathens are zealous of their superstitions and idolatries" (19, 63–64).

According to Miscellany 782, when natural men are "awakened and convinced," the Spirit of God gives them "an ideal apprehension of the things of religion with respect to what is natural in them, i.e. of that which is speculative in them, and that which pertains to a sensibleness of their natural good and evil" (18, 463). A little further on, in this same Miscellany, Edwards succinctly defined conviction as "an ideal and sensible apprehension of what is natural in the things of religion" (18, 465). These two definitions summarily present the issues surrounding religious knowledge that is both rigorous and engaged and yet still unregenerate. They indicate the contents of the awakened conscience, namely all that is natural in religion, their natural good and evil. They underline the sensible character of the awakened sinner's apprehensions and—by reiterating that only "an ideal apprehension" of the "things of religion" is present in "conviction"—also underscore the need for more clarification regarding the relationships between the speculative and the sensible.

Above and beyond mere speculative knowledge, which only consists in simple cogitation or an "ideal apprehension" of religious contents (see 18, 458), conviction also implies "a sensible apprehension" of "the things of religion" (18, 465). The awakened sinners of this world and the damned of the next are not limited to a notional knowledge of the doctrines of religion; they also have "a sense of the heart" (18, 358). This sense of the heart may be understood as a strong emotion but it also implies faith. Edwards preached in Newark that "unregenerate men may have a sense of the importance of . . . eternity, and the vanity of . . . time; the work of immortal souls . . . and the folly of . . . sin." The damned can have "a strong and most affecting sense of the awful greatness and majesty of God" (25, 627) and even the Devil has a sense of many divine things, which "deeply affects him, and is most strongly impressed on his heart" (25, 626). The damned have "terrors of conscience" that are infinitely greater than anything they ever experienced during their lifetime (25, 629) and Edwards emphasized the fact that his sermon's text, a verse from the Epistle of James, "has reference not only to the act of the understandings of devils in believing, but to that affection of their hearts which accompanies the views they have" (25, 630).

By virtue of their deep, religious emotion, "awakened sinners" have a fervent desire for God and Jesus Christ that appears to be satisfied because these sinners, like the devils, *have* faith. We read in one Miscellany that the Devil has as high a degree of assent as a real Christian to the articles of the faith (W 2, 637) in which, as we recall, he is "thoroughly established" (25, 617). Moreover, referring to a passage in Luke where the Devil bows down before Jesus (8, 28), Edwards stated: "The Devil is religious . . . he falls down before Christ . . . he prays earnestly" (21, 171). The Devil's piety, a classic Protestant criticism of "religion," appeared to be the ultimate refutation of any vague attempt to link the warmth and solidity of religious affections to regenerate faith. More precisely, it served as an *ad hominem* argument to counter attempts to identify pious exercises and feelings with the faith of the justified. Neither the fervor of our remorse nor the solidity of our assent to the articles of a *Credo* are criteria of true faith, and the sometimes hesitant but nonetheless systematic and consequent inclusion of sensible apprehensions in the description of conviction[107] is a reminder that the real demarcation line between natural and regenerate is not based on the speculation-sense duality but instead runs through the domain of the sensible. In particular, let's reiterate that the ultimate distinction is not metaphysical but ethico-epistemological in nature. The authentic criterion of real faith is not a psychologico-subjective factor, the strength of the mind's engagement, but the objective content of the spiritual reality reached by the mind.

In the language of Calvin, "what knowledge of God the wicked possess"[108] is the great question to which Edwards formulated his clearest answer in Miscellany 782. This text defined conviction as "an ideal apprehension" and "sensible knowledge" of "the things of religion with respect to what is natural in them" (18, 463). Further on, in a slightly simpler way, he mentioned a "common conviction, or an ideal and sensible apprehension of what is natural in the things of religion" (18, 465). But what exactly do we understand by these *naturalia* in a religious context? At first glance, it would seem to be a distinction based on the traditional opposition of reason and revelation. These *naturalia* are those aspects of God that fall under natural reason, whereas other truths about God—more specifically, those regarding the Trinity—are only accessible to minds informed by faith. Protestant dogmatics certainly maintained this basic distinction inherited from medieval theology, yet likewise held to another one, also of medieval origin, that no longer emphasized the opposition of the natural and the positive. Protestant theology made particular use of a distinction between natural and moral attributes in which the opposition is based less on criteria associated with knowing subjectivity than on the characteristics immanent in the Deity itself. Natural attributes can be roughly defined as those related to the Being and power of God, whereas moral attributes are related to his goodness. Edwards himself was content to appropriate this distinction and, as we will

---

107. "Sensible Knowledge . . . implies . . . an ideal apprehension" (18, 459); "ideal apprehension of . . . His greatness" (18, 460); "An ideal apprehension . . . with respect to . . . that which pertains to a sensibleness" (18, 463); "an ideal and sensible apprehension" (18, 465, etc.)

108. Calvin, *Institutes*, 3. 2. 9.

later see in more detail, he made frequent and creative use of it.[109] In his view, God's natural attributes are what an awakened and convinced mind conceives, although in this instance it seems less a question of ontological objectivity than of their religious significance. Edwards does not portray the *naturalia* of God as the proper contents of natural man's faith. They are not notional categories but effective and affective realities that exert a powerful influence on the life and destiny of the unregenerate. They are sources of fear and hope and, to the extent that natural man is a "convinced" sinner, they especially inspire fear.

God's greatness consists in his natural perfections (18, 463), and juxtaposing the sinner's infinite smallness and misery with God's immensity helps explain the subsumption of various ontological attributes under the attribute of greatness. In conviction, the Lord leads us "to a greater sense of the things of religion, as to their natural properties and qualities, and particularly of the natural perfections of God, such as his greatness, terrible majesty" (2, 311). This greatness of God is not so much the neutral notion of Being as it is the menacing aspect of such crushing power over a creature who is "worse than anything" (18, 223) and less than nothing, specifically in terms of transgressions. On the other hand—as Edwards noted—"there are many things exhibited in the gospel, concerning God and Christ, and the way of salvation, that have a natural good in them" (2, 277). In other words, the greatness of God, which most often appears menacing and opposed to natural self-love, can also seem to be a source of pleasure and profit for us. Expressed thus, i.e., in terms of their relationship to the events and course of human life, the *naturialia* of religion are reduced to two major categories, namely "natural good and evil" (18, 463). An outcome that should hardly come as a surprise is a thought where knowledge is not supposed to matter to us, unless it pertains to our will and heart (18, 465).

At first glance, subsuming the *naturalia* of religion under just two categories, namely good and evil, might seem like utilitarian or—at best—ethical reductionism, but as we will see later, it is nothing of the sort. Rather, it was the far-reaching requirements of an epistemology integrating the religious given within itself that led to this ultimate simplification. However, before we can fully describe this epistemology, we need to take a closer look at the knowledge that a man subject to the great test of conviction can obtain from good and evil or, more precisely, from the knowledge he has about evil, because "legal conviction" is first and foremost a state of remorse

---

109. See *infra*, p. 344 ss.

and terror, the realization of his sin, and an expectation of the punishment that must be incurred for sin.[110]

8. Natural knowledge of sin

In the great tradition of Calvinism, Edwards professed natural man's ability to discern moral good and evil[111]—although with precise limits on discernment, which prevents the regenerate man from understanding evil in itself, i.e., the very heinousness of sin, the hatefulness of evil, considered in and for itself—and then Edwards concluded with the existence of double knowledge. He wrote that, without the presence of a supernatural principle, "the mind of man . . . is capable of two things with respect to conviction of evil." It is capable of providing "a conviction of truth respecting evil" and "a sense of heart" of this evil (18, 358). This is natural evil, i.e., all that is repugnant to our external senses, all grief arising from hindrances and wounds inflicted on our self-love, and all terribleness arising from these various injuries (18, 462). As regards natural evil in the sphere of religion, Edwards primarily thought about the sufferings that natural, fallen man would have to endure because of his opposition to God. Likewise for his opposition's hateful character. In other words, the natural evil in religion consists as much in the punishment of sin as in sin itself. Edwards accordingly accepted that the conscience could discern evil, although more by a sort of natural instinct (see 17, 153) than by an adequate realization of moral evil in itself. These analyses tend to show that natural man's knowledge of the relationship between the fact of sin and the need for punishment is not essentially different from the "sense of heart" he can have of the pernicious character of evil itself. Both cases involve mechanical and necessary mental processes. We arrive at this demonstration of the continuity between (the unregenerate's) speculative and sensible knowledge primarily because of epistemological considerations.

According to an important sermon on Hosea 5:15, the feeling of guilt that assails natural man has two elements: (1) a sense of sin, and (2) a sense of the relationship between sin and punishment (17, 151–2); and, to a certain extent, we might even say that the latter explains the former. This "sense

---

110. "Common illumination" concerns (natural) good, whereas "legal conviction" concerns (natural) evil (18, 357–58). "A legal humiliation is all a mere farce. Men quit their own righteousness because they are driven and beaten from it. They despair of helping themselves" (22, 314). We can even say that "a legal spirit is attended with unbelief" (24, 269).

111. See 18, 357–59; 17, 152–53, etc.

of the relationship between sin and punishment" roughly corresponds to the judgment of the truth respecting evil, accessible to natural man reflecting on the anger of God which his transgression will not fail to provoke (see 18, 358). Man is conscious of his disobedience to God and of the offense he has committed against the Almighty, Most Holy Being. He understands that he deserves to be punished (17, 153–54) and also sees the inevitability of his condemnation. Edwards deduced this teaching on the demerits of sin and its condemnation from the immanent solidarity between the transgression and the sanction discerned by the conscience. The conscience is convinced that a man's moral and spiritual state corresponds to the quality of his willed acts and inclinations. Someone who does evil must also be subjected to it and in exact proportion to the evil he himself committed. Therefore, when a sinner is punished, he is merely getting what is due to him, i.e., in a manner of speaking, what properly belongs to him. Our conscience tells us that we reap what we sow. There is a rigorous connection in this world between one thing and another—depending on their nature—and it is this natural connection between sin and punishment that convicts our conscience of the immanent need for punishment (18, 436). This knowledge of evil stems virtually from a simple logico-mathematical reading of the relationships that prevail between a transgression against the Most High and the punishment for it. In a religious context, natural evil is primarily the punishment suffered by those who disobey God and—taught by reason, conscience and the Law (17, 155)—a man who knows that he himself is a transgressor clearly apprehends the evil his offenses entail. In the awakened and convinced state, these punishments will doubtless seem more vivid, frightening and terrifying to him. Nonetheless, this is still the same "notional" knowledge of evil (see 13, 400), although now made more lively and sensible by the sting of legal conviction (see 17, 410). The presentation of the truth concerning the evil of punishment, and the need for it, does not essentially differ from the consciousness these men had of them before their "conviction," but merely appear clearer and "more credible" to them (18, 464).

The knowledge that an awakened and convinced man obtains regarding the evil that transgression entails always remains natural in character, i.e., purely "speculative" (18, 463), although Edwards also spoke of "a sense of the heart of this evil," which is "something more than a mere conviction in the judgment" concerning the truth of these evils (18, 358). In other words, he appears to advocate a knowledge of evil that not only concerns its consequences but also its nature, and not only relates to the horror of punishment but also to that which is hateful in transgression. However, a more attentive reading of the Edwardsian texts shows that this concession—fairly traditional in Calvinism—to a natural sense of evil can or rather should be understood from the perspective of his teaching on self-love. Edwards attributed the surge in "a sensible apprehension of the heinousness of sin" (18, 463) to conviction. However, numerous passages that describe the modalities for accessing this "apprehension" show that, in and of itself, it isn't truly an apprehension of the evil of sin.

We read in the sermon on Hosea 5:15 that the damned "are sensible of the heinousness of sin" because they perceive "the awful greatness of that Being whom they have sinned against." At first glance, we might think that this is a sort of intuition, immediate knowledge or an intimate, existential apprehension of the greatness that makes sin so heinous. Edwards immediately stated that what makes sinners capable of being made sensible of that terrible majesty and greatness is also what makes them capable of hearing the thunder and seeing the flames that accompanied the giving of the Law on Mount Sinai (17, 155). In other words, even this apprehension of the *terribilia* of God—which engendered a sense of the heinousness of sin—was merely an empirical mental operation that originated from "external ideas." A sense of the heinousness of evil is not grasped and discerned immediately or by itself but is, as it were, deduced from realizing "the dreadfulness of God's displeasure," i.e., from the reactions of One other than ourselves. Moreover, even the "convinced" mind's accessing of this Other's representations is not portrayed as immediate but as if it was burdened with discursivity. An "awakened" man has a sense of the "dreadfulness" of the divine displeasure incurred by sin, yet this "sense" or "apprehension" refers only to "an idea of what God is supposed to feel in His own heart in having that displeasure" (18, 460). He does not immediately apprehend God's ideas, but is only accessing representations attributed to him by conjecture. He does not immediately intuit a sense of God, but instead accesses the eventual contents of his understanding indirectly by "reflection." Men do not apprehend God's ideas by "repeating" them as spiritual ideas, but instead attempt to put themselves, as it were, in his place by tending to "excite" similar ideas and placing them in their own imagination (18, 461). Once again, an unregenerate man's sensible, affective knowledge is reduced to mere notional knowledge and an external apprehension of religious contents.

These reflections of an epistemological nature help us understand that legal conviction, even with a lively impression of the terribleness of evil, still doesn't ensure anything more than indirect cognition. Conviction intensifies our apprehension of divine wrath, helping us better understand "the connection between . . . sin and punishment" (13, 509). Despite every insistence on the particular strength of this sense of the heinousness of sin, it is barely discernable from the sin itself, although understood from the wrath of God, the author of the punishment. The heinousness of the sin is therefore only conjectured from its relationship to the punishment. If this is so, we find ourselves in a Hobbesian position where the evil of a transgression is deduced from the sanction it provokes (*Bl.*, 138–9). In other words, if natural men can have a sense of the heinousness of sin, they do not get it from the sin itself (2, 311), but from its concomitants and consequences, i.e., by virtue of "hidden purposes."[112]

Puritan theologians elaborated on the subject of a purely indirect apprehension of sin, i.e., an apprehension by mere "discourse" that does not discern "the thing sin,"[113] but the deficiency of this indirect access to evil has less to do with the purely mediate, thoughtful character of the mental operation itself than with the imperfect notion of evil that it engenders. The mental operation itself doesn't lack precision, nor is it subject to uncertainty or arbitrariness. However, if it leads to inadequate results, that is because they are based on natural man's distorted epistemological state. T. Shepard said that the great misfortune of the wicked is that they are not able to see things as they are in themselves[114] and this strange powerlessness of the unregenerate intellect now gets an epistemological explanation.

The purely mediate, thoughtful character of the natural knowledge of good and evil does not, in any way, imply hesitancy, tentativeness or the presence of fortuitous or merely probable elements. On the contrary, the understanding becomes clearer and firmer as convictions become stronger. Edwards didn't think that the awakened state's strong emotions weakened or troubled the understanding of natural good and evil in any way. Rather, he taught that this understanding improves progressively. Yet—and this is key—no improvement in the logical understanding of good and evil can change the radically impersonal character of natural knowledge in the religious and moral domain. Awakened men have their sights set on sin. They apprehend it with clarity and certitude and—contrary to what so often happens during a scholarly sermon—"there will [be] no such thing as slumbering in Hell!" (25, 618).[115] Nevertheless, a clearer view of sin, strict correctness and the implacable logic of the knowledge of evil gained by the intellect do

---

112. See *supra*, p. 201. "Natural men in strictness see nothing of the proper deformity of wrong" (13, 514). They are certainly afflicted and mourn, though not for their sins but rather their sins' consequences, when they have to "freely" mourn their transgressions because of their "odious" nature and opposition to the "excellency of Christ" (*Bl.*, 185–87). The devils know their hatred of God is "unreasonable . . . but yet their hearts don't disrelish it and loath it: if they did, it would have no place in their hearts" (21, 317).

113. Shepard, *The Sound Believer*, *Works*, 1:127.

114. Shepard, *The Sound Believer*, *Works*, 1:144–45.

115. Regarding those who sleep during sermons, see V, 362.

not, in any way, ensure adequate discernment of the proper essence of evil. Partly a fruit of the conscience's natural, intuitive sense of good and evil and ultimately explained by the universe of egotistical self-love, this knowledge is primarily a mechanical and required reading of the relationships men maintain with evil, which is portrayed in terms of its consequences.

When subjected to the test of "legal conviction," natural man becomes more "sensible" to the relationship between sin and punishment, and between sin and the wrath of God. The conclusions of the wicked regarding their punishments are a result of strict logicity, although simply a faithful reflection of evidence imposed on their minds which they cannot necessarily ignore. Edwards emphasized the continuity between the knowledge of the unregenerate in this world and the clear knowledge of the damned on the Day of Judgment (2, 277). He did so for the good reason that the Day of the Lord will "manifest" the truth of which they became aware at the time of conviction, only with even greater clarity (see 25, 618–9). When awakened sinners are the subjects of great convictions, this is only "transacting the business of the Day of Judgment, in the conscience beforehand: God sits enthroned in the conscience, as at the Last Day, he will sit enthroned in the clouds of heaven . . . The sinner's iniquities are brought to light; his sins set in order before him . . . Many witnesses do, as it were, rise up against the sinner under convictions of conscience . . . as at the Day of Judgment. The conviction of a sinner . . . will be a work of the law, as well as the conviction of conscience" (25, 621).[116] The fire of judgment will make the evidence of evil and its punishment appear, just as characters written with orange juice become visible when exposed to heat.[117] This is merely explicitation of previously hidden and implicit contents and facts, and the necessarily mechanical unfolding of this process deprives it of any genuinely spiritual character.[118]

Since the Middle Ages, theologians have presented the Devil's faith, knowledge and feelings with respect to evil as something forced by the evidence and imposed on his mind and therefore devoid of any merit.[119]

---

116 The scope of the illuminated conscience is neither greater nor less than that of faith itself (8, 593–94).

117. Shepard, *The Sincere Convert*, Works, 1:38; see also, "By the aid of conscience things are so arranged that the judicial report follows at once upon every fault, and that the guilty one himself must write it. But it is written with sympathetic ink and only becomes thoroughly clear when in eternity it is held up to the light, while eternity holds audit over the consciences" (Kierkegaard, *Sickness Unto Death*, 203).

118. Edwards frequently recalls, with respect to "inferior affections," that there are affections "of the *same denomination* which are truly virtuous" (8, 616).

119. Saint Thomas Aquinas, *Summa Theologiæ*, 2-2. 5. 2 ad. 1–2. For Baader, "the weight of truth" under which a demonic mind bends was a paradigm for the "precise

For Edwards, emphasizing the exactitude of diabolical knowledge and the strength of the reprobate's remorse helped restate the contrast between spiritual knowledge—which alone is adequate—and its opposite, a notional or even sensible knowledge of good and evil. He wrote in a Miscellany that even devils can be "forced to speak the truth" of God (23, 84) and that, on the Day of Judgment, a clear vision of the extent of their sin will stop the mouths of sinners and thwart any vague attempt to contest the grounds of their condemnation (25, 621). Moreover, in this world, and "forced by the clear light of conscience" (25, 619), awakened sinners will be conscious of the justice of their punishment. In each of these cases, there is an immediate realization of the natural agreement between *opposing* Being in general and *being opposed by* Being in general (8, 595). The sinner's knowledge of his transgression does not penetrate his heart, and the silence to which he is reduced is hardly sincere remorse for having done wrong, but merely a clear realization that it is the order of things that requires him to be punished.

The radical insufficiency of the unregenerate's remorse and their purely legal repentance stem from the fact that the sinner can hardly protest against the grounds for his condemnation. Even though his understanding cannot but agree with them, this agreement still does not mean his inclination and heart are engaged (25, 620).[120] An understanding of the just and inexorable character of the Divine Judgment may very well co-exist, and effectively does co-exist, with continued hatred toward God. Devils—as we

---

knowledge" the mind requires if it hasn't freely internalized the truth (*Vorlesungen über Spekulative Dogmatik, Werke,* 9:178n.). This recalls the "tyranny of truth," denounced by Cicero and Mercier de la Rivière, and more recently by H. Arendt in *Between Past and Future,* 225, 240.

120. See "Les infidèles ... condamnent leurs forfaits par le propre jugement de leur conscience, estans sommez d'en répondre. Car toute intelligence n'est pas si entièrement esteinte en eux, que tousjours ils ne mettent quelque différence entre droiture et iniquité. Et quelque fois mesmes ils vienent jusques-là d'estre effrayez et tormentez de destresse pour le sentiment de leur mal et forfait, tellement que desjà en ceste vie ils soustienent une manière de damnation: mais néantmoins de tout leur cœur ils prenent plaisir à péché: et pourtant ils s'y addonnent, sans qu'en leur affection il y ait une vraye résistance. Car ces aiguillons de conscience, desquels ils sont picquez, procèdent plus-tost d'une contradiction de leur jugement, qui condamne ce qu'ils font, que non pas d'une affection contraire en leur volonté [The ungodly ... are reminded of their crimes, they condemn them in their own conscience; for knowledge is not so utterly extinguished in them, but that they still retain the difference between right and wrong; and sometimes they are shaken with such dread under a sense of their sin, that they bear a kind of condemnation even in this life: nevertheless, they approve of sin with all their heart, and hence give themselves up to it without any feeling of genuine repugnance; for those stings of conscience, by which they are harassed, proceed from opposition in the judgment, rather than from any contrary inclination in the will]" (Calvin, *Commentarius in Epistolam Pauli ad Romanos, Opera,* 49, 129–30).

read in a 1739 sermon—see their misery and sin and, consequently, their immense distance from God, but they are not reconciled to this distance and continue to hate God (8, 246).[121] In fact, hatred of God will not only continue in the next world but also grow. People who, while they were alive, doubted the existence of God or believed they could quite simply deny it, will end up hating it in hell. Atheism, which resulted in the vague, weak, and unreal feelings this world has about God, will be replaced by hate towards him. Natural man is inclined to vaguely think that God does not exist (see 8, 611), but when confronted with dazzling evidence of the terrible reality of God, this feeling switches to enmity against him. "A serpent will not bite, or spit poison at that which it sees at a great distance; which if it saw near, would do it immediately" (V, 299). Co-existence or, more precisely, a directly proportional relationship between a person's knowledge of God and the hatred he feels for him, is ultimately explained by the Calvinist religious epistemology because such hatred is the logical outcome of the operations of a mind imprisoned in sin. The paradox of conviction is that it provokes a violent apprehension of evil, yet only by an indirect, "non-spiritual" apprehension in which the true nature of evil remains alien to the mind. Now—and here is the crux of the paradox—this externality with regard to evil merely hides the powerlessness of the unregenerate's intellect to transcend the narrow limits of his fallen world.

At the beginning of his *Personal Narrative,* Edwards discusses his religious experiences prior to conversion. He tells of having felt a "kind of delight in religion . . . and had much self-righteous pleasure," of being in his "element" when "engaged in religious duties." And he added that many may be deceived by this kind of affection and delight in religion and ultimately "mistake it for [true] grace" (16, 791). Now, the fact that, prior to justification, a person can only feel that he is in *his* element indicates that he is still not regenerated, i.e., transferred outside of himself and into the objective world where things are seen as they are in themselves (2, 252–53).

In common illumination and legal conviction, good and evil are seen as imposing themselves from without. In fact, they impose themselves from without by virtue of our (subverted) epistemological state. Prior to justification, we are radically egotistical and can only experience good and evil in terms of this egotism. The natural attributes of God that the unregenerate

---

121. A man might understand and admit that he deserves damnation, yet continue to reproach God: Why did he create me? Why did he give me an existence determined towards sin? Why did he have me share in Adam's transgression and withhold his saving help? (13, 511). Such questions, which Edwards puts in the mouths of condemned sinners, are strangely reminiscent of the favorite Arminian and deist objections to Calvinist orthodoxy.

perceive are not derived from the universality of notions in what is called natural religion (see 23, 458); rather, they are the results of an inquiry bent by deviation and burdened by the weight of evil. The strict correctness of the conclusions regarding the *naturalia* of the Deity is not due to an adequate idea of God, but rather to an indirect idea considered from the perspective of the sinful will. The mental operations of the unregenerate are not founded on a spiritual idea that restates or represents God as he is in himself. The natural conscience only dreams of God (see MO, 394) and these dreams, like all others, are based on a subjective psychologism. The mind of the unregenerate does not understand God as he is in himself, but only as he appears to be from their point of view. Good and evil are not good and evil *in themselves*, but only good and evil *for ourselves*, creatures whose understanding and heart have been affected by evil.

6

The Knowledge of Spiritual Things

1. Knowledge and conversion

According to his *Personal Narrative,* Edwards prayed fervently as a child. He felt "in his element," experiencing "a kind of delight" and had "much self-righteous pleasure" and "affections" which many easily mistake for true "grace" (16, 791). On arriving at Yale, his fervor abated and it was only during his last year of college that religion became his central preoccupation. He devoted himself to practicing his "duties of religion," made repeated resolutions and made seeking his salvation "the main business" of his life. Although this period of reflections and resolutions, characterized by "great and violent inner struggles," didn't end with a sudden conversion at a particular point in time, the young man realized that a "wonderful alteration" had taken place in his mind. Though he had always been tormented by the "horrible doctrine" of sovereign election, Edwards now apprehended its just and reasonable character. His mind assented to this doctrine, which gave him "a delightful conviction."[1] However—and this is the essential point—he immediately remarked that the proper object of these "delightful convictions" was not the sovereignty of God but rather his excellency and glory. He experienced "a new sense" and "a new sort of affection" came into his soul for the excellency and glory of God. Thereafter he imagined the happiness of being "wrapt up to God in Heaven and be as it were swallowed up in Him" and experienced new perceptions and "apprehensions" of "the lovely way of salvation, by free grace" in Christ (16, 792–93).

---

1. See *infra,* Appendix 2, p. 409.

Edwards wrote his *Narrative* while rereading his *Resolutions* and *Diary*, written during his stay in New York City where he preached in 1722–1723 for a small Presbyterian congregation. In his *Diary* entry dated January 12, 1723, Edwards mentions the renewal of his "baptismal covenant" and self-dedication to God. "Henceforth," he wrote, "I am not . . . my own." "Neither have I any right to this body . . . no right to . . . these hands . . . these senses . . . I . . . have not retained any thing, as my own . . . I gave myself *wholly* to Him" (16, 792).[2] It was after three weeks of intense meditations, prayers and "experiences" that Edwards resolved to rededicate his entire being to God, a conversion process that follows a law that is diametrically opposed to the one underlying "legal conviction." Legal conviction begins with becoming conscious of the dreadful punishment due for sin and apprehending this evil leads to the notion of God. On the other hand, "saving conviction" (18, 465) begins with apprehending God's excellency and becoming conscious of it leads to an understanding of the heinousness of sin. At the beginning of this three-week period, Edwards wrote in his *Diary*: "This day revived by God's Spirit. Affected with the sense of the excellency of holiness. Felt more exercise of love to Christ than usual. Have also felt sensible repentance of sin, because it was committed against so merciful and good a God" (16, 759). And a little later: "Higher thoughts than usual of the excellency of Christ, and felt an unusual repentance of sin therefrom" (16, 761). First, there is a sense of the excellency of Christ and only then repentance for sins committed against such a merciful and good God. Instead of the horror of punishment leading us to conclude that God is angry and merciless, our ineffable experience of God's excellency and mercy leads us to discover the heinousness of sin.[3]

This reversed order of the spiritual path's essential moments expresses the justified, regenerated creature's transformed state. Torn from his natural, incarcerated state, the regenerated person finds himself transferred, in

2. Verbs in the first person and images of confinement predominate in *Personal Narrative* passages from the period prior to his conversion, whereas texts from his post-conversion period are characterized by passive verbs, "ecstatic metaphor and the language of epiphany" (Garrisson, "Teaching Early American Literature," in Lesser, *Jonathan Edwards*, 292).

3. In a New York sermon, Edwards illustrates the Christian teaching on spiritual illumination by resorting to the Cave allegory: "When a man is enlightened savingly by Christ, he is as it were, brought into a new world . . . he is like one that was born and brought up in a cave, where is nothing but darkness, but now is brought out into the lightsome world, enlightened by the beams of the sun. . . . He now sees things in their true shapes and colours . . . he sees his own vileness and filthiness, which he had often heard of before, but never believed" (10, 539). The odiousnesss of sin can only be understood in the light of the true God.

a manner of speaking, into the vast expanses of God's domain. The radical epistemological and other consequences of this new condition are to be understood from the soul's new reading of the Deity. Man leaves the straightjacket of his alienated self and finds himself in the presence of a God who no longer varies according to his own desires and terrors. Justification is like a second creation (see 20, 71), therefore God seems "new" (see 20, 436–37) with the creature's *"renewing of the mind."*[4] The Deity that the justified individual sees is still the same sovereign, all-powerful God, although this very sovereignty now seems to have absolutely different characteristics. It no longer seems arbitrary and vengeful, but merciful and saving. The crucial moment of conversion is realizing "the sufficiency of Jesus Christ," namely the fact that God is not obliged by any (immanent) necessity to condemn us for our sins, but is sufficiently powerful to remit them and sufficiently merciful to pardon and indeed save us. Calvinism undoubtedly teaches the irresistible power of God, although, in the final analysis, this power is not blind freedom because it is essentially merciful.

Unlike "legal conviction," which conjures up the immediate relationship between the transgression and the wrath that condemns it, "spiritual conviction" reveals our "freedom from damnation" (17, 152). But, at the same time, it also causes us to discover the heinousness of our sins which, in themselves, merit condemnation. In the best tradition of Christian preaching, Edwards professes that we can only imagine the heinousness of our sin by starting from the sufficiency of Jesus Christ and the infinite goodness of God, that the evil of our transgressions can only be truly understood in light of the very goodness of God. While there certainly is a profound asymmetry between good and evil, this doesn't hinder close solidarity between them in which good predominates. Taking this representation of natural good and evil in perfect reciprocity further brings us to an adequate understanding of "spiritual" good and evil. This adequate understanding, this "saving knowledge of good and evil" (15, 592), only comes when we realize who God is in himself and our understanding is completely renewed by the infusion of the "new simple idea" of grace (2, 205).

Christian preaching frequently succumbs to the temptation to explain the origin of our knowledge of God in light of our fear of his punishment, although dogmaticians have always emphasized the absolute priority of justification with respect to a true awareness of sin. In that regard, theologians think that a purely notional knowledge of sin isn't true knowledge and that true knowledge of transgressions always implies an "affective" (i.e., effective) understanding of their heinousness, an apprehension that is

---

4. Ephesians 4:23 in Calvin, *Institutes*, 3. 7. 1.

itself inseparable from repentance.[5] As a true "virtue," repentance can only properly arise from grace.[6] Luther thought that, without the illumination of the Spirit, man would never discern the supreme sin, namely unbelief in the divinity of Jesus Christ;[7] and because consideration and understanding of particular sin can only follow a general disposition to repent, repentance itself arises from seeing the love and wounds of Jesus Christ.[8] Though it occasionally seemed to confine itself to the proclamation of legal conviction, Puritan preaching at its best never ceased to restate that brilliant intuition of the Gospel: sinners only apprehend their sins when they comprehend the sufficiency and glory of Jesus Christ and only see the extent and horror of their transgressions when they discover the God who pardons their sins.[9] In New England, it was Thomas Shepard who forcefully explained that the essence of (spiritual) conviction is having "real" knowledge of our sin. "If you here ask," he wrote, "how the Lord makes sin real, I answer, by making God real; the real greatness of sin is seen by beholding really the greatness of God, who is smitten by sin."[10] Closer to Edwards, Solomon Stoddard thought that, prior to conversion, man might see some "moral evil" in sin but never "the great evil of sin."[11] New Theology stressed the strict parallelism between discovering the true God and understanding the proper evil of sin. "Without a sense of the supreme, infinite amiableness of the divine nature," wrote Joseph Bellamy "there can be no true sense of the infinite evil of sin."[12] A little later, he clarified this thought: there is a strict solidarity between a view of the glory of God and that of the infinite evil of sin, which are "naturally and inseparably connected; yea, they will be necessarily implied in each other."[13]

    5. See J. Hamon, "Comment saurais-je que vous êtes beau, si je ne sais que je suis difforme [How would I know that you are beautiful if I don't know that I am deformed]?" (*Soliloques sur le Psaume 118*, in Russier, *La foi selon Pascal*, 2:371n.2).

    6. Saint Thomas Aquinas, *Summa Theologiæ*, 3. 86. 2. co. See also, "Celui qui possède l'amour de Dieu, a, par là même, un regard absolu du péché [For whoever has divine love necessarily has perfect sorrow for his sins]" (Ruysbroeck the Admirable, *L'Ornement des noces spirituelles*, 21).

    7. Luther, *Enarratio in I. Cap. Genesin*, Werke, 52:291.

    8. Luther, *Grund und Ursach aller Artikel D. Martin Luthers, so durch Römische Bulle unrechtlich Verdammt sind*, Werke, 7:360.

    9. For this, see the exegesis of related biblical texts in Barth, *Kirchliche Dogmatik*, 4. 1. 433–34.

    10. Shepard, *The Sound Believer*, Works, 1:128.

    11. Stoddard, *Guide to Christ*, 54.

    12. Bellamy, *An Essay on the Nature and Glory of the Gospel of Jesus Christ*, Works, 2:381.

    13. Bellamy, *An Essay on the Nature and Glory of the Gospel of Jesus Christ*, Works,

Bellamy, an archetypal preacher of the Law, believed he was faithfully interpreting his master by teaching parallelism, not to mention the reciprocity of spiritual good and evil. Indeed, numerous Edwardsian texts seem to recommend that reading or, more precisely, make it possible to misunderstand the true link between these two ultimate categories. The Miscellanies define natural good and evil as objects of common illumination and legal conviction and present spiritual good and evil as the discoveries proper to spiritual illumination and conviction.[14] Spiritual good and evil seem to be in strict parallelism, where the realization of one goes hand in hand with the other. A passage in the *Treatise Concerning Religious Affections* echoes the Miscellanies: "the same eye that discerns the transcendent beauty of holiness, necessarily therein sees the exceeding odiousness of sin: the same taste which relishes the sweetness of true moral good, tastes the bitterness of moral evil" (2, 301). Other texts seem to involve more than mere parallelism, namely true reciprocity or a sort of interdependence: "he who sees the beauty of holiness, must necessarily see the hatefulness of sin, its contrary" (2, 274).[15] However, this apparent reciprocity and parallelism should not lead us into error. Jonathan Edwards was far too good a theologian and far too expert a metaphysician to fall into what is an attenuated form of Manicheism. Good and evil are never mere opposites and, on a purely "spiritual" level, their asymmetry is clear. Even if, from a metaphysical perspective, evil should not be deduced from good, at the level of the religious conscience, it can only be imagined from and after good.[16] Even though the evil of sin actually precedes the good of redemption, because "corruption is rooted deepest in us," at the level of the religious and moral conscience, the heinousness of sin is only apprehended from the absolutely amiable character of good. Of course, in the final analysis, the epistemological anteriority of good with respect to evil is founded on a soteriological and ontological anteriority. Awareness of the evil heinousness of sin follows our justification by God the savior, which tears us from our natural state. Finally, like Augustine, don't we need to remember that this world, though ruined and lost in sin, was created and is still sustained by a good God?

2:463.

14. See 18, 462–63; 18, 358.

15. Embracing Christ as savior implies a sense of, and rejection of, our sins (18, 216).

16. See "die Sünde sich nur an schon gewordenem Guten und vermöge desselben offenbart [Sin, accordingly, manifests itself only in connexion with and by means of already existent good, and what it obstructs is future good]" (Schleiermacher, *Der christliche Glaube*, 1. 68. 415).

2. The flesh and evil

At this point, before venturing into purely epistemological considerations about apprehending the heinousness of sin and the beauty of God's holiness, clarification is needed regarding the metaphysical status of evil, which has sin as its endpoint. Jonathan Edwards had two major preoccupations in his doctrine of evil: to never succumb to the temptation to make evil an ontological principle *sui generis* and to avoid its relativization, its Proclean "extermination from existence."[17] In fact, these two requirements call upon and mutually reinforce one another!

Calvin had already felt the need to denounce the Augustinian definition of evil as nothingness[18] and although Edwards himself stated that "divines are generally agreed, that sin radically and fundamentally consists in what is negative, or privative" (2, 118), he nonetheless professed the positivity of evil. He unambiguously stated that "suffering death, and failing of possible existence, are entirely different things," (3, 248–9)[19] and, to better define death as "a state of evil without any good," quoted Job's description of it as "a land of darkness . . . without any order . . . where the light is as darkness."[20] Evil—and especially moral evil—is not mere nonentity; it designates disorder and perversion. Likewise, our fallen, corrupt state is not mere nonentity (17, 205) but a positively "ungodly" condition (2, 197). Some might be tempted to consider the teaching on the divine constitution of the transmission of Adam's sin as a manifestation of Manicheism inherent in the Reformation, but Edwards would use this very doctrine to acquit God of the accusation that he was the author of evil. Calvin's God seems to propagate the corruption of Adam's descendants by his positive acts and

---

17. See *supra*, p. 67.

18. Calvin, *Consensus Genevensis*, in Niemeyer, *Collectio*, 305; see also, The libertines "interpret the 'devil,' the 'world,' and 'sin' as imagining something to be real that is nonexistent" (Calvin, "Against the Libertines," 234). Augustine's formulation is: "it cannot have an author, because it is nothing" (*Against Julian*, 1. 8. 38).

19. Edwards recalls that mankind has always had a horrible sense of death, beyond "a mere state of nonexistence" (18, 468). In hell, eternity "becomes an infinite positive evil, and so makes it infinitely worse than no existence" (*Ms. Book of Controversies*, 32). A purely "historic" faith and "common" religion are "worse than nothing" (25, 360); sinful man sinks below the beasts (10, 306) and the believer owning his sin confesses that he is "worse than nothing" (*Bl.*, 79). When the word of God proclaimed in preaching is treated carelessly, it is "lost" and—even "worse than lost"—it "hurts" (19, 48). Edwards knew about Persian dualism (20, 247), but his teaching on evil is ultimately theological. Sinners murdered the Son of God, for it is "the nature of all sin to kill God" (20, 182). In short, "All who are out of Christ are enemies to God and God is an enemy to them" (*Bl.*, 326).

20. Job 10:21 in 24, 670.

influence,[21] although resorting to the imputation or infusion of a bad quality isn't necessary for us to understand our original degradation. Corruption, let's recall, quite simply resulted from the withdrawal of supernatural and divine principles from the first man (3, 380-1). At creation, man received two kinds of principles: natural principles, which took sufficient account of his human constitution, and superior divine principles, which made him a "truly *virtuous, holy* and *spiritual*" creature (3, 381n.5). His natural tendency towards self-love, his inclination towards his own well-being, pleasure and honor are like fire in the house: a good servant while it is kept in its place, but an agent of destruction when it spreads throughout the whole house. Natural principles are good and legitimate in their proper role and under the control of superior principles, but when the latter are withdrawn, the former become independent and exercise unregulated dominion over the whole man. Adam's corruption need not be explained in terms of a positive, outside intervention; rather, the immanent change provoked by the withdrawal of supernatural gifts, the *superaddita* of God, is sufficient (3, 383).[22]

This interpretation of natural dependence leads us to view nature or, more specifically, man's fallen nature, as a moral principle. This metaphysical position is expressed in embryonic form in the *Treatise Concerning Religious Affections*. Light and darkness, love and lust are not stable realities, given once for all, but things that exist only in relation to one another. These two opposite principles can be compared to the two scales of a balance. When one rises, the other inevitably sinks. If divine love decays and falls asleep, dark lust and fear arise, but if love prevails and comes into lively exercise, this brings in the light of the Lord, "and drives away black lust, and fear with it" (2, 179). According to the Scottish moral philosopher, Henry Home (Lord Kames), the human body can be conceived of as a complex machine that functions harmoniously. However, if a spring or weight were removed, it would immediately and immanently disturb it. To this quotation, Edwards added: "by the withdrawnment of one kind of principle that balanced, limited and regulated others those others properly increase strength without any positive cause."[23]

This metaphysical model of the immanent deployment of a body, following the withdrawal of a principle that was previously part of it, recurs

---

21. See *supra*, p. 80.

22. This is a later version of the doctrine of the *dona superaddita* that Edwards may have found in P. van Mastricht, *Theoretico-Practica Theologia*, 4. cap. 1; see also 13, 382.

23. *Ms. Book of Controversies*, 252 in 3, 50n.8. For Edwards and Kames, see 1, 443-44. N. Fiering likens this to the image of a balance in Malebranche, *De la recherche de la vérité* 1. 5. 1, *Œuvres*, 1:48 in Fiering, *Edwards's Moral Thought*, 168n.46.

often in descriptions of the various "victories" of evil over good[24] and is strikingly formulated from the Pauline notion of "flesh." According to the teachings of the Apostle Paul, the spirit and the flesh are diametrically opposed, with flesh understood to mean more than simply the body and human faculties themselves. The flesh is not man's primitive constitution, but rather what man became as a result of sin. It expresses what he is "by nature," after the withdrawal of the superior principles (3, 279). "By flesh is here meant nature" (18, 234), the natural state of fallen man. According to the enduring tradition of Christian theology, this "nature," though henceforth immutable and necessary, is understood as a state that was nonetheless voluntarily chosen and assumed. Edwards recalls that the Apostle Paul gave the sense of "person or agent" to "flesh" (3, 277) and, in an important passage in his *Treatise on Grace*, Edwards went as far as to state "that by flesh and spirit are intended certain moral principles, natures, or qualities" (21, 154). For Jonathan Edwards, man's (fallen) nature—subsumed under the notion of "flesh," yet far from merely being a synonym for matter (see 24, 1086–87) or the given in general—is a moral condition, that of unregenerate man (18, 233–34) retreating into selfishness (8, 591).

The flesh is a moral category, i.e., something that *came about* and not an ontological principle, and the key, critical moment of evil. Evil is accordingly not to be understood as an ontological given. Some people think that to deny it has any "originating" character on a personal level is to relativize and minimize it, which is not at all the case. If evil were a primitive principle of our created universe, it would belong to the same ontological world as good, and the radicality of their opposition would consequently be lessened. The implacable opposition of good and evil, their condition of being true "contraries," is not confirmed by the fact of having come about, i.e., of not having originally belonged to the same world (21, 123). Nor when it comes to the apprehension of good and evil by the regenerate is their radical opposition affected by this asymmetry, this absence of a primitive "co-temporality," but is instead confirmed and deepened by it. Of course, Edwards frequently emphasized a kind of symmetry or rather reciprocity

---

24. Hypocrites pray zealously for a time, but then their prayer "naturally dies away in them" because it was only maintained by "a certain force put upon nature" and, when that force is gradually spent, nature prevails again (VII, 433). Of course, excommunication has positive aspects, but the Bible also describes it as "the Church *withdrawing* from a member" (VI, 514). When man falls into hell, it is simply because of his nature that God no longer graciously keeps him from perdition (22, 409; see also V, 307, 314, etc.). Edwards also explained the fall of angels by this abandonment to their own nature (13, 487) and a general reformulation of this doctrine can be found in his dissertation on *The Nature of True Virtue*: once detached from benevolence to Being in general, self-love immediately becomes a source of noxious egoism (8, 555–56).

in the perception of divine attributes. God should be understood in terms of his goodness and greatness, and his mercy is not experienced apart from his justice (17, 155).[25] Nonetheless, this symmetry and parallelism must not be regarded as questioning the actual hierarchy of causal relationships between these two apprehensions. According to many Edwardsian texts, the fact that we don't comprehend the beauty and goodness of God without also becoming aware of our own ugliness and wickedness still doesn't imply the dependence of the former on the latter, nor their effective reciprocity. That our sense of God's beauty is not without a sense of the heinousness of sin is because we see one in the other. This is moreover what is said in the above-mentioned text: "for the same eye that discerns the transcendent beauty of holiness, necessarily *therein* sees the exceeding odiousness of sin" (2, 301).[26] If a Miscellany from the beginning of the Northampton pastorate could say that "The sight of God's glory is sufficient to convince of the heinousness ... of sin" (13, 400), if Edwards could record in his *Personal Narrative* that, since his conversion, he felt "a vastly greater sense of my own wickedness" than he ever had before (16, 802), his preaching clearly explained that this sense of the heinousness of sin originates from the apprehension of God's glory: "The saints in heaven," wrote Edwards in 1734, "have as much greater a sense of their unworthiness in their natural state ... as they have a greater sense of God's glorious excellency" (X, 385).[27] "The light that gives evangelical humiliation and that makes men sensible of the hateful and odious nature of sin is a discovery of God's glory and excellency and grace" (17, 154). And lastly, to conclude with *True Grace*, that great sermon in Newark: "The light of God's beauty, and that alone, truly shows the soul its own deformity, and effectually inclines it to exalt God, and abase itself" (25, 637).

---

25. We must not forget that "as God is love, so also is He wrath ... Neither the love nor wrath of God are different from His essence" (25, 217). Moses saw "some token of divine glory ... some extraordinary luster or effulgence that had an appearance of exceeding awful majesty; and also surpassing pleasantness and sweetness" (24, 209). The light of which Revelation speaks shall be "immensely strong and glorious, yet infinitely sweet and pleasant" (24, 1243).

26. Italics mine.

27. See 14, 105. No one has ever had a greater sense of distance from God than Christ Jesus (19, 568; see also 16, 803). Devils recognize this distance but are unwilling to accept it (8, 244).

3. The epistemological consequences of conversion

Some people would be amazed that spiritual illumination and conviction depend on the discovery of God's beauty, although the beauty of which Edwards speaks is not a mere divine attribute but rather the very splendor of his merciful sovereignty. Because the ugliness of sin is only discerned from and after seeing God's beauty and glory, apprehending evil depends on perceiving the "amiable sufficiency" of God in Jesus Christ, i.e., comprehending how God is in himself. And so, contrary to what happens with unregenerate knowledge, that which is "holy" originates from God and not from us (see 2, 251–52), its illumination not only clarifying the givens of our natural state by immanent analysis, but starting from an external given that transcends this state. Natural man cannot procure this external, transcendent given at will; he can only receive it from outside. This once again bears out the profound asymmetry of good and evil at its most essential level. The phenomena of evil propagate themselves in an immanent way, whereas good requires "a new establishment" (3, 386). There is continuity between the mental operations that enable natural man to represent himself and God, but only a metaphysical rupture brings redeemed knowledge of God and oneself. When we objectively observe the extent of our sin, we conclude that God must punish it out of a true necessity for immanent justice and yet, by ourselves, we cannot envisage a merciful God, as he truly is in himself, nor have a genuine understanding of our own unworthiness. Spiritual writers in every age have emphasized the need to purify our soul and empty it of every attachment in order to welcome the presence of God, but we should not think that we ourselves can clean and prepare our soul to receive its guest. If God wants to visit a soul, he will prepare a place of welcome for himself in it. In other words, if the sanctification of a soul requires preparation, then that preparation can only be a work of God alone. We certainly need to disown and empty ourselves in order to receive the fullness of God (18, 242), although we are only made empty by the most proper action of that same fullness. We need to know that "the beginning of regeneration consists in the abolition of what is ours,"[28] but the self and its world cannot be eliminated from without.

Spiritual knowledge—the apprehension of God's excellency and the heinousness of sin—is born of an epistemological rupture which, in turn, is the immediate consequence of a metaphysical rupture, namely forensic justification. The knowledge imparted to us in this way surpasses the natural *episteme*—as though formed from the perspective of the redemption—and

---

28. Calvin, *Institutes*, 2. 5. 15.

it is precisely as this redeemed conscience appearing suddenly out of this spiritual, saved situation that it can claim objectivity. Along with an entire Christian tradition, Edwards regards our renewed mind as a restoration of our primitive understanding corrupted by the fall of man but, in a novel way, handles the claims of this regenerated knowledge at a purely epistemological level. The Puritan poet, Edward Taylor, wrote that the prayers of the unregenerate were mere "tautologies,"[29] i.e., restricted to the analytical immanence of our natural condition. On the contrary, true prayers—those of the justified—exhibit the new things of God impressed on minds captivated by love and faith (see 2, 215). Moreover, and this is a fundamental teaching of Edwardsian theology, a mind informed by faith is not simply transposed to some other particular perspective, but is instead brought back to the proper perspective of God himself. This merciful, sufficient God is only revealed by the Gospel of Jesus Christ, the revelation that testifies faithfully to him and shows him as he truly is.

The spiritual illumination that enables us to grasp the "sufficiency and excellency" of God follows the logic of forensic justification and is moreover an immediate consequence of it. It comes about in a quasi-instanteous way and expresses a continuing spiritualization of the creature which, although radical, does not amount to an ontological assimilation of the justified with the Spirit. Edwards, who even seems ready to question the existence of any innate idea of God in the human mind (23, 434), taught that God imparts spiritual knowledge to us immediately, without making use of any intermediate natural causes (17, 409). According to the great metaphysical principle which says that, in the spiritual realm, God's action is immediate and his causality undivided, the activity of all second causes—either the spiritually illuminated person or another creature—is excluded (17, 421–22). Grace melts on man from without (see 2, 132–33) and takes possession of his mind before any act of his own will (13, 463). In other words—and this is the *leitmotiv* of Calvinist preaching—there cannot be any preparation for it and therefore no continuity between natural and spiritual knowledge.

Spiritual knowledge is the privilege of the justified, converted man and conversion is "a great and universal change of the man, turning him from sin to God" (2, 341). It signifies regeneration, i.e., the fundamental change in man from the natural to the supernatural (W 2, 633), a state in which his conscience is filled with principles that are entirely different from those it formerly held (W 2, 569). Edwards emphasized the "adding" or "making" of "a new soul" in the sanctified person (13, 342) and the birth of "a new, divine and holy nature" in him (3, 278). Christian preaching has always stressed

---

29. Taylor, *Poems*, 422.

the radical scope of the new birth that makes us participants in the Deity. Jonathan Edwards himself also made abundant use of this terminology. The regenerate participate in the Holy Spirit (21, 124), in "God's bounty" (2, 210), in the "divine nature" (25, 639) and in his "fullness" (21, 187). Illuminated by the Holy Spirit, Christians shine with the same light as the sun of righteousness (2, 347) and "not only does the sun shine in the saints, but they also become little suns, partaking of the nature of the fountain of their light" (2, 343). Edwards continues to exalt the justified creature's state, yet his language of participation is not pantheistic in any way. It is not a matter of changing the creature's being, but of grace indwelling the creature (21, 194). We need to affirm and reaffirm that this is not a matter of "divinization" in the ontological sense of that term (2, 203), because the creature's "participation of God" equates to being penetrated and transformed by him. Nonetheless—and this is where the discussion gets complicated—this participation is not a "divinization" and this "vital union between Christ and the soul of a believer, which orthodox divines speak so much of" (21, 195) is not a transfer *of* the creature to some other level of being but rather the deployment of a transcendent Power *within* the creature, where the gracious state seems to be portrayed in terms of an appropriation of grace by the creature and even as a genuine naturalization of grace. More precisely, although grace indeed continues to transform creatures according to *God's* own nature (*ibid.*), it evidently shows itself as a principle of *their* nature (see 4, 453-4). Of course, in justification, we go outside of ourselves but, once outside, we seem to establish our own new, autonomous state.

4. Grace as a natural principle

To better understand the issues involved, we turn to Edwards's explanation of grace. Grace, he explained, can be understood as signifying either the operations of the Spirit on the heart or the fruits and effects of those operations. Grace can mean either actions the Spirit exercises on us or religious or moral attainments, which are "virtues" of the godly and the fruits of those actions. Edwards concluded that the latter was the mostly commonly accepted meaning of this term and the one he himself used. Saving grace is therefore saving virtue, i.e., the truly sanctified state of the regenerate (21, 153). At the end of his *Treatise on Grace,* Edwards remarked that the Holy Scriptures speak of the Spirit of God as becoming "a quality of the persons" in whom the Spirit resides. Therefore, being virtuous is the same as being spiritual (21, 197). Throughout these developments, Edwards not only referred to saving grace but also to common grace. The latter "virtue" belongs only to the carnal state, whereas the former—saving grace—is the virtue of the spiritual, regenerate state. Let's remember that, just as the flesh and the Spirit are opposites, these two "graces" or "virtues" are fundamentally contrary to one another and must likewise be understood as opposing moral principles (21, 154). Common grace is just a moral principle, like the natural sincerity that cannot save a person from damnation, whereas saving grace is ultimately portrayed as the true virtue of the regenerate, sanctified man.[30]

Here Edwards appears, in a certain way, to "naturalize" the work of grace as a principle that is proper to the human condition, although the telos of his developments was to maintain God's unlimited sovereignty and hold the creature fully responsible for all of his moral and religious actions and operations. This was why Edwards, who emphasized the fact that God not only sustains our being at all times but also our will, portrayed man as one who appropriated grace for himself and made it his own. In short, having become a moral principle of human existence, the spirit and its works, in the Pauline sense of that term, are henceforth treated as a human condition, specifically that of the regenerate, and without reference to the action of the Spirit underlying them.

At a deeper level, and expressed in terms of our existential condition, we then find the ancient question of the causality of our will. Although a core paradox of Christian dogmatics, it nonetheless seems not to have been given adequate conceptual formulation before Jonathan Edwards. God has willed, wrote Saint Augustine, that "the power to will . . . should be both his and ours"[31] and Saint Bernard admirably explained that a work of grace is produced by the will of God and the free will of man: "It is not that grace doeth part and free choice doeth part; but each doeth the entire work by its individual energy."[32] This doctrine of double causality comes up again later in covenant theology, in which the actions of people are also those of God.[33] When Edwards now says that "all that men do in real religion is entirely their own act and yet every tittle is wrought by the Spirit of God" (13, 240) and "God does all and we do all" (21, 251), he seems only to be repeating what his predecessors said. That Edwards was capable of expressing—with hitherto unknown clarity—how "something could simultaneously be a

---

30. This treatment of grace—relatively speaking—recalls Kant for whom the notion of justifying grace was just another expression for the same "practical idea" that he also represented as moral conversion, ("Religion within Boundaries of Reason," 6:119).

31. Saint Augustine, "To Simplician," 1. 2. 10.

32. Saint Bernard, *Grace and Free Will*, 82.

33. Miller, *New England Mind*, 1:421.

work of God and human self-determination,"[34] was not due to theological considerations but because of philosophical arguments. More specifically, the fact that Edwards succeeded in explaining Christian teaching on the double causality (i.e., divine and human) of all religious-moral acts in a more consequent manner than his great precursors was only because of his phenomenological doctrine of the will and his theory of a spiritual idea.

Whether they are describing vices or virtues, guilty acts or gracious exercises, theologians want to understand human behaviors as they are in themselves, i.e., to get an idea of them. "Repeating" or "copying" acts or exercises—not studying what precedes them—is the only way to get an idea of them. Instead of having to scrutinize the order where they appear, judging the quality and authenticity of religious affections means considering their nature,[35] i.e., how they are in themselves at the very moment they occur. Knowing a thing means having to form an idea of it and to do this we shouldn't concern ourselves with an idea's "antecedents" (13, 353) but rather with the idea itself. Spiritual knowledge, the only cognition that fully and adequately represents ideas, essentially reproduces a thing as it actually is right now and therefore doesn't invite us to regress to its origins. The theory of a spiritual idea is itself phenomenological in character. It consequently reinforces or rather provides secondary grounds for the doctrine of the will as a description of willing and sets aside the search for causes. In seeking spiritual knowledge, we are not striving to gain knowledge *about* things but rather to grasp their *nucleus* or kernel (2, 208). We therefore consider the thing itself, not its circumstances. Strictly speaking, "the thing itself"— which happens to be the will that is now willing—its "concomitants and effects," and its "antecedents" (13, 353) do not belong to the act of willing. This act takes place at the present moment and only concerns the subject who is willing at this present moment. The current evil will might well be a direct and inevitable consequence of the divine institution of man's sinful state in the past, yet what counts is that it is this will that is currently willing evil. Likewise, although a regenerate person's good intentions might stem from the forensic justification that made him righteous, it is nonetheless the regenerate person who is currently willing good and it is the current "intention" of his will that matters.[36]

34. Hirsch, *Geschichte der neueren evangelischen Theologie*, 3:353.

35. This principle is even found in trinitarian theology: "Though in the Trinity there is such a thing as prior and later in order, yet there is no such thing as degrees of dignity or excellence" (14, 378).

36. The Edwardsians do not seem to have wanted to take advantage of their master's epistemology. For a remarkably original formulation of dual causality from the Edwardsian School, we can cite E. Griffin: "men sustain two relations to God. As creatures

Of course, these parallelisms still do not exclude asymmetries. By withdrawing his supernatural principles from the creature, God becomes the "author" of evil (1, 399). He is only its author on the physical or ontological level. On the other hand, and albeit in a different way, God is the author of good because he "indwells" the justified and performs holy and virtuous acts in and through them. However, in both cases, theologians set aside the causal relationship linking human behavior to God. For the world of the evil will, this setting aside resolves the problem of divine responsibility for moral evil. In the realm of regenerate willing, it inhibits ontological questioning that might resurrect the problematic issue of pantheism in what is now the second creation, i.e., the redeemed, regenerated world. Of course, it is God the Holy Spirit who is the cause and source of the sanctified will and, more directly and immediately, not the cause of the sinful will that is bent on evil (see 23, 211). Nevertheless, it is always sanctified creatures that will "saintly" because they "spiritually" apprehend good and evil from the divine perspective to which they were transposed by justifying grace. In portraying this situation, one in which man wills and acts from God's perspective, the theologian is satisfied with describing the operations of the creature and trying to shed light on his changed, renewed character, yet never seeks to discuss and analyze the relationships between grace that became human virtue and grace as divine action.

5. The new spiritual sense

In his great *Treatise Concerning Religious Affections*, a Christian manual on experimental religion,[37] Edwards resolutely describes conversion in

---

they are necessarily dependent upon Him for holiness, as they are for existence, and as such they passively receive His sanctifying impressions; and they are moral agents." But "their moral agency is in no degree impaired or affected by their dependence and passiveness, nor their passiveness and dependence by their moral agency.... Their obligations rest upon their capacity to exercise, not on their power to originate; on their being rational, not on their being independent ... the action of the Spirit does not abate their freedom. The soul of man is that wonderful substance which is none the less active for being acted upon, none the less free for being controlled. It is a wheel within a wheel, which has complete motion in itself while moved by the machinery from without. While made *willing*, it is itself voluntary, and of course free" (*Extent of the Atonement*, in Park, *The Atonement*, 264–65).

37. "Edwards on Charity and Fruits," 227. Notwithstanding its flawed style (Miller, *Jonathan Edwards*, 215–16), it is an unsurpassable reference work on the theology of spirituality (Tracy, *Great Awakening*, 404). It contains an "admirably rich and delicate description of the supernaturally infused condition" (James, *Varieties of Religious Experience*, 196) and "lays down more intelligible and definite rules to distinguish true from false religion, and to ascertain, by distinct characters, the genuine spirit of vital piety,

epistemological terms. In gracious exercises, he writes, there is "something that is new, not only in degree and circumstances, but in its whole nature, and that which could be produced by no exalting, varying or compounding of what was there before, or by adding anything of the like kind; I say, if God produces something thus new in a mind, that is a perceiving, thinking, conscious thing; then doubtless something entirely new is felt, or perceived, or thought; or, which is the same thing, there is some new sensation or perception of the mind, which is entirely of a new sort, and which could be produced by no exalting, varying or compounding of that kind of perceptions or sensations which the mind had before; or there is what some metaphysicians call a new *simple idea*" (2, 205). The infusion of grace is therefore presented as the introduction of a new, simple idea in the mind—the ultimate avatar of an Edwardsian "dematerialization" of Locke[38]—and this presentation of regeneration is of very great importance. On the one hand, opting for the term "simple idea" to connote such a complex idea as grace, which has infinite conceptual implications, laid the foundations of a doctrine that sought to deploy all spiritual content from a single idea. On the other hand—and this relates to the Edwardsian understanding of an idea as the double of its object, which was itself made possible by the revelation of an affinity between the realities of ideas and the minds that conceived them—meant that religious knowledge was presented as the immanent articulation of the regenerated mind's total condition rather than as the sum of disparate content.

Along with his entire tradition, Edwards insisted on the radically novel character of justification in the realm of knowledge. Conversion, "that strange and wonderful transformation of man" (7, 525), is compared to creation (23, 211), to the resurrection of the dead and to opening the eyes of the blind (2, 204). According to the book of Revelation, God will give the sanctified a white stone on which is written a new name.[39] This new name symbolizes the creature's radical change and total renewal of mind. In his *Personal Narrative*, Edwards portrayed his conversion as having brought "new dispositions" and a "new sense of things" (16, 790). His thoughts were

---

separated from all fanatical delusions, than any other book which has yet been given to the world" (Moncreiff-Wellwood, *John Erskine*, 197). It was the "gentlest and the most human work" Jonathan Edwards "ever accomplished" (Baritz, *City on a Hill*, 66), and, of all his works, the one "which perhaps will longest endure" (Kingman, *Jonathan Edwards*, 12). This book contains "the theology of Edwards" (Byington, "Theology of Edwards," 201). It is his "Confessions" (Allen, *Jonathan Edwards*, 220) and if a great cataclysm were to destroy the earth and only one book other than the Bible could be saved, it should be this treatise (*Dw.*, I, 223).

38. See Kretzöi, *Az Amerikai Irodalom Kezdetei, 1607–1750*, 68.
39. Revelation 2:17 in 2, 231.

now filled with "a new sort of affection" and he experienced "a new kind of apprehensions and ideas of Christ" (16, 793). In legal conviction, the Spirit of God only assists the natural principles already present in man, whereas in "special" conviction, he is "infusing" them with "new [supernatural] principles" (18, 155). This is not merely a reorganization or recomposition of old, pre-existing ideas, nor an intensification or reinforcement of our natural perceptions and sensations, but rather "perceptions and sensations" that are "entirely of a new sort" (2, 205) and imply the rise of "a new nature" (25, 625).[40]

The purely epistemological character of this renewal is shown by the fact that the key "alteration" which the creature undergoes in conversion – the one that legitimizes the very use of the term "new nature" – is primarily an "alteration of *temper* and disposition" (13, 462). In any event, the use of the word *temper* is highly significant. In Miscellany #397, *temper* is practically equivalent to the presence of the Spirit of God in the regenerated soul and denotes a new spiritual sense or understanding (13, 462–63). However, in the context of a discussion that is purely dogmatic, Edwards is going to refine this notion. Taking advantage of the option available to him in English of using the terms *spirit* and *mind* in a quasi-interchangeable way, Edwards made a distinction between two senses of *mind*. The term *mind* is either "the spiritual substance or *mind* itself" or "the disposition, inclination or *temper of the mind.*" He concluded that, within the context of regeneration, "Spirit of God" referred specifically to this disposition, inclination or "temper" of the Spirit, while references to those who are "gentle in spirit" are always allusions to their *temper* (21, 123). Temper, a general and rather imprecise term, serves to highlight the epistemological connotations of the novel change wrought in us by grace and underlines the global, general, durable and permanent character of this new disposition. Edwardsian terminology provides us with even more opportunities to improve and refine our description of this new condition. In his short treatise on the Trinity,

---

40. A 1740 sermon titled "They Sing A New Song" (22, 227) speaks of the incarnation and passion as "new things" (22, 230), glorious perfections of God in "that new ... manifestation of them ... in the face of Christ" (22, 236), "new mercies," a new "melody of the heart," (22, 233) and that "sweet and excellent melody of the new song" (22, 238). Those who are redeemed by Christ receive "a new word of life ... a new ability ... to sing praise to God" (22, 232). They are "new creatures," "new men" with "new bodies" (22, 232) and "new eyes, new tongues, new hands" (24, 393). The saints, having become "new men" (25, 528–29), live in "a new world" (24, 865) where they drink "new wine" with Christ (25, 589). The risen Christ himself sings "a new song" and gives "a new name" to his saints (22, 241), and even "a new glory" in heaven (24, 491). Let's also remember that the revelation of the Trinity changes our moral duties "so that they are as it were new" (13, 416; see also *supra*, p. 303).

Edwards noted that the Spirit, the third person of the Trinity, is "denominated Holy" (21, 122). By "denomination" is meant the contrary of mere naming or calling, of partial or superficial attribution. Instead, it is more of a qualification or an essential, total determination. Because the Spirit of God assists but does not indwell natural men,[41] they are not "denominated" with a new name. Conversely, the regenerate do not only drink the water of eternal life, but themselves become never-ending springs of water and are "properly denominated . . . spiritual" (2, 200–1)[42] This complete change—this new "denomination" that regeneration brings about in man—penetrates to the very depths of his spirit but should not be considered a change of his faculties. This new spiritual sense, and the dispositions that flow from it, are not new mental faculties, but new principles of nature. These new principles do not simply multiply our habitual ideas but express themselves in radically new ideas. These old, natural ideas and new ideas are not related in the way that ideas of the same sense may differ from one another, but rather as ideas of different senses differ. So this new spiritual sense is not a new faculty of understanding or of the will, but is "a new foundation laid in the nature of the soul, for a new kind of exercises of the same faculty [of understanding]" (2, 206).[43] In other words, the change that natural man undergoes in regeneration cannot be expressed in terms of psychological change, but instead are expressed in terms of metaphysical transposition. The new simple idea of grace does not give rise to a series of new representations, but rather to a new understanding of reality (2, 202).[44]

The refusal to identify this new epistemological framework for the regenerate with any change in their psychological faculties is not only the result of Edwardsian observations and reflections on the great religious emotions of the Great Awakening, but also a logical outcome of the

---

41. "The Spirit of God . . . may . . . act upon the mind of a natural man, but he acts in the mind of a saint as an indwelling vital principle" (17, 411).

42. See also 17, 411.

43. Because a regenerate man does not obtain new psychological principles, the ideal society of Edwardsian "politics" does not require the overthrow of existing institutions but the advent of a new spiritual principle of community life (Davidson, *Logic of Millennial Thought*, 218–19).

44. See also J. Owen, "The new creature . . . does not consist in a new course of actions but in renewed faculties with new dispositions, powers and abilities," (*Pneumatologia*, 184). Edwards referred to this work in 20, 389. According to T. Hooker, mental faculties after regeneration are "the same in their essence afterwards, than they were before, but are renewed according to the gracious qualities & principles which are put into them." Hooker also wrote that "when a sinner comes to be renewed, there needs not new faculties, but those he hath, to be set in frame" (*Covenant of Grace Opened*, 31; see Willard, *Divinity*, 493).

Reformed theology of conversion. Calvinist writers have always liked to present schemes showing the various structural moments of the conversion process. They enumerate these moments in strict order, in an *armilla aurea* (golden chain) stretching from the abyss of man's natural condition to the peaks of regeneration and sanctification.[45] A veritable "morphology" of conversion developed from this combination of observation and speculation.[46] Edwards, who didn't seem to have personally followed the typical sequence of great moments of *metanoia* (repentance) and wrote that he had never felt terror (16, 791), very quickly questioned the exclusive validity of any such sequential order in conversion. The great Thomas Hooker had already said that it wasn't knowing the "history" of religious phenomena that mattered, but rather understanding their profound "nature."[47] At the beginning of his pastorate in New York, after duly enumerating the typical moments of a conversion process culminating in regeneration, Edwards makes this admission: "I do not say that a true penitent's thoughts always run exactly in this order, but I say that they are of this nature, and do arise from this principle" (10, 512), i.e., from spiritual conviction. A quarter of a century later, he remarked that David Brainerd likewise considered the nature of religious experiences to be more important than their order (7, 511). The great problem with "experimental religion" is distinguishing gracious affections from their perverted counterfeits and any morphology of conversion is but a mediocre instrument in the hands of those attempting this task. We know that imitating the order in which divine things appear is easier for the Devil than imitating their nature.[48] It is easier for him to bring about a certain sequence of religious phenomena than to produce affections with the same solidity, stability and "practical" character as those born of a truly regenerate disposition. During the Great Awakening's intense moments of religious elation, certain people concluded that their affections were spiritual in character and taste because they descended upon them so suddenly, unexpectedly and irresistibly. Now, just as the sequential order of certain phenomena is only an external, contingent thing, the sudden and violent way in which such emotions can seize us does not in any way prove that they are spiritual in origin (2, 220–1). In a "truly spiritual sensation, not only is the manner of its coming into the mind extraordinary, but the sensation itself is totally diverse" from all that men have, or can have, in a state of nature (2, 214). It is not the persuasive strength of the argument, nor the brilliant

---

45. See *supra*, p. 159.

46. See *supra*, p. 54.

47. Hooker, *Application of Redemption*, in Miller and Johnson, *Puritans*, 1:293.

48. See *supra*, p. 275.

clarity of the sensation, but rather the profound nature of ideas born of "a holy and divine temper of soul" that matters (8, 167–68). But what is this new disposition of soul, this radical novelty of ideas infused by grace?

Edwards refuses to explain the new nature engendered by grace in terms of a simple change of our mental faculties or even in terms of the various ways we receive these representations. He justifies his refusal to consider the speed or extraordinary circumstances with which the words of Scripture are brought to mind by the fact that "the Scripture speaks just the same thing at one time that it does at another. The words have the same meaning when they are read in course as they have when they are suddenly brought to the mind" (8, 168–69). There isn't any "notional" difference between natural knowledge and spiritual knowledge, for the very good reason that this new simple idea of grace is not a new religious representation. For Christians, the biblical text remains an unalterable fact which no experience—not even conversion—calls into question. When a young farmer, H. Husband, author of an interesting account on the Great Awakening, ran to hear the "great itinerant," George Whitefield, he overheard one man ask another: "What does this man preach? Anything that is news? The other answered: "No, but what you may read every day in your Bible."[49] This is not just about the material identity of a text for the regenerate and the natural man, but also about the fact that these are not, generally speaking, the representations and concepts that separate carnal knowledge from regenerate knowledge. In 1741, a critic of the revival's enthusiasm wrote that "they had only to put the *same* words, which from his [Whitefield's] mouth produced the boasted effects, into the mouth of an *ordinary* speaker, and see whether the same *effects* would be the consequence."[50] Now, it was precisely this proposition that showed the extent to which the moderate Calvinism of that era was unable to understand how the revival experienced and developed Protestantism's great traditional doctrines on illumination[51] and the inner witness.[52] The spiritual understanding imparted to the regenerated

---

49. Heimert and Miller, *Great Awakening*, 638.

50. Heimert, *Religion and the American Mind*, 20.

51. Samuel Johnson, a Berkeleyan Anglican, exhibited similar incomprehension. Schneider and Schneider, *Samuel Johnson*, 3:447–48.

52. For Calvinist texts on "le tesmoignage intérieur de l'Esprit [the inner witness of the Spirit]," see Vincent, *L'herméneutique du discours théologique*, 658–59. This is the witness which the Spirit of God gives to the true and profound meaning of Spirit-inspired texts: "the light of the Word, and the light in our souls are twins . . . and agree like brethren" (Rous, *Works*, 721, in Nuttall, *Puritan Faith and Experience*, 24n.1). Edwards explains the witness of the Spirit (2, 239) by starting from the presence of "spiritual ideas," which create a disposition in the mind that "raises such a series and succession of thoughts, as sweetly corresponds and harmonizes with the expressions of

conscience is neither a new type of "doctrinal knowledge" nor new theological "propositions" and here is a very rare instance when, in that regard, Edwards quotes Calvin: "the Spirit . . . is not to form new and unheard-of revelations, or to coin a new form of doctrine, by which we may be led away from the received doctrine of the gospel, but to seal on our minds the very doctrine which the gospel recommends."[53] Regeneration has little to do with changing our notions of religious knowledge; it is instead a new way that this knowledge can be acquired, understood and explained.

6. A new light

In his *Treatise Concerning Religious Affections*, Edwards remarks that no external, objective criterion enables natural man to discern the truly spiritual gifts of God, because it would be like "giving a man rules, how to distinguish visible objects in the dark" (2, 195). This amounts to saying that the transition from the natural to the regenerate state does not consist in the appearance of new, more intelligent and clearer concepts but in the communication of new light.[54] Here is Baxter's vigorous formulation of it: "The Spirit is not given to make our religion reasonable, but to make sinners reasonable. . . . The Spirit, therefore, is not first any objective cause of our belief . . . but it is the efficient cause"[55] The Spirit's role is not on the side of the content, but rather on that of the container. The Spirit does not make our representations more intelligible, but instead enables us to better represent them. After his conversion, Edwards did not have any new revelations regarding the doctrine of divine sovereignty, but only, as he wrote, "that now I saw further, and my reason apprehended the justice and reasonableness of it" (16, 792). During his first "harvest" in Northampton, Edwards witnessed the conversion of certain parishioners. These conversions brought about profound changes in their behavior and spiritual life. "There are no new doctrines embraced, but people have been abundantly established in those that we account orthodox" (4, 108). People who had heard the same Bible passages many times before now suddenly understood them in a radically different way. The word of God, which had previously been just a "dead

---

God's Word" (13, 290). The notion itself appears in a very early Miscellany (13, 177–78; see *supra*, p. 266 n.55).

53. Calvin, *Institutes*, 1. 9. 1.

54. See "une clarté nouvelle [a new clarity]" (Calvin, *Sermons sur le Livre de Job, Opera*, 34, 506).

55. Baxter, *Practical Works*, 20:32, in Nuttall, *Puritan Faith and Experience*, 46. Here Baxter uses "objective cause" in the Aristotelian sense of "material cause."

letter," now seemed like a "continual conversation" (13, 340). Prior to their conversion, natural men who spoke "the language of sin" (W 2, 587) could not grasp the words of God. Now they understood them (24, 191).[56]

Edwards had been able to observe the exercise of these renewed faculties during the Great Awakening and he provides a systematic interpretation of them in his *Treatise Concerning Religious Affections*. However, his teaching—the doctrine of Calvinist orthodoxy and the experimental theology of the Puritans—was already formulated in that great 1734 sermon, *A Divine and Supernatural Light*. In spiritual conviction—as "that most important of the Edwardsian sermons" explains it[57]—no new truth is suggested to the mind but only new light, which gives the mind "a due apprehension of the same truths that are revealed in the Word of God" (17, 416), is imparted to it. The word of God, the text of Scripture, is the incomparable means of communicating that light, although ultimately only a *means*. The biblical word is not the proper, material cause of illumination; it is "only made use of to convey to the mind the subject matter of this saving instruction." It conveys the teachings of the Gospel to the mind and "is the cause of the notion of them in our heads, but not of the sense of the divine excellency of them in our hearts." In other words, "the notions that are the subject matter of this light, are conveyed to the mind by the Word of God; but that due sense of the heart, wherein this light formally consists, is immediately by the Spirit of God" (17, 417).[58]

---

56 At Sinai, "God's word then was like thunder and lightning and devouring fire," whereas "God's voice is now gentle . . . revealing not only His wrath, but also His great mercy" (24, 304; see also 14, 382). According to the Talmud, "Before Adam sinned, God's voice sounded sweet and intimate; after his sin, it sounded harsh and stern" (Kasher, *Encyclopedia of Biblical Interpretation*, 1:125). This change of voice is not due to chronological differences between successive dispensations but instead to the difference between the system based on the Law versus the one based on the Gospel (see 10, 441).

57. M. Curtis, "Kantean Elements in Jonathan Edwards," in *Philosophische Abhandlungen für Max Heinze*, 35.

58 Regeneration doesn't change the "content" of our knowledge but merely allows us to better understand it. The Law contains virtually the same precepts and dispositions as the Gospel (13, 416), although the Gospel reveals them in a new and deeper way (20, 367–69). "Les choses sont maintenant beaucoup mieux vues mais il n'y a rien ajouté [matters are more clearly set forth to us: but yet there is nothing added]" (Calvin, *Sermons sur 2 Timothée, Opera*, 54, 924). The distinction between natural knowledge and regenerate knowledge does not result from the order of the contents (Hirsch, *Geschichte der neueren evangelischen Theologie*, 2:176–7). The light of the Spirit only makes the "content" of Scripture explicit: "The truths which I am to believe lie in Scripture, as colors in the wall. The Spirit is, as the light; I see the colored wall by the light, for that enlightens it, accentuates its shape and colors, brings them, unites them to my eye, enlightening and actuating that also" (Sterry, *Teachings of Christ*, 33 in Emerson,

In his sermon on *A Divine and Supernatural Light* and also in a great Miscellany (782) from around that same period, Edwards was still using the expression "sense of the heart," although by then he seemed to realize the unsatisfactory character of this terminology and qualified it as "a *due* sense of heart." In fact, "sense of heart"—a term *par excellence* for designating "sensible knowledge"— is not an adequate way to "translate" the regenerate soul's "holy temper." After all, like the sincerity of the Arminians, a heart can be good or bad and the "sense" of a bad heart has nothing to do with the holy disposition of a mind that discerns the new simple idea of grace. Edwards found himself grappling with an old problem, one that was more than just terminology and well-known to his predecessors. Calvin spoke of "a sense common to all the godly,"[59] John Smith of a "spiritual sensation" and of "reason . . . turned into sense,"[60] while Richard Baxter wrote that "reason hath in it more of eminent sensation."[61] Edwards himself summarized the regenerate's new epistemological framework as the advent of "a new supernatural sense" (2, 259). Although he never truly standardized his terminology, Edwards continually referred to this new spiritual sense to explain the regenerate's radically changed knowledge. In his first published sermon, he defined faith as "a sensibleness of what is real in the work of redemption" and emphasized "a sensibleness of our great dependence on God" (17, 213). Later on, he would speak of that "sense" of the goodness and reality of Christ that accompanies true faith (21, 434). Like all practitioners of "experimental religion," Edwards never questioned the sensible character of gracious affections. Although he remained convinced that he should assign the discernment of the new simple idea of grace to a new spiritual sense,[62] he found it difficult to precisely define the adjective "sensible" with an evidently broader meaning than the noun (i.e., "sense") from which it is derived. He wrote that, under the influence of the Holy Spirit, multitudes experienced "a sensible, strong and sweet love to God" (4, 328). Instead of a mere *natural* understanding of God, the poor in spirit mentioned in the Gospel according to Matthew have "an immediate and certain understanding of God's glorious excellency and love" (17, 64) and, during the "harvest"

John Cotton, 105). It is the unction of the Spirit that "teaches the truth, because it is the taste of the truth that holds the attention of the mind" (Malebranche, *Réflexions sur la prémotion physique*, *Œuvres*, 16:50), although attention adds nothing new, but only makes an object appear such as it is in itself. See Ricœur, *Freedom and Nature*, 155–56.

59. Calvin, *Commentarius in Epistolam Pauli ad Romanos, Opera*, 99, 164.

60. Smith, *Select Discourses*, 16.

61. Baxter, *Poetical Fragments*, 2, in Murdock, *Literature and Theology*, 52.

62. See "a discerning heart, which is the same with a new heart" (Hopkins, *System of Doctrines, Works*, 1:371).

at Northampton, others thought that their ineffable experiences were better expressed by "realizing conviction, or a lively or feeling sense of heart" (4, 172). This "sensible" knowledge—to the extent that it is "sensible"—appears to possess the following characteristics: vigor and vivacity, immediacy and certitude—which are expressions of what is within—and, lastly, the "realizing" power that enables us to definitively go beyond a purely subjective view of this new sense and reach an epistemological-objective understanding of it.

The most superficial and also the most spectacular and obvious of these characteristics is vivacity. The great religious experiences of regeneration are always marked by an intensification of sensations. Generally speaking, "there is a holy ardor in everything that belongs to true grace" (25, 91) and, just as the sensations of the blessed will be infinitely intensified in heaven (18, 350), the mental activities of those on earth are intensified by grace. After all, it is a matter of being given a "divine temper" and God himself is "infinitely the most intelligent and sensible being of all" (18, 396)! The sensible and vigorous character of the phenomena of regeneration finds expression, either at the psycho-physiological level or at the level of man's understanding and discernment, *stricto sensu,* of religious things. With respect to man's psycho-physiological status, Edwards, who knew and deplored the excesses of the revival, nonetheless defended the legitimacy of the natural reactions provoked by regeneration's great, transforming storms. He considered it entirely reasonable that those delivered from sin and the terrible peril of eternal damnation should have a lively sense of their deliverance, of the sufficiency of Christ and of the mercy of God (2, 151) and saw "no reason, why a being affected with a view of God's glory should not cause the body to faint" (2, 132). For the most part, it's best to restrain the visible expression of our emotions, although Edwards wrote that "if God is pleased to convince the consciences of persons, so that they can't avoid great outward manifestations, even to the interrupting and breaking off those public means they were attending, I don't think this is confusion, or an unhappy interruption, any more than if a company should meet on the field to pray for rain, and should be broken off from their exercise by a plentiful shower" (4, 267). However, aside from psycho-physiological epiphenomena, which are often inevitable but insignificant in themselves, the vivacity and vigor of spiritual illumination primarily impacts the discernment of divine things and the understanding of religious content. We read in Miscellany284—from those early years at Northampton—that "the will . . . follows . . . [the soul's sense of] good" and therefore the change of disposition known as conversion is the same as having a more lively idea of good (13, 380–1).⁶³ In other words, it is a matter of expanding, i.e., intensifying, a sense of good that was previously only superficial, abstract and obscure. Moreover, like this sense of good, regeneration strengthens the mind's sense of evil, giving it a foretaste of the knowledge of the blessed, who have "a truer and more lively apprehension of the evil of sin" (18, 101).⁶⁴

New spiritual knowledge intensifies this sense of good and evil. However, as we will see later, intensification is not restricted to a simple quantitative increase but is also accompanied by a more acute perception of the notional content of faith. The Spirit's supernatural operations also include assisting the soul's natural faculties. By restoring the imbalance of the soul's principles, regeneration removes the obstacle to a better understanding of the doctrines of the faith (17, 414–5). "For grace is of the nature of light, and brings truth to view" (2, 325).⁶⁵ It removes "sins spectacles,"⁶⁶ i.e., removes "blinding prejudices" so that "the mind becomes susceptive of the due force of rational arguments" for the truth of divine things (17, 414). This increased attention to divine things and greater sharpness of mind with respect to the truths of the faith must not only be expressed in external terms—as consequences of the heart being flooded by warmth and the mind by light—because they derive from a profound inner change. In an admirable letter that gave the first account of the "harvest" at Northampton and in which he spoke of converts who believed that they had never heard the Word of God preached before—even though we know that their pastor preached two long homilies every week!—Edwards reported that "there have been some instances of persons that by only an accidental sight of the Bible, have been as much moved . . . as a lover by the sight of his sweetheart"

---

63. During his conversion, Edwards "felt more exercises of love to Christ, than usual" (16, 759) and, a little later, "regarded the doctrines of Election, Free Grace . . . with greater pleasure than ever before" (16, 767).

64. The regenerate experience a "constant and ever increasing sense of sin" (Hopkins, *System of Doctrines*, *Works*, 1:163).

65. "Divine grace . . . itself is a pleasure which gives light" (Leibniz, *New Essays*, 2. 21. 35). In the Augustinian tradition, the love that grace infuses powerfully assists knowledge: "selon Saint Augustin . . . la charité . . . ouvre la porte de l'esprit que la cupidité tenait fermée. . . . Dieu . . . dans la foi . . . mêle la douceur de la charité; et cette douceur ne sert qu'à faire entrer les lumières très certaines de la vérité [according to Saint Augustine . . . charity . . . opens the door of the mind that cupidity holds closed. . . . God . . . in faith . . . mingles charity and sweetness; and this sweetness serves only to introduce the very sure light of truth]" (Arnauld, *Apologie pour les religieuses de Port-Royal, Œuvres*, 23:228–9).

66. Taylor, *Poems*, 206.

(4, 105).⁶⁷ Simply seeing our sweetheart can provoke overflowing emotion because it comes from a deep, emotional disposition towards that person that is firmly anchored in our inner nature. The "inward" character of the Spirit's operations seems contrary to "Satan's devices" (25, 93), which can only influence the imagination by interjecting external ideas (2, 288–90) because they are incapable of acting directly on the mind. Conversion involves a "new inward apprehension or view of God" (7, 138), although its essence is less about the immediacy, familiarity or even the proximity of the relationships between a "divine and spiritual sense" and "the life and soul of divine truth"⁶⁸ than that men truly "rest" on the judgment which puts an end to "their [evanescent] knowledge of God."⁶⁹

Contrary to an egotistical creature's "fleshly apprehensions," which are "of a fleeting and fading nature," the "signs" of "true goodness" have a more "enduring and constant" character.⁷⁰ However, even constant, lasting dispositions are only a subjective phenomenon and the unregenerate can also be solidly convinced of their religious ideas. Let's remember that the Devil is firmly established in the articles of his faith! To overcome considerations which, in the final analysis, are always subjective, we have to closely review Edwardsian terminology. In his great sermon, *A Divine and Supernatural Light*, the sense of divine things is contrary to the simple opinion that men might have of them (17, 414). In that context, "opinion" refers to the temporary nature of religious representation but, in Edwardsian epistemology, it generally refers to the imagination,⁷¹ i.e., the realm of external ideas where there is no truly adequate correspondence between the mental productions of the mind and the realities to which they are supposed to refer. Consequently, external ideas—and therefore ultimately the imagination—which we have subsumed under the speculative faculty in general, i.e., "the head,"⁷²

---

67. Luther, who was more vigorous, contrasted purely historic and notional faith, which is also the faith of the Devil, with the faith by which Adam knew his wife: "non speculative aut historice, sed experimentaliter [not speculative or historic, but experimental]" (*Enarratio 53, Capitel Esaie, Werke*, 40. 3. 738). Hegel compared the mutual relations between the mind and nature to those linking Adam and Eve (*Enzyklopädie der philosophischen Wissenschaften im Grundrisse, Werke*, 9:23). In an entirely different context, these impulses of the Devil on the soul are compared to a "carnal commerce" with him (Saint John of the Cross, *Noche Oscura de la Subida del Monto Carmelo*, 1. 4, *Obras Completas*, 528). For his part, J. Bunyan spoke of a "mystical but hellish copulation with the devil" (*Grace Abounding*, 193).

68. Smith, *Select Discourses*, 286.

69. Calvin, *Institutes*, 1. 7. 5; 2. 6. 4.

70. Smith, *Select Discourses*, 370–72 in 2, 217n.6.

71. See 2, 245; 2, 306, etc.

72. See *supra*, p. 279 ss.

precisely characterize a "conviction" that is not truly spiritual. As natural man's process of cognition, the imagination is opposed to the true sense of divine things which the new spiritual light perceives. We perceive the new light—said Edwards—when we have a "spiritual sense" and "a Reallizing apprehension" of the excellency of divine things.[73] And the term "Reallizing" is the decisive one! At first glance, the adjective seems to denote something subjective, the more profound character of the apprehension or perhaps the added vigor of the cognition. In reality, it is something else. When Edwards said that sinners "cannot realize it" (VII, 378), he doesn't simply mean that they have a faint vision of hell, but rather that they don't have a true representation of it. Although the regenerate have only a "very imperfect" sense of the excellency of God, they nonetheless possess "a realizing view" that enables them to understand that God is amiable, in and of himself (3, 146). Of course, an essential component of the term "realizing" is certainty which, according to Newman, is primarily a reflexive state—the result of "certification," i.e., confirmation[74] that adds nothing to the content—although the hidden implications of this "realizing sense" are broader in Edwards. When one of the best interpreters of Edwardsian thought commented that "the sense of the heart," which we understand here as a synonym for "spiritual sense," is not an unconscious state of feeling but a judgment,[75] he barely saw the full scope of his definition. A judgment never merely reaffirms previously perceived mental content in some vague way, but instead clarifies it. This means evoking all of its hidden implications and ultimately unfolding its elements and moments in detail. Finding himself struggling with the same issues as Edwards, French Jansenist writer Pierre Nicole thought he could say that "according to Saint Augustine, the growth of Christian lights does not consist in the scope and multiplication of the objects of our knowledge, nor of the truths we know, but in a clearer and livelier penetration of those same objects and truths. This is how the Holy Spirit taught the Apostles in all things: not by teaching them new truths that they did not know, but by making them understand what they knew in a new way."[76] However, if we look closely at the real meaning of this new way of understanding, we see that it is not just concerned with the knowing subject. More specifically, the transformation of the container will necessarily have an impact on the contents themselves. When we see the same thing under a different light, we can discern many previously unnoticed details and make out hidden

---

73. *Sermon on 2 Cor 13:5* in Miller, *Divine Things*, 31.
74. De Achaval and Holmes, *Newman on Faith and Certainty*, 126.
75. Cherry, *Theology of Edwards*, 23.
76. Nicole, *Essais de morale*, 7:151.

links that interconnect the various elements of the object in view. Seeing the same thing under a different light amounts to seeing it in another way and, ultimately, as a modification of that same thing. The big problem for Edwardsian epistemology was interpreting the nature of "spiritual sense" so that, even if it couldn't take knowledge regarding new spiritual realities into consideration, it would at least take account of an apprehension of new religious representations.

7. Spiritual tastes and distastes

Our analysis of the various characteristics of this new spiritual sense has shown us that this is not just an intensification of natural sensations or a better perception of the same contents, but the advent of a new "perceptual habitus"[77] with new contents as its objects. The regenerate have more acute discernment. Because they discern differently, they can also discern other things. After constantly searching for a better way to formulate his observations and reflections, Edwards finally adopted the terminology of "taste." He wrote that "there is given to those that are regenerated, a new supernatural sense, that is as it were a certain divine spiritual taste, which is in its whole nature diverse" [i.e., entirely different] from any of their previous sensations. "That something is perceived by a true saint in the exercise of this new sense of mind, in spiritual and divine things, as entirely different from anything that is perceived in them by natural men, as the sweet taste of honey is diverse from the ideas men get of honey by looking on it" (2, 259).[78] An important category of Edwardsian epistemology, "spiritual taste" is a notion where the themes of "experimental" religion and eighteenth-century philosophical reflections converge.

For many historians of ideas, the eighteenth century was the golden era in the development of this doctrine of taste. The old, intellectual or empirical aesthetics were gradually abandoned and there was a move towards a position where the autonomy and intelligibility *sui generis* of appreciating beauty make judging seem like sensing.[79] A third way—an intelligent grasp of singularity—was sought between the abstraction proper to rational

---

77. Schlaeger, "Edwards' Theory of Perception," 128.

78. The origins of this example, i.e., the taste of honey, in the context of gaining knowledge of divine things by direct experience, extend back to Saint Basil; see "Homily on Psalm 33," 258.

79. J. Addison used "judgment" with the meaning of "feeling," (*Spectator*, 160); see Helvétius, "*juger. . . est sentir* [judging . . . is feeling]" (*De l'esprit*, 210–1). For this topic, see Baeumler, *Das Irrationalitätsproblem in der Ästhetik und Logik des 18*, 2:85–87.

generality and the evanescent contingency of purely sensory particularity. The singular was envisaged as the quintessential place where the particular and the universal, the empirical and the rational, mutually resolved themselves, which subsequently led to the notion of intelligible, concrete totalities.[80] In philosophy, this approach led to the *Critique of Judgment* and then to absolute, post-Kantian metaphysics. Puritan theology—to quote an earlier author—said that "the understanding, as made spiritual, is the palate of the soul"[81] and talked about the "savoury sense . . . of the ways of God."[82] Aside from its totalizing and non-notional character, taste still has an essential connotation of the articulated discernment of spiritual realities. An existential grasp of an object, taste is rarely blind, but rather has an "acuity" discussed by spiritual writers from Augustine to Calvin.[83] In its proper, accepted, aesthetic sense, which closely approximates the "moral sense" of eighteenth-century English thinkers, taste is a universal faculty of discernment. However, for Edwards, the theologian of the regenerate's new spiritual sense, universality of discernment can only be *de jure* and not *de facto*. What this new spiritual sense discerns is indeed of absolutely essential value and validity, but it also takes eyes to see it, and that faculty is not given to everyone.[84] More specifically, natural man is given a notional understanding of the value and validity of divine things, not a realizing apprehension of their affective (and therefore their effective) character![85] In spiritual taste, the

80. Baeumler, *Das Irrationalitätsproblem in der Ästhetik und Logik des 18*, 219.

81. Goodwin, *Of Gospel Holiness Implanted in the Heart, and Continued in the Whole Conversation of Life*, Works, 7:143.

82. Miller, *New England Mind*, 1:83.

83. Balthasar, *Glory of the Lord*, 2:99. See also Erdt, *Sense of the Heart*, 8–9.

84. Notional knowledge amounts to an "ineffectual hearing" of God's word that "neither strikes with the sight of His glory nor with the sense and savour of His goodness" (Shepard, *Of Ineffectual Hearing of the Word*, Works, 3:366) because we "cannot see divine things but in a divine light" (Smith, *Select Discourses*, 412). "All creatures are dead cyphers, of no significance, except the influence of God adds a figure to them" (Willard, *Divinity*, 105); "When the power of the Word comes, the Scriptures are pregnant, arguments undeniable, counsels sweet, reproaches sharp and seasonable" (Hooker, *Application of Redemption*, bk. 9, in Hooker, *Three Sermons*, 62). Augustine had already observed, "For my part, I have spoken to all. But those to whom that anointing does not speak within, whom the Holy Spirit does not teach within, go back untaught" ("On the First Epistle of John," 3. 13).

85. Knowledge and saving faith are characterized by "confidence" which is lacking in purely notional, historic knowledge (Wollebius, *Abridgment of Christian Divinitie*, 3). The devils also know "the Passion story" of Christ but only the justified know that he suffered for them (Heppe, *Dogmatics*, 45). It is always a matter of believing in the word of God, not as the Law but as the Gospel, i.e., "something which is more than a piece of booklearning, or a historical narration of the free love of God" (Smith, *Select Discourses*, 313). As a metaphysical poet once wrote:

elements of totalization and discernment are present simultaneously and in an inseparable, organic way. Men can discern the holy beauty of divine things because they are regenerate, i.e., transformed, in their total state. The new, simple idea of grace gives a taste of divine things because it is as if we ourselves have become spiritualized by grace. The advent of spiritual taste was seen as a sovereign gift of God that abolished a degraded state or rather restored it to its primitive perfection. Taste itself is generally interpreted as a *habitus* where choice is irresistible and infallibly exercised, yet also cognitively grasped.[86]

Since Calvin, the advent of regeneration has been represented as illuminating the understanding so that "it begins to have a taste of those things which pertain to the kingdom of God; previously ... [being] too stupid and senseless to have any relish for them."[87] Edwards quickly adopts this notion and gives two main formulations of it. One is found in his *Treatise on Grace*: "The first effect of the power of God in the heart in regeneration, is to give the heart a divine taste or sense, to cause it to have a relish of the loveliness and sweetness of the supreme excellency of the divine nature" (21, 174). This definition, characterized as positive and affirmative, only concerns the

---

"when without tears I look on Christ, I see
Only a story of some passion,
Which any common eye may wonder on;
But if I look through tears Christ smiles on me."

(Story and Gardner, *Sonnets of William Alabaster*, 39 in Martz, *Poetry of Meditation*, 20.

86. Knowledge "per modum gustus [by way of taste]" (Sibbes, *Exposition of Second Corinthians Chapter IV, Works*, 4:335) is contrasted with notional knowledge. Calvin observed that, although "in the writings of the philosophers we meet occasionally with shrewd and apposite remarks ... not one of them even tasted [gousté] that assurance of divine benevolence [bonne volenté]" (Calvin, *Institutes*, 2. 2. 18, with modified translation to litarally reflect the original French where shown). On the other hand, "in the godly, holy truths are conveyed by way of a taste" (Sibbes, *The Bruised Reed and Smoking Flax, Works*, 1:60). When the preaching of the word is a "dead letter," it is "a sapless, tasteless, spiritless thing" (15, 359), whereas spiritual understanding conveys "a sense and taste" of the excellency of divine things (2, 297), and faith itself is defined as "a belief of truth ... from a spiritual taste and relish of what is excellent and divine" (21, 417). It is a "spiritual taste" that enables the regenerate to "discern the Lord's body in the sacrament" (12, 262), and "the felicity of friendship is tasted" in true moral "conversation" (23, 350); see "As for thy neighbour, whom thou art plainly obliged to love as thou lovest thyself, in order to appreciate him as he deserves, thou must estimate his worth not otherwise than as thou hast determined thine own. For he is what thou art" (Saint Bernard, *Sermons on the Canticle of Canticles*, 2:75 [Sermon 50]). At the summit of mystical knowledge, the soul receives "des goûts distincts et particuliers ... de chaque personne de la Trinité [distinct, individual tastes ... of each person of the Trinity]" (Surin, *Correspondance*, 1336).

87. Calvin, *Institutes*, 3. 2. 34.

appearance of a new sense that enables the heart to enjoy what it previously could not. Now, positive or affirmative definitions can be clarified or confirmed by formulations that emphasize the discerning character proper to the new taste: "Spiritual knowledge," we read in the *Treatise Concerning Religious Affections*, "primarily consists in a taste or relish of the amiableness and beauty of that which is truly good and holy: this holy relish is a thing that discerns and distinguishes between good and evil, between holy and unholy, without being at the trouble of a train of reasoning" (2, 281). Whether the affirmative formulation or the one about discernment, spiritual taste seems like a gracious gift to a destitute creature incapable of any existential perception of God.

The appearance of spiritual taste occurs at a point when the mind is deprived of all spiritual sense of good and evil,[88] or rather, when it experiences a taste for good and a distaste for evil. Natural man has "bad taste,"[89] or rather "a contrary taste,"[90] that prevents him from understanding the glorious character of the universal plan of divine government.[91] In fact, one of the most deplorable consequences of original sin is no longer having a taste or feeling for God, or that we taste and feel him with a kind of fear and horror.[92] This perversion of our spiritual faculties is expressed in a striking way by Edward Taylor, the Puritan poet who complained of losing the use of his nose ("*denos'de*," i.e., denosed) and bitterly exclaimed: "All things smell sweet to mee: Except thy sweetness, Lord."[93] By virtue of man's natural perfection, our experience ought to have been "that the mind should have the sweetest taste and most quick and exquisite delight of those things that are truly most delightful," but our present constitution is deprived of that power and the "things that are less beautiful and amiable in themselves, strike much quicker and deeper in with the sense and propension and constitution of the mind than things that have in themselves the highest excellence, most charming beauty and exquisite sweetness."[94] Rather than discerning and truly relishing the things of God, natural men

88. Bellamy, *True Religion Delineated*, Works, 1:95.

89. Bellamy, *The Wisdom of God in the Permission of Sin*, Works, 2:41.

90. Bellamy, *An Essay on the Nature and Glory of the Gospel of Jesus Christ*, Works, 2:501.

91. See Bellamy, *The Wisdom of God in the Permission of Sin*, Works, 2:53. Calvin wrote that "they have not the least relish for that special care in which alone the paternal favour of God is discerned" (*Institutes*, 1. 16. 1), where "they" refers to philosophers (*philosophi*) in the Latin text (Ref. p. 222n.2 in the 1957 French edition of the *Institutes*).

92. Malebranche, *De la recherche de la vérité, Œuvres*, 3:203–4.

93. Taylor, *Poems*, 8.

94. 13, 218. Miscellany 34, where these lines are found, is titled *Original Sin*.

have only a distaste and "disrelish" (18, 323) for them. They even have a genuine aversion to the happiness of heaven (X, 400) and demonstrate "an inbred distaste and disrelish of God's perfections" (V, 288). Let's remember: men hate God because of his perfections (25, 633–34)!

This inverted and perverted situation—one where there is distaste rather than a taste for genuine good—would be changed from top to bottom by a "taste rectification" (4, 437) in man that specifically restores "an holy taste, to discern and relish divine beauties" (2, 301).[95] This is not just a simple rectification of the situation, nor a partial improvement or correction, but a radical operation where, by virtue of eternal election,[96] "the Spirit of God . . . gives the soul a natural relish of the sweetness of that which is holy . . . and excites a disrelish and disgust of everything that is unholy" (2, 394).[97] This operation is indeed radical and completely reverses the facts of our state, because how could natural man bask in contemplation of the terrible majesty of God or love his electing and reproving sovereignty? Regeneration is characterized exactly by this profound change of our sensibility which, in the final analysis, is just a restoration of our original state, a return to normality and the advent of a perception of things and values as they themselves are.

95. For the traditional thesis of spiritual sense as the restoration of sensible knowledge from before the fall, see Stolz, *Théologie de la Mystique*, 231.

96. *Jansénisme, Dictionnaire de Théologie Catholique*, 8, 439.

97. In the same way that natural benevolence softens and sweetens the mind, making it more receptive to the influences of "gentler natural instincts" (8, 618), "the spirit of grace" implies "a relish" of true, supernatural "good" (25, 543). More specifically, "a true love to God must begin with a delight in His holiness" (2, 257), but this isn't given to us naturally, (see 2, 260–61). The entire Augustinian tradition—or rather every theology of grace—emphasizes the fact that grace can cause us to love the righteousness by which we would "conquer the inclination to sin" (Saint Augustine, *City of God*, 13. 5). "Since the Fall . . . we no longer naturally experience delight in His love" (Malebranche, *De la recherche de la vérité*, 5. 4, *Œuvres*, 2:163); consequently, although man partly sees the beauty in order, he isn't affected enough to prefer it above everything else unless God makes it "amiable" to him by the "sweetness" of his "grace" (*Méditations Chrétiennes et Métaphysiques*, *Œuvres*, 10:150). "La grâce nous enseigne cette délectation céleste qui nous est comme l'huile ou la graisse nécessaire pour faire tourner le gond de la volonté [Grace teaches us such heavenly delight, which is like the oil or grease needed to make the pivot hinge of the will turn]" (Jansenius, *Augustinus*, 4. 7. 176–78). We have an original "distaste" for divine things, which "grace alters" (Sibbes, *The Bruised Reed and Smoking Flax, Works*, 1:60), or rather, grace consists in "those perceptions . . . that cause us . . . to taste true good" (Malebranche, *Réflexion sur la prémotion physique*, *Œuvres*, 16:41). All of this is wonderfully summarized by Pascal, "God transforms the heart of man, by shedding abroad in it a heavenly sweetness, which, surmounting the delights of the flesh . . . makes him conceive a distaste for the pleasures of sin . . . Finding his chiefest joy in the God who charms him, his soul is drawn towards him infallibly, but of its own accord, by a motion perfectly free" (*Provincial Letters*, 448).

8. The sweetness of the things of God

Natural man finds his joys in what benefits him and delights in tasting everything that makes up and enriches his world. Let's remember that, prior to his conversion, Edwards "had much self-righteous pleasure" in the religious affections that arose, so to speak, naturally from his mind (16, 791). However, once converted and regenerated, he found everything that arose in himself to be nauseous (16, 803). He thereafter considered "the pleasures of humility" to be "the most refined, inward and exquisite delights in the world" (16, 767) and his entire religious outlook, in particular, underwent a radical transformation. Edwards considers the change in his inner attitude towards the Calvinist teaching on the sovereignty of God to be the decisive moment of his conversion. Previously "horrible," this doctrine became "delightful" (16, 792). Edwards constantly resorted to the words "delightful," "sweet," and "soft" to portray the wonders of the new regenerated state. "The pleasure of religion," he wrote, "begets a sweet, inexpressibly joyful smile" (13, 176) and it is the "sweet principle" of God's love that fills the heart of the regenerate here below (16, 795).[98] However, "sweet" and "sweetness" should not be understood as particular qualities or properties that simply happen and are therefore like "givens."[99] In fact, they connote a complete change of

---

98. A woman who loves her husband can "sweetly rest in him as a safeguard," while the soul that Christ considers his spouse has "a sweet confidence in Him" (13, 220–21). Spiritual experiences make earthly pleasures "sweet" and the exercise of religion can also "sweeten solitude . . . business and diversion" (19, 87). At the end of time, men shall "sweetly correspond with one another as brethren" (5, 339). In fact, "every saint there is as a note in a concert of music which sweetly harmonizes with every other note" (8, 386). Edwards asked his Indian parishioners to confess God as their "greatest and sweetest Good" (*Ms. Profession of Faith*, in S. J. Nichols, "Last of the Mohican Missionaries," in Hart et al., *Legacy of Jonathan Edwards*, 58). For young Edwards, "the love of Christ" fills the soul "with an inexpressible sweetness. It sweetens every thought" (10, 617). Indeed, the love of God is a "sweet, holy, and powerful affection" (24, 996) and, for the elect, the light of God "shall not be terrible . . . but . . . sweet" (24, 519). Grace—sovereign grace—is a "sweet attribute" (10, 395) that dispenses "sweet doctrines" (22, 314–15) and never forces wills but "sweetly inclines" them (14, 427). Edwards also spoke about God's "essential presence," as distinct from "the holy and sweet indwelling of His Spirit" (*Bl.*, 121), that "divinely sweet sensation in the soul" (24, 996), and he recalls that believers discern "the sweet harmony of the Old and New Testament" (24, 855). Lastly, even the happiness of the Deity is defined in terms of "the infinitely sweet and glorious society of the persons of the Trinity" (25, 153). See also "sweet," "excellent," and "new" in 22, 235, 238–40, and "sweet" and "full" in 22, 292. Note that "sweet" and "sweetness" appear fifty-seven times in the *Personal Narrative*, C. Hambrick-Stowe, "The 'Inward, Sweet Sense' of Christ in Jonathan Edwards," in Hart et al., *Legacy of Jonathan Edwards*, 85–7.

99. However, in itself, "all light is sweet" already (15, 215) and the "sweet order of the world" points back to "an intelligent willing agent" as its first principle (13, 452).

our religious and moral perception and its authentic spiritualization. Sweetness is not merely a quality that we just take for granted, but something that always represents an elevation, a breakaway or a transformation within our world.[100]

The most beautiful Edwardsian text on spiritual sweetness is a letter to Lady Pepperell, wife of the governor of Massachusetts, who was mourning the loss of her only son. Its purpose was to console by trying to bring her to a state of mind where sweetness prevailed, but Edwards scarcely exhorts his correspondent to do anything herself to bring about this state. He especially counsels her to see and contemplate the sweetness of Jesus Christ. God is majesty and greatness and therefore one for whom we have the utmost possible reverence; and yet, at the same time, our hearts are "drawn most sweetly and powerfully to the most free access, the most intimate embrace" (16, 416). That we respond with sweetness to the advances of Christ is because "his love to [us] sinners appeared like a sweet flame burning . . ." (16, 417); and yet, in himself, Christ, as a divine person, is not mild sweetness but a devouring fire. In condescending to the level of the work of his hands, God transcended himself, so to speak, so that the creature could transcend himself and know intimacy with him. "The effulgence of His glory is attempered to our sight. He is indeed a person of infinite majesty to fill our souls with the greatest reverence and adoration. But there is nothing in it that needs to terrify us. For His infinite majesty is joined with as it were infinite meekness, sweet condescension and humility." If the light of God appears soft on the face of Jesus Christ, it is because God, so to speak, has attenuated its strength. "But especially are the beams of Christ's glory infinitely softened and sweetened" by his love for men, and again, "his beams go forth with infinite strength, yet as they proceed from Christ in the character of the Lamb of God and shine through his meek and lowly humanity, they are infinitely gentle and mild" (16, 416). This frequent use of soft and sweet—adjectives that seem sensible in nature—is not a vague attempt in any way to underline the sensible character of religious experience, but instead a suggestive, visual way to express the mechanism by which the human mind conforms to the Spirit. Being "sweetened" or "softened"

---

100. The narratives of Scripture—those sweet, vivifying words that God in his mercy has gifted to men—exercised "a strange . . . enchantment" (13, 202). It was written of Sarah Pierrepont, Edwards's fiancée, that the great Being, who made and rules the world, at times filled her mind with "a strange sweetness" (16, 789–90). This sweetness was strange because it didn't seem to originate from anything clear or obvious, but evoked God's transcendence of this world. While gracious and arbitrary, this supernatural intrusion caused an immense change in her life and required constant effort on her part to cope with the "strange and wonderful transformation" brought about by her conversion (7, 525).

doesn't mean that someone is simply malleable, i.e., shapeless. When Christ "softens" the incandescent flame of his light, he thereby enables men to discern, taste, and as it were espouse its structures and form. The priestly anointing oil that ran down Aaron's beard, "by reason of its soft-flowing and diffusive nature, and its unparalleled sweetness and fragrancy, did most fitly represent divine love" (21, 184). The oil symbolized the anointing of the Spirit that softened the heart, enabling the creature to enter into the ways of God and taste his wonders. Its diffusive nature is not to be understood in terms of a mere flow or overflow, but rather as the "effusion" (13, 347) that communicates the Spirit's sweetness to the creature and enables the creature to welcome the Spirit. Just as "soft" does not refer to something sensible *per se*, the softening and diffusion that it implies should not be understood as a flow or subsidence. Softening does not mean to simply blur contours or abolish shapes, but instead expresses the results of that warm operation of the Spirit which melts the frosty frontiers of a being fixed and frozen into the structures of natural existence. Subject to the conditions of a purely notional knowledge and a merely speculative and external sense of the things of God, the human mind needs the sweetness of grace to respond and submit to the movements of the regenerating Spirit's power in him (see 13, 260). Softening and regeneration replaces the hardness of sin, allowing the return of the Spirit to the mind. In other words, regenerative totalization is manifested in the coming of a new "spiritual taste," the new holy disposition of the mind that enables it to rediscover its original harmony with the Spirit of God.

9. Wisdom and taste

It is helpful, at this point, to restate the rejection of a purely "sensible" interpretation of "sweetness" and "softness" and to underline their invincible reference to the content. The *Treatise Concerning Religious Affections* speaks of the "complacence" of a "gracious nature" that prizes God's commandments (2, 260), but these commandments always have a conceptual element. In his *Personal Narrative,* Edwards reported having "sweet complacency in God in views of his glorious perfections" (16, 799) and, in a letter to Lady Pepperell, wrote: "Let us think, dear Madam, a little of the loveliness of our blessed Redeemer . . . that we should . . . have sweet complacence" (16, 415). In this context, "complacence" expresses the state of a mind "in tune" with God and his commandments, and this concord is pleasing.

The distant goal of Edwardsian developments is to discern the harmony between the regenerated mind and the regenerating Spirit, although the use of the term "taste" ultimately did little to promote these vague concerns of speculative, idealistic theology. After all, it's a notion of a sensible and intuitive nature that hardly relates to conceptual structures. And yet, it was precisely so that he could lay the foundations of just such a theory that Jonathan Edwards tried to portray the new spiritual sense in terms of taste. His basic concern was to account for the regenerated Spirit's conformity to the things and commandments of God in such a way that it was not the result of a divine dictate, but an immanent deployment of our mind's auto-articulation. Edwards believed that justifying grace absolutely came from above, i.e., from God, but he also thought that the very sovereignty of grace itself required that it not dominate the human mind from without and with violence (see 2, 395-6), nor exert "tyrannical power" over it,[101] but instead penetrate and espouse its structures. Of course, there can be no real distinction between seeing the true hatefulness of an object and hating it (13, 527n.4).[102] Likewise, having a sense of the goodness and reality of Jesus as savior is the same as espousing and adhering to it.[103] Nevertheless, though our adherence to a spiritual reality that is delightful to us is immediate, it must still not be understood, i.e., be blind. While the use of the notion of taste—a faculty without "a medium between the object and the organ"[104]—serves to explain the non-discursive character of spiritual apprehension (see 2, 281), we shouldn't think that the non-discursivity of the mental act is a type of spiritual automatism. Edwards certainly discerned these implications in the notion of taste—turning them to advantage in his analyses and describing them admirably—yet he does not seem to have grasped the full metaphysical scope of this notion and his recourse to it is therefore without speculative consequences. His brilliant intuition regarding taste as a faculty *sui generis* of spiritual apprehension remains, but it does not get the proper conceptual deployment needed to be the keystone of a theologico-metaphysical system.

Taste is especially important in the *Treatise Concerning Religious Affections*, but even there isn't systematically developed at the epistemological level. If the first of the two essential elements of taste is the mind's immediate adherence to an object—the second being a sense of true goodness—the *Enquiry* (*Freedom of Will*), which came some seven years after the *Treatise*, completely subsumed this mental act of immediate apprehension-adhesion under the will. Analyzing the will's proper mechanism, Edwards explained

101. See Goodwin, *Of Gospel Holiness in the Heart and Life*, Works, 7:330.

102. See also 21, 432. The knowledge of the elect consists in the "taste of the heart by which he discerns the divine character with approbation" (Hopkins, *System of Doctrines*, Works, 1:405).

103. Hopkins, *Two Sermons*, Works, 3:531.

104. Dingley, *Spiritual Taste Described*, 45 in Erdt, *Sense of the Heart*, 17.

that good is what seems "agreeable" and "suits the mind," and the fact that a thing appears "agreeable" to the mind is the same as a preference of the mind for that "agreeable" thing (1, 143–44). However, in this case, this faculty's immediate option for its object is virtually blind or, more precisely, automatic. Good is indicated to the will by the understanding, i.e., by another faculty external to it, and the will follows its instructions like a robot. Taste only appears here in its primitive state, that of an external sense (1, 146–47), and we are therefore left with the two traditional faculties of the mind and the will. Latter-day Edwardsians would revisit this view to a certain extent,[105] but Jonathan Edwards himself didn't give any significant place to this notion in his great Stockbridge treatises. Even though the core questions in his dissertation on *The Nature of True Virtue* would seem to require and even impose a return to "taste," Edwards doesn't systematically use this term, or really develop it, but only speaks furtively of an inner sense for discerning spiritual beauty.[106] This absence of a systematic reflection on the proper faculty or sense of true goodness, i.e., of spiritual goodness, marks the incompleteness of Edwardsian thought and the limits of his attempt to unify metaphysical, aesthetic and ethical factors. This is not the case with his developments regarding immediate apprehension—an essential moment of taste—which represent lasting gains.

In the four pages he devoted to a somewhat systematic explanation of taste, which includes a lengthy quote from Ephraim Chambers, Edwards underlined the fact that the regenerate "easily distinguishes good and evil . . . and judges what is right, as it were spontaneously, and of himself, without a particular deduction." This spontaneity of judgment results from an instantaneous exercise of taste which, without resort to any series of arguments, "knows at once, what is a suitable amiable behavior towards God, and towards man" and with a first glance of the eye, as it were, discovers the qualities and properties of the things it encounters (2, 282–83). Both spontaneous and instantaneous, the judgment made relates to particular questions and situations. Taste is exercised with exactness and results in the discernment of an individual object. Nevertheless, the fundamental particularity that characterizes its universe is not portrayed at all in terms of a type of atomism. Taste doesn't hide a discontinuous succession of periodic impressions and judgments. A faculty that quite properly belongs to an individual, taste is rooted in each individual's own particular character. In other words, if taste only concerns individual objects, it can only be explained in terms

---

105. A. Burton portrayed taste as the essential faculty of the mind, the source of all moral choices (*Essays on Some First Principles*, 54–55, 253–55).

106. See *infra*, p. 359 ss.

of the mind's permanent dispositions and the very general rules that have become co-natural with the mind, i.e., that are embodied in and by it. "The saints," wrote Edwards, "in thus judging of actions by a spiritual taste, have not a particular recourse to the express rules of God's Word, with respect to every word and action that is before them . . . but yet their taste itself in general, is subject to the rule of God's Word. . . . As a man of a rectified palate judges of particular morsels by his taste: but yet his palate itself must be judged of . . . by certain rules and reasons." Unlike enthusiasts who, devoid of "any judgment or wisdom," periodically act according to "an immediate dictate," the regenerate discern the will of God by "taste or relish" exercised out of, and in accordance with, the conformity that grace established between their mind and the Spirit of God (2, 284–85).

This final convergence—between spiritual taste on the one hand and judgment and wisdom on the other—shows that taste, while preserving the original, immediate character of the sensation, should always be regarded as a synonym for an understanding that has become spiritual. Grasping something through spiritual taste is the same as contemplating it in an intuitive way (4, 179), because the true sense of the intuition is not its immediacy but rather its power to disclose the heretofore hidden elements and moments of a thing.[107] Nevertheless, we should avoid seeing spiritual taste as a "savoring" discursivity or confusing it with notional knowledge and faith that are simply made livelier and more subtle by the infusion of grace. In and by itself, taste is never theoretical reasoning and, even if shown to be an unbeatable reference to content, never has anything to do with dogmatic statements in the form of discursive expressions or conceptual explanations. We always have to underline that the proper object of spiritual taste is that "savor" of the things of God (17, 419), but while *sapor* has a positive relationship to *sapientia*,[108] it does not lend itself to thetic deployments. The "savor" that spiritual taste discerns is the sweetness of divine things that is

---

107. For this intuition in Edwards, see *infra*, p. 381 n.39.

108. Saint Gregory the Great wrote that "even though they may perceive hidden truths by their understanding . . . the proud are not able to experience their sweetness, and while they know about them they fail to know their relish" (*Morals*, 23. 31, in Saint Thomas Aquinas, *Summa Theologiæ*, 2–2. 162. 3. ad. 1), whereas the gift of true wisdom implies "such knowledge of God, His attributes and mysteries, as is full of flavour" (Lallemant, *Spiritual Doctrine*, 150). Puritan theologians knew that "in the learned languages, the words that do express wisdom imply likewise the general relish and savour of the whole soul" (Sibbes, *The Bruised Reed and Smoking Flax, Works*, 1:78). For *sapientia* and *sapor*, see Kraus, *Der Begriff der Dummheit bei Thomas von Aquin*, 28–29. See also Kant, "Anthropology from a Pragmatic View," 7:242; Nietzsche, *Philosophy in Tragic Age of Greeks*, 43.

not related to particular entities *per se* but rather to "the beauty of holiness," which is the beauty and excellency of divine things (2, 260).

7

THE TWO BEAUTIES

1. Consent, equality, proportion

JONATHAN EDWARDS CONTRASTED PURELY notional, doctrinal knowledge with an adequate spiritual understanding of good and evil and frequently called this understanding a "sense of the heart" to underline a person's total involvement in cognitive acquisition. However, highlighting the involvement aspect of spiritual knowledge still didn't satisfy this theologian, who sought to distinguish gracious affections from those that were merely natural. Edwards then used "taste" to describe this new spiritual sense. It wasn't just a matter of representing certain realities in an existential way, but also a question of exercising discrimination and discernment with regard to them. Although not related to any specific content, this new spiritual sense nonetheless referred to a reality that differed from those that are correlates of notional knowledge or imagination. Described as a taste, the "object" of this new spiritual sense is a particular level of reality, even if this particular determination is unrelated to conceptual discursivity. For Edwards, the level of reality in question is "beauty" or "excellence."

Beginning in 1734, Edwards explained that "spiritual and divine light" is the "sense of the divine excellency of the things revealed" in the word of God (17, 413); and, according to his great Miscellany 782, in "saving conviction," God gives the saints "a sensible knowledge of the things of religion, with respect to their spiritual good or evil" which does "originally consist in a sense of the spiritual excellency, beauty, or sweetness of divine things" (18, 464). Later, in his *Treatise Concerning Religious Affections*, he defined "the beauty and sweetness" of God's holiness as the "immediate" objects of this "spiritual taste" (2, 260). The *Treatise Concerning Religious Affections* certainly describes the beauty of divine things as "objects" of this "spiritual sense" in a most ample and admirable style. However, we think that, in the final analysis, his sermon at Newark on *True Grace* probably gives the most concise and striking formulation of the essential role that this perception of God's holy beauty played in Edwardsian doctrine. After focusing at length on the true riches of notional knowledge and faith, which even devils possess, Edwards ends by describing what distinguishes regenerate knowledge. The foundation of truly gracious affections is "an apprehension, or sense of the supreme holy beauty, and comeliness of divine things, as they are in themselves." The Devil perceives and knows all of God's attributes, although ever since the fall, he is altogether "blind" to the supreme beauty of the divine nature. He has a "strong sense of his awful majesty, but no idea of His beauty and comeliness." Observing the wonderful works of God for a thousand years still does not give the Devil the least sense of God's divine beauty. Moreover, God's holy beauty is what appears least beautiful to the Devil who, to the degree that he perceives it, hates God even more (25, 633–34). The absence of a spiritual idea of God's holy beauty hinders or rather distorts all knowledge we can acquire of God as he is in himself. Although an external view of God's majestic glory might, as it were, "submerge" the mind, it will still not affect the enmity of the heart. Only those who discern God's holy beauty in the person of Jesus Christ understand its cost and worth and therefore only they realize the sufficiency of his redemptorial mediation. Freed from the terror evoked by such a powerful and implacable righter of wrongs, the regenerate who contemplate the beauty proper to divine things turn to God with "free desires." However, even though contemplation of God's holy beauty "in the face of Jesus Christ" frees the creature from his terrors and reconciles him with his existence, this still does not mean that the creature may follow his own will or accept himself as he is. While "false experience is conceited of itself, and affected with itself," that "sense of the supreme, holy beauty and glory of God and Christ . . . truly humbles the soul." "The light of God's beauty, and that alone, truly shows the soul its own deformity, and effectually inclines it to exalt God, and abase itself" (25, 635–37). More precisely, a vision of God's holy beauty humbles the heart but also frees it, drawing its attention to God the savior and making it possible to live in and with him.

Edwardsian descriptions abound with terms from the world of beauty (and the sublime) and yet the beauty in question here is not exclusively aesthetic in nature but has profound moral connotations. Exegetes of Edwardsian thought have always been impressed by the highly unusual role it assigns to beauty in theology and metaphysics. Of course, the theme of the beauty of God and divine things is not absent from the Christian tradition.[1] Nevertheless, we had to wait until Jonathan Edwards to hear *expressis verbis* (in express terms) that what distinguishes God from all other beings is his divine beauty (2, 298)! The Holy Spirit, who is the location and source of gracious affections, is defined as the "infinite beauty" (6, 364)[2] of God; and because the beauty of this world is but a "communication," participation or reflection of God's "infinite beauty" (13, 384),[3] it is not surprising that even the most miserable of mortals greatly love this life and are so strongly attached to it: they cannot bear "to lose the sight of such a beautiful and lovely world" (6, 306). This sense of perception of the physical world's beauty is an existential moment in Edwards's mental universe but if, like Abigail Hutcheson, he had "a sense of the glory of God appearing in the trees" (4, 195), he knew for a fact that "the moral beauty and regularity" of the universe are infinitely superior to the "beauty and regularity" of its physical nature (20, 337).[4] Edwards always distinguished between these two types of beauty, although this distinction was only fully formulated in his treatise on *The Nature of True Virtue*.

This treatise begins by defining two types of beauty corresponding to two types of virtue, respectively. For spiritual virtue, we have general beauty; for natural virtue, we have particular beauty. Universal or "general" beauty is "that by which a thing appears beautiful when viewed most perfectly, comprehensively and universally, with regard to all its tendencies, and its connections with everything it stands related to." On the other hand, "particular" beauty is when a thing appears beautiful when considered only with respect to its connection with some particular things (8, 540). Further on, and based on their connections, Edwards distinguished these two beauties as spiritual and natural, respectively. Spiritual beauty is primitive, original and only defined in terms of relationships of a moral order, whereas secondary beauty—a simple image of the first—consists merely of physical or

---

1. For this theme, see what is probably the most important work of H. Urs von Balthasar, *Glory of the Lord*.

2. See also 13, 284, etc.

3. See also 6, 364; 8, 550–51.

4. See also "The beauty of the trees, plants and flowers, with which God has bespangled the face of the earth is delightful, the beautiful frame of the body of man, especially in its perfection, is astonishing; the beauty of the moon and the stars, is wonderful; the beauty of the highest heavens, is transcendent; the excellency of angels and the saints in light, is very glorious; but it is all deformity, and darkness in comparison of the higher glories and beauties of the Creator of all." And the young preacher exclaimed, "at the great day when God appears, the sun shall be turned into darkness, shall hide his face as if he were ashamed to see himself so much outshined" (10, 421).

physiological relationships (8, 564–65). In both cases, consent is designated the essential relationship of each beauty and the character of the consent determines which beauty is in question.

Consent is a key notion in Edwardsian thought and it was in *The Mind* that Edwards first made use of it. Though idealist, Edwardsian metaphysics served a theology whose fundamental challenge was to define religious affections. The most spectacular element of this idealism, i.e., the theory of the mental existence of all things, made a metaphysical explanation of justification and regeneration possible. The justified and regenerated creature, henceforth in the sphere of the Spirit, is spiritualized and conformed to God. Now, although this epistemological idealism helped, to a certain extent, to understand the metaphysical "place" of religious affections, moral idealism was needed to explain their actual structure. Jonathan Edwards was able to develop his natural theology—and, in a sense, the core of his positive theology—in terms of a metaphysic of beauty because his doctrine of beauty enabled the subjectivization of reality, although—and this is what matters—it was subjectivization of a moral order. Edwards discerned an entire scale of beauties in ascending order, from the humblest physical realities to the wonders of Trinitarian "relationships," because he conceived of beauty as a notion where the transition from the impersonal to the personal is almost imperceptible, where what is radically different in theology—namely nature and grace—appear in metaphysical continuity. By defining the excellency or beauty of beings in terms of consent, Jonathan Edwards satisfied the two great requirements of his system: on the one hand, explaining the continuity between God and the world he created and, on the other, highlighting the radical difference between nature and grace.

Edwards framed the question of beauty in terms of consent in an inquiry whose very imprecision had profound doctrinal implications. Speaking of excellency, he began his notes on *The Mind* with the remark that "we are concerned with nothing else. But what is this excellency? Wherein is one thing excellent and another evil, one beautiful and another deformed?" (6, 332). Excellency and beauty are, at first sight, contrasted with the deformity associated with evil, so that the natural and moral-spiritual aspects of beauty are immediately stated. Yet, what is the primitive sense of beauty, if we provisionally consider it as traditionally understood, i.e., without any spiritual-moral connotation? We will first try to present the conceptual elements of the notion of beauty as an aesthetic category, then move on to a systematic portrayal of moral beauty, the "holy beauty" of God. However, before commencing this presentation, it is necessary to explain that the moral will and action of the unregenerate involves the same kind of non-spiritual consent as that underlying the sublime greatness of the stars and the soft beauty of violets.

Edwards believed that he exhibited good sense, that common conscience of humanity, when he defined excellency as "harmony, symmetry or proportion." He later returned, more or less accidently, to the first two of these notions but dealt particularly with the last one. "Proportion," he wrote, "is pleasant to the mind, and disproportion is unpleasant." But what do we mean by "proportion"? Because proportion is "an equality, or likeness of ratios," it therefore follows that "equality" and—next to equality—"likeness" are essential elements of it. The mind naturally rejoices to see two equal things, two equal distances or two equal areas. Equality pleases us in an immediate, almost instinctive way. Simple equality is therefore the lowest form of beauty and only involves the mutual relations of very few things among themselves (6, 332-33). As the number of things perceived increases, equality disappears and is transposed, on another level, into proportion. Proportion reproduces, or rather expresses, identity at a higher level. It enables a multiplicity (i.e., of things or parts) to have virtually the same harmony as an equality. "By equality or likeness," wrote Edwards, "one part consents with but one part. But by proportion one part may sweetly consent to ten thousand different parts" (6, 380).[5] Once beyond mere simple equality, consent is "sweet." In proportion, various parts are in relation to and in agreement with one another, and these relations are regular, or rather, obey certain regularities. The brute fact of equality gives way to a kind of articulation, one where articulation and structuring are like the first, humblest expectations of a spiritual action.

Equality is the simplest form of beauty, with proportion the source of all complex beauty (6, 334-35). The natural world is primarily a place of complex beauty. The wonderful green of the plants, the blue of the sky, the white of the clouds and the complicated proportions that these colors maintain between themselves create harmonious views; and there is a sublime harmony—a "correspondence" *à la* Baudelaire—between the objects of different senses, such as the colors of plants, the smell of flowers, or the singing of birds. Such harmony is very likely attributable to a certain proportion between the vibrations made in our various sense organs (6, 305). A hidden, yet complex proportion is always at the source of our feeling of beauty; and this complexity will increase in the next world, that place of the most "exquisite spiritual proportions" (13, 328).[6]

---

5. For the metaphysical significance of "ten thousand," see *infra*, p. 386.

6. Already on earth, during the millennium, mankind will constitute "one orderly regular, beautiful society . . . all the members in beautiful proportion" (9, 484).

Edwards highlighted the increasing complexity of proportions as the reason for the intensification of our feelings of beauty and thereby detached beauty from its sensory vehicle, (13, 329)[7] the first step in a process that would lead to its complete spiritualization. He explained that, in the final analysis, every proportion can and should be reduced to relations of equality (6, 335) and that proportion consequently remains a reality of an arithmetic order. However, such idealistic inspiration almost imperatively led Edwardsian thought towards formulations where what was essentially just a brute arithmetic relation radiated like a "performed moral" act[8] or a symbol of the spiritual. The regularity of their difference, i.e., their equality of inequality, enables things to "consent to" and "oppose" one another. Using more abstract language, a draft Miscellany defined excellency as a synonym for beauty inasmuch as it "consists in correspondency and proportion" (13, 251n.7); and "correspondence" is a very useful word that gives more general metaphysical expression to a state which ultimately only concerns order and quality. Before speaking of how proportion enables one part to "sweetly consent to ten thousand different parts," colder, more severe language is used to express the mutual character concealed in a relation that can always be regarded as a simple composition of equalities. However, if correspondence is to express proportion in a way that accents the reciprocity of its relations, something that would be extremely valuable for the study of moral beauty *per se*, then proportion must first be developed along the lines of a multiple relation with an ethical connotation that is actually more basic than that of spiritual beauty.

Synonyms for proportion include "regularity," "uniformity," "order," and "harmony" (8, 561–2). Now, although each of these notions can be reduced to simple compositions of equalities, they nonetheless conceal and suggest moral meaning. As pluralities governed by unity, i.e., inasmuch as they are beauties (*ibid.*), these notions express arrangement in a certain direction or towards an end and, in that sense, go beyond simple intellectuality and refer to the world of wisdom. As unity submitting to order, accepting regularity and abandoning its particularity, a mathematical relation also anticipates ethical obedience. Unlike attempts by some of his contemporaries, such as Kames, who gave "carrying on commerce and procuring so many conveniencies to mankind"[9] as an example of moral beauty, Jonathan Edwards—author of a wonderful, natural typology and tireless investigator of the "images or shadows of divine things" in this world here

---

7. See "Music is feeling, not sound," Stevens, *Poems*, 94.
8. See Schelling, *Investigations into Human Freedom*, 43.
9. See Kames, *Morality and Natural Religion*, 46.

below—preferred to seek reflections of supreme spiritual beauty in the most primitive and simplest instances of natural beauty. In other words, rather than naturalizing spiritual beauty, his intent was to spiritualize physical beauty. He wrote that the highest beauty—spiritual beauty—is the union and consent found among spiritual beings, a primary beauty that has its reflection and even its image in inanimate things. "Such is the mutual agreement of the various sides of a square, or equilateral triangle, or of a regular polygon. Such is, as it were, the mutual consent of the different parts of the periphery of a circle, or surface of a sphere, and of the corresponding parts of an ellipse. Such is the agreement of the colors, figures, dimensions, and distances of the different spots on a chess board. Such is the beauty of the figures on a piece of chintz, or brocade. Such is the beautiful proportion of the various parts of an human body, or countenance. And such is the sweet mutual consent and agreement of the various notes of a melodious tune" (8, 562). All of these instances of harmony, from arithmetic figures to musical melodies, do not concern "the will, disposition, or affection of the heart" but only constitute natural beauty (8, 565). Now, although Edwards had a particularly acute sense of the beauties of nature, he advised only taking "a transient view" (17, 431) of them because, in the final analysis, they are only mere images of a higher beauty.

2. Wisdom and justice

Edwardsian idealism held that bodies are mere shadows of minds and that beings are essentially spiritual in nature. The deployment of the theory of beauty-excellency as consent provided this idealism with a wonderful explanation. Bodies are merely shadows of minds, because the consent that constitutes their "excellency" is not "cordial" but only natural. More precisely, natural consent is not true consent because it is only a reflection or distant analogy of the cordial consent proper to minds. Of course, the primitive kernel of all proportion is a simple mathematical relation but, even in the realm of material things, true beauty requires going beyond raw equality. The uniformity or likeness of a number of pillars scattered here and there does not constitute beauty in the same degree as the pillars of a particular building that are in proper relation to one another (8, 567). The true beauty of physical things derives from their structure, i.e., their "figure," because the agreement—in this instance, of the pillars—is not reduced to a mere relation of equality but is expressed in the form of a harmonious composition of elements which, in a striking manner, evoke the consent between minds. When one thing sweetly harmonizes with another, as happens with notes in music, they relate as if they love one another. "So the beauty of figures and motions is, when one part has such consonant proportion with the rest as represents a general agreeing and consenting together; which is very much the image of love in all the parts of a society united by a sweet consent and charity of heart" (6, 380).

Edwards recognized, in the elemental beauties of nature and art, an image or reflection of the beauties of order and agreement in society, although this social order and agreement aren't necessarily related to a metaphysical state other than that of the colorful splendor of flowers or the exquisite sweetness of a piece of music. Edwards, a Calvinist theologian who had always taught that so-called natural virtues only expressed a fallen nature, now strove to rediscover essential continuity between the beauty of natural things and the harmony of moral virtues. From a metaphysical point of view, the beings of this world are either material or immaterial, and yet, because the phenomenon of proportion is common to these two levels of reality, beauty asserts itself in both material and immaterial beings (8, 568). The beautiful proportion of material beings is, of course, supremely expressed in their mutual relations.

A key tradition in aesthetics, from Scalinger to Kant, has been to draw the suitable and beautiful closer[10] and thereby rediscover an essential moment of beauty in the phenomena of social life. We have only to think of Shaftesbury: "the elegant Passion or Love of Beauty, which is so advantageous to *Virtue*," and itself no other than, "the Love of Order and Beauty in society."[11] Though knowing that "a civil union" and "an harmonious agreement" among men are less "aimiable" than "a pious union, and sweet agreement" (5, 365), Jonathan Edwards persisted in rediscovering the ethico-social moment at the heart of natural beauty. Beauty is always a question of proportion and, as we saw, proportion can appear as either unity in diversity or as a mutual relation. In the former, it is perceived more as order or uniformity; in the latter, as correspondence or symmetry. The first kind of beautiful proportion concerns human relations at the level, so to speak, of the community; the second views them more from the perspective of mutuality and reciprocity.

Proportion between the parts of a whole gives an appearance of order. The beauty of a building depends particularly on the regular distribution of its elements: each one of its pillars, panels, cornices, and pilasters must be set in its proper place. Likewise, the beauty of order in society requires

---

10. For this, see Baeumler, *Das Irrationalitätsproblem in der Ästhetik und Logik des 18*, 285 and n.3.

11. Shaftesbury, *Characteristics*, 1:279.

that the various members of society "have all their appointed office, place and station, according to their several capacities and talents, and everyone keeps his place and continues in his proper business." The harmony between the elements of a material thing corresponds, in immaterial beings, to the natural virtue of wisdom, i.e., "the united tendency of thoughts, ideas, and particular volitions, to one general purpose" (8, 568). Designated as dependent on the thoughts and intentions of intelligent beings, "wisdom" falls half-way between the physical and the moral. Every teleological moment of beauty, which Edwards variously termed "fitness," "agreableness," "suitableness," "design," or "end" (8, 563–64), is to be subsumed under it: that entire sphere where free intention is only prefigured or preformed by the finality inherent in material things and free volition fades into collective design. As wisdom often has more to do with the cosmic than the moral, it was not by chance that Edwards composed a short text—purely scientific in nature—to celebrate "Wisdom in the Contrivance of the World" (6, 307–10). Given this naturalization, it might be tempting to believe that the social level of morality is incorporated in the sphere of secondary beauty and that individual morality or personal virtue is restricted to primary beauty. This is not at all the case. Edwards, a passionate reader and fervent exegete of the Revelation to John, assigns "the pious union, and sweet agreement" among men, i.e., among the regenerate in society, to the sphere of primary beauty (5, 365). Conversely, he never ceases to vigorously reaffirm the purely natural character of any excellency found in the acts performed by the unregenerate.

The supreme virtue of interhuman relations is justice, a notion that this eighteenth-century Calvinist writer inherited from the entire, ancient Christian tradition. Suffice it to say Augustine considered *iustitia* the very order and perfection of the soul's orientation. "Justice," he wrote, consists in "to love the better things more and the lesser things less"[12] and giving "to each what is due,"[13] because what we call justice is simply equity, and doesn't equity derive its name from equality?[14] Closer to Edwards, Henry More skillfully reintroduced proportion into justice,[15] and Edwards's own description of this notion was profoundly marked by the subject of proportion, even if—in this instance—"justice" had less to do with order in society than the structure of the relations between individuals, i.e., the structure of their "mutual" relations. A kind of secondary beauty, more moral and less "natural" in character and scarcely prefigured by physical

12. Saint Augustine, "True Religion," 273.
13. Saint Augustine, *On Order*, 1. 7. 19, 2. 7. 22.
14. Saint Augustine, *Magnitude of the Soul*, 9. 15.
15. Watts, "Edwards' 'True Virtue,'" 185.

things, justice—unlike wisdom—is portrayed by Edwards using examples drawn almost exclusively from interhuman relations: what we owe to our neighbor and what we may rightly expect from him (see 8, 569). However, for Edwards—and this is perhaps a second sign of approaching a higher moment of secondary beauty—it is no longer even instances of mutual justice nor just actions and behaviors that express secondary beauty in a truly ethical sense, but rather their "moral sense," i.e., the "sense of justice" or "conscience" we have with respect to their justness or sinfulness.[16]

The polemic design of the dissertation on *The Nature of True Virtue* refuted the doctrine of moral sense professed by many eighteenth-century thinkers. Jonathan Edwards certainly agreed with Shaftesbury, Hutcheson, Kames, and Hume that men have a moral sense, a natural conscience that almost infallibly discerns good and evil, yet he refused to give this sense the same metaphysical standing as the deistic moralists or skeptics. Edwards thought that this sense wasn't a striking manifestation of the heart's moral vocation, but only a kind of instinct that interprets subconscious reasonings and conveys reactions and agreements performed on a purely natural level.

According to the Edwardsian analysis, natural conscience is related to the sense of proportion on two levels. The conscience manifests itself by a sharp feeling of remorse when we act towards others as we would not want them to act towards us. We have a guilty conscience when we act with cruelty, injustice, or ingratitude. Guilty consciences may vary considerably in degree and strength, yet all manifest uneasiness originating from considerations of proportion.

The affection of love has a natural, innate tendency to reach out to others, to stand by them and, consequently, to desire and act as though they are at one with us. In self-love, we are inclined to feel like we are acting at one with ourselves, i.e., in solidarity with ourselves. When conflicted, i.e., when "inconsistent with ourselves," we feel uneasy. We deal with this very inconsistency whenever we treat our neighbor in a cruel or shabby way. "To do that to another which we should be angry with him for doing to us, and to hate a person for doing that to us which we should incline to and insist on doing to him . . . is to disagree with ourselves, and contradict ourselves" (8, 589-90). The individual's conscience is divided, so to speak; he examines his own will, yet acts as if it was the will of another. This inconsistency—the contradiction between the volitions and acts performed by this other (in fact, himself) and the volitions and acts he could rightly have expected of himself—highlights a rupture in mutuality and a transgression

---

16. For the origin and meaning of "conscience" in Edwards, see Fiering, *Edwards's Moral Thought*, 110-11.

against reciprocity. A guilty conscience expresses a particular form of injustice, one that a moral subject perpetrates against himself.

Analyzed in this way, a guilty conscience can be understood as a particular case of disorder and disproportion. We still need to ask this question: how does a purely theoretical observation of disorder and disproportion lead to troubled feelings or even violent remorse? Edwards gave two reasons for the actual outcome and practical expression of moral judgment. On the one hand, Edwards plainly attributed the work of the moral conscience to fallen nature and to self-love incapable of tolerating contradiction—an offense—even when the offence originated with us. On the other hand, he attributed the origin of moral judgment to a natural, moral sense—without any ethico-religious characterization of good and evil, reward and punishment—and these two reasons are largely interdependent.

When I realize, wrote Edwards, that I mistreat my neighbor, I don't just confine myself to a purely theoretical judgment of the contradiction in which I find myself embroiled, but also find my situation painful. This sharp feeling of inconsistency with oneself is actually a second constituent moment of a guilty conscience. In the first moment, I understand that my treatment of my neighbor is appalling, not just by virtue of my personal contradictions, but also in what might be termed an objective way. Independently of the self-contradictory character of my dealings and, as it were, preceding them, I have a sense, intuition and realization that they are reprehensible from "a natural agreement, proportion and harmony between malevolence or injury and resentment and punishment; or between loving and being loved, between showing kindness and being rewarded" (8, 593).

Here Edwards is considering good and evil at a very profound level, although still without engaging in a discussion about their meaning, i.e., how they are "in themselves." For the moment, he is content to clarify the relations that the natural mind discerns between good and its reward (virtue and happiness) and evil and its punishment (vice and misfortune). Edwards initially advocates a "primitive," natural sense for good and evil and scatters adjectives from the world of proportion throughout his presentation. He notes that, in justice, the approbation of the conscience is generally related to the "natural agreement . . . in manner and measure" of the sanction (8, 596–97). The purely natural virtue of gratitude is based on "a sense of uniformity and proportion" (8, 583) and, generally speaking, "a sense of equality" is the key moment of the operations of "the natural conscience" (8, 594).[17]

17. For the difference between "the approbation of conscience" and "the approbation of the heart, or relish, or love," see 21, 317; see also "the great difference between the dictates of Conscience and divine Taste," (*Ms. Book of Controversies*, 93).

The perfection of equality and proportion is therefore the ultimate motivation for the exercise of our moral sense. It is here, albeit transposed onto a higher level but essentially unchanged, that Edwards finds the category of the natural, mathematical order of consent. In spite of the immense difference separating the pleasure felt on seeing the symmetry of a chessboard's squares and the admiration that provoked David's sublime gratitude to Saul, Edwards emphasizes the continuity between primary beauty and the beauty of moral action, and he attempts to defend the essential affinity of all moments of natural beauty. On the other hand—and here we will see the subtlety of this metaphysic of Calvinism—it was from these natural moments, and without any reference to the spiritual benevolence that is the essence of true virtue, that Jonathan Edwards found a way to transition from natural good to spiritual good without calling their essential discontinuity into question.

3. Secondary beauty and greatness

In his discussion on the guilty conscience, Edwards frequently returns to the approbation that the natural conscience cannot but give to his own condemnation and, in particular, to his condemnation by God. In all moral sin consisting in malevolence and hate for our neighbor, we can easily see the natural agreement between hating men and being hated by them, between wronging them and being wronged in turn by them (8, 593). In the same way—and this is something awakened sinners know only too well—transgression against the Being of beings will unfailingly provoke this Being to respond with hate and punishment. When sinners hear their verdict at the Day of Judgment, they will only "justify God's anger and condemnation" (8, 590). The acquiescence of our conscience to its own condemnation is understood as the outworking of a simple reading of the relations that it maintains with God and our neighbor, which are manifested in terms of proportion. Having an idea of God's "greatness" enables consciences to understand the extent of God's wrath when offended (8, 590), while apprehending the degree to which they have "acted as enemies" of God makes them realize the extent of their demerit (8, 599).[18] This emphasis on God's greatness and our degree of hostility towards him powerfully illustrates the theme of proportion as a central notion in the sphere of natural good, although it might also lead to an ultimate reformulation of the domain of

---

18. See also "the degree of anger" that ought to be ascribed to the Judge (*Ms. Book of Controversies*, 93).

natural beauty itself based on the natural, unregenerate realization of the supreme moral-religious offense.

A careful reading of the Edwardsian texts lets us make a link between "secondary" beauty, in its broadest sense, and greatness. Firstly, we saw that evil's natural sense of demerit appears to be based on a perception of the proportion between God's greatness and the creature's opposition to it. Secondly, we will understand that it is indeed God who—as greatness—is the foundation for the sphere of beauty itself or, more generally speaking, that greatness, in the final analysis, *is* natural beauty. This greatness—not to be understood as a raw quality or intensity but instead limited to proportion—evokes a feeling analogous to what Burke and Kant termed the "sublime." On an explicitly terminological level, Edwards was certainly little inclined to link beauty to greatness, although in his general statement contrasting greatness and the excellence that is primary beauty, greatness plays the role of secondary beauty. We read that the demons and the damned see God's greatness, majesty, and wisdom, but not his excellence and amiability (8, 237–38). This is why they have a conviction that their condemnation is just, yet not "a sense of the harmony and beautiful congruity of punishment" (13, 439). When God's wisdom is linked to his greatness in this way, greatness takes the "place" of natural beauty; and it's the presence of this notion of wisdom that enables us to rediscover the underlying theme of beauty in portrayals that are seemingly only concerned with the world of nature, which is dominated by strength and quantity.

In a 1723 Miscellany (103), Edwards remarked that angels, created before the incarnation, "excel" unregenerate men "in strength and wisdom ... but not in grace and sweet holiness and love to God" (13, 271).[19] In this period of his reflection—one in which this young thinker had yet to clearly grasp the essential distinction between these two beauties—greatness and wisdom play the role of secondary beauty and Edwards was unable to subsume them under a general definition derived entirely from the world of proportion. For the young Edwards, the notion of greatness—often used in the texts from his mature years as a synonym for Being—was actually an essential component of Deity in general and he had problems confining it to the realm of *naturalia Dei*. In an important Miscellany (42) titled *Religion,* Edwards is elated by "the greatness ... immense distance ... and rapid motion" of the universe, yet he immediately noted that all of this "is but a little, trivial and childish greatness in comparison of the noble,

---

19. In comparison with the saints, "the angels will be superior in greatness, in strength and wisdom ... but ... not ... in beauty and amiableness" (18, 535). Again, we note that "the honor put upon faithful ministers is ... greater than that of the angels" (25, 344).

refined, exalted, divine, spiritual greatnesses." Edwards added that "these are but the shadows of greatness and are worthless, except as they conduce to true and real greatness and excellency, and manifest the power and wisdom of God." A little later, he remarked that, in comparison to the glories of this corporeal world, "the glories of religion" refer to "greater and more real worlds" (13, 224). Even though the rhetoric of the text should not be considered an adequate, systematic foreshadowing of the definitions in the treatise on *The Nature of True Virtue*, this duality of greatness and excellence nonetheless hints at the idea of a certain distinction, within the Deity itself, between a natural sphere and a spiritual one.

In another great Miscellany (782), Edwards explains that, in common conviction, awakened sinners view "God's natural perfections, wherein consists his greatness," whereas saving illumination is to be understood as "a sense of the spiritual excellency, beauty, or sweetness of divine things" (18, 463–64). This definition foreshadows the appearance of "two kinds of attributes" in God: on the one hand, his justice, authority, and majesty; on the other hand, his mercy, goodness, and grace (4, 463–65). As previously noted, Edwards revisited the traditional doctrine of God's natural and moral attributes,[20] which he would explicitly set forth in his *Treatise Concerning Religious Affections*. In this "insurpassable" treatise,[21] we read that God's moral attributes—his faithfulness and goodness or, in one word, his holiness—are distinguished from God's "natural attributes or perfections," which consist of his greatness, i.e., his power, omniscience, eternal being, and terrible majesty (2, 255). A little later, in the context of a discussion on the conviction of awakened sinners, Edwards explicitly describes God's natural perfections as "His awful and terrible greatness" (2, 276), although this shortcut, which bends God's *naturalia* in the direction of his *terribilia*, must not call into question the fact that natural perfections have two aspects: one evoking God's greatness as it is in itself, the other as it appears to fallen, natural man. However, this distinction depends, to a certain extent, on the creature's viewpoint. Peaceful and placid in itself and, in particular, of a purely ontological nature, God's greatness transposes into a righter of wrongs and an avenging sublimity for those who find themselves in opposition to it. It is very instructive to learn that this same terrifying vision of God's greatness as a source of punishment hides an essential element of proportion. We shouldn't think of God's offended nature as a heavy weight that crushes transgressors but as a reality, the Being against whom

---

20. See *supra*, p. 283; see the divine attributes of greatness and majesty as a terrifying "burning flame" (4, 463) vs. "that sweet attribute" of grace (10, 395).

21. See *supra*, p.306 n.37.

we are guilty of enmity to a high degree and, consequently, one who has "a high degree" of wrath towards us (8, 597). In other words, the punishment I should expect is not an expression of raw strength being unleashed but an act of justice that is appropriate for the relation. More specifically, the extent of the punishment that falls on sinners is merely the dramatic expression of a gap, a kind of disproportion, between them and God. Now, a disproportion can only exist between beings with an articulated structure and, to be precise, the internal proportion of a being is an articulated structure. We can therefore conceive of God's infinite wrath as an expression of greatness, which itself is a proportion.

Edwards's dissertation on *The Nature of True Virtue*—the distillation and culmination of an entire life of philosophical and theological reflection—very clearly disassociates greatness and secondary beauty in order to distinguish the natural and spiritual in metaphysics. Greatness, identified with existence, represents the *naturalia* of God. The author doesn't want to run the risk of confusing the spiritual with fallen nature. He therefore ensures that secondary beauty—the "false beauty" of *The Mind*[22]—is never explicitly predicated of God. Even alluding to any idea of real continuity between the most holy God and the sphere of nature, an integral part of which is the "virtue" of the unregenerate, is precluded. Now, while continuity of any sort between the spiritual and the natural, i.e., the finite, had to be avoided at all costs, a deeper, more essential continuity was claimed, namely the continuity between God's *naturalia* and his *spiritualia*.

As a Calvinist theologian, Jonathan Edwards knew perfectly well that those who don't recognize God in his word are ignorant of "his name,"[23] i.e., the God of truth and mercy,[24] and worship only idols.[25] Nonetheless, as a theologian-philosopher, he was very careful to maintain and mark the metaphysical continuity in God between greatness and beauty (see 6, 382). When giving many wonderful descriptions that compare God's moral attributes with his natural attributes, Edwards took care to show that, in themselves, these "two kinds of attributes" are in continuity, that the value of God's natural perfections derives from his moral perfections, and that moral perfections are the end and sense of natural perfections (2, 256–57).[26] Or

---

22. See 6, 344; see also "False affections . . . no beautifull proportion" (Affections Notebook, "No. 7") and the resemblance between "vice . . . deformity and disproportion" (8, 612), "deformity and demerit" (21, 368).

23. Calvin, *Institutes*, 3. 21. 7, 416 and n.3.

24. Calvin, *Institutes*, 3. 2. 7; 15–16.

25. For this, see the texts and references in Torrance, *Calvin's Doctrine of Man*, 161.

26. See also 2, 266. Conversely, "a sense of the beauty and wonderfulness of divine grace, does in great measure depend on a sense of the greatness and majesty of that

again, and more simply, that goodness is "the end of greatness" (18, 536). On a strictly metaphysical level, the hesitations of young Edwards—who was seemingly incapable of distinguishing the Deity's purely ontological moments from his "spiritual" ones—are explained by the fact that, in the created world, proportion (in bodies) can only be an analogy to the consent of minds,[27] whereas all perfection within the Deity is moral because it refers to spiritual consent. The supreme consent of God is undoubtedly to be found in Jesus Christ,[28] a consent which, at first sight, is distinctly superior to the proportion contained in the Being of God. But could we lose sight of the fact that the consent of Jesus Christ can only be understood in terms of the Trinitarian relations that, strictly speaking, constitute the consent that is the very being of the Personal God (see 13, 283–84)?

Veiled for a moment by fearful, avenging majesty, greatness essentially remains proportion and, in that sense, is in hidden yet close continuity with the Trinity, the culminating expression of which is the consent of Jesus Christ. On the other hand, regarding greatness as a synonym for secondary beauty, i.e., the beauty of the world of creatures, shows that there is no continuity within this sphere and that the natural may very well not be the first moment of the spiritual but rather its indomitable opposite. Whether within the Deity or in man, greatness can certainly enhance excellence. After all, a virtuous affection in two beings is of greater value than if it only involves one (8, 548–9). However, taken by itself and separately from primary beauty, greatness is opposed to goodness. In one Miscellany (107a), Edwards declared that "power and intellect . . . are not excellencies without holiness and grace, but only a capacity of more odiousness" (13, 277). In a later note from *The Mind,* we read that a being who dissents from universal being "is the more odious for his greatness" (6, 381). And furthermore: "The greater anyone is without goodness, so much the greater evil" (19, 588). Greatness, of course, should not be understood as weight or dimension, but rather as "power and wisdom" (13, 271). Yet again, this reaffirms the radical impossibility of any neutrality in religious and moral matters.

It goes without saying that, in this discussion on the greatness of God as secondary beauty, Edwards and the Edwardsians returned, on a metaphysical level, to the subject of fallen nature and attempted to portray it in a strictly conceptual manner. Fifteen years after the death of his master, Samuel Hopkins returned in force to this subject. He declared that holiness

---

being whose grace it is" (18, 465).

27. See 8, 564–65. There is a strict analogy here between the perception of physical things, including aesthetic phenomena, and the perfection of minds in the sphere of theoretical knowledge.

28. See Carse, *Visibility of God,* 137.

constitutes the true worth of intelligent beings and added "that without it they have no real excellence, nor any true worth; but they are, in themselves, odious, despicable, and worse than nothing." Because of the radical opposition between the mind and nature, all of our natural perfections and capacities that are not characterized by grace are instead turned against it, so that an intelligent being who is not holy is opposed to holiness to the same degree and extent as his natural faculties and capacities.[29] The Calvinist conviction regarding the impossibility of a third way—a nature that was neither good nor bad—returned with insistent force in propositions where the expression "worse than nothing" predominated. Here we find the deep subject of notional knowledge which, without a transforming change brought about by grace, seems only to aggravate the condemnation. A metaphysical exegesis of the two covenants of faith and grace does not allow the nothingness-being conceptual couple, but only dramatic oppositions between a negative being and a positive being, a "contrary" light" and a "holy" light. A Miscellany (41) from Edwards's youth states that fallen man is "as little or less . . . than nothing (13, 223)."[30] That is why it can be said of Jesus Christ that he raises souls captive to sin out of a situation that is "infinitely lower than a state of nonentity" (15, 600). Now, if the initial term of the work of redemption is "infinitely lower than a state of nonentity," its final term—heavenly bliss—is "a state infinitely better than mere being" (V, 333).[31] More generally, without the gracious mercy of God, the creature is "worse than nothing" (21, 290); and so we understand the apparent excess of the sermon on *True Grace*: without his holy beauty and amiability, God's other attributes are worse than nothing (25, 634). Without "the beauty of holiness . . . God himself (if that were possible to be) would be an infinite evil" (2, 274).

However, because it is not just the greatness of the creature which, without spiritual beauty, i.e., goodness, is worse than nothing, but also the greatness of God, we begin to see deep and troubling implications of this Calvinist metaphysic. The knowledge or sense that the awakened sinner gets from evil primarily concerns punishment. Now, punishment is proportionate to the scale of the transgression which, in turn, is measured in relation to the infinite Being against whom it was directed. The terrors of the conscience are inspired by realizing the horrors of the punishment that will express God's offended majesty; and the pain of punishment and wrath

---

29. Hopkins, *An Inquiry into the Nature of True Holiness, Works*, 3:10.

30. See *supra*, p. 287 ss.

31. There is a hint of bitterness in Edwards's comment that the Great Awakening, an extraordinary religious movement, "has . . . come to that which is worse than nothing" (7, 517).

of God are objects of the natural knowledge of evil or rather are natural evil itself. As for the natural knowledge of good, viz. natural good, the situation is as follows: the harmony of natural things and the virtue of unregenerate, intelligent creatures are subsumed under the notion of secondary beauty and thereby brought closer to God's greatness. Greatness therefore turns out to be the supreme object of the natural knowledge of good. In itself, greatness is the same thing as the anger of God, which is the supreme natural evil. This amounts to saying that good and evil, in their "natural" sense, are one and the same thing.

First of all, this conclusion is troubling in that it reminds us of the difficult inquiry regarding the relation between hellfire and the anger of God,[32] but it also raises serious questions, even if we resign ourselves to keeping it within what is, strictly speaking, the moral domain. More precisely, to the extent that the Calvinist concession on the unregenerate's natural aptitude to discern good and evil is being retracted, the very meaning of morality itself seems called into question. However, we think that there is another plausible interpretation of these developments. If Edwardsian doctrine seems to imply that natural good and evil are the same thing, it's because God's greatness and wrath—their respective matches—are but one and the same reality apprehended in a different manner. The identity of natural good and evil simply shows that natural knowledge has only one object: the natural being who appears either as joy and pleasure, i.e., natural good, or as fear and pain, i.e., natural evil. On the other hand, the proper object of spiritual knowledge is spiritual good, conceived in and for itself, and spiritual evil, conceived only after and from itself (see 18, 462–63). The proper object of natural knowledge is being, while that of spiritual knowledge is mind or grace. It is to these conclusions that Jonathan Edwards's aesthetic ultimately leads.

4. The beauty of true virtue

Drawing the good and the beautiful closer together is an authentic tradition in Western thought. In neo-Platonic thought, its crowning moment, beauty and good almost seem interchangeable on an ontological level. In parallel to these tautologising tendencies in ontology, although in a more modest way, we see an affinity between the good and the beautiful, properly speaking, at an ethical level. In his commentaries on the Psalms, Augustine stated that "all that is fair in a soul, is virtue."[33] In this, Augustine is only an heir to the

---

32. See *supra*, p. 184 ss.
33. Saint Augustine, *Expositions on Psalms 59*, 18.

ancients. Plato had already spoken about the beauty of justice,[34] but it was primarily Aristotle who designated ethical acts as beautiful and noble because they stem from an activity that is worthy in and of itself, unlike those produced by profitable or servile activities.[35] Cicero translated *akalos* as *honestum*, i.e., meriting praise for itself, without any regard to profitability or reward.[36] Christian thought adopted what Cicero realized about the resplendent beauty of a beautiful act, yet also stressed the fact that it was the *internal* act that merited praise.[37] This internalization of the *honestum* was accompanied by an enhancement of its theological standing. Saint Augustine distinguished the *honestum* from the profitable. The profitable denotes all that is only a means to a supreme end, while the *honestum* relates to what is to be enjoyed (*frui*) and not used (*uti*), i.e., which only properly denotes God.[38] The beauty of virtue therefore consists in the orientation of the soul towards God as an end in itself: an action is only beautiful when it is directed towards good and only intended for good.

In the great Christian tradition, we witness a profound change in the ancient idea of the beauty of virtue. For the ancients, virtue was beautiful in itself. For the Christian, virtue certainly continued to be beautiful in itself, but only insofar as it concerned what was to be enjoyed in and for itself. However, with the weakening of Christian theocentricity, the beauty proper to moral action was seen more and more in terms of its immanent amiability and the natural admiration and affection that the soul feels for moral perfection. For Shaftesbury, "the most natural beauty in the world is honesty and moral truth;"[39] and Hutcheson wrote that "the Author of Nature . . . has made Virtue a lovely Form, to excite our pursuit of it."[40]

While Edwards knew Shaftesbury and carefully read Hutcheson, he established his doctrine at an incomparably deeper level and, in particular, with a diametrically opposing finality. For the English moralists, bringing

34. Plato, *Laws*, 859d [Stephanus pagination].

35. Aristotle, *Nicomachean Ethics*, 1176b. This and what follows were inspired by the work of Gilson, *Spirit of Mediaeval Philosophy*, 304–6.

36. Cicero, *On Moral Ends*, 2. 45.

37. Saint Thomas Aquinas, *Summa Theologiæ*, 2-2. 145. 1. ad. 3. Kant himself identified the "(absolutely) good" with the "*honestum*" (*Critique of Judgement*, 5:266 [Academy pagination]).

38. Saint Augustine, *De Diversis Quaestionibus LXXXIII*, 30; see also "The grace of God may appear lovely two ways: either as *bonum utile*, a profitable good to me, that which greatly serves my interest, and so suits my self-love; or as *bonum formosum*, a beautiful good in itself, and part of the moral and spiritual excellency of the divine nature" (2, 262–63).

39. Shaftesbury, *Characteristics*, 1:94.

40. Hutcheson, *Beauty, Order, Harmony, Design*, 25.

the beautiful and the good closer together helped highlight the natural character of moral action and conscience; for this American theologian, the relation between the two beauties was similar to that of a body to its shadow. For Edwards, virtue wasn't just an instance of beauty—or even the most brilliant instance of beauty—but the only true beauty. He emphasized the fact that true consent, by itself, characterizes the relations that intelligent beings can have with one another and added that it is not just a matter of any intellectual relation between intelligent beings but of the dispositions and actions of their heart (see 8, 539). However, this resort to the heart as the only seat of true consent—and therefore as the sphere of true beauty—is not the outcome of moralizing reductionism but is defined at the deepest level of metaphysics. The supreme form of this consent, which is the essence of virtue, is not proper to man but rather to absolute Being. The paradigm of all spiritual consent is what absolute Being has for himself and for human virtue, with the latter only being beautiful if it participates, in some way, in this primitive consent. In other words, the object of moral virtue itself is ultimately none other than absolute Being. Consent for other intelligent beings is only beautiful if they are in a harmonious relation with absolute Being, i.e., "consent" to him.

Edwards established his teaching on the beauty of virtue at a strictly metaphysical level, and the full complexity of this issue is found, in concentrated form, in a passage from his biography of David Brainerd. His study on the life of this eminent servant of God shows "that that beauty, that sort of good, which was the great object of the new sense of his mind, the new relish and appetite given him in conversion, and thenceforward maintained and increased in his heart, was holiness, conformity to God, living to God, and glorifying him." In this remarkable passage, spiritual beauty is identified with holiness, i.e., piety, although a little later we read that the love of God which Brainerd "very often exercised"—even towards "his enemies" (7, 507)—is a "universal benevolence."

Primary beauty therefore means seemingly very different realities: piety, love of one's neighbor, and "the beauty" that emanates from these two perfections. We have already referred to the analyses in the treatise on *The Nature of True Virtue* that clarify the relations between piety and love,[41] but we still need to discuss the difficult and ambivalent notion of the beauty

---

41. See *supra*, p. 201 ss.; see also "Goodness or godliness" (18, 364); "grace or virtue" (7, 523); "holiness or true virtue" (24, 543). It is "special," justifying grace, see *infra*, p. 369 n.11. N.B. Even God's holiness implies his moral perfection (24, 288; 24, 345; etc.). This does not mean, however, that religion is reduced to morality. Christianity is ultimately not an outward form of morality or worship but a "sweet harmony between the soul and Jesus Christ" (19, 447).

of virtue as beauty. The beauty that seems like a condition or an objective quality of the converted person isn't really distinguished from the regenerate person's new taste and sense. In other words, spiritual beauty isn't just a metaphysical condition but also the perception of that same condition.[42] We ultimately realize that, as a condition, spiritual beauty is enriched or rather complemented by the perception of that same beauty.

To better understand the mutual relations of spiritual beauty's objective and subjective aspects, we will now describe them in terms of consent. Firstly, we explain, in metaphysical terms, how spiritual beauty *is consent*. Secondly, we realize that the perception of this consent *is also consent*. We see that the essence of spiritual beauty is consent to consent or rather love of love. Here we encounter one of those profound tautologies that crown the summits of metaphysics and speculative theology and also develop a growing appreciation for the legitimacy of using an aesthetic vocabulary. Unlike ethics, physics, or logic, aesthetics doesn't tolerate the duality of *noema* and *noesis*. Good and the sense of good are indivisible and inseparable, i.e., somewhat like the inseparability we see—after the eventful moments of consent—when benevolence addresses benevolence at the supreme moment of virtue.

Edwards defined excellence, in its proper sense, as "being's consent to being." He immediately added that proper consent is always conditional upon the will. He then concluded: "Wherefore all the primary and original beauty or excellence that is among minds is love" (6, 362). This sentence, which had to have been written in 1726, already contained the essential systematic developments of his dissertation on *The Nature of True Virtue*. In lieu of "union of minds," if we were to borrow the term "consent" to designate harmony, even in this corporeal world (6, 336), then consent, strictly speaking, would only designate the operations of spiritual beings[43] or, more specifically, the operations proper to these beings, i.e., those having to do with the will.[44]

"True virtue" is "benevolence to Being in general." To speak more accurately, it is that "consent, propensity and union of heart to Being in general, that is immediately exercised in a general good will" (8, 540). A little further on, the text clarifies that "Being in general" should be understood to mean "*intelligent* Being in general" (8, 542). Wanting to base his doctrine of virtue

---

42. See Delattre, *Beauty and Sensibility in Edwards*, 49.

43. For the central role of the notion of consent in Edwards, see Riforgiato, "Unified Thought of Edwards," 606–7.

44. It is the will, properly speaking, that differentiates men from beasts (6, 373–74). The connection between beauty and the will is a hidden outcome of Edwards's aesthetic ethics (13, 533).

on the most general level of metaphysics, Edwards sought to rediscover general benevolence at the level of Being, i.e., in "the Being of beings . . . the best of beings" (8, 550). The primary form of benevolence is the consent that God has with respect to himself. Consent involves a minimum of two beings and, to find it within the Deity, we have to understand that there must be "a plurality in God" (13, 284).[45] Excellence or beauty in a being consists in dispositions and actions. God has always been excellent, but before the coming of the creature, he could only be disposed or take action with respect to himself. This disposition or action consists in God's infinite love of himself. This "mutual love . . . makes . . . the personal Holy Spirit or the holiness of God, which is his infinite beauty . . . God's infinite consent to being in general" (6, 364).[46] The Holy Spirit, the very beauty of God, therefore designates "the divine love . . . the mutual love and friendship which subsists eternally and necessarily between the several persons in the Godhead" (8, 557). The Trinity, this "society or family" in God (21, 135), is therefore the primary and, so to speak, most striking manifestation of consent as moral beauty, yet God does not choose to only love himself nor limit his radiant beauty to the three Persons of the Godhead. In creation, the love of God is spread *ad extra*. And so, we need to understand that God consents to the being of the creature, yet the latter only follows this intradivine, Trinitarian consent and remains subordinate to it. God loves the creation only insofar as it is part of his own consent to himself (see 8, 421–2). Aside from God's overflowing generosity in creation and a certain emanation of his beauty in the creature, we can see that it is peculiar to God to have beauty within himself, i.e., "consenting with His own Being, or the love of Himself in His own Holy Spirit; whereas the excellence of others is in loving others" (6, 365). These "others," of course, are either God or the creature and—being a Christian theologian—Jonathan Edwards explained, with requisite clarity, that our love for other creatures can only be understood and justified by our love for God (see 8, 546–47).

True virtue is "the beauty of an intelligent being." It is benevolence towards God and all other beings and is only beautiful insofar as it is a reaffirmation of this primitive consent. The proper object of a good will in general is "intelligent Being in general." Various individual intelligent beings, for their part, can be loved insofar as they are in harmonious relation with God and consent to him, i.e., participate in his own consent (8, 541–42).

45. "One alone, without any reference to any more, cannot be excellent; for in such a case there can be no manner of relation . . . and therefore, no such thing as consent" (6, 337).

46. The Holy Spirit is "God's sweet consent to Himself," the pleasure he takes in his own "excellency" (13, 263).

Because consent is a matter of primary beauty, i.e., spiritual or moral beauty, we need to mention at this point that it doesn't fall under nature but rather under grace. God only delights in his creatures "according as they partake of more or less of excellence and beauty . . . that is, according as He communicates more or less of His Holy Spirit" (6, 364). God wills the happiness of moral beings (8, 422), but "it would be a grating, dissonant and deformed thing for a sinful creature to be happy in God's love." And so, "He therefore gives them holiness," a beauty that "delights" and pleases God, and one that induces him to give the gift of happiness to the creature (13, 395). As a later Miscellany (791) put it, the sacrifice of Christ means his "lovely virtue" is imputed to the saints and "the beauty of this robe recommends 'em to the favor and delight of God the Father" (18. 495).[47] By falling, the intelligent creature lost his spiritual beauty.[48] It can only be restored to him by way of "immediate emanation" from God's beauty. (13, 331) This spiritual beauty, let's remember, is consent to Being in general, and the insertion of the creature's consent into God's own consent can only be the fruit of a gracious operation, the one that follows justification. In other words, regenerate creatures are the only ones that have spiritual beauty.

Consent that constitutes benevolence—insofar as it does not conceal introversion, but instead turns outward—remains undivided and uninterrupted. This equates to saying that the authenticity of a consent depends on whether it is consent to another who is just a double of oneself or, conversely, for whom we are "a copy" (see V, 338). This is why only one of the two main kinds of affections towards others is truly virtuous. The most common form—a natural form of loving affection—is called love of complacence. It springs from the delight we feel with respect to the amiability of a being, the pleasure we take in their beauty. Love of complacence presupposes beauty in an object and has particular fondness for that object precisely because of its beauty. Love of benevolence, on the other hand, is "that affection or propensity of the heart to any being . . . which causes it to incline to its well-being." Not every affective disposition necessarily presupposes beauty, i.e., something that takes pleasure in its object. That another exists, whether benevolent or ugly, is all it takes for us to show selfless love, a love of general good will. Moreover, true benevolence, the primary and normative form of all good will found in God, doesn't even imply the simple existence of its correlate. God is the creator; it is his goodness that moves him to create, his

---

47. "The redeemed . . . are made excellent by a communication of God's excellency: God puts His own beauty . . . upon their souls. They are made 'partakers'. . . of the moral image of God" (17, 208).

48. Man also lost a physical diffraction of that beauty, namely "the beauty and that kind of luster that was on their bodies" (24, 136).

divine benevolence that gives an object its existence and beauty (8, 542). In creation, God gave being; in redemption, holy beauty. A natural love of complacence depends on what is amiable in its object; in contrast, virtuous love only has "Being simply considered," Being itself as its object. True virtue does not consist in love felt for any particular beings, because of their goodness, nor in gratitude, because they love us, but "in a propensity and union of heart to Being simply considered" (8, 544). If the object of virtuous benevolence is Being simply considered, the continuous propensity of this benevolence can only tend towards the supreme good of Being in general. More than anything else, the virtuous man desires the good of Being in general, which is God, "the Being of beings, infinitely the greatest and best of beings" (8, 550); and he can only oppose and reject any being he finds is implacably opposed to God (8, 545).

If the primary object, the primitive and natural correlate of benevolent love, is being in general, its secondary object is a being who is also benevolent. Edwards explained that, if "being's consent to being must needs be agreeable to perceiving being" in the case of excellence or secondary beauty, the fact that we are now in the spiritual sphere means we have to understand that "mind's love to mind must needs be lovely to beholding mind; and being's love to being in general must needs be agreeable to being that perceives it" (6, 362). What *The Mind* often conveys in ontological-aesthetic terms is expressed, albeit in a more profound, explicitly ethical way, in the treatise on *The Nature of True Virtue*. We read that perceiving a benevolent mind elicits greater benevolence in another mind than would be elicited by mere existence. In benevolence, it's as if he is, so to speak, enlarged and comprehends Being in general—whom he loves and, in a certain sense, even becomes—so that he cannot but attract the love of a heart that itself loves this Being. A benevolent heart loves another with benevolence, "as it were out of gratitude to him for his love to general existence." The second ground of benevolent love does not really differ from the first but is more in continuity with it: "For he that has a simple and pure good will to general entity or existence must love that temper in others that agrees and conspires with itself. A spirit of consent to Being must agree with consent to Being. That which truly and sincerely seeks the good of others must approve of, and love, that which joins with him in seeking the good of others" (8, 546–47).

Having first defined Being or God as the primary and most general object of benevolence, we now clarify and develop our analysis. A benevolent being, i.e., benevolence in a being, is the secondary object of virtuous benevolence or, rather, its supreme object. It is always a matter of deepening the great doctrine of consent, with the maximum degree of consent being that which a mind—having itself become consent, so to speak—has towards another mind, which is also consent. In any event, only those with this particular disposition of general benevolence can effectively discern it in others. Once they have discerned it, they can no longer not love it. The discernment of spiritual beauty is not the result of reasoning, but the object of a judgment of taste that only judges, i.e., savors, to the extent that it tastes. As Joseph Bellamy wrote: "To see the holy beauty of God's moral character, to see the beauty of holiness, to have holiness appear beautiful and seem lovely to the soul, is of the same nature as to love holiness."[49]

5. Moral sense

If Edwardsian metaphysics expressed itself in terms of ethical connotations, it was precisely to take account of the essential affinity between the discernment of spiritual beauty and the love felt for it. The moralists of that era also compared "moral sense" to aesthetic perfection in order to highlight the natural, immediate character of moral discernment. Henry More had already spoken of the "*Boniform Faculty*" that "enables us to distinguish not only what is simply and absolutely the best, but to relish it, and to have pleasure in that alone."[50] For this Cambridge Platonist, discernment had to do with spiritual beauty and good; for Shaftesbury, this disposition was already situated on a more natural level. He wrote that there exists a moral sense in man that is "a real affection or love towards equity and right for its own sake and on the account of its own natural beauty and worth."[51] However, the greatest theoretician of this moral sense, the one who most consciously relates it to the sense of beauty and develops this deduction in greatest detail, is Hutcheson.

Hutcheson vigorously taught the existence of a "superior sense" or "moral sense" that causes us to feel pleasure when we contemplate virtuous actions and "excites" us to take such actions without appealing to self-love or interest. Some said that our appreciations and judgments of rational beings or inanimate things vary according to the profit or pleasure that we believe we can gain from them. Now, if this was the case, "Had we no *Sense* of *Good*, distinct from the *Advantage* or *Interest* arising from the external Senses, and the Perceptions of *Beauty* and *Harmony*; the Sensations and Affections toward a *fruitful Field*, or *commodious Habitation*, would be

---

49. Bellamy, *An Essay on the Nature and Glory of the Gospel of Jesus Christ*, Works, 2:503.

50. More, *Enchiridion Ethicum*, 1. 2. 5, in Lichtenstein, *Henry More*, 67; see also Fiering, *Moral Philosophy at Seventeenth Century Harvard*, 261–62.

51. Shaftesbury, *Characteristics*, 1:178.

much the same with what we have towards a *generous Friend*, or any *noble Character*; for both are, or may be *advantageous* to us." In fact, however, it is evident that we are clearly conscious of an essential difference between our appreciation of the moral beauty of rational agents and our perception of the natural excellence of physical beings. We have, properly speaking, a "moral sense" that causes us to admire and rejoice in beautiful actions, which "makes rational Actions appear *Beautiful*, or *Deform'd*."[52] In solidarity with this natural moral sense is that instinctive approval we give to virtuous actions. We have a profound inclination to desire the good of our neighbor and to suffer with him when he is afflicted.

Hutcheson spoke about "this secret Chain" between each person and mankind,[53] the compassion that is the supreme sign of man's inner goodness. Compassion—in its literal, emotional sense—was a major theme of preaching in that era. It was thought that it could be said "of the generality of men" that "their hearts are so tender an[d] their natural affections so humane, that they cannot but pity an[d] commiserate the afflicted with a kind of fatal and mechanical Sympathy."[54] Or, to quote an English sermon from 1709: "We are all Counterparts one of another; the Instruments tun'd Unison: the doleful Cry of one in extreme Distress, makes the Strings tremble at our very Hearts."[55] Lastly, and this is central, we have what Calvinists dare assign only to the regenerate: disinterested benevolence and a taste for altruistic action, which Arminian preachers all too indiscriminately attribute to natural man. In 1671, Isaac Barrow, who was known to Edwards (20, 280), wrote that nature had "made the communication of benefits to others to be accompanied with a very delicious relish upon the mind of him who practices it; nothing indeed carrying with it a more pure and savoury than beneficence. A man may be virtuously voluptuous, and a laudable epicure by doing much good."[56] On the other hand, for an Augustinian theologian, virtuous benevolence to our neighbor springs from a taste and relish of the divine excellence that only an immediate act of sovereign grace can give. Yet, before considering the critical moment when the taste of holy beauty and that of natural harmony separate from one another, we need to hear young Edwards's question once more: How natural men have a taste of and delight in that external beauty that is a resemblance to love (6, 390)? This will help

52. Hutcheson, *Ideas of Beauty and Virtue*, 107–8.

53. Hutcheson, *Ideas of Beauty and Virtue*, 111; compare with "all generations of men, from the beginning to the end of the world, are morally concerned one with another" (20, 339).

54. Crane, "Man of Feeling," 224.

55. Crane, "Man of Feeling," 225.

56. Barrow, *Theological Works*, 2:225 in Crane, "Man of Feeling," 228.

us answer the question that immediately precedes it: What moral sense is natural (6, 389)? More precisely, we have to see the affinity, on the one hand, between the aesthetic perception of beauty and natural knowledge and, on the other, between the discovery of the transcendent excellence and amiability of divine things (see 2, 256).

Edwards used aesthetic categories when describing the discernment of spiritual beauty because the analysis of aesthetic perception gave him valuable tools to formulate his own metaphysical-theological theory. The judgment of taste is not based on reasoning; it is immediate, also involves the discernment of content—or at least content in general—and is accompanied by intense pleasure. Here again, it is Hutcheson who makes the strongest contribution to the Edwardsian formulations, because it is he who explained, with the greatest conceptual rigor, that even though the perceptions arising from this moral sense are not in opposition to the conclusions of reason, they are not the facts of ratiocination. They are more of an "approbation" that is not changed by any "previous *Volition*, or Choice." Moral sense is defined as a "Determination of our Minds to receive Ideas independently on our Will, and to have Perceptions of Pleasure and Pain."[57] Thanks to the wise dispositions of "the Author of our nature," we do not have to resort to "long Deductions" but have "quick and powerful Instructions" that help us discern virtue and especially inspire us to act virtuously, because—let's remember—God has "made Virtue a lovely form, that we might easily distinguish it from its contrary, and be made happy by the pursuit of it."[58] The pleasure we feel when performing a virtuous act "necessarily arises from the Contemplation of the Idea, which is then present to our Minds."[59] It is an immediate sensation and not "any Knowledge of Principles, Proportions, Causes, or of the Usefulness of the Object." Pleasure "strikes us . . . with the Idea of Beauty" and this "Pleasure of Beauty" is not increased by even the most accurate knowledge of an object.[60]

Edwards also emphasized the non-discursive, immediate and intuitive character of any apprehension of moral beauty. Of course, at the root of any feeling of natural, secondary beauty, of any pleasure we might experience when contemplating a beautiful thing or action, we find a certain proportion, order and harmony which, on an objective level, are basic forms or rather analogies of true consent. However, minds that experience pleasure "don't reflect on that particular agreement and proportion, which according

---

57. Hutcheson, *Passions and Affections*, 243; 4.
58. Hutcheson, *Beauty, Order, Harmony, Design*, 25.
59. Hutcheson, *Beauty, Order, Harmony, Design*, 24.
60. Hutcheson, *Beauty, Order, Harmony, Design*, 36.

to the law of nature is the ground and rule of beauty in the case; yea, are ignorant of it. Thus, a man may be pleased with the harmony of the notes in a tune and yet know nothing of that proportion or adjustment of the notes, which by the law of nature is the ground of the melody." A man may be attracted by the beautiful proportions of a human face, "and yet not know what that proportion is, or what measures, quantities, and distances it consists in" (8, 556).[61]

Edwards emphasized the absence of any calculation or discursive character in the perception of beauty, although this wasn't a vague sign of some kind of irrationalism. By returning forcefully to the immediate, necessary character of this upsurge of pleasure, he was instead trying to highlight the autonomy and autarchy of aesthetic perception. A form or quality that appears agreeable and gracious in itself seems beautiful to us. What matters is that the "idea" in question immediately pleases me by itself. Whatever pleases me does so by itself and not indirectly in terms of something else. Of course, there are things that attract us because of their potential to give us pleasure or be useful to us, but these things are not truly beautiful. Likewise, when we taste the sweetness of honey, we discern "by immediate sensation of the gratefulness of the idea called *beautiful*" and not in terms of a discursive argument. Beauty accordingly "depends" on "the *frame of our minds*, whereby they are so made, that such an idea, as soon as we have it, is grateful, or appears beautiful" (18, 618). For Edwards, the perception of secondary beauty is thus derived from a "certain condition" and frame of mind. This disposition is subjective, of course, but it is only exercised if certain objective proportions are met (8, 602–3). Only one particular configuration of the comtemplative mind—an upsurge of pleasure—generates natural approbation. This natural disposition, the source of our perception of the harmony of physical things, is what makes us discern the beauty of natural

---

61. What we have here, of course, is the discernment of secondary beauty in the human face. Indeed, "when we see beautiful airs of look and gesture, we naturally think the mind that resides within is beautiful" (13, 330) but, in fact, "beauty of face, and sweet airs in men are not always the effect of the corresponding excellencies of mind" (13, 279). See also 6, 346; 13, 301. On the other hand, in paradise, "the beauty of the bodies of the saints . . . shall . . . consist . . . in a semblance of the excellency of their minds . . . their air and mien will be such as will necessarily result from the wisdom, purity, and love of the soul and shall denote and hold forth an inexpressible sweetness, benevolence, and complacence" (X, 327). This is a return to their state before the fall when "the affections of the mind had a more quick, easy and notable influence upon the whole body, as it has on the face now" (13, 325). After Christ's transfiguration, "there was an ineffable beauty, majesty, and brightness in His countenance that held forth and naturally represented the excellencies of His mind, His holiness, His heavenly meekness, and grace, and love" (15, 214). See "sweet and full in 22, 292; see also *supra*, p. 324 n.98.

things. This disposition—a sense of beauty or moral sense, aesthetic taste or natural conscience—varies widely in detail and seems to be present in every person. This is not the case with the discernment of spiritual beauty which, according to this theologian, also requires a certain temper or disposition, albeit one that is lacking in all who are unregenerate.

6. Sense of spiritual beauty

Always seeking to ground and portray Christian doctrine in a more satisfactory manner, Edwards resorted to the theory of moral sense to integrate—or reintegrate—it into his theology.[62] However, precisely because of his theological preoccupations, he successfully transcended even the best formulation of this theory that Hutcheson had given him. Hutcheson proposed—only to reject—the notion of "a desire without inclination and a choice that precedes all inclination."[63] He then formulated the notion of hardcore, primitive, moral knowledge independent of all empirical preoccupations. Now, as Kant taught, moral sentiment is only moral if it is based on the representation of the law. In other words, the originality and autarchy of the moral sense are only conceivable in the presence of an objective, primitive content that alone can keep it from arbitrariness and falling back into a hidden utilitarianism.[64] Edwards avoided the pitfall of an inadequate foundation for the moral sense, i.e., the spiritual sense, because of his theology of grace. In the *Treatise Concerning Religious Affections*, we read of some who said that if contemplation of God's glory and excellence gives us pleasure, this is only an offshoot of self-love.[65] Of course, once the apprehension of God's glory and the contemplation of his perfections have become so agreeable to a man's mind that he finds his highest happiness in them, he cannot but desire them, as he would his own happiness, and

62. Fiering, *Edwards's Moral Thought*, 106.

63. See Henrich, "Hutcheson und Kant," 63.

64. ⊠One must first value the importance of what we call duty, the authority of the moral law, and the immediate worth that compliance with it gives a person in his own eyes, in order to feel that satisfaction in consciousness of one's conformity with it" (Kant, "Critique of Practical Reason," 5:38 [Academy pagination]). And, generally speaking, "Alles moralische Gefühl setzt ein sittliches Urtheil durch den Verstand voraus [All moral sentiment presupposes ethical judgment through understanding]" (*Moralphilosophie, Rechtsphilosophie und Religionsphilosophie, Schriften, Ak.*, 19:152). See also Henrich, "Hutcheson und Kant," *passim*.

65. We are reminded that, for Edwards, even a "cordial" acceptance of God's transcendent grace implied a sight of his holy beauty (21, 101). The saints first see that God is glorious and lovely, "and then, *consequentially*, they see God's love . . . for them" (2, 246).

cannot but include them in the circuit of his self-love. The key question, however, is this: How does a man get to that state where these things become so agreeable to him, that he finds his highest happiness in them? Because God's good is already our sovereign good, because his glory is already what is most precious to us, and because we already love his excellence and grace, contemplating such excellence and grace rejoices our heart. Then, and only then, are we able to admit that the pleasure felt when contemplating God's beauty might be motivated by self-love. If any man regards God as his greatest good, it is because that man's own self-love and desire for his own happiness compels him to glorify God. The new spiritual sense that enables the regenerate to joyously contemplate the excellence of divine things does not issue from the natural desires of the heart, but from discovering the "beauty, glory, and supreme good, in God's nature, as it is in itself" (2, 241).

The correlate of this new spiritual sense is God's excellence or beauty, a reality to do with the order of content, an objective reality, otherwise notional in nature. An apprehension of this reality is only given to the regenerate creature. To paraphrase John Smith, philosophers, with their natural minds, "unfold the garment of truth, but they cannot behold the lovely form of it."[66] Reason does not know beauty *stricto sensu*, but only notional truth (17, 413); excellence has no place in the realm of "our heads" and can only enter the kingdom of "our hearts" (17, 416)! The Edwardsians constantly taught that while natural, wicked men know who God is, they have no sense of his beauty or his glory[67] and, more generally speaking, "Orthodox speculations and notions in theory about God, Christ, and things divine, tho' ever so exact, give not those amiable apprehensions of divine objects,which the divinely enlightned soul is the subject of."[68] Jonathan Parsons would end by declaring that hell is a place of darkness and torments precisely because the devils have lost their internal sense of God's moral glory.[69] According to a justly famous passage in the *Treatise Concerning Religious Affections*, the devils have a very great knowledge of the glory of God, but have lost "a sense of the amiableness of His moral perfections" and "are perfectly destitute of any sense or relish" of spiritual beauty (2, 263).

---

66. Smith, *Select Discourses*, 8.

67. Bellamy, *True Religion Delineated*, Works, 1:55–57. "A man may from rational arguments be convinced in his conscience, that God is lovely; and yet have no sense of his loveliness in his heart" (Bellamy, *An Essay on the Nature and Glory of the Gospel of Jesus Christ*, Works, 2:504n.z).

68. Buell, *Spiritual Knowlege [sic] of God*, 40. This is why "no natural man can form so much as one amiable apprehension of God" (Buell, *Spiritual Knowlege [sic] of God*, 40).

69. Parsons, *Sixty Sermons*, 1:460.

As always, the devil is a paradigm of the unregenerate creature and, generally speaking, of all those ensnared in sin who find themselves deprived of the particular means of savoring the taste of God's excellence (X, 113). Whereas knowledge of notional truth is accessible to any finite mind and the perception of secondary beauty only arises from a disposition common to all men, the amiable character of the excellence of spiritual things and the beauty of God's holiness should not be capable of being perceived by the natural mind (2, 263).[70] According to the very orthodox and very speculative Jonathan Edwards the Younger, divine omniscience itself—a purely natural attribute of the Deity—does not extend to moral beauty![71]

Tasting the beauty of God is never an affair of the natural mind, but "the first effect of the power of God... in regeneration, is to give the heart a divine taste or sense, to cause it to have a relish of the loveliness and sweetness of the supreme excellency of the divine nature" (21, 174). Edwards emphasized the fact that, because supernatural taste concerns the highest order of spiritual realities, it could only be an immediate gift of the Holy Spirit. "'Tis rational to suppose," he wrote in 1734, that this blessing, i.e., "relish or sense of divine beauty, or excellency," would be beyond the natural scope of the human mind, that it would be "immediately from God; for there is no gift or benefit that is in itself so nearly related to the divine nature... 'tis a kind of emanation of God's beauty" itself (17, 421). Edwards, let's recall, had already discussed in a Miscellany (187) from his youth about restoring the spiritual beauty in the regenerate by way of "immediate emanation" from God's beauty (13, 331). Here again, this immediately communicated beauty doesn't merely designate spiritual beauty, the only moral benevolence, but also its discernment. In the realm of supremely amiable things, discernment cannot be distinguished from enjoyment which, precisely because we are in the sphere of the purely spiritual, is identical to love. These Edwardsian descriptions culminated in a theory where spiritual beauty was understood to immediately imply or rather, to simultaneously be, both virtue itself and discernment, i.e., the love of that virtue. Or again: the beauty of the regenerated creature is benevolent and benevolently loves the benevolent God in whom it takes pleasure. Readers of *The Life of David Brainerd* know that "beauty"—the proper object of his new, regenerated sense—was "the new

---

70. Because of original sin, "man... has become... ignorant of the excellency of God" (X, 113). Natural men have never had the slightest idea of God's holy beauty (Bellamy, *An Essay on the Nature and Glory of the Gospel of Jesus Christ*, Works, 2:508–9).

71. Edwards, "Liberty and Necessity," in Edwards, *Works*, 1:473. Jonathan Edwards himself wrote that—in the context of the Final Judgment—hidden sins would be revealed by the penetrating light of "God's omniscience" (25, 476). Apparently, this was only notional knowledge.

relish and appetite" for the good that is holiness itself (7, 506). However, it was the dense, vibrant language of a Miscellany (791) from the 1730s that most vividly described the reciprocal deployment of the two constituent moments of spiritual beauty. The terminology is still hesitant—"excellence" is translated by "greatness"—but the sense is very clear. The saints, we read, "see the transcendent greatness of his love shining forth in the same act that they see the transcendent greatness of his loveliness shining forth, and his loveliness to shine in his love; so that 'tis most lovely love. Their seeing his loveliness tends to make them desire his love, but the sight of his loveliness brings satisfaction to this desire with it, because the appearance of his loveliness as they behold it, mainly consists in the marvelous exercise of his love to them. It being thus, his excellency both endears his love, and his love endears his excellency" (18, 495).

This dialectic of love and amability illustrates the essential reciprocity between, on the one hand, discernment and the love of true virtue and, on the other hand, true virtue itself. The true virtue that is holiness is an immediate gift of God and implies the discernment of his amiable excellence and, following discernment, a love of this excellence. While unbelievers "see no form or comeliness in Christ, and hence they have no love at all to Him" (VII, 399), the regenerate apprehend the supreme beauty of Christ and the rest, namely love for God and obedience to his commandments, immediately follows it (21, 174). Perceiving the "moral and spiritual glory of God" softens and melts the heart, turning it towards God in a manner "which nothing can withstand" (2, 265). The "result" of justification by a holy God is the sanctification of man: "a holy nature must be . . . agreeable to holy nature" (2, 261).[72]

---

72. Likewise, whenever a benevolent "heart" discerns true benevolence in a neighbor, this results in love for that neighbor (8, 545–56).

8

THE WHOLE AND THE ESSENTIAL

1. The heart and excellence

EDWARDS PROFESSED THE RADICAL superiority of heart knowledge over all mere head knowledge, yet this superiority should not be construed as being exercised at the cost of the mind's being faithfully conformed to what is known. On the contrary, what favorably distinguishes a spiritual idea from a purely external idea is the fact that it faithfully copies or reproduces its object; and this epistemology culminates with the highly significant opposition of the respective perceptions of primary and secondary beauty. Whenever the mind perceives secondary beauty, it is ignorant of the proportional relationships that constitute the ground of that beauty. On the other hand, whenever primary beauty is apprehended, there is "an immediate view" of the "spiritual union and agreement" underlying that beauty (8, 566). This immediacy of spiritual apprehension not only indicates a thing's existential presence but also the intelligence of its structure.[1] God's holy beauty is ineffable, of course, and yet this very ineffability implies specific moments. It was the epistemological fact of this implication that enabled Edwards to open up new metaphysical perspectives on Calvinist thought.

Like any speculative thinking that seeks to capture the ineffable, Edwardsian Calvinism also seemed vulnerable to accusations of irrationality. They said it would create an impassable rift, an insurmountable

---

1. "The infinite greatness . . . of God, in *general*, ravishes the heart; the infinite moral beauty of the divine goodness and grace, in particular, ravishes the heart" (Bellamy, *True Religion Delineated*, *Works*, 1:135).

duality between the supremely ineffable and the interconnected system of beliefs and thereby dissociate spiritual intuition from doctrinal knowledge. Moreover, this accusation made a strong comeback at the moral level. The doctrine of justification teaches that the soul is completely seized by an irresistible external force that leads to a faith without works, religious piety without moral action. However, the great claim of this theology is precisely that it refutes all of these accusations and Edwards unceasingly advocated the existence of an organic link between the supreme idea—the correlate of a regenerated sense—and the particular contents that can be expressed in notional terms. In the realm of doctrinal theology, Edwards wanted to show that if new light was cast on the essential doctrines of Christianity, i.e., if these doctrines were made understandable in a new way by the illumination of the new simple idea of grace, then it would be as if they were contained by it. In terms of piety and morality—and contrary to what was said by the Arminians—the great doctrine of justification by faith alone and prior to any works implied immaculate, perfect, moral, and religious conduct. On the one hand, all moral and religious precepts and laws can be deduced from justifying faith. On the other hand, the spirit of love and obedience that grace plants in our heart is what actually causes us to conform to each of these laws and precepts.

Here we are faced with a particular issue of speculative theology, i.e., working out the relations between the Absolute conceived by superior knowledge and the various thetic declarations of metaphysics and theology. It wasn't possible to explicitly address this issue prior to the coming of post-Kantian idealism, although the seeds of it are present in the thought of Jonathan Edwards. In one of his very first Miscellanies (aa), devoted to analyzing the notion of "the testimony of the Spirit," i.e., the certainty and clarity that emanate from content apprehended by faith, Edwards addressed this subject in the form of a discussion on the relations between God and his attributes. He explained that, under the influence of the Holy Spirit, the mind conceives "ideas of religion" and may "feel divinity in them." "The notion of God . . . is that complex idea of such power, holiness, purity, majesty, love, excellency, beauty, loveliness," etc. Certain of what it sees, the mind "annexes the term God" to them because these things amount to its "idea of God." But then—and this is the conclusion—"God and religion are the same!" (13, 177)

This is an important statement regarding the relations between an "idea of God" and the other ideas subsumed under it, because these relations cannot be discovered "by intuition as other intuition" but only by an intuition proper to them that is different from all others. This amounts to saying that if we advocate the conceptual deduction of particular ideas from the supreme idea of God—from the "divinity" (13, 178)—such deduction is only conceivable when dependent on a spiritual apprehension. An idea of God is not merely the sum of various attributes or particular truths, but a whole where the latter can be represented as moments, on condition that the whole itself is subject to an overall spiritual apprehension. In this way, Edwards assigned the grasping of particular truths to our heads while attributing the comprehension of "divine excellency"—which enlightens by subsuming all truths under itself—to our hearts (17, 416). Now, the ultimate significance of these statements regarding our hearts can only be understood from the general context of the whole and its moments. This reference back to the heart is not an insistence on the emotional *per se*, i.e., as emotion, but is rather a vision of an essential moment of a mind whose engagement implies the engagement of the whole man. Edwards required "visible Christians" to "make a profession of a *hearty* believing the truth of the gospel" (13, 413) and later defined faith in Christ to mean that a person was "*heartily* applying himself to the Savior for salvation" (21, 424). In this instance, "hearty" doesn't really have its usual sense of "vigorous," a meaning which the anti-Arminian controversy has taught us to distrust.[2] Rather it expresses a man's most profound commitment, one that engages the whole man and unites him completely to Christ. However, this complete commitment of the heart isn't just existential in nature and lacking moral justification, but is to be understood as an adherence to spiritual beauty. The heart mentioned here is one that has become good through regeneration, a stony heart that has become a heart of flesh. To further emphasize that this total commitment is a good one, i.e., a commitment to goodness, Edwards quite often uses *cordial*, the original Latin form of the adjective, in place of "hearty."

In his treatise on *Qualifications for Communion*, Edwards wrote that it was not enough for the saints to have a purely notional faith, because even if this were sufficient to "animate" the mind, it still does not engage the heart; and "he that keeps back his heart, does in effect keep back all" (12, 207). The Gospel requires us to believe "with all the heart" and such believing "with the whole heart" signifies justifying faith. This is why the saints are to believe "cordially," i.e., "with his whole heart" (12, 237). Saving faith implies a cordial inclination of the heart to "Christ as a Savior" or a "hearty conviction and acknowledgement . . . of Christ Jesus" (21, 428). We must not forget that, in contrast to the "natural union" characteristic of "secondary beauty" in which "the will, disposition or affect of the heart" play no part, "cordial union" constitutes "spiritual beauty" (8, 565). Like Pascal before

---

2. See *supra*, p. 198.

him, Edwards did not use heart terminology in a pre-romantic, sentimentalist sense, but instead echoed the use of heart in the Scriptures to designate the whole man.[3] Like some of his Puritan predecessors, Edwards made correlations between the will and the heart[4] and between taste and the heart.[5] Since taste and the will are not definitively designated as central faculties of man, the heart cannot be identified with any given faculty and instead remains a visual picture of man's total engagement, not in terms of his material totality but rather in terms of his formal totality. In other words, we see man's engagement at a particular level of his being, yet nonetheless a summary of its essence.

As we have seen, Edwards used "excellency" as a synonym for "beauty." In fact, the term "excellency" predominates in *The Mind*. In his treatise on *The Nature of True Virtue*, "beauty" is used more often. From a conceptual standpoint, excellency plays a vital role in helping us understand the proper meaning of the primary beauty that constitutes cordial union. At the beginning of *The Mind*, Edwards said that we are more concerned with excellency than with anything else whatsoever and, in fact, we are concerned with nothing else (6, 332). In his *Treatise Concerning Religious Affections*, Edwards wrote that the very ground of our gracious affections is "the transcendently excellent and amiable nature of divine things, as they are in themselves" (2, 240). On the pages following this definition, we note a certain parallelism or synonymy between beauty and excellency. Conversely, in an important statement in this same work, excellency is not a synonym for beauty and amiability but rather its source. What makes a creature amiable, we read, is his excellency (2, 242). Further on, when Edwards explains that excellency is "the first objective ground of all holy affections," he refers to "their moral excellency" (2, 256). The fact that "good" and "excellent" are used from time to time as synonymous, interchangeable terms, or that excellency sometimes appears to be the ground of all spiritual qualities, is not a sign of confused terminology, but rather flows from the intimate nature of the notion itself. Excellency can be viewed as a particular spiritual attribute—among others—of an intelligent, voluntary being or as an attribute where, so to speak, a being's entire virtue is exposed, albeit only externally. In the strictest sense, excellency is therefore a synonym of what

---

3. "As the man's heart is, so is the man" (Cotton, *Way of Life*, 220. For a more elaborate definition: "the Heart . . . is the actual compliance of the Will and the Affections with the Mind and understanding with respect unto the objects proposed by them" (Owen, *Pneumatologia*, 212).

4. See *supra*, p. 103.

5. See 20, 509–10. See also the teaching of Edwardsian A. Burton, *supra*, p. 328 n.105.

is beautiful.[6] Though excellency might very well be seen as a particular or determined attribute, it nonetheless expresses the very essence of the spiritual reality in question. Excellency is not the entire sum of a being's parts, nor does it bring all of its elements together, and yet it summarizes what is essential. The essence of spiritual reality *per se* is moral goodness and true virtue. Excellency is therefore perceived as representing the whole being, according to what is most proper to it (2, 274).[7] It's in this sense, and in this context, that "excellency" is used with respect to the heart: either the heart is viewed as the excellency of a spiritual being, or the heart of a spiritual being is represented as adhering to what is excellent. In one Miscellany (370), the Holy Spirit is defined as the "amiable excellency" of God and, a little further on, in a psychologizing analogy of the Trinity, this same Spirit, this excellency of God, corresponds to the heart.[8] Because the heart is said to represent what constitutes the excellency of a being, a man's highest spiritual manifestations are therefore those in which he cordially adheres to what is excellent.

A late Miscellany (1352) explains that, in faith—which, we remember, is a "cordial reception of Christ"—the soul receives the revelation of Christ "as worthy and excellent."[9] Saving faith is based on our sense that Christ is "sufficient," although the "sufficiency" of Christ is explained by his "excellency" (21, 428–9). We can rely on Jesus Christ because he is as excellent as he is "sufficient" (2, 173); and he is not only sufficiently powerful to be able to save us, but he actually saves us. That he indeed saves

6. See 10, 157; 8, 442, etc.

7. The excellency that is true moral beauty is "the fullness of all things, without which all the world is empty, no better than nothing, yea, worse than nothing" (2, 274). The essence of regeneration is to relish the "excellency of the divine nature" (21, 173)—an excellency denied to natural men because of the fall (X, 113), yet one that God communicates to the "redeemed" (17, 208). Elsewhere, excellency is a synonym for God's glory (24, 1181), his "all-sufficiency" (24, 267), and even "His divinity" itself (MO, 399). Indeed, God is "nothing but excellency" (13, 252). According to T. Erdt (*Sense of the Heart*, 17), the comparison of excellence to "sweetness" (starting from 6, 365) may be due to the English translation of J. Wollebius (*Abridgment of Christian Divinity*, 247). For the antecedents of the Edwardsian notion of "excellence" in the works of Puritan theologians, see Morris, *Young Jonathan Edwards*, 368.

8. 13, 442. Elsewhere, God's excellency or divinity concerns the heart (MO 399ff.).

9. W 2, 606. "[T]he beauties of nature are really emanations, or shadows, of the excellencies of the Son of God" (13, 279). This is why nothing excellent is seen "before Christ is found" (22, 289). However, "natural man . . . sees . . . no divine excellency . . . in the face of Jesus Christ" (*Bl.*, 350), but instead "we fly from Him as we would from a mortal enemy" (10, 456). The excellency of the Savior is not a "chiefly legal" discourse but rather a proper "evangelical subject" (19, 797). The "discovery of the spiritual excellency of Christ" is the "most excellent gift" of God (19, 133).

us is because he is good. The sufficiency of Christ ultimately demonstrates his goodness (21, 425–26). Elsewhere, the *Notes on Scripture* identify the excellency of a man, his good, and his fullness (15, 185–86). Fullness is a notion of ontological origin that designates the diffusive disposition in God to communicate his goodness and bestow existence (8, 433–35); and thus, through the notion of excellency, the sufficiency of Christ is brought closer to the sovereignty of God (19, 363), which becomes a good sovereignty, a merciful sovereignty and the free consent that God extends to his creatures. This being so, we can easily understand that it is precisely because of his excellency that the devils hate God (25, 633–34)! Hatred of spiritual and moral excellency is the extreme point of discord in the universe, whereas agreement with God's spiritual beauty, the most "immediate" work of the Holy Spirit, is the highest form of consent in the creature. Justifying faith—whose essence very much lies in "the approbation and acceptance of the heart" (20, 510), i.e., the engagement of what is of greatest worth in us—is a "sense and conviction of the reality, the excellency and sufficiency of Jesus Christ as a Savior" (21, 64). All of this was already very clear in 1723. Edwards defined excellency as "being's consent to entity" (13, 253). Is there any manifestation of the cordial union superior to the justifying faith alone by which intelligent creatures consent to Jesus Christ?

2. Knowing God as he is and obeying him completely

As a correlate of cordial union, excellency is a part or moment of spiritual reality that, so to speak, represents and summarizes it as a whole, and emphasizing the cordial nature of our agreement with excellency therefore highlights our entire understanding and acceptance of it. This amounts to saying that justifying faith implies an adequate knowledge of God in Jesus Christ and results in total adherence to him,[10] an adherence manifested by "full obedience" and a flawless observation of the Law. The great assertion of Edwards against all practical or theoretical Pelagianism is that only the Protestant doctrine of justification by faith involves complete obedience to the Commandments, i.e., comprehensive morality (see 7, 526), and only immediate spiritual enlightenment creates the new spiritual sense that allows divine things to be adequately known.

Edwards thought that the true martyrs of Jesus Christ are not those who simply have an opinion that the gospel of Christ is true, but rather those who have also seen and know the truth of it (2, 306). The Devil

---

10. Justifying faith is "the harmonizing of the whole soul with Jesus Christ" (19, 448).

can only conjecture excellency, the true "divinity of Divinity" (2, 274).[11] Conversely, the "saving instruction" communicated to the regenerate gives them sure knowledge. It not only gives a vigorous apprehension but also more exact knowledge than that of which natural men are capable (2, 283). Spiritual knowledge is not merely sweet but also more exact because it is comprehensive and consequently objective. The wicked would truly like to "have a part of Christ," yet they refuse cordially to "accept" of "the whole of Christ," for that would mean accepting him "as He is" (X, 399). Expressed in the simplest terms, the difference between the regenerate and those who continue in their carnal state is this: the former know reality and the latter do not. "For this is the great plague of the wicked," exclaimed Thomas Shepard, "they see nothing as it is." Conversely, "the saving knowledge of Christ" is "to see the Lord in His glory as He is."[12]

Edwards constantly uses terms such as "seeing" or "knowing" God "as He is" or "as it is" when referring to his goodness and everything pertaining to him. In our carnal state, our fallen subjectivity sees things from our particular perspective and not as they truly are. Because our sight is corrupted, we are "by nature totally blind" to the holy beauty in divine things (2, 276); we cannot access them "by reason of the alienation of the inclinations & natural dispositions of the soul from those things as they are."[13] On the other hand, what characterizes the heavenly state is the fact that it makes "the wonderful works of God ... appear as they are" to the regenerate consciousness (X, 341). Even if, in this world here below, our sympathies might be determined by fear of our neighbor's hypocrisy, we will be able to welcome and accept the affections of others in heaven, "as much as if there were a window in all their breasts, that they could see each other's hearts" (8, 378). "In heaven," we will appear as we truly are.

This heavenly correspondence of being and appearance is anticipated here below by spiritual knowledge, which is ultimately a knowledge of things as they are in themselves. Unlike the allegorizing excesses of certain exegetes, who played with Scripture "as with a ball,"[14] and the liberties that the enthusiasts took with the letter of the Bible, Jonathan Edwards thought that "spiritually to understand the Scripture, is rightly to understand what *is in* the Scripture" (2, 280). Thomas Hooker was undoubtedly right: "when the power of the Word comes, the Scriptures are pregnant, Arguments

---

11. See *supra*, p. 271 n.86.
12. Shepard, *The Parable of the Ten Virgins, Works*, 2:145; 123.
13. See *supra*, p. 262.
14. Calvin, *Commentary on Corinthians*, 2:163.

undeniable, Counsels sweet,"[15] but that doesn't in any way mean that gracious inspiration causes things to appear as other than they are in reality. If Edwards defended the "affectionate" preachers of the Great Awakening, it was only to the extent that their sermons enabled their hearers to have a better understanding of Christian truths (see 4, 386). True saints have a spiritual conviction of the truth and certainty of spiritual things because they see the reality of them (2, 291–2). Conversely, those who refuse to accept the doctrine of sovereign predestination thereby show they do not know that "God is God" (VI, 484). The proper object of the saints' knowledge is the transcendent excellency of God, which is found only in him. In comparison to it, the harmony and attraction of everything else seem to fade away or be wiped out. This is why anyone who has a "realizing" sense of divine excellency cannot but love God. Now "he that truly loves God, loves him as God" (3, 146). And again: The true test of the gracious nature of an affection is when a person finds within himself a "heart to treat God as God" (2, 452), just as a true love of the brethren means "a love to saints *as* saints" (12, 253).

The great claim for the objectivity of spiritual knowledge specifies that the subject, who is regenerate and endowed with a new spiritual sense, must resolutely free himself from the subjective limits of his perspective, be more outgoing and emigrate, as it were, towards his object. The goal of all spiritual effort is to apprehend the excellency of God, something we can only do by seeing and considering it as it is in itself. Firmly anchored in the Protestant Christian tradition, Edwards taught that the Gospel "has its highest and most proper evidence in itself" (2, 307) and that the Scripture must be taken "as an whole, and in itself" (4, 296). In fact, the dialectic underlying Edwardsian thought involves the development of metaphysical and theological relations between the whole and the essential—between "a profession of Christianity" and whatsoever "is essential in the profession of Christianity" itself (2, 413)—and this dialectic was developed by clarifying the meaning of the phrase "as it is in itself."

The great definition leading into the description of the second distinctive sign of gracious affections states: "The first objective ground of gracious affections, is the transcendently excellent and amiable nature of divine things, as they are in themselves" (2, 240). The unjustified do not grasp the glory, nor any other excellency "in God's nature, as it is in itself" (2, 241). The regenerate, on the other hand, apprehend the beauty, glory, and supreme good in God's nature "as it is in itself" (2, 258). This is a deepening of the objective nature of spiritual knowledge, an emphasis on the perfect cognitive apprehension of spiritual things, albeit one that transcends the purely

---

15. Hooker, *Application of Redemption*, bk. 9, in Hooker, *Three Sermons*, 62.

theoretical and ends in the sphere of the practical. When envisaged in all its dimensions and as that which enables the excellency of divine things to be apprehended, spiritual knowledge cannot but result in virtue and devotion. Though justifying grace gives us "a saving instruction" (2, 276), it is always understood as *assensu practico sed fiduciali*[16] [a practical yet trusting consent]. This cordial apprehension of spiritual things as they are in themselves invariably results in virtuous action. The three gifts of the Spirit, "faith, hope and charity . . . into which all Christianity, as a principle in the [regenerate] mind, is to be resolved" when "joined together and united into one, constituteth saving faith," i.e., "justifying faith" (15, 277). In other words, in vigorous opposition to critics of the Calvinist system, we can declare that "justifying faith is nothing else but true virtue" (21, 463). Whereas optimism in the thought of antiquity resulted in the calm conviction that the knowledge of good rendered man incapable of opting for evil, Christian optimism firmly professes that the sight of spiritual beauty leads the mind to join and unite with it.

The core of Edwardsian thought lies in its analysis of that essential moment when a cognitive grasp of spiritual things leads to love, when understanding of the sweetness of Jesus Christ frees the soul to follow his law.[17] Joseph Bellamy expressed this crucial connection between the theoretical and the practical, that great moment when faith becomes "universal benevolence," with this simple definition: "To view beings and things as they are, and to be affected and act accordingly, is the sum of moral virtue."[18] Closer to his master's terminology, Samuel Hopkins said: "Right views and exercises of heart respecting God, considered as being what He is in Himself, is *love*.[19] Edwards very often used the expression "as they are in themselves" to indicate that access to the essential reality of divine things

---

16. *Declaratio Thoruniensis*, in Niemeyer, *Collectio*, 675.

17. From a metaphysical point of view, this Edwardsian thought is a draft outline of practical knowledge, i.e., knowledge whose objects are defined according to the inclination of the mind. The saint has "a principle in his heart that directs and governs him, that abhors sin, and relishes and delights in righteousness, by which principle he is led and directed in the right way, as by a spiritual scent, distinguishing good from bad, and inclining him to that which is right" (24, 559). The glory that shines from the face of God gives a right knowledge of his divine excellency and "of the way of duty . . . and inclines us to walk in it" (24, 531–32). The thing believed is received as "good and agreeable . . . embracing . . . the inclination . . . of the soul (25, 513) and this is the sense in which Scripture teaches that "all that know Him do love Him" (25, 525). Conversely, to know your sins means to own them (14, 241; 17, 152). Suffice it to say that he that thus sees the evil of sin and its desert of hell, he destroys it; his heart is divorced from it (24, 1080).

18. Bellamy, *An Election Sermon*, *Works*, 1:578.

19. Hopkins, *System of Doctrines*, *Works*, 1:447.

amounted to a practical engagement in their favor because, when seen as they are in themselves, divine things invariably become motives of my volition (see 2, 394). The joy of the saints, "the spring of all their delights, and the cream of all their pleasures, is to contemplate divine things as they are in themselves" (2, 250); and, on a purely conceptual level, Edwards declared and explained the identity of this sight of holy beauty as it is in itself with true virtue. True virtue is related to Being in general, simply considered, i.e., as he is in himself; and its "object" is that which "is beautiful by a *general* beauty, or beautiful in a comprehensive view as it is in itself" (8, 540). True virtue is universal benevolence to the extent that its object is Being in general as he is in himself. The formulation "in himself" denotes a whole or totality which "private systems" (i.e., only "partial" ones) cannot attain, and even oppose, because they are merely objects of a particular, limited benevolence (8, 610).[20]

This vision of true virtue, one in which engagement to Being in general as he is in himself was equated with engagement to a "universal system"—that of Being in general and every (intelligent) being in some way related to Being in general (see 8, 541–42)—enabled Jonathan Edwards to present a moral doctrine in which full, comprehensive consent to true goodness became *eo ipso* total consent. In other words, a theology in which cordial adherence to Jesus Christ implied obedience to all his Law. Criticizing Calvinism for professing the absolute primacy of faith over works by saying that it annihilates all human morality, Arminians preach the sovereign efficacy of "moral sincerity" in ethical matters. On the contrary, Edwards thought that only Augustinian-Calvinist theology was capable of portraying authentic morality for the very reason that only it could transcend "moral sincerity" and its bad faith accompanied by vague, powerless desires. Only those to whom God gives a heart for heavenly things can make "earnest and firm resolutions" to press into the kingdom. The firmness of resolution "lies in the fullness of the disposition of the heart" to do what must be done. This entire disposition requires a constant inclination of the mind to perform all the required actions. A cordial agreement is therefore a complete engagement—not periodic but for its entire duration—and one in which fullness implies totality, namely obedience to every commandment. The essential elements of a cordial engagement to follow Christ are detailed in a Miscellany (462) on the qualifications for communion. Communicants had to be "heartily convinced" of the truth of Scripture, i.e., believe it "with

---

20. Before the fall, the soul of man was "enlarged to a kind of comprehension of all his fellow creatures." After man had transgressed, "this excellent enlargedness of his soul was gone and he thenceforward shrunk into a little point, circumscribed and closely shut up within itself to the exclusion of others" (8, 253).

all their heart," which implied "universally forsaking sin." Cordial engagement required a "fixed determination of mind" to will and to act to the very end, and to do so perfectly. Such all-encompassing, ongoing action meant having to forsake all ways of sin, to deny every lust, and live in the performance of all Christ's commands universally (13, 503). "Grace," we read in an earlier Miscellany (164), "is to turn from every wicked way to every good one" (13, 321). It means keeping all of the Law, something of which only the saints, and never hypocrites, are capable (2, 402).[21]

Edwardsian texts overflow with passages in which cordial agreement is described in terms of total commitment. Spiritual knowledge touches the heart and makes it disposed to "universal obedience (20, 510). Real faith makes us "sensible" of the infinite detestableness of sin, causing us to be "fully approving" of the law itself . . . and renouncing sin" (20, 509). Faith is the soul "entirely embracing the revelation of Jesus Christ," which is "adhering to and acquiescing in" and entirely "believing" it. This entails the engagement of our entire "inclination" (21, 424), not merely momentarily or temporarily, but permanently. In his discussion on the twelfth distinctive sign of gracious affections, Edwards stated that virtuous practice implies the "strict, universal and constant obedience" of the Church to the Commandments (2, 396). Whereas many hypocrites are like "comets, that appear for a while with a mighty blaze; but are very unsteady and irregular in their motion (and are therefore called wandering stars, *Jude 13*)," true saints are like "the fixed stars, which, though they rise and set, and are often clouded, yet are steadfast in their orb, and may truly be said to shine with a constant light" (2, 373–74). There was an abiding change in the Northampton converts who, after the end of the 1734–1735 revival, "still remained a reformed people" in terms of their life and faith (4, 208–9). More generally speaking, truly gracious experiences are those that "are attended with the most amiable behavior, and will bring forth the most solid and sweet fruits . . . and will have the greatest effect on the abiding *temper* of the soul" (4, 466), one of "permanent sobriety" and "unmoveable stability" (7, 521).[22]

However, the stability and permanence that characterize a regenerate mind should not be represented in a static sense, but instead in a dynamic

---

21. See 21, 309. "There is a certain measure, source, degree, plenitude or fullness of the Spirit of grace in the heart of the faithful of which the unsound professors fall . . . short" (2, 262). As Henry Smith, a Presbyterian, once said: "Now if we be almost Christian, let us see what it is to be almost a Christian. Almost a son is a bastard; almost sweet, is unsavory, almost hot is lukewarm, which God spueth out of His mouth Rev. 3:16. So almost a Christian is not a Christian" (Pattison, *History of Christian Preaching*, 168 in Stoeffler, *Rise of Evangelical Pietism*, 16).

22. 7, 521. See "an universal and persevering obedience" (25, 416) of the soul that has a "perpetual dwelling" in the light of grace (25, 708).

one. Just as God's "holy immutability" is not "inflexible obstinacy" (2, 257), the coming of a new, abiding spiritual sense does not exclude change. It certainly allows for temporary slowdowns and periods of obscurity, but inscribed into it, so to speak, is an inherent tendency to constantly become more intense. Justification, a unique act at a given time, takes place all at once, as with creation or the resurrection of Jesus Christ (see 18, 232), whereas regeneration, which expresses justification as moral behavior, is spread over time. From God's perspective, justification is imparted in full measure. On man's part, it is followed by an ongoing effort of assimilation and a constant process of moral and religious maturation. Grace invites man to constant renewal. Grace is the "most active" and fruitful kind of life "in heaven and earth" (2, 398) and—by its very exercise—endlessly enlarges and enriches. Edwards quoted Thomas Shepard: "There is in true grace an infinite circle: a man by thirsting receives, and receiving thirsts for more" because "true grace as it comforts, so it never fills, but puts an edge on the appetite."[23] Unlike hypocrites, who never having crossed the borders of their fallen ipseity, drink only from one particular, "limited" spring and, as a result, grow weary and abandon the practice of virtue (VII, 430-1), true saints, having become "spiritual," drink the living and inexhaustible waters of the Spirit, and ever long after "further attainments in religion" (2, 397). Cordial engagement accordingly implies permanence and perseverance, as well as growth (13, 337). It is therefore comprehensive and, more especially, integrating, or rather, totalizing.

3. Perfect virtue and the sum of the Commandments

Arminians do not want to accept that only a flawless attachment to sanctifying faith can save us. Although they don't fully believe it themselves, they think that moral sincerity, efforts and vague desires of the heart nonetheless constitute a kind of faith that will suffice for salvation. Edwards plainly said that those who do not fully and cordially believe "may be said not to believe at all" (W, 2, 633). This is not a matter of contrasting one degree of "moral sincerity" that would suffice for salvation with another that would prove insufficient. "Saving sincerity" is distinct—not only in degree, but also in nature—from sincerity that is still of the flesh. "Saving sincerity" can only be perfect (see 21, 308). Edwards sternly observed: "The thing that the law exacts is *perfect*, and not *sincere*, obedience" (15, 111). Such perfection means unlimited adherence to God in Jesus Christ and, consequently, obedience to all his commandments. An appropriate example of Arminian sincerity is the

---

23. Shepard, *The Parable of the Ten Virgins*, Works, 2:288; 350 in 2, 376n.6.

parable of the rich young man who believed he was ready to do everything that Jesus would ask of him. However, when he heard the call enjoining him to sell all he had and give his money to the poor, he realized that he had no sincere willingness at all for any such thing. It follows that he did not want to do everything asked in order to be saved (12, 415).

The moral sincerity of which the Arminians speak is merely an imperfect, deceptive sincerity, because anyone who truly wants to obey God is ready to obey all his commandments. Notwithstanding all of their "moral sincerity," however, the unjustified never stop sinning and thereby refuse complete obedience. Just as it wouldn't be enough, in the case of a complete crossing of the Atlantic, to have covered most of the distance, we shouldn't think that any who are "sincere in endeavors to do more than half their duty, though they sincerely neglect the rest," will be saved (21, 308)[24]. Just as a man's volitions are not isolated atoms but moments in a complete configuration, the commandments of the Gospel are not the dust of scattered precepts but form a connected whole animated by a common spirit. An intimate intention is not like some distant impulse found separate from the succession of volitions; the will is merely the woven fabric of its volitions, each of which is immanent to it. We are under the ever-present threat of a brutal attack by the evil one and must therefore constantly "put on the whole armor of God" (2, 388). The ancestor of our race in the Garden of Eden had a spiritual relationship with God because he had "the whole of moral rectitude in every part of it" (3, 230). After his conversion, young Edwards felt "a burning desire to be in everything a complete Christian; and conformed to the blessed image of Christ: and that I might live in all things, according to the pure, sweet and blessed rules of the gospel" (16, 795). It is therefore by resolutely rejecting mere moral sincerity and works that we can keep all the Commandments. Yet how do we explain the strict, logical relations between the whole and its parts, between the total engagement of the heart and the exhaustive accomplishment of every precept? Edwards was persuaded that there was a rational relation between every precept of the Law and every commandment of the Gospel (see 13, 416–17), yet he still needed to demonstrate how the regenerate could actually understand the mutual dependence of the particular moments of true religion. He began this task by describing God's excellency and moral beauty as a spiritual idea involving a multitude of other ideas. In other words, he taught that conceiving of grace as an idea simply opened the mind's eyes to relations and connections that objectively existed but which the mind would never have

---

24. See "moral sincerity" (25, 368)—"a transient thing, a morning cloud or early dew" (25, 369)—is but "a short-lived qualification" (25, 370); see also "temporary faith" (*supra*, p. 230).

been able to discover or understand without an infusion of grace. Precisely because this understanding is a work of grace, it doesn't end up as a theoretical goal but as a cordial adhesion to every element of spiritual reality and to each of these divine things.

4. Universal and cordial obedience

Jonathan Edwards attributed the decoding and comprehension of the organic connections between moral and religious ideas to the spiritual knowledge proper to the sanctified state. The ecclesial discipline position that would cost the Northampton pastor his position is a brilliant illustration of this theologico-metaphysical theory. Edwards, as we know, initially continued the practice of his famous predecessor Solomon Stoddard by admitting Christians to the Lord's Supper who were incapable of making a gracious profession of faith or a confession of cordial acquiescence to Christ as savior and to all the articles of his religion! However, his growing disagreement with Stoddard's practice eventually led Edwards to reject it once and for all.[25] The Church is "the fullness" of Christ" (8, 439), the "ornament" he is pleased to receive (15, 186). It is "the whole company or society of . . . real and true saints,"[26] and only those who are "by profession and in visibility a part of that heavenly and divine family" (12, 248) can be members "in complete standing" of it (12, 175). Those who desire to partake in the Lord's Supper ought to profess "an hearty embracing [of] Christ . . . as the Savior" (20, 114), and "believe the Gospel with all their hearts" (13, 503). If they don't, they are true "murderers" of Christ who only share "the body and blood" as "blood thirsty cannibals."[27] Of course, to know the heart is ultimately a "divine prerogative" (25, 301), although our actions remain visible to our neighbor. Consequently, the profession of a gracious faith must be accompanied by a moral life and conduct that is virtuous "in the eye of a reasonable judgment."[28] Without falling into the errors of "a works righteousness, good moral practice is a *sine qua non* of full ecclesial

---

25. "I have had difficulties . . . for many years, with regard to admission of members into the church who made no pretense to real godliness. These gradually increased, and at length to such a degree, that I found I could not with an easy conscience be active in admitting any more members in our former manner" (12, 507).

26. Sermon on Eph. 5:25–27, *Ms.*, in Sweeney, "The Church," 168.

27. "Sermon on I Cor 10:16," *Ms.*, Marsden, *Jonathan Edwards*, 354.

28. "Sermon on Ezek 44:9," Edwards mss. collection, Andover-Newton Theological School, in Sweeney, "The Church," 183.

communion.[29] It is a genuine acceptance of the Law of God that implies obedience to all of his commandments.

The grand design of Edwardsian developments is to show that, because it affects the whole man, regeneration concerns conformity to the whole Law, i.e., in its entirety. Partial obedience is characteristic of hypocrites (10, 635), when the change that God demands cannot be "partial" but has to be "complete" (*Bl.*, 253). It is not enough to only accept Christ as our Savior "in part" (*Bl.*, 221); we have to give our heart "wholly" to him (19, 604) and must not keep back a part for ourselves (10, 553–4).[30] Arminians celebrate those who "do more than half their duty, though they sincerely neglect the rest" (21, 308); and yet a duty that is even more than half accomplished is still not done.[31] The regenerate lives by righteousness, but "an imperfect righteousness . . . is no righteousness" (19, 189). Like most of the great Christian theologians, Edwards taught that a single sin would tear the coat of sanctification. There is "a concatenation of the graces of Christianity . . . so that if one link be broken, all falls" (8, 327). Conversely, "he who allows himself in the breach of one command is as if he broke all" (*Bl.*, 105). "Our obedience should be universal; and he that offends on one point is guilty of all" (22, 118). Every moment, "every degree of sin," the Calvinist preacher said, "is devilish in its nature" (19, 692).[32]

This intransigent position regarding the decisive implications of a single transgression should not be attributed to an unhealthy rigorism, because it simply expresses the great Protestant doctrine of justification. Justification doesn't just touch parts or elements of our being, but affects it fully and completely and radically transforms it. The peace of God sanctifies us "wholly" (*Bl.*, 297), while conversion is "a renewing of the whole man" (*Bl.*, 302). "The corruption and death which came by Adam" must be "wholly removed" (20, 71) and Christ is to be accepted "with the whole man: soul, spirit and body" (20, 324). This involves a "willingness with the whole

---

29. As a sermon preached to the Indians of Stockbridge once put it: "So none ought to come into the Christian church but good men" (25, 578).

30. Since God is like the soul's spouse, how can anyone enter into marriage while reserving their heart for others (25, 363)? Men are to give themselves up to God "with all their heart and all their soul" (25, 366) and "to give God a blank that He may write what He pleases" (24, 236). As long as converts don't deliver up everything they have to God but instead hold back something for themselves, God will look upon them "as enemies" (24, 191).

31. "Partial obedience" is only "conformity without grace" (24, 287).

32. Though they hate "strictness" (10, 375), this is why sinners should strive to be as "particular" as they can (19, 267) when examining their conscience.

heart" (21, 357), a cordial receiving of Christ that implies "the whole soul's compliance with the holiness and moral excellency of God" (21, 358).[33]

The adherence of the whole man to the moral excellency of God can only be comprehensive, i.e. comprehensive with respect to the human subject and comprehensive with regard to its object or objects, namely divine laws and commandments. The obedience of the sanctified person is perfect and universal, and it extends to the totality of moral-religious precepts. Just as Adam had a disposition "to do all his duty, and that perfectly,"[34] we also, in our day, must perfectly agree with the "eternal rule of rectitude or righteousness" and its "perfect fulfillment""(20, 482). In fact, it's "the natural appetite of a gracious soul to be . . . perfectly conformed to God" (19, 685) whose "law is perfect" (19, 690). Perfect acquiescence to the will of God the Savior implies "universal and willing obedience to all His commandments" (14, 427). Whereas "universal observance of outward moral duties" was required under the old dispensation, i.e., the Old Testament (21, 493), it is now "Christ's commandments" that we are to "universally" keep (21, 87). We must "be alienated from sin . . . universally" (*Bl.*, 145) and live in "gracious and universal obedience" (17, 425). In short, what is required of the regenerate Christian is "a life of universal holiness" (14, 429).

The universal and the perfect are *formal* categories, and yet they constitute the counterpart to the notion that everything is *material*. Perfect obedience and universal holiness are proper to the justified Christian and they imply the accomplishment of all laws. The preacher reminded his congregation that we cannot divide our love and affections for God with others: "Our love to Him must govern all our love; our desires after Him must govern all our desires; our joy in Him must be above all our joy" (10, 555n.3). We aspire to holiness, but we are only holy when "all God's laws without exception are written in our hearts" (10, 473). What is required of us is that we strive to do all our duties (19, 699). In short, there must be "universal . . . obedience . . . to all His commandments" (14, 427).

Edwards emphasized this attitude of universal submission—to all laws without exception—although the complete text reads: "universal and *willing* obedience" (14, 427). These descendants of the Puritans—the Congregationalists of Northampton—weren't merely asked to obey all the commandments of God, but to do so "willingly."[35] Moreover, the require-

---

33. True believers must "be willing to be wholly Christ's, to be only Christ's, and to be forever Christ's" (*Bl.*, 369).

34. *Ms. Book of Controversies*, 78.

35. Just as the "justified man"—on a "theoretical" level — is "thoroughly convinced" of the truth of the Gospel, he must be ready—on a "practical" level (25, 535)—to "freely and readily" give everything he has (24, 408). Likewise, if spiritual knowledge

ment to be willing wasn't simply added to the universal extension of the compliance required but was an indispensable complement to it and even solely responsible for making it possible. People had long been pleased to compare the freedom of God's children—or even just that of men of good will—to the miserable requirements of a narrow legalism, to an obsession with detail, or to the maniac preoccupations of theoretical or practical, dogmatic or moral-ritual orthodoxy. For Jonathan Edwards, this great Christian theologian and moralist, the gracious liberty of love and obedience to all the commandments seemed to go together and even to have mutual, organic connections. The Northampton pastor ultimately required his parishioners to exhibit impeccable moral conduct and have a gracious profession of faith that lovingly agreed with Christ the Savior. Now, these requirements are the two sides of the great doctrine formulated as follows: "Justifying faith is nothing else but true virtue" (21, 463). The young preacher called for a "strict and hearty religion" (14, 499), i.e., one concerned about compliance with all the commandments, albeit a willing compliance. Twenty-five years later, this theologian wrote of "an hearty and thorough consent" to everything implied by holiness (21, 361). The commandments of Jesus Christ are a whole: spiritual knowledge enables their reciprocal connections to be discerned, while sanctifying faith engenders willing obedience to them.

5. Compossibility

In a Miscellany (646) in which he discussed the "strictness of the Law," Edwards, citing James 2:10, wrote that "He that offends in one point, is guilty of all" and quoted the Apostle Paul: "Cursed *is* every one that continueth not in all things which are written in the book of the law to do them" (Galationa 3:10) to prove that a single transgression was enough to be condemned (18, 179–80). The severity of this view wasn't ordered by the obsession of a servile mind blindly attached to the minutest prohibition of the Law, desiring to want and to do what was right in each particular case. It is instead explained by the reasonable and resolute conviction that every transgression of a commandment is a transgression against God himself because the commandments form an organic whole. Edwards professed this doctrine as a biblical theologian, but his teaching had more general conceptual foundations. A scientific "observer" of the great regularity and precision

---

of God as God implies knowledge of all his attributes (24, 1157), then love of holiness for itself and viewing "holiness" as our "happiness" will help us obey all the commandments of God and "practically prefer God to the world" (25, 535).

of "the frame and composition" of things in the universe (20, 128),[36] he surmised that there must be a "universal attraction in the whole system of things from the beginning of the world to the end." Only the limitations of our understanding prevent us from perceiving "the series of things—to speak more strictly, the series of ideas" (6, 357) at any moment. "'Tis only for want of sufficient accurateness, strength and comprehension of mind, that from the motion of any one particular atom we can't tell all that ever has been, [all] that now is in the whole extent of the creation . . . and everything that ever shall be." With a sigh of envy and pleasure, Edwards added: "What room for improvement of reason is there, for angels and glorified minds!" (13, 374). We are filled with envious wonder when we think of how an improvement of our understanding would expand our knowledge of the connections between the things in the universe, yet these connections themselves are ultimately just a faithful expression and highly exact formulation of logico-metaphysical structures. God has distributed things in species and designed that particular things be together in the mind. He made "the soul of such a nature that those particulars which He thus made to agree are unavoidably together in the mind, one naturally exciting and including the others" (6, 362).

As a philosopher from the post-Cartesian metaphysics movement that culminated with Leibnitz's doctrine of compossibility, Edwards firmly believed in a logico-metaphysical link between the things in the world.[37] The "association" between our ideas, that "mutual attraction" between them (6, 391) observed by introspection, is not in the least random or contingent: the articulation of our thoughts merely reproduces the articulation of the world, while a properly functioning mind merely discovers the objective structure of the being. Reasoning does not absolutely differ from perception, because it too is ultimately just "the knowledge of self-evident truths" (6, 373), although our mind's temporal and spatial states make it impossible to immediately grasp the relations between these truths. "Therefore, if we had perfect ideas of all things at once, that is, could have all in one view, we should know all truth at the same moment, and there would be no such thing as ratiocination or finding out truth. And reasoning is only of use to us in consequence of the paucity of our ideas, and because we can have but very few in view at once" (6, 342). If the author of a particular sin feels justified in protesting against a general condemnation, it's because his fallen

---

36. "The world was made to have all parts of it nicely hanging together, and sweetly harmonizing and corresponding" (13, 189–90).

37. This topic is further discussed in M. Veto, "Beauté et Compossibilité: L'épistémologie Théologique de Jonathan Edwards," in Veto, *Philosophie et religion*, 153–67.

mind doesn't allow him to discern the correspondence and connection between one particular law and all laws. It is not so for God, before whom the things of this world appear "in their mutual respects and relations," and it is this same "comprehensive view" (see 13, 288) that spiritual regeneration infuses into the mind of the justified sinner.

In his *Faithful Narrative*, Edwards observed that, after conversion, arguments heard many times before that had no impact or outcome now seemed exceedingly "rational" (4, 180). Grace attracts our attention, sheds light on ideas and makes their mutual relations plainly visible (2, 308). A Miscellany (408) compares the situation of a natural mind to that of a man walking at night who only sees the trees as "fainting, fading shadows." But "when the light comes to shine upon them, then the ideas appear with strength and distinctness; and he has that sense of the beauty of the trees and fields given him in a moment, which he would not have obtained by going about amongst them in the dark in a long time. A man that sets himself to reason without divine light is like a man that goes in the dark into a garden full of the most beautiful plants, and most artfully ordered, and compares things together by going from one thing to another, to feel of them and to measure the distances; but he that sees by divine light is like a man that views the garden when the sun shines upon it" (13, 470).[38] Edwards emphasized the inherent rationality of the relations between things which the infusion of grace highlights and makes more clearly discernible. Illuminated by divine light, the mind immediately embraces these relations, so to speak, and sees or grasps them intuitively. Edwards called this superior form of knowledge without a string of arguments[39] "intuition," because it derives from intui-

---

38. Of course, the "light" that unifies but also distinguishes and differentiates contents can only be discerned by a man who "has the stream of his affections wholly towards God, and so has but one inclination to serve." He looks on objects "through a single clear eye that represents objects single, and distinct, and each one in his true state" (24, 837).

39. Unlike ratiocination (6, 370), demonstration (1, 182), or all knowledge from signs, intuitive knowledge is immediate (18, 427). This notion appears in one of Edwards's very first texts: it is "intuitively evident" to us that "nothing . . . could not be" (6, 202), and so there must be an infinite, "eternal Being" (1, 182). Moreover, intuition implies knowledge of existence (6, 370). However, Edwards generally used this notion in the context of spiritual knowledge. In his early Miscellanies, he called the certainty that the Spirit gives in faith "intuitive," albeit a very particular "intuition" that differs from all others (13, 177–78). Knowledge proper to prophetic inspiration is "intuitive" (6, 346). They who have "seen and tasted" the excellency of the Spirit's operations, have "intuitively beheld . . . the powerful evidence of divinity in them" (4, 179). The saints "intuitively" see the bond of love that unites them to God (2, 239), and those who apprehend the "transcendent, supreme glory of those things which are divine . . . know their divinity intuitively" (2, 298). Present at the transfiguration, Saint Peter was "irresistibly . . . and . . . intuitively certain" of the divinity of Jesus (13, 471). Finally, only

tive perception rather than the far more traditional ratiocination and also glimpses the totalizing unity of the relations within a whole that is not of a metaphysico-logical order.

In his letter of acceptance for the presidency of the College of New Jersey (later Princeton University), Edwards mentioned his plan to write a "great work" titled *The History of the Work of Redemption* in which he would consider "the affair of Christian Theology, as the whole of it, in each part, stands in reference to the great work of redemption by Jesus Christ." His method would be historical. This history would consider the successive events connected with "all three worlds, Heaven, Earth and Hell" and, by using this "method," the author hoped that "every divine doctrine will appear to the greatest advantage, in the brightest light, in the most striking manner, showing the admirable contexture and harmony of the whole." A little further on, he mentioned *The Harmony of the Old and New Testaments*, a work which would study the fulfillment of the prophecies to show "the universal, precise, and admirable correspondence between predictions and events" (16, 728).[40] It seemed as though Edwards wanted to represent the temporal succession of history in terms of logical relations and connections, because the unity linking biblical events and teachings is narrative rather than discursive. In a Miscellany (6) from 1723, Edwards wrote with delight of "a strange and unaccountable type of enchantment" found in "Scripture history." Recalling and recounting the minutest facts in detail makes us seem actually present at those events, in a manner of speaking, and "we insensibly fancy not that we are readers but spectators, yea actors in the business." However, we shouldn't think that the purpose of including details or recalling the circumstances of the minutest event is to provide an exhaustive description—a complete, literal presentation—of past events. The only circumstances mentioned are those that continue to "brighten the ideas of the more principal parts of the history" and "the whole story and illustrate, nobody knows how, every part of it. So the story is told very fully, and

---

the man Jesus "is admitted to know God immediately," i.e., intuitively (18, 428). The essence of all this stems from "tradition," namely that intuitive knowledge apprehends things as they are in themselves (Shepard, *The Parable of the Ten Virgins*, *Works*, 2:127); intuitive knowledge is "irresistible" (Locke, *Essay*, 2. 2. 1) and it alone can discern the presence of grace (Stoddard, *Defects of Preachers Reproved*, 17). The source of these theories is a great axiom professed by metaphysicians from the Scholastics to Kant: "Deus omne intuitive cognoscit [God knows all things intuitively]" (Wolff, *Theologia Naturalis*, 1. § 207. 181).

40. Once the "grand design" of God in that "great scheme" known as "The Work of Redemption" has brought history to its consummation, its events and specific moments will be seen as part of "a glorious structure that will then stand forth in its proper perfection" (9, 121–22).

without the least crowding or jumbling things together." This subtle dose of great conciseness and minute evocation of details gives us the sensation of following the natural rhythm of the story. Accounts often consist of "but two or three negligent words," yet communicate a whole chain of ideas and "the story is so told that one's mind, although the things are not mentioned, yet naturally traces the whole transaction" (13, 202–3).

The evocative power of the biblical narrative to seemingly reconstitute missing moments—unspoken events—for us is certainly not without discursive pretention, and the relations between the whole and its parts still have a fairly rationalist coloration. But what is essential is that everything involving the parts is of a narrative rather than a logical order, i.e., there are rationalities other than deductive ones. However, while non-discursive rationality—as witnessed in the narrative coherence of Scripture—is important for distinguishing Edwardsian thought from other natural theologies of classical dogmatics, it must still be made clear that this "strange enchantment" is not evoked by the biblical story as a summary of events, but arises instead from the narrative form itself.[41] The "raw" story itself—its set of events—is not what we admire, but rather the narrative constructed from them; and it's the law and rationality proper to each narrative that allow us to track its unspoken events, i.e., its missing moments. Grasping the totality of the narrative allows us to access its individual missing moments, although this totality is not a sum of events but rather a quality that is the nerve, spring, and medium underlying the dialectic of the relations between the whole and its parts.

6. The spiritual idea of God

The crucial instant of this religious epistemology, based on the infusion of the new simple idea of grace, is found in the attempt to explain the transition from the proper content of the spiritual enlightenment itself to the other contents that are supposed to flow from it. Emphasizing the quality of the biblical narrative that allows us to grasp every moment of Scripture history shows that it is a particular content, albeit a very particular one in being representative of other particular contents. Though only the beauty or the moral and spiritual excellency of divine things, strictly speaking, can provide such content, we already see an attempt here, in the form of a theoretical apologetic, to rediscover what is essential in Christianity by starting from a particular doctrine. In a critical reference to John Locke in one of

---

41. For this issue, see Frei, *Eclipse of Biblical Narrative* and Laurence, "Religious Experience in Edwards," 21–22.

his earliest Miscellanies (*ee*), Edwards stated that those who think that only one article of faith—a profession that Jesus Christ was a person sent from God—is necessary and sufficient for a Christian, and that all the rest follows, are indeed right, although for reasons other than those they themselves put forward. Belief in the affirmation that "Jesus Christ was a person sent from God" is only sufficient as the sole article of our religion insofar as it implies other articles. If we believe that Jesus Christ was sent by God, then we have to profess that every one of his teachings is true. Especially as the motive for sending him had to be the mercy of God, who foresaw and ordained it by his wisdom and accomplished it by his omnipotence, believing in Jesus as the messiah obliges us to believe in God's other divine perfections. Consequently, faith in that one article concerning the messianic status of Jesus Christ implies belief in the entire scheme (or system) of Scripture and a profession of almost "all the articles . . . which good Protestants all along have said to be necessary" (13, 183).

This deduction of God's various perfections from belief in the messianic status of Jesus Christ is an example of the derivation of several notional contents from a single, essential content that nonetheless remains particular. The dialectic that plays out—between "a profession of Christianity" and whatsoever "is essential in the profession of Christianity" itself (2, 413)—requires a content that is not simply the primitive source, i.e., the first link of the deduction, but penetrates, so to speak, every content in the series, or rather, contains and involves them. We can discern such instances of involvement in the main subjects and notions of Edwards's work: we have only to think of love and sin or, more especially, the sin against the Holy Spirit! In a sense, love is but one of the sanctified man's virtues, although it could equally be considered his main virtue, the one underlying all the others. Love is "the essence and soul" of religion, the "chief" of religious affections, the fountain from which all others "necessarily" flow (2, 106–8). Love is a particular affection, of course, but it is also the source of all virtuous affections because it signifies engagement and agreement with others—whether God or our neighbor—that is the condition and soul of all virtuous feelings and behaviors towards them. Now, if love is the source and fountain of all affections, then hatred for God underlies and penetrates all vices, i.e., all bad actions. The "sin against the Holy Spirit" is what theologians call the essential moment of this hatred. It is not only the most grievous of all sins, but we can even conceive of it as being present in every sin. All sin is opposition to the will of God. The sin against the Holy Spirit has always been understood as open, explicit opposition, done with full knowledge and therefore "the most willful" of sins (18, 324). Moreover, because every transgression is ultimately and at least indirectly against God, the object of the sin against the Holy Spirit is therefore God as God, i.e., "as He is in Himself." It is not against the Holy Spirit as one of the three divine Persons, but the Holy Spirit as the representative of the Trinitarian God's supreme work of redemption. The sin against the Holy Spirit is committed against God's grace, goodness and amiableness (13, 519–20), against the very excellency of God (18, 327).[42]

This interpretation of love and hate as particular-universal contents that underlie other contents of the same order is, in the end, entirely traditional. On the other hand, Edwards is more novel in discussing the particular-universal in the realm of divine attributes or truths of the Christian religion. At the end of his treatise on *The Nature of True Virtue*, he observed that, because men have "a perception of that moral excellency," they have "that true knowledge of God, which greatly enlightens the mind in the knowledge of divine things in general" (8, 623) and the biblical formulation of "ten thousand"[43] allowed him to highlight the various moments of his reasoning regarding the relations between "the divine" and the other religious truths (see 13, 177).

Miscellany 201 speaks of things that appear real to us because we have "a clear idea of them in all their various mutual relations, concurring circumstances, order and dispositions," i.e., "the consent of the simple ideas" among themselves, "which consents and harmony consists in ten thousand little relations and mutual agreements that are ineffable" (13, 338). Of course, the thing that appears real when we understand the hidden, implicit consent of its elementary moments is religion. As we have seen, Edwards conceded that a man's idea of religion "amounted to" (i.e., equates to) his idea of God. He spoke of "the notion of God, or idea I have of Him" as identical to "that complex idea of such power, holiness, purity, majesty, love, excellency, beauty, loveliness, and ten thousand other things" (13, 177). In both of these Miscellanies, the "ten thousand" appear to be undifferentiated, particular contents at the same level and Edwards only mentions them to illustrate the huge number of elements that constitute man's idea of God. At this point, we only seem to be dealing with a multitude of particular contents that fit together and no mention is made of any one element playing a totalizing or unifying role. However, a kind of totalizing element, one that is representative of the other elements, is indeed present in Edwards's theologico-metaphysical thinking. We read in a previously cited passage from *The Mind* that the most simple kind of beauty is equality, by which one part consents

---

42. Although the persecution of Christians is an aspect of the sin against the Spirit, it is provoked by the very "excellence" of the grace that penetrates them, by their "holiness" (13, 331). See *supra*, p. 223 ss.

43. See *supra*, p. 335.

with one other. "But by proportion," Edwards added, "one part can sweetly consent to ten thousand different parts, all the parts may consent with all the rest, and . . . the parts taken singly may consent with the whole taken together.""Proportion is a moment of excellency, a herald of primary beauty in the universe of secondary beauty, and it is because of this relation to the properly spiritual that its consent is "sweet." The "ten thousand" continue to form the mass of particular contents, but the representative of beauty—proportion—appears in the role of mediator, like an "image of love" (6, 380). Lastly, two other texts prove that Edwards resolutely transcended the notion of an infinite chain, formed by the simple "mutual attraction" of contents, in favor of representing that same chain as being made from both a particular and a universal element. First of all, a passage in his *Personal Narrative* mentions a sense of "the excellent fullness of Christ" whereby He appeared to him to be "far above all, the chief of ten thousands" (16, 801). Then, in the *Treatise Concerning Religious Affections*, we find Edwards affirming Christ's holiness and moral perfection as the "amiableness and beauty of the Lord Jesus, whereby He is the chief among ten thousands" (2, 258).

Their "chief" makes mutual relations between the ten thousand others possible, and therefore it is Christ who is the source and principle of all other religious virtues. As J. Bellamy observed: "he who rightly sees God, as He has manifested Himself in the gospel, does virtually know the whole of Christianity." When we are enlightened by grace, "the whole gospel plan will naturally open to view, and appear to contain a complete system of religious sentiments, harmonious and consistent throughout, perfect in glory and beauty."[44] Bellamy seemed to want to derive all religious contents from one particular content—"God . . . manifested . . . in the gospel"—but this conclusion is not derived from it as notional content. The "God . . . manifested . . . in the gospel" must be seen rightly by a mind enlightened by grace. In other words, the particular-universal content that opens the way to understanding the various particular contents isn't used in accordance with its simple notional acceptance. We have only to recall that, according to Edwards, Christ does not sweetly mediate ten thousand relations by virtue of his natural ontological state, but according to his fullness, glory, excellency, and moral beauty.

That the dialectic underlying the notion of cordial knowledge is not a simple theoretical deduction can be shown from the examples of involvement found in Edwardsian writings. Regeneration doesn't implant a multitude of scattered graces in the heart. It only implants one: saving grace.

---

44. Bellamy, *An Essay on the Nature and Glory of the Gospel of Jesus Christ*, Works, 2:415; 275.

Because the various graces or virtues are not only attached to one another but originate from a common source and fountain, they are mutually "involved" with one another (21, 16).[45] Saving grace is essentially divine love indwelling the soul, and the first and most fundamental moment of this indwelling is the relish of divine sweetness and excellency. Once this relish has been acquired, i.e., once we love God as God, as he is in himself, everything else that belongs to divine love "naturally and necessarily proceeds" from it. "When once the soul is brought to relish the excellency of the divine nature, then it will naturally, and of course, incline to God every way" (21, 173).

Cordial union, that loving acquiescence to God's beauty and moral character, is therefore a practical, effective condition, which doesn't nonetheless prevent it from also deploying itself in terms of properly cognitive implications. The great sermon on *A Divine and Supernatural Light* explains that discovering the excellency of the divine things of religion "sanctifies" the reason, enabling it to better understand their mutual relations and apprehend the evidence of their truth (17, 414–5). The particular-universal content here is excellency which, so to speak, emanates from religious things and appears like their brilliance. However, in his *Treatise Concerning Religious Affections*, Edwards modifies and clarifies his position. It is not so much a particular quality or attribute of religious things, but a quality or reality that penetrates each one of them. They are excellent in themselves, of course, although this excellency is only theirs because they belong to the primordial reality that is their source and foundation. Attempts have always been made to better define "spiritual understanding" and Edwards said that it "consists in a sense of the heart, of the supreme beauty and sweetness of the holiness or moral perfection of divine things, together with all that discerning and knowledge of things of religion, that depends upon, and flows from such a sense" (2, 272). This concerns, of course, the excellency of divine things and Edwards observed a little further on that from the "sense of true divine beauty being given to the soul, the soul discerns the beauty of every part of the gospel scheme" (2, 302). It is this sense of the excellency of divine things that allows us to see their truth; and this excellency—we cannot repeat it enough—is not merely particular. A sort of universality, one that is implicative and not totalizing, is hidden within it. As soon as we are able "to behold the holy beauty and amiableness that is in divine things, a multitude of most important doctrines of the gospel, that depend upon it (which all appear strange and dark to natural men), are at once seen to be true." And a little further on: "Men by seeing the true excellency of holiness,

---

45. For the meaning and significance of this "involvement," see Ramsey, "Introduction," 8, 80n.4.

do see the glory of all those things, which both reason and Scripture shew to be in the Divine Being." And lastly: "And this sense of spiritual beauty ... enables the soul to see the glory of those things which the gospel reveals concerning the person of Christ" (2, 301–2). Throughout this important passage in which Jonathan Edwards reiterates the mutual interdependencies of religious truths and their common dependence on the central truth of God's holy beauty and excellency, this theologian is not developing a work of apologetics but rather promoting a position in which the rational relations between religious notions are projected and updated to the level of their active reception by faith. While the terms "notion" and "idea" were almost identical in his early Miscellanies (see 13, 177), Edwards mainly used "idea" in his mature years because the mutual involvement of religious truths only takes place at the level of an "idea," i.e., an affective content of the mind.

We cannot overemphasize the exceptional importance of the formula that designates regeneration as the divine production of something absolutely new, i.e., the presence of a new simple idea of grace in the mind. This is much more than a translation of a Calvinist *theologoumenon* into Lockean terms. Edwards explained that the human mind would never be able to conjure up this idea from within itself, nor be able—to use the language of the *Essay*—to "compose" (make) it from other ideas.[46] It can only receive and welcome it as something granted and directly infused by God. Moreover, the "simple idea" designation in no way implies that grace is a sort of meteor that falls into the mind or an indivisible spiritual atom. It is instead intended to highlight the radical homogeneity of grace and its autarky, i.e., a not being based on any composition of prior data. A simple idea is a spiritual idea and, as we saw above, a spiritual idea can and may indeed contain other ideas within it. The fact that it is not composed from other ideas does not prevent the new simple idea of grace from concealing or virtually containing other ideas within itself. After all, the object of our "faith ... this complex act of the mind" (21, 462) is our "idea of God," which is "that complex idea of such power, holiness, purity ... and ten thousand other things!" (13, 177). Represented in this way, our idea of God amounts to an extremely complex "idea of religion" (13, 338)![47]

Understanding the correspondence between a spiritual idea of God and an extremely complex idea of religion marks the high point of efforts to explain the compossibility of particular contents using a particular-universal content. We can only achieve this by means of "the new simple idea of grace." This amounts to saying that the supreme speculative notion of metaphysics

---

46. See 13, 287. See Locke, *Essay*, 2. 12. 1.
47. See *supra*, p. 364.

can only be developed from a level that, *stricto sensu*, transcends the speculative. The excellency of God, which allows us to understand compossibility, is sweetness; it is not a notional category but a spiritual idea that only a soul regenerated and renewed by grace can get. In other words, contents are only adequately subsumed under a totalizing or key content to the extent that it is spiritually apprehended. Only the subsuming of all content under the main content, i.e., the excellency of God—which is, so to speak, God as God—allows us to adequately understand compossibility. Consequently, the supposedly speculative notion of compossibility can only be deployed at the spiritual level. The contents proper to the head only truly become clear by the light of the heart. In the more sober language of the dissertation on *The Nature of True Virtue*, true knowledge, i.e., spiritual knowledge from God, enlightens the mind in the knowledge of "divine things in general" (8, 623). Spiritual knowledge assists and especially perfects notional knowledge. The end of notional knowledge is compossibility. However, according to the requirements of theistic metaphysics, God—who is this compossibility—cannot be presented as the mere sum of the contents or the logical number of their mutual relations. The idea of God must take precedence over and transcend the contents that flow from it. This transcendent primacy is based on the spiritual enlightenment that follows justification, i.e., on the new illumination that bursts into the mind, regenerates it, and makes it expand the idea of God until it seems to consist of ten thousand different ideas. And yet even this fertile transcendence, shown by the unique efficacy of the spiritual in the realm of the notional, does not result in full enlightenment. A spiritual idea of God clarifies the complex contents of religion. Now, in the final analysis, this idea is not denominated "spiritual" for the manner in which the mind receives it, but because of the object towards which it is directed. An idea of God is spiritual insofar as it is directed towards God as a spirit. However, affirming that God himself is a spirit still doesn't imply any kind of neutrality regarding his moral character. God is not spirit "in general" but as "sovereign good." Knowledge of an idea of God allows the mind to have "knowledge of . . . divine things in general. But this knowledge also gives "a sense of the importance of things of religion in general," which implies "a sensibleness of their natural good and evil" (18, 463), i.e., of natural good and evil *per se*. However, the advent of this true knowledge of God not only broadens and clarifies our theoretical knowledge of religious truths but also spiritualizes it. This true knowledge of God, as we saw earlier, is essentially an apprehension of his spiritual-moral goodness that leads to a renewed understanding of evil, not only in terms of its physical and logical structure but also its spiritual essence. Whereas a natural knowledge of evil only reveals its theoretical elements, concomitants and consequences—in a word, its "greatness"—a "sense of the spiritual excellency" of divine things allows us to discern the very essence of evil and its spiritual nature (18, 464).

In its final conclusions, Edwardsian thought shows that the compossibility of contents is only clarified and deployed by means of a particular-universal content, i.e., a spiritual idea of God, just as evil's true nature can only be understood in light of the holy beauty of God, who is goodness itself. These conclusions might lead to the consideration of a model of knowing in which the inferior is explained by the superior, or to a metaphysical interpretation of the radical primacy of religious experience with respect to all theologico-philosophical knowledge. However, the essential lesson learned from studying the work of Edwards can be formulated in another way. Critics believed they could say that Edwards had succeeded in shifting the center of gravity of theological enquiries from the doctrine of eternal decrees towards conversion or, in other words, from the transcendence of God to the interiority of the religious man. Even though the most original part of Edwardsian speculative thinking wasn't, in fact, concerned with election or reprobation—and notwithstanding phenomenological analyses that left aside efficient causes—it was no less theocentric and had the transcendence of God as its starting point on every level.

In the first note of *The Mind*, Edwards remarked that nothing really interests us more than excellency (6, 332). Excellency is only a philosophical term for God. Not the "God of the philosophers," but the one of redeeming mercy. The excellency of God, as opposed to his greatness, concerns the divinity as a communication of himself, i.e., goodness. The creature only perceives excellency insofar as his mind receives a new simple idea of grace as a result of free justification. The transcendence of God is therefore the basis of human knowledge. It is its formal cause: the "ten thousand" ideas as the true essence of evil can only be understood on seeing the excellency of God. It is also its efficient cause. We only apprehend the holy beauty of God that opens our eyes to the truth about our world because of the sovereign revelation of God's moral character in the sufficiency of Jesus Christ. The holy beauty of the Deity—primary beauty—only concerns God in Jesus Christ (*Bl.*, 165). This is ultimately why the knowledge of any theological truth only has importance for us insofar as it relates to "Christ as Mediator" (18, 53).

Conclusion

1

AMERICA HAS ALWAYS REGARDED Jonathan Edwards as the iconic figure of the Great Awakening and author of the Enfield sermon, as a bard of sweet religious affections, and as a hellfire preacher. Of course, Edwards not only celebrated religious experience, but also practiced the "critique of religious appearances."[1] Conversely, his 1741 homily spoke more about the mercy that prevents sinners from falling into the flames than about their effective damnation. In any event, rather than a simplistic and artificial opposition of sweetness and severity, it is more about discerning the duality between a theory of Pietism and orthodox Calvinist dogmatics. This duality primarily harks back to that great synthesis with which this New England thinker attempted speculative theology, namely a metaphysical reconstruction of Christian dogma. In this reconstruction, philosophy helped theology but was also, so to speak, broadened by it.

In one of his earliest surviving texts, Edwards exclaims: "How, where, and by what means may God be found?" (10, 380), and it is no exaggeration to say that the ultimate end of his writings is to find the answer to this question. His *Notes on the Bible*, *Types*, *The Mind*, Miscellanies, as well as his *Sermons and Discourses*, were but various ways to conduct this search, various paths to follow in pursuit of this quest. The question of religious experience, the discernment of true and false affections, and the complex and complicated relationship between historic-notional knowledge and spiritual knowledge were major themes of young Edwards's reflection, but they also form part of a whole in which other themes of an exegetical, dogmatic or philosophical order are perhaps even more important. This is especially

---

1. Jenson, *America's Theologian*, 12.

so where matters of religious epistemology are to be understood in light of the exegetical and dogmatic elements of this whole.

As the Awakening reclaimed the lands of American Christianity, it found in the pastor from Northampton a well-informed theoretician who knew how to read and evaluate spiritual experience in terms of Calvinist dogmatics. Pietism was a response of Christians to that century's attack on the Christian tradition. Pietists were not only opposed to Deism, Natural Religion and all those forerunners of the Enlightenment, but also had little regard for the dogmatic structure inherited from orthodoxy. Of course, Pietism did not directly or explicitly attack ecclesial dogmas, but preferred to set them aside. It celebrated spiritual experience and the Christian life, while scarcely caring about ecclesial structures and doctrines. The Pietism of Protestant Europe—of Germany, England and Holland—attests to the vitality of the Christian message in the very middle of the Enlightment, although the cost of this spiritual renewal seems to have been a devaluing and effacement of dogma. The situation in British North America was different, especially in New England, where the work of the Awakening was not accomplished at the expense of doctrine. While Awakenings continued to punctuate life in America, the emotional charge and spiritual inspiration of these seasons of fervor was assumed and articulated by Jonathan Edwards, and then by his disciples and successors, the New Divinity men and the proponents of New England Theology. The originality of American Pietism is its harmonious synthesis, on the one hand, of feeling and life, and on the other hand, of doctrine. Jonathan Edwards was the ultimate practitioner of this synthesis. His first Miscellany, titled *Of Holiness,* speaks of man's holiness; his second, *Of Christ's Mediation and Satisfaction.* His two posthumous dissertations deal respectively with *The Nature of True Virtue* and *The End for Which God Created the World.*

2

The constant interaction of piety and the Christian life with dogmatic themes is characteristic of Edwardsian thought, although not enough to adequately portray it. Rather, this interaction is itself dependent on the fundamental goal of Edwardsian thought, which was not content to simply pursue the theological discourse of orthodox Calvinism but sought to broaden it. Reformation theology was always wary of patristic and Scholastic compromises with Natural (i.e., pagan) Reason. Its fundamental desire was the proclamation and exegesis of the word. Of course, in the seventeenth and early eighteenth century, Protestant dogmaticians ultimately drew inspiration from the great Scholastic tradition's conceptual formulation of Christian doctrines. Edwards was their student and disciple, yet he also went much further than Reformed theologians like Turretin or Mastrict. Scholastics, whether Roman Catholic or Protestant, fervently devoted themselves to the metaphysical formulation of Christian theses that also appeared to be based on Natural Reason, striving to apply their distinctions even in matters of positive theology, although they would never have dreamed to think of them as metaphysical truths. The deduction of dogmas did not appear at the level of Christian Reason prior to the speculation of the post-Kantians. Once the Kantian revolution opened a way to conceptually handle a positive fact in the historical sphere, the idealists were able to rethink dogmas as metaphysical categories. From then on, the Trinity and the incarnation would be seen as the fundamental principles of reason, the keystone of great speculative systems like those of Schelling or Hegel.

Jonathan Edwards didn't have access to theories of knowledge, time and history that could have helped him deduce Christian dogmas. Notwithstanding this, he labored throughout his life on a discourse in which the mysteries of the incarnation, the Trinity, and grace were given a unique type of metaphysical formulation. This Protestant preacher studied the Bible "more than all other books,"[2] and most of his works exegete, explain, or comment on this marvellous "epistle" that "Christ . . . has written to us" (10, 477). However, he wasn't afraid to say "twenty things about the Trinity which the Scripture never said" and even ventured to declare this mystery to be within the reach of "naked reason" (13, 257)! Notwithstanding their profound sense of, and belief in, the fallen nature of our understanding, the great theologians of Christianity never tired of repeating what was revealed by means of natural reason. Edwards was one such figure, but he also wanted to go further. He wasn't satisfied with just using logic and metaphysics as a means of expressing and reformulating Christian teaching, but sought to rethink these mysteries in terms of their immanent conceptual potentialities. Edwards was convinced of the "perfect harmony between the doctrines of the Christian religion and human reason" (26, 120) and of the ultimate simularity of the truths of these two worlds (14, 231). However, he illustrates and unfolds this simularity-harmony in a reflection in which these mysteries lead to a reorientation and broadening of metaphysical conceptuality.

There has always been speculation about the theological shift that Jonathan Edwards might have sparked with *A History of the Work of Redemption*, that great work which he intended to be like a historical reformulation (*more historico*) of the entire body of Christian doctrine (16, 727–8).

---

2. Hopkins, *Life*, 40.

However, because Edwards died at Princeton before he could undertake this project, we don't really know in what sense he envisaged the intelligibility of the historical or how, prior to Hegel, he might have integrated history into theological-metaphysical conceptuality. On the other hand, we do know and can deduce how he managed to explain core Christian doctrines in metaphysical terms. We also know how he perceived an immanent metaphysical logic in and between the central doctrines of the Trinity, the incarnation, and grace that enables thinking about ethical, aesthetic and epistemological matters.

In classical Western theology, natural reason—whose ultimate intentional object is Being—cannot conceive of the Trinity. The Scholastics taught that God is Being *per se*, the Absolute Being, with perfect actuality, necessity, and unity. Originating from the descendants of Parmenides, this metaphysical theology rejected *alterity* (otherness), i.e., the possibility of any relationship within the divinity, because this would mean that *becoming* would undermine *being*. This fundamental notion of *being* or, more precisely, a fissured, inflected form of that notion, is what we find in Edwardsian thought. God is Being (6, 346), of course, though no longer the immutable present nor the perfectly immobile. God is movement, yet not crude *kinesis* but pouring forth and overflowing. The pouring forth and overflowing of this God-Being has nothing to do with the ancient notion of *becoming*, which is a primitive, random principle of change. Even though it springs from being's own essence, being is nevertheless not subject to it as if it were a destiny or necessity.

The pouring forth at the heart of Being leads to the manifestation that theology finds in and through the Son, the image of the Father. This repetition or duplication is not the advent of a duality of beings in opposition to one another, but is instead a communion of persons, an archetype, and principle for the resurgence of every complete plurality. In other words, ontology is decisively impacted by the notion of the Trinity, which provides an opening for Being without necessarily precipitating a flight or exodus. The Trinity is a central theme of Edwardsian thought, which perceives in and through it "the supreme harmony of all" (13, 329). Now if this dogma of dogmas is to permit a genuine reworking of theology and metaphysics, the kingpin notion of that operation will be the second person, the Son. Christ, the Son and Word of God, is the paradigm of all repetitions/duplications and manifestations. He is also the conceptual outcome of a metaphysic that managed to think of something new without subjecting it to becoming. It is by the light of Christ's historic coming that theology and philosophy will be brought to restate the positivity of evil, rethink beauty, stake out a new epistemology, and recast "the science of the will."

As the primary repetition/duplication, the Son opens up hitherto unknown metaphysical dimensions of newness and beauty. Classical ontology didn't care for newness—which it subsumed under the condemned becoming—nor was it able to think of beauty in terms of its originarity and metaphysical autarchy. With its metaphysical interpretation of the *theologoumenon* of the incarnate Son, Edwardsian thought set being free from confinement within self and began reflecting deeply on the specific intelligibility of the beautiful.

The pouring forth perfected in repetition/duplication is the metaphysical expression of everything new that comes, but before dealing with newness, Edwards prepared the ground for it by rethinking classical ontology. He borrowed the notion of actuality—a synonym for being—from the Aristotelian tradition, yet redirected it to mean an act whose accomplishment is announced in an entirely dynamic way. In contrast to idle, ontological quietisms, this speculation disassociates immobility and rest, inaction, and perfect happiness (17, 258). True perfection is not a particular state that is acquired forever, nor does it extinguish desire. Someone who finds Christ will still yearn to continue to "possess" him in ever-greater measure. Nevertheless, such yearning is not a desire for change (17, 136). The act exists as actualization which, in turn, implies enrichment and depth. While the theologian-philosopher couldn't overemphasize the "growing" state of our knowledge and joys, this growth isn't an alteration. Edwards succeeded in going beyond the ontological vision of an immobile perfection, of a self-enclosed actuality, although not at the cost of absorbing becoming in being, i.e., of slipping towards a monistic metaphysic. Action and increase are integrated within being to the same extent that being is perceived to yearn for expression. Expression, which is being's true life, is communion. Classic Western metaphysics has always wanted to identify being with good. Jonathan Edwards himself conceived of their identity in terms of this movement of expression, of self-diffusion leading to another's position. First, an eternal, immanent other: the Son, the image of the Father; then an external, finite other: the creature.

God created the world by his Word, and even though nature obeys perfectly rational laws and is ruled by necessity, it is no less the fruit of divine goodness, which is not motivated by anything pre-existent (8, 542). Moreover, having been created *ex nihilo*, the world continues in subjection to the sovereign power of the creator. The resistance of bodies that constitutes matter is an "immediate exercise of God's power" (6, 215). Nature's being and order are dependent on the free work of continuous creation. The continuous maintenance of the identity of all beings—including that of man, a rational creature—hangs on the will of God (3, 400–402). The entire universe remains "in absolute dependance" upon the creator whose unlimited sovereignty isn't confined to the created world but also extends, of course, to the universe of grace. God is the absolute master of the grace he freely bestows: election is free, and even man's perseverence in the grace received depends entirely on God, the giver of grace.

The pouring forth or repetition/duplication represented by the coming of the Son, his trinitarian generation, is being-act metaphysically expressed as desire and increase, although only arising from creation, i.e., from an "immediate" relationship with other living things. To better express the mystery of something new that doesn't involve change, Edwards thought deeply about the Son's state as the image of the Father. The Son is the image of the Father, but not as a separate copy or reflection falling outside of him. He is "the brightness of his Father" (*Bl.*, 157), his "beauty" (22, 294). Brightness and beauty are "a plus" that add nothing to a being, but nevertheless renew how it is in reality. The Son "repeats" the Father or, in a manner of speaking, shows us a new order of the Divinity. The new order established by the Son not only concerns the order of existence but also that of essence. One traditional view was content to read the Old Testament as a universe of strength, majesty and severity, with the New Testament as one of love and gentleness. Although this portrayal of Scripture is only a very general one, it nonetheless conveys an important truth. Theology teaches that, in the Son—who is the Father's brightness and excellence—God is other than in the Father. This *theologoumenon* has decisive significance in philosophy, inspiring a new view of being. The ontological unlocking practiced in the Edwardsian discourse didn't just lead to the essential breakthrough where becoming was transposed into pouring forth. Going beyond Parmenides wasn't just a matter of including alterity in being, but also meant the appearance or revelation of a new metaphysical condition. Indeed, all of this newness of existence and essence only finds ultimate fulfillment in the testing of the newness who is the incarnation of the redeemer, the answer to another newness, sin.

3

The incarnation is possible because of the metaphysical logic of pouring forth. This fact—the coming of the Son in the flesh—is, in a manner of speaking, the matching half of another fact, that of original sin. Edwards wrote a treatise on *The Great Christian Doctrine of Original Sin Defended*, a theory he considered "agreeable" to human experience (23, 61). He believed it possible to discern "the natural blindness, in which all men are enveloped"

(20, 250) and "man's natural emnity against God" (10, 455). This Calvinist theologian vigorously proclaimed the positivity of evil. Evil is not just an absence or deficiency, i.e., non-being, but something "worse than nothingness"; not just an imperfection, but a radical opposition to good. Sinners are totally depraved because of their roots, something which should be understood in a literal sense. Original sin is hereditary and everyone is subject to it from birth, i.e., we ourselves don't choose it but rather inherit it. We inherit it by virtue of a sovereign decree of God that constitutes our identity in continuity with our ancestor. Edwards performed feats of dialetical prowess to demonstrate that the decisions we take by virtue of our relationship to Adam—one that we ourselves did not choose—are nonetheless genuinely our decisions. The ultimate end of this line of argument was to establish man's entire responsibility for a condition to which he is subject because of a prior, external determination of God. By using paradoxes in his rebuttal of "moral sincerity," Edwards managed to present a doctrine in which the truth of the will is reduced to its effective act of volition. The will's goodness or wickedness doesn't depend on whether or not external or prior causal factors determined its condition. When willing in continuity with Adam, and as Adam willed, man's will is as guilty as that of his ancestor. The truth of the will has nothing to do with what might have led it to will as it wants; it is simply a question of its present, effective will.

The metaphysical defence for the doctrine of original sin starts out with the conceptual notion of an attack on causal determination and ends up by reducing the will to its present volition, i.e., intention. This Calvinist theologian worked to demonstrate the plausability and truth of a position where the native heteronomy of our moral actions is not only compatible with our autonomy but even becomes one of its conceptual assumptions. Augustine's heirs constantly struggled with the paradoxes of a dogmatic which, notwithstanding the material goodness of actions, judged them as pernicious when performed by the unjustified. A theory of this sort seemed to dissociate the good and evil of a moral action itself, only to then read and evaluate it according to a criterion established by an external force, namely the will of God. Edwards himself brilliantly professed this position and the theses that flow from it, although he reinterpreted it from the perspective of his theory of the will. Although our justified state was certainly constituted by God, its corresponding moral will is nonetheless ours. Conversely, the fallen state of those outside the grace of election is determined by the divine constitution of their union with their ancestor. They continue to will in and with Adam and therefore can only will evil. Though determined towards evil, this will nonetheless remains that of its agent. It may spur acts that are useful or praiseworthy, yet none that are morally good.

In essence, the Edwardsian position can be summarized by this thesis: the materially good acts of the unjustified are, in reality, evil. The virtues of heathens are only "splendid sins" (2, 316n.6), the good works of the unjustified only hidden transgressions. The moral truth of an action or conduct depends on the will of its agent and, without God's grace, a creature's will can only be evil. What fifteen centuries of anti-Augustinian criticism had regarded as particularly virulent manifestations of theological heteronomy, this American thinker explained in terms of a theory of intention. This absolutely sovereign, autonomous intention does not depend on any external or prior circumstance or condition. This reduction *ad absurdum* of the wilful person's essence doesn't just take account of the metaphysical logic that underpins forensic justification, but ultimately appears to become the keystone of the entire Edwardsian ethical and metaphysical theory.

Edwards designed Christ as "the beauty of God" and historiography has always emphasized the extreme importance of this aesthetic vision of the good and the spiritual. For the young preacher, "holiness ... is the highest beauty that shines in the creation" (10, 423). This theoretician of "religious affections" didn't hesitate to state that "God is god, and distinguished from all other beings ... chiefly by his divine beauty" (2, 298). "The missionary to Stockbridge" gave this reminder to his Indian congregation: a good man must "love God above all for his own beauty."[3] This conception has metaphysical logic, yet the beauty of which he speaks is merely a transcendental of Scholastic philosophy. It can only be imagined in terms of a dualism. Now, if the first outcome of this dualism is the trinitarian repetition/duplication, the rift that sin brought into the world is also one of its founding moments. The principle and root of all beauty is well and truly the trinitarian God; and even an elementary analysis would differentiate the *Pulchritude* (23, 659) into primary beauty and secondary beauty. Distinguishing between these two beauties is a matter of the mind discerning what can only be explained by epistemological considerations that, in turn, are dependant on an understanding of duality characterized by sin and redemption.

Jonathan Edwards constrasted secondary beauty with primary beauty. Secondary beauty is the beauty of equality, of proportion, of harmony between faces and things, i.e., realities of a natural order. Primary beauty is only seen in actions and intentions or, more precisely, in actions and intentions that conform to, and are inspired by, the moral-religious order, namely by love for God in Jesus Christ. Secondary beauty emanates from the world's structures; primary beauty is the halo of authentically virtuous actions. The

---

3. *Lecture before the sacrement, Ms.* in McDermott, *Edwards Confronts the Gods*, 201.

beauty of proportions and harmonies certainly inspires, yet all minds—independently of their moral condition—can experience it. On the other hand, to experience sweetness in the face of true virtue, it is not enough to determine an action's "objective" conformity to God's law; the soul itself also has to share that state. Beauty, Edwards said, is a matter of consent. In secondary beauty, there is consent between structures; in primary beauty, between intentions. An action has true moral beauty when the intention of its agent agrees with another intention—that of our God and saviour—and only a soul that lovingly consents with another soul really perceives this moral beauty. In other words, to see the moral beauty of another being, we ourselves have to be morally beautiful.

Edwardsian ethics and epistemology can justly be characterized as aesthetic, although the term "aesthetic" in this context doesn't connote any artistic experience or attitude of moral non-engagement. Although the sweetness that accompanies the perception of excellence and the taste of primary beauty that spiritual knowledge discerns certainly denote a quality or a psychological factor of a cognitive operation, they particularly indicate the existential state of the mind. When going about its job of perceiving, the mind tends to assume the mode of being of its object. This American thinker seemed to announce some very original things, and yet, in the final analysis, his aesthetic is just an admirable variant of an ancient doctrine that defined truth as the mind conforming to something. Only the benevolent soul can know benevolence because getting to the truth of something requires conformity to it. Having real knowledge means "to realize a thing" (see 14, 201–3), and repetition/duplication is true realization. The central notion of Edwardsian epistemology is that of a spiritual idea. Now, a spiritual idea is not a distant approximation, summary draft or schema but a true double of its original. The Son is like the repetition/duplication of the Father, his adequate image; and this image is adequate because the very being of the Son is loving consent to the Father.

A spiritual idea is proper knowledge through taste, the aesthetic perception of an object. The conformity that alone permits an understanding of sense and moral truth is also the key to full knowledge, to a knowledge of compossibility. Spiritual knowledge is like the vision of a man walking in a garden bathed in light, glancing from tree to neighbouring tree and then to more distant trees, without discontinuity, or without being stopped or interrupted by opaqueness or obscurity (13, 470). A spiritual idea of an object is a true copy, its authentic presentification: it makes everything that is in the object appear and reveals the object like the beginning of a road that leads to other objects. In other words, spiritual knowledge is, properly speaking, intuitive and sees its object in itself. Now, an object "in itself" isn't an isolated structure enclosed within itself but rather a moment of a whole that allows the deployment of that whole.

The theory of compossibility as a metaphysical-epistemological thesis is only implicit in Edwardsian discourse, yet explicitly stated and expounded in ethics and theology. Only a benevolent soul can discern benevolence, which is only one virtue among others. Edwards wrote that "all the virtues are derived from pure benevolence" (21, 326n.6) and "charity is the sum of all saving virtue" (15, 277). Love is the moral principle from which the other moral principles flow in a clear, obvious way. The ancient thesis of the unity of virtue—reworked by Christian theology—therefore finds itself confirmed by epistemological-metaphysical considerations, while analogous considerations also lead to an attempt at systematic theology. The justified who consents to Christ as his savior, also adheres to all the articles of the Christian faith. These articles are not isolated lights. They are all taught by, and relate to, the Son. Those who trust in the Son by theoretical faith alone do not recognize the mutual harmony between these articles, namely their organic dependence on the principle of our salvation. On the other hand, faith which is cordial consent to the savior will make all of these themes and theses appear as implied by the primordial truth it embodies.

4

Edwards wrote throughout his life and his immense body of work covers many areas of theology and philosophy. So what are the enduring results of his work? What actual "benefit" has been gained from this work of over 100,000 handwritten pages? Having attempted to reconstruct the essential moments of Edwards's thought according to its own logic, we ought to consider his core contribution to the history of thought. Aside from Franklin, Jonathan Edwards was certainly the most important intellectual figure of colonial America. Many consider him to be one of the most profound English-speaking thinkers of all time, and another Protestant theologian of his calibre was scarcely seen in the entire eighteenth century. So what did Edwards contribute to theology and philosophy? What ideas, themes and theses make us want to read and study him?

Talking about results or new contributions isn't necessarily the best way to evaluate accomplishments in theology and metaphysics. In theology, it is more a matter of restating what has been revealed in order to bring out its hidden implications. As for metaphysics, if a thinker presents something new, it will certainly not be because of a more insightful demonstration of those themes than what his predecessors gave. Such cautions are especially appropriate for a writer who is a theologian-philosopher or philosopher-theologian, i.e., one who uses philosophy to shed light on hidden meanings in doctrines or, conversely, who enriches conceptual metaphysics by applying theology to themes that are proper to philosophy.

Meditating on the doctrine of the Trinity gave this American thinker unprecedented ontological perspectives. A doctrine of being that rescued becoming and succeeded in reconciling eternity and newness. A vision of the divinity, quite unlike that which shows it as self-diffusion but with goodness as the truth of that diffusiveness. The role played by that other fundamental Christian mystery—Jesus Christ, Son and Word—is perhaps even more important in the treatises, Miscellanies and sermons than that of the Trinity. While Jonathan Edwards undoubtedly never tried to reformulate christological doctrines, his work nonetheless appears to be an authentic Christology. The theologian from Stockbridge who brought to mind and brilliantly expressed the great intuitions of Christian dogmatics to "defend [the doctrine of] the proper deity of Christ" (16, 699) nonetheless used an innovative apologetic that deepened our understanding of the role of the Second Person within the life of the Trinity and re-centered our piety on the one who is "the darling of heaven"(14, 417). Aside from its purely theological riches, this Christology is also exceptionally rich in metaphysics. The Son, who is the image of the Father, becomes the powerful paradigm of the great "duplications" proper to Edwardsian thought: natural beauty and moral beauty, the notional concept and the spiritual idea.

These Edwardsian duplications are original and profoundly philosophical statements and *theologomena*, although they ultimately point beyond themselves to a renewal of metaphysical knowledge. Primary beauty and spiritual ideas are discerned or grasped by noetic operations accompanying the sense of sweetness which not only analyze their objects as concepts but also capture their taste and discern what is morally or spiritually abhorrent or aimiable in them. This knowledge though taste—this realizing grasp—is like the preliminary outline of a doctrine of aesthetic-moral reason. Here Edwards is aligning himself with those thinkers of his century who anticipated Kantism by elevating sense and taste as principles of knowledge, i.e., by giving non-theoretical ways of knowing and making sense of things their rightful place. Although the doctrine of aesthetic-moral reason, which emerges from a very diverse range of his writings, might well have been how Jonathan Edwards announced the renewal of metaphysics that would fulfill Kantian idealism, it was ultimately with his "science of the will" (1, 133) that he brought about a conceptual revolution. The *sui generis* metaphysical outcome and message of Kantian teaching on practical reason was the radical autonomy of the will, a faculty with irrevocable principles and laws that are proper to the structures of theoretical reason. The phenomenological setting aside by Edwards of any external or prior determination underlined the perfect homogeneity of the will and therefore, like the German philosopher, its *sui generis* intelligibility. A great number of readers and exegetes have identified the American thinker's greatest accomplishment as the "science of the will," which he essentially developed within the strict limits of philosophical argument. And yet, the genesis of the *Enquiry* is well and truly theological, since it is also "a defense of the great Christian doctrine of original sin."

There are innumerable examples of the interpenetration of philosophy and theology in the *Treatises* and Miscellanies, in the *Sermons and Discourses*—far too many, in fact, for them to be listed. They would only serve to illustrate and confirm the lesson that seems to emerge from studying Edwards's thought, namely that philosophy and religion cannot be separated, read and understood in isolation from one another. Someone interested in his dogmatics or analysis of religious experience can scarcely separate the philosophy from his theological developments. Conversely, how can we understand his philosophical issues if we skip over their theological context? Philosophy and religion are definitely different paths to the truth and may well target different intentional objects. The work of Jonathan Edwards, "that moral Newton, and that second Paul,"[4] eloquently attests to that fact that these two discourses are inseparable.

---

4. Dwight, *Triumph of Infidelity*, 22.

Appendix 1

Can Man Wish to be Damned?

Jonathan Edwards's reflection is the source of a theology that, in a belated and quasi-unconscious manner, harkens back to the quietist challenge to accept and desire our own damnation,[1] an idea addressed by a great many studies over the centuries. The source of this speculation is a statement by the Apostle Paul: "For I could wish that I myself were accursed and cut off from Christ for the sake of my brethren, my kinsmen by race" (Rom. 9:3). This Pauline passage was interpreted to imply that, with respect to their salvation, believers could opt to separate from Jesus Christ. Its theological corollary is a hypothetical dissociation between man's happiness and his knowledge and love for God. Clement of Alexandria taught that if eternal salvation and the knowledge of God were at all separable, the Gnostic would choose knowledge (*gnosis*), "deeming that property of faith, which from love ascends to knowledge, desirable, for its own sake."[2] Saint Augustine would later reformulate this idea in another style: "And if, God forbid, there seems no hope of this great boon, we should still prefer to remain in the turmoil of these battles."[3] Now, what appears here in the form of a simple school hypothesis would have even more real implications, i.e., which would challenge a servile fear of hell.[4] "The pious mind," wrote Calvin, "guarding, with the utmost diligence, against transgressing . . . not [by] the mere fear of punishment," but would honor God "although there

---

1. Post, *Christian Love and Self-Denial.*
2. Clement of Alexandria, "The Miscellanies," 4. 22.
3. Saint Augustine, *City of God*, 21. 15.
4. See *supra*, p. 211.

were no hell."⁵ Of course, this still doesn't mean that filial love for the Father implies an effective willingness to separate from him. Rather, punishment in hell is set aside as a motive for Christian obedience and seeking God remains inseparable from the desire for blessing.⁶ However, the development of Christian religious sentiment pushed writers towards sharper, more dramatic formulations: "God's good pleasure is the supreme object of the indifferent soul," wrote Saint Francis de Sales, which "would prefer hell with God's will to paradise without God's will. . . . Therefore, to imagine something impossible, if the soul knew that damnation would be a little more pleasing to God than salvation, it would forsake salvation and run after its own damnation."⁷ As for nascent Protestantism, Luther—under Tauler's influence—advocated *resignatio ad infernum*,⁸ declaring that Christ wouldn't want to be the savior of those who weren't ready to be damned for him.⁹ Yet these are essentially pathetic expressions of a spirituality of tension and paradox, not proper doctrinal positions.¹⁰ Nonetheless, the Calvinist-Puritan tradition seems to have intermittently developed along these lines. Thomas Hooker thought that man should serenely accept damnation if God so decrees it for his greater glory¹¹ and Thomas Shepard wrote that even the

---

5. Calvin, *Institutes*, 1. 2. 2. A man with a true love for God would not want to enter heaven if that were not the will of God, because he does good "nitt auss lautter furcht des todts odder helle, und auch nitt auss geniess des hymells, sondern auss freyem geyst, lust und liebe der gerechtigkeyt [not through fear of death or Hell, or for the sake of enjoying Heaven, but through a free spirit, a desire and love for righteousness]" (Luther, *Kirchenpostille*, Werke, 10. 1. 1. 453). Such a man wills and does good "as if there were neither Heaven nor Hell," (Perkins, *A Treatise of God's Free Grace and Man's Free Will*, Workes, 1:730, 746).

6. Calvin, *Commentarius in Epistolam Pauli ad Romanos*, Opera, 49, 34.

7. Saint Francis de Sales, *On the Love of God*, 9. 4. It is not proposed to elaborate further on this topic, which has a rich historiography, especially for the French School. For a complete history of its place in Christian thought, refer to the excellent article, "Charité," *Dictionnaire de Spiritualité Chrétienne*, 2:530–691.

8. Luther, *Epistola ad Romanos*, Werke, 56:88; see Gandillac, *Valeur du temps dans la pédagogie spirituelle de Jean Tauler*, 74–75.

9. Luther, *Epistola ad Romanos*, Werke, 56:303.

10. For an interpretation of Luther's position, see Iwand, *Rechtfertigungslehre und Christusglaube*, 29–30.

11. Hooker, *Soules Vocation*, 212, in Levy, *Preaching in New England*, 31–32. A very different formulation of this question—one in which the consent to his own damnation is stated in a non-dogmatic manner—is found in J. Bunyan: "I was bound, but he was free: yea, it was my dutie to stand to his Word, whether he would ever look upon me or no ... *if* God doth not come in, thought I, I will leap *off* the Ladder even blindfold into Eternitie, sink or swim, come heaven, come hell, Lord Jesus, if thou will catch me, do; if not, I will venture for thy Name," (*Grace Abounding*, 103).

wicked will bless the Lord who sent them to hell.[12] All of this, however, is but a prelude of sorts to the teaching of Samuel Hopkins.

Hopkins dramatically denounced the sordid egoism of those who cannot rejoice in the glory of God without being certain of their own happiness. Instead of considering whether their own personal interest is secure or not, Hopkins exhorted believers to realize that God, who knows how to bring all things to an end, will save everyone who can be saved for "the greatest happiness of His church . . . without considering your own personal interest, whether this is secure or not."[13] On the contrary, when a man has a "benevolent" heart, even "if he could know that God designed, for his own glory and the general good, to cast him into endless destruction, this would not make him cease to approve of his character; he would continue to be a friend of God, and to be pleased with his moral perfection."[14] It's in his *Dialogue between a Calvinist and a Semi-Calvinist* that Hopkins fully develops this doctrine. It would certainly be inadmissible to suppose that anyone might desire damnation to be eternally miserable. On the other hand, and although it would be a horrible evil, someone might accept it to avoid an even greater evil. Better one man endure even eternal suffering than that a multitude should suffer. Likewise, if the glory of God and the universal good require it, a man ought to be able to desire his own damnation. If the Apostle Paul could desire to be accursed for his brothers, then a Christian who, in any event, "is seeking more important objects and events than his own salvation"[15] can desire to be damned for others. Knowing that the glory of God requires the damnation of certain creatures, we cannot but consent to this. Because there is no essential difference between myself and others, there is therefore no reason why I cannot or should not consent to my ultimate damnation.[16] This doctrine "shocks" and "perplexes" the Semi-Calvinist, yet the Calvinist ultimately shows him that sincerely accepting his damnation is not only a way to avoid a greater evil but also the way to accomplish the greatest good. Man can only be saved if he does the will of

---

12. Shepard, *The Parable of the Ten Virgins, Works*, 2:338.

13. Hopkins, *Two Sermons, Works*, 3:739-40. In any event, as Emmons said, "If I never get to heaven, others will" (Park, *Memoir of Nathanael Emmons*, 401).

14. Hopkins, *System of Doctrines, Works*, 1:389; see also "If God does not love sinners before they love Him, then they must love Him, while they know that He hates them, and is disposed to punish them forever" (Emmons, *Works*, 6:465).

15. Hopkins, *System of Doctrines, Works*, 1:533.

16. Hopkins, *A Dialogue between a Calvinist and a Semi-Calvinist, Works*, 3:143-44. In a Romantic version of the Hopkinsian theory, Mary, a heroine of Harriet Beecher-Stowe, responded to the idea "of suffering eternal pains for the glory of God and the good of being in general . . . with a sort of sublime thrill" (*Minister's Wooing*, 25).

God, and if this will entails my damnation, I must accept it, precisely in order not to be damned. Inasmuch as a man accepts his abandonment to sin and misery—if that is God's will—he cannot effectively be abandoned to it. However, the moment when, in a sudden burst of self-love, he refuses such consent, he will find himself abandoned. Expressed in the impoverished, stereotypical language of this Newport minister, this supreme, Kierkegaardian paradox is simply this: "No man can know that he loves God until he does really love him; that is, until he . . . is disposed to say, 'Let God be glorified, whatever may be necessary in order to it,' . . . and this is to be willing to be damned, if this be necessary for the glory of God. And as he cannot know that he loves God till he has this disposition, which is necessarily implied in love to God, he does not know that it is not necessary for the glory of God that he should be damned. He therefore cannot know that he loves God, and shall be saved, until he knows he has this disposition which implies a willingness to be damned, if it be not most for the glory of God that he should be saved."[17]

As an Edwardsian, Hopkins believed that he had to profess this doctrine, yet Jonathan Edwards himself had never subscribed to it.[18] Unlike Hopkins, whose theory of benevolent love led posterity to discern "a striking resemblance" between him and Fénelon,[19] Edwards, a metaphysician with a "hedonist" morality, was more in the line of Bossuet or Malebranche.[20] During the great "harvest" in Northampton, Edwards—for whom a true

---

17. Hopkins, *A Dialogue between a Calvinist and a Semi-Calvinist*, Works, 3:148. See also "by self-renouncement a heaven of which he [i.e., man] had no conceptions, begins at once in his heart" (McGiffert, *Young Emerson Speaks*, 210). For the dialectic and paradoxes of the Hopkinsian theory, see Breitenbach, "Unregenerate Doings," 479–502.

18. In *Resolutions* from his youth, Edwards advocated the performance of duty independently of heaven and hell (16, 797), but his mature thought emphasized the fact that "the saints love their own happiness" (8, 254). During highly religious experiences, Sarah Edwards felt "a holy indifference" for the rage of devils (*Dw.*, I, 173) and was ready to die "in darkness and horror" for the glory of God (*Dw.*, I, 181) or live "a thousand years an hell," albeit a hell "on earth" (*Dw.*, I, 182). Jonathan Edwards summarized the condition of his spouse as "a willingness to suffer the hidings of God's face" (4, 337) and not as an acceptance of her damnation. The converts in Northampton, for their part, would frequently just forget to rejoice in their deliverance from the perils of hell (4, 183). However, it should be noted that, in his edition of Brainerd's diary, Edwards deleted the passages that spoke of Brainerd's refusing to accept his damnation (7, 125–27).

19. Park, *Samuel Hopkins*, 21, in Hopkins, *Works*, vol 1.

20. Edwards also had numerous predecessors from the Puritan tradition. For example, S. Willard rejected the possibility of accepting his own condemnation because he thought that, without the "means" to pursue proper happiness, the glorification of God could not be "an effective end" of man (*Divinity*, 4). For S. Stoddard, such acceptance was quite simply incompatible with self-love (*Guide to Christ*, 64–65).

Christian is "a mortal enemy" to his own sins (19, 688)—certainly wrote in his *Faithful Narrative* that "some have declared themselves to be in the hands of God" so that God may glorify himself in their damnation. He also mentioned how some of his parishioners were ready to think that if they are damned, they could take part with God against themselves; and they experienced a kind of indignation against themselves, almost "a willingness to be damned" (4, 170). In a preparatory notebook for his *Treatise Concerning Religious Affections*, Edwards noted that "the great Mr. Hooker and Mr. Shepard supposed it absolutely necessary that there should be a work of the Spirit making men willing to be damned."[21] He made no comments on his observations in Northampton, however, and the opinions of Hooker and Shepard were not reproduced in the *Treatise Concerning Religious Affections* itself. In fact, long before the "harvest" in Northampton, Edwards resolved this problem in terms of and by means of his metaphysical doctrine of love.

Edwards questioned whether God's love could arise in a heart without self-love and answered this question by making a number of distinctions. Taken in the most extensive sense of that term, self-love is only a capacity of enjoyment. It hardly makes sense to state that a man's love to God is superior to his self-love. Love to God means to desire and delight in God's good, and yet a man's delight in God's good cannot be superior to his love to delight in general. Starting from this observation, we can say that self-love is a man's love to his own good in two senses: (1) any good whatsoever that a man enjoys may be said to be his own good and it is impossible that a man should delight in any good that is not his own. In this sense, love to God can be superior to self-love. (2) a person's good may be said to be his own good, which is proper to him and separate from the general good. In this sense, and in this sense only, love to God can and ought to be superior to self-love (18, 73-4). Edwards also distinguished a "simple self-love arising from the nature of a perceiving willing being," and a "compounded self-love" exercised in the delight that a man has in the good of another. Compounded self-love also arises from the nature of a perceiving being who, insofar as he is perceiving, finds himself united to another being, so that the good of that other being becomes his own. In this sense, self-love may imply love to

---

21. *Ms.* A separation between our love of God and desire for happiness amounts to a separation of our knowledge of God and desire for God. This distinction seems theoretically possible in Edwardsian theology, with its vigorous contrast between a purely notional knowledge of God and an affective and effective knowledge of God. In reality, however, it is nothing of the sort. Notional knowledge is proper to natural, fallen man who, deprived of that taste for God which only justifying grace can impart, cannot submit and abandon himself to the will of God. Presuming that anyone is capable of selfless love for God without his redeeming grace, moreover, amounts to pure Pelagianism. See Montcheuil, *Malebranche et le quiétisme*, 309.

God, although here we understand the logical impossibility for any person to be perfectly and finally miserable for God's sake. It may be possible, that a man may be willing to be deprived of all his own separate good for God's sake; but then he is not perfectly miserable because he takes greater delight in God's good, for the sake of which he parts with his own, than he did in his own. He has greater delight in what is obtained than in what was lost; in reality, he has only exchanged a lesser joy for a greater. But if a man is willing to be perfectly miserable for God, he should be willing to part with all his own separate good and even with that which is indirectly his own, i.e., God's good. This requirement is inconsistent with itself, "for to be willing to be deprived of this latter sort of good is opposite to that principle of love to God itself, from whence such a willingness is supposed to arise." In conclusion, if love to God is superior to any other principle of our soul, then it will make it absolutely impossible for us to be deprived of this part of our happiness, which we have "in God's being blessed and glorified" (18, 75).

Appendix 2

Saints and Damned

Edwardsian theology seeks to justify the damnation of the wicked. Damnation is not merely plausible but, in a certain way, also necessary and even contributes to the glory of God. What then is God's attitude towards those he damns and how do the blessed relate to the damned? God and his blessed ones, both angels and men, possess immaculate charity and yet because God—and therefore God's good—is the object of love, it cannot extend to God's enemies. God loves Judas with benevolence but not with complacence.[1] Now, such benevolence "will give a particular weight and pungency to the punishment of the finally impenitent."[2] And, generally speaking, God's hatred of the wicked "is not only consistent with His benevolence towards them, but necessarily flows from it."[3] If this is so, there is no reason to suppose that God will have pity on the damned; and Samuel Willard went so far as to say that "He will laugh at their calamity."[4] As for the elect creatures, it would be criminal on their part to have compassion on those whom the Lord has so justly condemned.[5] To love God's enemies means to oppose him,[6] which is why the misfortunate inhabitants of hell cannot expect any compassion, not even from their next of kin on Earth. The most popular poem in New England sings soberly of the terrible rejection of the damned by their spouses and parents:

1. Emmons, *The Plea of Sinners against Endless Punishment*, *Works*, 5:595. For love of benevolence and love of complacence, see *supra*, p. 353.
2. Emmons, *God's Hatred of Sinners*, *Works*, 6:121.
3. Emmons, *The Death of Sinners Not Pleasing to God*, *Works*, 6:68.
4. Willard, *Divinity*, 241.
5. See Dante, *Inferno*, 20.29–30.
6. Norris, *Theory and Resolution of Love*, 120, in Walker, *Decline of Hell*, 32n.1.

> The godly wife conceives no grief
> nor can she shed a tear
> for the sad state of her dear Mate
> when she his doom doth hear. . . .
>
> The tender Mother will own no other
> of all her numerous brood
> But such as stand at Christ's right hand
> acquitted through his Blood.
> The pious Father had now much rather
> his graceless Son should lie
> In Hell with Devils, for all his evils,
> burning eternally.

And the poet continues:

> The Saints behold with courage bold,
> and thankful wonderment,
> To see all those that were their foes
> Thus sent to punishment[7]

As for Edwards, he would return to this theme throughout his works. His doctrinal point of departure was that, in Scripture, "the works of God's vindictive justice and wrath are spoken of as works of mercy to his people" (8, 509). He thought that hatred has "no inconsiderable part of true religion" and quoted the Psalmist: "Do I not hate them, O Lord, that hate thee?" (Ps 139:21 in 2, 104). Edwards taught that "the view of the misery of the damned will double the ardor of the love and gratitude of the saints in Heaven" (VII, 480).[8] He sees "the glorious inhabitants" of paradise "fall down and adore that great power and majesty" of God when they behold the suffering of the damned (22, 415)—those manifestations of wrath that will increase their sense of God's love for them (20, 513)—and hears the heavens resound with the praise of God's justice (VI, 543). In a sermon from the 1730s, *The End of the Wicked Contemplated by the Righteous; Or the Torments of the Wicked in Hell, No Occasion of Grief to the Saints in Heaven*, Edwards returned to a well-known theme: the total absence of pity felt by pious parents faced with the terrible fate of their children. And he went one step further. Even faithful pastors would themselves turn against their

---

7. Wigglesworth, *Day of Doom*, 58–59, 64. The echoes of this *theologoumenon* continued into the twentieth century: "watching the contortions of the damned is supposed to be a favourite sport of the angels" (Wharton, *Age of Innocence*, 140).

8. See also 13, 379. The eternal damnation of the wicked serves "the happiness of God's people" (8, 509). Conversely, contemplating the happiness of the blessed aggravates the suffering of the damned (10, 321).

former parishioners and, as Edwards was speaking in Northampton, he felt constrained to warn his hearers with these words: "Consider ye that have lived under Mr. Stoddard's ministry. . . . How dreadfull it will be to you when you shall see him . . . that was so tenderly Concernd for the Good of your souls . . . Rising up in Judgmt against you" (IV, 518–9).

What does this doctrine, which one nineteenth century Anglican writer termed "an abominable fancy," actually say?[9] First of all, some clarification is needed. The saved are not called to rejoice in "having their revenge glutted" but to understand and rejoice in "the justice of God executed." The joy of the blessed is not motivated by the sufferings of the damned, nor do they take pleasure in their misfortune "for its own sake" (IV, 509–10).[10] The reactions of the saints to the fate of the damned are not due to contingent feelings, but are to be understood in terms of their submission to the will of God. Edwards begins by explaining that, while we are on earth, we must love our neighbors, including those who appear to us to be inveterate sinners, but the situation changes in the next world. The two worlds of heaven and hell are mutually transparent and the saints clearly see and understand the judgment of the damned (IV, 507).[11] "Then there will be No remaining difficulties . . . Pertaining to God's dispensations towards men . . . but Gods Justice then in the destruction of the wicked will appear then As Light without darkness" (IV, 510). This is no mere factual understanding of the guilt of the wicked, but "a more lively apprehension of the evil of sin" that allows the blessed to consent to the afflictions of the damned (18, 101)

---

9. Farrar, *Eternal Hope*, 61, in Walker, *Decline of Hell*, 31. The source of this *theologoumenon* is Tertullian (*Of Public Shows*, 30), whose teaching is brought up in, among others, Gibbon, *Decline and Fall*, vol. 2, cap. 15. 34, and Nietzsche, *Genealogy of Morality*, 1. 15 [indicating essay and section]. The critics of Edwardsian theology frequently targeted the profession of this doctrine, but as J. DeWitt once remarked, Dante wasn't reproached for it (*Jonathan Edwards: a Study*, 107).

10. Edwards did not approve of this suffering as good in itself, but simply accepted it as a seeming reality of the "constitution wherewith God governs the world" (Haroutunian, *Piety versus Moralism*, 44). It is the vindicating character of divine justice—not the punishment—that we ought to love (Bellamy, *A Careful and Strict Examination of the External Covenant, Works*, 3:325). See also S. Finley, "They who are so highly delighted with the dreadful Executions of divine Justice, are not turbulent, cruel and revengeful Spirits, but Saints and Angels . . . Justice has an inexpressible Excellency, and a most charming *Beauty* to *upright Minds*. To be pleased with its executions *is* only to be pleased, that things are as they ought to be" (*Curse of Meroz*, 20, in Heimert, *Religion and the American Mind*, 337).

11. The pleasure and joy which the blessed experience on seeing the torments of the damned obeys an immanent logic. If the punishment of the wicked wasn't "agreeable to this sight and sense they have of God's glory, and the evil of sin, there will be a visible defect, an unharmoniousness, an unanswerableness in the things which they see, one to another" (20, 107).

and makes the justice of God appear "agreeable" (IV, 510). Knowing the guilt of the damned perfectly, understanding the hateful character of their transgressions, and freed of all the "natural affection" that linked them to their neighbor in this world (X, 340), the blessed will faithfully conform themselves to the will of God. However, God condemns sinners because he doesn't want them to be objects of compassion. "The language of Christ for the damned is that of an enemy," so we shouldn't pray for them (23, 584)![12] The preaching of the word doesn't reach the damned; the Gospel isn't preached in hell.[13] True love is to love God's good and conform ourselves to God's love of himself; therefore, by hating the damned, we conform to God (IV, 509). Indeed, the obligation to hate God's enemies is not just a positive stipulation of biblical religion, but is also required by metaphysical considerations. There is a natural proportionality between doing evil and suffering it. He "whose heart opposes the general system" of Being not only provokes opposition in "the heart of the Head and Ruler of the system," but also in "the hearts of the system" (8, 569). Or again, in the case of "any being that is . . . irreclaimably opposite and an enemy to Being in general," i.e., God, then consent and adherence "to Being in general will induce the truly virtuous heart to forsake that being, and to oppose it"[14] (8, 545).

The world's divine order therefore implies the rejection of any compassion for the damned, but what is the finality of this hatred for the blessed who are supposed to feel it? According to Edwards, the fate of the reprobate satisfies our sense of justice and reinforces our gratitude with respect to the sovereign mercy of God. Leibniz had already thought that "restoring order" by means of chastisement provided "a certain compensation of the mind" that was prejudicial to his sense of justice and without any regard to the usefulness of the chastisement itself.[15] Since men, as "the eye of the creation," desire nothing more than to contemplate the moral beauty of the world, the rectification of all disorder and deformity would only be sovereignly pleasing to them (20, 337). Edwards emphasized the fact that men have a tendency to acquiesce in the pain or suffering of the ill-deserving,

12. "if they cry to God to have mercy on 'em, He won't hear 'em" (25, 595).

13. Edwards, *Selections from the Unpublished Writings*, 204. More specifically, the preaching of Christ in hell was "nicht evangelica, sondern legalis [only legal and not evangelical]" (Güder, *Die Lehre von der Erscheinung Jesu Christi unter den Todten*, 240). The damned shall not only be hated by "excellent beings" (13, 350), but also tortured by their own violent wickedness (X, 263) and the other damned souls (8, 391); (see *supra*, p. 71); "all things round about will look grim and dreadful with the appearances of God's anger in them" (13, 350).

14. An annotation in the *Blank Bible* (24, 1237) provides a veritable recap of the reasons for the rejection of the damned by the elect.

15. Leibniz, *Theodicy*, 1. 73.

not merely out of a natural desire for their own good or the good of others, but also out of a natural gratification of the sense of merit and demerit that God implants in the heart (23, 599). However, the real explanation for this absence of compassion, this delight at seeing God execute his terrible, vindicative justice that sweetly constrains the blessed to sing, "Amen, Alleluia," while they behold the smoke of the torments of the damned,[16] is that seeing such dreadful misery gives them an ever-increasing appreciation of "God's electing love" (13, 428). The elect are similar to the damned in every respect; it is only "the sovereign grace" of God that makes them different (IV, 512). If the doctrine of the elect's rejection of the damned has any non-literal meaning, then it is in God's sovereign mercy to those who are its objects that we should look for it.[17]

---

16. Emmons, *Submission to Divine Sovereignty, Works*, 3:125.

17. See Eckley, *Divine Glory*, 33–4. For another vision, we quote Saint Isaac the Syrian: "And what is a merciful heart? It is the heart's burning for the sake of the entire creation, for men, for birds, for animals, for demons."

Chronology

Historical events	The life and works of Jonathan Edwards
1534 Henry VIII breaks with the Holy See	
1536 Calvin: *Institutes of the Christian Religion*	
1620 Pilgrims arrive in Plymouth, Massachusetts	
1636 Foundation of Harvard College	
1648 The Cambridge Platform	
1662 The Half-way Covenant	
1669 Solomon Stoddard (born 1643) begins preaching in Northampton, Massachusetts	
1701 Foundation of Yale College	
	1703 (October 5) Birth of Jonathan Edwards, son of Timothy Edwards (1669–1758) and Esther Stoddard (1672–1770), in East Windsor, Connecticut
1706 Birth of Benjamin Franklin	
	1716–1722 Studies at Yale College
	1722–1723 Preaches to Presbyterian congregation in New York City
	1722 (December)–1723 (January) Experiences conversion
	1722 Begins the *Miscellanies*
	1723 Begins *The Mind* and *Notes on the Apocalypse*

Historical events	The life and works of Jonathan Edwards
	1723 Preaches *A Spiritual Understanding of Divine Things Denied to the Unregenerate*
	1723 Begins *Notes on the Apocalypse*
	1723–1724 Serves as pastor in Bolton, Connecticut
	1724–1726 Elected tutor at Yale College
	1727 (February 15) Ordained assistant minister at Northampton, Massachusetts and serves under his grandfather Solomon Stoddard
	1727 (July 28) Marries Sarah Pierrepont (born January 9, 1710)
1728 Death of Cotton Mather	
	1729 Becomes minister at Northampton following the death of Solomon Stoddard
	1731 Preaches *God Glorified in the Work of Redemption* in Boston
	1733 Preaches *A Divine and Supernatural Light*
	1734–1735 Experiences first "harvest" in Northampton
	1737 Publishes excerpt from *A Faithful Narrative*
	1738 Publishes *Five Discourses*, including *Justification by Faith alone*
	1738 Preaches *Charity and Its Fruits* (published 1852)
	1739 Preaches *History of the Work of Redemption* (published 1774)
1741–1742 Great Awakening	1741 Preaches sermon in Enfield
1743 Charles Chauncy: *Seasonable Thoughts*	1742 *Thoughts on the Revival*
1744–1748 King George's War	
	1746 Publishes *Treatise Concerning Religious Affections*
	1747 Death of David Brainerd
	1748 Publishes *The Life of David Brainerd*

Historical events	The life and works of Jonathan Edwards
	1749 Writes *Qualifications for Communion*
	1750 Dismissed by congregation in Northampton
	1751 Becomes missionary to the Indians in Stockbridge, Massachusetts
	1751 Writes *Letter to Lady Pepperell*
	1754 Publishes *Freedom of the Will*
	1755 Completes *The End for Which God Created the World* (published 1765)
	1757 Completes *The Nature of True Virtue* (published 1765)
	1758 (February 16) Becomes President of the College of New Jersey in Princeton
	1758 (March 22) Death of Jonathan Edwards in Princeton
	1758 (October 2) Death of Sarah Pierrepont Edwards in Princeton
	1758 Publication of the treatise on *Original Sin*
	1765 Biography of Jonathan Edwards published by Samuel Hopkins
	1765 *The Nature of True Virtue* and *The End for which God Created the World* published by Samuel Hopkins
1776 United States Declaration of Independence	
	1793 Publication of *Miscellaneous Observations on important theological subjects*, Edinburgh
	1796 Publication of *Remarks On Important Theological Controversies*, Edinburgh
	1806–1811 Publication of *The works of President Edwards*, Leeds (reprinted London, 1817; supplement, Edinburgh, 1847)
	1808 Publication of *The works of President Edwards*, Worcester, Massachusetts

Historical events	The life and works of Jonathan Edwards
	1829–1830 Publication of *The works of President Edwards*, New York (Dwight edition)
	1881 Final reprint of the *Works* (New York edition)
	1903 Bicentenary of Edwards's birth
	1935 Publication of *Representative selections* (T. H. Johnson and C. Faust edition)
	1949 Perry Miller: *Jonathan Edwards*
	1957–2008 Yale edition
	2003 Tercentenary of Edwards's birth

Bibliographic Notice[1]

1. Literature on the religious and philosophical thought of the American Puritans.[2]

THE BEST GUIDE TO the vast body of literature devoted to seventeenth and eighteenth century New England is U. Brumm, *Puritanismus und Literatur in Amerika*, (Darmstadt, 1973). Bibliographies on the various branches of Puritan studies are found in P. Miller and T. H. Johnson, eds., *The Puritans*, 2 vols. (1938; New York, 1963) and, more recently, in F. J. Bremer, *John Winthrop: America's Forgotten Founding Father* (New York, 2003). Only a few of the most important works are mentioned here.

History of religious thought:

S. Ahlstrom. *A Religious History of the American People.* New Haven, 1972.

M. J. Crawford. *Seasons of Grace: Colonial New England's Revival Tradition in its British Context.* New York, 1991.

H. Dexter. *The Congregationalism of the Last Three Hundred Years as Seen in Its Literature.* New York, 1880; Westmead, 1970.

D. D. Hall. *Worlds of Wonder, Days of Judgment: Popular Religious Belief in Early New England.* New York, 1989.

---

1. No works, dated after 2007, the year of publication of the French original, are given.

2. The literature cited in this work is confined to works published in or before 2007, the year in which the French original appeared, with exception to the final volume of *The Works of Jonathan Edwards*, printed in 2008, and a few English translations of philosophical texts.

A. Heimert. *Religion and the American Mind.* Cambridge, 1966.

J. W. Jones. *The Shattered Synthesis: New England Puritanism before the Great Awakening.* New Haven, 1973.

M. A. Noll. *America's God, From Jonathan Edwards to Abraham Lincoln.* New York, 2002.

H. S. Stout. *The New England Soul: Preaching and Religious Culture in Colonial New England.* New York, 1986.

H. S. Stout. *The Divine Dramatist: George Whitefield and the Rise of Modern Evangelicalism.* Grand Rapids, 1991.

Theology of the Edwardsians:

F. H. Foster. *A Genetic History of the New England Theology.* Chicago, 1907; New York, 1963.

A. C. Guelzo. *Edwards on the Will: A Century of American Theological Debate.* Middletown, 1989.

J. Haroutunian. *Piety versus Moralism: The Passing of the New England Theology.* 1932; New York, 1970.

History of philosophy:

E. F. Flower, M. G. Murphey. *A History of Philosophy in America.* Vol. 1. New York, 1977.

N. Fiering. *Moral Philosophy at Seventeenth Century Harvard.* Chapel Hill, 1981.

Anthologies of texts:

W. Walker, ed. *The Creeds and Platforms of Congregationalism.* 1893; Philadelphia, 1960.

S. Ahlstrom, ed. *Theology in America.* Indianapolis, 1967.

P. Miller, A. Heimert, eds. *The Great Awakening.* Indianapolis, 1967.

2. Works by Edwards

The vast majority of unpublished works by Jonathan Edwards are found in the Beineke Rare Book and Manuscript Library at Yale University. There are also a certain number of manuscripts in the Andover-Newton (Massachusetts) seminary library.

A list of published works by Edwards can be compiled from T. H. Johnson, *The Printed Writings of Jonathan Edwards, 1703–1758: A Bibliography*, rev. ed. by M. X. Lesser (Princeton, 2003). Only major editions and key individual publications are mentioned here.

There are five old editions of the *Works*:

The Works of President Edwards, in Eight Volumes. Worcester, 1808.

The Works of President Edwards, 10 vols. London,[3] Edinburgh, 1817, 1847; New York, 1968.

The Works of President Edwards: With a Memoir of his Life. In Ten Volumes. Ed. S. E. Dwight. New York, 1829.

The Works of Jonathan Edwards, With an Essay on His Genius and Writings, by Henry Rogers . . . In Two Volumes. E. Hickman, ed. London, 1834.

The Works of President Edwards, In Four Volumes. A Reprint of the Worcester Edition. New York and Boston, 1843.

The great critical edition, the Yale Edition, is *The Works of Jonathan Edwards*, 26 vols. New Haven, 1957–2008. (Additional online volumes are at WJE web site.)

For the content of these editions, see *Concordance infra*, 433ff.

As for the *Miscellanies*, which were published in their entirety in the Yale Edition, two important selections have appeared since the 18th century:

Miscellaneous Observations on Important Theological Subjects, Original and Collected. Edinburgh, 1793.

Remarks on Important Theological Controversies. Edinburgh, 1796. This volume was reprinted virtually *in extensis* in the New York edition.

A third collection of *Miscellanies* is found in Volume 9 of the Dwight edition and in Volume 10 of the London-Edinburgh edition. More recently, an anthology of specifically philosophical (or philosophico-theological) *Miscellanies* was published by H. G. Townsend: *The Philosophy of Jonathan*

---

3. The first eight volumes (London, 1817) are basically a reprint of an earlier Leeds edition (1806–1811).

Edwards from His Private Notebooks, (Eugene, 1955; Westport, 1974). Other important *Miscellanies* were transcribed by E. S. Smyth in Appendix 1 of *Exercises Commemorating the 200th Anniversary of the Birth of Jonathan Edwards,* (Andover, 1904) 1–60, and in *Observations Concerning the Scripture Economy of the Trinity and Covenant of Redemption,* (New York, 1880).

Other key texts have appeared in the following volumes:

Charity and Its Fruits: or, Christian Love as Manifested in the Heart and Life. Ed. T. Edwards. London 1852; rpt. 1969.

Images or Shadows of Divine Things. Ed. Perry Miller. New Haven, 1948.

Treatise on Grace and Other Posthumously Published Writings by Jonathan Edwards. Ed. P. Helm. London, 1971.

The Blessing of God: Previously Unpublished Sermons of Jonathan Edwards. Ed. M. D. McMullen. Nashville, 2003.

The Salvation of Souls: Nine Previously Unpublished Sermons on the Call of Ministry and the Gospel by Jonathan Edwards. Ed. R. A. Bailey and G. A. Wills. Wheaton, 2002.

Along with the *Works,* we should also mention the anthologies: the very noteworthy *Jonathan Edwards: Representative Selections,* ed. C. Faust and T. H. Johnson (1935; New York, 1962) and *The Sermons of Jonathan Edwards: A Reader,* ed. W. H. Kimnach, K. P. Minkema & D. A. Sweeney (New Haven, 1999).

3. Writings on Edwards

There are some excellent bibliographies available for the secondary literature:

M. X. Lesser. *Jonathan Edwards: A Reference Guide.* Boston, 1981.

N. Manspeaker. *Jonathan Edwards: Bibliographical Synopses.* New York, 1981.

M. X. Lesser. *Jonathan Edwards: An Annotated Bibliography, 1979–1993.* Westport, 1994.

M. X. Lesser. *Reading Jonathan Edwards: An Annotated Bibliography in Three Parts,* 1729–2005. Grand Rapids, 2008. This volume incorporates and completes two earlier bibliographies by M. X. Lesser.

The above works make any additional bibliographical efforts superfluous. We therefore limit ourselves to mentioning just a few key titles. Biographies of Edwards include the classic work by S. Hopkins, *The Life and Character of the Late Reverend Mr. Jonathan Edwards* (in *Jonathan Edwards:*

A Profile, ed. D. Levin (New York, 1968) 1–86), as well as the immense compilation by S. E. Dwight, *The Works of President Edwards, with a Memoir of His Life*, vol. 1 (New York, 1829).

- O. E. Winslow. *Jonathan Edwards, 1703–1758: a Biography.* New York, 1940.
- P. J. Tracy. *Jonathan Edwards, Pastor: Religion and Society in Eighteenth-Century Northampton.* New York, 1979.
- I. Murray. *Jonathan Edwards: A New Biography.* Grand Rapids, 1987.
- G. M. Marsden. *Jonathan Edwards: A Life.* New Haven, 2003.

Overview of the life and work of Jonathan Edwards:

Perry Miller. *Jonathan Edwards.* New York, 1949.

Works dealing with the thought of Jonathan Edwards:

- A. V. G. Allen. *Jonathan Edwards.* Boston, 1889.
- C. W. Bogue. *Jonathan Edwards and the Covenant of Grace.* Cherry Hill, 1975.
- R. E. Brown. *Jonathan Edwards and the Bible.* Bloomington, 2002.
- J. P. Carse. *Jonathan Edwards & The Visibility of God.* New York, 1967.
- C. Cherry. *The Theology of Jonathan Edwards: A Reappraisal.* 1966; Gloucester, 1974.
- S. H. Daniel. *The Philosophy of Jonathan Edwards: A Study in Divine Semiotics.* Bloomington, 1994.
- R. A. Delattre. *Beauty and Sensibility in the Thought of Jonathan Edwards: An Essay in Aesthetics and Theological Ethics.* New Haven, 1968.
- T. Erdt. *Jonathan Edwards: Art and the Sense of the Heart.* Amherst, 1980.
- N. Fiering. *Jonathan Edwards's Moral Thought and Its British Context.* 1981; 2nd ed. Eugene, 2006.
- J. Gerstner. *The Rational Biblical Theology of Jonathan Edwards.* 3 vols. Orlando, 1991–1993.
- R. W. Jenson. *America's Theologian: A Recommendation of Jonathan Edwards.* New York, 1988.

M. J. McClymond. *Encounters with God: An Approach to the Theology of Jonathan Edwards*. New York, 1998.

G. R. McDermott. *One Holy and Happy Society: The Public Theology of Jonathan Edwards*. University Park, 1992.

G. R. McDermott. *Jonathan Edwards Confronts the Gods: Christian Theology, Enlightenment Religion, and Non-Christian Faiths*. New York, 2000.

A. Plantinga Pauw. *The Supreme Harmony of All: The Trinitarian Theology of Jonathan Edwards*. Grand Rapids, 2002.

J. Ridderbos. *De Theologie van Jonathan Edwards*. The Hague, 1907.

H. Westra. *The Minister's Task and Calling in the Sermons of Jonathan Edwards*. Lewiston, 1986.

S. A. Wilson. *Virtue Reformed*. Leiden, 2005.

Collected Articles:

W. J. Scheick, ed. *Critical Essays on Jonathan Edwards*. Boston, 1980.

Concordance

THERE ARE FIVE KNOWN editions of the *Works* of Jonathan Edwards, all dating from the first half of the nineteenth century. A sixth, critical edition—in progress since 1957—has extended into the twenty-first century. In any event, the older editions it references have to be consulted in order to use the secondary literature on Edwards. Because even large U.S. libraries don't always have all of these editions, we are often stuck with the thankless task of guessing where a reference might be found in an edition available to us. It therefore seemed useful to us to prepare a preliminary concordance for these six editions. This initiative has a number of limitations. First of all, this concordance isn't based on page numbers, but instead tries to identify matches by chapter or sub-chapter. Second, it doesn't take account of the fact that several volumes of the old editions were recombined or reprinted in the nineteenth century with variations which—with the notable exception of the Rodgers edition—were actually insignificant and mainly concerned tables of contents or title pages. However, with the exception of the Leeds 1806–1811 edition reprinted in London and Edinburgh, our inevitable choice in every other case was the first printing. For all of the variants and details on these "collected works," see M. X. Lesser, *The Printed Writings of Jonathan Edwards, 1703–1758: A Bibliography*, (Princeton, 2003). Lastly, it should be noted that, aside from differences in how chapters and sub-chapters are divided, the texts reproduced from the various editions are not exactly alike. Older editors regularly "cleaned up," mutilated and rewrote texts; and these processes produced texts that were markedly different from one another. In some works, and especially in the *Miscellanies*, the cuts were significant enough in certain places that the references to them in this concordance are only approximate.

The following six editions are referenced by this concordance:

Abbreviation	Edition
London	*The Works of President Edwards.* 10 vols. London, Edinburgh, 1817, 1847; New York, 1968.
Yale	*The Works of Jonathan Edwards.* New Haven, 1957–2008.
Worc.	*The Works of President Edwards, in Eight Volumes.* Worcester, 1808.
Dwight	*The Works of President Edwards: With a Memoir of His Life. In Ten Volumes.* New York, 1829.
Rogers	*The Works of Jonathan Edwards, A.M., With an Essay on His Genius and Writings,* by Henry Rogers. 2 vols. London, 1834.
N.Y.	*The Works of President Edwards. In Four Volumes. A Reprint of the Worcester Edition.* 4 vols. New York and Boston, 1843.[1]

There are no references to texts that were only published in one edition. The columns on page 415 and following contain references to several texts from the Dwight, Worcester, and New York editions that do not appear in the London-Leeds edition.

This concordance of six major editions is complemented by another one that, among others, includes references to several important texts published after the five old editions and not always included in the Yale Edition (p. 442).

Abbreviation	Edition
Grosart	*Selections from the Unpublished Writings of Jonathan Edwards, of America.* Ed. A. B. Grosart. Edinburgh, 1865.
Helm	Jonathan Edwards: *Treatise on Grace and Other Posthumously Published Writings.* Ed. P. Helm. Cambridge and London, 1971.
Fisher	G. P. Fisher. *An Unpublished Essay of Edwards on the Trinity, with Remarks on Edwards and His Theology.* New York, 1903.
Charity	Jonathan Edwards: *Charity and Its Fruits.* Ed. T. Edwards. New York, 1852; London, 1969.
Images	Jonathan Edwards: *Images or Shadows of Divine Things.* Ed. Perry Miller. New Haven, 1948.

The principles governing the creation of this concordance are few in number. Titles were frequently abbreviated for reasons of economy and space. They very often didn't come from Edwards himself and are not even reproduced faithfully in the various editions. This concordance follows the divisions of the London edition, the only one recently reprinted, and only

1. Notwithstanding its title, the New York edition not only reproduced the Worcester edition but also corrected and, more especially, supplemented it.

very rarely adds to it—most notably in the case of a long discourse titled *Justification by Faith Alone*—and, in such cases, no numbers or titles appear in the first column. In general, only the last page of a volume is indicated. However, the last page of a work is always provided whenever that work is not immediately followed in a given volume by a division matching the division found in the London edition (1st column).

	London	Yale	Worc.	Dwight	Rogers	New York
Memoir of the life of Jonathan Edwards by S. Hopkins, revised						
Preface	1 7		1 vii			1 5
I.	9		9			7
II.i. Resolutions	12	16 753	13	1 68	1 XLIII	7
ii. Diary	16	759	18	76–94	LXV	10
iii. (Personal Narrative)	24 28 32 36 36–41	781 790 794 798 799–804	29	99–106 58–62 64–67 98–99 131–36	XLVIII	17
III.	41		47			27
IV.	57		62			35
V.i.	75		82			46
ii.	77		85			48
(Letter to the Trustees of Princeton)	78–82	725–30		568–71		
VI.	85		93–9			53–55
Appendix I.	91					
II.	98					
III.	103					
Enquiry into Freedom of the Will						

CONCORDANCE

	London		Yale		Worc.		Dwight		Rogers		New York	
Preface	1	123	1	129	5	III	2	II	1	3	2	VII
I.i.		127		135		9		15		4		1
ii.		131		141		12		18		5		3
iii.		139		149		22		26		8		8
iv.	1	145	1	156	5	31	2	32	1	10	2	13
v.		152		163		38		38		11		17
II.i.		156		171		43		42		13		20
ii.		160		175		47		45		14		22
iii.		164		180		53		50		15		26
iv.		171		186		61		55		17		30
v.		174		190		65		59		18		32
vi.		178		195		70		62		19		35
vii.		185		203		78		68		21		39
viii.		194		213		89		77		23		45
ix		197		217		92		80		24		48
x.		204		225		101		86		26		52
xi.		217		239		116		98		30		61
xii.		235		257		137		114		35		73
xiii.		249		270		152		127		40		81
III.i.		255		277		156		133		41		83
ii.		258		281		160		136		42		86
iii.		271		295		176		148		46		94
iv.		278		302		183		154		47		99
v.		291		312		195		166		51		105
vi.		298		320		204		173		53		110
vii.		306		328		212		179		55		115
IV.i.		313		337		219		186		57		119
ii.		323		343		226		195		60		122
iii.		333		350		234		204		63		127
iv.		339		357		241		210		65		131
v.		346		365		250		217		67		136
vi.		353		372		258		223		69		142
vii.		355		375		261		226		69		142
viii.		363		384		271		233		72		147
ix.		376		397		285		244		75		155

	London		Yale		Worc.		Dwight		Rogers		New York
x.		392		413		303		258		80		169
xi.		399		415		306		265		82		166
xii.		406		420		311		272		84		169
xiii.		409		423		315		274		85		171
xiv.	1	415	1	431	5	323	2	280	1	86	2	177
Appendix		426–37		453–70		335–48		290–300		89–93		183–90
A Dissertation Concerning the End for Which God Created the World												
Preface	1	441	8	401	6	III	3	3	1	94	2	191
Introduction		443	8	405		95		5		95		193
I.i.		451		417		20		12		97		199
ii.		457		428		29		18		99		204
iii.		461		436		34		21		100		207
iv.		467		445		42		27		102		211
II.i.		481		467		61		40		106		222
ii.		482		469		62		41		106		222
iii.		486		475		68		44		107		226
iv.		502		493		87		59		112		236
v.		510		503		95		66		114		242
vi.		515		512		104		71		116		246
vii.		526–35		526–32		116–24		81–90		119–120		252–57
A Dissertation Concerning the Nature of True Virtue												
I.	2	7	8	539	2	395	3	93	1	123	2	261
II.		15		550		404		101		125		266
III.		25		561		413		110		127		271
IV.		34		575		424		118		130		277
V.		46		589		437		128		133		285
VI.		54		606		447		135		135		290
VII.		59		609		455		141		137		291

	London	Yale	Worc.	Dwight	Rogers	New York
VIII.	68	609–27	464–70	148–57	140–43	300–304
The Great Christian Doctrine of Original Sin Defended						
Preface	2 84	3 102	6 127	2 307	1 145	2 307
I.I.i.	84	107	129	309	146	309
ii.	99	120	144	320	149	317
iii.	106	128	153	327	151	322
iv.	111	134	159	332	153	326
v.	116	139	165	336	154	329
vi.	123	147	174	343	156	334
vii.	133	158	186	352	159	341
viii.	144	169	199	361	162	348
ix.	162	189	221	378	169	361
II.	179	206	241	393	173	372
II.I.i.	193	223	258	406	177	381
ii.	206	237	273	418	180	390
iii.	213	245	282	424	182	395
II.	229	262	301	439	187	405
III.i.	246	274	315	449	190	413
ii.	248	283	325	456	193	419
iii.	257	292	336	464	195	425
IV.i.	270	306	352	476	199	434
ii.	295	335	384	500	207	451
III.I.	309	353	401	512	211	461
II.	316	361	409	529	213	468
IV.i.	326	375	422	528	216	473
ii.	330	380	427	532	217	476
iii.	342	389	436	542	220	481
iv.	364	413	463	563	227	495
Conclusion	384	434–37	487–90	581–83	232–33	509–10
Men's Natural Blindness						
I.	391			7 3	2 247	16

	London	Yale	Worc.	Dwight	Rogers	New York
II.	395			5	247	17
III.	405			16	251	25
IV.	411			21	253	29
V.	413			27–30	255–56	33–35
An Humble Attempt						
Advertisement	2 425			3 439	2 278	
Pref. Engl. Editor	427			441	278	
Pref. Amer. Editor	429	5 309		443	279	
I.i.	431	312	3 355	445	280	3 429
ii.	433	314	358	447	281	431
iii.	440	321	365	453	282	435
iv.	444	324	370	457	284	437
II.i.	447	329	373	460	284	439
ii.	456	337	383	468	287	445
iii.	459	341	387	471	288	447
iv.	463	344	391	474	289	450
v.	466	347	395	477	290	451
vi.	475	357	406	486	293	468
vii.	481	364	414	492	295	462
III.i.	485	368	418	495	296	465
ii.	488	370	421	498	297	467
iii.	495	378	430	504	299	471
iv.	508	394	449	516	302	482
v.	534	427	488	540	310	504
vi.	537–41	432–36	489–94	543–47	311–12	505–8
A Faithful Narrative						
Preface I. ed.	3 III	4 130–37	3 III	4 XI	1 344	3 III
I.	9	144	9	17	346	251
II.	23	160	25	30	350	240
III.	53	191–211	61–82	57–74	359–64	260–72

CONCORDANCE

	London	Yale	Worc.	Dwight	Rogers	New York
Life and Diary of the Rev. David Brainerd						
Preface	3　75	7　89		10　27	2　312　(1)	
I.	81	99		33	316	
II.	99	157		52	321	
III.	115	175		67	326	
IV.	128	189		79	330	
V.	3　140	7　202		10　91	2　333	
VI.	185	253		143	346	
				194, 196		
VII.	225	298		307	359–368	
	257–73	410–28		252–367		
VIII.	3　273	7　429–76	3　499–519 (3)	1　0 367–413	2　373	3　645–46
Mr. Brainerd's Journal						
Advertisement	315				387	
Preface	317			194–96 (1)	387	
I.	319–54	300–338		196	388	
II.	364	340–410 (2)		10　244–307　(4)	401	
1. Appendix	415			308	416	
2. Appendix	433			321–51	420	
3. Appendix	471			162–71	431–35	
Mr. Brainerd's remains	487	483		94–96	435–36	
	489	486		177	436	
	490	487		119–20	436	
	492	489		152–54	436–37	
	494	490		178–79	437	
	495	491		255	437	
	495	492		375	437	
	496	493		387	438	

	London	Yale	Worc.	Dwight	Rogers	New York
	498	494		389		
	500	496–499		390–92		
Detached papers	503	477		124–29	440	
	3 508	7 482		10 42	2 441	
	508	483		45	441	
Sermon by E. Pemberton	511	543–59		11–25	442	
Reflections and observations	533–73	500–541	520–48	414–51	447–58	1 657–72
A Treatise Concerning Religious Affections						
Preface	4 III	2 84	4 III	5 1	1 234	3 IX
I.i.	7	93	9	7	236	1
ii.	13	99	16	12	237	5
iii.	31	119	39	30	243	18
II.i.	37	127	46	35	245	22
ii.	41	131	51	39	245	25
iii.	45	135	55	42	246	27
iv.	47	138	58	44	247	29
v.	51	142	64	49	248	32
vi.	54	146	67	51	249	34
vii.	56	147	69	53	250	35
viii.	60	151	74	57	250	37
ix.	71	163	88	67	252	45
x.	73	165	90	69	255	47
xi.	75	167	93	71	257	48
xii.	88	181	109	83	260	57
III. (Introductory remarks)	97	193	119	91	262	63
i.	101	197	124	95	264	65
ii.	138	240	171	129	274	91
iii.	151	253	187	140	278	100

CONCORDANCE

	London		Yale		Worc.		Dwight		Rogers		New York	
iv.		163		264		201		151		281		108
v.		186		291		230		172		288		124
vi.		205		311		253		190		294		137
vii.		233		340		286		215		302		155
viii.		238		344		291		219		303		159
ix.		250		357		307		230		307		167
x.	4	257	2	365	4	314	5	237	1	309	1	171
xi.		269		376		326		247		312		178
xii.		275		383		332		253		314		182
xiii.		298		407		353		273		321		193
xiv.		311		420		369–416		285		324		202–28
Appendix												
Letter 1 from Gillespie				470		1		224–30				
Letter 1 to Gillespie		352		478		5		322–33		336		
Letter 2 from Gillespie				490		1		252–61				
Letter 2 to Gillespie		364		501–13		5		333–44		340–43		
Christian Caution												
Introduction	4	379			8	66	6	328	2	173	4	502
I.		381				68		329		174		503
II.		385				74		334		175		506
III.		390				79		337		176		509
IV.		397				87		344		178		513
V.		401				93		348		180		516
VI.		403				94		349		180		517
VII.		405				96		351		181		519
IX.		416				109–14		361–64		184–85		527
A Warning to Professors												
Introduction	4	423					6	365	2	185	4	529
I.		425						367		186		530
II.		427						368		186		531
III.		431						373		188		534

434 CONCORDANCE

	London	Yale	Worc.	Dwight	Rogers	New York
IV.	437			378	189–92	538–39
The Final Judgment						
Introduction	443	14 509		381	190	202
I.	445	511		383	191	203
II.	4 448	14 513	6	385	2 192	4 205
III.	452	517		389	193	207
IV.	456	522		393	194	210
V.	465	531		401	197	217
VI.	466	532		402	197	217
VII.	469	534		404–13	198	219–25
Sinners in Zion						
I.	481	22 265	8 153	6 440	201	488
II.	484	268	156	442	202	489
III.	490	275	165	449	204	494
IV.	494	278	169	452	205	496
V.	496	280	171–77	453–57	205	497–501
The End of the Wicked						
Introduction	503			466	207	287
I.	506			468	208	288
II.	508			473	208	290
III.	512			476	209	293
IV.	515–22			479–85	210–12	294–99
A History of the Work of Redemption						
Preface	5 7		2 V	3 161	1 532	296
Advertisement	9		IV	163	532	295
General Introduction	11	9 113	9	165	533	296
Period I.	21	128	24	175	536	305
I.	22	129	25	176	536	306
II.	35	149	44	189	540	317
III.	42	157	54	196	542	322

	London	Yale	Worc.	Dwight	Rogers	New York
IV.	53	175	69	207	546	332
V.	72	203	96	226	553	348
VI.	97	240	131	251	560	367
VII.	124	281	168	278	569	388
	London	Yale	Worc	Dwight	Rogers	New York
Period II.	5 133	9 294	2 180	3 287	1 572	1 395
I.	134	295	181	288	572	396
II.	140	303	190	294	574	401
III.	159	337	217	313	580	416
Period III.	166	343	229	323	582	423
I.	167	344	231	323	583	424
IV.	183	371	253	337	588	437
I.	185	372	256	339	588	439
II.	192	387	266	346	590	445
III.	203	403	281	357	594	453
IV.	206	410	285	360	595	456
V.	213	427	295	367	597	461
VI.	217	447	315	381	602	472
VII.	236	455	328	390	604	480
VIII.	250	479	346	404	609	490
IX.	259	492	358	413	612	497
X.	270	510	375–92	424–36	615–19	507–16
Men Naturally God's Enemies	285		7 159	7 31	2 130	4 36
I.	287		161	33	131	37
II.	290		166	36	131	40
III.	293		170	39	132	42
IV.	297		175	42	134	45
V.	303		184	48	136	50
VI.	307		188	52	137	53
VII.	312		195	57	138	57
VIII.	317		203	62	140	61
IX.	319		205–7	64	141	63

	London		Yale		Worc.		Dwight		Rogers		New York
The Wisdom of God, displayed in the way of Salvation	323						66		141	4	133
I.	326						68		142		135
II.	332						75		144		139
III.	335						78		145		142
IV.	341						84		147		146
V.	5	345					7	88	2	148	4	149
VI.	349						91		149		151
VII.	356						98		151		156
VIII.	359						101		153		159
XI.	369						111–14		156		166–68
Christian Knowledge											
Introduction	375	22	83	8	3	6	265		157		1
I.	377		85				267		157		2
II.	378		87		8		268		158		4
III.	379		87		9		269		158		4
IV.	381		89		12		271		159		6
V.	389		97		22		278		161		11
VI.	393				27–28		282–83		162		14–15
Christian Charity											
I.	397	17	321			6	536		163		
II.	401		375				540		164		
III.	404		379				543		165		
IV.	415		390–404				554–68		169–73		
Seven Discourses											
I. Christ exalted	434							2	213		
II. Self-Flatteries	448				115–28		414–24		217		322–29

	London	Yale	Worc.	Dwight	Rogers	New York
III. *Dishonesty; or, the Sin of Theft and Injustice*	458		481–506	517–35	220	601–14
IV. *Temptation and Deliverance*	477		7 131–58	115–34	226	585–600
V. *The Preciousness of Time*	5 499	19 246–60		6 486–97	2 233	
VI. *Procrastination*	511		178–203	498–516	237	4 347–60
VII. *The Christian Pilgrim*	5 530–42	17 429–60	7 208–27	7 135–46	2 243–6	4 573–84
Some Thoughts Concerning the Present Revival of Religion in New England						
Preface	6 IV	4 291	3 87	4 77	1 365	3 275
I.i.	5	293	89	79	366	277
ii.	8	296	92	82	367	279
iii.	21	314	110	95	370	289
iv.	31	325	122	105	374	296
v.	36	331	130	110	376	300
vi.	44	341	141	118	378	306
II.i.	50	348	147	124	380	310
ii.	54	353	152	128	381	313
iii.	59	358	159	133	383	316
iv.	70	370	173	144	386	324
III.	82	384	188	156	390	333
IV.	104	409	217	178	397	349
i.	108	414	223	182	398	353
ii.	124	432	243	198	404	364

	London	Yale	Worc.	Dwight	Rogers	New York
iii.	146	458	273	220	411	381
iv.	159	474	290	233	415	391
v.	167	483	300	241	417	397
vi.	172	489	307	246	419	401
V.	178	496	314	252	421	405
i.	178	496	315	252	421	405
ii.	183	502	320	257	422	408
iii.	6 194	4 513	3 335–51	4 268–80	1 426–30	3 416–25
Five Discourses						
Preface	6 209	19 793–98		5 347	1 620	
Justification by Faith alone	213	147	7 9	351	622	4 64
	232	161	26	370	628	73
	255	183	54	392	635	90
	272	207	77	409	640	102
	296	225	108–30	433	648	120–32
Pressing into the Kingdom of God	316	274		453	654	381–402
Ruth's Resolution	347	19 307	7 308	5 484	1 664	4 412–21
The Justice of God in the Damnation of Sinners	361	339–76	326–74	498	668	226–53
The Excellency of Christ	399	563–94	267–307	535–66	680–89	179–201
Two Sermons						
Advertisement	433				2 2	
God glorified in Man's Dependence	435	1 7 196–216	7 467	7 149	3	169–78
Sinners in the Hands of an Angry God	450	22 404–18	486–502	163–77	7–12	313–21

CONCORDANCE

	London	Yale	Worc.	Dwight	Rogers	New York
Seven Sermons on Important Subjects						
I. *The Best Portion*	467		8　29–43	6　284	104	540
II. *God's Sovereignty*	6　477			6　293	2　107	4　548–60
III. *Pardon for Sinners*	488			304	110	422–28
IV. *A Prayer-Hearing God*	498		44–65	314–27	113	561–72
V. *The Nature and End of Excommunication*	512		461–80	569–80	118	638–49
VI. *Wrath upon the Wicked to the Uttermost*	525			458–67	2　122	280–86
VII. *Wicked Men useful in their Destruction only*	535–50		129–52	424–39	125–29	300–312
Inquiry Concerning Qualifications for Communion (Citation highlighted)	7　2				1　431	
The Author's Preface	3	12　167	1　147	4　283	431	1　85
Preface by the Author's American friends	7	12　172		287	433	
Advertisement	9			289	433	
I.	11	174	1　153	291	434	89
II.i.	18	184	162	298	436	94
ii.	34	199	182	314	441	105

	London	Yale	Worc.	Dwight	Rogers	New York
iii.		40	205	189	320	443	109
iv.		53	219	206	333	447	119
v.		59	225	214	339	449	123
vi.		65	230	220	344	451	127
vii.		71	237	228	351	453	132
viii.		85	251	246	365	457	142
ix.	7 89	12 256	1 251	4 369	1 458	1 145
III.i.		95	263	259	375	460	149
ii.		98	266	262	378	461	151
iii.		105	274	272	385	464	157
iv.		113	283	283	393	466	163
v.		115	285	286	395	467	164
vi.		117	286	288	397	468	166
vii.		118	288	290	398	469	167
viii.		121	251	293	401	469	168
ix.		122	291	294	402	469	169
x.		127	297	301	407	471	173
xi.		129	299	303	409	471	174
xii.		131	302	306	411	472	176
xiii.		133	304	309	413	473	177
xiv.		136	307	313	416	474	179
xv.		137	308	314	417	474	180
xvi.		139	310	317	419	474	182
xvii.		140	311	318	420	475	182
xviii.		142	313	320	422	475	184
xiv.		143	314	321	423	476	184
xx.		148	319	328–35	428	477	188–92
Appendix	154	326		434–51	479–84	
Misrepresentations Corrected . . . in Reply to Rev. Mr. Solomon Williams						
Preface	175	351	339	455	484	195
I.i.	179	359	343	459	486	197

CONCORDANCE 441

	London		Yale		Worc.		Dwight		Rogers		New York
ii.	184		355		349		464		488		200
II.i.	196		373		364		476		491		209
ii.	199		376		369		479		492		211
iii.	206		384		378		486		495		216
iv.	210		386		383		490		496		219
v.	216		395		391		496		498		223
vi.	224		404		401		504		500		229
vii.	227		407		405		507		501		231
viii.	7	230	12	410	1	409	4	510	1	502	1	234
ix.	241		422		423		521		503		241
III.i.	252		434		437		532		506		249
ii.	257		439		444		537		509		253
iii.	259		441		446		539		511		254
iv.	264		447		453		544		513		258
v.	267		450		456		547		514		260
vi.	268		451		458		548		514		261
vii.	270		457		461		550		515		263
viii.	274		458		466		554		516		266
ix.	278		462		471		558		518		268
x.	283		468		478		563		519		272
xi.	286		471		482		566		520		274
xii.	290		475		487		570		521		277
xiii.	293		478		491		573		522		279
xiv.	295		480		493		574		523		281
xv.	301		486		501		581		525		285
xvi.	305		491		507		585		526		288
xvii.	309		494		511		589		526		290–92
Appendix	317		499–03				597–612		529–31		
Farewell Sermon											
Preface	325			1	103	1	626			4	59
(sermon)	329	25	462–93		109		630–651	1	1 CCXL–CCXLIX		61

CONCORDANCE

	London	Yale	Worc.	Dwight	Rogers	New York
Result of a Council of Nine Churches	355		142–44	399–401		81–82
Fifteen Sermons						
Preface	363			6 3	2 51	
I. *The Manner in Which Salvation is to be Sought*	7 365			6 5	2 51	4 368–80
II. *Unreasonableness of Indetermination in Religion*	383	19 93–106	7 422	23	57	4 338–46
III. *Unbelievers Contemn the Glory and Excellency of Christ*	395		438	35	61	361–67
IV. *The Folly of Looking Back in Fleeing out of Sodom*	405	323–95	451	45	64	403
V. *The Folly of Looking Back in Fleeing out of Sodom*	413		461–66	53	66	408–11
VI. *The Warnings of Scripture*	418			58	68	330–37
VII. *Hypocrites Deficient in the Duty of Prayer*	429		8 204	69	71	474

	London	Yale	Worc.	Dwight	Rogers	New York
VIII. *Hypocrites Deficient in the Duty of Prayer*	439		7 217–29	79	74	481–87
IX. *Future Punishment of the Wicked*	449		375	89	78	254
X. *Future Punishment of the Wicked*	457		385	97	80	259
XI. *Future Punishment of the Wicked*	7 466		7 396–421	6 106	2 83	4 266
XII. *The Peace Which Christ Gives His True Followers*	486	25 538–52	8 230	125	89	429–37
XIII. *The Perpetuity and Change of the Sabbath*	499	17 220	248	138	93	615
XIV. *The Perpetuity and Change of the Sabbath*	510	230	262	148	96	622
XV. *The Perpetuity and Change of the Sabbath*	525–33	242–80	279–89	162–70	100–103	632–37
Five Sermons on Different Occasions						
I. *A Divine and Supernatural Light*	8 3	408–26	290	171	12	483–50
II. *The Church's Marriage*	21	25 167–96	313–50	189–216	17 3	559–79

	London	Yale	Worc.	Dwight	Rogers	New York
III. *True Saints, When Absent From The Body, Are Present with the Lord*	50	225–56	412–40 10	456–83	26	624–39
IV. *God's Awful Judgment*	81	315–29	441–60 6	217	36	604–14
V. *True Grace Distinguished from the Experience of Devils*	8 96	25 608–40	7 228–66	6 232–61	2 41–50	4 451–73
Miscellaneous Observations on Important Theological Subjects						
Preface (5)	8 129			7 199	2 459	
Advertisement	131			198	460	
I.i.	133			201	460	
ii.	154			221	466	
iii.	161			228	468	
iv.	167			233	470	
v.	175			240	473	
vi.	179			244	474	
vii.	196			261	479	
viii.	214			277	485	
ix.	236			298	491	
x.	242			303	493	
II.	248		2 475–91	7 310	2 495	3 537–46
III.	262			323	499–510	
Remarks on Important Theological Controversies						
I. (6)	8 303			7 360		1 565
II.	318			374		612–42

	London	Yale	Worc.	Dwight	Rogers	New York
III.	351		5 351	405		2 513
IV.	388	21 204–12 227–37 240–80	413–504	440		547–97
V.	434			483		3 509–32
VI.	458			505		1 582–611
VII.	491	417–68	4 419–90	536–72		2 601–41
Distinguishing Marks						
Preface by William Cooper	533	4 215		3 550	2 257	1 519
Introduction	8 541	4 226		3 559	2 260	1 525
I.	543	228		561	261	526
II.	560	248		578	266	538
III.	570–94	260–88		588–612	269–77	546–62
Notes on the Bible (7)						
The Pentateuch	9 1	15		9 115		
Genesis	37			155		
Exodus	109			235		
Leviticus	143			274		
Matthew	143			274		
Luke	143			274		
Numbers	144			275		
Deuteronomy	150			281		
Joshua	155			287		
Judges	162			295		
Ruth	174			309		
1 Samuel	175			309		
2 Samuel	175			310		
1 Chronicles	179					
1 Kings	180			315		
2 Kings	182			319		
2 Chronicles	188			324		
Nehemiah	190			327		

	London	Yale	Worc.	Dwight	Rogers	New York
Esther	191			328		
Job	193			331		
Psalms	198			336		
Proverbs	216			357		
Ecclesiastes	217			357		
Song of Solomon	218			358		
Isaiah	231			373		
Jeremiah	246			391		
Ezekiel	254			400		
Daniel	265			412		
Hosea	269			416		
Amos	271			419		
Jonah	272			420		
Micah	9 274			9 422		
Habakkuk	277			425		
Zechariah	280			429		
Malachi	283			433		
Matthew	285			435		
Mark	314			467		
Luke	318			472		
John	325			480		
Acts	336			492		
Romans	340			497		
1 Corinthians	349			508		
2 Corinthians	353			512		
Galatians	358			518		
Ephesians	366			527		
Philippians	372			534		
Colossians	372			534		
2 Thessalonians	372			534		
2 Timothy	373			535		
Hebrews	373			535		
James	383			547		
1 Peter	383			547		

CONCORDANCE

	London	Yale	Worc.	Dwight	Rogers	New York
2 Peter	386			550		
1 John	391			556		
Jude	392			557		
Revelation	394			559–563		
Types of the Messiah	401–94	1 1 157–328		9–111		
Miscellaneous Observations (8)						
1.	10 1			8 485		
2.	11			496		
3.	10 23			8 509		
4.	24			511		
5.	38			526–604		
Seventeen Occasional Sermons						
1. Natural Men	111			5	2 817	
2. God Makes Men Sensible	10 146	17 142–72		8 44	2 830	
3. Hope and Comfort	170			70	838	
4. God's Sovereignty	201			105	849	
5. The Character of Paul	10 216			8 123	2 855	
6. Christ's Agony	248			159	866	
7. The Portion of the Wicked	281			195	878	
8. The Portion of the Righteous	309	58–86		227	888	
9. The Pure in Heart Blessed	357			281	905	
10. Praise	379			305	913	

	London	Yale	Worc.	Dwight	Rogers	New York
11. Wicked Men Inconsistent	393			320	918	
12. Safety	424			355	929	
13. Christians a Chosen Generation	445	272–328		379	936	
14. Jesus Christ	480			418	949	
15. The True Excellency	496	25 84–102	8 351	437	955	3 580
16. Christ the Example of Ministers	512	25 333–48	375	455	960	593–603
17. The Sorrows of the Bereaved	526–36		396–411	471–82	965–69	614–23
Letter to William McCulloch		4 539–41		1 196–88		
Letter to Thomas Prince		4 544–57		1 160–70		
Letter to William McCulloch		558–60		211–19		
		1 6 65–66 (9)		1 139–40		
		105–7 108–10 111–12		196–98		
		115–27		160–70		
		127–33		204–9		
		134–42 180–97 199–03		211–19		
		16 219–21		230–32		
		224–35 241–4		232–42		
		248–50		255–2		

CONCORDANCE

London	Yale	Worc.	Dwight	Rogers	New York
	16 259–65		1 265–76		
	268–71		273–76		
	272–74		276–78		
	275–81		279–83		
	288–90		285–86		
	327–39		287–97		
	294–95		322–23		
	295		324–26		
	302–7		327–33		
	310–11		334–35		
	311–15		335–38		
	316–17		367–68		
	317–18		369–70		
	347–56		405–13		
	357–58		413–14		
	363–67		415–18		
	646–54		421–27		
	16 370–74		1 453–56		
	16 375–80		1 458–62		
	380–87		462–68		
	388–90		469–71		
	400–414		474–81		
	414–19		481–85		
	420–21		485–87		
	422–30		489–92 (excerpts)		
	471–77		493–94 (parts)		
	479–84		597–609		
	489–93		496–99		
	537–42		507–22		
	545–49		513–6		
	542–45		516–28		
	578–80		525–27		
	594–95		533–34		
	609–10		535–37		

	London	Yale	Worc.	Dwight	Rogers	New York
		657–58		544–45		
		16 679–81		1 550–52		
		684–87		553–55		
		688–89		555–56		
		701–02 706–18		557–58		
		718–24		558–63		
		725–30		568–71		
		341–47		627–28 (excerpts)		
Cover-Leaf Memoranda		6 192		702		
Of the Prejudices of Imagination		196		703		
Of Being		202		706		
Of Atoms		208		708		
Things to be Considered (10)		219–95		715–61		
The Mind (11)		332–87		668–702	1 CCVI–CCLXXIII	
Subjects to be Handled		393		664–68		
The Soul		405		20–21		
"Spider" Letter-Draft		409–15		23–28		
Against Dr. Watts		23 89–92	2 492–96			3 533–36
Observations upon Particular Passages of the Scripture			6 494–504			3 547 (12)
Theological Questions			505–08		690–91	554–56
Great Concern of a Watchman		25 62–81		7 178–96		

	Grosart	Yale	Helm
Treatise on Grace I	I 19	21 153	25
II	30	165	39
III	39–56	176–97	51–74
Annotations on Passages of the Bible (13)	57–179		
Directions for Judging	183–85	522–24	
On the Trinity	Fisher 77–133	113–48	99–133
Charity and Its Fruits			
	Charity	Yale	
Introduction	III	8 125	
I	1	129	
II	26	149	
III	50	174	
IV	66	185	
V	96	207	
VI	111	218	
VII	128	232	
VIII	157	252	
IX	186	272	
X	204	283	
XI	221	293	
XII	251	313	
XIII	268	326	
XIV	285	351	
XV	323	368	
Images and Shadows	**Images** 43–137	11 50–135	

Notes

(1) For an explanation of the way in which the text is presented, see London III. pp. 225 and 80.

(2) The text that the London edition divides as Private Journal (pp. 225–57) and Public Journal (pp. 319–64), the latter published by Brainerd himself, is presented as one continuous text (pp. 298–410) in the Yale Edition.

(3) Corresponds to London III. pp. 296–311.

(4) The text which the London edition divides as Private Journal (pp. 225–57) and Public Journal (pp. 319–64), the latter published by Brainerd himself, is presented as one continuous text in the Dwight edition.

(5) This text reproduces the *Miscellanies* published in *Miscellaneous Observations on Important Theological Subjects*, although often in a truncated manner and apparently with certain unidentified additions. See 13, 546–7.

(6) These texts—with additions—publish various *Miscellanies* (several of which are truncated) that were first published in *Remarks on Important Theological Controversies*. See 13, 551–2. The various editions correspond with one another in a partial, fragmented way.

(7) Unlike the five older editions, the Yale Edition publishes the *Notes* in their chronological order of writing. It is possible to cross-reference these editions by looking up the relevant Bible verse in the *Index of Biblical Passages*. See 15, 639–40.

(8) The *Miscellanies*, each of which is numbered, begin from 13, 551.

(9) The headings that follow relate exclusively to letters written by Edwards and do not mention their recipients. A certain number of letters in the Dwight edition have already been reprinted in other volumes of the Yale Edition, although references are only provided up to volume 16 of the final edition.

(10) The Yale Edition rearranged the order of the texts.

(11) The Yale Edition completely rearranged the order of the texts.

(12) These *Observations* come from the *Blank Bible*. See Yale Edition, vol. 24, p. 1251.

(13) All of the texts in the *Blank Bible* from which this selection of notes was taken are published in the Yale Edition. See vol. 24, pp. 1251–55.

Bibliography

Aaron, Richard I. *John Locke*. 3rd ed. Oxford: Oxford University Press, 1971.
Adams, Brooks. *The Emancipation of Massachusetts*. Boston: Houghton Mifflin, 1887.
Addison, Joseph. *The Spectator* 160 (3 September 1711). In *The Spectator*, edited by H. Morley, 2:126–30. London: Routledge, 1891.
Ahlstrom, Sydney. *A Religious History of the American People*. New Haven: Yale University Press, 1972.
Ahlstrom, Sydney, ed. *Theology in America: The Major Protestant Voices from Puritanism to Neo-Orthodoxy*. Indianapolis: Bobbs-Merrill, 1967.
Aldridge, Alfred Owen. "Edwards and Hutcheson." *Harvard Theological Review* 44, no. 1 (1951) 35–53.
———. "Jonathan Edwards and William Godwin on Virtue." *American Literature* 18, no. 4 (1947) 308–18.
Allen, Alexander Viets Griswold. *Jonathan Edwards*. Boston: Riverside, 1889.
Althaus, Paul. *Die Prinzipien der deutschen reformierten Dogmatik im Zeitalter der aristotelischen Scholastik*. Leipzig: Deichert, 1914.
Ambrose. "Hexameron." In *Hexameron, Paradise, and Cain and Abel*, translated by John J. Savage, 3–284. The Fathers of the Church: A New Translation. Washington, DC: Catholic University of America Press, 2003.
Amesius, Guilielmus. *Medulla Sacrae Theologiae*. London, 1623 (*Medulla Theologica*).
Anderson, Wilbert L. "The Preaching Power of Jonathan Edwards." *Congregationalist and Christian World* 88 (1903) 463–66.
Angoff, Charles. *A Literary History of the American People*. New York: A. A. Knopf, 1931.
Anselm of Canterbury. *Why God Became Man*. In *The Major Works*, edited by Brian Davies and G. R. Evans and translated by Janet Fairweather, 260–356. Oxford World's Classics. New York: Oxford University Press, 2008.
Aquinas, Thomas. *Summa Theologiæ*. Translated by Jordan Aumann et al. 61 vols. Cambridge: Cambridge University Press, 2006.
Araud, Régis. «Quidquid non est ex fide peccatum est. Quelques interprétations patristiques.» In *L'homme devant Dieu. Mélanges offerts au P.H. de Lubac. I. Exégèse et patristique*, 127–45. Paris: Auber, 1964.
Arendt, Hannah. *Between Past and Future: Eight Exercises in Political Thought*. New York: Penguin, 1973.
———. *The Life of the Mind*. Vol. 2. New York: Harcourt Brace Jovanovich, 1978.

Aristotle. *Nicomachean Ethics*. In *The Complete Works of Aristotle*, edited by Jonathan Barnes and translated by W. D. Ross and J. O. Urmson, 1729-867. Princeton: Princeton University Press, 1995.

Arnauld, Antoine. *Œuvres de Messire Antoine Arnauld*. Paris: Sigismond d'Arnay & Compagnie, 1775-83.

Arnauld, Antoine, and Pierre Nicole. *Logic, or the Art of Thinking: Being the Port-Royal Logic*. Translated by Thomas Spencer Baynes. Edinburgh: Sutherland and Knox, 1850.

The Articles of the Synod of Dort. Philadelphia: Presbyterian Board, 1841.

Atwater, Lyman H. "Jonathan Edwards and the Successive Forms of the New Divinity." *The Biblical Repertory and Princeton Review* 30, no. 4 (1858) 585-620.

Augustine. "Admonition and Grace." Translated by John Courtney Murray. In *Christian Instruction; Admonition and Grace; the Christian Combat; Faith, Hope and Charity*, 237-306. The Fathers of the Church: A New Translation. Washington, DC: Catholic University of America Press, 2002.

———. *Against Julian*. Translated by Matthew A. Schumacher. The Fathers of the Church: A New Translation. Edited by Hermigild Dressler et al. Washington, DC: Catholic University of America Press, 2004.

———. "Answer to the Two Letters of the Pelagians." In *Answer to the Pelagians II: Marriage and Desire, Answer to the Two Letters of the Pelagians, Answer to Julian*, edited by John E. Rotelle and translated by Roland J. Teske, 97-219. The Works of Saint Augustine: A Translation for the 21st Century. New York: New City, 1998.

———. *City of God*. Translated by Demetrius B. Zema et al. The Fathers of the Church: A New Translation. Edited by Hermigild Dressler et al. Washington, DC: Catholic University of America Press, 2008.

———. *Confessions*. Translated by Vernon J. Bourke. The Fathers of the Church: A New Translation. Washington, DC: Catholic University of America Press, 2008.

———. *De Diversis Quaestionibus LXXXIII*. Bibliothèque Augustinienne 10. Paris: Desclée De Brouwer, 1952.

———. *Expositions on the Book of Psalms: Translated, with Notes and Indices in Six Volumes*. Translated by Members of the English Church. A Library of Fathers of the Holy Catholic Church, Anterior to the Division of the East and West. Oxford: John Henry Parker, 1847-57.

———. "Grace and Free Will." In *The Teacher, the Free Choice of the Will, Grace and Free Will*, translated by Robert P. Russell, 243-308. The Fathers of the Church: A New Translation. Washington, DC: Catholic University of America Press, 2004.

———. *Letters (6 Volumes)*. Translated by Wilfrid Parsons and Robert B. Eno. The Fathers of the Church: A New Translation. Edited by Roy Joseph Deferrari et al. Washington, DC: Catholic University of America Press, 1981-2008.

———. "Marriage and Desire." In *Answer to the Pelagians II: Marriage and Desire, Answer to the Two Letters of the Pelagians, Answer to Julian*, edited by John E. Rotelle and translated by Roland J. Teske, 11-96. The Works of Saint Augustine: A Translation for the 21st Century. New York: New City, 1998.

———. "Of True Religion." In *Augustine: Earlier Writings*, edited and translated by John H. S. Burleigh, 218-83. A Library of Christian Classics: Ichthus Edition. Philadelphia: Westminster, 1953.

———. "On Nature and Grace." In *Four Anti-Pelagian Writings*, translated by John A. Mourant and William J. Collinge, 1–90. The Fathers of the Church: A New Translation. Washington, DC: Catholic University of America Press, 2001.

———. *On Order.* Translated by Silvano Borruso. South Bend: St. Augustine's, 2007.

———. "On the Literal Interpretation of Genesis: An Unfinished Book." In *On Genesis*, translated by Roland J. Teske, 143–88. The Fathers of the Church: A New Translation. Washington, DC: Catholic University of America Press, 2001.

———. "On the Proceedings of Pelagius." In *Four Anti-Pelagian Writings*, translated by John A. Mourant and William J. Collinge, 91–178. The Fathers of the Church: A New Translation. Washington, DC: Catholic University of America Press, 2001.

———. "The Enchiridion of Augustine, Addressed to Laurentius; Being a Treatise on Faith, Hope, and Love." In *On Christian Doctrine; the Enchiridion; on Catechising; and on Faith and the Creed*, edited by Marcus Dods and translated by J. F. Shaw and S. D. Salmond, 173–260. The Works of Aurelius Augustine, Bishop of Hippo: A New Translation. Edinburgh: T. & T. Clark, 1873.

———. "The Free Choice of the Will." In *The Teacher, the Free Choice of the Will, Grace and Free Will*, translated by Robert P. Russell, 63–242. The Fathers of the Church: A New Translation. Washington, DC: Catholic University of America Press, 2004.

———. "The Magnitude of the Soul." In *The Immortality of the Soul, the Magnitude of the Soul, on Music, the Advantage of Believing, on Faith in Things Unseen*, translated by John J. McMahon, 49–150. The Fathers of the Church: A New Translation. Washington, DC: Catholic University of America Press, 2002.

———. *The Retractions.* Translated by Mary Inez Bogan. The Fathers of the Church: A New Translation. Edited by Roy Joseph Deferrari et al. Washington, DC: Catholic University of America Press, 1999.

———. "The Soliloquies." In *The Happy Life, Answer to Sceptics, Divine Providence and the Problem of Evil, Soliloquies*, translated by Thomas F. Gilligan, 333–426. The Fathers of the Church: A New Translation. Washington, DC: Catholic University of America Press, 2008.

———. "The Spirit and the Letter." In *Augustine: Later Works*, translated by John Burnaby, 182–250. Philadelphia: Westminister, 1955.

———. "To Simplician." In *Augustine: Earlier Writings*, edited and translated by John H. S. Burleigh, 370–406. A Library of Christian Classics: Ichthus Edition. Philadelphia: Westminister, 1953.

———. "Tractates on the First Epistle of John." In *Tractates on the First Epistle of John*, translated by John W. Rettig, 112–24. The Fathers of the Church: A New Translation. Washington, DC: Catholic University of America Press, 1995.

Baader, Franz Xaver von. *Sämtliche Werke.* Leipzig: Verlag von Herrmann Bethmann, 1851–1860.

Baeumler, Alfred. *Das Irrationalitätsproblem in der Ästhetik und Logik des 18. Jahrhunderts bis zur Kritik der Urteilskraft.* Vol. 2. Tübingen: Wissenschaftliche Buchgesellschaft WBG, 1967.

Balthasar, Hans Urs von. *The Glory of the Lord: A Theological Aesthetics.* Translated by Erasmo Leiva-Merikakis et al. 7 vols. San Francisco: Ignatius, 1982–91.

Baritz, Loren. *City on a Hill: A History of Ideas and Myths in America.* New York: John Wiley & Sons, 1964.

Barrow, Isaac. *The Theological Works of Isaac Barrow, D. D: Volume 2.* 8 vols. Oxford: Oxford University Press, 1830.

Barth, Karl. *Kirchliche Dogmatik.* 5 vols. Zollikon: Verlag der Evangelischen Buchhandlung, 1932–67.

———. *Protestant Theology in the Nineteenth Century: Its Background and History.* Translated by Brian Cozens and John Bowden. London: SMC, 1972.

Basil. "Homily 16: A Psalm of David When He Changed His Countenance before Abimelech and Being Dismissed by Him Went Away (on Psalm 33)." In *Exegetic Homilies*, translated by Agnes Clare Way, 247–74. The Fathers of the Church: A New Translation. Washington, DC: Catholic University of America Press, 2003.

Baxter, Richard. *The Poetical Fragments of Richard Baxter.* London: Pickering, 1821.

———. *The Practical Works of the Late Reverend and Pious Mr. Richard Baxter.* Vol. 2. London: Thomas Parkhurst, Jonathan Robinson, and John Lawrence, 1707.

———. *The Practical Works of the Reverend Richard Baxter.* Vol. 20. London: Duncan, 1830.

Bayle, Pierre. *Mr Bayle's Historical and Critical Dictionary.* 5 vols. Edited by D. Midwinter et al. London, 1734–38.

———. *Œuvres diverses de Mr. Pierre Bayle, contenant tout ce que cet auteur a publié sur ses matières de théologie, de philosophie, de critique, d'histoire et de littérature, excepté son dictionnaire historique et critique.* Edited by P. Husson et al. La Haye, 1727.

Bede, Venerable. *In Lucae Evangelium Expositio.* Patrologia Latina 92. Opera Omnia 3. Edited by Jacques-Paul Migne. Paris, 1862.

Beecher, Edward. *The Conflict of Ages: Or, the Great Debate on the Moral Relations of God and Man.* Boston: Phillips, Sampson, 1853.

Beecher, Lyman. *A Reformation of Morals Practicable and Indispensable.* 2nd ed. Utica: Merrell & Camp, 1813.

———. "Future Punishment of Infants Never a Doctrine of the Calvinistic Churches." *The Spirit of the Pilgrims* 1 (1828) 78–95.

Beecher-Stowe, Harriet. *Sunny Memories of Foreign Lands.* Boston: Sampson Low, Son, 1854.

———. *The Minister's Wooing.* New York, 1959.

Bellamy, Joseph. *The Works of the Rev. Joseph Bellamy.* 3 vols. New York: Stephen Dodge, 1811–12.

Bercovitch, Sacvan. *The Puritan Origins of the American Self.* New Haven: Yale University Press, 1975.

Berkeley, George. *The Works of George Berkeley.* 9 vols. Edited by A. A. Luce and T. E. Jessop. London, 1948–57.

Bernard. *Concerning Grace and Free Will.* Translated by Watkin W. Williams. New York: Macmillan, 1920.

———. "Letter XXVIII (Circa A.D. 1130): To the Abbots Assembled at Soissons." Translated by Samuel J. Eales. In *Some Letters of Saint Bernard Abbot of Clairvaux*, 117–20. London: John Hodges, 1904.

———. *St. Bernard's Sermons on the Canticle of Canticles.* Translated by a priest of Mount Melleray. 2 vols. Dublin: Brown and Nolan, 1920.

Beumer, Johannes. "Et daemones credunt (Iac. 2, 19): Ein Beitrag zur positiven Bewertung der fides informis." *Gregorianum* 22, no. 2 (1941) 231–51.

Blakey, R. *History of the Philosophy of Mind: Embracing the Opinions of All Writers on Mental Science from the Earliest Period to the Present Time.* Vol. 4, London: Saunders, 1848.

Bledsoe, Albert Taylor. *An Examination of President Edwards' Inquiry*. Philadelphia: H. Hooker, 1845.

———. *A Theodicy, or, Vindication of the Divine Glory, as Manifested in the Constitution and Government of the Moral World*. New York: Carlton & Phillips, 1853.

Bogue, Carl W. *Jonathan Edwards and the Covenant of Grace*. Cherry Hill: Mack, 1975.

Boileau-Despréaux, Nicolas. *Satire XII*. Œuvres complètes. Paris: Hachette, 1934.

Boller, Paul F. *Freedom and Fate in American Thought*. Translated by Freedom and Fate. Dallas: Southern Methodist University Press, 1978.

Borges, Jorge Luis. *Obra Poetica*. Madrid, 1972.

———. *Poetic Works*. Madrid, 1972.

Bossuet. *Défense de la tradition et des saints pères*. Œuvres 4. Paris: Vivès, 1862.

Bradford, William. *History of Plymouth Plantation 1606-1646*. New York: Scribner's, 1908.

Bradstreet, Anne. *The Works of Anne Bradstreet*. Gloucester: Peter Smith, 1962.

Breitenbach, William Kern. "New Divinity Theology and the Idea of Moral Accountability." Yale University, 1978.

———. "Unregenerate Doings: Selflessness and Selfishness in New Divinity Theology." *American Quarterly* 34, no. 5 (1982) 479–502.

Bremer, Francis J. *John Winthrop: America's Forgotten Founding Father*. New York: Oxford University Press, 2003.

Brémond, Henri. *Histoire littéraire du sentiment religieux en France*. 12 vols. Paris: Bloud et Gay, 1924–1936.

Brown, Robert E. *Jonathan Edwards and the Bible*. Bloomington: Indiana University Press, 2002.

Browne, Thomas. *The Works of Sir Thomas Browne*. Vol. 1. London: Faber & Gwyer, 1928.

Brumm, Ursula. *Puritanismus und Literatur in Amerika*. Darmstadt: Wissenschaftliche Buchgesellschaft, 1973.

Buell, Samuel. *A Spiritual Knowlege* [sic] *of God in Christ, Comprehensive of All Good and Blessedness*. New London: Timothy Green, 1771.

Bulkeley, Peter. *The Gospel-Covenant*. London: Matthew Simmons, 1651.

Bunyan, John. *Grace Abounding and the Life and Death of Mr. Badman*. London, 1964.

Burton, Asa. *Essays on Some of the First Principles of Metaphysicks, Ethicks and Theology*. Portland: Arthur Shirley, 1854.

Bushnell, Horace. *Christian Nurture*. New Haven: Yale University Press, 1967.

Butler, Joseph. "Dissertation II.—of the Nature of Virtue." In *British Moralists*, edited by L. A. Selby-Bigge, 244–50. Oxford: Clarendon, 1897.

Byington, Ezra Hoyt. "The Theology of Edwards, as Shown in His Treatise Concerning Religious Affections." *American Theological Review* 1, no. 2 (1859) 199–220.

Cady, Edwin H. "The Artistry of Jonathan Edwards." *New England Quarterly* 22, no. 1 (1949) 61–72.

Calvin, John. *A Harmony of the Gospels: Matthew, Mark and Luke (Volume I)*. Translated by A. W. Morrison. Calvin's New Testament Commentaries. Edited by David W. Torrance and Thomas F. Torrance. Grand Rapids: Eerdmans, 1994.

———. *A Harmony of the Gospels: Matthew, Mark and Luke (Volume II)*. Translated by T. H. L. Parker. Calvin's New Testament Commentaries. Edited by David W. Torrance and Thomas F. Torrance. Grand Rapids: Eerdmans, 1995.

———. "Against the Fantastic and Furious Sect of the Libertines Who Are Called 'Spirituals.'" In *Treatises against the Anabaptists and against the Libertines*, edited and translated by Benjamin Wirt Farley, 159–326. Grand Rapids: Baker, 1982.

———. "Commentaries on the Epistle of Paul to the Ephesians." In *Commentaries on the Epistles of Paul to the Galatians and Ephesians*, translated by William Pringle, 189–364. Edinburgh: Calvin Translation Society, 1854.

———. *Commentaries on the First Book of Moses Called Genesis*. Translated by John King. Grand Rapids: Eerdmans, 1948.

———. *Commentary on the Epistles of Paul the Apostle to the Corinthians*. Translated by John Pringle. 2 vols. Edinburgh: T. Constable, 1848–49.

———. *Concerning the Eternal Predestination of God*. Translated by J. K. S. Reid. London: James Clark, 1961.

———. *Institutes of the Christian Religion*. Translated by Henry Beveridge. Grand Rapids: Eerdmans, 1993.

———. *Institution de la religion chrestienne*. 5 vols. Edited by J.-D. Benoît. Paris: Vrin, 1957–60.

———. *Opera Quae Supersunt Omnia. Corpus Reformatorum*. 59 vols. Edited by G. Baum et al. Berlin: Brunswick, 1863–90.

———. *Sermons on Deuteronomy*. Translated by Arthur Golding. Oxford: Banner of Truth, 1987.

———. *The Gospel According to St John 1–10*. Translated by T. H. L. Parker. Calvin's New Testament Commentaries. Edited by David W. Torrance and Thomas F. Torrance. Grand Rapids: Eerdmans, 1995.

———. *The Gospel According to St John 11–21 and the First Epistle of John*. Translated by T. H. L. Parker. Calvin's New Testament Commentaries. Edited by David W. Torrance and Thomas F. Torrance. Grand Rapids: Eerdmans, 1994.

Carse, James P. *Jonathan Edwards and the Visibility of God*. New York: Scribner's, 1967.

Cassirer, Ernst. *The Platonic Renaissance in England*. Translated by James P. Pettegrove. New York: Gordian, 1970.

Channing, William Ellery. *The Moral Argument against Calvinism*. The Works of William E. Channing. Boston: American Unitarian Association, 1900.

Channing, William Henry. "Jonathan Edwards and the Revivalists." *The Christian Examiner* 43, no. 11 (1847) 374–94.

Chauncy, Charles. *The Benevolence of the Deity, Fairly and Impartially Considered*. Boston: Powers and Willis, 1784.

———. *Five Dissertations on the Scripture Account of the Fall; and Its Consequences*. London: C. Dilly, 1785.

Cheever, George B. "Review of Professor Tappan's Works on the Will." *American Biblical Repository* 7, no. 13–4 (1842) 411–40.

Cherry, Conrad. *Nature and Religious Imagination from Edwards to Bushnell*. Philadelphia: Fortress, 1980.

———. *The Theology of Jonathan Edwards: A Reappraisal*. Gloucester: Peter Smith, 1974.

Chesne, J.-B. du. *Le prédestianisme, ou les hérésies sur la prédestination et la réprobation*. Paris, 1724.

Chesterton, Gilbert Keith. *Orthodoxy*. London: John Lane, 1909.

The Christian Book of Concord, or Symbolical Books of the Evangelical Lutheran Church. Translated by C. P. Krauth et al. 2nd ed. Newmarket: S. D. Henkel & Brs., 1854.

The Christian History. Vol. 1. Boston, 1744.
Cicero. *On Moral Ends.* Translated by Raphael Woolf. Cambridge: Cambridge University Press, 2011.
Clebsch, William A. *American Religious Thought: A History.* Chicago: The University of Chicago Press, 1973.
Clement of Alexandria. "The Miscellanies." In *The Writings of Clement of Alexandria,* edited by Alexander Roberts and James Donaldson and translated by W. Wilson, 1–514. Ante-Nicene Christian Library: Translations of the Writings of the Fathers Down to A.D. 325. Edinburgh: T. & T. Clark, 1869.
Colacurcio, R. "The Perception of Excellency as the Glory of God in Jonathan Edwards." New York: Fordham University, 1972.
Coleridge, Samuel Taylor. *Aids to Reflection in the Formation of a Manly Character on the Several Grounds of Prudence, Morality and Religion.* Burlington: Chaunvey Goodrich, 1829.
Colwell, John E. "The Glory of God's Justice and the Glory of God's Grace: Contemporary Reflections on the Doctrine of Hell in the Teaching of Jonathan Edwards." *Evangelical Quarterly* 67 (1995) 291–308.
Cotton, John. *Christ the Fountaine of Life; or, Sundry Choyce Sermons on Part of the Fift Chapter of the First Epistle of St. John.* London: Robert Ibbitson, 1651.
———. *The New Covenant; or, a Treatise Unfolding the Order and Manner of the Giving and Receiving of the Covenant of Grace to the Elect.* London: Francis Eglesfield & John Allen, 1654.
———. *The Way of Life: Or, Gods Way and Course, in Bringing the Soule into, Keeping It in, and Carrying It on, in the Wayes of Life and Peace. Laid Downe in Foure Severall Treatises on Foure Texts of Scripture.* London: M. F., 1641.
Crabtree, Arthur B. *Jonathan Edwards' View of Man: A Study in Eighteenth Century Calvinism.* Wellington: Religious Education, 1948.
Crane, R. S. "Suggestions toward a Genealogy of the 'Man of Feeling.'" *A Journal of English Literary History* 1, no. 3 (1934) 205–30.
Crawford, Michael J. *Seasons of Grace: Colonial New England's Revival Tradition in its British Context.* New York: Oxford University Press, 1991.
Cremin, Lawrence A. *American Education: The Colonial Experience, 1607–1783.* New York: Harper & Row, 1970.
Cromwell, Oliver. *Letters and Speeches.* London: J. M. Dent, 1908.
Crusius, Christian August. *Weg zur Gewißheit und Zuverlässigkeit der menschlichen Erkenntnis.* Leipzig: Verlag Johann Friedrich Gleditsch, 1747.
Cushman, Rorbert E., and Grislis, Egil, eds. *The Heritage of Christian Thought: Essays in Honour of Robert Lowry Calhoun.* New York: Harper and Row, 1965.
Daniel, Stephen H. *The Philosophy of Jonathan Edwards: A Study in Divine Semiotics.* Bloomington: Indiana University Press, 1994.
Dante (Alighieri). *The Divine Comedy of Dante Alighieri: Inferno.* New York: Oxford University Press, 1997.
Davidson, Edward H. "From Locke to Edwards." *Journal of the History of Ideas* 24, no. 3 (1963) 355–72.
Davidson, James W. *The Logic of Millennial Thought: Eighteenth-Century New England.* New Haven: Yale University Press, 1977.
Davis, Thomas M., and Davis, Virginia L. "Edward Taylor on the Day of Judgment." *American Literature* 43, no. 4 (1972) 525–47.

Davis, Thomas M., and Davis, Virginia L., eds. *Edward Taylor Vs. Solomon Stoddard: The Nature of the Lord's Supper*. The Unpublished Writings of Edward Taylor 2. Boston: Twayne, 1981.

Day, Jeremiah. *An Examination of President Edward's Inquiry on the Freedom of the Will*. New Haven: Durrie & Peck, 1841.

De Achaval, Hugo M., and J. Derick Holmes, eds. *The Theological Papers of John Henry Newman on Faith and Certainty*. Oxford: Clarendon, 1976.

Delattre, Roland A. *Beauty and Sensibility in the Thought of Jonathan Edwards: An Essay in Aesthetics and Theological Ethics*. New Haven: Yale University Press, 1968.

Denzinger, H. *Enchiridion symbolorum definitionum et declarationum de rebus fidei et morum*. 37 ed. Freiburg im Breisgau, 1991.

———. *Symboles et définitions de la foi catholique*. Paris: Cerf, 1996.

Descartes, René. "Author's Replies to the Second Set of Objections." In *The Philosophical Writings of Descartes*, translated by John Cottingham et al., 93–120. New York: Cambridge University Press, 2008.

———. *Œuvres de Descartes*. 12 vols. Edited by C. Adam and P. Tannery. Paris: Vrin, 1964–74.

———. *Œuvres philosophiques*. Vol. 2. Paris: Garnier, 1967.

———. "Third Set of Objections with the Author's Replies." In *The Philosophical Writings of Descartes*, translated by John Cottingham et al., 121–37. New York: Cambridge University Press, 2008.

———. "To Princess Elizabeth, 6 October 1645." In *The Philosophical Writings of Descartes: The Correspondence*, translated by John Cottingham et al., 268–73. Cambridge: Cambridge University Press, 1997.

———. "To Princess Elizabeth, January 1646." In *The Philosophical Writings of Descartes: The Correspondence*, translated by John Cottingham et al., 281–83. Cambridge: Cambridge University Press, 1997.

DeWitt, John. *Jonathan Edwards: A Study. An Address Delivered at Stockbridge, Massachusetts, October 5, 1903*. Stockbridge: Berkshire Conferences, 1903.

Dexter, Franklin Bowditch. *Biographical Sketches of the Graduates of Yale College, with Annals of the College History, October, 1701-May, 1745*. New York: Holt, 1885.

———. *The Literary Diary of Ezra Stiles*. 2 vols. New York: Scribner's, 1901.

Dexter, Henry Martyn. *The Congregationalism of the Last Three Hundred Years as Seen in Its Literature*. Westmead: Gregg, 1970.

Dingley, Robert. *The Spiritual Taste Described; and a Glimpse of Christ Discovered*. London: Matthew Simmons, 1649.

Donne, John. *The Poems of John Donne*. Vol. 1. Oxford: Oxford University Press, 1912.

———. *The Works of John Donne*. 6 vols. London: John W. Parker, 1839.

"Dr. Beecher against the Calvinistic Doctrine of Infant Damnation." *The Christian Examiner* 5 (1828) 229–63, 316–40, 506–42.

Dwight, Timothy. *The Triumph of Infidelity: A Poem*. London, 1788.

Eckley, Joseph. *Divine Glory Brought to View in the Condemnation of the Ungodly*. Boston: Robert Hodge, 1782.

Edwards, Jonathan. *Charity and Its Fruits: or, Christian Love as Manifested in the Heart and Life*. Edited by T. Edwards. 1852. Reprint, London: Banner of Truth Trust, 1969.

———. "Manuscript." The Beinecke Rare Book & Manuscript Library, Yale University.

---. *Miscellaneous Observations on Important Theological Subjects, Original and Collected, by the Late Reverend Mr. Jonathan Edwards*. Edinburgh: M. Gray, Vernor & Hood, Ogilvie & Speare, 1793.

---. *Observations Concerning the Scripture Economy of the Trinity and Covenant of Redemption*. New York: Scribner's, 1880.

---. *Remarks on Important Theological Controversies*. Edinburgh, 1796.

---. *Representative Selections*. Edited by C. Faust and T. H. Johnson. New York: American Book, 1935.

---. *Selections from the Unpublished Writings of Jonathan Edwards, of America*. Edited by A. B. Grosart. Edinburgh: Ballantyne, 1865.

---. *The Blessing of God. Previously Unpublished Sermons of Jonathan Edwards*. Edited by M. D. McMullen. Nashville: Broadman and Holman, 2003.

---. *The Salvation of Souls: Nine Previously Unpublished Sermons on the Call of Ministry and the Gospel by Jonathan Edwards*. Edited by R. A. Bailey and G. A. Wills. Wheaton: Good News, 2002.

---. *The Sermons of Jonathan Edwards: A Reader*. Edited by W. H. Kimnach, K. P. Minkema, and D. A. Sweeney. New Haven: Yale University Press, 1999.

---. *The Works of Jonathan Edwards, With an Essay on His Genius and Writings by Henry Rogers. In Two Volumes*. Edited by E. Hickman. London: Westley, 1834.

---. *The Works of Jonathan Edwards*. 73 vols. New Have: Yale University Press, 1743.

---. *The Works of Jonathan Edwards*. 26 vols. New Haven: Yale University Press, 1957–2008.

---. "The Works of Jonathan Edwards Online." Vols. 27–73. Edited by the Jonathan Edwards Center at Yale University. http://edwards.yale.edu.

---. *The Works of Jonathan Edwards, D. D., Late President of Union College, with a Memoir of His Life and Character by Tryon Edwards*. Boston: Doctrinal Tract and Book Society, 1850.

---. *The Works of President Edwards*. 10 vols. 1817–47. Reprint, New York: Burt Franklin, 1968.

---. *The Works of President Edwards, in Eight Volumes*. Worcester: Isaiah Thomas, 1808.

---. *The Works of President Edwards, in Four Volumes. A Reprint of the Worcester Edition*. 4 vols. Boston: Crocker & Brewster, 1843.

---. *The Works of President Edwards with a Memoir of His Life. In Ten Volumes*. Edited by S. E. Dwight. New York: S. Converse, 1829.

---. *Treatise on Grace and Other Posthumously Published Writings by Jonathan Edwards*. Edited by P. Helm. Cambridge: James Clarke, 1971.

Edwards, Jonathan, Jr. *The Works of Jonathan Edwards, D. D.: Late President of Union College, with a Memoir of His Life and Character*. 2 vols. Andover: Allen, Morrill & Wardwell, 1842.

Elwood, Douglas J. *The Philosophical Theology of Jonathan Edwards*. New York: Columbia University Press, 1960.

Emerson, Everett H. *John Cotton*. New Haven: Twayne, 1965.

Emmons, Nathanael. *The Works*. 6 vols. Boston: Crocker and Brewster, 1842.

Erdt, Terrence. *Jonathan Edwards: Art and the Sense of the Heart*. Amherst: University of Massachusetts Press, 1980.

Eusden, John Dykstra. "Introduction." In *The Marrow of Theology*, edited by John Dykstra Eusden, 1–66. Grand Rapids: Baker, 1968.
Evans, W. Glyn. "Jonathan Edwards — Puritan Paradox." *Bibliotheca Sacra* 124 (1967) 51–65.
Exercises Commemorating the 200th Anniversary of the Birth of Jonathan Edwards. Andover: Franklin, 1904.
Farrar, Frederic William. *Eternal Hope: Five Sermons*. London: Macmillan, 1878.
Fénelon. *Lettres et opuscules spirituelles*. Œuvres 1. Paris: Gallimard, 1983.
Ferm, Robert L. *A Colonial Pastor: Jonathan Edwards the Younger, 1745–1801*. Grand Rapids: Eerdmans, 1976.
Fiering, Norman. *Jonathan Edwards's Moral Thought and Its British Context*. Chapel Hill: The University of North Carolina Press, 1981.
———. *Moral Philosophy at Seventeenth Century Harvard: A Discipline in Transition*. Chapel Hill: University of North Carolina Press, 1981.
Finley, Samuel. *The Curse of Meroz; or, the Danger of Neutrality, in the Cause of God, and Our Country*. Philadelphia: James Chattin, 1757.
Fisher, George Park. *An Unpublished Essay of Edwards on the Trinity, with Remarks on Edwards and His Theology*. New York: Scribner's, 1903.
Fleming, Sandford. *Children and Puritanism*. New York: Arno, 1969.
Flower, Elizabeth F., and Murphey, Murray G. *A History of Philosophy in America*. Vol. 1. New York: Putnam's, 1977.
Foster, Frank Hugh. *A Genetic History of the New England Theology*. Chicago: University of Chicago Press, 1907.
Francis de Sales. *Treatise on the Love of God*. Translated by John K. Ryan. Vol. 2. Rockford: Tan Books, 1975.
Frank, Gustav. *Geschichte der protestantischen Theologie*. Leipzig: Breitkopf und Härtel, 1862.
Frei, Hans W. *The Eclipse of Biblical Narrative: A Study in Eighteenth and Nineteenth Century Hermeneutics*. New Haven: Yale University Press, 1974.
Gale, Theophilus. *The Court of the Gentiles*. 4 vols. London: A. Maxwell and R. Roberts, 1669–1678.
Gandillac, Maurice de. *Valeur du temps dans la pédagogie spirituelle de Jean Tauler*. Montréal: Institut d'Études médiévales; Paris: Vrin, 1956.
Gardiner, H. N. "The Early Idealism of Jonathan Edwards." *Philosophical Review* 9, no. 6 (1900) 573–96.
Garrison, Joseph M., Jr. "Teaching Early American Literature: Some Suggestions." *College English* 31, no. 5 (1970) 487–97.
Gaustad, Edwin S. *The Great Awakening in New England*. Chicago: Quadrangle, 1968.
Gay, Peter. *A Loss of Mastery: Puritan Historians in Colonial America*. Berkeley: University of California Press, 1966.
Gerstner, John. *Jonathan Edwards on Heaven and Hell*. Grand Rapids: Baker Book House, 1980.
———. *Steps to Salvation: The Evangelistic Message of Jonathan Edwards*. Philadelphia: Westminster, 1960.
———. *The Rational Biblical Theology of Jonathan Edwards*. 3 vols. Orlando: Berea, 1991–1993.
Gibbon, Edward. *The History of the Decline and Fall of the Roman Empire*. London: Henry G. Bohn, 1854.

Gibson, James. *Locke's Theory of Knowledge and Its Historical Relations*. Cambridge: Cambridge University Press, 1917.
Gilson, Étienne. *L'esprit de la philosophie médiévale*. Vol. 2. Paris: Vrin, 1948.
———. *La liberté chez Descartes et la théologie*. Paris: Alcan, 1913.
———. *The Spirit of Mediaeval Philosophy (Gifford Lectures 1931-1932)*. Translated by A. H. C. Downes. Notre Dame: University of Notre Dame Press, 1991.
Gohdes, Clarence. "Aspects of Idealism in Early New England." *The Philosophical Review* 39, no. 6 (1930) 537-55.
Goodwin, Thomas. *The Works of Thomas Goodwin, D. D.* 12 vols. Edinburgh: James Nichol, 1861-1866.
"The Great Christian Doctrine of Original Sin Defended." *The Monthly Review* 36 (1767) 17-21.
Gregory of Nyssa, *The Life of Moses*. Translated by A. Halherbe and E. Ferguson. New York: Paulist Press, 1978.
Gregory the Great. *Morals on the Book of Job*. 3 vols. Oxford: John Henry Parker, 1844-1850.
Griffin, Edward D. *An Humble Attempt to Reconcile the Differences of Christians Respecting the Extent of the Atonement*. New York: Stephen Dodge, 1819.
Güder, Eduard. *Die Lehre von der Erscheinung Jesu Christi unter den Todten*. Bern: Jent & Reinert, 1854.
Gueroult, Martial. *Berkeley*. Paris: Aubier, 1956.
Guelzo, Allen Carl. *Edwards on the Will: A Century of American Theological Debate*. Middletown: Wesleyan University Press, 1989.
Guillaume de Saint-Thierry. *La contemplation de Dieu. L'oraison de Dom Guillaume*. Paris: Cerf, 1959.
Guilloré, François. *Le progrès de la vie spirituelle*. Paris: Étienne Michallet, 1675.
Hall, David D. *Worlds of Wonder, Days of Judgment: Popular Religious Belief in Early New England*. New York: Harvard University Press, 1989.
Haller, William. *The Rise of Puritanism*. Philadelphia: University of Pennsylvania Press, 1972.
Hamon, Jean. *Soliloques sur le psaume 118*. Paris, 1685.
Hankamer, Ernst Wolfram. *Das politische Denken von Jonathan Edwards*. Munich: Ludwig Maximilians Universität, 1972.
Haroutunian, Joseph. *Piety Versus Moralism: The Passing of the New England Theology*. New York: Harper & Row, 1970.
Hart, Darryl G., Lucas, Sean Michael, and Nichols, Stephen J., eds. *The Legacy of Jonathan Edwards: American Religion and the Evangelical Tradition*. Grand Rapids: Baker, 2003.
Hart, William. *Remarks on President Edwards's Dissertations Concerning the Nature of True Virtue*. New Haven: T. and S. Green, 1771.
Hawthorne, Nathaniel. *The Centenary Edition of the Works of Nathaniel Hawthorne*. Edited by William Charvat, Roy Harvey Pearce, and Claude M. Simpson. Columbus: Ohio State University Press, 1962-.
Hegel, Georg Wilhelm Friedrich. *Elements of the Philosophy of Right*. Translated by H. B. Nisbet. Cambridge: Cambridge University Press, 2003.
———. *Enzyklopädie der philosophischen Wissenschaften im Grundrisse*. Gesammelte Werke 20. Hamburg: Felix Meiner Verlag, 1992.

———. *Enzyklopädie der philosophischen Wissenschaften im Grundrisse*. Werke 9. Frankfurt am Main: Suhrkamp Verlag, 1970.
———. *Lectures on the Philosophy of Religion*. Translated by R. F. Brown, P. C. Hodgson, J. M. Stewart, and H. S. Harris. 3 vols. Oxford: Oxford University Press, 2011–2012.
———. *Lectures on the Proofs for the Existence of God*. Edited and Translated by Peter C. Hodgson. New York: Oxford University Press, 2011.
———. *Phänomenologie des Geistes*. Gesammelte Werke 9. Hamburg: Felix Meiner Verlag, 1980.
———. *Vorlesungen über Rechtsphilosophie*. Vol. 2. Stuttgart: Frommann-Holzboog, 1974.
Heidelberg Catechism. Cleveland: Reformed Church, 1877.
Heimert, Alan. "Puritanism, the Wilderness, and the Frontier." *The New England Quarterly* 26, no. 3 (1953) 361–82.
———. *Religion and the American Mind*. Cambridge: Harvard University Press, 1966.
Heimert, Alan, and Miller, Perry, eds. *The Great Awakening: Documents Illustrating the Crisis and Its Consequences*. Indianapolis: Bobbs-Merrill, 1967.
Heinze, Max, ed. *Philosophische Abhandlungen Für Max Heinze*. Berlin: Ernst Siegfried und Sohn, 1906.
Helvétius. *De l'esprit*. Œuvres complètes 1. Hildesheim: Georg Olms Verlag, 1969.
Henrich, Dieter. „Hutcheson und Kant." *Kant-Studien* 49, no. 1–4 (1957) 49–69.
Heppe, Heinrich. *Die Dogmatik der Evangelisch-Reformierten Kirche*. Edited by E. Bizer. Neukirchen, 1935.
———. *Reformed Dogmatics Set out and Illustrated from the Sources*. Translated by G. T. Thomson. London: George Allen and Unwin, 1950.
Hill, George. *Lectures in Divinity*. Vol. 2. Edinburgh: Waugh, 1821.
Hincmar of Rheims. *De Praedestinatione Dei et Libero Arbitrio*. Patrologia Latina 125. Opera Omnia 1. Edited by Jacques-Paul Migne. Paris, 1852.
Hirsch, Emanuel. *Geschichte der neueren evangelischen Theologie*. 5 vols. Gütersloh: Bertelsmann, 1949–1954.
Hodge, Charles. *Systematic Theology*. New York: Scribner's, 1872.
Homer. *The Odyssey*. Translated by William Cooper. 5th ed. London: Baldwin, Cradock, and Joy, 1820.
Hooker, Richard. *Of the Laws of Ecclesiastical Polity: Attack and Response*. The Folger Edition of the Works of Richard Hooker 4. Cambridge: Harvard University Press, 1982.
Hooker, Thomas. *Redemption: Three Sermons, 1637–1656*. Gainsville: Scholars' Facsimiles & Reprints, 1956.
———. *The Application of Redemption by the Effectual Work of the Word, and Spirit of Christ, for the Bringing Home of Lost Sinners to God*. London: Peter Cole, 1656.
———. *The Covenant of Grace Opened*. London: G. Dawson, 1649.
———. *The Saints Dignitie and Dutie, Together with the Danger of Ignorance and Hardnesse*. London: Francis Eglesfield, 1651.
———. *The Soules Humiliation*. London: Andrew Crooke, 1638.
———. *The Soules Vocation or Effectual Calling to Christ*. London: John Haviland, 1638.
———. *The Unbeleevers Preparing for Christ*. London: Thomas Cotes, 1638.

———. *Writings in England and Holland, 1626–1633.* Cambridge: Harvard University Press, 1975.
Hopkins, Samuel. *System of Doctrines.* Vol. 1. Boston: Lincoln & Edmands, 1811.
———. "The Life and Character of the Late Reverend Mr. Jonathan Edwards." In *Jonathan Edwards: A Profile,* edited by David Levin. New York: Hill and Wang, 1969.
———. *The Works of Samuel Hopkins, D. D.* 3 vols. Boston, 1854.
Howard, Leon. *"The Mind" of Jonathan Edwards: A Reconstructed Text.* Berkeley: University of California Press, 1963.
Hume, David. *An Enquiry Concerning Human Understanding.* Indianapolis: Bobbs-Merrill, 1955.
Hutcheson, Francis. *An Essay on the Nature and Conduct of the Passions and Affections.* London: J. Darby and T. Browne, 1728.
———. *An Inquiry Concerning Beauty, Order, Harmony, Design.* The Hague: Martinus Nijhoff, 1973.
———. *An Inquiry into the Original of Our Ideas of Beauty and Virtue.* Edited by J. Darby et al.. London, 1726.
Huxley, Thomas Henry. *Hume.* London: Macmillan, 1879.
Inge, William Ralph. *The Platonic Tradition in English Religious Thought: The Hulsean Lectures at Cambridge 1925–1926.* London: Longmans, Green, 1926.
Isaac the Syrian. *Discours ascétiques.* Translated by Jacques Touraille. Œuvres Spirituelles 84. Paris: Desclée de Brouwer, 1981.
Isidore of Seville. *Sententiarum Libri Tres.* Patrologia Latina 83. Opera Omnia 5. Edited by Jacques-Paul Migne. Paris, 1862.
Iwand, Hans Joachim. *Rechtfertigungslehre und Christusglaube.* Vol. 3. Munich: Kaiser, 1966.
Jacobs, Paul. *Institution: Prädestination und Verantwortlichkeit bei Calvin.* Darmstadt, 1973.
James, William. *The Varieties of Religious Experience.* New York: Macmillan, 1961.
Jansenius, Cornelius. *Augustinus.* 3 vols. Rouen: Jean Berthelin, 1643.
Jenson, Robert W. *America's Theologian: A Recommendation of Jonathan Edwards.* New York: Oxford University Press, 1988.
Jenyns, Soame. *A Free Inquiry into the Nature and Origin of Evil.* London: R. and J. Dodsley, 1757.
Jerome. *Commentariorum in Isaiam.* Patrologia Latina 24. Opera Omnia 4. Edited by Jacques-Paul Migne. Paris, 1863.
John of the Cross. *Noche Oscura de la Subida del Monto Carmelo.* In *Obras Completas* 2. Madrid, 1980.
———. "The Dark Night." In *The Collected Works of St. John of the Cross,* translated by Kieran Kavanaugh and Otilio Rodriguez. Washington, DC: Institute of Carmelite Studies, 1979.
John of Damascus. "An Exact Exposition of the Orthodox Faith." In *Writings,* edited by Hermigild Dressler et al. and translated by Frederic H. Chase Jr., 165–406. The Fathers of the Church: A New Translation. Washington, DC: Catholic University of America Press, 1999.
Johnson, Edward. *The Wonder-Working Providence 1628–1651.* New York: Scribner's, 1910.
Johnson, Samuel. *The Works of Samuel Johnson, LLD.* London: George Cowie, 1825.

Johnson, Thomas H. *The Printed Writings of Jonathan Edwards, 1703–1758: A Bibliography*. Edited by M. X. Lesser. Princeton: Princeton University Press, 2003.

Jones, James W. *The Shattered Synthesis: New England Puritanism before the Great Awakening*. New Haven: Yale University Press, 1973.

Kames, Henry Home. *Essays on the Principles of Morality and Natural Religion*. Edinburgh: R. Fleming, 1751.

Kant, Immanuel. "Anthropology from a Pragmatic Point of View." In *Anthropology, History, and Education*, edited by Günter Zöller and Robert B. Louden and translated by Robert B. Louden, 227–429. The Cambridge Edition of the Works of Immanuel Kant. New York: Cambridge University Press, 2007.

———. "Conjectural Beginning of Human History." In *Anthropology, History, and Education*, edited by Günter Zöller and Robert B. Louden and translated by Allen W. Wood, 160–75. The Cambridge Edition of the Works of Immanuel Kant. New York: Cambridge University Press, 2007.

———. *Correspondence*. Edited and Translated by Arnulf Zweig. The Cambridge Edition of the Works of Immanuel Kant. Edited by Paul Guyer and Allen W. Wood. New York: Cambridge University Press, 1999.

———. "Critique of Practical Reason." In *Practical Philosophy*, edited and translated by Mary J. Gregor, 133–272. The Cambridge Edition of the Works of Immanuel Kant. New York: Cambridge University Press, 1999.

———. *Critique of Pure Reason*. Translated by Paul Guyer and Allen W. Wood. The Cambridge Edition of the Works of Immanuel Kant. Edited by Paul Guyer and Allen W. Wood. New York: Cambridge University Press, 2009.

———. *Critique of the Power of Judgement*. Translated by Paul Guyer and Eric Matthews. The Cambridge Edition of the Works of Immanuel Kant. Edited by Paul Guyer and Allen W. Wood. New York: Cambridge University Press, 2000.

———. *Gesammelte Schriften*. Ausgabe der Königlichen Preussischen Academie ed. 29 vols. Berlin, 1902–.

———. "Groundwork of the Metaphysics of Morals." In *Practical Philosophy*, edited and translated by Mary J. Gregor, 37–108. The Cambridge Edition of the Works of Immanuel Kant. New York: Cambridge University Press, 1999.

———. "Lectures on the Philosophical Doctrine of Religion." In *Religion and Rational Theology*, edited by Allen W. Wood and George di Giovanni and translated by Allen W. Wood, 335–452. The Cambridge Edition of the Works of Immanuel Kant. New York: Cambridge University Press, 2001.

———. "Moral Philosophy: Collins's Lecture Notes." In *Lectures on Ethics*, edited by Peter Heath and J. B. Schneewind and translated by Peter Heath, 37–222. The Cambridge Edition of the Works of Immanuel Kant. New York: Cambridge University Press, 1997.

———. *Œuvres philosophiques*. 3 vols. Paris: Gallimard, 1980–86.

———. "On the Causes of Earthquakes on the Occasion of the Calamity that Befell the Western Countries of Europe Towards the End of Last Year." In *Natural Science*, edited by Eric Watkins and translated by Olaf Reinhardt, 327–37. The Cambridge Edition of the Works of Immanuel Kant. New York: Cambridge University Press, 2013.

———. "Religion within the Boundaries of Mere Reason." In *Religion and Rational Theology*, edited by Allen W. Wood and George di Giovanni and translated by

George di Giovanni, 39–216. The Cambridge Edition of the Works of Immanuel Kant. New York: Cambridge University Press, 2001.

———. "Review of Schulz's Attempt at Introduction to a Doctrine of Morals for All Human Beings Regardless of Different Religions." In *Practical Philosophy*, edited and translated by Mary J. Gregor, 1–11. The Cambridge Edition of the Works of Immanuel Kant. New York: Cambridge University Press, 1999.

———. "The Conflict of the Faculties." In *Religion and Rational Theology*, edited by Allen W. Wood and George di Giovanni and translated by Major J. Gregor and Robert Anchor, 233–328. The Cambridge Edition of the Works of Immanuel Kant. New York: Cambridge University Press, 2001.

———. "The Metaphysics of Morals." In *Practical Philosophy*, edited and translated by Mary J. Gregor, 353–604. The Cambridge Edition of the Works of Immanuel Kant. New York: Cambridge University Press, 1999.

Kasher, Menahem M. *Encyclopedia of Biblical Interpretation*. Vol. 1. New York: American Biblical Encyclopedia Society, 1953.

Kierkegaard, Sören. *Journal 2*. Translated by Knud Ferlov and Jean-Jacques Gateau. Paris: Gallimard, 1954.

———. *Journal 5*. Translated by Knud Ferlov and Jean-Jacques Gateau. Paris: Gallimard, 1961.

———. *Philosophical Fragments*. Translated by David Swensen and Howard V. Hong. Princeton: Princeton University Press, 1962.

———. *The Sickness Unto Death*. Translated by Walter Lowrie. Princeton: Princeton University Press, 1941.

Kimnach, Wilson Henry. "The Literary Techniques of Jonathan Edwards." Dissertation. University of Pennsylvania, 1971.

King, H. C. "Jonathan Edwards as Philosopher and Theologian." *Hartford Seminary Record* 14, no. 1 (1903) 22–57.

Kingman, Henry. *Jonathan Edwards: A Commemorative Address in Observance of the Bicentenary of His Birth, at First Congregational Church, Berkeley, California, October 5, 1903*. San Francisco: Pacific Theological Seminary, 1904.

Kittel, Gerhard, ed. *Theologisches Wörterbuch zum Neuen Testament*. Vol. 5. Stuttgart: W. Kohlhammer, 1954.

Knight, Janice. "Typology." In *The Princeton Companion to Jonathan Edwards*, edited by Sang Hyun Lee. Princeton: Princeton University Press, 2005.

Köstlin, Julius. *The Theology of Luther in Its Historical Development and Inner Harmony*. Translated by Charles E. Hay. Vol. 2. Philadelphia: Lutheran Publication Society, 1897.

Kraus, Anni. *Der Begriff der Dummheit bei Thomas von Aquin und seine Spiegelung in Sprache und Kultur*. Münster: Münster Aschendorff, 1971.

Kretzöi, Mikósné. *Az amerikai irodalom kezdetei, 1607–1750*. Budapest, 1976.

Lallemant, Louis. *Spiritual Doctrine*. Translated by Frederick William Faber. London: Burns & Lambert, 1855.

Laporte, Jean. *La doctrine de Port-Royal*. Paris: Presses Universitaires de France, 1923.

Laurence, David Ernst. "Religious Experience in the Biblical World of Jonathan Edwards." PhD diss., Yale University, 1976.

Lecky, William Edward Hartpole. *History of the Rise and Influence of the Spirit of Rationalism in Europe*. New York: Appleton, 1871.

Lee, Sang Hyun. *The Philosophical Theology of Jonathan Edwards*. Princeton: Princeton University Press, 1988.

Leibniz, Gottfried W. *Confessio Philosophi*. Translated by Yvon Belaval. Paris: Vrin, 1970.

———. "Discourse on Metaphysics." In *Philosophical Essays*, edited and translated by Roger Andrew and Daniel Garber, 35–68. Indianapolis: Hackett, 1989.

———. "Letter to Magnus Wedderkopf, May 1671." In *Philosophical Papers and Letters*, edited and translated by Leroy E. Loemker, 146–47. The New Synthese Historical Library: Texts and Studies in the History of Philosophy. Dordrecht: Kluwer, 1989.

———. *New Essays Concerning Human Understanding*. Translated by Alfred Gideon Langley. New York: Macmillan, 1896.

———. *Philosophische Schriften*. 7 vols. Edited by C. J. Gerhardt. Berlin, 1875–90.

———. *Textes inédits, d'après les manuscrits de la bibliothèque provinciale de Hanovre*. Paris: Presses Universitaires de France, 1948.

———. "The Principles of Philosophy, or, the Monadology." In *Philosophical Essays*, edited and translated by Roger Andrew and Daniel Garber, 213–25. Indianapolis: Hackett, 1989.

———. *Theodicy: Essays on the Goodness of God, the Freedom of Man and the Origin of Evil*. Translated by E. M. Huggard. New York: Cosimo Classics, 2009.

Leroux, Emmanuel. "Le développement de la pensée philosophique aux États-Unis." *Revue de synthèse historique* 29 (1919) 125–49.

Lesser, M. X. *Jonathan Edwards: A Reference Guide*. Boston: G. K. Hall, 1981.

———. *Jonathan Edwards: An Annotated Bibliography, 1979–1993*. Westport: Greenwood Press, 1994.

———. *Reading Jonathan Edwards: An Annotated Bibliography in Three Parts, 1729–2005*. Grand Rapids: Eerdmans, 2008.

Levin, David, ed. *Jonathan Edwards: A Profile*. New York: Hill and Wang, 1969.

Levy, Babette M. *Preaching in the First Half Century of New England History*. Hartford: American Society of Church History, 1945.

Lewis, C. S. *English Literature in the Sixteenth Century Excluding Drama*. Oxford: Oxford University Press, 1954.

Lichtenstein, Aharon. *Henry More: The Rational Theology of a Cambridge Platonist*. Cambridge: Harvard University Press, 1962.

Locke, John. *An Essay Concerning Human Understanding*. Edited by P. H. Nidditch. Oxford: Clarendon, 1973.

Lombard, Peter. *The Sentences: Book 2: On Creation*. Translated by Giulio Silano. Medieval Sources in Translation. Edited by Joeseph Goering and Giulio Silano. Toronto: Pontifical Institute of Medieval Studies, 2012.

———. *The Sentences: Book 3: On the Incarnation of the Word*. Translated by Giulio Silano. Medieval Sources in Translation. Edited by Joeseph Goering and Giulio Silano. Toronto: Pontifical Institute of Medieval Studies, 2010.

Loring, Israel. *Serious Thoughts on the Miseries of Hell*. Boston: J. Phillips, 1732.

Lowell, Robert. "Jonathan Edwards in Western Massachusetts." In *For the Union Dead*, 40–44. New York: Farrar, Straus & Giroux, 1964.

Lowrie, Ernest Benson. *The Shape of the Puritan Mind: The Thought of Samuel Willard*. New Haven: Yale University Press, 1974.

Luther, Martin. *D. Martin Luthers Werke: kritische Gesamtausgabe*. 62 vols. Weimar, 1883–2009.

———. *In Oseam Prophetam*. Exegetica Opera Latina 24. Frankfurt, 1870.
———. *Lectures on Galatians (1519)*. Luther's Works 27. St Louis: Concordia, 1964.
MacCracken, Henry Mitchell. "The Hall of Fame." *American Monthly Review of Reviews* 22 (1900) 563–71.
MacPhail, Andrew. "Jonathan Edwards." In *Essays in Puritanism*, 1–68. London: T. Fisher Unwin, 1905.
Malebranche, Nicolas. *Œuvres complètes*. 21 vols. Paris: Vrin, 1962–1970.
Manspeaker, Nancy. *Jonathan Edwards: Bibliographical Synopses*. Lewiston: Edwin Mellen, 1981.
Marsden, George M. *Jonathan Edwards: A Life*. New Haven: Yale University Press, 2003.
Martz, Louis L. *The Poetry of Meditation*. 2nd ed. New Haven: Yale University Press, 1962.
Mastricht, Peter van. *Theoretico-Practica Theologia*. Utrecht: Thomae Appels, 1699.
Mather, Cotton. *Magnalia Christi Americana: Or, the Ecclesiastical History of New-England*. Hartford: Andrus, 1855.
Mather, Increase. *A Sermon Occasioned by the Execution of a Man Found Guilty of Murder*. Boston: Richard Pierce, 1687.
———. *Discourse Concerning the Danger of Apostasy*. Boston: Richard Pierce, 1685.
Maurice, Frederick Denison. *Modern Philosophy; or, Moral and Metaphysical Philosophy*. Vol. 4. London: Griffin, Bohn, 1862.
Mausbach, Joseph. *Die Ethik des heiligen Augustinus*. 2nd ed. 2 vols. Freiburg im Breisgau: Herder, 1929.
May, Henry F. *The Enlightenment in America*. New York: Oxford University Press, 1976.
McClelland, G. *Predestination and Election Vindicated from Dependence on Moral Necessity, and Reconciled with Free-Will and Universal Atonement*. Edinburgh, 1848.
McClymond, Michael J. *Encounters with God: An Approach to the Theology of Jonathan Edwards*. New York: Oxford University Press, 1998.
McDermott, Gerald R. *Jonathan Edwards Confronts the Gods: Christian Theology, Enlightenment Religion, and Non-Christian Faiths*. Oxford: Oxford University Press, 2000.
———. *One Holy and Happy Society: The Public Theology of Jonathan Edwards*. University Park: Pennsylvania State University Press, 1992.
McGiffert, Arthur C., Jr., ed. *Young Emerson Speaks: Unpublished Discourses on Many Subjects*. Boston: Houghton Mifflin, 1938.
McGiffert, Michael. "American Puritan Studies in the 1960's." *The William and Mary Quarterly* 27, no. 1 (1970) 36–67.
McGinley, Phyllis. *Times Three: Selected Verse from Three Decades with Seventy New Poems*. New York: Viking, 1961.
Melanchthon, Philip. *Commonplaces: Loci Communes 1521*. Translated by Christian Preus. Saint Louis: Concordia, 2014.
Melville, Herman. *The Works of Herman Melville*. 16 vols. New York: Russell and Russell, 1963.
Miller, Perry. *Errand into the Wilderness*. Cambridge: Harvard University Press, 1956.
———. *Jonathan Edwards*. New York: Meridian, 1959.
———. "Jonathan Edwards on the Sense of the Heart." *Harvard Theological Review* 41, no. 2 (1948) 123–45.
———. *Orthodoxy in Massachusetts, 1630–1650*. Boston: Beacon, 1959.

———. *The New England Mind.* 2 vols. Boston: Beacon, 1961.
Miller, Perry, ed. *Images or Shadows of Divine Things.* New Haven: Yale University Press, 1948.
Miller, Perry, and Thomas H. Johnson, eds. *The Puritans.* 2 vols. New York: Harper Torchbooks, 1963.
Miller, Samuel. *A Brief Retrospect of the Eighteenth Century.* New York: T. and J. Swords, 1803.
———. *Jonathan Edwards.* New York: Harper, 1902.
Milton, John. *A Treatise on Christian Doctrine.* Translated by Charles R. Sumner. Cambridge: J. Smith, 1825.
———. *The Works of John Milton.* 18 vols. New York: Columbia University Press, 1931–42.
Möhler, Johann Adam. *Symbolik oder Darstellung der dogmatischen Gegensätze der Katholiken und Protestanten.* Vol. 3. Mainz: Florian Kupferberg, 1834.
Moltmann, Jürgen. *Prädestination und Perseveranz : Geschichte und Bedeutung der reformierten Lehre „de perseverantia sanctorum."* Neukirchen: Neukirchener Verlag der Buchhandlung des Erziehungsvereins, 1961.
Moncreiff-Wellwood, Henry. *Account of the Life and Writings of John Erskine, D. D.* Edinburgh: Constable, 1818.
Montcheuil, Yves de. *Malebranche et le quiétisme.* Paris: Aubier, 1946.
"Monthly Catalogue: For September, 1774." *The Monthly Review* (1774) 234–46.
More, Henry. *Enchiridion Ethicum.* Translated by Edward Southwell. New York: Facsimile Text Society, 1930.
Morgan, Edmund S. *The Gentle Puritan: A Life of Ezra Stiles.* New Haven: Yale University Press, 1962.
———. *Visible Saints: The History of a Puritan Idea.* New York: New York University Press, 1963.
Morris, William Sparks. "The Reappraisal of Edwards." *The New England Quarterly* 30, no. 4 (1957) 515–25.
———. *The Young Jonathan Edwards: A Reconstruction.* Eugene: Wipf & Stock, 2005.
Muirhead, John H. *The Platonic Tradition in Anglo-Saxon Philosophy.* London: G. Allen & Unwin, 1931 .
Müller, Julius. *The Christian Doctrine of Sin.* Translated by William Urwick. Vol. 2. Edinburgh: T. & T. Clark, 1885.
Murdock, Kenneth. *Literature and Theology in Colonial New England.* Cambridge: Harvard University Press, 1949.
Murray, Iain Hamish. *Jonathan Edwards: A New Biography.* Grand Rapids: Banner of Truth Trust, 1987.
Newtoun, B. *A Preservative against the Doctrine of Fate.* Boston, 1770.
Nicole, Pierre. *Essais de morale.* Vol. 7. Paris, 1730.
———. *Instructions théologiques et morales sur le symbole.* Paris: Guillaume Desprez et Jean Desessartz, 1725.
Niebuhr, H. Richard. *The Kingdom of God in America.* New York: Harper Torchbook, 1959.
Niemeyer, Hermann A. *Collectio Confessionum in Ecclesiis Reformatis Publicatarum.* Leipzig, 1840.
Nietzsche, Friedrich. *On the Genealogy of Morality.* Translated by Carol Diethe. New York: Cambridge University Press, 2006.

———. *Philosophy in the Tragic Age of the Greeks*. Translated by Marianne Cowan. Washington, DC: Regnery, 1998.

De Normandie, James. "Jonathan Edwards at Portsmouth, New Hampshire." *Proceedings of the Massachusetts Historical Society* 15 (1901) 16–20.

Noll, Mark A. *America's God, From Jonathan Edwards to Abraham Lincoln*. New York: Oxford University Press, 2002.

Norris, John. *The Theory and Resolution of Love*. Oxford: Clements, 1688.

Nuttall, Geoffrey F. *The Holy Spirit in Puritan Faith and Experience*. Chicago: The University of Chicago Press, 1992.

Opie, John, ed. *Jonathan Edwards and the Enlightenment*. Lexington: Heath, 1969.

Orcibal, Jean. *Les origines du jansénisme*. Vol. 5. Paris: Vrin, 1962.

Osgood, Samuel. "Jonathan Edwards." *The Christian Examiner* 44, no. 9 (1848) 367–86.

Owen, John. *Pneumatologia; or, a Discourse Concerning the Holy Spirit Wherein an Account Is Given of His Name, Nature, Personality, Dispensation, Operations, and Effects*. London: J. Darby, 1674.

———. *The Death of Death in the Death of Christ*. London: Banner of Truth, 1959.

Pancoast, Henry Spackman. *An Introduction to American Literature*. New York: Holt, 1898.

Parain, Brice, ed. *Histoire de la philosophie* Vol. 2. Paris: Gallimard, 1973.

Park, Edwards. A., ed. *Memoir of Nathanael Emmons; with Sketches of His Friends and Pupils*. Boston: Congregational Board of Publication, 1861.

———. *Memoir of the Life and Character of Samuel Hopkins, D. D*. Boston: Doctrinal Tract and Book Society, 1852.

———. "New England Theology." *Bibliotheca Sacra* 9, no. 33 (1852) 170–220.

———. *The Atonement: Discourses and Treatises*. Boston: Congregational Board of Publication, 1859.

Parker, Alexander A. *The Theology of the Devil in the Drama of Calderon*. London: Blackfriars, 1958.

Parrington, Vernon Louis. *Main Currents in American Thought: An Interpretation of American Literature from the Beginnings to 1920*. New York: Harcourt, Brace and World, 1958.

Parsons, Jonathan. *Sixty Sermons on Various Subjects*. Newbury-Port, 1780.

Parton, James. *The Life and Times of Aaron Burr*. Vol. 1. New York: Houghton Mifflin, 1898.

———. *The Life and Times of Aaron Burr*. 2 vols. New York: Mason, 1864.

Pascal, Blaise. *Œuvres complètes*. Paris: Seuil, 1963.

———. *Penseés*. Translated by A. J. Krailsheimer. London: Penguin, 1966.

———. *The Provincial Letters of Blaise Pascal*. Translated by Thomas M'Crie. Cambridge: Osgood, 1880.

———. "Writings on Grace." In *Pensées and Other Writings*, edited by Anthony Levi, 205–26. New York: Oxford University Press, 1995.

Pattison, T. Harwood. *The History of Christian Preaching*. Philadelphia: American Baptist Publication Society, 1909.

Pauw, Amy Plantinga. *The Supreme Harmony of All: The Trinitarian Theology of Jonathan Edwards*. Grand Rapids: Eerdmans, 2002.

Perkins, William. *The Workes of That Famous and Worthy Minister of Christ in the Vniversitie of Cambridge, M. William Perkins*. 3 vols. London: John Legatt, 1616–18.

Personal Reminiscences of the Life and Times of Gardiner Spring. Vol. 1. New York: Scribner's, 1866.
Pettit, Norman. *The Heart Prepared: Grace and Conversation in Puritan Spiritual Life.* New Haven: Yale University Press, 1966.
Phillips, Samuel. *The Orthodox Christian; or, a Child Well Instructed in the Principles of the Christian Religion.* Boston: S. Kneeland, and T. Green, for D. Henchman, 1738.
Plato. *Laws.* In *Plato: Complete Works,* edited by John M. Cooper and D. S. Hutchinson and translated by Trevor J. Saunders, 1318–616. Indianapolis: Hackett, 1997.
———. *Republic.* In *Plato: Complete Works,* edited by John M. Cooper and D. S. Hutchinson and translated by G. M. A. Grube and C. D. C. Reeve, 971–1223. Indianapolis: Hackett, 1997.
Pliny the Elder. *Natural History.* Translated by H. Rackham and W. H. S. Jones. Cambridge: Harvard University Press, 1960–67.
Plues, Robert. *The Rev. C. H. Spurgeon and His Brethren.* London, 1862.
Plutarch. "Common Conceptions against the Stoics." In *Essays and Miscellanies: Volume Three.* The Complete Works of Plutarch, 357–403. New York: Thomas Y. Crowell, 1909.
Pope, Elizabeth Marie. *Paradise Regained: The Tradition and the Poem.* Baltimore: Johns Hopkins, 1947.
Post, Stephen G. *Christian Love and Self-Denial: An Historical and Normative Study of Jonathan Edwards, Samuel Hopkins and American Theological Ethics.* Lanham: University Press of America, 1987.
Potterie, Ignace de la. *La vérité dans saint Jean.* Vol. 2. Rome: Biblical Institute Press, 1977.
"President Edwards on Charity and Its Fruits." *New Englander* 10, no. 37 (1852) 222–36.
Preston, John. *The New Covenant.* London: Nicholas Bourne, 1629.
Prosper of Aquitaine. *Liber Sententiarum ex Augustino Delibatarum.* Patrologia Latina 51. Opera Omnia. Edited by Jacques-Paul Migne. Paris, 1861.
———. *Responsiones ad Capitula Objectionum Vincentianarum,* Patrologia Latina 51. Opera Omnia. Edited by Jacques-Paul Migne. Paris, 1861.
Ratzinger, Joseph. *Jesus of Nazareth: From Baptism in the Jordan to the Transfiguration.* Translated by Adrian J. Walker. London: Bloomsbury, 2008.
"Recension: *A History of the Work of Redemption.*" *The Monthly Review* 52 (1775) 117–20.
"Review of '*Freedom of the Will.*'" *The Monthly Review* 27 (1762) 434–38.
Ridderbos, Jan. *De Theologie van Jonathan Edwards.* The Hague: Johan A. Nederbragt, 1907.
Ricœur, Paul. *Freedom and Nature: The Voluntary and the Involuntary.* Translated by Erazim V. Kohak. Evanston: Northwestern University Press, 1987.
Riforgiato, Leonard R. "The Unified Thought of Jonathan Edwards." *Thought: Fordham University Quarterly* 47, no. 4 (1972) 599–610.
Riley, I. W. *American Philosophy: The Early Schools.* New York: Dodd Mead, 1907.
Rist, John M. "Augustine on Free Will and Predestination." In *Augustine: A Collection of Critical Essays,* edited by Robert A. Markus, 218–52. Garden City: Doubleday Anchor, 1972.
Ritschl, O. *Dogmengeschichte des Protestantismus.* Vol. 3. Göttingen: Vandenhoeck and Ruprecht, 1926.

Rogers, Henry. "An Essay on the Genius and Writings of Jonathan Edwards." In *The Works of Jonathan Edwards*, edited by Edward Hickman, i–lii. London: Westley and Davis, 1834.
Rous, Francis. *The Works of Francis Rous, Esq.; or, Treatises and Meditations Dedicated to the Saints, and to the Excellent Throughout the Three Nations*. London: Robert White, 1657.
Royce, Josiah. *The Basic Writings of Josiah Royce*. Chicago: University of Chicago Press, 1991.
Russier, Jeanne. *La foi selon Pascal*. 2 vols. Paris: Presses Universitaires de France, 1949.
Ruysbroeck the Admirable. *L'ornement des noces spirituelles*. Translated by The Benedictines of Saint-Paul de Wisques. Paris: Éditions universitaires, 1966.
Ryland, John. "Preface." In *The Excellency of Christ*, 3–6. Northampton: Thomas Dicey, 1780.
Sainte-Beuve, Charles-Augustin. *Port-Royal*. Paris: Gallimard, 1952–54.
Santayana, George. *Character and Opinion in the United States*. New York: Scribner's, 1920.
Schafer, Thomas A. "The Concept of Being in the Thought of Jonathan Edwards." PhD diss., Duke University, 1951.
Schaff, Philip. *The Creeds of Christendom, with a History and Critical Notes*. Vol. 3. New York: Harper, 1877.
Scheeben, Matthias. *Die Mysterien des Christentums*. Freiburg im Breisgau: Herder, 1912.
———. *Handbuch der katholischen Dogmatik*. Vol. 4. Freiburg im Breisgau: Herder, 1903.
Scheick, William J., ed. *Critical Essays on Jonathan Edwards*. Boston: G. K. Hall, 1980.
———. *The Will and the Word: The Poetry of Edward Taylor*. Athens: The University of Georgia Press, 1974.
Schelling, Friedrich Wilhelm Joseph von. *Clara: Or, on Nature's Connection to the Spirit World*. Translated by Fiona Steinkamp. Suny Series in Contemporary Continental Philosophy. Albany: The State University of New York Press, 2002.
———. *Contribution à l'histoire de la philosophie moderne*. Translated by Jean-François Marquet. Paris: Presses Universitaires de France, 1983.
———. *Philosophical Investigations into the Essence of Human Freedom*. Translated by Jeff Love and Johannes Schmidt. Suny Series in Contemporary Continental Philosophy. Albany: The State University of New York Press, 2006.
Schlaeger, Margaret Clare. "Jonathan Edwards' Theory of Perception." PhD diss., University of Illinois, 1964.
Schleiermacher, Friedrich. *Der christliche Glaube: Nach den Grundsätzen der evangelischen Kirche im Zusammenhange dargestellt*. 2nd ed. Berlin: Walter de Gruyter, 2003.
———. *On Religion: Speeches to Its Cultured Despisers*. Edited and translated by Richard Crouter. New York: Cambridge University Press, 2012.
Schneider, Herbert W. *The Puritan Mind*. New York: Holt, 1930.
Schneider, Herbert W., and Carol Schneider, eds. *Samuel Johnson, President of King's College: His Career and Writings*. Vol. 3. New York: Columbia University Press, 1929.
Sévigné, Madame de. *The Letters of Madame de Sévigné to Her Daughter and Friends*. Boston: Roberts, 1878.

Shaftesbury (Anthony Ashley Cooper, Earl of). *Characteristics of Men, Manners, Opinions, Times*. 2 vols. Edited by J. M. Robertson. Indianapolis: Library of Liberal Arts, 1964.

Shedd, William Greenough Thayer. *Dogmatic Theology*. Vol. 2. New York: Scribner's, 1888.

Shepard, Thomas. *The Works of Thomas Shepard*. 3 vols. Boston: AMS, 1967.

Sibbes, Richard. *The Complete Works of Richard Sibbes, D. D.* Edinburgh: James Nichol, 1862–64.

Slotkin, Richard. *Regeneration through Violence: The Mythology of the American Frontier 1660–1860*. Middletown: Wesleyan University Press, 1973.

Smalley, John. *The Consistency of the Sinner's Inability to Comply with the Gospel; with His Inexcusable Guilt in Not Complying with It*. Hartford: Green & Watson, 1769.

———. *The Works of John Smalley D.D.* Vol. 2. n.d.

Smith, Elias. *An Essay on the Fall of Angels and Men*. Wilmington: Brynberg and Andrews, 1793.

Smith, H. Shelton. *Changing Conceptions of Original Sin: A Study in American Theology since 1750*. New York: Scribner's, 1955.

Smith, John. *Select Discourses*. London: J. Flesher, 1660.

Sola Pinto, Vivian de. *Peter Sterry: Platonist and Puritan, 1613–1672*. Cambridge: Cambridge University Press, 1939.

Spanheim, Friedrich. *Opera Omnia in Tres Tomos Divisa*. Vol. 3. Leiden: Cornelius Boutestein, 1703.

Spinoza, Benedict de. "The Letters." In *Spinoza: Complete Works*, edited by Michael L. Morgan and translated by Samuel Shirley. Indianapolis: Hackett, 2002.

Stephen, Leslie. "Jonathan Edwards." *Littell's Living Age* 120 (1874) 219–36.

Sterry, Peter. *The Teachings of Christ in the Soule*. London: R. Dawlman, 1648.

Stevens, Wallace. *The Collected Poems of Wallace Stevens*. New York: Knopf, 1954.

Stewart, Dugald. *Dissertation Exhibiting the Progress of Metaphysical, Ethical and Political Philosophy, since the Revival of Letters in Europe*. The Collected Works of Dugald Stewart 1. Edinburgh: Constable, 1854.

Stoddard, Solomon. *A Guide to Christ; or, the Way of Directing Souls That Are under the Work of Conversion*. 1714. Reprint, Northampton: Andrew Wright, 1816.

———. *A Treatise Concerning Conversion*. Boston: James Franklin, 1719.

———. *The Defects of Preachers Reproved: In a Sermon Preached at Northampton, May 19th 1723*. 1724. Reprint, Boston: Kneeland and Green, 1747.

———. *The Efficacy of the Fear of Hell to Restrain Men from Sin: Showed in a Sermon before the Inferiour Court in Northampton, December 3d, 1712*. Boston: Thomas Fleet, 1713.

———. *The Presence of Christ with the Ministers of the Gospel*. Boston: B. Green, 1718.

———. *The Safety of Appearing at the Day of Judgment in the Righteousness of Christ, Opened and Applied*. Boston: Samuel Green, 1687.

Stoeffler, F. Ernest. *The Rise of Evangelical Pietism*. Leiden: Brill, 1965.

Stolz, Dom Anselm. *Théologie de la mystique*. Vol. 2. Chèvetogne: Éditions des bénédictins d'Amay, 1947.

Story, G. M., and Helen Gardner, eds. *The Sonnets of William Alabaster*. Oxford: Oxford University Press, 1959.

Stout, Harry S. *The Divine Dramatist: George Whitefield and the Rise of Modern Evangelicalism*. Grand Rapids: Eerdmans, 1991.

———. *The New England Soul: Preaching and Religious Culture in Colonial New England*. New York: Oxford University Press, 1986.

Strack, Hermann, and Paul Billerbeck. *Kommentar zum Neuen Testament aus Talmud und Midrasch*. Vol. 3. Munich: Verlag C. H. Beck, 1926.

Surin, Jean-Joseph. *Correspondance*. Paris: Desclée de Brouwer, 1966.

Suter, Rufus. "An American Pascal: Jonathan Edwards." *The Scientific Monthly* 68, no. 5 (1949) 338–42.

Sweeney, Douglas A. "The Church." In *The Princeton Companion to Jonathan Edwards*, edited by Sang Hyun Lee. Princeton: Princeton University Press, 2005.

Sweet, William Warren. *Revivalism in America: Its Origin, Growth and Decline*. Gloucester: Peter Smith, 1965.

Tappan, Henry Philip. *A Review of Edward's "Inquiry into the Freedom of the Will."* New York: J. S. Taylor, 1839.

Taylor, Edward. *Christographia*. New Haven: Yale University Press, 1962.

———. "God's Determinations." In *The Poems of Edward Taylor*, edited by Donald E. Stanford, 261–336. New Haven: Yale University Press, 1963.

———. *The Poems of Edward Taylor*. New Haven: Yale University Press, 1963.

Taylor, Isaac. *Logic in Theology and Other Essays*. New York: William Gowans, 1860.

Taylor, Jeremy. *Ductor Dubitantium; or, the Rule of Conscience in All Her Measures*. The Whole of the Works of the Right Reverend Jeremy Taylor, D.D. 9. London: Longman, Brown, Green, and Longmans, 1850–54.

Taylor, Thomas. *The Fragments That Remain of the Lost Writings of Proclus*. London: Thomas Taylor, 1825.

Tertullian. *Of Public Shows*. In *Apologetic and Practical Treatises*, translated by C. Dodgson, 187–219. A Library of Fathers of the Holy Catholic Church, Anterior to the Division of the East and West. Oxford: John Henry Parker, 1842.

Thomas, Keith. *Religion and the Decline of Magic*. New York: Scribner's, 1971.

Thompson, Joseph P. "Jonathan Edwards, His Character, Teaching, and Influence." *Bibliotheca Sacra* 18, no. 72 (1861) 809–39.

Toland, John. *Christianity Not Mysterious*. London: Sam. Buckley, 1696.

Torrance, Thomas F. *Calvin's Doctrine of Man*. London: Lutterworth, 1949.

Townsend, Harvey G. *The Philosophy of Jonathan Edwards from His Private Notebooks*. 1955. Reprint, Westport: Greenwood, 1974.

Tracy, Joseph. *The Great Awakening: A History of the Revival of Religion in the Time of Edwards and Whitefield*. Boston: Tappan and Dennet, 1842.

Tracy, Patricia J. *Jonathan Edwards, Pastor: Religion and Society in Eighteenth-Century Northampton*. New York: Hill and Wang, 1979.

Trefz, Edward K. "Satan in Puritan Preaching." *Boston Public Library Quarterly* 8 (1956) 71–84, 148–59.

Tulloch, John. *Rational Theology and Christian Philosophy in England in the Seventeenth Century*. Vol. 2. Edinburgh: Blackwood, 1872.

Turnbull, George. *The Principles of Moral Philosophy*. London: John Noon, 1740.

Tyndale, William. "The Exposition of the Fyrste Epistle of Seynt Jhon." In *English Reformers*, edited by T. H. L. Parker. Philadelphia: Westminster, 1966.

Vacant, J.-M. Alfred, et al, eds. *Dictionnaire de Théologie Catholique*, 30 vols. Paris: Letouzey-Ané, 1899–1950.

Vail, Eugène. *De la littérature et des hommes de lettres des États-Unis d'Amérique*. Paris: Charles Gosselin, 1841.

Valeri, Mark. "The Economic Thought of Jonathan Edwards." *Church History* 60, no. 1 (1991) 37–54.
Veto, Miklos. *From Budapest to Paris (1936–1957). An Autobiography.* Eugene, OR: Resource, 2020.
———. *La naissance de la volonté.* Paris: Harmattan, 2002.
———. *La pensée de Jonathan Edwards.* Paris: Harmattan, 2007.
———. *Le fondement selon Schelling.* 2nd ed. Paris: Harmattan, 2002.
———. *Le mal: essais et études.* Paris: Harmattan, 2000.
———. *Philosophie et religion: Essais et études.* Paris: Harmattan, 2006.
———. *The Religious Metaphysics of Simone Weil.* Translated by Joan Dargan. Albany: The State University of New York Press, 1994.
Vignaux, Paul. *Justification et prédestination au XIVe siècle.* Paris: E. Leroux, 1934.
Viller, M. et al, eds. *Dictionnaire de Spiritualité. Ascétique et mystique. Doctrine et histoire.* Vol. 2. Paris: Beauchesne, 1937.
Vincent de Paul. *Correspondance, Entretiens, Documents.* Vol. 3. Paris: Lecoffre J. Gabalda, 1921.
Vincent, Gilbert. «L'herméneutique du discours théologique : Calvin et la rupture de l'onto-théologie.» PhD diss., Université de Paris X, 1980.
Voltaire. *Extraits de la bibliothèque raisonnée. Œuvres 39.* Edited by M. Beuchot. Paris: Lefèvre, 1830.
Wadsworth, Benjamin. "The Nature of Early Piety as It Respects God." In *A Course of Sermons on Early Piety.* Boston, 1721.
Walker, Daniel Pickering. *The Decline of Hell: Seventeenth-Century Discussions of Eternal Torment.* Chicago: The University of Chicago Press, 1964.
Walker, Williston. *The Creeds and Platforms of Congregationalism.* Philadelphia: Pilgrim, 1960.
Wang Tch'ang Tche, J. *Saint Augustin et les vertus des païens.* Paris: Beauchesne, 1938.
Warfield, Benjamin B. *Studies in Theology.* New York: Oxford University Press, 1932.
Watts, Emily Stipes. "The Neoplatonic Basis of Jonathan Edwards' 'True Virtue.'" *Early American Literature* 10, no. 2 (1975) 179–89.
Weil, Simone. *Cahiers. Œuvres Complètes 6.* Paris: Gallimard, 2005.
Wencelius, Léon. *L'esthétique de Calvin.* Paris: Les Belles lettres, 1937.
West, Stephen. *An Essay on Moral Agency.* New Haven: T. & S. Green, 1772.
———. *The Impotency of Sinners, with Respect to Repentance and Faith, No Excuse.* Hartford: E. Watson, 1777.
Westra, Helen. *The Minister's Task and Calling in the Sermons of Jonathan Edwards.* Lewiston: Edwin Mellen, 1986.
Wharton, Edith. *The Age of Innocence.* New York: Dover, 1997.
Wheeler, Rachel. "'Friends to Your Souls': Jonathan Edwards' Indian Pastorate and the Doctrine of Original Sin." *Church History* 72, no. 4 (2003) 736–65.
Whichcote, Benjamin. *Moral and Religious Aphorisms.* London: J. Payne, 1753.
White, Eugene E. "Solomon Stoddard's Theories of Persuasion." *Speech Monographs* 29, no. 4 (1962) 235–59.
White, John. *A Way to the Tree of Life: Discovered in Sundry Directions for the Profitable Reading of the Scriptures.* London: R. Royston, 1647.
Whittemore, Robert C. "Jonathan Edwards and the Theology of the Sixth Way." *Church History* 35, no. 1 (1966) 60–75.
Wigglesworth, Michael. *The Day of Doom.* New York: Russell and Russell, 1966.

Willard, Samuel. *A Brief Reply to Mr. George Keith, in Answer to a Script of His, Entitled, a Refutation to a Dangerous and Hurtful Opinion, Maintained by Mr. Samuel Willard, &C.* Boston: Samuel Phillips, 1703.

———. *A Compleat Body of Divinity.* New York: Johnson, 1969.

———. *Morality Not to Be Relied on for Life; or, a Brief Discourse, Discovering the One Thing Wanting, Which Leaves the Legalist Short of Life Eternal.* Boston: B. Green and J. Allen, 1700.

———. *Spiritual Desertions.* Boston: B. Green and J. Allen, 1691.

Willey, Basil. *The Eighteenth Century Background: Studies on the Idea of Nature in the Thought of the Period.* London: Chatto & Windus, 1957.

Wilson, Stephen A. *Virtue Reformed: Rereading Jonathan Edwards's Ethics.* Leiden: Brill, 2005.

Winslow, Ola Elizabeth. *Jonathan Edwards, 1703-1758: a Biography.* New York: Macmillan, 1940.

———. *Meetinghouse Hill, 1630-1783.* New York: Macmillan, 1952.

Wise, John. *Vindication of the Government of New England Churches.* Boston: J. Allen, 1717.

Wolff, Christian Friedrich von. *Theologia naturalis methodo scientifica pertractata.* Frankfurt: Rengerische Buchhandlung, 1739.

Wollebius, Johannes. *The Abridgment of Christian Divinity.* London: T. Mabb, 1660.

Woodbridge, Jonathan Edwards. *The Memorial Volume of the Edwards Family Meeting at Stockbridge, Mass., September 6-7 A.D.* Boston: Congregational Publishing Society, 1871.

Wright, Conrad. *The Beginnings of Unitarianism in America.* Boston: Beacon, 1955.

Wynne, James. *Lives of Eminent Literary and Scientific Men of America.* New York: D. Appleton, 1850.

Youngs, J. William T. "The Indian Saints of Early New England." *Early American Literature* 16, no. 3 (1981-1982) 241-56.

Scripture Index

Old Testament

Genesis, Gen, 47, 113
Exodus, Ex, 11, 169, 366
Leviticus, Lev, 176, 243
Deuteronomy, Deut, 105, 176, 192
1 Samuel, 1 Sam, 259
2 Kings, 2 Ki, 116
Isaiah, Isa, 134, 145, 161
Jeremiah, Jer, 103, 113
Ezekiel, Ezek, 51, 138, 376
Hosea, Hos, 163, 284–86
Amos, 135
Psalms, Ps, 31, 133, 161, 181, 190, 191, 198, 216, 234, 242, 319, 348, 410
Proverbs, Prov, 36, 70, 103, 109, 135, 165, 227
Job, Jb, 66, 109, 113, 184, 187, 269, 271, 297, 312, 399
Song of Solomon, Song (Sol), 259
Ecclesiastes, Ecc, 113
Daniel, 271

New Testament

Matthew, Mt, 103, 223, 314
Luke, Lk, 103, 189, 281
John, Jn, 54
Romans, Rom, 58, 103, 137, 167, 183, 227, 403
2 Corinthians, 2 Cor, 54, 321
Ephesians, Eph, 113, 156
2 Thessalonians, 2 Thess, 168
1 Timothy, 1 Tim, 141
2 Timothy, 2 Tim, 25, 313
Hebrews, Heb, 178
James, Jas, 270, 279, 379
1 Peter, 1 Pet, 44
2 Peter, 2 Pet, 11
1 John, 1 Jn, 193, 229
Revelation, Rev, 307, 339

Name Index

A

Aaron, 31, 326
Aaron R., 249
Abihu, 237
Abraham, 145
Absalom, 136, 144
Adam, 19–23, 73–80, 85, 102–4, 114–16, 127, 152, 196, 218, 221, 290, 297–98, 313, 317, 377–78 , 397
Adams B., 173
Addison J., 319
Ahlstrom S., 77, 114
Aldridge A. O., 97, 215
Allen A. V. G., xix, 7, 88, 194
Alquié F., 227
Althaus P., 279
Ambrose, Saint, 168
Amesius G., 54, 149, 163, 187
Anderson W. L., 2–3, 9, 178, 248
Angoff C., xviii
Anselm of Canterbury, Saint, 72
Apostles, 318
Aquinas T. See Thomas Aquinas, Saint.
Araud R., 192
Arendt H., 90, 289
Aristotle, Aristotelian, xviii, 108, 124, 220–222, 349
Aristotle, pseudo-Aristotelian, 36
Arminian, 86–87, 110, 117–24, 139, 194–97, 229, 290, 356, 374
Arminianism, 86–87, 158, 272
Arminians, 56, 86–88, 92–93, 104–5, 118, 122, 139, 144, 160, 171, 197–200, 222, 229, 314, 364, 372–77
Arminian (anti-), 161, 365
Arminius J., 86–87
Arnauld A., 118, 135, 142, 175, 191, 215–17, 316
Atwater L. H., xix, 102, 135
Augustine, Saint, 135, 139–40, 149–78, 189–98, 208–31, 237, 242, 270, 296–97, 304, 316–23, 339, 38–349, 397, 403
Augustinian, xxii, 15–16, 23, 56, 63, 99, 101, 105, 109, 116, 356, 372, 398

B

Baader F. X. von, 97, 154–55, 288
Baeumler A., 319–20, 338
Baius M., 72, 99
Balaam, 232, 276–78
Balthasar H. Urs von, 320, 333
Baritz L., 307
Barrow I., 356
Barth K., Barthian, xxi, 51–53, 58, 68, 149, 159–60, 168, 227, 266, 295
Bartlett P., 115
Basil, Saint, 319
Baudelaire C., 335
Baxter A., 117
Baxter R., 205, 223, 267, 312–14
Bayle P., 118, 271
Bede, Venerable, 211

Beecher E., 53
Beecher L., 65–66, 80, 113–16, 158
Beecher-Stowe H., 65, 405
Bellamy J., 59, 86, 102, 121, 129–32, 157, 167, 175–80, 194, 213–16, 295–96, 322, 355, 360, 371, 386, 411
Bercovitch S., 205
Berkeley G., Berkeleyan, 2–5, 16, 23, 135, 256, 311
Bernard, Saint, 96, 219, 304, 321
Beumer J., 270
Bèze T. de, 114
Billerbeck P., 241
Blakey R., 89
Bledsoe A., 88–89, 94–97, 128
Boethius, 135
Bogue C. W., 26, 422
Boileau-Despréaux N., 212
Boller P. F., 89
Borges J. L., 176
Bossuet J.-B., 169, 406
Bradford W., 50
Bradstreet A., 213
Brainerd D., 57, 310, 350, 361, 406
Breitenbach W. K., 102, 406
Brémond H., 87, 212–14
Brown R. F., xx, 45, 422
Browne, Sir Thomas, 171, 213
Brumm U., xix
Buell S., 360
Bulkeley P., 25
Bunyan J., 122, 241, 317, 404
Burke E., 343
Burr A., xxii, 88
Burton A., 328, 366
Bushnell H., 60, 115
Butler J., 72
Byington E., 307

C

Cady E., 178
Calvin J., xxi–xxiii, 24, 27, 50–56, 70, 72, 82, 101, 105, 128, 134–35, 145, 148, 154–55, 160–68, 175, 192–95, 212, 216–30, 238, 242, 247, 264, 269, 279, 297, 314, 321

Calvinism, xvi-xix, xxiii, 1, 22–25, 33, 56, 63–67, 76, 84–88, 104, 106, 124, 128–30, 134, 140, 155, 157, 171, 186, 284–85, 294, 311, 342, 363, 372, 392
Calvinist, calvinistic xvi-xxiii, 8, 10, 14–19, 75, 80, 90–92, 98, 104, 111–18, 121–47, 158, 198, 215–16, 233–35, 240–248, 262, 266, 270, 179, 302, 310–313, 338–39, 345–48, 356, 371–72, 377, 388–92, 397, 404–6
Anti-Calvinist, 147
Camus J.-P., 212
Carse J. P., xx, 100, 111, 346
Cassirer E., 101
Chalmers T., 88
Chambers E., 328
Channing W. E., 171, 106, 128, 138
Channing W. H., xvii, 88, 164, 177
Charnier D., 195
Charybdis, 28
Chauncy C., xvii, 80, 87, 174
Cheever G., 88
Cherry C., xx, 53, 74, 318
Chesne J.-B. du, 156
Chesterton G. K., 75
Cicero, 171, 289, 349
Clarke S., 94, 117
Clebsch W. A., 111
Clement of Alexandria, Saint, 403
Cloyne, Bishop of. *See* Berkeley.
Coccejus J., 25, 187
Colacurcio R., 250
Coleridge S. T., 75, 94
Colwell J., 182
Cotton J., 73, 103–4, 222, 232, 238, 314, 366
Crabtree A. B., 70
Crane R., 356
Cremin L., 69
Cromwell O., 267
Crusius C. A., 254
Cudworth R., 154
Cunitz E.
Curtis M., 469
Cushman R., 212

NAME INDEX 483

D

Daniel S., xx
Dante (Alighieri), 409
David, 136, 278, 342,
Davidson E., 100
Davidson J. W., 309
Davies S., 212
Davis T. M., 174
Davis V. L., 174
Day J., 118
De Achaval H. M., 318
De Normandie J., xvii
Delattre R. A., xx, 351
Denzinger H., 159, 214
Descartes R., Cartesian, xxiii, 16, 21–23, 85, 92–93, 141–42, 169, 227,
Descartes R., post-Cartesian, xxiii, 23, 124, 380
DeWitt J., 411
Dexter F. B., xix, 128, 238
Dingley R., 327
Donne J., 55, 69
Dwight S. E., 2
Dwight T., 114, 402

E

Eckley J., 413
Edwards J. (the Younger), 88, 133, 183, 361
Edwards S., xviii
Elliott J., 69
Elwood D., 33
Emerson E., 73, 313, 406
Emmons N., 15, 35, 54, 102–5, 133, 116, 121, 131–35, 147, 157, 160, 168, 178–80, 198, 216, 231, 237, 240, 268, 271–72, 405–13
Enlightenment, Age of, xvi, xxiii, 16, 66–68, 88, 108, 131, 135–36, 146, 248, 392
Erdt T., 176, 320, 327, 367
Erskine J., 86, 119, 307
Euclide, 8
Eusden J., 157
Evans W. G., xviii
Eve, 317

Evodius, 174

F

Farrar F. W., 411
Faust C., 16
Fénelon F., 83, 181, 242, 406
Ferm R., 158
Fiering N., xxiii, 2, 94, 173, 176, 248, 298, 340, 355, 359,
Finley S., 411
Finney C. G., 238
Fisher G. P., xix
Flaccus I., 70
Fleming S., 114–16
Flower E. F., 252
Foster F. H., 72, 88, 175, 215
Francis de Sales, Saint, 145, 404
Frank G., 128
Franklin B., xviii, 400
Frei H. W., 383

G

Gale T., xxiii, 11, 70, 94, 108, 215, 271
Gardner H., 321
Gardiner H. N., 33
Garrisson J. M., 293
Gaustad E., 174
Gay P., xvii
Gerstner J., 26, 172, 177, 184, 187, 237–39, 243
Gibbon E., 411
Gibson G., 249
Gilson E., 92, 142, 190, 222, 349
Gohdes C., 87
Goodwin T., 33, 44, 219, 241–44, 320, 327
Godwin W., 97
Gottschalk, 160
Gregory of Nyssa, Saint, 220
Gregory of Rimini, 115
Gregory the Great, Saint, 329
Griffin E., 138, 153, 305
Grislis E., 136
Grosart A. B., 146
Güder E., 412
Gueroult M., 4

Guillaume de Saint-Thierry, 210
Guilloré F., 262

H

Hall D. D.
Hall R., 215
Haller W., 51, 219
Hambrick-Stowe C., 324
Hamilton W., 215
Hamon J., 295
Hankamer E. W., 71
Haroutunian J., 35, 89, 182, 411
Hart D. G., 324
Hart W., 206, 215
Hawthorne N., 65, 184, 240
Hegel F., Hegelian, xxi, 118, 151, 154, 189, 222–23, 264–66, 317, 393–94
Heidelberg Catechism, 66
Heimert A., xxi, 33, 52, 73, 87, 174, 311, 411
Helvétius C.-A., 319
Henrich D., 359
Henshaw S. E. T., wviii
Heppe H., 24, 54, 72, 76–77, 95, 131, 139–43, 149, 157–58, 163–71, 187, 194, 209, 223–32, 247, 264, 270, 274, 320
Herod, 270
Hill G., 75
Hincmar of Rheims, 160
Hirsch E., 305, 313
Hobbes T., Hobbesian, 71, 128, 155, 287
Hodge C., 80, 238
Holbrook C., 74, 116, 136
Holmes J. D., 318
Homer, 171
Hooker R., 106, 143, 165, 165, 170–71, 210
Hooker T., 66–67, 71, 103, 200, 218, 228–29, 309–10, 320, 369–70, 404, 407
Hopkins S., xvi, 16, 29, 66, 72–73, 76, 81, 87, 102, 114, 120, 129–33, 153–58, 173, 175, 215–17, 227, 237, 239–48, 269, 271, 279, 314, 327, 346–47, 371, 393, 405–6
Horace, 70, 216
Howard L., 248
Hume D., 18–19, 87, 92, 101, 340
Husband H., 311
Hutcheson A., 333
Hutcheson F., 215, 5340, 349, 355–59
Huxley T., 87

I

Isaac the Syrian, Saint, 181, 413
Isidore of Seville, Saint, 159–60
Iwand H., 404

J

Jacobs P., 163
Jamblique, 11
Jansenists, xxiii, 109, 217, 270, 318
Jansenius C., 70, 99, 212, 217, 230, 240, 323
Jenson R. W., xx, 391, 422
Jenyns S., 135–36
Jerome, Saint, 238
James W., 306
John of Damascus, Saint, 141
John of the Cross, Saint, 232, 317
John the Evangelist, Saint, 229
Johnson E., 50
Johnson S., 104, 131, 136, 144, 311
Johnson T. H., 222, 310
Jones J. W., 182, 229
Joseph, 136
Judah, 232
Judas Iscariot, 95, 180, 210
Jurieu P., 131

K

Kaballah, 149
Kames H. H., Lord, 298, 336
Kant I., Kantian, ix, xi, xiii, xix, xxiv, 18, 49, 63, 72, 81, 87, 99, 100–101, 107, 114, 124, 136, 151, 164, 188, 195–98, 205, 211, 214, 216, 220, 256, 260, 265, 270, 279,

NAME INDEX

304, 313, 329, 338, 343, 349, 359, 364, 382, 393, 401
Kant I., Post-kantian, xi, 5, 320, 364, 393
Kasher M., 313
Keckermann B., 163
Kierkegaard S., Kierkegaardian, 35, 107, 124, 240, 288, 406
Kimnach W. H., iii, xi, 32, 187, 421
King H., 88
Kingman H., 177, 307
Kittel, G., 113
Knight J., 45
Köstlin J., 211
Kraus A., 109, 270, 329
Kretzöi M., 307

L

Lallemant L., 220, 329
Laporte J., xxiv, 70, 109, 142, 155, 163, 191, 195, 230
Laurence D. E., 248, 383
Laurent, Saint, 195
Le Mercier de la Rivière P.-P., 289
Lecky W. E. H., 75
Lee S. H., 36, 416
Leibniz G., Leibnizian, xix, xxiii, 5, 59, 67, 87, 92–95, 112, 131, 134, 138, 142, 171, 179, 185, 199, 227, 244, 254, 412
Leo X, Pope., 137
Leroux L., xix
Lesser M. X., xix, 88, 113, 118, 140 176, 215, 218, 224, 245, 293, 339, 408, 420–424
Levin D., 75, 229
Levy B. M., 404
Lewis C. S., 113
Lichtenstein A., 355
Locke J., Lockean, xx, 7, 9, 18, 67, 78–79, 87, 89–90, 93, 100, 105, 108, 117, 248–55, 261, 267, 307, 382–83, 388
Lombard P., 68, 96, 211
Loring I., 173
Lowell R., 3
Lowrie E. B., 17, 95

Luther M., 51–56, 68, 75, 98, 101, 134, 39, 145, 149, 154, 156, 171, 178, 181, 193, 211–12, 216, 218, 223, 228, 270, 295, 317, 404

M

MacPhail A., xviii
Mahomet, 271
Malebranche N., xxiii, 58, 62, 135, 174, 181, 238–42, 262, 298, 314, 322–23, 406–7
Manspeaker N., xviii, 115
Manton T., 113
Marsden G. M., 73, 376
Martz L. L., 321
Mastricht P. van, 144, 229, 298
Mather C., xviii, 73
Mather I., 68–69, 174, 415
Maurice F. D., 8
Mausbach J., 211
May H. F.
Mayhew J., xvii
McClelland G., 97
McClymond M. J., 3
McDermott G. R., 398
McGiffert A. C., 406
McGiffert M., xix
McGinley P., 115
Melanchthon P., 76, 227
Melville H., 65
Miller P., xix-xxi, 9, 25, 33, 54, 60, 67–71, 87, 110, 144, 174, 177, 215, 222, 232, 238, 248, 256, 266, 270, 304, 306, 310, 318, 320, 417–25
Miller S., 87
Milton J., 16, 25, 65, 144, 149, 153, 156, 170–71, 213, 215, 219, 243, 271
Minkema K. P., x, xi
Möhler J.-A., 230
Moltmann J., 72
Moncreiff-Wellwood H., 307
Montcheuil Y. de, 407
More H., 9, 355
Morgan E. S., 53, 239
Morris W., 2, 100, 367

NAME INDEX

Moses, 11, 80, 220, 232, 270, 300
Muirhead J. H., xviii
Müller J., 169, 228
Murdock K., 314
Murphey M. G., 252, 419

N

Nadab, 237
New Divinity, xvi
New England Theology, xvi
New Theology, 88, 128, 131–33, 153–55, 216, 237, 239, 295
Newman J. H., 318
Newton I., Newtonian, xx, 5, 9, 15, 24, 27, 116, 376, 402
Newtoun B., 89
Nichols S. J., 324
Nicole P., 109, 215, 318
Niebuhr H. R., 69, 174
Niemeyer H., 24, 72, 148, 156, 160–63, 242, 297, 371
Nietzsche F., 329, 411
Norris J., 2
Nouilleau J.-B., 214
Nutall G., 267–70, 311–12

O

Opie J., 16
Orcibal J., 261
Osgood S., xvii
Ovid, 216
Owen J., 103, 158, 260, 309

P

Paley W., 74
Pancoast H. S., xix
Parain, B., 87
Park E. A., 75, 138, 153, 168, 215, 248, 306, 406
Parker, A. A., 109
Parmenides, 37, 394–96
Parrington V., 177
Parsons J., 229, 241, 360
Parton J., xxi, 88

Pascal B., xviii, xxiii, 16, 99, 108–9, 118, 124, 168, 231, 269–71, 295, 323, 365
Pattison T. H., 373
Paul, Saint, 19, 58, 113, 116, 137, 141, 167, 220, 227, 299, 379, 402–5,
Pelagianism, 87, 368
Pelagianizing, 154
Pelagians, 56, 86–87, 113, 154, 192, 198, 272, 368, 407
Pelagius, Pelagian, 70, 115, 151
Pepperell, Lady, 325–26
Perkins W., 66–68, 77, 113, 149, 157, 159, 161, 220, 231–32, 247, 404
Pettit N., 103
Pharaoh, 144, 167–69, 232
Phillips S., 229
Pierrepont S. *See* Edwards, S.
Plato, Platonist, xviii, 11, 32, 69, 108, 154, 205, 213, 271, 349, 355
Platonist (Neo), 2, 33, 63, 348
Pliny the Elder, 271
Plues R., 88
Plutarch, 74
Polanus A., 158, 223
Pope E. M., 271
Post S. G., 403
Potterie I. de la, 210
Preston J., 25
Proclus, Proclean, 67, 173, 297
Prosper of Aquitaine, Saint, 159, 215

Q

Quesnel P., 212

R

Ramsey P., xx, 36, 87, 100, 387
Ratzinger J., 214
Ricœur P., 314
Riforgiato L., 351
Riley I. W., 1
Rist J., 103
Ritschl O., 70, 161
Rogers H., 75, 87
Royce J., xvi, xviii
Russier J., 270, 295

Ruysbroeck the Admirable, 295
Ryland J., xix

S

Saint-Cyran, Jean Duvergier de, 261
Saint-Thierry, William, 210
Sainte-Beuve C. A., xxiii, 114, 230
Santayana G., xx
Satan, 70, 155–56, 168, 171, 174, 181, 213–14, 219, 231, 236, 268, 317
Saul. *See* Paul, Saint.
Scalinger J.-C., 337
Schafer T. A., xxi, 2, 13
Schaff P., 157, 164
Scheeben M., 159, 184
Scheick W. J., 103–4
Schelling F., ix, 134, 140, 146, 181, 220, 254, 260, 336, 393
Schlaeger M. C., 87, 137, 319
Schleiermacher F., 72, 98, 147, 296
Schneider H., xviii
Scotus, John Duns. *See* Duns Scotus J.
Scylla, 28
Seneca, 271
Sévigné, Madame de, 58
Shaftesbury, Earl of, 67–68, 131, 338, 349, 355
Shedd W. G. T., 99
Shepard T., 67, 73, 146, 175, 178, 209–10, 231–35, 239, 263, 266, 270, 287, 295, 320, 369, 374, 382, 404–7
Sibbes R., 216, 321, 329
Slotkin R., 73, 176
Smalley J., 120
Smith E., 88, 165
Smith H. S., 373
Smith J., 32, 114, 181, 213, 132, 241, 314–20, 360
Smyth E., xix
Socrates, 79, 108, 124, 271
Sola Pinto V. de, 146, 213
Solomon, 175
Soto D., 232
Spanheim E., 142
Spanheim F., 114
Spinoza B., xvii, 8, 11, 87, 112, 128

Spring G., 112
Stephen L., xvii, 8, 248
Sterry P., 146, 181, 213, 313
Stevens W., 336
Stewart D., 2
Stiles E., 128, 238
Stoddard E. *See* Edwards E.
Stoddard S., 14, 58, 60, 67, 96, 105, 174, 212, 231, 237, 295, 376, 382, 406, 411
Stoeffler F. E., 373
Stolz A., 323
Stout H. S., iii-vii
Strack H., 241
Suter R., xviii
Sweeney D. A., 39, 376
Sweet W. W., 213

T

Talmud, 241, 313
Tappan H. P., 88, 91
Tauler J., 404
Taylor E., 10, 53, 60, 110, 162, 163, 237, 244, 302, 316, 322,
Taylor I., 88
Taylor Jeremy, 143
Taylor John, 75, 128
Taylor N. W., 77, 114
Taylor T., 67
Tennent G., 87, 174
Tertullian, 411
Thomas Aquinas, Saint, xxi, xxiii, 76, 81, 109, 130, 141, 151, 161, 163, 170, 186, 189–93, 197, 211, 214, 220–24, 240, 242, 270, 288, 295, 329, 349
Toland J., 67
Torquemada T. de, xvii
Torrance T., 274, 345
Tracy J., 177, 406
Trefz E., 174
Tulloch J., 70
Turnbull G., 74, 146, 215
Turretin F., 144, 393
Tyndale W., 193, 195

U

Ursinus, D.-Z., 70

V

Vail E., 87
Valeri M., 71
Veto M., 68, 85n 89, 103, 146, 181, 198, 201, 209, 259, 265, 380
Vignaux P., 160
Vincent de Paul, Saint, 155
Vincent G., 69, 163, 192, 231, 311
Virgil, 175
Voltaire, 74

W

Wadsworth B., 114
Walker D., 131, 181
Walker W., 53, 56, 73, 75, 131, 154, 157, 162, 171, 181, 216, 221, 229, 238, 243, 409, 411
Wang Tch'ang Tche J., 191
Warfield B. B., xix, 8, 114, 154, 161
Washington G., xviii
Watts E. S., 339
Weil S., ix, 15, 174, 209
Wencelius L., 216
West S., 88, 121, 132, 146, 179
Wharton E., 410
Wheeler R., 73
Whichcote B., 70, 213
White E. E., 60, 212
White J., 270
Whitefield G., 311, 419
Whittemore R. C., 2, 128
Wigglesworth M., 114
Willard S., 16, 17, 32, 53–55, 68, 77, 95, 113, 115, 131, 135, 149, 157–61, 167, 178, 181, 186, 216, 229, 233, 235, 309, 320, 406, 409
Willey B., 136
Williams Rev. S., 236
Winslow E., 184
Wise J., 67
Whitacker W., 77
Wolff C. F. von, 382
Wollebius J., 32, 72, 76, 171, 320, 367
Woodbridge J. E., xviii, 177
Woolsey T., 177
Wright C., 86
Wynne J., 194
Wyttenbach D., 264

Y

Youngs J. W. T., 73

Z

Zanchius J., 113

Subject Index

A

Asymmetry of causality with respect to evil, 144–51, 162, 294–301
Attribute of God, 385

B

Benevolence, 353–54
    Affection detached from general, 84
    Assurance, 321
    At the level of Being, 352
    Complex idea, 254–55
    Complex spiritual idea, 254
    Consent, 354
    Deity, 87
    Disinterested, 356
    Disposition of general, 355
    Divine, 354
    Eliciting greater, 354
    Essence of God's moral perfection, 29
    Formulation of, 202
    General, 84
    General love of, 201
    God's overflowing, 39
    Idea of, 255
    In a being, 354
    Inseparability of, 351
    JE sought to rediscover general, 352
    Lacking, 267
    Limited, 372
    Love another with, 354
    Love of, 180, 201–3, 353
    Mankind, 132
    Mere, 238
    Modern religion, 267
    Moral, 361
    Most general object of, 354
    Natural, 323
    Object of general, 84
    Object of ultimate propensity, 202
    Object of virtuous, 202, 354
    Opposed to general, 205
    Particular, 372
    Primary form of, 352
    Primary object of, 354
    Private affection and general, 84
    Propensity, 354
    Saints in Paradise, 362
    Secondary object of virtuous, 354
    Spiritual, 342
    Spiritual beauty, 361
    Spiritual idea, 273
    Sweet harmony, 255
    Tender, 177
    To Being in general, 267, 350
    True, 202, 255, 353, 362
    True virtue, 350–352, 372
    Universal, 350, 372
    Virtuous, 356
Benevolent
    Attention to little children, 115
    Beauty of regenerated creature, 361
    Being, 353–54
    Disposition, 255
    Existence of another, 353

Benevolent *(continued)*
  God, 361
  Heart, 354, 405
  Love, 353–54
  Love of God, 240
  Man, 132
  Mind, 273, 354

C

Common grace, 227–36, 303
Compossibility, 379–89, 399–400
Conversion, 292
  Bartlett P., 115
  Brainerd D., 350
  Consequences, 301
  Crucial moment, 294
  Decisive moment for Edwards, 324
  Description, 54, 307, 316
  Edwards, xviii, 46, 292, 293, 307
  Edwards after, 293, 300, 312, 375, 381
  Edwards and the Indians, 73
  Edwards during, 316
  Edwards prior to, 290, 293, 324
  Edwards S., 325
  Emmons N., 54
  Essence, 317
  Experience, 236–37, 311–15
  False, 231, 238
  From death to life, 53
  From God, 63
  Great and universal change, 302
  Holy Spirit, 87
  Improper designation, 238
  Kant, 304
  Key alteration, 308
  Leap, 54
  Man prior to, 313
  Meaning, 119
  Means, 60–62
  Morphology, 53, 310
  Order, 310
  Poem, 162
  Prior to, 313
  Process, 293–310
  Reformed theology of, 310
  Renewing of whole man, 377
  Sinners prior to, 121
  Study, 246
  Theological enquiries affected by Edwards, 583
  Transformation of man, 307
  Treatise, 14, 67,
Conviction (belief)
  Calm, 371
  Calvinist, 347
  Condemnation is just, 343
  Eternal nature of Hell, 183
  False, 210
  Infinite offense and punishment, 72
  Strong belief not necessarily right, 197
  Stronger, 287
Conviction (sense), 279
  Common sense 99, 104, 125–27
  Conscience, 315
  Defined by Edwards, 282
  Definition, 282, 315
  Delightful, 292
  Description, 282
  Divine wrath, 286
  Evil, 316
  False, 285
  Hawthorne N., 240
  Heart, 368
  Heart not open, 240
  Heinousness of sin, 300
  In-depth analysis of, 234
  Jesus Christ as Savior, 368
  Legal, 283–95, 308
  Lord's leading, 283
  Man's will necessitated by, 96
  More than mere, 285
  Natural man, 280
  Not truly spiritual, 318
  Paradox, 290
  Process, 54
  Saving, 293, 331
  Sensible apprehension, 281
  Sin, 370
  Sinner, 288, 344
  Sins, 136
  Special, 308
  Spiritual, 294, 310–313
  Test, 288

SUBJECT INDEX 491

Time of, 288
Truth respecting evil, 284
Corruption, 65–85, 101, 116, 128–30,
    172–84, 234, 239, 269, 296
  Adam, 22, 80, 152, 298, 377
  Author, 128
  Children, 113
  Diversity among creatures, 130
  Divine responsibility, 80
  Explaining, 81, 85, 152, 298
  Extent, 66, 71, 72, 239, 296
  Fallen creature, 55, 173
  Fallen man, 70, 269
  Heart, 173, 182, 244
  Hereditary, 75–76
  Human nature, 65
  Man, 22, 70, 80, 85
  Mind, 183
  Natural man, 56, 66–72
  Propagation, 297
  Residual, 56
  Voluntary, 65, 79, 81
  Wicked, 177
Creation, 13
  Creator distinct from, 13
  Deity, 47
  Direct act of God, 20
  Divine action, 20
  Divine foundation, 2
  Expression of divine glory, 48
  First exercise of divine power, 17
  General revelation, 45
  God and, 13
  God delights in, 41
  God's self-communication, 47
  God's sovereignty, 31
  Immediacy, 14
  Immediate, 20
  Implied by sovereignty, 14, 35–38
  Intelligent, 44–48
  Intelligent beings, 20
  Key to understanding, 32
  Man, 21
  Man is the end of, 41
  Material world, 20
  Mysterious work, 271
  Not necessary for God, 28, 30
  Not self-perpetuating, 19

  Notion, 32
  Pinnacle of, 44
  Providence, 48
  Purpose, 6, 29, 42
  Redemption, 48
  Redemption greater, 49
  Seeing hand of God in, 20
  Serves men's wickedness, 71
  Sustained by God, 15, 16
  To glorify the Creator, 30
  Trinity, 27
Creation (continuous), 49
  Doctrine, 17
  Identity, 22
  Mental, 7
  Physical, 7

D

Damnation, xvii, 26, 72, 113–16, 131,
    139, 151–89, 198, 214, 221, 226,
    239, 247, 289–90, 294, 304, 315,
    391, 404–10
Divine arbitrariness, 154

E

Election, 157–66, 179, 241, 292, 316,
    323, 371, 390, 396–97
Evil
  Act, 117, 119
  Augustine, Saint, 72
  Author, 120, 128
  Cause of, 150
  Discerning, 284, 287
  Disposition, 82, 120, 122
  Edwards' doctrine, 297
  Existence of, 129
  God, 128, 129, 137, 138
  Good and, 25, 72, 81, 100, 119, 138,
      147, 257
  Good from, 54, 142
  Good vs., 53
  Hypocrites sink into, 239
  Imagination, 82
  Indivisible, 72
  Intention, 228
  Leibniz, 67

Evil *(continued)*
  Man, 150
  Man and his works, 193
  Man responsible, 107, 150
  Man's nature, 65, 73
  Man's will, 77
  Moral, 127, 130, 167, 216, 297
  Moral good and, 99–105, 116, 123
  Natural good and, 62
  Origin of, 134, 147
  Original sin, 75
  Producing vs. permitting, 139
  Punishment, 178, 284–89
  *Shaftesbury, Earl of, 68
  Sin, 75, 183–87, 287
  Subjugation of fallen will, 2
  Wicked, 242
  Will, 81, 100, 122, 153, 162, 185–88, 189 Willing good and, 147
Excellence, 6, 39, 60, 222–24, 264, 276, 305, 314, 322, 331, 343–67, 385, 396, 399
External idea, 274–75, 286, 317, 363

F

Faith of devils, xv, 198, 205, 213, 270, 279, 281, 287–89, 320, 332, 360
Fall. *See* Original sin
Freedom, xv-xvi, 25–27, 30, 34, 59, 61, 85–102, 107–11, 118–27, 140, 155, 161, 164, 181, 194, 197, 294, 306, 314, 327, 336,
  Children of God, 194, 379
  Definition, 90, 91–94
  God, 25, 27, 30, 34, 59, 93, 117, 128
  Grace, 61
  Kant, 124
  Will, xv, xvi, 85–88, 90, 100, 107, 111, 327

G

Glory of God, 26, 30, 40, 43, 46, 58, 129–33, 147, 180–82, 206, 209, 250, 275, 292, 295, 332, 405–9
Goodness of God, 27, 49, 53, 117, 294, 300

Grace, 14, 15, 21, 47, 45–63, 68, 70, 73, 86, 109, 113, 118–19, 122, 124, 133, 152, 153, 157, 162–66, 168–69, 170, 188, 191, 193–98, 212, 216–18, 227–45, 248–51, 253, 255, 270, 292, 300–306, 307–11, 314–16, 321, 323–24, 326, 327, 343–47, 350, 356, 358–60, 360, 363, 364, 373, 376, 377, 381–83, 385, 386–90
  Aquinas T., Saint, 191
  Augustine, Saint, 97, 168
  Covenant, 25, 165, 194, 309
  Definition, 55
  Doctrines of, 133, 270
  Edwards, 31, 47, 49, 300, 303, 324
  Efficacious, xviii
  Election, 163
  Explanation, 311
  Free, 15, 55, 57, 248, 292, 316
  From God, 15, 20
  God, 158, 174, 217, 243–45, 300, 316, 345, 349, 360, 364, 386
  Irresistible, 54, 124, 243
  Kant, 195
  Means of, 60, 62, 221, 229, 236, 239–40, 243
  Metaphor, 57
  Paradox, 217
  Pascal B., xxiii
  Perseverance, 54, 229
  Prevenient, 240
  Redemptive, 2, 21
  Saving, 229, 234, 236
  Simple idea, 232, 260, 262, 294, 309, 311, 314, 321, 364, 383, 388
  Sinner redeemed by, 124
  Spiritual, 230
  To the elect, 136
  True, xv, 270, 279, 290, 292, 300, 315, 332, 347, 374
  Withdrawal, 170
  Work, 14, 304
Great Awakening, 52, 56, 73, 1722–177, 221, 233, 274, 306, 309–13, 347, 370, 391, 415
Greatness, 342–48
  Angels, 343

Attribute of God, 283, 346–47
Beauty, 347–50
Creature, 347
Dreadful, 132
End of, 346
Excellence, 343
God, 6, 13, 37, 130, 259, 280–283, 286, 295, 342–54, 390
God's infinite wrath, 345
God's natural perfections, 283, 344–47
God's power, 395
God's wisdom linked to, 343
Infinite, 363
Lacking, 39
Naturalia of God, 345
Notion, 343
Opposition to God's, 343
Power and wisdom, 346
Proportion, 344, 346
Redemption, 51
Secondary beauty, 342–54
Shadows of, 336
Sin, 286, 295
Sinners, 286
Stars, 335
Taken by itself, 346
Terrible, 259
Transcendent, 370
True, 293
Universe, 343
Wrath of God, 149, 156, 176, 183–87, 286–88, 300

H

Hardening, 146, 151, 167–73, 188, 253
Hatred of God, 71, 121, 287, 290
Head, 6, 201, 272, 278, 363, 389, 412
Heart, 120–23, 125, 126, 132, 144, 151, 152, 167–77
    Afflicted, 115
    Arrow, 176
    Christ, 39
    Definition, 103–6
    Depravity, 71–76
    Devil, 70

Disposition, 74, 77
Emmons, 105
Evil, 104–7, 112, 123, 239
Evil imagination, 82
Examining, 110
Gladness, 74
God, 25, 31, 39
God-given, 104
Good, 104–8
Hardened, 106
Iniquity, 109
Man, 39, 70, 103
Move, 46
Music, 60
Panting, 12
Propensity, 119
Reading, 104
Savior, 61
Scripture, 103
Sin, 70
Strings, 106
Subterfuges, 109
Term, 103–6
Wicked, 104
Heart, Sense of the, 103, 176, 257–58, 281, 313–20, 327, 331, 387
Hell. *See* Damnation
Historic faith, 263–68
Hypocrisy, 222
    Contrary to truth, 222
    Corrupt human nature, 216
    Definition, 222
    Difficult to discern, 222
    Gospel, 228
    Legal, 222
    Neighbor, 369
    Notion, 222

I

Idealism, 3–6, 44
    Continuity, 35
    Edwards, 1–4, 32, 35, 40, 259, 268, 334, 337
    Epistemological, 334
    Form of, 256
    German, 398
    Intuition, 9

Idealism *(continued)*
  Moral, 334
  New England, 87
  Of divine understanding, 6
  Philosophical, 21, 22
  Post-Kantian, 364
  Subjective, 6
Imagination, 17, 113, 271, 272–78, 317, 331
  Content might be false, 278
  Description, 275
  Devil's influence, 274, 317
  Edwards, 371
  Evil, 82, 113
  External ideas, 274
  Ideas, 286
  Ideas rooted in our mind, 276
  Imaginary vs. spiritual, 276
  Imagination vs. Heart, 277
  Impressions, 277
  Mirages, 277
  Notion, 276
  Overheated, 274
  Paradox, 273
  Perception by a conscious being, 5
  Process of cognition, 318
  Religious, 69, 74, 274
  Religious enthusiasm, 277
  Theological, 271
Immediacy of divine action, 13–15, 20–21, 261
  Edwards, 15
Incarnation, 37–39, 271, 393–96, 468

J

Justification, 21, 49–63, 123, 154, 160, 188, 193–97, 201, 215, 216, 218, 238, 271, 294, 296, 302–3, 305, 307, 334, 353, 362, 364, 362, 368, 374, 389–90
  Act of, 53
  After, 56
  By faith alone, xxii, 51–52, 59, 193–95, 364
  Calvin J., 52
  Distinctly Christian, 52
  Doctrine, xx, 52, 194

Essential doctrine, 52, 271
Grounded in Christ, 59
Immediacy, 54
Importance, 52
Luther M., 51
Prior to, 56, 57, 195
Reformed dogmatics, 52
Roles in salvation, 52
Romans, Chapter 8, 51

L

Liberty of indifference, 92–94, 116–17, 123–25

M

Mercenary love, 208–14, 265, 276
Moral inability, 105–21
Moral responsibility, 90–95, 105, 113, 120, 138
Moral sense, 320, 340–342, 355–59
Moral sincerity, 197–98, 201–5, 215, 232, 235–36, 372–75, 397
Moral subject, 89, 101–2, 126, 140, 217, 244, 341

N

Nature (physical), 26, 45–46, 105
Natural beauty, 337–43, 349, 355, 401, *See* Particular beauty
Natural condition
  Man, 740 81–84, 175, 207, 302, 310
Natural evil, 284–85, 348
Natural knowledge of evil. *See* Natural evil
Necessity, 84–88, 91–97
  Calvin, 96
  Edwards, 91–97
  Existence, 8
  God, 28, 36, 88, 93, 301, 394
  Hobbesian, 155
  Hypothetical, 95
  Moral, 95–97, 105, 108, 125
  Natural, 96–97, 100, 105
  Opposite of, 96
New sense. *See* Spiritual sense

SUBJECT INDEX

New simple idea of grace. *See* Grace - Simple idea
Nominalism, 7, 17, 100–102, 122
    Late Middle Ages, 101
    Of the will, 122
Notional faith, 268, 317, 365, *See* Historic faith
Notional knowledge, 261, 267, 280–281, 320–321, 329–32, 347, 361, 389, 391, 407 *See* Notional faith

O

Original sin, ix, xv-xxi, 18, 22, 65, 67, 74–87, 102, 114–15, 123, 127–28, 136, 151, 155, 163, 196–97, 262, 322, 361, 396–97, 402

P

Pantheism, 1–2, 8–9, 11, 22, 35–40, 306
Particular beauty, 333
Plenitude, 32, 373, *See* Sufficiency of God, of Jesus Christ
Positive evil, 152
Predestination, 23, 49, 97, 101–3, 127, 130, 157–68, 370,
    Augustine, Saint, 160
    Doctrine, 155
    Double, 154–68
    Elect, 160, 163
    Impious, 160
Primary beauty, 2, 337–43, 350, 353, 363, 366, 386, 390, 398–401
Pulchritude, 398

R

Reprobation, xxii, 23, 104, 130, 151–72, 179, 189, 243, 390

S

Saving grace, 45, 53, 229–36, 245, 303–4, 386–87
    Absence, 233

Secondary beauty, 339–48, 354, 357–63, 386, 398 Greatness and, 345
Self-love, 71, 83–84, 152, 193, 201–10, 238, 276, 283–88, 298–99, 340–341, 349, 355, 359–60, 406–7
Servile fear, 211, *See* Mercenary love
    Can keep man from evil, 211
    Not useless, 211
    Of God, 211
    Of Hell, 211
    Rejection of, 214
Sin against the Spirit, 223–28, 385
Sovereignty of God, xvii, 8, 16, 24–27, 58, 61–62, 80, 86, 102, 105, 140, 147, 157, 161, 292, 324, 368
Speculative knowledge, 233, 258, 262, 268–72, 277–81
Spiritual idea, 206, 245, 305, 311, 332, 363, 375, 388–90, 399–401
    Archetypal, 260
    Benevolence, 254, 273
    Complex, 254
    Continuity, 254
    Development, 254
    Doctrine, 261
    Excellency of God, 390
    God, 332, 383, 388–90
    God's holy beauty, 332
    Immediate knowledge, 259
    Mediate knowledge, 262
    Notion, 253
    Relationship to the mind, 275
    Represented by signs, 262
    Require attention, 262
    Simple, 388
    True, 260
    Vividness of representations, 256
Spiritual knowledge, 301
Spiritual sense, 306–9, 314–23, 327, 331–32, 359–60, 368, 370, 374
Sufficiency of God, of Jesus Christ, 294, 315, 332, 368, 390

T

Taste, 112, 216, 242–49, 296, 310–329, 351–66, 401, 407

Taste *(continued)*
  Augustine, Saint, 242
  Bad taste, 322
  Contrary taste, 322
  Distaste, 323
  Divine things, 329
  Doctrine, 319
  Essential elements, 327
  Esthetic, 401
  Explanation, 328
  Faculty of spiritual apprehension, 327
  For God, 407
  God's excellence, 361
  God's will, 329
  Holy, 323
  Natural man, 322
  Notion, 327
  Object, 329
  Spiritual, 319–22, 326–32, 460
  Spiritual knowledge, 322
  Spiritual sense, 327
  Term, 326–28
  Wisdom, 326
Theodicy, 79–80, 124, 127–39, 147, 150
Trinity, 27, 30–36, 48, 52–53, 115, 154, 224, 233, 249–50, 274, 282, 305, 308–9, 321, 324, 346, 352, 367, 393–94, 401
True virtue, xv, xviii, 33, 201–8, 215, 304, 328, 333, 339, 340, 342–54, 362, 366, 371–72, 379, 385, 389, 392, 399,

V

Virtue of pagans, 191, 215, 227, 236

W

Will, 65
  Act, 89
  Augustine, 103
  Character, 86
  Choice, 90
  Definition, 82
  Determination, 76, 104
  Doctrine, 88, 103
  Edwards, 87
  Ethic, 82
  Fall an act of, 65
  Fallen, 2, 64, 66
  Free, 86, 89
  Free or not, xviii
  Freedom, 111
  God, 16, 23–27, 50, 59, 134
  God's free will, 25
  God's saving will, 53
  God's sovereign will, 19, 20, 24, 58
  Heart, 277
  Indifferent, 59
  Judging the, 196
  Moral necessity, 95
  Motive, 82
  Natural inclination, 82
  Object, 80, 82, 91
  Opposing models, 101
  Realism, 101, 121
  Science of the, 80, 89
  Sin, 384
  Under bondage, 86, 89, 94, 107, 108, 115, 123, 124, 137, 245
Will (faculty), 65, 89, 93, 98, 101, 103, 107, 199, 203, 309, 328
Will (immediacy), 98, 125

www.ingramcontent.com/pod-product-compliance
Lightning Source LLC
Chambersburg PA
CBHW052046290426
44111CB00011B/1632